Chinese Civil-Military Relations in the Post-Deng Era

Implications for Crisis Management
and Naval Modernization

Nan Li

CHINA MARITIME STUDIES INSTITUTE
U.S. NAVAL WAR COLLEGE
Newport, Rhode Island

www.usnwc.edu/Research---Gaming/China-Maritime-Studies-Institute.aspx

Naval War College

Newport, Rhode Island
Center for Naval Warfare Studies
China Maritime Study No. 4
January 2010

President, Naval War College
Rear Admiral James P. Wisecup, U.S. Navy

Provost
Amb. Mary Ann Peters

Dean of Naval Warfare Studies
Robert C. Rubel

Director of China Maritime Studies Institute
Dr. Lyle J. Goldstein

Naval War College Press

Director: Dr. Carnes Lord
Managing Editor: Pelham G. Boyer

Telephone: 401.841.2236
Fax: 401.841.3579
DSN exchange: 948
E-mail: press@usnwc.edu
Web: www.usnwc.edu/press
www.twitter.com/NavalWarCollege

Printed in the United States of America

The China Maritime Studies are extended research projects that the editor, the Dean of Naval Warfare Studies, and the President of the Naval War College consider of particular interest to policy makers, scholars, and analysts.

Correspondence concerning the China Maritime Studies may be addressed to the director of the China Maritime Studies Institute, www.usnwc.edu/Research---Gaming/China-Maritime-Studies-Institute.aspx. To request additional copies or subscription consideration, please direct inquiries to the President, Code 32A, Naval War College, 686 Cushing Road, Newport, Rhode Island 02841-1207, or contact the Press staff at the telephone, fax, or e-mail addresses given.

ISSN 1943-0817

ISBN 978-1-884733-73-4

The views elaborated herein are those of the author alone and do not represent the official viewpoints of the U.S. Navy or any other agency of the U.S. government. The author thanks Pelham Boyer, Andrew Erickson, Lyle Goldstein, and Jonathan Pollack for their helpful comments, but he is solely responsible for any shortcomings in the monograph.

Photographs are from *People's Daily, Liberation Army Pictorials,* and *Modern Navy,* all publications of the Chinese government.

Chinese Civil-Military Relations in the Post-Deng Era

Implications for Crisis Management and Naval Modernization

Analytical Questions

This study addresses two analytical questions: What has changed in Chinese civil-military relations during the post–Deng Xiaoping era? What are the implications of this change for China's crisis management and its naval modernization?

Why Important?

Addressing these questions is important for three major reasons. First, because the People's Liberation Army (PLA) is a party army, it is commonly assumed that its primary function is domestic politics—that is, to participate in party leadership factional politics and to defend the Chinese Communist Party (CCP) against political opposition from Chinese society. For the past twenty years, however, the PLA has not been employed by such party leaders as Jiang Zemin and Hu Jintao against political opposition from either the CCP or Chinese society. The PLA's ground force, which is manpower-intensive and therefore the most appropriate service for domestic politics, has been continuously downsized. Technology and capital-intensive services that are appropriate for force projection to the margins of China and beyond and for strategic deterrence but are inappropriate for domestic politics—such as the PLA Navy (PLAN), the PLA Air Force (PLAAF), and the Second Artillery (the strategic missile force)—have been more privileged in China's military modernization drive.[1] This study, by examining change in Chinese civil-military relations, undertakes to resolve this analytical puzzle.

Second, China's civil-military interagency coordination in crisis management during the post-Deng era has remained an area of speculation, for lack of both information and careful analysis. By analyzing change in Chinese civil-military relations, this study aims to shed some light on this analytical puzzle as well.

Finally, the PLAN was previously marginalized within the PLA, partly because the latter was largely preoccupied with domestic issues and politics, where the PLAN is not especially useful. By exploring change in Chinese civil-military relations, this study also attempts to explain why during the post-Deng era the PLAN has become more important in China's military policy.

Background: Legacies of Mao and Deng

Traditional analysis of China's civil-military relations assumes that the relationship between the CCP and the PLA remains symbiotic, without functional differentiation or technical specialization–based institutional boundaries. Such a symbiosis has been attributed to Mao Zedong's reliance on a strategy of manpower-based mass mobilization rather than functional and technical specialization–based expertise and administrative efficacy for his revolutionary agenda and post-revolutionary development. A product of civil war and revolution, the PLA was naturally an integral part of Mao's strategy. Party-army "symbiosis" did not imply the lack of political dynamics; on the contrary, political rivalries and alignments were rampant in the Mao years and immediately after. But rather than party-army institutional boundaries, highly personalized leadership factions defined these rivalries and allegiances, which cut across and weakened further the party-army boundaries. That is, a few political-military factions engaged in a zero-sum struggle for political power.[2]

Photo 1. *Mao met with PLAN sailors in 1953. But the PLAN was largely neglected by Mao because he wanted "politics to take command" in the PLA.*

The rise of Deng Xiaoping in the late 1970s, however, led to the replacement of Mao's revolutionary agenda with a nation-building project of "four modernizations"— modernizing industry, agriculture, science and technology, and national defense. It was recognized that technical expertise and administrative efficiency based on a division of labor are indispensable for such tasks. As a result, functional differentiation and technical specialization have been promoted. Institutional boundaries between the party and the army became clearer, so that the latter could enjoy more institutional autonomy to pursue its functional and technical expertise. This trend was reflected in the downsizing of the PLA by a million billets during 1985–87, the reduction of its role in domestic party and societal politics, the decline of cross-boundary circulation of elites, and the concentration of the armed forces on the military-technical tasks of modernization.[3]

Photo 2. *Deng reviewing PLA troops on 1 October 1984.*

There was, however, one caveat. At the top leadership level, such as the Central Military Commission (CMC), Deng's informal and personal influence remained substantial and institutional prerequisites were not so important. Deng, for instance, held the position of CMC chair from 1981 to 1989, though he did not hold the position of the CCP general secretary from 1981 to 1987 or any party or state portfolio between 1987 and 1989. Deng's command of the military was based largely on his revolutionary and military credentials, as well as his status and prestige as one of the founders of the People's Republic of China and the PLA. Moreover, Deng appointed to key CMC positions close allies, like Yang Shangkun (CMC vice chair from 1981 to 1992 and CMC secretary general from 1981 to 1989) and such pre-1949 Second Field Army (where Deng served as political commissar) comrades as Qin Jiwei (CMC member and defense minister from 1987 to 1992), Liu Huaqing (CMC deputy secretary general 1987–89 and CMC vice chair 1989–97), and Yang Baibin (CMC member 1987–89 and CMC secretary general 1989–92). These personal factors prompted Deng to employ the PLA covertly against political opponents within the party, such as Hu Yaobang and Zhao Ziyang, and explicitly against threats from society such as the popular rebellion in Beijing in the summer of 1989. The

PLA's intervention in 1989 led some scholars to argue that the emphasis of China's civil-military relations had shifted from military tasks to politics.[4] Based on similar logic, the conventional wisdom suggests that Jiang Zemin, as the CMC chair 1989–2004, employed the PLA largely for factional struggle against political opponents within the CCP leadership, particularly in times of power transition.[5]

Useful Concepts

The mobilization of armed forces against domestic political opposition or inserting them into domestic politics constitutes what Samuel Huntington calls "subjective control," which aims to enhance civilian power by a "divide and rule" strategy of "politicizing" the military. It is also intended to preempt such major military interventions as coups. Subjective control is based on the premise that undesirable military intervention in politics is caused not by weak or failed civilian governance but rather by excessive institutional autonomy and professionalism of the military, fostering managerial ability, an ethos of public service, and internal cohesiveness and inculcating with the "military mind" skepticism regarding politicians.[6]

"Objective control," in contrast, intends to enhance the institutional autonomy and professionalism of the military. It is based on the premise that coups and the like are in fact caused by weak or failed civilian governance or by the inability of civilian authorities to resolve major socioeconomic, political, or foreign-policy crises. It is not a product of military professionalism, because the military is mainly a conservative organization that prefers narrow functional and technical expertise to the broad and complex area of politics.[7] In that view, the best strategy to preempt undesirable military intervention in politics is to enhance civilian governance, not to "politicize" the military.

Central Argument

This study argues that rather than employing the PLA against political opponents from within the CCP and Chinese society as suggested by the conventional wisdom, post-Deng leaders—Jiang and Hu—have prevented the PLA from intervening in intra-CCP and intra-societal political struggle, by changing the dominant paradigm of Chinese civil-military relations from subjective control to "objective control with Chinese characteristics." Such a change, in turn, has major implications for Chinese crisis management and naval modernization.

To flesh out the central argument, this study makes four specific subarguments. First, Jiang's policies with regard to the PLA were similar to what Huntington calls "objective control"—that is, tending on the civilian side to enhance civilian governance, or the CCP's legitimacy to rule, and on the military side promoting functional and technical expertise, or professionalization of the PLA. Both policies helped to maintain civil-military boundaries and contributed to the PLA's internal cohesion. While there is an element of subjective control in employing the PLA for power transition and consolidation, mobilizing it into factional rivalries among the CCP central leadership and in Chinese society, which would have eroded civil-military boundaries and fractured the military's cohesion, was clearly not the primary purpose of Jiang's approach to managing the Chinese armed forces.

Second, Hu Jintao's policies regarding the PLA, since he succeeded Jiang as the CMC chair in 2004, have represented not only continuity with Jiang's policies but also a significant step in the trend toward objective control, mainly in terms of externalizing the PLA.[8] That is, Hu has required the military to fulfill *externally oriented* missions that were absent under Jiang: to secure China's newly emerging interests in outer, maritime, and electromagnetic space, and to contribute to world peace by participating in peace-keeping and humanitarian assistance.

Third, while clearer institutional boundaries may have contributed significantly to the cohesion and professionalization of the PLA, increased civil-military bifurcation has also led to pronounced tensions in interagency coordination for crisis management. Such tensions were more or less evident in such foreign policy crises or events as the EP-3 incident in 2001, China's antisatellite (ASAT) test in early 2007, the intrusion of a Chinese submarine into Japanese territorial waters while submerged, China's refusal to allow the U.S. aircraft carrier *Kitty Hawk* to visit Hong Kong in late 2007, and the USNS *Impeccable* incident in 2009. They became particularly acute, however, in a domestic crisis of 2009, the Sichuan earthquake. That situation was further exacerbated by a lack of appropriate PLA force structure, equipment, and training for nonwar military operations. Remedies have been introduced to correct these deficiencies, but major issues remain unresolved.

Finally, the PLA Navy is probably the biggest institutional beneficiary of the shift toward objective control and "externalization," partly because it is one of the most technology-intensive services, and partly because of the specific environment in which it operates and the functions it is supposed to fulfill. The promotion of the PLAN by the central civilian leadership and the PLAN's skillful leveraging of that promotion are also likely to contribute to its increased importance in China's military modernization.

Organization

This study has six sections, of which the first is the present introduction. The second and third sections address Jiang's and Hu's policies with regard to the PLA. The fourth discusses civil-military tensions in interagency coordination in crisis management stemming from increasing civil-military bifurcation, as well as the prospects for remedies. The fifth section examines the naval implications of objective control and externalization. The concluding section summarizes the findings and discusses the analytical implications.

Jiang and the PLA

Analysts agree that though he had no service experience and few close connections in the PLA, Jiang was quite successful in consolidating his power, by exploiting his position as the CMC chair. The CMC chair has the final say regarding all major military decisions, including appointing senior officers, allocating the budget, deploying troops, and controlling the employment of nuclear weapons. Jiang was able to win support from PLA senior officers mainly because he was able to employ his formal position to promote many of them to higher ranks and to increase the defense budget, which translated into higher salaries and better living conditions for the military. Jiang was also quite adept in cultivating and maintaining good relations with all the informal groupings within the PLA leadership, as well as with lower levels, by showing respect for PLA elders, listening to officers' concerns on major issues, honoring PLA heroes and traditions, and conducting regular inspection tours of basic-level PLA units.[9]

Photo 3. *Jiang visits with PLAN sailors and officers on 23 December 2000.*

Why Power Consolidation?

Some argue that the primary purpose of Jiang's power consolidation in the PLA was to employ the military against political threats and opponents from within the CCP

Table 1. *Central Military Commission of the Fifteenth CCP Congress (1997–2002)*

Name	Position	Date of Birth	Provincial Origin	Education	Unit Origin	Military Expertise/ Combat Experience
Jiang Zemin	Chair	1926	Jiangsu	Shanghai Jiaotong University	None	None
Hu Jintao	First vice chair since 1999	1942	Anhui	Qinghua University	None	None
Zhang Wannian	Vice chair	1928	Shandong	Nanjing Military College	41st Army, Guangzhou Military Region (MR)	Command and staff, infantry/Civil War
Chi Haotian	Vice chair	1929	Shandong	PLA General Advanced Infantry School	27th Army, Beijing MR	Command and staff, infantry/Civil War and Korean War
Fu Quanyou	Chief of General Staff Department (GSD)	1930	Shanxi	Nanjing Military College	1st Army, Wuhan MR	Command and staff, infantry/Civil War and Korean War
Yu Yongbo	Director of General Political Department (GPD)	1931	Liaoning	PLA Fourth Political Cadre School	42nd Army, Guangzhou MR	Political work/Civil War and Korean War
Wang Ke	Director of General Logistics Department (GLD)	1931	Anhui	PLA Military College	21st Army, Lanzhou MR	Command and staff, infantry/Civil War and Korean War
Cao Gangchuan	Director of General Armament Department (GAD)	1935	Henan	Artillery Engineering School, Soviet Union	General departments	Military engineering and administration
Wang Ruilin	Deputy GPD director	1930	Shandong	High school	Confidential staff, Fourth Field Army	Confidential work
Guo Boxiong	Deputy chief of GSD and member since 1999	1942	Shaanxi	PLA Military College, Beijing	19th Army, Lanzhou MR	Command and staff, infantry
Xu Caihou	Deputy GPD director and member since 1999	1943	Liaoning	Harbin Military Engineering Institute	Jilin Military District, Shenyang MR	Political work

leadership and from Chinese society, lessons learned from the power struggles under Mao and from the military suppression of the popular rebellion in Tian'anmen of 1989. Such an argument, however, produces an analytical puzzle. During Jiang's fifteen years as the CMC chair (1989–2004), the PLA was in fact not employed to suppress domestic social unrest, the major type of threat from society.[10] Regarding political threats and opponents from within the CCP leadership, evidence of PLA intervention in intraparty factionalism struggles at Jiang's invitation is sketchy. The only evidence produced so far is the alleged collective support by senior officers of Jiang's retention of the CMC chair position at the Sixteenth CCP Congress of November 2002. In this instance, Hu Jintao, who succeeded Jiang as the CCP general secretary, was assumed to be a potential political threat and opponent to Jiang.[11] Some also suggest power struggles between Jiang and Hu over the role of the PLA in the SARS crisis and with respect to a submarine accident that occurred in 2003.[12] Jiang's promotion of a few senior officers, including his chief bodyguard You Xigui, to the rank of general in June 2004 was also interpreted as preparation for a power struggle against Hu.[13]

Though plausible, such evidence is inconclusive. The alleged collective petition by senior officers for Jiang to stay as the CMC chair is highly unlikely, for several reasons. Most of the uniformed CMC members—Zhang Wannian, Chi Haotian, Fu Quanyou, Yu Yongbo, Wang Ke, and Wang Ruilin, for instance—were to retire at the Sixteenth Congress. They had no special incentive to sponsor a petition to keep Jiang as the CMC chair or to encourage their subordinates to do so. New uniformed members, such as Liang Guanglie, Liao Xilong, and Li Ji'nai, were too new to sponsor such a petition.[14] Also, military and CCP discipline forbid senior officers (who are also party members) from organizing such a "collective action"; it is doubtful that anyone would want to risk his career to engage in politically incorrect behavior. Complaints from senior officers about the "two power centers" have been reported.[15] This contradicts the assertion that senior officers preferred Jiang to stay on as CMC chair while Hu took over as the CCP general secretary.

It was actually Hu who proposed to the CCP Politburo that Jiang stay on, to help him make a successful transition.[16] It is likely that Hu, as the first CMC vice chair since 1999, consulted the remaining military professionals in the CMC (such as Cao Gangchuan, Guo Boxiong, and Xu Caihou) and gained their support before he made the proposal. Jiang stayed on also to push for what he calls "new military revolution" (新军事革命), or a revolution in military affairs (RMA)–based transformation of the PLA, against the vested interests.[17] Not yet equipped with the political capital that Jiang enjoyed with the PLA, Hu would have found this agenda more difficult to accomplish had he become the CMC chair in 2002. This suggests Jiang actually stayed on for two more years to help Hu, not compete against him.

Table 2. *Central Military Commission of the Sixteenth CCP Congress (2002–September 2004)*

Name	Position	Date of Birth	Provincial Origin	Education	Unit Origin	Military Expertise/ Combat Experience
Jiang Zemin (see table 1 for information)	Chair					
Hu Jintao (see table 1 for information)	First vice chair					
Guo Boxiong (see table 1 for information)	Vice chair					
Cao Gangchuan (see table 1 for information)	Vice chair					
Liang Guanglie	GSD chief	1940	Sichuan	PLA Military College, Beijing	1st Army, Wuhan MR	Command and staff, infantry/War with Vietnam (1979–89)
Xu Caihou (see table 1 for information)	GPD director					
Liao Xilong	GLD director	1940	Guizhou	PLA Military College, Beijing	11th Army, Kunming MR	Command and staff, infantry/War with Vietnam
Li Ji'nai	GAD director	1942	Shandong	Harbin Polytechnic University	Base 52 (Anhui), Second Artillery	Political work

There were other institutional limits on the extent of Jiang's power consolidation in the PLA and on his use of this power. It is usually argued that Jiang won personal loyalty by appointing a large number of senior officers. But these appointments can be attributed to reasons other than Jiang's intention to consolidate power. *PLA Officers' Service Regulations* requires authorization by the CMC chair for the appointment of officers at and above the divisional command, or senior colonel, level. As a result, Jiang would inevitably have been responsible for a large number of such appointments; he served as the CMC chair for fifteen years, the PLA is a large bureaucracy with many senior positions to be filled in so long a period, and higher personnel turnover has resulted from new term and age limits. Also, the candidates for these appointments were recommended by the military professionals in the CMC, not picked by Jiang.[18] He interviewed some of the senior candidates, but his knowledge of them was limited by the little time they spent together. As a result, personal ties were not especially strong. Officers would fulfill military tasks on Jiang's orders; however, without Deng's credentials, Jiang might have been unsure that they would follow an order from him to shoot unarmed civilians in another crisis on the scale of Tian'anmen.

From the officers' perspective, Jiang was to be supported and obeyed because he was the commander in chief. But when Hu became the CMC chair in September 2004, their support and obedience shifted to Hu, as shown by the behavior of Cao Gangchuan, Guo Boxiong, and Xu Caihou.[19] Guo and Xu are alleged Jiang "loyalists" but have not been replaced by a new entourage of Hu "loyalists"; to that extent, retention, removal, and new appointments of senior PLA officers are apparently more regularized by institutional and professional criteria (such as term and age limits and performance) than by the personal connections with and loyalty to individual party leaders. Finally, because rank affects remuneration and privileges after retirement, sometimes a decision by the commander in chief to promote officers to higher rank simply expresses appreciation of their services, by offering better material conditions for retirement. This can particularly explain such June 2004 appointments as You Xigui. Also, that announcement was made jointly by Jiang and Hu. This indicates that the transfer of power would take place soon, but not that there would be a power struggle between Jiang and Hu.

Photo 4. *Jiang and Hu speak to PLA delegates attending the second annual meeting of the 10th National People's Congress on 11 March 2004.*

Defense budget increases also cannot be explained by power consolidation alone. The 1991 Gulf War showed how large the technological gap had become between the most advanced militaries and the PLA, a gap that could be narrowed only by budget increases. The 1996 Taiwan Strait crisis and the possibility of U.S. intervention added a degree of urgency to the need to upgrade PLA capabilities, which would cost money. The post-1998 divestiture of the PLA from business activities led to a shortfall in income that had to be offset by budget increases. In late 2002, the CMC endorsed a shift in emphasis of military modernization from mechanization to RMA-based informatization. This made digitized operational platforms the top priorities for acquisition. Because these items are technology-intensive, they are also capital-intensive and therefore require more financial investment. In the meantime, the Chinese economy had been growing rapidly since the early 1990s, which made it easier to argue for more spending on national defense. All these points were articulated and socialized by China's military planners in lobbying civilian leaders for defense budget increases. The resulting budget growth has continued since the retirement of Jiang from the CMC in 2004, suggesting that the policy has broader roots than would a crude ploy by Jiang to win support from military leaders.

Objective Control: The Civilian Side

If power struggle is not the primary purpose of power consolidation in the PLA, what is? Jiang's power consolidation aimed at implementing two types of policies. The first was to enhance party-state governance, or the legitimacy of CCP rule, by promoting economic growth and social stability. This would reduce the need to mobilize the PLA into domestic politics. The second was to confine the PLA to narrow military-technical tasks. Both approaches helped to maintain civil-military boundaries and enhance the cohesion of the PLA. In his writings, Jiang particularly stressed the importance of the functional specialization–based division of labor as society developed.[20] This was also a major lesson from the 1989 Tian'anmen incident and the collapse of communism in the Soviet Union and Eastern Europe between 1989 and 1991.

The CCP's dependence on military force in Tian'anmen for its survival, for instance, indicated the failure of the party-state to resolve major socioeconomic crises and implied its inability to manage social protests other than by such lethal means as tanks and submachine guns. This had contributed to a decline of the CCP's legitimacy to rule. Also, there are indications that the PLA was reluctant to get involved in the suppression of the rebellion, mainly because its image would be damaged.[21] Even for Deng, the task of persuading the PLA to intervene may have been far from easy, and it is likely that he had to exhaust much of his political capital to accomplish it. As we have noted, new leaders like Jiang do not possess the revolutionary and military credentials that Deng did, so they are not confident that the military would take their side in another such crisis. In the popular revolts that ended communist rule in the Soviet Union and Eastern Europe, rather than taking the party's side, the military mostly defied its orders.[22] This means the party's reliance on military force for its survival may not necessarily guarantee success but may quicken the demise of party rule instead.

These concerns explain why, at the Fourteenth CCP Congress of 1992, Jiang replaced the post-1989 policy of military control and ideological indoctrination with a new policy of economic growth, a policy also associated with Deng's southern tour in early 1992.[23] It was intended to enhance the legitimacy of CCP rule by increasing income, improving living standards, and providing employment opportunities for the millions of people joining the labor force every year. It also helped to generate revenue needed for preventing and preempting crises. Strategies have been developed to manage social protests stemming from the downsides of rapid economic growth, such as massive urban unemployment due to reform of state-owned enterprises, overtaxation of the peasants, rampant corruption, wealth polarization, and environmental degradation. These strategies range from soft approaches (such as meeting the demands of the protesters and improving institutions for monitoring, expressing, and resolving grievances before they escalate) to hard ones (arresting politically conscious organizers and isolating and containing protests to prevent them from evolving into larger, better organized movements that challenge the CCP). Similarly, the People's Armed Police (PAP), which is primarily responsible for maintaining domestic social stability, has been substantially strengthened, and riot-control units with nonlethal weapons like tear gas and rubber bullets have been developed and deployed.[24] All these have reduced the need to mobilize the PLA against domestic political opposition.

Objective Control: The Military Side

On the military side, Jiang aimed to confine the PLA to military-technical tasks. For instance, he endorsed in 1993 the new PLA strategic principle of preparing for local war under high-tech conditions, in 1995 operationalizing the principle into a policy to transform the PLA from a manpower-intensive force to a technology-based one. He introduced the concept of "leapfrogging development" (跨越式发展) in 1997, shifting, as noted above, the emphasis of military modernization from mechanization (that is, adding new hardware platforms) to informatization (developing information technologies–based network and software) to narrow the technological gap with the more advanced militaries of the world. This led to the CMC's endorsement of a policy of "dual construction" (双化建设), referring to mechanization and informatization, in late 2002.[25] These technology-centric policies led to decisions to downsize the PLA by five hundred thousand billets in 1997 and another two hundred thousand in 2002.

Because bureaucracies and the ground force, or the elements most likely to become involved in domestic politics, suffered the most from the cuts, these decisions erected more technological barriers between the PLA and domestic politics. It is, for instance, more difficult to employ in situations of domestic turbulence such technology-intensive services as the PLAN, the PLAAF, and Second Artillery. The cuts, however, were unpopular in the PLA, because they eliminated numerous billets, particularly in sectors that believed in manpower-based people's war and mechanized warfare. Jiang was able to make these decisions after 1997 mainly because he felt his power was more secure than it had been, as support from the top PLA leadership had become more solid with the death of Deng and the retirement of "old guards" like Liu Huaqing and Zhang Zhen from the CMC in 1997. By removing major bureaucratic obstacles, these decisions made it easier for Hu, in his turn, to consolidate power in the PLA when he assumed power. This shows that the relationship between Jiang and Hu was actually more cooperative than competitive.

Another major decision endorsed by Jiang and supervised by Hu for implementation after 1997 was to divest the PLA from its business activities, in 1998. This policy significantly reduced the domestic role of the PLA, so that it could focus on its military-technical tasks. Jiang has written that from the day he became the CMC chair, he wanted to get the PLA out of commercial business.[26] He was unable at first to do so, apparently because it had been more or less Deng's decision to allow the PLA to go into business;[27] many children of the PLA elders were involved, and military units were poorly funded otherwise. But after 1997 Jiang felt sufficiently secure to introduce this policy without fear of displeasing Deng and the PLA elders; also, the PLA's business had grown to the extent that it began to negatively affect the normal functioning of the national economy, and Zhu Rongji, the then premier, was particularly concerned. Furthermore, rapid economic growth had made it possible to allocate more funding to the PLA. Moreover, the policy presented itself as a good political strategy to control the PLA through control of the purse, by cutting off its extrabudgetary income. The policy would also help to reduce bickering over distribution of funds and the incidence of corruption cases among officers, thus enhancing the internal cohesion of the PLA. Finally, the policy resolved a thorny issue that may have complicated Hu's journey to power. This is clearly another example of cooperation between Jiang and Hu to develop military policy.

Hu and the PLA

Like Jiang, Hu took over, in 2002, the position of CCP general secretary with weak military credentials, having no service experience and few close connections in the PLA. Hu, however, had been the first CMC vice chair since 1999 and therefore had developed good relations with Jiang and the military professionals in the commission. His strategy initially was to employ Jiang to help him to deal with the PLA. In a "grand bargain," he invited Jiang to continue as CMC chair after shedding his other party-state positions. Hu needed more experience in running the state and the economy and therefore wanted Jiang to preside over military affairs and foreign policy, where Jiang had more experience.[28] Deng had set a precedent of serving as CMC chair without other party or state portfolios for two years, beginning in 1987.

The strategy also represented a goodwill gesture to Jiang, who seemed eager to show that he was just as competent a commander in chief as his predecessors, if not more so. Partly to return the favor, Jiang endorsed the RMA-based transformation, leading to the elimination of a large number of senior billets. This benefited Hu, because it made it easier for him to consolidate power in the PLA in the near future. Jiang stayed rather low-key and refrained from interfering in Hu's running of state affairs. By 2003, Jiang had handed over the foreign-affairs and Taiwan-affairs leadership positions to Hu. Hu had also begun to preside over major CMC decisions. At a CCP plenum in September 2004, Jiang volunteered to resign from the CMC chair, and Hu took over. More or less as a reciprocal gesture, Hu codified Jiang's theory of "three represents" (the party as representing the most advanced productive forces, culture, and the interests of the broadest masses) into the state constitution and published the *Selected Works of Jiang Zemin* for all CCP members to study.

Partly because Jiang held the CMC chair until 2004, and partly because the PLA had become more professional under Jiang and therefore less politically inclined, Hu did not focus particularly on consolidating his position in the PLA after 2002 by cultivating personalized relations with senior officers or making personnel changes. Instead, Hu's policies have largely centered on objective control—that is, enhancing civilian governance, thus the CCP's legitimacy to rule, and endorsing programs that confine the PLA to its military-technical and external tasks. Both have helped him consolidate power in the PLA.

Objective Control: The Civilian Side

On the civilian side, Hu has attempted to reverse the excesses of single-minded economic growth, such as the widening of the income gap (which has led to serious social tension), lack of social security for large numbers of marginalized groups, official graft, and environmental damage. Hu believes that these issues cannot be resolved by more economic growth or riot-control techniques alone but rather require dedicated social policies. Otherwise, they could render economic growth unsustainable, thus undermining the CCP's legitimacy to rule, possibly triggering socioeconomic and political crises and military intervention. Hu has worked closely with the premier, Wen Jiabao, to divert investment from the rich coastal regions to the less developed heartland and the west, reduce tax burdens on farmers, remove restrictive regulations on migrant workers, develop basic social and medical safety nets for the poor and unemployed, fight corruption on a more substantial scale, and require "green" gross-domestic-product growth as a criterion for the career advancement of local officials.

It is still too early to determine the success of these policies, because vested interests at both the central and local levels have been recalcitrant, and some measures cannot succeed without genuine political reform. The 2008 financial crisis has also cast a shadow, by making job creation the top priority. But Hu and Wen's policies have proved immensely popular among the ordinary people in China, and contributed to the image of the CCP leadership as having a heart and a human touch. The perception of fair and competent governance has clearly enhanced the CCP's legitimacy. This has helped to consolidate Hu's control over the PLA as well, because it has enhanced Hu's popularity among PLA officers and in the ranks.[29] Also the image of competent civilian governance reduces the preconditions needed for PLA intervention in politics.

As to maintaining social stability, Hu has continued Jiang's policy of minimizing the use of force. To deal with the numerous "mass incidents" (群体事件) concerning land and property compensation and environmental grievances, officials at various levels are required to increase transparency, conduct "face to face" explanation, employ persuasion, avoid "politicization" of reasonable economic and livelihood-related demands but meet them, and refrain from employing public security and PAP forces, which tend to escalate tension. Officials are also required, after resolution of incidents, to draw lessons from them, penalize accountable individuals, and formulate new "rectification plans."[30] To implement this policy, about 2,800 party secretaries and two thousand secretaries of party disciplinary inspection commissions, all at the county level, were brought to Beijing's Central Party School, the State Administration College, and the CCP Central Disciplinary Inspection Commission (CDIC) training center for instruction in investigating graft and abuse of power by basic-level (township and village) officials—offenses that are major triggers of mass incidents. Similarly, 3,080 public security bureau directors and 3,500 prosecutors, also from the county level, traveled to Beijing for training in how to prevent and control, and not escalate, mass incidents and how to "harmonize police-people relations."[31] Moreover, the CCP Central Committee and the State Council have recently issued regulations on penalizing and removing officials for major cases of misconduct, including mismanagement practices that trigger mass incidents.[32] Similarly, the CCP CDIC has recently issued regulations on inspection and supervision at the county level, aimed at bureaucratic misconduct.[33] Furthermore, domestic surveillance apparatuses, such as the First Bureau (domestic security) of the Ministry of Public Security and the Ministry of State Security, have been strengthened to preempt mass incidents.[34] Millions of surveillance cameras are also planned for China's rural communities.[35] Similarly, the PAP has continuously been reinforced to deal with domestic security threats. As the PLA continues to downsize, more infantry divisions are likely to be converted into PAP quick-reaction units.[36] All these measures have reduced the need to employ the military against domestic political threats and opposition.

A caveat to the PLA's relative detachment from handling domestic security threats concerns its involvement in suppressing the unrest in Tibet in March 2008. It is important, however, to note that the military units involved were relatively few and small in size and that their involvements were brief. Also, these units deliberately stayed in the background so that the PAP units could take the lead, mainly providing protected transportation to the PAP personnel with their armored personnel carriers. Also, the denial of Chinese government spokesmen of the presence of military personnel in Lhasa and the effort made to conceal the license plates of military vehicles at the site showed that the regime is concerned about the negative image of employing the PLA against domestic political opposition.[37] Moreover, in the eyes of many both in and outside China, the unsettled issues concerning Tibet have both domestic and external, not purely domestic, origins, particularly as compared with hinterland provinces. Finally, in the most recent riot, in Ürümqi of Xinjiang Uighur Autonomous Region, on 5 July 2009, PAP reinforcement was transported or airlifted by civilian airlines from provinces of Gansu, Jiangsu, Henan, and Fujian to Ürümqi to "maintain stability" (维稳). No evidence, however, shows that any PLA active-service unit was directly employed.[38]

These policies could not have been possible without a high level of consensus, based on power consolidation, among the CCP leadership. This consolidation and consensus are possible mainly because without a strongman like Deng, institutional positions become especially important, and Hu, holding the positions of CCP general secretary and state president, is "the first among equals." Hu is also assisted by Wen, who heads the State Council, the most influential institution dealing with nonmilitary affairs in China. Jiang, though he still held the CMC chair position for a time, was not comparable to Deng in credentials, status, or prestige; therefore, the position confined him narrowly to military affairs. Also, Hu's policies are articulated as a further development of Jiang's policy of economic growth, not as an affront to Jiang's legacy. Both Jiang and Hu want economic growth to sustain the CCP's legitimacy to rule. But Hu wants to add a "human face" to the growth so that it can be more balanced and better sustained. These policies are also popular. Both made it more difficult for Jiang to mobilize his Shanghai colleagues in the Politburo Standing Committee against these policies.

Also, Zeng Qinghong, an alleged loyalist of Jiang from Shanghai, jumped on Hu's bandwagon, because Hu holds formal leadership positions, is popular, and thus represents the future.[39] Jiang's other allies, like Wu Bangguo and Jia Qinglin, are of mediocre political acumen and not likely to challenge Hu, and the institutions they head, the National People's Congress and the National People's Political Consultative Conference, are not highly influential over policies. Jiang's inability to salvage his Shanghai colleagues, such as Chen Liangyu, in the countergraft investigations reduced even more the credibility of a coherent and robust "Shanghai faction" assisting Jiang in his power struggle against Hu. Most important, Hu's success in power consolidation within the CCP leadership has made a significant impact on the PLA's perception of him. It is likely that most PLA senior officers see Hu as a prudent and competent leader, and this should contribute to Hu's power consolidation to control the PLA.

Objective Control: The Military Side

On the military side, Hu has continued Jiang's program of RMA-based transformation of the PLA. In May 2003, he presided over a Politburo study session where researchers from the Academy of Military Science (AMS) lectured the members on world trends in RMA and priorities for China's military modernization.[40] Hu met with Chinese astronauts and watched the whole processes of launching three manned spacecraft, in October 2003, October 2005, and September 2008, respectively. He has initiated a campaign to study RMA-related subjects in the PLA and has supported personnel reform to appoint officers who understand the RMA to higher ranks and key positions. For instance, Li Ji'nai and Chen Bingde, who ran the *Shenzhou V* and *Shenzhou VI* programs, respectively, now hold the positions of the director of the PLA's General Political Department and chief of the PLA's General Staff Department.[41] Hu has stressed regular military training and exercises, rules and regulations, and effective management as major ways to regulate behavior.[42] All these clearly aim to confine the PLA to its functional and technical expertise—a good political strategy to enhance the objective, or institutional, control of the PLA.

More important, however, at a CMC expanded conference in late 2004 Hu introduced a new military policy that defined the four missions of the PLA: to "serve as an important source of strength for consolidating the party's governing position" (为党巩固执政地位提供重要的力量保证); to "provide a strong security guarantee for the important period of strategic opportunity for national development" (为维护国家发展的重要战略机遇期提供坚强的安全保障); to "serve as a forceful strategic support for safeguarding national interests" (为维护国家利益提供有力的战略支撑); and to "play an important role in upholding world peace and promoting common development" (为维护世界和平与促进共同发展发挥重要作用).[43]

The first mission may contradict somewhat objective control, or alternatively it may reflect the "Chinese characteristics" aspect of objective control. But it is the politically correct thing to say for any new CCP leader, and it really refers to the "party's absolute leadership of the army" (党对军队的绝对领导), enshrining civilian control. Party leadership of the PLA, however, may be largely nominal, mainly because the political commissar system, the ostensible tool by which the party controls the PLA, is an integral component of the military command structure, not external to it. As a result, the true incentive for political commissars is to perform well within this structure so that they can advance their careers. They are therefore unlikely to investigate deviations and report on military commanders to outside party authorities. A critical test of the political orientation of the political commissars is a crisis, such as Tian'anmen in 1989. If political commissars are more loyal to the party than to the PLA, then one should find that the majority of political commissars followed the order of the party leaders to suppress the students but that the majority of commanders refused to do so. Instead, there were significant numbers of political commissars and commanders on both sides of the issue. As argued in the introduction of this study, the central reasons for the PLA following the party order in 1989 was not enforcement of political commissars but Deng's prestige-based political capital and his loyalists' control of the CMC.

Also, the post-Mao objectives of the party and the PLA are consistent: to promote national economic and technological development and national defense modernization. This is very different from Mao's time, when pursuit of military expertise was criticized as practicing a "bourgeois military line" that undermined the chairman's "proletarian revolutionary line," leading to a continuous witch hunt for class enemies in the PLA and causing severe political divisions there. Finally, the new *PLA Political Work Regulations,* issued in late 2003, contained important revisions. One is that political officers are to "uphold the legal rights and interests of the military and military personnel" (维护军队和军人的合法权益). They are also to "give full play to the operational function of political work" (发挥政治工作作战功能), characterized mainly in terms of information operations, such as "opinion warfare," "psychological warfare," and "law warfare."[44] These revisions were clearly aimed to integrate political officers into the PLA by redefining their objectives and functional expertise in ways more in line with those of the PLA. All these indicators show that the best way for the PLA to help in consolidating the CCP's governing position is not to intervene in civilian governance but to develop and perfect its own functional and technical expertise.

The other three missions are more in line with objective control. The second, for instance, refers to continued military modernization to enhance the credibility of deterrence against threats, such as formal Taiwan independence. Strategic stability ensures a peaceful external environment for economic development at a time when China can benefit from the U.S. concentration on countering terrorism, from globalization, and also from the integration of China into the global economy.[45]

The third and fourth missions were not only absent under Jiang Zemin but unprecedented in PLA history. The third calls on the PLA to secure China's newly emerging interests in outer, maritime, and electromagnetic space in addition to its traditional security interests, such as its sovereign territories, airspace, and waters.[46] The fourth is for the PLA to participate in United Nations peacekeeping operations and international humanitarian assistance. What is remarkable is that these new missions are externally oriented. Externalization of the PLA is clearly a good political strategy for Hu, if he is to control the PLA. This is because, as the end of the Cold War showed, a declining focus of the military on external threats tends to make civil-military relations more difficult to manage.[47]

Power Consolidation

In June 2006, Hu promoted ten senior officers to three-star general and many more to lower ranks. By July, PLA officers had received a 100 percent increase in their salaries, and better-quality uniforms had been issued. As early as since 1999, Hu has regularly received briefings on major military policy issues and attended CMC meetings. He has also paid many visits to basic-level units, attended and delivered speeches at party congresses of major PLA institutions, and maintained good relations with senior officers. While these can be interpreted as efforts to consolidate power in the PLA, as discussed earlier, there are strict limits on how far the new generations of CCP leaders can go to do so and how they can use such power. In comparison with Deng's and Jiang's years, the promotion rate of senior officers under Hu to the rank of general is not high.[48] CMC membership at the Seventeenth CCP Congress in the fall of 2007 involved only minor changes (compare tables 3 and 4). Cao Gangchuan was retired because he was seventy-two, exceeding the normative retirement age of sixty-eight for CMC members. Wu Shengli and Xu Qiliang, who succeeded the deceased Zhang Dingfa and the sixty-eight-year-old Qiao Qingchen as the new PLAN and PLAAF commanders, became new members because the navy and air force commanders have been CMC members since 2004.

Jiang was lenient on disciplinary issues in his early years as the CMC chair, for fear of offending Deng and the PLA elders, but Hu has been bolder. Wang Shouye, a deputy navy commander, was dismissed from his office and court-martialed in early 2006 for taking bribes of millions of dollars and keeping mistresses. Also in 2006, the CMC appointed a small leading group to audit the financial conditions of a thousand senior officers.[49] Similarly, in June 2006 disciplinary actions were taken against four senior and seven lower-ranking air force officers as the result of a crash of an airborne warning and control plane that killed forty people in Anhui. The penalties ranged from recording demerits, serious warnings, and demotions to dismissal from office.[50]

There are several reasons why Hu has felt secure enough to enforce discipline against senior officers soon after becoming the CMC chair. Because Jiang's credentials, status, and prestige are not comparable to those of Deng and PLA elders, his influence over Hu is much less than Deng's and PLA elders' influence over Jiang. Also, Hu has accumulated some political capital in the PLA, having been in the CMC since 1999. His objective-control measures have also contributed to the accumulation of this capital. Finally, the professionalizing trend within the PLA has had a dampening effect on the political aspiration of senior officers. Because these disciplinary measures were driven by specific issues, it may be inappropriate to treat them as stratagems meant to politicize and divide the officer corps in a power struggle against political opponents. In any case, Hu's no-nonsense style enhanced his authority as the new commander in chief of the PLA.

Table 3. *Central Military Commission of the Sixteenth CCP Congress (September 2004–2007)*

Name	Position	Date of Birth	Provincial Origin	Education	Unit Origin	Military Expertise/ Combat Experience
Hu Jintao (see table 1 for information)	Chair					
Guo Boxiong (see table 1 for information)	Vice chair					
Cao Gangchuan (see table 1 for information)	Vice chair and defense minister					
Xu Caihou (see table 1 for information)	Vice chair					
Liang Guanglie (see table 2 for information)	GSD chief					
Li Ji'nai (see table 2 for information)	GPD director					
Liao Xilong (see table 2 for information)	GLD director					
Chen Bingde	GAD director	1941	Jiangsu	PLA Military College, Beijing	60th Army, Nanjing MR	Command and staff, infantry
Zhang Dingfa	Navy commander	1943	Shanghai	Qingdao Naval Submarine Academy	North Sea Fleet	Command and staff, submarine force
Qiao Qingchen	Air Force commander	1939	Henan	PLAAF 6th Aviation School	4th Air Corps, Nanjing MR Air Force	Aviator, command and staff, Air Force
Jin Zhiyuan	Second Artillery commander	1944	Hubei	Wuwei Artillery School, Gansu Province	Base 56 (Qinghai), Second Artillery	Command and staff, strategic missile force

Table 4. *Central Military Commission of the Seventeenth CCP Congress (2007)*

Name	Position	Date of Birth	Provincial Origin	Education	Unit Origin	Military Expertise/ Combat Experience
Hu Jintao (see table 1 for information)	Chair					
Guo Boxiong (see table 1 for information)	Vice chair					
Xu Caihou (see table 1 for information)	Vice chair					
Liang Guanglie (see table 2 for information)	Defense minister					
Chen Bingde (see table 3 for information)	GSD chief					
Li Ji'nai (see table 2 for information)	GPD director					
Liao Xilong (see table 2 for information)	GLD director					
Chang Wanquan	GAD director	1949	Henan	Wei'nan Teachers College, Shaanxi Province	47th Army, Lanzhou MR	Command and staff, infantry
Wu Shengli	Navy commander	1945	Hebei	PLA Measuring and Mapping College	6th Destroyer Flotilla, East Sea Fleet	Sea measuring and mapping, command and staff, Navy
Xu Qiliang	Air Force commander	1950	Shandong	PLAAF 5th Aviation School	8th Air Corps, Nanjing MR Air Force	Aviator, command and staff, Air Force
Jin Zhiyuan (see table 3 for information)	Second Artillery commander					

Implications of Civil-Military Bifurcation for Crisis Management

While objective control, or allowing more institutional autonomy for military professionalization, may substantially benefit military modernization, it has also reinforced
civil-military bifurcation, which has produced the unintended consequence of difficulty
in interagency cooperation and coordination in the management of crises. The old
party-army symbiosis, based on personal relationships, may have been characterized by
political infighting among political-military factions, but in times of crisis, such as the
Korean War and the 1979 war with Vietnam, it enabled charismatic political-military
leaders like Mao and Deng to make quick decisions without much institutional hin-
drance. Since then, the institutionalization of civil-military boundaries that began under
Deng has made it increasingly difficult for the new generations of uncharismatic techno-
crats like Jiang and Hu to do so.[51]

Foreign-Policy Crisis Management

There have been several major cases where a lack of interagency coordination appears
to have incurred high costs, at least in terms of diplomacy and image, on China. In
April 2001 a patrolling Chinese jet interceptor collided with a U.S. EP-3 reconnaissance
aircraft seventy miles off the coast of Hainan Island, leading to the loss of the Chinese
aircraft, the death of its pilot, and the crash landing of the American aircraft on Hainan,
where the crew was detained. The crisis remained unresolved for about eleven days.[52]
One major reason for the delay seems to have been that the PLA took a much harder
line than China's Ministry of Foreign Affairs (MFA), insisting that the United States be
required to terminate its reconnaissance activities in China's exclusive economic zone
(EEZ) and compensate the Chinese losses. This hard line reportedly made it difficult for
Jiang Zemin to build quickly a civil-military consensus on resolving the issue—whereas
a quick resolution is presumably what Jiang desired, to maintain a good and stable U.S.-
Chinese relationship so he could focus on issues of economic development.

Similarly, in November 2004 a Chinese nuclear-powered attack submarine intruded,
while submerged, in Japanese territorial waters southwest of Okinawa for two hours. It
was about a week before the MFA acknowledged the incident, attributing the intrusion
to a technical error, and expressed regret.[53] This happened at a time when Hu was preparing to attend an Asia-Pacific Cooperation Forum summit in Chile, where he was to
meet with Japanese prime minister Junichiro Koizumi to find ways to improve strained
Sino-Japanese relations. The incident seems not only to have caught the MFA by surprise
but to have added difficulty to Hu's effort to improve Sino-Japanese relations. It was
even suggested that Hu, the new CMC chair, had not even been aware of the operation.

In January 2007, China launched a ground-based ballistic missile carrying a kinetic-kill
vehicle. It impacted and destroyed an aging Chinese weather satellite orbiting 537 miles

above the earth. The United States, Japan, Australia, and Britain asked Beijing for an explanation but met with prolonged silence. Only after twelve days did the MFA officially acknowledge the test. China's space program is largely managed by the PLA's General Armament Department; such a belated response suggests that the MFA may not have been informed of the test. Nonetheless, the test contradicted the image of China as a rising power committed to peaceful development that Hu wanted to project to the world. The test produced numerous pieces of debris that could interfere with space activities for years to come, and, more important, might have triggered an arms race in space.[54]

Just before the Thanksgiving holiday of 2007, the U.S. aircraft carrier *Kitty Hawk* and accompanying ships approached Hong Kong to make a long-planned port visit. Without warning, China suddenly denied them entry; the decision was reversed abruptly, again without explanation, but the ships were already on their way to Japan. This incident again seems to indicate a lack of coordination between the PLA and the MFA; apparently the soldiers wanted to turn the U.S. ships away while the diplomats tried unsuccessfully to neutralize the fallout. It also implies Chinese insensitivity, in thwarting the planned family reunion of American sailors. Moreover, this happened only weeks after a visit to China by Secretary of Defense Robert Gates, who had aimed to initiate a long-term dialogue. Again, the disruption seems to have made it more difficult to maintain a stable U.S.-Chinese relationship, which Hu is understood to have wanted badly.[55]

In early March 2009, five Chinese ships—two trawlers, two Fisheries Administration patrol vessels, and a naval intelligence ship—blocked and surrounded the U.S. ocean surveillance ship USNS *Impeccable* (T-AGOS 23) seventy-five miles south of Hainan. The trawlers attempted to snag the towing cable of *Impeccable*'s sonar array with a grappling hook. The incident led to the exchange of protests between the two governments. It happened only eight days after the two countries had agreed to restore a military-to-military dialogue; Secretary of State Hillary Clinton had just visited China, and China's foreign minister, Yang Jieshi, was just about to visit Washington, D.C.[56] Once more, the incident clearly made it more difficult to improve U.S.-Chinese relations as China's civilian leadership appears to have desired.

In these incidents a lack of civil-military interagency coordination may have been the cause of diplomatic and image costs to China, but several caveats are in order. First, other related but different factors may have caused delay. The indecision about the EP-3 incident, for instance, may be attributable in part to Jiang's absence at the time on a state visit to Latin American countries, to frustration stemming from the PLA's failure to recover the lost pilot, or to the absence of a more forthcoming American apology. Moreover, China's civilian leader might sometimes prefer the more hawkish positions of the military, to enhance his bargaining leverage with foreign counterparts in negotiating a resolution. In the case of the EP-3 incident, this bargaining power was further enhanced by the fact that China held the crew, which made it difficult for the United States to retaliate. While China might have paid a high cost if it had indefinitely delayed resolution of the crisis, China's civilian leader had no incentive to resolve it too quickly, on U.S. terms.

In addition, China's civilian leader may calculate that the benefits of building domestic consensus outweigh the diplomatic and image penalties of not reacting quickly. This is particularly the case if these costs are symbolic and difficult to measure or if the chance of escalation to a real military conflict is low (either because the other side may be uncertain about the effects of escalation or because China could retaliate effectively). Collective decision making and consensus building, for instance, have become the new norms with the end of the era of charismatic leaders. One of the often-cited benefits of these norms is that they can minimize the chance of such arbitrary and costly decisions as another costly war or another Cultural Revolution, particularly under a condition of high uncertainty. As a result, China's civilian leader has an incentive to abide by these internal norms in a crisis, because doing so will enhance domestic credibility and legitimacy. This also seems a rational choice under conditions of highly imperfect information.

Similarly, one of the new missions Hu assigned to the PLA since becoming the CMC chair in 2004, as we have seen, was to secure China's newly emerging interests in outer, maritime, and electromagnetic space; Hu has also promoted PLA informatization. In both instances, space capabilities are essential. So Hu had a reason to endorse the ASAT test, and thereby match his words with deeds, which would enhance his credibility and legitimacy in the eyes of the PLA high command. In comparison, space debris may be a minor issue; it did not cause a problem in earlier, non-Chinese ASAT tests. It was also unclear that the Chinese test would trigger a space arms race, because the military space programs of other major powers were ahead of the Chinese test; China still has a long way to go to operationalize its space war-fighting capabilities. Finally, the prolonged silence and lack of an explanation about the ASAT test were consistent with Chinese behavior with respect to the testing of strategic weapon systems, where secrecy is intended to aggravate the sense of uncertainty for China's opponents, thus enhancing the deterrent effect.[57]

There are other incentives as well for China's civilian leader not to resolve foreign-policy crises too quickly on the terms of foreign states. He, for instance, does not want to be perceived by domestic constituencies as compromising Chinese national interests, particularly at the time of power transition when he may still be relatively inexperienced and therefore politically vulnerable. He may also leverage foreign-policy crises to foster populism and nationalism and to enhance his domestic popularity by scapegoating foreigners. Jiang and Hu desired a stable U.S.-Chinese relationship, but not at all costs. If they were to make too many concessions, their domestic legitimacy may have been hurt and therefore their rule destabilized.

Furthermore, it may be wrong to interpret some of the cited incidents as instances of poor interagency coordination. The *Impeccable* incident, for instance, might actually show good Chinese civil-military coordination. The two fishing boats that confronted the U.S. ship directly constituted the first line, backed up by two of China's Fisheries Administration patrol ships, which constituted the second line, while a naval intelligence ship formed the third line. Employing civilian ships to confront the American ship directly seems to have been a well-thought-out interagency plan, calculated to gain publicity points by showing China as the weak and victimized side. Also, Jin Yi'nan, the strategic studies director at China's National Defense University, complains that U.S. reconnaissance in China's EEZ has been a long-standing thorn in the side of Sino-U.S. military relations. The issue was raised in the PLA's Beijing meeting with Deputy Assistant Secretary of Defense for East Asia David Sedney in late February 2009, an event that was intended to resume the U.S.-Chinese military-to-military dialogue.[58] The MFA would have helped to arrange for the meeting and so would have been notified of the agenda. The CMC and Hu should be aware of the major issues to be discussed in similar meetings. Finally, making U.S. reconnaissance activities in China's EEZ difficult is consistent with Hu's requirement on the PLA to defend China's newly emerging interests in China's maritime space and with the call by China's central leadership over the years to "develop the national maritime consciousness." As a result, Hu has reason to endorse such a plan to enhance his credibility and popularity as the commander in chief of the PLA.

Even the November 2007 *Kitty Hawk* incident may actually reflect a well coordinated plan. The decision to refuse the carrier's visit to Hong Kong can be interpreted as an exhibition of MFA displeasure over a visit by the Dalai Lama to the White House and of PLA disapproval of a recent American decision to upgrade Taiwan's missile system. The quick reversal of the decision would have been meant to show that the demonstration was measured and limited, that China was still willing to maintain workable relations with the United States.

The only incident that convincingly shows weak central and civil-military interagency coordination seems to be the Chinese nuclear submarine's two-hour, submerged intrusion into the Japanese territorial waters. It is still unclear what caused the intrusion, but it is highly unlikely that Hu ordered it. Also, the MFA is unlikely to have been aware of the operation; it would have objected to it as likely to produce a major diplomatic incident.

Because the costs of these incidents are largely symbolic rather than substantial, there seems to be no sense of urgency to introduce corrective measures. A central, integrated interagency coordinating institution similar to the U.S. National Security Council has been in discussion for many years, but there is no evidence that one has been fully established. Also, detailed information about the Chinese foreign-policy processes is generally lacking. Both factors suggest that any assumption that weak civil-military interagency coordination is causing Chinese delay or dysfunction in crisis response would be premature.

However, and in contrast to foreign-policy cases, wherein information remains highly speculative, a domestic crisis offers concrete and convincing indicators on the relationship between civil-military interagency coordination and crisis management. This is because the stakes are much higher in these crises, where there could be huge material and human losses, which in turn puts the competence and legitimacy of major leaders and institutions to a critical test. Moreover, more information has become available about these domestic crises. Finally, such crises are usually followed by observable remedial mechanisms and measures for prevention and preemption. The Chinese management of the Sichuan earthquake relief in May 2009 is a case in point.

Domestic Crisis Management: Sichuan Earthquake Relief

On the early afternoon of 12 May 2008, an earthquake of Richter magnitude 8 hit northern Sichuan Province, which has about eleven million inhabitants. The first seventy-two hours after an earthquake are critical, and most of the PLA troops deployed for earthquake relief arrived within this time, with the central objective of "saving lives" (救人). Within three hours of the earthquake, for instance, the PLA had mobilized and deployed sixteen thousand troops from the Chengdu Military Region (MR), the PLAAF, and the Sichuan provincial PAP. Within twelve hours another thirty-four thousand were mobilized from the more distant Ji'nan MR and the PLAAF airborne army in Hubei Province. On 14 May another 32,600 troops were mobilized, including a marine brigade from Guangdong Province and sixty-one helicopters from army aviation and the PLAAF. In total, China deployed 137,000 troops (including more than twenty thousand PAP men) for the Sichuan earthquake relief. It is important to note that this employment was mostly requested and authorized by Hu Jintao.[59] It is likely Hu was in close contact with Wen Jiabao, who reached the scene of the quake within two hours after it occurred. This contact is likely to have shaped decisions about the type and scale of the troop deployment.

The PLA transferred more than a million people in distress to safer areas and provided extensive aids in terms of tents, temporary quarters, food, potable water, medical treatment, and disease control. Nonetheless, the central indicator of "saving lives" was not impressive: only 3,336 people were saved from the ruins of the earthquake by the PLA.[60] In the end, over sixty-nine thousand were confirmed killed, with over eighteen thousand reported missing. A more careful examination of the case shows that weak civil-military interagency coordination was a major reason why the PLA was not able to save more lives. The episode raises major new issues in China's civil-military relations, mainly in terms of interagency coordination–based command and control and also regarding force structure, equipment, and training in crisis management.

For higher command and control in the Sichuan earthquake-relief operation, a two-level structure was established: the Army Command Group for Resisting Quake and Relieving Disaster (军队抗震救灾指挥组), headed by the PLA chief of General Staff Chen Bingde, which is responsible for deploying out-of-area troops to the earthquake region; and the Chengdu MR Joint Command Department for Resisting Quake and Relieving Disaster (成都军区抗震救灾联合指挥部), headed by Chengdu MR commander Li Shimin, which is responsible for deploying all the troops within the earthquake region. For interagency coordination, the two-level PLA structure was to follow the orders of the State Council Command Department for Resisting Quake and Relieving Disaster (国务院抗震救灾指挥部), headed by Wen, who was at the scene of the earthquake.[61]

Photo 5. *Wen Jiaobao issuing orders to a PLA senior officer at the site of the Sichuan earthquake.*

As a result partly of the urgent desire to save the lives of the hundred thousand people trapped in the epicenter of the earthquake, Wenchuan County, and partly of his lack of understanding of the PLA (stemming from the fact that he had never served in the military), Wen somewhat hastily ordered the PLA to reach the epicenter within thirty-four hours of the earthquake. The commanders on the scene, however, saw reaching Wenchuan on such short notice as almost impossible; Wenchuan, although only one hundred kilometers from the city of Dujiangyan, where most of the PLA troops had gathered, is surrounded by impassable mountains, and all the roads were now blocked by massive rock slides and debris. Efforts to clear the landslides were hampered by incessant rain, minor quakes, and a shortage of heavy road construction equipment. Wen also requested the PLA to send helicopters or air-drop troops into Wenchuan. To the PLA commanders, however, because of the rain, quakes, four-thousand-meter-high mountains, and a visibility of less than twenty meters, such an order amounted to a reckless risking of the lives of their soldiers. The tension between Wen and the PLA commanders grew to the point where Wen allegedly snapped, "It is the people who have raised you. It's up to you to see what to do! Even with two legs, you must walk in there" (是人民养育了你们, 你们自己看着办! 你们就是靠双腿走, 也要给我走进去).[62]

A PLA helicopter attempted six times to reach Wenchuan but failed. As the sky cleared on 14 May, one hundred paratroopers were airborne; fifteen of them, having left wills behind, jumped at a height of five thousand meters, with no ground command or guidance, no ground signposts, and no meteorological information. The plan to air-drop the rest of the paratroopers was aborted when the fifteen, who landed safely, reported that the terrain was too treacherous for a massive airdrop. In any case, late the night before a PAP unit had reached Wenchuan by foot, only to find the damage there not as serious as had been believed. By 16 May Hu had to replace Wen as the commander in chief on the earthquake scene, partly because it had became difficult for Wen and the PLA commanders to coordinate, as a result of the mutual mistrust that had developed.[63]

Photo 6. *Hu talks with a PLA medical officer at the site of Sichuan earthquake on 16 May 2008.*

For lower-level interagency coordination in command and control, the central difficulty was the lack of collateral coordination between the PLA units and the county, township, and village government authorities. This is because most of the troops deployed were centrally or MR-controlled quick reaction forces (快反部队) and strategic reserve forces (战略预备队), which have no regular or institutional interactions and relationship with the local government authorities. As a result, any coordinated tasks had to go up and down their own chain of command before approval. This cumbersome and time-consuming process contributed to a situation where some units idled while none were available where relief work needed to be done; the units could not adapt well to the rapidly changing circumstances on the ground.[64] A high cost was incurred as a result of this inability to take timely action.

One major indicator of this weak local interagency coordination was the postearthquake call by PLA analysts to employ reserve elements (预备役部队) controlled by provincial military districts (MDs) and local militia for disaster relief. The reserve and the militia units are more familiar with local geographical, social, and cultural conditions and are closer to crisis locations. But most important, these local units are under the dual leadership (双重领导) of the PLA and civilian chains of command; provincial and local party secretaries serve as first political commissars of these units. This institutionalized relationship would facilitate local civil-military interagency coordination in managing crises, thus contributing to lower costs and higher effectiveness.[65]

Another major civil-military issue arising from the PLA's Sichuan earthquake relief experience concerns force structure, equipment, and training. Except for a few small support units specializing in engineering, road construction, transportation, and medicine, which are highly applicable to civil disaster-relief work, the troops deployed for the Sichuan earthquake were armed and trained to fight conventional wars. Their arms and equipment could not be used for disaster relief. Some heavy machinery, such as excavators and bulldozers, was issued to the involved units at the last moment, but the troops were not trained to handle it. The majority of the troops were issued light tools, such as spades and picks. The attempt to remove large concrete pieces of collapsed buildings with light tools and bare hands turned out to be ineffective and lost time that was precious for saving lives. Inappropriate force structure and equipment and lack of specialized training significantly increased the costs of the Sichuan earthquake relief.[66]

Again, a major indicator of the relative ineffectiveness of the PLA in the Sichuan episode was the postquake endorsement of remedies to correct these deficiencies. For instance, at the CMC meeting held in December 2008 Hu requested the PLA to adopt for civil-military interagency coordination in command and control a new core-value concept (核心价值观): "Be loyal to the party, love the people, render service to the state, dedicate to mission, and uphold honor" (忠于党, 热爱人民, 报效国家, 献身使命, 崇尚

Photo 7. *PLA paratroopers with picks and shovels await transport to the site of the Sichuan earthquake.*

荣誉).[67] What Hu really means by requiring the PLA to "be loyal to the party" is that the CMC and other senior PLA officers are to follow the orders of the CCP Politburo Standing Committee, of which Wen Jiabao is the second-ranking member. In the same way, by requesting the PLA to render service to the state, he means that the PLA officers are to coordinate well with state authorities, including the State Council (headed by Wen) at the highest level, in fulfilling nonwar military operations, including disaster relief. Similarly, there has been extensive discussion on how to institutionalize, and formalize in law, civil-military interagency coordination in command and control, particularly in terms of who issues orders, who follows orders, and what the legal accountability is of various parties involved concerning these orders.[68]

With regard to force structure, equipment, and training, Hu reiterated his instruction to the PLA to "enhance the capabilities of the military to cope with multiple types of security threat and fulfill diversified military missions" (提高军队应对多种安全威胁、完成多样化军事任务的能力), outlined in his report to the Seventeenth CCP Congress of October 2007. This means that the central criteria of PLA combat effectiveness needed to be expanded from traditional preparation for war fighting, narrowly defined, to the broader areas of counterterrorism, stability operations, and emergency and natural-disaster relief. As a result, major changes needed to be brought about in the areas of strategic guidance, interagency coordination–based command and control, unit specialization, armament and equipment development, and training.[69] This call for a fundamental shift in military missions, however, was implicitly criticized by various

PLA analysts. PLAAF colonel Dai Xu, for instance, argues that the primary mission of the elite forces controlled by the services and MRs is defense against foreign invasion. As a result, they are not organized, armed, or trained for disaster relief. China is prone to natural disasters, he noted, and using these forces regularly for such a mission will not only prove ineffective but could harm national security, at a time when China's external security environment is still quite grim.[70]

Toward the end of 2008 and, particularly, in a session with the PLA delegates to the National People's Congress annual meeting on 12 March 2009, Hu modified his earlier instruction to the PLA, seemingly taking into consideration the implicit criticisms of fundamentally shifting its missions. Hu now instructed the PLA to place "emphasis on enhancing *core military capabilities* construction, while at the same time [to] handle well nonwar military capabilities construction in overall planning" (重点加强核心军事能力建设，同时统筹搞好非战争军事能力建设). That is, the PLA was to continue to emphasize preparation to fight and win "local war under informatized conditions."[71]

Photo 8. *Hu receives PLA delegates attending the second annual meeting of the 11th National People's Congress on 11 March 2009.*

This modification of policy has two implications. First, rather than requiring the PLA to shift its missions fundamentally, it points to a division of labor among the elite forces, the provincial MD–controlled reserve and militia forces, and the PAP. The elite forces would concentrate on traditional security missions, which also lay a solid basis for an ability to support nontraditional security missions. The MD reserves and militias would focus on preparation for nontraditional security missions or nonwar military operations, including emergency and natural-disaster relief.[72] The elite forces, however, would support these operations, particularly with transportation and logistics. Moreover, because the elite forces have become more technology-intensive and therefore need more systematic, lengthy, and uninterrupted training to translate informatized platforms into combat effectiveness, the PAP would take full responsibility for operations to maintain domestic social stability. As a result, more motorized infantry units of the PLA will likely be transferred to the PAP to reinforce its mobile units (机动部队).[73] Second, the elite forces would designate units with appropriate specializations and expertise, arms, equipment, and training (those specializing in engineering, medicine, road construction, transportation, and nuclear, biological, and chemical defense) for nonwar military operations (flood and earthquake relief; nuclear, biological, and chemical disaster relief; transportation disaster relief; and international peacekeeping).[74]

The Gulf of Aden Mission: A Success Story?

The PLA's participation in fighting piracy in the Gulf of Aden appeared to be more successful in terms of civil-military interagency coordination. The fact that no sudden, unexpected incident (突发事件) was involved allowed more time for planning and preparation. Also, the PLAN seems to be interested in opportunities to expose itself to genuine maritime conditions in more distant seas, in order to gain operational experience. Both factors contributed to this success, but more forthcoming PLA cooperation and coordination with the state authorities to remedy deficiencies revealed in the Sichuan earthquake relief were clearly also important.

The Ministry of Transportation (MT) of China's State Council first raised the issue of deploying naval ships to escort Chinese merchant ships against pirates in Gulf of Aden, at a meeting of the MT and MFA in mid-October 2008. The MT had two concerns. One was that the piracy issue had become so disruptive that Chinese shipping firms might have had to breach contracts and so lose global market share; relatedly, four hundred thousand Chinese merchant mariners needed to be protected. The second was that diplomatic efforts to resolve the issue through foreign governments and international organizations had been difficult and ineffective. The MT, MFA, and PLAN quickly reached consensus on the urgency and importance of the issue after intensive coordination and research on three key issues: capacity, logistic supply, and international law. The PLAN Military Art Studies Institute (海军军事学术研究所) in Beijing, for instance, analyzed legal issues concerning counterpiracy naval operations: whether it is legal to deploy naval ships against pirates; what they can do and how much force they can use; legal accountability if a warship fails to rescue a vessel under pirate attack; and what must be done if Chinese naval ships enter Somali territorial waters.[75] By 26 December 2008 a naval escort group had set sail for the Gulf of Aden.

Photo 9. *A Chinese warship patrols the sea-lanes against pirates in the Gulf of Aden.*

A circular coordination chain has been introduced for interagency coordination in command and control in counterpiracy operations. It begins with voluntary applications of concerned ships, seven days in advance, to the China Ship Owners Association. The applications are forwarded to the MT, which analyzes the capacities of the ships involved, holds coordination conferences, and makes escort recommendations to the PLAN. The PLAN command decides on a final escort plan; the MT coordinates with the merchant ships, directing them to designated sea areas where the naval ships are deployed. To enhance effectiveness, a highly advanced maritime satellite–based ship-movement tracking system (船舶动态跟踪系统) has been deployed with newly developed software that provides all-dimensional tracking (全方位跟踪) and video-based communications among all concerned ships.[76]

Room for Improvement

The PLAN's counterpiracy operation in the Gulf of Aden appears to be a success of civil-military interagency coordination. The PLAN's cooperative behavior here is in contrast to its earlier reluctance to get involved in the 2004 Indian Ocean tsunami relief and in the evacuation of Chinese nationals threatened by civil unrest in the Solomon Islands in late April 2006.[77] But major issues still exist and need to be resolved in order to reduce the cost of future crisis management. For instance, the issue of who pays for nonwar military operations remains unresolved. "Military budgets do not cover nonwar military operations. But under emergency, the military budget has to be used, and the equipment can be very expensive. If there is no compensation afterward, routine war preparation and training would be negatively affected." Also, if they do not have to compensate the PLA, civilian authorities may develop the habit of considering military assistance in crises a "free ride," making it more difficult for the PLA to cooperate in the future.[78]

Also, the role of the Ministry of National Defense (MND) of the State Council is ceremonial. It has no real organization or personnel; the putative functions are fulfilled by the PLA's four general departments (staff, political, logistics, and armament). However, those departments answer to the CMC and its chair, not the premier of the State Council. There may be coordination conferences with State Council ministries, but the senior officers who represent the PLA general departments are likely not to follow the instructions of the State Council but simply report the proceedings of these conferences to the CMC, if only for fear of being suspected of institutional disloyalty. Also, the State Council premier, Wen Jiabao, has no control over the career advancement of senior PLA officers, so the latter have little incentive to follow his orders. This partly explains why it is difficult for Wen to order the PLA to do things on his own authority; he has to go through Hu Jintao. Similarly, his predecessor, Zhu Rongji, had to go through Jiang Zemin to get the PLA out of business activities when they began to impact the national economy.

Figure 1. *China's Civil-Military Bureaucratic Hierachy*

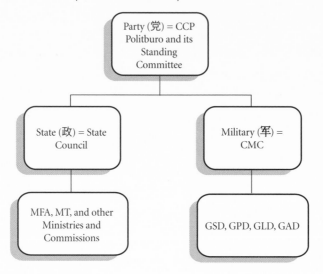

Because the CMC is at the same bureaucratic level as the State Council, it is external to the State Council, answering only to the CCP Politburo and its Standing Committee (see figure 1).[79] But the latter do not meet regularly to manage daily state affairs, and the State Council, which does, has no administrative jurisdiction over the PLA, making routine civilian oversight over PLA affairs clearly more difficult. Such a difficulty, however, can be eased by establishing a genuine, more civilianized MND, one within the State Council and answering to the premier. A real MND could absorb the majority of the PLA's four general departments, which would in turn help streamline the PLA command structure and turn the CMC into a central, joint command institution of chiefs of services.

Naval Implications of Objective Control and Externalization

As discussed earlier, the sense of insecurity in dealing with military matters, arising from lack of personal military credentials and their technocratic backgrounds, have generally motivated new leaders like Jiang and Hu toward objective control and externalization of the PLA. The PLAN is clearly the biggest beneficiary of this trend, partly because it is one of the most technology-intensive services and partly because of the specific environment in which it operates and of the functions it fulfills. Also, the promotion of the PLAN by Jiang and Hu and the leveraging of this promotion by the PLAN have combined to elevate the importance of the navy.

Technology, Environment, and Functions

Objective control allows for more institutional autonomy and military professionalism. To the extent that the PLAN is much more technology and capital-intensive than the ground force and therefore requires more systematic, intensive, lengthy, and uninterrupted training to translate technologies into combat effectiveness, institutional autonomy without major political interference clearly benefits the PLAN more than it does the ground force.[80] It is certainly true that objective control should also benefit greatly the PLAAF and the Second Artillery, because both are also technology and capital-based. Externalization, however, should benefit the PLAN more than the PLAAF and the Second Artillery, for two major reasons.

One has to do with the operational environments of these services. The environment in which the PLAAF and Second Artillery operate is mostly nonphysical or one or two-"dimensional." The second reason is a result of the first reason—that is, the functions of the PLAAF and the Second Artillery tend to be fewer and narrower, mainly in terms of providing operational support and strategic deterrence. But the environment that the PLAN operates in is mostly physical and multidimensional, involving the sea surface, the ocean depths, the air, space, the littoral, and the shore. As a result, the functions that the PLAN fulfills are more numerous and also broader, which explains why the PLAN is a *comprehensive* (综合性) service possessing its own surface combatant, submarine, air, sea-based strategic deterrence, amphibious assault, and coastal-defense arms. But whereas the physical environment of the PLA ground force is largely internal, that of the PLAN is often the high seas—that is, external to national territories—and therefore necessarily more *international* (国际性). Because of its comprehensive and international nature, the PLAN is also a versatile service that can be employed on its own for multiple tasks in distant areas. They range from traditional security tasks, such as strategic and local deterrence, sea control and denial operations, and surveillance and countersurveillance, to nontraditional security tasks, such as sea-lane security and counterpiracy operations, naval diplomacy, and international humanitarian assistance and disaster relief. As a result, the PLAN is also a *strategic* (战略性) service.[81] On the whole, the PLAN is clearly more useful in fulfilling the "new historical missions" assigned by Hu to the PLA generally, missions that aim to externalize the PLA.

Civil-Military Interactive Dynamics

The PLAN benefits from objective control and externalization also because Jiang and Hu have actively promoted the PLAN, which in turn has leveraged this priority position. Both Jiang and Hu have promoted the PLAN, though for different strategic priorities.

For Jiang the top strategic priority, particularly after the 1996 Taiwan Strait crisis, was to deter Taiwan from declaring formal independence and the United States from intervening militarily in a conflict over Taiwan. As a result, he promoted the PLAN by acquiring *Sovremenny*-class destroyers and *Kilo*-class submarines from Russia, as well as indigenously developed more advanced surface and undersea combatants. He paid particular attention to the East Sea Fleet, deploying the heavy, Russian-built antiship platforms in that fleet. Because air superiority in any military conflict over Taiwan can be gained by land-based combat aircraft, Jiang did not endorse the aircraft carrier program for which Admiral Liu Huaqing, who served as the PLAN commander from 1982 to 1988 and CMC vice chair from 1989 to 1997, had actively lobbied, to provide air cover for naval operations over the more distant Spratlys, in the South China Sea.[82] Instead, Jiang pursued diplomacy with Southeast Asian countries under his "new security concept," leading to China's signing of the Treaty of Amity and Cooperation with the Association of Southeast Asian Nations (ASEAN) and of the Declaration of Code of Conduct with ASEAN with regard to the South China Sea. Jiang even removed a commanding officer of the South Sea Fleet for advocating, directly to him during an inspection tour of the fleet, aircraft carriers to resolve the Spratlys issue.[83]

By the time Hu took over, the naval capabilities thought necessary to deter a formal declaration of independence by Taiwan and U.S. military intervention in its support were largely in place. As shown in the second of his four new historical missions for the PLA, Hu wants the military to deter flash points on China's margins such as the Taiwan issue from escalating into military conflict, so that China can leverage the twenty-year window of strategic opportunity from 2001 to 2020 to develop its economy.[84] But as shown in the third and fourth historical missions, Hu has other strategic priorities on his mind as well. The election of the anti-independence candidate Ma Ying-jeou as Taiwan's new president in March 2008 made it easier for the PLA to fulfill the second historical mission, making it possible for Hu to concentrate on the other two historical missions, in which the PLAN would play a major role, because these missions are largely external.

Hu, for instance, has been particularly concerned about China's newly emerging national interests in terms of energy security. As early as at the Central Economic Work Conference held in November 2003, Hu, as the new CCP general secretary, advanced the concept of oil security (石油安全), and stressed the need to develop a new energy-development strategy from a "strategic overall height" (战略全局高度) to achieve national energy security.[85] Because the South China Sea has potentially rich deposits of fossil fuels and natural gas and straddles major sea-lanes through the Strait of Malacca into the Indian Ocean, Hu seems to favor particularly the development of the South Sea Fleet.

The first PLA unit that Hu inspected after becoming the CCP general secretary, for instance, was a destroyer flotilla of the South Sea Fleet, and this took place as early as 11 April 2003.[86] On 9 April 2008 he inspected the South Sea Fleet again. This time he visited the naval base at Sanya on Hainan Island, where he instructed: "The navy is a strategic, comprehensive, and international service. It holds an important position and plays an important role in safeguarding the security of state sovereignty and territorial integ-

Photo 10. *Hu visits PLAN officers and sailors at Sanya Naval Base of Hainan on 9 April 2008.*

rity and national maritime interests." He particularly requested the PLAN to strive to develop "powerful" capabilities for accomplishing the new "historical missions" that he had assigned to the PLA.[87] It is also important to note that the first two escort groups for the Gulf of Aden deployment in the first six months of the mission came from the South Sea Fleet.

The special attention that Hu has paid to the PLAN is also reflected in his other endeavors. In December 2006, Hu attended the inauguration ceremony for a new-type nuclear submarine and conferred a PLA flag upon the captain of the boat.[88] Finally, Hu attended the naval parade in Qingdao to commemorate the sixtieth anniversary of the PLAN, on 22 April 2009.[89]

Another indicator of naval promotion by both Jiang and Hu is the increased naval representation in China's party and PLA central institutions under their rules. In September 2004, for instance, the PLAN commander gained membership in the powerful CMC, together with the PLAAF and the Second Artillery commanders. This membership has surely enhanced the PLAN's bargaining position (as well as those of the PLAAF and the Second Artillery) in negotiating budgetary allocations, force restructuring, senior personnel appointments, and weapons acquisition.

Moreover, the navy's representation in the CCP Central Committee has also increased under Hu's tenure. Counting both full and alternate members and excluding the PAP members, PLA membership constitutes about 17 percent, or sixty-two out of 356, of the membership of the CCP Central Committee elected at the Sixteenth CCP Congress of November 2002.[90] Out of sixty-two, five (8 percent of the PLA delegation) came from the PLAN. PLA membership declined to 15.6 percent of the membership of the CCP Central Committee elected at the Seventeenth CCP Congress of October 2007, or fifty-eight out of 371. Naval membership, however, grew from five to seven out of the fifty-eight, or 12 percent of the PLA delegation.[91]

Finally, many senior positions within PLA central institutions have opened up to senior PLAN officers under Jiang and Hu. Vice Admiral Sun Jianguo, for instance, now holds the position of deputy chief of the PLA General Staff, while Vice Admirals Tong Shiping and Xu Yitian hold the positions of NDU political commissar and National Defense Science and Technology University political commissar, respectively. Rear Admiral Wang Zhaohai, on the other hand, held the position of vice president of AMS.[92]

While Jiang and Hu have actively promoted the PLAN, the PLAN has also leveraged this promotion well to advance its own institutional interests. Only one month after Hu became CMC chair in September 2004, researchers from the Navy Military Art Studies Institute in Beijing published several articles in the October issue of the prestigious *Military Art Journal* of AMS, arguing for shifting the PLAN strategy from one of "near-sea active defense" to "far-seas operations." Their argument was based on the need to secure newly emerging Chinese interests with respect to increased dependence on maritime resources, energy imports, external trade and investment, merchant fleets, and sea-lanes, as well as on the need to improve China's unfavorable maritime strategic posture by breaking out of the narrow, long, and blocked "near seas" in order to gain the initiative.[93] This was clearly an institutional effort of the PLAN to operationalize both Jiang's and Hu's naval aspirations and promotions, and perhaps even more a response to Hu's concern about China's energy security.

Similarly, in response to Hu's instruction, given during his inspection tour of Sanya in April 2008, that senior naval officers follow his neo-Confucian concept of "taking people as the foremost" (以人为本) by paying particular attention to basic-level units, the PLAN launched a "Project of Warming Hearts and Benefiting Soldiers" (暖心惠兵工程), meant to improve the quality of life for PLAN sailors and officers. The project involves construction on shore of living quarters, study facilities, libraries, sports facilities, psychological counseling facilities, and battlefield-acclimatization facilities in all naval bases, with an emphasis on humanistic concerns, ecology, and personal privacy. Moving sailors from ships to land has helped to improve their health, because quarters on board are smaller, hotter, more humid, more crowded and noisy, and more subject to electromagnetic radiation, and as a result are more likely to make sailors physically and psychologically ill. The project has also saved energy costs and lengthened the service lives of ships, because generating energy on board ship is costly and takes a high toll on power plants. Moreover, it has helped to protect the environment, because trash disposal on land is easier to manage; there is less trash to pollute harbors and waterways. Finally, the project has helped to enhance morale, because sailors can eat and rest well on shore after long and exhausting sea tours.[94] Undoubtedly, this quality-of-life improvement effort closely aligns with Hu's priorities to improve genuinely both living standards and the environment.

Finally, among all PLA services, the PLAN appears to be most responsive to Hu's call to cope with multiple types of threats and fulfill diverse missions, partly because, as discussed above, the PLAN is more versatile and therefore more appropriate for these missions. Senior naval officers, for instance, have published major analytical pieces to operationalize the PLAN role in these missions.[95] But more important, the PLAN is clearly much more amenable to complex interagency cooperation and coordination, as demonstrated in the counterpiracy operations in the Gulf of Aden, and as compared to the PLA's role in the Sichuan earthquake relief.

Generally speaking, the civil-military interactive dynamics stemming from naval promotion by the central civilian leadership and the PLAN's skillful leveraging of this promotion are likely to enhance the PLAN's importance in China's military modernization.

Conclusions and Analytical Implications

This study shows that even though Jiang was successful in consolidating his power in the PLA, there is little evidence that he employed the PLA against domestic threats, from either Chinese society or within the CCP leadership. There were also major institutional limits on the extent of this power consolidation and on Jiang's use of this power.

Personnel appointments and budget increases, for instance, may have been driven by reasons other than an intention to consolidate power in the PLA, and Jiang may have been unsure that the military would follow his orders to fulfill functions other than its usual tasks. As a result, the central thrust of his policies to control the PLA was to enhance civilian governance or the CCP's legitimacy to rule, through promoting economic growth, and to confine the PLA to narrow, military-technical tasks. These policies prevented and preempted domestic crises and threats that might have provided excuses for the PLA to intervene in domestic politics. Jiang's policies in this regard helped to maintain civil-military institutional boundaries and therefore increased the internal cohesion and combat effectiveness of the PLA.

Hu's policies are similar to Jiang's. One exception is that Hu has not particularly focused on consolidating his power in the PLA. While inviting Jiang to help him to deal with the military, Hu has concentrated on enhancing the CCP's legitimacy to govern, by promoting more equitable income distribution and sustainable economic growth, and on adopting programs that confine the PLA to its narrow military-technical tasks. But more important, he has directed the military to fulfill new external missions, such as defending China's newly emerging interests in outer, maritime, and electromagnetic space, and in international peacekeeping and humanitarian assistance. These policies have also helped him to consolidate power in the PLA.

While objective control benefits PLA modernization, it has also contributed to civil-military bifurcation, which has complicated interagency coordination in managing crises and, as a result, increased the cost of crises. This complication is reflected in both foreign-policy and domestic crisis cases, including particularly the Sichuan earthquake-relief episode. While policies have been adopted to remedy deficiencies, apparently with some success, unresolved issues remain.

Finally, the PLA Navy is the biggest beneficiary of objective control and externalization, partly because it is one of the most technology-intensive services, and partly because the specific environment in which it operates is mostly physical, multidimensional, and external, as a result of which its functions are highly diverse. Also, the promotion of the PLAN by the central civilian leadership and the service's leveraging of this promotion are also likely to contribute to the increased importance of the navy in China's military modernization.

The findings of this study have three analytical implications. One is that the conventional wisdom on party-army relations in China may be flawed. According to this view, the CCP leaders, highly insecure in the face of domestic threats both from within the party and from society, attempt to buy off the military with higher ranks and more money. In this way, it is often said, the leaders can consolidate their power by controlling the military (or part of it) in order to employ it in power struggles against political threats and opponents; as a result, they can feel more secure. However, such linear thinking neglects the possibility that by employing the military against domestic political opponents CCP leaders would no doubt reveal their own weaknesses or incompetence, which could be exploited by the military. As a result, they actually would create a new threat—the military itself—and thus make themselves feel even less secure.

Roman emperors established the Praetorian Guard to protect them from domestic unrest. Over time, the unit gained independent power and became instrumental in installing and deposing emperors. As its domestic political role increased, its effectiveness in war waned. The newer generations of CCP leaders may not be students of Greco-Roman history, but their sense of insecurity—arising from lack of charisma, military credentials, or close ties with the military—may have convinced them that there are major limits on how far they can go to consolidate power in the PLA and how they can use this power. They seem to have adopted an additional way to control the military—that is, enhancing civilian governance and thereby the CCP's legitimacy to rule, to prevent and preempt domestic threats, on the one hand, and to confine the PLA to narrow functional-technical and external tasks, on the other. In this way the chances of undesirable military intervention in politics decline, and as a result the leaders should feel more secure.

Second, as the findings of this study show, an unintended consequence of a Leninist party-army structure is that if the military is given institutional autonomy and allowed to increase its professionalism, routine civilian oversight becomes difficult, mainly because state authorities have no administrative jurisdiction over the military, whereas the party, which controls the military, does not manage daily state affairs. The effects are particularly pronounced in unexpected crises. Accordingly, the extent of efforts to introduce new institutional arrangements to ease this difficulty should be carefully analyzed; they may have important implications for China's future crisis management.

Finally, the extent of military involvement in domestic politics is closely related to the degree of the military's institutional autonomy and level and types of its technological development. If this is true, research should continue to focus on the evolving relationship between these two key variables in China. This is because such a focus may help to reveal both the level of civilian governance–based political and social stability and the degree and types of technological development of the military. But more important, if domestic political and social stability can be achieved and maintained in China, more analytical attention should be paid to technological development in the PLA. This development has widened and deepened during the past twenty years, and it may have major implications for Asian and global security.

Notes

1. Recently, for instance, China announced plans to cut its ground force by another seven hundred thousand billets and boost naval and air force personnel in the next two to three years. See "China to Cut Army by 700,000 Troops: Sources," Reuters, 30 September 2009.

2. See William Whitson, "The Field Army in Chinese Communist Military Politics," *China Quarterly*, no. 37 (1969), and *The Chinese High Command: A History of Communist Military Politics, 1927–1971* (New York: Praeger, 1973). For a more rigorous discussion of factional explanation of Chinese political-military politics, see William Parish, Jr., "Factions in Chinese Military Politics," *China Quarterly*, no. 56 (December 1973).

3. See Nan Li, "Political-Military Changes in China, 1979–1989," *Security Studies* 2, no. 4 (Winter 1994/1995).

4. David Shambaugh, "The Soldier and the State in China: The Political Work System in the People's Liberation Army," *China Quarterly*, no. 129 (September 1991), pp. 551–68, and *Modernizing China's Military: Progress, Problems, and Prospects* (Berkeley: Univ. of California Press, 2002), pp. 11, 20–31.

5. See Andrew Scobell and Larry Wortzel, eds., *Civil-Military Change in China: Elites, Institutes, and Ideas after the 16th Party Congress* (Carlisle, Pa.: U.S. Army War College, 2004), mainly chapters by James Mulvenon and John Tkacik.

6. For the underlying premise, see Morris Janowitz, *The Military in the Political Development of New Nations* (Chicago: Univ. of Chicago Press, 1964), pp. 1, 27–29; and W. H. Morris Jones, "Armed Forces and the State," *Public Administration*, no. 25 (Winter 1957), pp. 411–16.

7. See Samuel Huntington, *The Soldier and the State* (Cambridge, Mass.: Harvard Univ. Press, 1957), pp. 80–85, and *Political Order in Changing Society* (New Haven, Conn.: Yale Univ. Press, 1968), pp. 193–94.

8. For a theoretical argument that a military focus on external threats makes civil-military relations easier to manage, see Michael Desch, *Civilian Control of the Military: The Changing Security Environment* (Baltimore, Md.: Johns Hopkins Univ. Press, 1999). Desch's prediction on China, however, reflects the conventional wisdom and contradicts the findings of this study.

9. You Ji, "Jiang Zemin's Command of the Military," *China Journal*, no. 45 (January 2001); and James Mulvenon, "China: Conditional Compliance," in *Coercion and Governance: The Declining Political Role of the Military in Asia*, ed. Muthiah Alagappa

10. See Dennis Blasko, "Servant of Two Masters: The People's Liberation Army, the People, and the Party," in *Chinese Civil-Military Relations*, ed. Nan Li (New York: Routledge, 2006). In 1999, the Chinese government labeled Falun Gong an "evil cult" and began a campaign to eliminate the movement. While such a campaign was also waged within the PLA, no evidence exists that it was mobilized to suppress Falun Gong outside the service by force.

11. You Ji, "Hu Jintao's Consolidation of Power and His Command of the Gun," in *China into the Hu-Wen Era: Policy Initiatives and Challenges*, ed. John Wong and Lai Hongyi (Singapore: World Scientific, 2006), p. 59.

12. James Mulvenon, "Party-Army Relations since the 16th Party Congress: The Battle of the 'Two Centers'?" in *Civil-Military Change in China*, ed. Scobell and Wortzel, pp. 27–38. SARS (severe acute respiratory syndrome), which spread from Guangdong Province in early 2003, reached near-pandemic status by that summer.

13. Wang Chu, "Power Struggle in Beijing: Hu vs. Jiang," *Asia Times*, 8 July 2004.

14. Compare tables 1 and 2 for changes in the CMC membership at the Sixteenth CCP Congress.

15. Mulvenon, "Party-Army Relations since the 16th Party Congress."

16. Conversations with the Chinese security and military analysts and officials during trips to China in 2003. The Chinese term for such a cooperative leadership transition is 扶上马, 送一程—the predecessor assisting the successor to "mount the horse and accompanying his journey for a short while."

17. This is discussed in detail in a following section.

18. Appointments of senior officers had largely been worked out by Zhang Zhen (CMC vice chair), Liu Huaqing (CMC vice chair), and Yu Yongbo (CMC member and director of the General Political Department) and approved by Jiang during the 1992–97 period. See 张震[Zhang Zhen], 张震回忆录, 下册 [Zhang Zhen's Memoirs, Book 2] (Beijing: Liberation Army Press, 2003), pp. 377–78.

19. Willy Lam, "Hu Moves to Exert Added Control over PLA," *China Brief*, 20 September 2006.

20. See 国防大学军队建设研究所 [Army Construction Studies Institute of National Defense University (NDU)], 江泽民国防和军队建设

(Stanford, Calif.: Stanford Univ. Press, 2001), p. 318.

思想学习读本 [A Reader for Studying Jiang Zemin's Thought on National Defense and Army Construction] (Beijing: CCP History Press, 2002), p. 309.

21. See Blasko, "Servant of Two Masters," pp. 118–19.

22. The military, for instance, may insist on staying out of the dispute between the party and society. Or it may decline to intervene to suppress social protest but instead join the protesters against the party. Also, the military, disappointed with the way the party handles a crisis, may even attempt to overthrow party rule through a military coup. Finally, if the party leadership fractures over how to handle a crisis, the chances are that the military may fracture as well if it is ordered to intervene. This may lead to a civil-war situation, where different political-military factions fight one another to seize state power. For instance, while the execution of the Romanian communist dictator Nicolae Ceausescu and his wife in late December 1989 was largely the result of a military decision to stay out of conflict between the party leader and society, the failed August 1991 Soviet coup and the subsequent collapse of the Soviet Union show what serious consequences a fractured military mobilized along different political persuasions can cause.

23. See 郭德宏 [Guo Dehong] and 李玲玉 [Li Lingyu], eds., 中共党史重大事件述评 [Review of Major Events in CCP History] (Beijing: Central Party School Press, 2005), pp. 310–19.

24. For the PAP, see Blasko, "Servant of Two Masters," pp. 126–27.

25. See Army Construction Studies Institute of NDU, *A Reader for Studying Jiang Zemin's Thought*, pp. 56, 232–44.

26. 江泽民 [Jiang Zemin], "军队必须停止一切经商活动" [The Army Must Stop All Its Business Activities] (speech, 21 July 1998, at a CMC meeting), in Jiang Zemin, 论国防和军队建设 [On National Defense and Army Construction] (Beijing: Liberation Army Press, 2002), pp. 321–34.

27. The policy was formally endorsed by Zhao Ziyang (first CMC vice chair) in 1988. But Zhao was likely to have consulted Deng, the CMC chair at the time. See Zhang, *Zhang Zhen's Memoirs*, p. 399.

28. Conversations with the Chinese security and military analysts and officials during trips to China in 2003.

29. Conversations with the Chinese security and military analysts and officials during trips to China in 2005.

30. 陈锡文 [Chen Xiwen], cited in "中央三措施应对群体事件, 原则上不使用警力" [Three

Measures of the Central to Cope with Mass Incidents, Not to Use Force in Principle], 中国评论社 [China Review News], 2 February 2009. Chen is the deputy director of the State Council Office of Central Finance and Economics Leadership Small Group and director of the State Council Office of Central Rural Work Leadership Small Group. See also "群体性事件应对之忧" [Worries about How to Cope with Mass Incidents], 瞭望新闻周刊 [Outlook News Weekly], 30 June 2009.

31. See 杨章怀 [Yang Zhanghuai] and 陈雨 [Chen Yu], "中纪委集训2,000县纪委书记, 主要内容是群体事件" [CDIC Assembles 2,000 County-Level Disciplinary Inspection Commission Secretaries for Training, Mass Incidents Being the Primary Content], 南方都市报 [Southern Metropolis News], 14 May 2009; Shi Shan, "China Trains 3,000 Public Security Bureau Directors to Cope with Mass Incidents," *Radio Free Asia*, 19 February 2009; and "中国首次大规模培训基层检察长" [China for the First Time Trains Basic-Level Prosecutors on a Large Scale], 新华网 [Xinhua Net], 17 June 2009.

32. "中办国办印发 '关于实行党政领导干部问责的暂行规定'" [CCP Central General Office and State Council General Office Issue "Provisional Regulations on Interrogating Accountability of Party and Government Leading Cadres"], Xinhua Net, 12 July 2009.

33. "中共中央印发 '中国共产党巡视工作条例 (试行)'" [CCP Central Issues "Regulations on CCP Inspection and Supervision Work (Trial Implementation)"], Xinhua Net, 13 July 2009."

34. Public security bureaus at the provincial, city, and county levels, for instance, have specialized units, known as "state security teams" (国保大队), for domestic political surveillance.

35. So far, China has installed 2.75 million surveillance cameras in public areas across the country, mostly in urban communities. See "Rural Areas to Get Surveillance Cameras," *Shanghai Daily*, 11 August 2009, p. A8.

36. Many of the seven hundred thousand PLA billets to be downsized in the near future are likely to be transferred to the PAP.

37. For a detailed account of civil-military issues in the 2008 unrest in Tibet, see Edward Cody, "Backstage Role of China's Army in Tibet Unrest Reflects Heed for Reaction Abroad," *Washington Post*, 13 April 2008, p. A17.

38. For an example, see "乌维稳部队换防, 南京武警接替兰州武警" [Change of Guard in Ürümqi's Stability-Maintaining Force: Nanjing PAP Replacing Lanzhou PAP], 大公报 [Ta Kung Pao (Hong Kong)], 11 July 2009.

39. For Zeng Qinghong's evolving behavior, see Joseph Kahn, "Former Rival Helps Hu Solidify Grip
on China," *New York Times,* 25 September 2005.

40. Lyman Miller, "More Already on Politburo
Procedures under Hu Jintao," *China Leadership
Monitor,* no. 17 (Winter 2006), p. 22.

41. "航天功臣多获要职" [Many Space Heroes Hold
Vital Positions], *Ta Kung Pao,* 9 September 2009.
Among many reasons, familiarity with the role
of space in future military operations was clearly
important in the appointment of Li and Chen to
their current positions.

42. 张建军 [Zhang Jianjun], "树立新观念, 履行
新使命" [Develop New Concepts, Accomplish
New Missions], 国防大学学报 [Journal of the
National Defense University], no. 12 (2005); 龙
义和 [Long Yihe] (Senior Col.), "新世纪新阶
段我军创新的治军思想" [Creative Thought of
Our Army to Manage the Army at the New Stage
of the New Century], 军事学术 [Military Art
Journal], no. 3 (2006).

43. See 杨春长 [Yang Chunchang] (Maj. Gen.) and
刘义焕 [Liu Yihuan] (Senior Col.), "科学认
识和把握我军新的历史使命" [Scientifically
Comprehend and Handle the New Historical
Missions of Our Army], *Military Art Journal,* no.
11 (2005).

44. Yang Chunchang, "'政工条例' 的一次重大修
改"[A Major Revision of *Political Work Regulations*], *Liberation Army Daily,* 19 October 2008, p.
3, available at www.chinamil.com.

45. For an explanation of "important period of
strategic opportunity," see 徐根初 [Xu Genchu]
(Lt. Gen.), "对我军维护国家发展重要战略机
遇期的思考" [Reflections on Safeguarding the
Important Period of Strategic Opportunity for
State Development by Our Army], *Military Art
Journal,* no. 11 (2005).

46. Hu, cited in 陈振阳 [Chen Zhenyang] and 孙艳
红 [Sun Yanhong], "贯彻落实科学发展观与全
面提高我军的威慑和实战能力" [Implement
Scientific Development Concept and Compre-
hensively Enhance the Deterrence and Real War-
fighting Capabilities of Our Army], *Liberation
Army Daily,* 28 February 2006, available at www
.chinamil.com.

47. See Desch, *Civilian Control of the Military.*

48. The military rank system was restored in 1988.
Seventeen senior officers were given the rank of
general by Deng in September 1988. Between
1989 and 2004, Jiang's fifteen years as the CMC
chair, eighty-one officers gained the rank of
general, an average of slightly fewer than eleven
every two years. Hu's promotion of ten to general
rank in slightly less than two years as the CMC
chair is a promotion rate quite similar to Jiang's.

Hu presided over the ceremony to promote
Zhang Dingfa (navy commander) and Jin
Zhiyuan (commander of the Second Artillery) to
the rank of general several days after he became
the CMC chair. The two were counted as Jiang's
appointments, because he had approved their
promotions. By 2006, only thirty-six generals
were on active duty. See "胡锦涛主席授予十
位将军上将" [Chairman Hu Jintao Confers the
Rank of General on Ten Senior Officers], 南方周
末 [Southern Weekend], 6 July 2006.

49. See "全军领导干部经济责任审计领导小组成
立" [Economic Accountability Auditing Leader-
ship Small Group for All-Army Leading Cadres
Is Established], Xinhua Net, 20 July 2006; James
Mulvenon, "So Crooked They Have to Screw
Their Pants On: New Trends in Chinese Military
Corruption," *China Leadership Monitor,* no. 19
(Fall 2006).

50. See "中央军委通报: 空军运输机失事责任人已
严肃处理" [CMC Circulates the Notice: People
Responsible for Loss of Air Force Transport
Plane Have Been Dealt with Seriously], Xinhua
Net, 7 September 2006.

51. In Mao's time, party-army symbiosis was
pervasive not only at the highest level but also
at the provincial and local levels. A major
reason why Mao had to mobilize the centrally
controlled field armies (野战军) to "support the
left" during the Cultural Revolution (1966–76)
at provincial and local levels is that provincial
military district–controlled local units (地方部
队) tended to protect the provincial and local
party secretaries and governors, or "those who
took the capitalist road." That was because most
military-district (MD) commanding officers had
developed highly personal relationships with
provincial and local party and state officials over
time. This had happened mainly because most
civilian party and state officials had served in
the PLA and most MD officers had local civilian
working experience during the war years, as well
as because of a lack of career mobility stemming
from a lack of age and term limits and retirement
requirements. In the post-Mao era, however, the
relationship between the provincial and local
party secretaries and governors and MD commanding officers has become highly impersonal,
formal, and bifurcated. This has happened
mainly because officials on both sides are regularly rotated within their own systems, because
of the introduction of age and term limits and
retirement requirements. In the meantime, little
cross-boundary circulation of elites occurs—that
is, few military officers have had any civilian
experience, and few civilian officials have had any
military experience. Provincial party secretaries
also serve as first party secretaries of provincial
MDs, but they are largely part-timers, and their

ties to the military are only nominal. For this post-Mao change at the provincial and local levels, see Zhiyue Bo, "The PLA and the Provinces: Military District and Local Issues," in *Civil-Military Relations in Today's China: Swimming in a New Sea,* ed. David Finkelstein and Kristen Gunness (Armonk, N.Y.: M. E. Sharpe, 2006).

52. See "Hainan Island Incident," Wikipedia.com; and "Chinese Poker," *Economist,* 17 April 2001.

53. See "Chinese Submarine Enters Japanese Waters," Wikinews.org, 18 November 2004; and Sean Curtin, "Hu Warns Koizumi against Going to Yasukuni," *Asia Times,* 23 November 2004.

54. See "2007 Chinese Anti-satellite Missile Test," Wikipedia.com; and "Space to Maneuver: Satellite Attack Upsets U.S. Space Supremacy," *Jane's Intelligence Review,* 7 February 2007.

55. See James Pomfret, "China Opens Hong Kong to U.S. Carrier," Reuters, 22 November 2007; and Richard Halloran, "Looking beyond the *Kitty Hawk* Incident," *Honolulu Advertiser,* 10 December 2007.

56. "U.S. Navy Provoked South China Sea Incident, China Says," *New York Times,* 10 March 2009.

57. See Chong-Pin Lin, *China's Nuclear Weapons Strategy: Tradition within Evolution* (Lexington, Mass.: Lexington Books, 1988).

58. 金一南 [Jin Yi'nan], "美在南海活动严重破坏中国国家安全" [U.S. Activities in the South China Sea Seriously Harm China's National Security], 中国广播网 [China Broadcast Net], 13 March 2009.

59. See 陈炳德 [Chen Bingde], "回忆汶川地震救灾决策指挥过程" [Recollect Command and Decision Processes for Wenchuan Earthquake Relief], *Liberation Army Daily,* 9 December 2008, available at www.chinamil.com; and "国防部: 解放军四级指挥体系确保地震高效救援" [Ministry of National Defense: PLA's Four-Level Command System Ensures Highly Effective Earthquake Relief], 中国新闻网 [China News Net], 11 June 2008.

60. See "Ministry of National Defense: PLA's Four-Level Command System Ensures Highly Effective Earthquake Relief."

61. Chen, "Recollect Command and Decision Processes for Wenchuan Earthquake Relief."

62. This paragraph is largely based on conversations with informed sources in Beijing in late December 2008 and with Chinese scholars and officials in Shanghai in early August 2009. For an example of various interpretations of Wen's famous quotation from major Chinese websites, see blog.sina.com.cn/.

63. For these events, see "地震救援13.7万军队是如何调配?" [How Were 137,000 Earthquake Rescue and Relief Troops Deployed?], 中国新闻周刊 [China Newsweek], 6 June 2008; and Chen, "Recollect Command and Decision Processes for Wenchuan Earthquake Relief."

64. Conversations with informed sources in Beijing in late December 2008.

65. See 戴旭 [Dai Xu] (Col., PLAAF), "中国应建立常备救难体系" [China Should Establish Permanent Disaster Relief System], 环球时报 [Global Times], 2 July 2008; and 刘世青 [Liu Shiqing] and 潘杰昌 [Pan Jiechang], "提高预备役部队执行处置突发事件任务的能力" [Enhance the Ability of the Reserve Units in Executing Tasks in Handling Emergency Incidents], 27 May 2008, in *Liberation Army Daily,* available at www.chinamil.com.

66. For issuing different types of equipment, see Chen, "Recollect Command and Decision Processes for Wenchuan Earthquake Relief." For inappropriate equipment and lack of training, see "李运之: 关注非战争军事行动装备建设" [Li Yunzi: Show Concern for Equipment Construction of Nonwar Military Operations], *Liberation Army Daily,* 11 March 2009, p. 1; and Dai, "China Should Establish Permanent Disaster Relief System." Li Yunzi is a former deputy political commissar of the Shenyang MR.

67. For PLA interpretations of the new core-value concept and ways to internalize it, see 李亚萍 [Li Yaping] and 张涛 [Zhang Tao], "我军核心价值观的精辟概括" [An Incisive Summary of the Core-Value Concept of Our Army], *Liberation Army Daily,* 2 February 2009, p. 7; and 占国桥 [Zhan Guoqiao], "把握军人核心价值观的内在逻辑" [Grasp the Internal Logics of the Core-Value Concept for Military Men], *Liberation Army Daily,* 29 March 2009, p. 7.

68. "兵马未动, 军法先行—中国军队也需要法律'掩护'" [Military Law Precedes Movement of Troops and Horses: The Chinese Military Also Needs "Cover" of Law], *Southern Weekend,* 2 April 2009. According to this story, on 28 March 2009 a research seminar was held at China Politics and Law University in Beijing involving legal experts from the CMC Legal Bureau, AMS, NDU, PLA Science and Engineering University, PLA Xian Political College, and the PLAN.

69. See 霍小勇 [Huo Xiaoyong], "锻造有多样化能力的现代化军队" [Forge a Modern Military with Diversified Capabilities], *Liberation Army Daily,* 24 June 2008, p. 11; and 韩志庆 [Han Zhiqing], "'能战度'—非战争军事行动新课题" ["The Levels of Ability to Fight": New Issue for Nonwar Military Operations], *Liberation Army Daily,* 24 June 2008, p. 11.

70. See Dai, "China Should Establish Permanent Disaster Relief System." It is important to note that Dai's article was published on 2 July 2008.

71. Hu, cited in 张兆垠 [Zhang Zhaoyin] (Maj. Gen.), "坚持不懈地加强我军核心军事能力建设" [Resolutely and Steadily Strengthen the Core Military Capabilities Construction of Our Army], *Liberation Army Daily*, 2 December 2008; and "胡锦涛强调军队重点加强核心军事能力建设" [Hu Jintao Stresses That the Military Should Place Emphasis on Enhancing Core Military Capabilities Construction], Xinhua Net, 12 March 2009. Zhang is deputy commander of the Fourteenth Group Army, stationed in Yun'nan Province.

72. See 陈学武 [Chen Xuewu], "科学推进核心军事能力建设" [Scientifically Move Forward Core Military Capabilities Construction], *Liberation Army Daily*, 12 March 2009, p. 10; and 王西欣 [Wang Xixin], "打造与时代同步的核心军事能力" [Forge Core Military Capabilities in Step with the Time], *Liberation Army Daily*, 2 May 2009, p. 6.

73. See 李飞 [Li Fei], "中国需强大内卫力量，增强对内维稳能力" [China Needs Powerful Domestic Security Force to Enhance Ability to Maintain Domestic Stability], *Global Times*, 5 June 2009. Li, a PAP major, is a doctoral student at NDU in Beijing.

74. See "非战争军事行动有精兵" [Nonwar Military Operations Have Elite Forces], *Liberation Army Daily*, 16 September 2009.

75. See "交通部国际合作司长透露海军护航决策由来" [Head of International Cooperation Department of Ministry of Transportation Reveals Origins of Decision on Naval Escort], 三联生活周刊 [Sanlian Life Weekly], 16 January 2009; and "Military Law Precedes Movement of Troops and Horses."

76. See "Head of International Cooperation Department of Ministry of Transportation Reveals Origins of Decision on Naval Escort."

77. Conversation with Chinese scholar visiting the U.S. Naval War College on 16 September 2009.

78. See "Military Law Precedes Movement of Troops and Horses."

79. Nominally, the CMC also answers to China's legislature, the National People's Congress.

80. It is important to note, however, the PLA ground force is also undergoing transformation in terms of "mechanization" and "informatization."

81. For a discussion of the special characteristics of the PLAN, see also 田中 [Tian Zhong], "海军非战争军事行动的特点，类型及能力建设" [Characteristics, Types, and Capability Development of Naval Nonwar Military Operations], 中国军事科学 [China Military Science], no. 3 (2008). Tian is the commander of the PLAN's North Sea Fleet.

82. For Liu's advocacy of an aircraft carrier program, see Liu Huaqing, 刘华清回忆录 [Liu Huaqing's Memoirs] (Beijing: Liberation Army Press, 2004), pp. 477–81.

83. Conversation with informed sources in Guangzhou in 2003. See also "凤凰网专访马辛春: 十年前就该造航母" [Phoenix Net's Special Interview with Ma Xinchun (former PLAN North Sea Fleet commander): Aircraft Carrier Should Have Been Developed 10 Years Ago], *Phoenix Net*, 14 October 2009. In the interview, Ma makes the point that someone was criticized for advocating aircraft carriers ten years ago. He actually refers to an incident where a North Sea Fleet senior officer was reprimanded by Jiang at a National People's Congress annual meeting for advocating aircraft carriers.

84. See note 45.

85. Hu, cited in 瞿健文 [Qu Jianwen] (deputy dean of International Relations Research Institute of Yunnan University), "中缅油气管道, 两国人心所向" [Sino-Burmese Oil and Gas Pipeline Is Favored by the People of Both Countries], 中国青年参考 [China Youth Reference], 1 July 2009.

86. "碧海铸剑: 党中央, 中央军委为海军现代化建设科学决策" [Forge Sword in Blue Seas: Party Central and CMC Make Scientific Decisions for Navy Modernization Construction], Xinhua Net, 18 May 2009.

87. See "远征索马里背后: 中国海军为国家利益挺进深蓝" [Behind the Expedition to Somalia: The Chinese Navy Advances to Deep Blue for National Interests], *China Newsweek*, 1 February 2009; and "海军2006年服役两艘新型核潜艇, 胡主席亲自授旗" [Two New-Type Nuclear Submarines Entered Service in 2006: Chairman Hu Personally Conferred the Flag], 人民日报 [People's Daily], 18 May 2009.

88. See "Two New-Type Nuclear Submarines Entered Service in 2006."

89. "China Parades Naval Might," Agence France-Presse, 23 April 2009.

90. PAP members are excluded from the PLA membership mainly because the PAP has a separate budget and its senior officers are not represented in the CMC or the PLA's four general departments.

91. PLAN members are 吴胜利 (Wu Shengli, PLAN commander), 刘小江 (Liu Xiaojiang, PLAN political commissar), 童世平 (Tong Shiping, NDU political commissar), 孙建国

(Sun Jianguo, deputy chief of PLA General Staff), 苏世亮 (Su Shiliang, PLAN chief of staff), 徐一天 (Xu Yitian, National Defense Science and Technology University political commissar), and 丁一平 (Ding Yiping, deputy PLAN commander). This paragraph is based on materials from 军政在线 (Military and Politics Online), www.chinajunzheng.com, a Chinese website on military and political personalities in China. Similarly, PLAAF members grew from five to eight and Second Artillery members from two to three. PLAAF has one more member than the PLAN, because Yang Liwei, China's first astronaut, became a member.

92. "中国海军四化舰长将领领航, 清一色科班出身" [Ship Captain Admirals of the Chinese Navy in Command, All Having Professional Origins], *Ta Kung Pao,* 7 April 2009. Wang Zhaohai, however, recently became the director of PLAN Political Department, and his AMS billet was filled by Rear Adm. Xu Lili, former political commissar of PLAN Logistics Department.

93. See Nan Li, "The Evolution of China's Naval Strategy and Capabilities: From 'Near Coast' and 'Near Seas' to 'Far Seas,'" *Asian Security* 5, no. 2 (May–August 2009), pp. 161–63.

94. See Wu Shengli, "万里海疆推进暖心惠兵工程" [Move Forward the Project of Warming Hearts and Benefiting Soldiers along the 10,000 Li Sea Frontier], *Liberation Army Daily,* 20 January 2009, p. 11, available at www.chinamil.com.

95. For examples, see Tian, "Characteristics, Types, and Capability Development of Naval Nonwar Military Operations"; and 沈金龙 [Shen Jinlong], "海军非军事行动面临的挑战及对策" [Naval Nonwar Military Operations: Challenges Faced and Coping Strategies], 人民海军 [People's Navy], 20 January 2009, p. 4. Shen is commander of a North Sea Fleet support base.

Abbreviations and Definitions

A **AMS** Academy of Military Science

ASAT antisatellite

ASEAN Association of Southeast Asian Nations

C **CCP** Chinese Communist Party

CDIC Central Disciplinary Inspection Commission

CMC Central Military Commission

E **EEZ** exclusive economic zone

G **GAD** General Armament Department

GLD General Logistics Department

GPD General Political Department

GSD General Staff Department

M **MD** military district

MFA Ministry of Foreign Affairs

MND Ministry of National Defense (of the State Council)

MR military region

MT Ministry of Transportation

N **NDU** National Defense University

P **PAP** People's Armed Police

PLA People's Liberation Army

PLAAF People's Liberation Army Air Force

PLAN People's Liberation Army Navy

R **RMA** revolution in military affairs

About the Author

Nan Li is an associate professor at the China Maritime Studies Institute, in the Strategic Research Department, Center for Naval Warfare Studies, of the U.S. Naval War College. He has published extensively on Chinese security and military policy. His writings have appeared in *Security Studies, China Quarterly, China Journal, Armed Forces & Society, Issues and Studies,* and many other journals. He has contributed to edited volumes from RAND Corporation, the National Defense University Press, Clarendon Press, M. E. Sharpe, U.S. Army War College, and National Bureau of Asian Research. He has also published a monograph with the United States Institute of Peace. He is the editor of *Chinese Civil-Military Relations* (Routledge, 2006). His most recent publication is "The Evolution of China's Naval Strategy and Capabilities: From 'Near Coast' and 'Near Seas' to 'Far Seas'" in *Asian Security* (Spring 2009). Nan Li holds a PhD in political science from the Johns Hopkins University.

UPDATED
1994
EDITION

THE DYNAMICS OF MASS COMMUNICATION

THE DYNAMICS OF MASS COMMUNICATION

JOSEPH R. DOMINICK

University of Georgia, Athens

McGRAW-HILL, INC.

New York   St. Louis   San Francisco   Auckland   Bogotá   Caracas   Lisbon   London   Madrid
Mexico City   Milan   Montreal   New Delhi   San Juan   Singapore   Sydney   Tokyo   Toronto

THE DYNAMICS OF MASS COMMUNICATION
Updated 1994 Edition

Copyright © 1994, 1993, 1990, 1987, 1983 by McGraw-Hill, Inc. All rights reserved. Printed in the United States of America. Except as permitted under the United States Copyright Act of 1976, no part of this publication may be reproduced or distributed in any form or by any means, or stored in a data base or retrieval system, without the prior written permission of the publisher.

1 2 3 4 5 6 7 8 9 0 VNH VNH 9 0 9 8 7 6 5 4

ISBN 0-07-017882-8

This book was set in Janson Text by Monotype Composition Company.
The editors were Hilary Jackson, Fran Marino, and James R. Belser;
the design was done by Circa 86;
the production supervisor was Kathryn Porzio.
The photo editor was Elyse Rieder.
Von Hoffmann Press, Inc., was printer and binder.

Library of Congress Cataloging-in-Publication Data

Dominick, Joseph R.
    The dynamics of mass communication / Joseph R. Dominick. —
Updated 1994 ed.
        p.   cm.
    Includes bibliographical references and index.
    ISBN 0-07-017882-8
    1. Mass media.   I. Title.
P90.D59   1994
302.23—dc20   93-47900

ABOUT THE AUTHOR

JOSEPH R. DOMINICK received his undergraduate degree from the University of Illinois and his Ph.D. from Michigan State University in 1970. He taught for four years at Queens College of the City University of New York before coming to the College of Journalism and Mass Communication at the University of Georgia where, from 1980 to 1985, he served as head of the Radio-TV-Film Sequence. He currently serves as the college's Director of Graduate Studies. Dr. Dominick is the author of three books in addition to *The Dynamics of Mass Communication* and has published more than thirty articles in scholarly journals. From 1976 to 1980, Dr. Dominick served as editor of the *Journal of Broadcasting*. He has received research grants from the National Association of Broadcasters and from the American Broadcasting Company and has consulted for such organizations as the Robert Wood Johnson Foundation and the American Chemical Society.

To Joan and Meaghan

CONTENTS

PART *TWO*   THE PRINT MEDIA   77

PART *THREE*   **THE ELECTRONIC MEDIA   171**

SPECIAL MASS MEDIA PROFESSIONS   335   PART *FOUR*

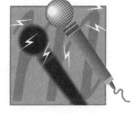

PREFACE

Why an updated edition? Consider the following. In the year and a half or so since the fourth edition of *The Dynamics of Mass Communication* appeared, the following events have happened: Congress passed the 1992 Cable Act; NBC got burned by a rigged news report; TCI paved the way for a 500-channel cable TV system; the courts allowed Bell Atlantic to provide video service in its own market; the two New York City tabloid papers nearly went under and changed ownership; and, finally, both Viacom and QVC were trying to buy Paramount Communication. These are just some of the new developments that are covered in the updated edition. Moreover, I have provided updated tables and data where possible. As first noted in the original preface to the fourth edition, mass communication is truly a dynamic process. Changes are happening faster and faster. This updated edition strives to keep up with them.

In the first place, I have maintained the strong emphasis on economics found in the first three editions. In a time when most magazines and newspapers are struggling to stay alive, when the traditional TV networks and local stations are implementing drastic cost-cutting measures, and when many big media corporations are struggling under debt acquired during the merger mania of the 1980s, the impact of the bottom line is an important thing for students to understand.

Second, I have continued to stress the interrelationships among the various media. It is not unusual for a book based on newspaper stories to be made into a movie (with a soundtrack that is released on CD) which is later available on home video and then shown on cable and broadcast TV. Further, newspapers, books, and magazines share similar content and production techniques. Radio stations depend heavily on recorded music. The same companies produce television shows and movies. Home video further blurs the line between film and TV. All in all, the symbiosis among media persists as an important feature of this edition.

Third, this edition preserves the emphasis on the social effects of the media. The last few years have seen media violence escalate to unprecedented heights of explicitness. In addition, the couch potato concept has taken firm root in American culture, and politics has entered the age of the sound bite. Given the continuing concern over the effects of the mass media on antisocial behavior, politics, and intellectual skills, this material seems crucial for students.

As in earlier editions, I have tried to keep the writing style conversational and informal. Technical terms are boldfaced and defined in the glossary. I have tried to give a sufficient number of contemporary examples to illustrate key concepts. Every chapter contains boxed inserts that highlight, amplify or illuminate points in the text. The book also contains a large number of tables, figures, charts, and other illustrations to further enhance understanding.

Those who have previously used the third edition will notice some improvements. First and most striking is the more colorful and eye-catching design. It is hoped that this new layout will make the book easier and more pleasant to read while enhancing its educational impact. Second, the emphasis on international media and the globalization of mass communication has been increased. Chapter 3 ("The Global Village:

nized. Additionally, boxed inserts with the international perspective have been added to almost every chapter. Third, many users of the third edition suggested that more discussion of the social consequences of mass communication would be helpful. In response, a section labeled "Issues" has been added to twelve chapters. This section examines some of the current controversies that surround the various media and their functions.

Further, I have added new information to several chapters. Chapter 9 ("Structure of the Radio Industry") now contains a discussion of digital audio broadcasting. Chapter 13 ("Structure of the Television Industry") considers the dwindling network audience and the financial-syndication rules while Chapter 17 ("Formal Controls") includes a new section on invasion of privacy. A discussion of TV's impact on behavior disorders has been added to Chapter 22 ("The Effects of Mass Communication on Behavior"), and Chapter 23 ("Mass Media in the Future") has a new section in virtual reality.

Moreover, every chapter has been updated and revised to reflect the drastic changes of the last three years. All tables have been revised to reflect the latest available data. More than eighty new boxed inserts have been added to this edition to illustrate the dynamic world of mass communication.

Finally, I wish to thank all of the faculty and students who have used the first three editions and were kind enough to provide me with suggestions for improvement. As noted in the text, feedback in mass communication is difficult and these comments were greatly appreciated.

• • • •
ACKNOWLEDGMENTS

Once again I wish to thank all those people who helped me make the first three editions successful. Several people deserve special mention for their help with the fourth edition. Colleagues Barry Sherman, Dean Krugman, Len Reid, Tom Russell, John English, and Kent Middleton graciously shared their professional libraries, clipping files, archives, and general knowledge with me. Terri Frye, Kristen Smith, and Denise DeLorme helped me track down a great deal of arcane information. Myrna Powell provided invaluable assistance at several stages of the project.

Additionally, I would like to acknowledge the reviewers and questionnaire respondents who provided me with valuable feedback and guidance through the course of another revision. Thanks to Thomas Berg, Creighton University; Mary Cassata, SUNY—Buffalo; David Clark, Colorado State University; Jeremy Cohen, Stanford University; R. Ferrell Ervin, Southeast Missouri State University; Doug Ferguson, Bowling Green State University; Harvey Jassem, University of Hartford; Robert McGaughey, Murray State University; Larry Mason, Syracuse University; Jerry Pinkham, College of Lake County; Emery Sasser, West Virginia University; and Kim Walsh-Childers, University of Florida.

And of course I want to thank Hilary Jackson, Jim Belser, and the editorial staff at McGraw-Hill for their assiduous efforts.

In closing, I'd like to reiterate the sentiment mentioned in the preface to the first edition: The mass media are a ubiquitous, vital, and influential force in our society; I hope this book will help promote better understanding of their inner workings and impact.

JOSEPH R. DOMINICK

UPDATED
1994
EDITION

THE DYNAMICS
OF MASS
COMMUNICATION

THE NATURE
AND FUNCTION
OF MASS
COMMUNICATION
SYSTEMS

COMMUNICATION: MASS AND OTHER FORMS

Communication is a fragile thing. It's hard enough for two people to communicate face-to-face; it's even harder when machines get in the way. Consider the following:

In January of 1990, most of the nation's long distance phone callers were unable to reach out and touch someone because of a massive busy signal. The problem was a bug in a machine.

The people who work in AT&T's Network Operations Center look like they have the easiest job in the world. They are supposed to monitor AT&T's long distance system, which handles more than a hundred million phone calls a day, about 70 percent of the nation's long distance traffic. Although this may sound like a big job, the system really runs itself. One hundred and fourteen computerized switching devices scattered across the country automatically monitor the volume of calls on each long distance trunk line. If one line gets crowded, the computers are programmed to reroute the calls to some other line that is not so congested. A two-story array of video monitors that looks like it belongs in the Pentagon's War Room displays maps of the U.S. with AT&T's trunk lines delineated by different colors calibrated to the volume of calls they are carrying. All the workers have to do is watch the displays and make minor adjustments.

The job seemed even easier on January 15, 1990. It was Martin Luther King's birthday, a holiday, and phone traffic was down about 20 percent. Moreover, just a few months before, AT&T had installed a faster, more reliable switching computer which actually examined itself every few minutes and fixed any minor problems it discovered. Not surprisingly, the AT&T personnel were pretty relaxed when something went wrong.

It started in New York City. The lines on the video map of the area glared red and blue, showing the circuits were overloaded. No one panicked. Little problems like this happened all the time. The computers were programmed to search for another path and reroute calls. The predicament would clear itself up in a couple of seconds. AT&T customers wouldn't even know there was a problem.

Five minutes later, however, New York was still overloaded. Worse still, the display now showed the switching computers in Atlanta, Detroit, and St. Louis were also overloaded. That had never happened before. AT&T workers now knew they had a big problem.

As they watched helplessly, the video map of the U.S. glowed with red and blue lines as other switching computers became overloaded. Whatever the fault, it was cascading through the whole system, threatening to shut the whole thing down.

Calls were turned away by the millions. Travel agents couldn't make reservations. Brokers couldn't buy or sell stocks. Catalog sales were stopped. Faxes of important legal documents couldn't go through. Telemarketing companies shut down. Almost everybody who tried to make an AT&T long distance call got a busy signal or the annoying "All circuits are busy" message.

AT&T's Network Operations Center at Bedminster, New Jersey, can process more than 100 million long distance calls a day . . . when everything works right. (© Courtesy AT&T Archives)

AT&T's technicians hurriedly called the scientists at Bell Labs to see if they knew what was going on. The call never got through—the circuits were busy. The situation was getting more puzzling by the minute. Some switching computers were coming back to normal but as soon as they came back on line, other computers, previously unaffected, would show that they were overloaded. It was like watching one gigantic electronic pinball game.

It might have been worse. Luckily, the problem didn't affect the other long distance services, Sprint and MCI, so some calls did get through. It was bad enough, however, as it took AT&T nine hours to trace the problem to a software bug and rig a temporary solution.

The AT&T breakdown highlighted a dilemma in modern telecommunications. The software that drives today's complicated computers has become so complex that it is virtually impossible to anticipate every eventuality. Some of you may have written computer programs that were a couple of dozen lines long. If you've used a common word processing program, that program has about 30,000 to 50,000 lines of instructions. In contrast, the AT&T switching program uses up to ten million lines of coded instructions. Somewhere in those millions of lines, something was wrong. Searching for the bug would be a long and tedious job, sort of like combing through the Sunday *New York Times* for a sentence without a period. Eventually, however, the bug was located. One line in the program was out of place. A switching computer that had temporarily shut itself down to repair a minor fault in its workings received a flurry of calls just as it came back on line and sent out a false busy signal to another. Since all the computers used the same software, they all started sending false busy signals to one another. It was an occurrence that might happen only once in a decade. AT&T has since corrected this software problem.

AT&T's software difficulties pointed out others that have cropped up in other sectors. A radiation machine delivered a lethal dose of radiation to a cancer patient because of a software error. A guidance system in an F-16 jet contained a programming error that would cause the plane to flip upside down if it crossed the equator. An automatic teller machine's faulty software let it give unlimited cash withdrawals to customers regardless of the amount in their accounts.

The total damage caused by the AT&T incident will probably never be known. AT&T itself estimates it lost $75 million in revenue. As a goodwill gesture, the company made up for its error by offering reduced long distance rates on Valentine's Day. Bad as the AT&T breakdown was, perhaps we were lucky. The air traffic control system uses software equally as complicated as AT&T's. What if there's a bug in it?

High technology is only one factor that adds to the fragile nature of communication. Consider some other examples:

A passenger on a Greyhound bus traveling from Baltimore to Washington, D.C., opened the rest room door in the back of the bus and yelled, "There's a bum in the bathroom." A passenger sitting in the middle of the bus didn't quite hear the message correctly and shouted to the bus driver, "There's a bomb in the bathroom!" The bus driver slammed on the brakes and evacuated the bus. The police were called and searched the bus with bomb-sniffing dogs. Traffic on the expressway was backed up for 15 miles. When the police finally searched the back of the bus, they found a vagrant hiding in the bathroom.

Gourmet magazine published a recipe for Aunt Vertie's sugar cookies that called for wintergreen oil instead of wintergreen extract. Wintergreen oil can be toxic. The magazine had to send out 750,000 letters warning readers of the mistake.

You can't call anybody named Young in Dublin unless you already know their number. The Irish Telephone Company totally omitted names starting with *X*, *Y*, and *Z* from their new telephone directory. The company planned to issue a supplement.

The Fresno *Bee* recently announced a new editorial policy. Black citizens would henceforth be referred to as African-Americans. A computer program that changed all mentions of black or blacks to African-American or African-Americans was run on all newspaper copy. The next day a story reported that new taxes had put the state budget back in the African-American.

Customers at the Check-X-Change check cashing store in Spokane, Washington, were watching a TV monitor when all of a sudden the picture showed a man with a gun creeping behind a counter. One customer quickly called the police, who swarmed all over the store. No man with a gun was found. It was later discovered that an employee had tuned in an episode of *General Hospital* which showed an actor creeping along with a gun.

A banner welcoming visiting Philippine dignitaries to the San Jose, California, public library was supposed to say "Welcome" in the native dialect of the visitors. A printing error made the banner read, "You are circumcised."

The 1990 graduating class of the U.S. Naval Academy at Annapolis got diplomas reading, "The seal of the Navel Academy is hereunto affixed."

A recent promotion for Kraft Cheese promised a free Dodge minivan to anyone who got a winning game piece in a package of Kraft Singles American cheese. Consumers were supposed to match the game piece in the cheese package with another printed in newspaper ads. Kraft had planned to print one winning game piece and about 499,999 losing ones. Instead, due to a printing slip-up, Kraft printed 499,999 winning pieces and one losing one. When they discovered their error, Kraft marketing executives canceled the contest but not before 21,000 winning entries were mailed to the company. The company offered to compensate the "winners" with $250 each but this did not satisfy everybody. A class action lawsuit was filed against Kraft in Illinois by 500 contestants who wanted their minivan. Kraft finally satisfied all disgruntled "winners" in an out of court settlement that cost the company about $4 to $5 million.

A recent McDonald's sales promotion offered customers a videocassette of *Mr. Mom* as part of their "Meal and a Movie Deal." Because of a labeling problem, some patrons received a copy of the slasher movie, *Edge of the Axe*, instead.

In an incident that eerily foreshadowed history, TV viewers watching a regional Spanish TV station in Barcelona, Spain, were shocked to hear that a coup in the Soviet

Union had overthrown Mikhail Gorbachev. The program showed tanks rolling through the streets of Moscow and carried a "CNM" report from Washington stating the U.S. was severing normal diplomatic ties with the U.S.S.R. The fascinating thing is that this report was aired in April of 1991, several months before an aborted Soviet coup actually took place. At the end of this April report, it was announced that the whole thing was a spoof engineered by the station's program director as part of a documentary series on how easily TV can distort reality. Viewers were not amused and besieged the station with irate phone calls. When tanks actually rolled through Moscow during the August, 1991, aborted coup, the program director was not around to cover the story. He had been fired the day after the bogus story ran.

These seemingly unrelated examples illustrate different types of human communication. They range from the relatively simple—dialing a phone number—to the relatively complicated—publishing a newspaper. Despite their apparent lack of similarity, these illustrations share certain elements common to communication. A glance at these elements will serve as a starting point for our examination of the differences between mass and other forms of communication.

● ● ● ●
ELEMENTS IN THE COMMUNICATION PROCESS

At a general level, comunication events involve the following:

1. a source

2. a process of encoding

3. a message

4. a channel

5. a process of decoding

6. a receiver

7. the potential for feedback

8. the chance of noise

Figure 1-1 on page 7 is a rough sketch of this process. We will refer back to this figure as we examine the process more fully.

Transmitting the Message

To begin with, the **source** initiates the process by having a thought or an idea that he or she wishes to transmit to some other entity. Naturally, sources differ in their communication skills ("Garçon . . . I will have du Boeuf Haché Grillé au Charbon de Bois" versus "Gimmeahamburger"). The source may or may not have knowledge about the receiver of the message. If you are in a conversation with your roommate, you probably know there are some topics that might send him or her up the wall. So you avoid bringing them up (most of the time). Conversely, as I write these lines I have only a general notion about the kind of people who will read them, and I have absolutely no idea of what you'll be doing while you're reading them (that's probably for the best). Sources can be single individuals, groups, or even organizations. For example, in the illustration dealing with *Gourmet*, the magazine was the source. In the AT&T example, the source is harder to pin down. At first glance it appears that the computer was the source of the errant busy signals. Upon closer examination, the computer was programmed by human beings, so perhaps those persons are the ultimate source.

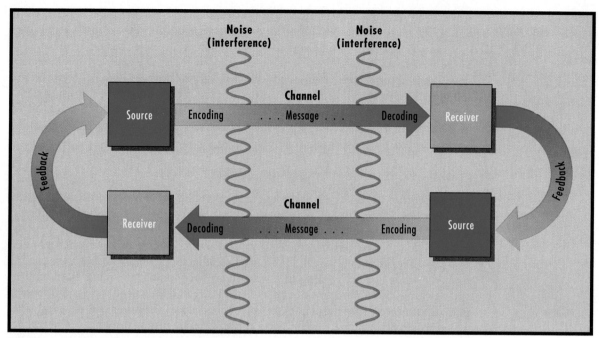

FIGURE 1-1 *Elements of the communication process.*

Encoding refers to the activities that a source goes through to translate thoughts and ideas into a form that may be perceived by the senses. When you have something to say, your brain and your tongue work together (usually) to form words and spoken sentences. When you write a letter, your brain and your fingers cooperate to produce patterns of ink or some other substance on paper that can be seen. If you were trying to communicate with someone who has impaired vision, you might produce a series of pinholes in a piece of paper that can be experienced by touch. If you were a Hollywood director, you would point your camera at a scene that re-creates the image you had in your mind, and you would capture light rays with photosensitive chemicals. Encoding in a communication setting can take place one or more times. In a face-to-face conversation, the speaker encodes thoughts into words. Over the telephone, this phase is repeated, but the mechanism in the phone subsequently takes sound waves and encodes them into electrical energy. Some people are better encoders than others; in like manner, some machines are better encoders than others as well. Music recorded on a $40,000 audio console in a sound studio will probably sound better than that recorded on a pocket cassette recorder.

The **message** is the actual physical product that the source encodes. When we talk, our speech is the message. When we write a letter home, what we put on the paper is the message. When a television network presents *Home Improvement* or *Roseanne*, the programs are the message. Human beings usually have a large number of messages at their disposal from which they can choose to send, ranging from the simple but effective "No!" to something as complicated as Darwin's *On the Origin of Species*. Messages can be directed at one specific individual ("You turkey!") or at millions (*People* magazine). Messages can be cheap to produce (the spoken word) or very expensive (this book). Some messages are more under the control of the receiver than others. For example, think about how hard or easy it is for you to break off communication in (1) a face-to-face conversation with another person, (2) a telephone call, and (3) a TV commercial.

Channels refer to the ways in which the message travels to the receiver. Sound waves carry spoken words; light waves carry visual messages. Air currents can also serve as an olfactory channel carrying messages to our noses—messages that are subtle but nonetheless significant. What kind of message do you get from someone who reeks of Chanel No. 5? Of Brut? Of garlic? Touch is also a channel (e.g., braille). Some messages use more than one channel to travel to the receiver. Radio signals travel by electromagnetic radiation until they are transformed by receiving sets into sound waves that travel through the air to our ears. A rock song starts out using sound waves and is then transformed into patterns of ferrous oxide particles that are sealed in a plastic tape. A cassette player then transforms these patterns back into sound waves that use the air as their channel.

Receiving the Message

The **decoding** process is the opposite of the encoding process. It consists of activities that translate or interpret physical messages into a form that has eventual meaning for a receiver. As you read these lines, you are decoding a message. If you are playing the radio while you are reading these lines, you are decoding two messages simultaneously—one aural, one visual. If you are listening to a friend while you are playing the radio while you are reading this, you are probably doing too much. Both humans and machines can be thought of as decoders. The radio is a decoder; so is a videotape playback unit; so is the telephone (one end encodes and the other end decodes); so is a film projector. A single communication event can involve many stages of decoding. A reporter sits in on a city council meeting and takes notes (decoding); he or she phones in a story to the rewrite desk where another reporter types the story as it is read (decoding). The story is read by an editor (decoding). Eventually it is printed and read by the audience (decoding). What we said earlier about encoding also applies to decoding: Some people are better at it than others. Many of you will not be able to decode "¿Dónde está el baño?"; others will. Some people are able to read 1500 words a minute; others struggle along at 200. There are some messages that may never be decoded because the encoder put the message in the wrong channel. A letter will have no meaning if the receiver lacks the ability to read. A telephone call may not be decoded by someone with impaired hearing.

Nose Pollution

As mentioned in the text, smell can be a significant channel of communication. Manufacturers of cosmetics, toiletries, and fragrances seized upon this fact and with the help of chemists, developed the now famous scent-strip. This strip could be bound in magazines, books, and catalogs and would release a sample sniff of the product when scratched. This sounds good in principle but in practice the strips were often activated accidentally when the publication was jolted around during delivery. If a magazine or other publication contained more than one of the strips, the odors could mingle and create a smell that was altogether unpleasant. Many consumers, angered by reeking magazines, asked for relief.

Never fear. In 1991, federal legislation was enacted that preserved your freedom to smell . . . or actually it preserved your freedom from unwanted smells. The new guidelines specified minimum paper porosity and mandated that samples be activated only after a glued flap was removed. That helped a bit, but some microcapsules that held the scent still broke during delivery. Not satisfied, the state of New York considered even stricter regulation: a prohibition against delivering any magazine that didn't unconditionally lock in odors. The stink over this issue has yet to subside.

The **receiver** is the target of the message—its ultimate goal. The receiver can be a single person, a group, an institution, or even a large, anonymous collection of people. In today's environment, people are more often the receivers of communication messages than the sources. Most of us see more billboards than we put up and listen to more radio programs than we broadcast. In addition, most college students receive more mail than they send—thanks in part to subscription offers from magazines and special deals from insurance agents. The receivers of the message can be determined by the source, as in a telephone call, or they can self-select themselves into the audience, as would be the case with the audience for a TV show. It should also be clear that in some situations the source and receiver can be in each other's immediate presence while in other situations they can be separated by both space and time.

Now let us examine the bottom half of Figure 1-1. This portion of the figure represents the potential for **feedback** to occur. Feedback refers to those responses of the receiver that shape and alter the subsequent messages of the source. Feedback represents a reversal of the flow of communication. The original source becomes the receiver; the original receiver becomes the new source. Feedback is useful to the source because it allows the source to answer the question, "How am I doing?" Feedback is important to the receiver because it allows the receiver to attempt to change some element in the communication process. Communication scholars have traditionally identified two different kinds of feedback—positive and negative. In general terms, positive feedback from the receiver usually encourages the communication behavior in progress; negative feedback usually attempts to change the communication or even to terminate it.

Consider the following telephone call:

"Bambi?"

"Yes."

"This is Harold. I sit in front of you in econ class."

"Are you the one who keeps scratching your head with a pencil?"

". . . Gee, I never noticed it. I guess I do it unconsciously. Say, I was wondering if you would like to have coffee with me sometime after class?"

"Are you kidding?"

Click.

Negative feedback. The original receiver terminated the message. Another conversation:

"Bambi, this is Rod."

"Oh, hi Rod. Has your leg healed up from the last game yet?"

"Yeh."

"How are your classes going?"

"I can't get econ."

"I'll be over in 20 minutes to give you some help. OK?"

"OK."

Click.

Positive feedback. The original receiver encouraged the communication.

Feedback can be immediate or delayed. Immediate feedback occurs when the reactions of the receiver are directly perceived by the source. A speechmaker who

Feedback reverses the flow of communication, sending a message back to the original source. Here David Lee Roth coaxes some positive feedback from a willing audience. (Theo Westenberger/Sygma)

hears the audience boo and hiss while he or she is talking is getting immediate feedback. On the other hand, if after reading this chapter you decide it was the silliest thing you've ever read, it would take a while for you to communicate that evaluation to me. You would first have to double-check my name, find an address or a phone number, and write or call. By the time your letter or call got to me, at least several hours, more probably several days, would have passed.*

The last factor we will consider is **noise**. Communication scholars define noise as anything that interferes with the delivery of the message. A little noise might pass unnoticed, while too much noise might prevent the message from reaching its destination in the first place. There are at least three different types of noise: semantic, mechanical, and environmental.

Semantic noise occurs when different people have different meanings for different words and phrases. If you ask a New Yorker for a "soda" and expect to receive something that has ice cream in it, you'll be disappointed. The New Yorker will give you a bottle of what is called "pop" in the Midwest. A leading national shoe company premiered this slogan in 1987: "We'll only sell you the right shoe." Semantic noise again. A colleague reported that on the first day of his class he asked his students to sit in alphabetical order because then, as he put it, "I'll be able to get to know you by looking at your seats." More semantic noise. In another conversation, a female colleague was displeased about the way she looked. She didn't like her clothes, her makeup, or her hair. A male colleague said to her, "Why don't you dye it?" meaning her hair. The female colleague thought he said, "Why don't you diet?" She didn't speak to him again for a month. The male colleague never realized that semantic noise was the reason for her coolness.

Noise can also be mechanical. This type of noise occurs when there is a problem with a machine that is being used to assist communication. A TV set with a broken focus knob, a pen running out of ink, a static-filled radio, a typewriterwithabroken-

---

*The speed of modern communications may have made this example obsolete. One student at a college in New York claims it took him just three minutes to reach me by phone. I think he was just lucky.

Semantic noise is bad enough in a person's own language, but imagine some of the problems that crop up when messages are translated into a foreign tongue.

- During President Jimmy Carter's visit to Poland, a sentence in his greeting speech, "I have a deep affection for the Polish people," was somehow translated into Polish as "I lust after the Polish people."

- When Chevrolet introduced its Nova model into South America it was puzzled by sluggish sales. Someone then pointed out that "no va" was Spanish for "it doesn't go."

- When Braniff Airlines introduced a Spanish-language advertising campaign touting its new comfy leather seats, Braniff used the headline "Sentado in cuero," thinking it meant "seats of leather." Unknown to Braniff, the words "Sentado en cuero" constituted a slang phrase translated by most Hispanics as "sit naked" —not exactly the meaning that Braniff intended.

- A sign in a Norwegian cocktail lounge: "Ladies are requested not to have children in the bar."

- Another sign, this one at an airport in Denmark: "We take your bags and send them in all directions."

- One last sign, this one in a Japanese hotel: "Please take advantage of the chambermaid."

spacebar are all examples of mechanical noise. In addition, problems that are caused by people encoding messages to machines can also be thought of as a type of mechanical noise. Thus the typographical error in the Naval Academy example and the printing error in the Kraft promotion are examples of mechanical noise.

A third form of noise can be called environmental. This type refers to sources of noise that are external to the communication process but that nonetheless interfere with it. Some environmental noise might be out of the communicator's control: a noisy restaurant, for example, where the communicator is trying to hold a conversation. Some environmental noise might be introduced by the source or the receiver; for example, you might try to talk to somebody who keeps drumming his or her fingers on the table. A reporter not getting a story right because of a noisy room is an example of someone subjected to environmental noise.

As noise increases, message fidelity (how closely the message that is sent resembles the message that is received) goes down. As noise is eliminated, message fidelity goes up. Clearly, feedback is important in reducing the effects of noise. The greater the potential for immediate feedback—that is, the more interplay between source and receiver—the greater the chance that semantic noise will be overcome ("Did you say bomb or bum?"), that mechanical noise will be corrected ("Isn't it Naval?"), and that environmental noise will be brought under control ("Turn down that stereo. I'm trying to talk.").

COMMUNICATION SETTINGS

Interpersonal Communication

Having looked at the key elements in the communication process, we next examine three common communication settings or situations and explore how these elements vary from setting to setting. The first and perhaps the most common setting is called **interpersonal communication**. In this situation, one person (or group) is interacting with another person (or group) without the aid of a mechanical device. The source and receiver in this form of communication are within one another's physical presence. Talking to your roommate, participating in a class discussion, and conversing with your professor after class are all examples of interpersonal communication. The source in this communication setting can be one or more individuals, as can the receiver. Encoding is usually a one-step process as the source transforms thoughts into speech and/or gestures. A variety of channels are available for use. The receiver can see, hear, and perhaps even smell and touch the source. Messages are relatively difficult for the receiver to terminate and are produced at little expense. In addition, interpersonal messages can be private ("I've fallen and I can't get up.") or public (a proclamation that the end of the world is near from a person standing on a street corner). Messages can also be pinpointed to their specific targets. For example, you might ask the following of your English professor: "Excuse me, Dr. Iamb, but I was wondering if you had finished perusing my term paper?" The very same message directed at your roommate might be put another way: "Hey Space Cadet! Aren't you done with my paper yet?" Decoding is also a one-step process performed by those receivers who can perceive the message. Feedback is immediate and makes use of visual and auditory channels. Noise can be either semantic or environmental. Interpersonal communication is far from simple, but in this classification it represents the least complicated situation.

Machine-Assisted Interpersonal Communication

Machine-assisted interpersonal communication combines characteristics of both the interpersonal and mass communication situations. In this setting, one or more people are communicating by means of a mechanical device (or devices) with one or more receivers. The source and receiver may or may not be in each other's immediate physical presence. In fact, one of the important characteristics of machine-assisted interpersonal communication is that it allows the source and receiver to be separated by both time and space. The machine can give a message permanence by storing it on paper, magnetic tape, or some other material. The machine can also extend the range of the message by amplifying it and/or transmitting it over large distances. Without a microphone, one person can talk only to those who can hear the unaided human voice; with a public address system, assembled thousands can hear. The telephone allows two people to converse even though they are hundreds, even thousands of miles apart (Richard Nixon placed a person-to-person call to the Apollo 11 astronauts while they were on the moon). A pen and a piece of paper, which make up what we might consider a very simple machine, allow us to send a message over great distances and across time. A letter can be reread several years after it was written and communicate anew.

A tremendous variety of modern communication falls into this category. Here are some diverse examples of machine-assisted communication:

1. Banks have an automated "teller," which (who?) allows a customer to make withdrawals and deposits and to conduct other transactions by inserting a magnetically striped card and then punching an access code and a few buttons on a machine.

2. In Las Vegas, computerized slot machines flash the following electronic message to gamblers as they pull the handles: "Too bad. Better luck next time."

3. There are machines that play chess by displaying their moves electronically. Some even have a built-in voice, which (who?) talks to you while you play: "I was expecting that."

4. Telephone companies offer 900- or 976-lines, where for a fee, people can hear recorded horoscopes, erotic fantasies, or the latest Elvis sightings. (One 976 service is Dial-a-Chant, where callers can hear recordings of Tibetan, East Indian, or Native American chants. Cost per call: $99.99! O-o-o-o-o-o-m-m-m-m-m-m.)

5. In New York, people who feel guilty can call the Apology Line and hear a taped message of various people saying they're sorry. At the tone, the caller gets a chance to apologize for something he or she has done.

6. Dilk's Creative Tombstones, Inc., sells a solar-powered headstone with a video display screen so that a person can tape messages to loved ones left behind. (For a few dollars more, Dilk's will add such options as sensors to detect when visitors are present or when the flowers need watering and a mechanical arm to cut the grass.)

7. Hand-held, go anywhere, cellular phones are now so popular that some restaurants have a "phone-check person" who guards patrons' electronic equipment while they eat.

Let's examine how each of the eight major elements of communication functions in the machine-assisted interpersonal situation.

The source in the machine-assisted situation is easy to identify in some instances, harder in others. The person on the other end of the phone, the person who wrote the letter, the person behind the microphone—all of these are fairly easy examples. But what about messages from automated tellers, chess machines, and tombstones? In these examples, the source of the message is the human being or beings who actually programmed these devices in the first place. To sum up, the source in the machine-assisted setting can be a single person or group of persons. The source may or may not have firsthand knowledge of the receiver.

Encoding can also take several forms in this setting. It might be as complicated as writing a computer program or as a simple as speaking into a telephone. There are at least two separate stages of encoding in machine-assisted communication. The first involves the source translating his or her thoughts into words or other appropriate symbols, while the second occurs when the machine encodes the message for transmission or storage. Thus when you are typing a term paper, the first encoding stage occurs when you form your thoughts into words and sentences ("It will be the purpose of this paper to examine the pros and cons of fraternity and sorority membership in today's college world."). The second stage occurs as your fingers fly over the keyboard to produce a permanent message ("It will be the porpoise of thispaper to examin the prose and cones of fraternity and sorrity mem bership in todays colleg world."). As you can see, some noise might get into the message. In other forms of machine-assisted communication, there may be several stages (e.g., writing a computer program on paper, keying it in, debugging it, testing it, and loading the finished program into the machine).

Channels are more restricted in machine-assisted communication. Whereas interpersonal communication can make use of several channels, machine-assisted settings generally restrict the message to one or two. The telephone relies on sound waves and electrical energy. CB radio does the same. A written document uses light rays to convey the message. A closed-circuit TV system makes use of light waves, electromagnetic energy, and sound waves. Furthermore, as is implied by the definition, machine-assisted interpersonal communication has at least one machine interposed between source and receiver.

Messages vary widely in machine-assisted communication. They can range from messages that can be altered and tailor-made for the receiver, as is the case with a telephone call, to a small number of predetermined messages that cannot be altered once they are encoded. An automatic bank teller, for example, can send no more than two dozen or so messages. If you accidentally got your necktie or scarf caught in the machinery, the machine could only print: "Ineligible transaction. Please contact customer service." Messages are relatively cheap to send in most forms of machine-assisted communication. A telephone call costs a small amount (unless you're talking to your sweetheart who happens to live in Brazil) and, of course, there is also the cost of installing the phone. Writing a letter is a fairly cheap way to send a message, even when the postage is included. On the other hand, using a computer-assisted instruction machine might be quite costly if you figured in the cost of the machine and the labor that went into programming. Talking over a cellular phone is fairly cheap once the necessary equipment is purchased. Showing home videos is a little more expensive. Using closed-circuit TV is quite costly.

Messages can be both private and public, depending on the circumstances. A letter, a phone call, a telegram are examples of private machine-assisted messages. A sound truck broadcasting an election-day message, a person handing out pamphlets, a poster nailed to a telephone pole are all examples of public messages. The ease with which the message can be terminated is also variable but, by and large, people need little effort to end communication. Throwing away the pamphlet, hanging up the phone, closing your window to avoid the sound truck are all accomplished with ease. Walking out on a speaker while he or she is at the microphone is a little harder, but the interposition of a machine between source and receiver tends to increase what we might call the psychological distance between these two elements. Consequently, the transaction can be terminated by the receiver much more easily than in interpersonal communication settings, where the source has a bit more control over the situation.

Decoding in machine-assisted communication can go through one or more stages, similar to the encoding process. Reading a letter requires a single phase of decoding. Hearing a hit song on the radio requires two phases: one for the machine to decode the electrical energy into sound waves and another for your ear to decode the sound waves into words or symbols that have meaning.

The receiver in the machine-assisted setting can be a single person or it can be a small or large group. The receivers can be in the physical presence of the source, as would be the case if you were attending a political convention and were listening to the amplified speeches of the people on the podium. Or the receivers can be out of physical view (as was the case with Nixon's call to the moon). The receivers can be selected by the source, as would be the case for a letter or a telephone call, or they can self-select themselves into the audience, as would happen if you took a pamphlet from a person on a street corner.

Feedback can be immediate or delayed. When the source and receiver are in close proximity, then feedback will be immediate. The speaker at a political convention will hear the applause immediately. If the source and the receiver are separated by geography, then feedback may or may not be immediate. A telephone call is a situation in which feedback would be nearly instantaneous. Answering a letter, leaving a message with an automatic phone-answering device, and inserting your plastic card into an automated machine and having it disappear without a sound would be examples of situations in which feedback would be delayed, if it occurred at all. The person who plays back the tape on the answering machine may not want to call back, the letter might not be answered, and so on. The extent of possible feedback is dependent on the actual circumstances surrounding the machine-assisted setting. Although some circumstances allow for a great deal of feedback (the speaker at the political rally can see and hear the audience react), it is never as abundant as it is in the interpersonal setting. To return to our example of the somewhat long-winded speaker at the political rally (he or she has been talking for several pages now), in an interpersonal setting it might be possible for the speaker to seek out reactions from some or perhaps all of the audience. The speaker in front of an audience of thousands may not have that opportunity. In other situations, feedback is limited. In a telephone conversation feedback is limited to the audio channel. Feedback in the form of written communication is limited to the visual channel. In some situations, as we have mentioned before, feedback may be virtually impossible. When the Las Vegas slot machine smugly flashes "Too bad," there is little the unlucky gambler can do to show the machine (or whoever programmed it) exactly what he or she thinks of that message, short of physical violence. If the automatic teller gives you a coded message that says "Insufficient funds," you cannot tell it "Well, I just made a deposit this morning. Look it up."

Noise in machine-assisted communication can be semantic and environmental, as in interpersonal communication, but it can also be mechanical, since interference with the message might be due in part to difficulties with the machine involved.

The recent appearance of new personal communication media ensures that machine-assisted interpersonal communication will continue to grow. The two innovations that have had the most impact are the facsimile (fax) machine and computerized data bases. First let's examine the fax.

Facsimile. Facsimile transmission is an old idea, first invented in the 1840s. It wasn't until the late 1980s, however, that it caught on, thanks to the development of low cost fax machines that used the phone lines to transmit documents. About 100,000 fax units were sold in 1991 as prices dropped to below $300 a machine. The business world accounted for most of these sales but home fax machines are becoming more popular. About seven million homes had fax devices in 1992 and the number was expected to grow to sixty million by the end of the century. In addition, computer companies are offering cards or boards that turn personal computers into fax machines. Faxes are becoming so popular that they might one day replace the U.S. Postal Service for personal mail. On the international scene, the political implications of faxes are significant. When China's government cracked down on student dissidents and ordered a news blackout, sympathizers overseas started faxing news reports to their counterparts in China. Recently, the Israeli government, fearing that they might be used to inflame violence, has banned fax machines in the Gaza Strip.

The Essential Fax

Fax machines have been in widespread use for only a few years but many people wonder how they ever got along without them. Here are some common and not-so-common uses for fax:

- Office workers commonly fax their lunch orders to nearby restaurants.

- Radio stations now have fax request lines in addition to regular telephone request lines.

- In many states, it is acceptable to serve legal documents by fax.

- A new craft called "fax art," sparked by artist Peter Max, whe sends Max Fax, is growing in popularity.

- Fax has even come to the North Pole. A communications and marketing company called Faxnet will fax kids' Christmas lists to Santa. The company promises that Santa will fax back a reply the next day.

- Many newspapers now publish "faxpapers," news summaries sent before the paper hits the street.

- Many Japanese now have fax machines in their cars. Donald Trump had a fax machine in his boat.

- An expedition climbing Mount Everest sent back progress reports by fax.

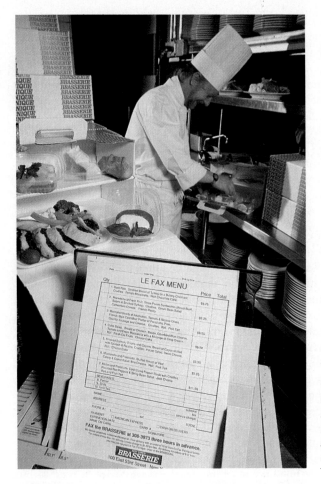

One of the many creative uses of the fax machine is the fax menu. Faxing your order may be more efficient, but you can't ask your food server "How's the corned beef today?" (Louie Psihoyos/Matrix)

Faxes are a further example of how machine-assisted communication blends together the characteristics of mass and interpersonal communication. Like interpersonal communications, faxes can be directed at one person known to the source. (You can fax a request for cash to your parents.) Or, like mass communication, they can be directed at a large number of people unknown to the source. (Many direct marketing companies now send out fax advertisements instead of mailing a flyer. The companies figure that most people will just throw away something that looks like junk mail but almost everybody will read a fax. The situation has gotten to the point that some states have laws regulating what is now called "junk fax.") Additionally, like interpersonal communication, faxes are relatively cheap to send. Similar to mass communication, however, faxes are public. Whoever is in charge of the fax machine can simply lift up a cover page and read it. As you are probably aware, consumers have found a host of uses for fax (see box on page 15).

Computer Data Bases. There are four major companies that provide information and other services to their subscribers through a computerized data base: CompuServe, Prodigy, Genie, and Delphi. About two million Americans subscribe to these services, which allow them to read electronic newspapers, play games, buy products and services, look up information in electronic encyclopedias, book airline tickets, send electronic mail, and leave messages for one another on electronic bulletin boards by using a computer and phone lines. The cost for all of this is highly variable and might range from $10 to $50 or more per month.

From the standpoint of machine-assisted interpersonal communication, the computer bulletin board system (BBS) is the most intriguing. The BBS works a little like a telephone conference call but you type instead of talk. Once you enter the system, or go "online," you may post a message for all to see or, if you're the shy type, you may just read what others are saying. (Using a BBS requires knowing a new language. (See the box below). In addition to chitchat about the latest game and new hardware options, some BBSs have been put to novel use. After the 1989 California earthquake, CompuServe set up a bulletin board that allowed subscribers to exchange earthquake information through its global network. Names and telephone numbers of people looking for news of friends and relatives in the quake area were posted and anyone who knew of their whereabouts was asked to post a message. There are about 50 Alcoholics Anonymous BBSs throughout the country where users can get help and encouragement. At the other end of the spectrum, some systems have an "adult channel" where users can get to know one another on a more personal basis. A new term, "compusex," has been coined to describe some of the more intimate online encounters.

Like fax, these computerized information systems combine some of the features of interpersonal and mass communication. Someone using Prodigy to look up the day's stock activity or the latest sports scores engages in an activity that is very much like mass communication. Using a BBS, however, is a little complicated. Like interpersonal communication, a message can be directed at a single person. Like mass communication, however, the person sending the message and the person receiving it can be anonymous and unknown to one another. In fact, some BBS users invent whole new personas for themselves and use fictitious names. In one well-known case, a male invented a female persona for a BBS and used the imaginary woman to fix him up with female BBS users. Moreover, like interpersonal communication, the message can be easily altered and tailored to fit an individual receiver. On the other hand, like mass communication, feedback in a BBS is limited. The usual clues from personal appearance, tone of voice, and gestures are not present. Further, much like mass communication, the online conversations are easily terminated.

Are You a Newbie Lurker?

To get the most enjoyment out of a computer bulletin board system (BBS), you need to know a rather specialized vocabulary. Here are some of the key terms:

BCNU: Be seeing you. Means the same as CU L8TR.

BRB: Be right back.

GA: Go ahead.

Lurker: Somebody who just reads a service and doesn't post messages.

Newbie: Somebody new to the system.

Nytol: Good night all.

ROTFL: Rolling on the floor laughing.

Spam: Information that might be false, e.g., this report may have a high Spam count.

TNX: Thanks.

Then there are "emoticons," graphic faces used to express emotions in or about messages. They use standard computer graphic codes and are difficult to reproduce in a typeset book, but here are a few:

:-)   (Smiley face)

:-((Frowning face)

:-\   (Wry face)

:-#   (Nothing-to-say face. Mouth taped shut)

BCNU.

Before we close, it's also important to note how new forms of machine-assisted interpersonal communication have altered some of the functions and customs of traditional interpersonal communication. The new personal media allow for communication that is distanced both physically and psychologically. By faxing your order, it is now possible to have lunch without talking to anybody. 900-numbers that promise erotic conversations provide intimacy on demand but at a distance and in isolation. Online computer conversations also give the illusion of closeness, but the participants have total control over the amount and kind of information that they disclose. People interested in meaningful communication but too shy to cultivate interpersonal contacts might turn to computer chat lines as a substitute and encounter imposters. Cellular phones keep people in constant communication but also are a new source of interruptions to face-to-face communication. It's safe to say that the new personal media increase our range of contacts and experience but they do so at a price.

Mass Communication

The third major communication setting is the one that we will be most interested in. Although the differences between machine-assisted communication and unaided interpersonal communication are fairly easily seen, the differences between machine-assisted interpersonal communication and mass communication are not that clear. A working definition of what we mean by **mass communication** may be appropriate at this point. Mass communication refers to the process by which a complex organization with the aid of one or more machines produces and transmits public messages that are directed at large, heterogeneous, and scattered audiences. This definition, while slightly cumbersome, will serve us adequately in most instances. There are, of course, situations that will fall into a gray area. How large does the audience have to be before we call it mass communication? How scattered? How heterogeneous? How complex must the organization be? The boundaries are a little blurry. For example, a billboard is constructed on a busy street in a small town. Obviously, this would qualify as machine-assisted communication (a machine was used to print the billboard), but is this example better defined as mass communication? An automatic letter-writing device can write thousands of similar letters. Is this mass communication? There are no "correct" answers to these questions. The dividing line between what we have labeled machine-assisted interpersonal communication and mass communication is not a distinct one. The degree of "massness" involved in any particular situation should be viewed as a continuum where one setting shades into another. True, there are some clear examples at both extremes, but the middle contains a large gray area. Perhaps if we examine our eight communication elements as they occur in settings that should obviously be labeled mass communication, our definition will become clearer.

The source in the mass communication situation is a group of individuals who usually act within predetermined roles in an organizational setting. That sentence is a rather complicated observation of a simple fact: Mass communication is the end product of more than one person. Think about how a newspaper is put together. Reporters gather news; writers draft editorials; a cartoonist may draw an editorial cartoon; the advertising department lays out ads; editors lay out all of these things together on a sample page; technicians transfer this page to a master, which is taken to a press where other technicians produce the final paper; the finished copies are given to the delivery staff who distribute them; and, of course, behind all of this is a publisher who has the money to pay for a building, presses, staff, trucks, paper, ink, and so on. As you can see, this particular newspaper is not the product of a single individual but of an organization. This institutional nature of mass communication has several consequences that we will consider later in this book.

Mass communication sources have little detailed information about their particular audience. They may have collective data, but these will be expressed as gross audience characteristics. The newspaper editor, for example, may know that 40 percent of the readers are between twenty-five and forty years old and that 30 percent earn between $20,000 and $50,000, but the editor has no idea about the individual tastes, preferences, quirks, or individual identities of these people. They are an anonymous group, known only by summary statistics.

Encoding in mass communication is always a multistage process. A film producer has an idea. He or she explains it to a screenwriter. The writer goes off and produces a script. The script goes to a director, who translates it for the camera. Cinematographers capture the scenes on film. The raw film goes to an editor, who splices together the final version. The film is copied and sent to motion picture theaters, where a projector displays it on the screen, where the audience watches it. How many examples of encoding can you find in that oversimplified version of movie-making?

Mass communication channels are characterized by the imposition of at least one and usually more than one machine in the process of sending the message. These machines translate the message from one channel to another. Television makes use of complicated devices that transform light energy into electrical energy and back again. Radio does the same with sound energy. Unlike interpersonal communication, in which many channels are available, mass communication is usually restricted to one or two.

Messages in mass communication are public. Anyone who can afford the cost of a newspaper or a tape deck or a TV set (or who can borrow them from a friend) can receive the message. Additionally, the same message is sent to all receivers. In a sense, mass communication is addressed "to whom it may concern." These messages are also expensive. A typical half-hour TV show might cost $750,000 or more; a film might run into the tens of millions. Of all the various settings, message termination is easiest in mass communication. The TV set goes dark at the flick of a switch, an automatic

The director as encoder: Jodie Foster on the set of Little Man Tate. *A motion picture goes through several stages of encoding (idea, story, script, shooting script, filming, and editing) before it gets to the receiver. (Photofest)*

timer can turn off the radio, the newspaper is quickly put aside, and so forth. There is little the source can do to prevent these sudden terminations, other than bullying the audience ("Don't touch that dial!") or trying to stay interesting at all times ("We'll be back after these important messages.").

Mass communication typically involves multiple decoding before the message is received. The tape deck decodes patterns of magnetic particles into sound waves for our hearing mechanism. The TV receiver decodes both sight and sound transmissions.

One of the prime distinguishing characteristics of mass communication is the audience. In the first place, the mass communication audience is a large one, sometimes numbering in the millions of people. Second, the audience is also heterogeneous; that is, it is made up of several dissimilar groups who may differ in age intelligence, political beliefs, ethnic backgrounds, and so on. Even in situations where the mass communication audience is somewhat well defined, heterogeneity is still present. (For example, consider the publication *Turkey Grower's Monthly*. At first glance, the audience for this publication might appear to be pretty much the same, but upon closer examination we might discover that it differs in intelligence, social class, income age, political party, education, place of residence, and so on. The only thing we know that the audience has in common is an interest in growing turkeys.) Third, the audience is spread out over a wide geographic area; source and receiver are not in each other's immediate physical presence. The large size of the audience and its geographic separation both contribute to a fourth distinguishing factor: The audience is anonymous to one another. The person watching the *CBS Evening News* is unaware of the several million others who might also be in the audience. Lastly, in keeping with the idea of a public message, the audience in mass communication is self-defined. The receiver chooses what film to see, what paper to read, and what program to watch. In the interpersonal and machine-assisted settings, sources may search you out and select you as the receiver of the message ("Hey you! What's in that bag?"), but in mass communication, the receiver is the key to the process. If the receiver chooses not to attend to the message, the message is not received. Consequently, the various mass communication sources spend a great deal of time and effort to get your attention so that you will include yourself in the audience.

Feedback is another area where mass communication contrasts greatly with interpersonal communication. The message flow in mass communication is generally in one direction only, from source to receiver, and feedback is minimal. In fact, in many mass communication settings, feedback between receiver and source is quite difficult to achieve. If, for example, you were offended by the content of a TV program, you might call the station immediately after viewing. If you got through, you would probably be instructed to call back during business hours when the manager was in. The next day, assuming you got in touch with the manager, he or she might refer you to the network, since what you saw was probably a network show. If you chose to call the network (a long-distance call for most people), you might be connected to a receptionist, who might graciously suggest that if you put your complaint in writing, "someone will get back to you." Eventually, someone probably will respond with a form letter. This hypothetical example illustrates the difficulty in achieving feedback and the fact that feedback is typically delayed. It might be hours or even days before the source of the message is aware of the receiver's response. The delayed nature of feedback in mass communication is further pronounced because, as we shall see in a later chapter, much of it is indirect and must travel through a third party before it returns to the source.

Finally, noise in the mass communication setting can be semantic, environmental, or mechanical. In fact, since there may be more than one machine involved in the process, mechanical noise can be compounded (watching a scratchy copy of an old film on a snowy TV set).

ELEMENT	SETTING		
	Interpersonal	Machine-assisted interpersonal	Mass
Source	Single person; has knowledge of receiver	Single person or group; great deal of knowledge or no knowledge of receiver	Organizations; little knowledge of receivers
Encoding	Single stage	Single or multiple stage	Multiple stages
Message	Private or public; cheap; hard to terminate; altered to fit receivers	Private or public; low to moderate expense; relatively easy to terminate; can be altered to fit receivers in some situations	Public; expensive; easily terminated; same message to everybody
Channel	Potential for many; no machines interposed	Restricted to one or two; at least one machine interposed	Restricted to one or two; usually more than one machine interposed
Decoding	Single stage	Single or multiple stage	Multiple stages
Receiver	One or a relatively small number; in physical presence of source; selected by source	One person or a small or large group; within or outside of physical presence of source; selected by source or self-defined	Large numbers; out of physical presence of source; self-selected
Feedback	Plentiful; immediate	Somewhat limited; immediate or delayed	Highly limited; delayed
Noise	Semantic; environmental	Semantic; environmental; mechanical	Semantic; environmental; mechanical

FIGURE 1-2 *Differences in communication settings.*

As a review, Figure 1-2 summarizes some of the differences among the three communication settings that we have talked about.

• • • •

NATURE OF THE MASS COMMUNICATOR

Since a large portion of this book will examine the institutions that are in the business of mass communication, it will be to our advantage to consider some common characteristics that typify "mass communicators." We will list them first and then elaborate.

1. Mass communication is produced by complex and formal organizations.

2. Mass communication organizations have multiple gatekeepers.

3. Mass communication organizations need a great deal of money to operate.

4. Mass communication organizations exist to make a profit.

5. Mass communication organizations are highly competitive.

Formal Organizations

Publishing a newspaper or operating a TV station requires control of money, management of personnel, coordination of activities, and application of authority. To accomplish all of these tasks, a well-defined organizational structure characterized by specialization, division of labor, and focused areas of responsibility is necessary. Consequently, this means that mass communication will be the product of a bureaucracy. As in most bureaucracies, decision making will take place at several different levels of management, and channels of communication within the organization will be formalized. Thus many of the decisions about what gets included in a newspaper or in a TV program will be the result of committee or group decisions. Further, this means that decisions will have to be made by several different individuals in ascending levels of the bureaucracy and that communication will follow predetermined and predictable patterns within the organization. On occasion, this leads to communication problems and misunderstandings (see the *Heidi* example in the accompanying boxed material). On other occasions, decisions will be made that have to satisfy various individuals at several different levels of the bureaucracy, and this results in end products that seldom resemble the original idea of the creator. For example, TV writer Merle Miller describes one such experience in his book *Only You Dick Daring or How to Write One Television Script and Make $50,000,000.* Miller's idea for a TV show about a Peace Corps worker had to be approved by the vice president of the production company, the vice president of CBS Program Development, the vice president of CBS Programming, the president of CBS, the producer, the director, and the research department. When everything had settled, the show was about a county agent working in the Southwest, and Miller, totally frustrated, quit the project.

The Gatekeepers

Another important factor that characterizes the mass communicator is the presence of multiple **gatekeepers**. A gatekeeper is any person (or group) who has control over what material eventually reaches the public. Gatekeepers exist in large numbers in all mass communication organizations. Some are more obvious than others, for example, the editor of a newspaper or the news director at a TV station. Some gatekeepers are less visible. To illustrate, let's imagine that you have the world's greatest idea for a TV series, an idea that will make *M*A*S*H* and *The Cosby Show* look like mediocre successes. You write the script, check possible production companies, and mail it off to Universal Studios in California. A clerk in the mailroom judges by the envelope that it is a script and sees by the return address that it has come from an amateur writer. The clerk has been instructed to return all such packages unopened with a note saying that Universal does not consider unsolicited material. Gate closed.

Frustrated, you decide to go to Los Angeles in person and hand deliver your work. You rush in from the airport to the office of Universal's vice president in charge of production, where a receptionist politely tells you that Universal never looks at scripts that were not submitted through an agent. Gate closed. You rush out to a phone booth and start calling agents. Fourteen secretaries tell you that their agencies are not accepting new writers. Fourteen closed gates. Finally, you find an agent who will see you (gate open!). You rush to the agent's office where he or she glances through your

Mass communication organizations are complex bureaucracies with formal lines of communication and distinct layers of authority. Occasionally, this complexity causes problems, such as the one that occurred on Sunday evening, November 17, 1968.

Pregame

The National Broadcasting Company (NBC) was televising the Oakland Raiders–New York Jets pro football game from California. The game was crucial in determining who made the playoffs.

The Lineups

1. Julian Goodman, President of NBC.

2. Carl Lindemann, Vice President, NBC Sports.

3. Scotty Connal, Manager of NBC Sports Programs.

4. Don Ellis, Producer for NBC Sports in Oakland.

5. An assistant director at NBC studios in Burbank, California.

6. The head engineer at NBC Broadcast Operations Control in New York.

The Situation

It was the policy of NBC sports to broadcast all sports events to their conclusion, but Broadcast Operations Control had to get approval from Julian Goodman to run overtime. At 7 P.M. this particular evening, NBC had scheduled *Heidi*, a high-priced TV version of the classic story about the little Swiss girl and her grandfather. At 6:40 P.M., Scotty Connal was watching the game in his Connecticut home. Don Ellis was watching the game on his monitor in the NBC remote truck in Oakland. The Jets were ahead 32–29.

The Play by Play

6:41 P.M.   Lindemann phoned Connal and told him it looked as if the game wouldn't be finished by 7 P.M.

Lindemann said he would call NBC president Goodman to get permission to run over.

6:55 P.M.   Lindemann phoned Connal and told him that Goodman said the game must stay on until it was over. The beginning of *Heidi* would be delayed.

6:56 P.M.   Connal called NBC Operations Control in New York. He could not reach them. (It turned out that hundreds of parents had tied up the NBC switchboard to ask whether the network would show *Heidi* or keep televising that dumb football game.) Connal momentarily panicked.

6:57 P.M.   Connal remembered that the NBC studios in Burbank had a direct open line to NBC in New York. He decided to call Don Ellis in the truck in Oakland. Ellis could pass the message to Burbank, which, in turn, could pass it on to New York.

6:58 P.M.   Connal told Ellis: "Don, call NBC in Burbank. Tell them to tell New York that Julian Goodman says to continue with the game until conclusion."

Ellis told Burbank: "Call NBC in New York and tell them Goodman says to stay with the game."

An anonymous assistant director in Burbank told the head engineer at Broadcast Operations Control in New York: "The guys in the truck at Oakland say we should keep the game on the air."

6:59 P.M.   The head engineer in New York, unused to this irregular channel of communication, decided that he wasn't going to take orders from the guys in the truck at Oakland. There were still fifty seconds left to play and the Jets were still leading 32–29 as the image of Oakland stadium faded into shots of the Swiss Alps on TV screens all over America.

7:00 P.M. Don Ellis in Oakland sat dumbfounded as New York took the game off the air. Scotty Connal shouted helplessly at his TV set.

7:01 P.M. Don Ellis on the phone to Scotty Connal: "Scotty," gasped Ellis, "Oakland just scored!"

Postgame

The Oakland Raiders scored fourteen points in those final fifty seconds after the game went off the air to beat the Jets 43–32. The switchboard at NBC in New York was so deluged with calls from enraged fans that the entire CIrcle 7 telephone exchange in Manhattan broke down. Heidi, however, lived happily ever after.

Postgame Postscript

The ghost of Heidi is alive and well at NBC. In November of 1984, during a broadcast of *The Skins Game*, a high-stakes golf match, NBC infuriated golf fans all over the country by cutting away from pro golfer Jack Nicklaus' attempt to win $240,000 by making a single putt. The network preempted Jack's putt and went instead to the beginning of a professional football pregame show, leaving golf fans in the dark. Somewhere, Heidi was smiling.

script and says, "No thanks" (gate closed). By now the point is probably clear. Many people serve as gatekeepers. In our hypothetical example, even if an agent agreed to represent you, the agent would then have to sell your script to a producer who, in turn, might have to sell it to a production company which, in turn, might have to sell it to a network. There are many gates to pass through, and you can begin to appreciate some of Merle Miller's frustration.

In the newsroom, an assignment editor decides whether to send a reporter to cover a certain event. The reporter then decides if anything about the event is worth reporting. An editor may subsequently shorten the story, if submitted, or delete it altogether. Obviously, gatekeepers abound in mass communication. The more complex the organization, the more gatekeepers will be found.

Operating Expenses

It costs a large sum of money to start a mass communication organization and to keep it running. Recently, the *Houston Chronicle* was sold for more than $400 million. A dozen magazines formerly owned by CBS were sold to a French company for about $700 million. *U.S. News and World Report* brought $167 million. In Los Angeles an FM station was sold for nearly $110 million and a TV station was bought for $510 million.

Once the organization is in operation, expenses are also sizable. In the early 1990s, it cost approximately $4 to 5 million annually to run a small daily (one with a circulation of about 35,000 to 40,000). A radio station in a medium-sized urban market might spend $700,000 annually in operating expenses. A TV station in the top ten markets might need more than $10 million to keep it going. These economic facts mean that only those organizations that have the money necessary to institute and maintain these levels of support are able to enter into the production of mass communication.

Media economics have contributed to another trend that made itself evident at the end of the decade: consolidation of ownership. Companies that have strong financial resources are the likeliest to survive high operating expenses and are better

TABLE 1-1 Global Media Giants	
COMPANY (HOME COUNTRY)	1992 REVENUE (IN BILLIONS)
Sony (Japan)	$28.7
Time Warner (USA)	13.0
Bertelsmann A.G. (Germany)	9.3
Matsushita (Japan)	7.4
Hachette, S.A. (France)	5.7
News Corp. (Australia)	8.6

In 1993, Paramount was planning to merge with Viacom or QVC. If the deal were consumated, the new company would be part of this list.

able to compete in the marketplace. Consequently, by 1991 a number of global media giants had emerged that dominated the field. The biggest of these companies is Time Warner Inc., formed in 1989 by the merger of Time, Inc., with Warner Communications. Table 1-1, lists other "mega-media" companies. Note that the names listed in the table will frequently turn up in succeeding chapters.

Competing for Profits

Since we are talking about money, we should also note that most mass communication organizations exist to make a profit. Although there may be some exceptions to this generalization (the public broadcasting system, for example), most newspapers, magazines, record companies, and TV and radio stations in the United States strive to produce a profit for their owners and stockholders. Although it is true that radio and television stations are licensed to serve in the public interest and that newspapers commonly assume a "watchdog" role on behalf of their readers, if they do not make money, they go out of business. The consumer is the ultimate source of this profit. When you buy an album or a movie ticket, part of the price includes the profit. Newspapers, TV, magazines, and radio earn most of their profits by selling their audiences to advertisers. The cost of advertising, in turn, is passed on by the manufacturers to the consumer. Thus, although the process may be direct or indirect, the audience eventually pays the bills. The economics of mass communication is an important topic, and we will have more to say about it later in this book.

Since the audience is the source of profits, mass communication organizations compete with one another as they attempt to attract an audience. This should come as no surprise to anyone who has ever watched television or passed a magazine stand. The major TV networks compete with one another to get high ratings. Millions of dollars are spent each year in promoting the new fall season. Radio stations compete with other stations that have similar formats. Some even give away prizes for listening; others play more music. Record companies spend large sums promoting their records, hoping to outsell their competitors. Daily newspapers compete with weeklies and radio and television. *Time* competes with *Newsweek*. Motion picture companies gamble millions on films in an effort to compete successfully. This fierce competition has several consequences, and this will be a topic that we will return to time and again.

● ● ● ●
MODELS FOR STUDYING MASS COMMUNICATION

Figure 1-1 outlines the elements present in the general process of communication. When we want to talk about mass communication, however, we need to construct a new model that adequately represents its distinctive features. But first a word about models. At a basic level models try to show the main elements of any structure or process and the relationship between these main elements. Models are helpful for several reasons:

1. They help us *organize* by ordering and relating various elements and concepts to one another.

2. They help us *explain* things by illustrating in simplified form information that might otherwise be complicated or ambiguous.

3. They help us *predict* outcomes or the end processes of events.

At the same time, there are some risks in using models. Inevitably, models are incomplete and oversimplified. There is no single model that is appropriate for all purposes and situations. Models are aids to help us understand the mass communication process. We need to be careful to choose the proper model for the purpose we have in mind.

Now let's examine a model that seems useful in our study of the dynamics of communication. This is the Westley–MacLean model and is presented in Figure 1-3. At first glance the model seems complicated, but closer examination shows that it is straightforward.

FIGURE 1-3 *Westley and MacLean's conceptual model of mass communication in which a second type of communicator, C (channel role), is introduced. (From Bruce Westley and Mal MacLean, "A Conceptual Model for Mass Communication Research,"* Journalism Quarterly, *34: 31–38, 1957. Reprinted by permission of* Journalism Quarterly.*)*

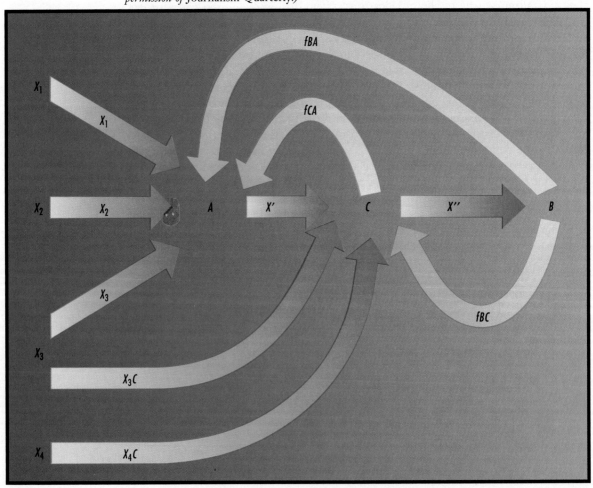

Let's begin our discussion by starting at the left side and working to the right. The X's in the model (X_1, X_2, X_3) stand for events or objects in the social environment. They may be election results, earthquakes, a new album by R.E.M., baseball scores, or another Star Trek movie. The A in the model refers to *advocates*. These are individuals or organizations that have something to say about the X's to the general public. The A's might be politicians ("Vote for me"), public relations agencies ("We'd like to tell you what our company is doing to clean up pollution"), advertisers ("Buy our jeans"), news sources ("I'm announcing my resignation"), or special-interest groups ("We must save the sparrows"). In short, they are purposive communicators.

The C in the model stands for the channel. More precisely, the C stands for the individual or individuals within a media organization who select from the messages offered by the A's those that they (the C's) think are of interest to the audience ("We'd better cover the resignation, but let's ignore the save the sparrows people"). Also note that the C's can select directly from the X's in the environment and communicate information about them to the audience as well ("Events in eastern Europe make up our lead story"). The C's are seen as neutral; they are nonpurposive communicators. Turning back to the model, X' represents a message coming from A that is selected by the media organization to be communicated to the audience (for example, a resignation speech). X_3C represents the observation of an event made directly by the media without the intervention of an A (for example, a reporter covering a city council meeting). The X'' represents the message as modified by the media organization for transmission. The resignation speech, for example, might have lasted fifteen minutes, but the evening TV news might contain only a ninety-second summary.

The B in the model stands for a behavioral role, an individual or group or even a social system. In other words, the B's are the audience, people like you and me, at whom the messages from media organizations are aimed. The arrows going from right to left in the model represent the channels of feedback. For example, fBC is the feedback from audience member to the communication organization, either by way of direct contact, such as a letter to the editor, or indirectly, through audience research. The notation fBA represents the feedback from a member of the audience (B) to the original source (A). For example, this might be a vote for a candidate or the purchase (or nonpurchase) of some product. The feedback from communicator to advocate is fCA. This might take the form of additional coverage in the future or other attempts to somehow change or modify A's purposive communications.

In addition, the model helps us predict certain things about the process. For example, let's say that the unemployment rate in a certain state has fallen dramatically in the last six months (an example of X, an event in the environment), and a local politician (an A role) holds a new conference to take credit for it. The news conference is covered by the local TV news crew (a C role) and from a thirty-minute press conference (X') a sixty-second story (X'') is carried on the evening news. The model suggests that the news story (X'') may be significantly different from the original event (X) and the interpretation offered by the politician (X'). The news story might point out that the drop in unemployment is really just a statistical quirk or that the politician had little to do with the decline. In short, the model alerts us to the fact that messages will be altered as they pass through the various communication stages.

This model is useful in drawing our attention to several distinctive features of mass communication:

1. the several stages at which selection (gatekeeping) takes place

2. the self-regulating nature of the system since a large number of C roles compete for B's

3. the importance of feedback in the total process

Of course, the model is not perfect. One of the things it does not portray is the relationship of the communicators and audience members to society. *A* and *C* are influenced by the political and economic climate as well as their own organizational arrangements. Audience members (*B*) are also part of the larger social environment. They belong to families, have friends, classmates, or co-workers, belong to political parties, and are part of the social fabric. In sum, the impact of social processes should not be overlooked.

The remainder of this book can be organized according to the Westley–MacLean model. Parts Two and Three concentrate on the *C* roles in the model. Part Four includes a look at the *A*'s, as exemplified by advertising and public relations, and the *X*'s, as seen in news gathering and reporting. Part Five looks at the social implications of the media as illustrated by controls, rules, and regulations. Parts Six and Seven look at the audience, the *B* roles, and the various feedback channels used by the audience.

● ● ● ●
MASS COMMUNICATION MEDIA

Defining Mass Media

In the broadest sense of the word, a medium is the channel through which a message travels from the source to the receiver ("medium" is singular; "media" is plural). Thus in our discussion, we have pointed to sound and light waves as media of communication. When we talk about mass communication, we also need channels to carry the message. **Mass media** use these channels to carry the message. Our definition of a mass medium will include not only the mechanical devices that transmit and sometimes store the message (TV cameras, radio microphones, printing presses), but also the institutions that use these machines to transmit messages. When we talk about the mass media of television, radio, newspapers, magazines, sound recording, and film, we will be referring to the people, the policies, the organizations, and the technology that go into producing mass communication. A **media vehicle** is a single component of the mass media, such as a newspaper, radio station, TV network, magazine, etc.

In this book we will examine seven different mass media: radio, television, film, book publishing, sound recording, newspapers, and magazines. Of course, these seven are not the only mass media that exist. If we choose, we might also include billboards, comic books, posters, direct mail, matchbooks, and buttons in our discussion. To do that, however, would require a volume much larger than this. In an effort to conserve space (and to make the book easier to carry), we will limit ourselves to the seven we have mentioned. These seven tend to be the ones that have the largest audiences, employ the most people, and have the greatest impact. They are also the ones with which most of us are familiar.

The End of Mass Communication As We Know It?

The last two decades have seen a basic change in the mass communication process: it's gotten less mass and more selective. In the 1930s, for example, almost everybody tuned their radios to *Amos 'n' Andy*. Other top-rated shows might attract about 40 percent of all people in the U.S. Today the top-rated network radio show gets about 2 or 3 percent of the audience. In the 1950s, virtually everybody watched Milton Berle on TV. The typical top-rated shows would attract about 45 percent of all TV households. This figure dropped to about 33 percent in the 1960s and 31 percent in the 1970s. Currently, top-rated shows get about 24–28 percent of the audience. The three TV networks' share of the audience was 90 percent in the 1960s. Now, thanks to competition from cable, the Fox network, VCRs, and independent stations, the three nets get less than 65 percent.

In the 1940s and 1950s, general interest, mass circulation magazines, such as *Life*, *Look*, and *Collier's* were popular. Today *Reader's Digest*, the most widely read general interest magazine, is down from its all-time high of 18.4 million readers in 1977 to about 16 million in 1991. *TV Guide* lost about four million readers in the same period. In 1960, about 75 percent of the adult population read a newspaper. In 1990, that figure was down to about 55 percent.

What we are seeing is the "fractionalization" or "segmentation" of the mass media audience. What are the forces behind this fundamental change? First, today's audiences are different. There has been an increase in one-parent families. A record number of women are now working outside the home. In many households both the husband and wife bring home paychecks. Time has become a scarce commodity and much of it is devoted to commuting, working, and child-raising. All of this means less time devoted to the media, and when audience members do spend time with the media, they look for content geared to their own special interests. Secondly, the emergence of new media such as VCRs, cable TV, computers, and direct broadcast satellites has given today's consumers more media to choose from. Consequently, the audience for any one media vehicle is divided into smaller and smaller segments.

Finally, manufacturers and service organizations have turned from mass to target marketing as they discovered that it was more efficient and ultimately more profitable to concentrate on well-defined consumer groups instead of the mass audience ("niche-picking" as some have called it). This has led to an era where Americans now have more choices than ever before. In the retail arena, specialty shops and mail order catalogs have taken customers from Sears and J. C. Penney. Even in the breakfast cereal market, mass appeal products like corn flakes and oatmeal have lost ground to distinctive brands such as Just Right, Special K, and Mueslix. The same trend has carried through in the media. Large movie theaters with a single screen have given way to four- or eight-screen multiplexes. Instead of a handful of radio stations, most big cities now have a couple dozen. There are magazines for seemingly every demographic and special interest group. Back in the 1960s, most households could get an average of just four TV channels. Now most get more than thirty and some get sixty or more.

Does all of this mean that mass communication no longer is a meaningful term? Should this book be retitled *The Dynamics of Segmented Communication*? Well, not quite yet. In the first place, the definition of mass communication given earlier still applies to the current situation. Complex organizations still use machines to transmit public messages aimed at large, heterogeneous, and scattered audiences. Of course, the audiences reached by mass media are becoming smaller and more specialized, but they are still large (even a flop TV show can reach four million households), scattered, and heterogeneous enough to qualify as mass communication.

Secondly, we need to make a distinction among the terms mentioned above. The *channels* of mass communication are still unchanged. There are, however, more and more *mass media* using these channels: almost 11,000 radio stations today compared with half that number a couple of decades ago, more than 3000 new magazines in the last decade, a record number of TV stations, etc. Further, the *messages* sent by these mass media through the channels of mass communication have become more specialized. Magazines, newspapers, radio, TV, etc., are aiming their content at more defined audience niches, in part to meet the demands of advertisers and in part because it's more cost efficient. Consequently, it's harder for any one media vehicle to reach a large number of the audience. Nonetheless, the potential is still there for the right message in the right medium to transcend the limits of specialized content and to attract a mass audience in the broadest sense of the term. This has happened, for example, with *Roots*, the farewell episode of *Cheers*, *The Cosby Show*, *Star Wars*, *Home Alone*, and coverage of the opening hostilities of the Gulf War. And who knows, perhaps with the right formula a new mass-appeal magazine might just catch on.

Mass Media Symbiosis

If we can borrow a term from biology, we can easily see that the mass media have evolved a system of **symbiotic relationships.** In biology, symbiosis is defined as the association of two organisms for mutual benefit. To draw an analogy, in mass media, the television and film industries demonstrate what we might call a form of symbiosis. The same companies produce works for both media; films that originally played in the theaters find their way to television in videocassettes, over cable, and over network and local stations. Film actors and actresses make TV shows and vice versa; executives from one industry sometime cross over into the other. The sound recording and radio industries demonstrate another symbiotic relationship. Most radio stations depend on recordings to fill their air time; most records need air play to sell. MTV demonstrates a three-way symbiosis: Record companies use it as a promotional tool; MTV uses videos supplied by the record companies as their programming source; and radio stations use MTV as a sounding board for new releases. Similar relationships exist between newspapers and magazines. Most Sunday editions carry a magazine insert; the same writers contribute to both media and both employ the same audience measurement and marketing techniques. Some intermedia relationships have crossed traditional boundaries. Many local newspapers also operate a local cable TV channel. Best-selling books are made into theatrical and TV movies, while movie scripts are transformed into books. There are TV shows that review films. Although the following chapters discuss the various media individually, it should be kept in mind that they do not exist in a vacuum. In the future, we are likely to see more examples of the synergy that exists among all communication media.

Lastly, it's becoming harder and harder to tell the media apart. Motion pictures are transferred to videotape and played over the home TV set. Made-for-TV movies are released as theatrical movies overseas. Some radio stations now carry the audio portion of a local TV station's newscast. Newspapers exist in electronic and fax versions. There are magazines that are distributed on videotape. In addition, the

Leonardo, Donatello, Raphael, and Michelangelo (missing in this scene from Secret of the Ooze) *probably don't realize that they are part of media symbiosis. Their TV cartoon characters have spawned three movies, several records, dozens of books, stage performances, and a whole line of toys.* **Talk about turtle power.** *(Globe Photos)*

dividing lines among media are blurring with regard to their functions (more about functions in the next chapter). Radio used to be the place where most young people heard new music. Now they can tune into MTV or one of the other dozens of outlets for music videos. Taking a date to a movie used to mean leaving the home and going somewhere special. Now it's perfectly possible to watch a movie in the comfort of home. Some experts have labeled this coming together of media as *convergence*. It is also a trend that should continue in the future.

• • • •
SUGGESTIONS FOR FURTHER READING

The books listed below are good sources to consult for further information about the concepts discussed in this chapter.

BERLO, DAVID K., *The Process of Communication*, New York: Holt, Rinehart and Winston, 1960.

BRODY, E.W., *Communication Tomorrow: New Audiences, New Technologies, New Media*, New York: Praeger, 1990.

DEFLEUR, MELVIN, AND SANDRA BALL-ROKEACH, *Theories of Mass Communication*, New York: Longman, 1989.

GUMPERT, GARY, *Talking Tombstones and Other Tales of the Media Age*, New York: Oxford University Press, 1987.

HARMS, L.S., *Human Communication: The New Fundamentals*, New York: Harper & Row, 1974.

LEDERMAN, LINDA COSTIGAN, *New Dimensions: An Introduction to Human Communication*, Dubuque, Iowa: William C. Brown, 1977.

MCQUAIL, DENIS, AND SVEN WINDAHL, *Communication Models*, New York: Longman, 1981.

MEYROWITZ, JOSHUA, *No Sense of Place*, New York: Oxford University Press, 1985.

SCHRAMM, WILBUR, *Men, Women, Messages, and Media*, New York: Harper & Row, 1982.

USES AND FUNCTIONS OF MASS COMMUNICATION

here are several methods that we can use to describe the relationship among media, society, and individuals. We might, for example, look at the persuasive aspect of mass communication or the sociological environment of the media. Or we might take a critical look at how the media affect our lives and our culture. Of the many that we might discuss, the **functional approach** seems the most advantageous. Specifically, this technique:

- provides us with a perspective from which to examine mass communication

- generates concepts that are helpful in understanding media behavior

- makes us aware of the diversity of gratifications provided by the media

In its simplest form, the functional approach holds that something is best understood by examining how it is used. In mass communication, this means examining the use that audiences make of their interactions with the media.

By way of introduction, below are some more or less typical responses that were given by college students to the following questions:

1. Why do you watch TV?
   "I like to vegetate sometimes."
   "I like to watch when there's nothing else to do."

2. Why do you go to movies?
   "I enjoy going to the theater with someone I like. I also enjoy the buttered popcorn"
   "I like to go to movies because they afford an opportunity to lose two hours in someone else's life."

3. Why do you listen to records and tapes?
   "I listen because music can make a room more comfortable."
   "I like music and it takes my mind off what I'm doing (work, driving, etc.)."

4. Why do you watch TV soap operas?
   "I watch them because I like to see just how bizarre they can get in terms of smut."
   "I watch them because I feel as if I know the characters personally and as if I'm actually involved in their lives."

Responses like these have led to several generalizations about the functions that media have for a society and for its individual members. This chapter will focus on cataloging and describing those functions.

THE ROLE OF MASS COMMUNICATION

Maybe the best way to appreciate the role that mass communication plays in our society would be to imagine what it would be like if, all of a sudden, the whole system never existed. How would we find out what was on sale at the local supermarket? How would we know what songs are most popular? How would we know Cher's current love interest? (Would there *be* a Cher?) How could we find out what was happening in the Middle East? How would we find out the real story behind the resignation of a prominent cabinet member? How could we avoid the traffic jams during rush hour? How would we spend our evenings? Obviously, the mass media are a pervasive part of our life. Just how pervasive might become clear if we charted the various functions the media perform for us. Before we do this, however, we need to realize that different media have different primary uses. Not many people, for example, listen to records to find out the latest news. Even fewer people read the newspaper while driving their cars. Moreover, different groups of people make use of the same mass media content for different reasons. History professors, for example, might read articles in scholarly journals in order to keep up with their profession. Others who pursue history as a hobby might read the same journals in order to relax and be diverted from their normal routine.

One more qualification needs to be mentioned before we begin examining the functions and uses of mass communication. It is possible to conduct this analysis on at least two different levels. On the one hand, we could take the perspective of a sociologist and look through a wide-angle lens and consider the functions performed by the mass media for the entire society (this approach is sometimes called **macro-analysis**).

This viewpoint focuses on the apparent intention of the mass communicator and emphasizes the manifest purpose inherent in the media content. On the other hand, we could look through a close-up lens at the individual receivers of the content, the audience, and ask them to report how they use mass media (this approach is called **microanalysis**). Sometimes the end results of these two methods are similar in that the consumer uses the content in the way that the source intended. Sometimes they are not similar, and the consumer uses the media in a way not anticipated by the mass communicator. Let's begin our analysis by using the wide-angle lens.

● ● ● ●
FUNCTIONS OF MASS COMMUNICATION FOR SOCIETY

For a society to exist, certain communication needs must be met. These needs existed long before Gutenberg bolted together his printing press and Morse started sending dots and dashes. Primitive tribes had sentinels who scanned the environment and reported dangers. Councils of elders interpreted facts and made decisions. Tribal meetings were used to transmit these decisions to the rest of the group. Other members of the tribe may have been storytellers and jesters who functioned to entertain the group. As society became larger and more complex, these jobs grew too big to be handled by single individuals. With the advent of a technology that allowed the development of mass communication, these jobs were taken over by the mass media. This change was an important one, and throughout the following discussion we will examine the consequences of performing these communication functions by means of mass communication as opposed to interpersonal communication. Furthermore, there may be instances where these consequences are undesirable from the point of view of the welfare of the society. These harmful or negative consequences are called **dysfunctions**. We will mention some of these as well. Lastly, these functions are not mutually exclusive. A given example might illustrate several different categories.

Surveillance

Of all the media functions, this one is probably the most obvious. **Surveillance** refers to what we popularly call the news and information role of the media. The media have taken the place of sentinels and lookouts. Correspondents for wire services, TV networks, and newspapers are located across the globe. These individuals gather information for us that we couldn't get for ourselves. Their reports are funneled back to mass media organizations that, in turn, produce a radio or TV newscast or print a paper or magazine. The size of this surveillance apparatus is impressive; in the early 1990s, more than 90,000 people were employed in news-gathering jobs in radio, television, newspapers, news magazines, and wire services. The output is also substantial. The three national television networks provide approximately 600 hours annually of regularly scheduled news programs. CNN provides a twenty-four-hour news service to cable subscribers. Many radio stations broadcast nothing but news. News magazines reach nearly 10 million people. There are approximately 1650 daily newspapers and around 7500 weeklies that also spread the news. Surveillance is apparently an important function, and the degree of audience dependence on the media for news supports this observation. In any given day, approximately 50 million to 60 million Americans are exposed to mass-communicated news. About 90 percent of the American public report that they receive most of their news from either the electronic media or newspapers.

The surveillance function can be divided further into two main types. **Warning** or **beware surveillance** occurs when the media inform us about threats from hurricanes, erupting volcanoes, depressed economic conditions, increasing inflation, or military attack. These warnings can be about immediate threats (a television station interrupts programming to broadcast a tornado warning), or they can be about long-term or chronic threats (a newspaper series about air pollution or unemployment). There is, however, much information that is not particularly threatening to society that people might like to know about. The second type, called **instrumental surveillance**, has to do with the transmission of information that is useful and helpful in everyday life. News about what films are playing at the local theaters, stock market prices, new products, fashion ideas, recipes, teen fads, and so on, are examples of instrumental surveillance. Note also that not all examples of surveillance occur in what we tradition-ally label the news media. *People* magazine and *Reader's Digest* perform a surveillance function (most of it instrumental); so does *Modern Screen* ("Find Out Madonna's New Love!!!!!"). Smaller, more specialized publications such as technical journals also perform the job of surveillance. In fact, the surveillance function can be found in content that is primarily meant to entertain. A soap opera might perform an instrumen-tal surveillance function by portraying new hair styles and furniture arrangements.

What are some of the consequences of relying on the mass media to perform this surveillance function? In the first place, news travels much faster, especially since the advent of the electronic media. It took months for the news of the end of the War of 1812 to travel across the Atlantic. The famous Battle of New Orleans was actually fought after peace had been declared. It took weeks for news of Lincoln's assassination to spread to the rural Midwest. In contrast, when John Kennedy was assassinated, 90 percent of the U.S. population knew about it within one hour. And the beginning of the air war against Iraq was carried live by CNN. This speed sometimes leads to problems. Inaccuracies and distortions travel just as fast as truthful statements. During the 1980 Republican convention in Detroit, the anchorman for one TV network reported that former President Gerald Ford would be the vice-presidential nominee. The *Chicago Sun Times* carried a front-page banner headline: "It's Reagan–Ford."

The warning function: this antidrug message was one of the most remembered public service campaigns in the last ten years. (Courtesy, Partnership for a Drug-Free America) ▶

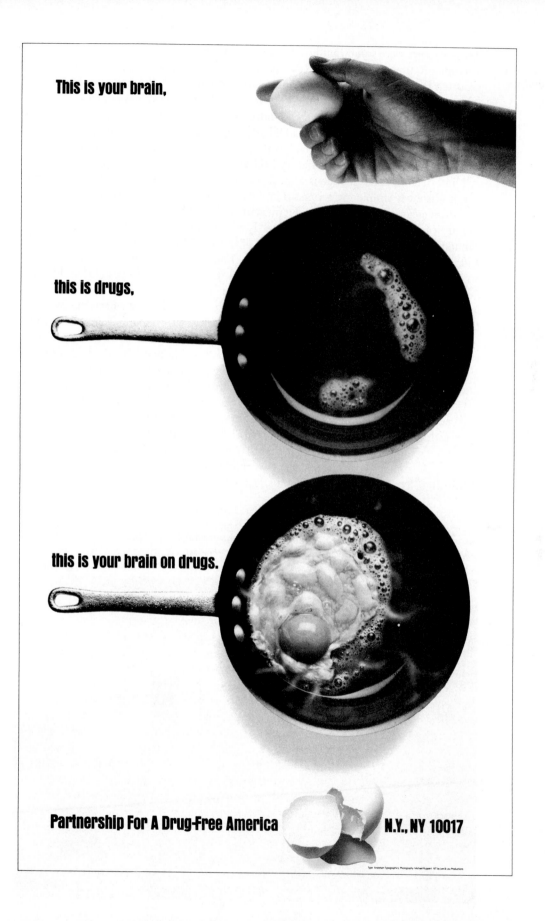

This is your brain,

this is drugs,

this is your brain on drugs.

Partnership For A Drug-Free America   N.Y., NY 10017

35

These reports were somewhat premature. During the live coverage of the assassination attempt on President Ronald Reagan, one of the television networks erroneously reported that Press Secretary James Brady had been killed. Brady had been seriously wounded. The live coverage of the Persian Gulf War was also marked by inaccuracies which might have been corrected had more time been available for fact checking. One television network reported that Israel had been attacked by Iraqi Scud missiles which contained nerve gas. No such attack had occurred. Another report erroneously stated that Israel had mounted a retaliatory raid against Iraq.

The second consequence is a bit more subtle. In prehistoric times, if war broke out, it was fairly simple for people to find out about it. A stranger would appear at the mouth of a cave and belt the inhabitant with a club. There was little doubt about the validity of this information; it was directly observable. The world of early men and women was small and easily surveyed. All of it was within the range of their eyesight, and seldom did it extend over the next hill. Today, thanks to the mass media, there aren't any more hills. Our world now extends well beyond our eyesight, and we can no longer observe all of it directly. The media relay to us news from environments beyond our immediate senses that we cannot easily verify. Much of what we know about the world is machine-processed, hand-me-down information. News is prescreened for us by a complex arrangement of reporters and editors, and our conception of reality is based on this second-generation information, whose authenticity we do not usually question. For example, human beings have allegedly walked on the moon. Millions saw it—on TV. Not many saw it in person. Instead, we took the word of the TV networks that what we were seeing was fact, not fiction. The creative people in TV and movies, however, were perfectly capable of fabricating the whole event. In fact (interesting expression), many of the networks' simulations looked more convincing than the "real thing." (Some people feel that television staged the whole thing some-where in Arizona as part of a massive, government-inspired publicity stunt.) The point is this: In today's world, with its sophisticated system of mass communication, we are

Surveillance function: Judge Clarence Thomas being questioned by the Senate Judiciary Committee. Thanks to coverage by CNN, the networks, and C-Span, these sessions attracted the biggest audience for a Senate hearing since the Watergate investigation of the 1970s. (Brad Markell/Gamma Liaison)

highly dependent on others for news. Much of this news is difficult to verify firsthand, so we must rely on what others tell us. Consequently, we have to put a certain amount of trust in the media that do our surveillance. This trust, called **credibility**, is an important factor in determining which news medium people find the most believable. We will discuss the concept at length in Chapter 14.

Media surveillance can cause needless anxiety. In late 1990 a small army of reporters descended on the town of New Madrid, Missouri, when an "expert" predicted that an earthquake would strike the area around December 4th. It seemed to matter little that the expert's predictions had been wrong before and that the technique used to predict the quake was ridiculed by other scientists. In New Madrid, sales of earthquake insurance jumped 50 percent; newspapers published special pull-out sections detailing what to do in the case of a quake; many schools announced that they would be closed on that date; and a significant number of residents left town on the predicted day. No earthquake happened and the media wound up doing stories about the media coverage the nonevent prompted.

By the same token, media coverage can be dysfunctional by generating false hopes. In the early 1990s, a possible cure for AIDS that involved heating the blood was given extensive coverage by the media even though only one patient had been ostensibly helped by the treatment and there was little scientific evidence to suggest that the technique was effective. A lot less attention was given to the subsequent developments in the story that suggested the person "cured" of AIDS had really been misdiagnosed and that the treatment proved of little value for other patients.

Lastly, the fact that certain individuals or issues receive media attention means that they achieve a certain amount of prominence. Sociologists call this process **status conferral**. At the basis of this phenomenon is a rather circular belief that audiences seem to endorse. The audience evidently believes that if you *really* matter, you will be at the focus of mass media attention, and if you are the focus of media attention, then you *really* matter. Knowing this fact, many individuals and groups go to extreme measures to get media coverage for themselves and their causes so that this status-conferral effect will occur. Parades, demonstrations, publicity stunts, and outlandish

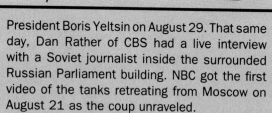

Covering the Coup

Covering the aborted 1991 coup in the U.S.S.R. was made easier thanks to a policy of noninterference by the Soviet government. Unlike the Tiananmen Square violence, during which the Chinese government shut down the broadcasting facilities, reporters in Moscow were generally given freedom to report what they chose. In addition, the three networks were able to fly in extra equipment and personnel to help them get the story out faster.

CNN broke the story first, at 11:27 P.M. on Sunday, August 18. Half an hour later, CNN's Moscow Bureau Chief was providing live reports over the telephone. The three networks also contributed some major scoops. ABC's Diane Sawyer got an exclusive interview with Russian President Boris Yeltsin on August 29. That same day, Dan Rather of CBS had a live interview with a Soviet journalist inside the surrounded Russian Parliament building. NBC got the first video of the tanks retreating from Moscow on August 21 as the coup unraveled.

One question that went unanswered was how much money the financially beleaguered nets were willing to commit to the story. In the wake of the $150 million or so the networks lost in advertising revenue during the Persian Gulf War, many thought the networks would eventually have to skimp on their coverage of the events in Moscow. Since the coup only lasted three days, cost did not become a factor.

Even entertainment programs can perform the surveillance function, sometimes with unforeseen results. For example, on December 19, 1973, the writers for NBC's *Tonight Show* starring Johnny Carson noticed a short newspaper item that quoted a Wisconsin congressman as saying that the federal government had fallen behind in getting bids from its toilet-paper suppliers. Immediately sensing the humor in such a situation, the writers put together a couple of gags for Carson's opening monologue. Later that night Johnny Carson jokingly informed his millions of viewers that the United States was facing an acute toilet-paper shortage.

Unfortunately, some people confused the *Tonight Show* with the *NBC Nightly News*, and when the supermarkets opened the next morning the rush was on. People didn't want to be caught empty-handed, and roll after roll was snatched from the shelves. Some people appeared at checkout counters with as much as twenty dollars' worth of the stuff. In Flushing, New York, one woman bought a case of sixty-four rolls. The hoarding got so bad that some grocery stores started rationing toilet paper, four rolls to a customer. The paper companies that produce toilet tissue were caught off guard; they never anticipated such a run on their product. They geared up to meet the abnormal demand, but it would take time to get their shipments to the stores. Meanwhile, customers, in their eagerness to stockpile, had wiped out the supermarkets' supply. Other consumers, seeing the empty shelves, were convinced that Carson was right about the shortage and scrambled quickly to other stores.

Carson tried to stem the tide. He announced that he was only joking. The news item referred to the production of low-grade, government-issued paper. There was no shortage of the squeezably soft, high-grade consumer type. This helped a little, but since panic feeds on itself, it took another three weeks before the shelves were back to normal.

Jay Leno, Carson's replacement, almost suffered through a similar incident in 1991. In his opening monologue, Leno recounted a newspaper story in which it was reported that the Lionel Corporation was going bankrupt. Leno then did some jokes about the loss of Lionel toy trains. Unfortunately, Lionel Trains was still in business and had no connection to the Lionel Corporation. The next day, Lionel Trains national headquarters was flooded with calls from retailers who were ordering trains for the holiday season. Leno corrected the statement at the beginning of the next show and reassured children and their parents that Santa could still bring them a Lionel train for Christmas. All the while he was saying this, a Lionel train was chugging along a track at his feet.

behavior are commonly employed to capture air time or column inches. Those concerned about nuclear war stage "die-ins" to capture attention. Those who favor the legalization of marijuana sponsor "smoke-ins" to attract media attention. In the early 1990s, the Ku Klux Klan staged a march in Washington, D.C. Only about forty people participated in the march, but it still garnered the group extensive coverage on TV and in the print media.

The media can even convey status to topics that may have been dead and buried—literally. In mid-1991, thanks in part to the media interest generated by an author with an upcoming book on the topic, the body of former President Zachary Taylor, who died in 1850, was exhumed and tested for traces of arsenic in an attempt to discover if he was murdered. The exhumation and subsequent analysis of the remains got top story coverage on TV and a three-page spread in *Newsweek*. As it turns out, Taylor's death was not the result of foul play.

Closely allied with the surveillance function is the interpretation function. The mass media do not supply just facts and data. They also provide information on the ultimate meaning and significance of those events. One form of interpretation is so obvious that many people overlook it. Not everything that happens in the world on any given day can be included in the newspaper or in a TV or radio newscast. Media organizations select those events that are to be given time or space and decide how much prominence they are to be given. Those stories that are given page-one space and eight-column headlines are obviously judged to be more important than those items that are given two paragraphs on page twelve. In a TV newscast, those stories that are given two minutes at the beginning of the show are deemed more newsworthy than the item that gets two minutes toward the end. Stories that ultimately make it into the paper or the newscast have been judged by the various gatekeepers involved to be more important that those that didn't make it.

The most obvious example of this function can be found on the editorial pages of a newspaper. Interpretation, comment, and opinion are provided for the reader so that he or she gains an added perspective on the news stories carried on other pages. Perhaps an elected official has committed some impropriety. An editorial might call for that person's resignation, thus demonstrating that the management of the newspaper considers this impropriety to be serious. A newspaper might endorse one candidate for public office over another, thereby indicating that at least in the paper's opinion, the available information indicates that this individual is more qualified than the other.

Interpretation is not confined to editorials. Articles devoted to an analysis of the causes behind a particular event or a discussion of implications of a new government policy are also examples of the interpretation function. Why is the price of gasoline going up? What impact will a prolonged dry spell have on food prices? Treatment of these topics may deal with more than the factual information that might be contained in a straight news story. Radio and television also carry programs or segments of programs that fall under this heading. An editorial by David Brinkley or by the manager of the local TV or radio station are two such examples. TV documentaries such as *Eyes on the Prize* or *Common Threads: Stories from the Quilt* are others. When the president broadcasts a major political address, network correspondents usually appear afterward to tell us what the president "really said." At special events such as political conventions, rocket launches, and elections, commentators are on hand to interpret for us the meaning behind what is going on. During the Gulf War, CNN and the networks brought in dozens of experts on topics ranging from military hardware to oil field operation to interpret the meaning of the day's events.

Interpretation, as is probably obvious by now, can take various forms. Editorial cartoons, which originated in 1754, may be the most popular form. Other examples are less obvious but no less important. Critics are employed by the various media to rate motion pictures, plays, books, and records. Restaurants, cars, architecture, and even religious services are reviewed by some newspapers and magazines. One entire magazine, *Consumer Reports*, is devoted to analysis and evaluation of a wide range of general products.

The interpretation function can also be found in media content that at first glance might appear to be purely entertainment. *Free Willy* conveyed a certain viewpoint about ecology and the ethics of keeping wild animals in captivity. *Rising Sun* contained an interpretation of Japanese culture. Public Enemy's rap songs relate a certain viewpoint toward authority. Attitudes about the role of women in society are presented in *Thelma and Louise*, *Designing Women*, and *Roseanne*. (Even the classic comic strip "Blondie" has taken a point of view about this topic as the title character rejoined the work force over her husband's objections.)

After spending decades picking up after Dagwood, Blondie joined the work force in 1991 by opening a catering business. (Reprinted with special permission of King Features Syndicate.)

Editorial statements about race relations can be found in episodes of *The Fresh Prince* and *In Living Color*.

What are the consequences of the mass media's performing this function? First, the individual is exposed to a large number of different points of view, probably far more than he or she could come in contact with through personal channels. Because of this, a person (with some effort) can evaluate all sides of an issue before arriving at an opinion. Additionally, the media make available to the individual a wide range of expertise that he or she might not have access to through interpersonal communication. Should we change the funding structure of Social Security? Thanks to the media, a person can read or hear the views of various economists, political scientists, politicians, and government workers.

There are, however, certain dysfunctions that might occur. Since media content is public, any criticism or praise of a certain individual or group is also public and might have positive or negative consequences for the medium involved. For example, when the television networks were carrying damaging news-analysis programs examining the Nixon administration's involvement in the Watergate affair, the White House threatened the networks with economic reprisals. Frank Stanton, then the president of CBS, claimed that a Nixon aide told him that the White House would bring CBS "to its knees on Wall Street and on Madison Avenue." A similar event occurred in 1986 when the Justice Department considered prosecuting five news organizations for publishing an analysis of the United States' code-breaking abilities. A newspaper that carries an interpretive piece critical of the insurance industry might prompt these companies to switch their advertising to a competitor. In 1976, when *The Atlantic Monthly* carried a cover story entitled "Rip-Off at the Supermarket," a number of store managers for a large supermarket chain pulled the copies of the magazine from their shelves. The public nature of interpretation and its possible negative consequences might discourage critical evaluation of controversial topics.

On another level, there is also the danger that an individual may in the long run come to rely too heavily on the views carried in the media and lose his or her critical

Suppose you were running in an election in a state where your name wasn't even on the ballot and where you never made a single personal appearance. Suppose further that when the votes were counted, you had received 49.4 percent while your nearest opponent had tallied only 42.2 percent. You would probably consider it a clear-cut victory. Interestingly enough, that is exactly the situation that occurred when incumbent President Lyndon Johnson outpolled Eugene McCarthy in the 1968 New Hampshire Democratic primary. Even more interesting is the way the mass media interpreted the results of the election. Despite what it seemed on the surface, the media called it a great victory for McCarthy. *Time* put him on the cover of its next issue. Inside, the magazine called his showing a victory in "all but the figures." "McCarthy Strong in N.H. Voting" said a headline in the *Washington Post*. "Senator Exceeds Top Primary Predictions . . ." said a headline in the *New York Times*. The media interpreted the results in such a way that McCarthy came out on top. A few weeks later, Lyndon Johnson withdrew from the race.

In 1972, Senator Edmund Muskie received 48 percent of the New Hampshire Democratic vote while Senator George McGovern, his nearest challenger, got only 37 percent. A big victory for Muskie? The media did not interpret it that way. "Ed Muskie's Underwhelming Victory," read a headline in *Newsweek*; "Disappointing," wrote *Time* about Muskie's vote total. McGovern went on to win the nomination.

By now you probably are thinking that the front-runner in the New Hampshire election is always perceived to be the loser by the mass media. Not exactly. In 1976, Jimmy Carter got only 30 percent of the Democratic vote, just six percentage points ahead of his nearest rival, Representative Morris Udall. A great showing for Udall? No. NBC called Carter "the man to beat." *Time* said his campaign was the only one "with real possibilities of breaking far ahead of the pack." Both *Time* and *Newsweek* put Carter on the cover. *Time* gave Carter more than 2600 lines of coverage; all of the other candidates

got only 300 lines total. Carter went on to win the nomination.

The room for interpretation was much narrower in 1980 as Ronald Reagan collected 50 percent of the Republican vote while his nearest pursuer collected only 23 percent. On the Democratic side incumbent Jimmy Carter collected 49 percent of the vote without even appearing in the state.

In 1984, the media, now more conscious of their role as political interpreters, were more cautious. The Democratic primary saw Gary Hart upset preelection favorite Walter Mondale by nine percentage points. The media gave more coverage to Hart (the number of reporters following his campaign increased from six to about seventy-five), but Mondale was not counted out. "Now It's a Race" was the headline in *Time* and both candidates were featured on the cover. The two-man race theme was featured throughout the next few months until Mondale won enough delegates to become the clear front-runner.

In 1988, the New Hampshire primary was upstaged by the Iowa caucuses, where instead of voting, people merely stood up in a group to support their candidates. Nonetheless, according to the *Media Monitor*, Iowa—with a total of eighty-nine delegates at stake—was the focus of 105 network TV stories. New Hampshire, with forty total delegates, was the subject of eighty-four stories. (In contrast, the "Super Tuesday" primaries, where 2056 delegates were up for grabs, were the focus of only 53 stories. Obviously, as far as the electronic media are concerned, the first contest is the most important.) The dangers of placing too much faith in caucus results were vividly illustrated by the interpretation of the Iowa aftermath. On the Democratic side, Congressman Richard Gephardt won and was dubbed the front-runner. On the Republican side, Senator Bob Dole won but the media paid more attention to the surprising showing of TV preacher Pat Robertson, labeling him a strong and viable candidate, and the weak showing of Vice President George Bush. A week later, Bush and Massachusetts Governor Michael Dukakis won in New Hampshire and each

(Continued)

went on to win his party's nomination. "Front-runner" Gephardt and "viable candidate" Robertson were out of the race shortly thereafter.

In 1992, Republican Pat Buchanan's 37 percent of the vote was interpreted as a severe blow to President George Bush's reelection campaign and Buchanan received increased media attention as a result.

ability. Accepting without question the views of the *New York Times* or David Brinkley may be easier than forming individual opinions, but it might lead to the dysfunctional situation in which the individual becomes passive and allows others to think for him or her.

Linkage

The mass media are able to join together by interpersonal channels different elements of society that are not directly connected. For example, mass advertising attempts to link the needs of buyers with the products of sellers. Legislators in Washington may try to keep in touch with constituents' feelings by reading their hometown papers. Voters, in turn, learn about the doings of their elected officials through newspapers, TV, and radio. Telethons that attempt to raise money for the treatment of certain diseases are another example of this **linkage** function. The needs of those suffering from the disease are matched with the desires of others who wish to see the problem eliminated.

Another type of linkage occurs when geographically separated groups that share a common interest are linked by the media. The outbreak of hostilities in the Persian Gulf linked together a whole nation concerned about the safety of their friends and relatives in the armed forces. Media usage reached record levels during the war as people turned to TV, radio, newspapers, and magazines to learn the latest war news. In mid-1991, a photo surfaced showing what many believed to be three American servicemen reported missing in action (MIA) during the Vietnam War. The public release and subsequent media coverage of the photograph linked together families of the missing, members of MIA activist groups, and sympathetic citizens, a coalition which eventually prompted Senate hearings on the issue. (It was later discovered that the photograph itself was apparently the work of a hoaxer, but this fact did not lessen the linkage impact of the coverage. Interest in renewing the search for MIAs continued strong.) Television coverage on the Tiananmen Square violence in Beijing linked together students in the United States who started their own protests in support of the Chinese students.

On a less somber note, other examples of the linkage function can be seen in the 1985 Live Aid Concert for Famine Relief and the 1988 Freedomfest concert against apartheid. The media coverage of these two events provided informational as well as emotional linkage among listeners and viewers and helped foster a general feeling that they were part of a worldwide movement. This linkage function is present at other levels as well. People who wear "No Nukes" buttons and T-shirts are advertising their feelings so that others with similar concerns might "link up" with them. The magazine *Gambling Times* allows a person who is interested in games of chance to be linked to others with similar interest. *The General*, a publication devoted to those who play board war games, contains a classified ad section where readers advertise for opponents. If a partner is found, then the two people turn to another channel, the postal system, to solidify the linkage. *Swinger*, a publication for those with "emancipated" attitudes toward sex, also contains a section where readers advertise to meet other swingers. Some firms, with the help of the local phone company, are offering "party lines" or "gab lines." A person dials a number and is linked up with similarly minded folks.

Linkage: These dramatic pictures from Beijing inspired Chinese students in the United States as well as American students to demonstrate in sympathy with their colleagues in China. (Sygma)

Most users of this service are looking for dates, and if two people hit it off, they can ask the operator to transfer them to a private line. One New York–based party line logged about 100,000 minutes in calls a day.

Of course, it is entirely possible that the media can create totally new social groups by linking members of society who have not previously recognized that others have similar interests. Some writers call this function the "public-making" ability of the mass media. In the movie *Network*, for example, newscaster/guru Howard Beal urges people to stand up for their rights by shouting, "I'm mad as hell and I'm not going to take it anymore!" The next scenes show people all over the country throwing open their windows and shouting this line into the night. Pretty soon, an organized I'm-Not-Going-To-Take-It-Any-More movement is born. A new group has been formed, with the media acting as linkage. This same phenomenon may account for the growth of the ecology movement in the 1970s and the antinuclear and antiapartheid movements in the mid-1980s.

When the media perform in this role, one obvious consequence is that societal groups can be mobilized quickly. For example, in 1993 more than 55 million people saw the dinosaur thriller *Jurassic Park*. Not surprisingly, the movie created a new audience interested in dinosaurs. Attendance at natural history museums skyrocketed as did the sales of dinosaur-based toys. The *Wall Street Journal* and *Newsweek* ran special articles about the huge beasts. The movie even rekindled scientific debate over what made the dinosaurs extinct.

On the other hand, this linkage function may have negative consequences. Persons with antisocial interests can be linked as easily as dinosaur buffs. Thus media attention to terrorists and other extremist groups might prompt others in the same direction.

Transmission of Values

The transmission of values is a subtle but nonetheless important function of the mass media. It has also been called the **socialization** function. Socialization refers to the ways in which an individual comes to adopt the behavior and values of a group. The mass media present portrayals of our society, and by watching, listening, and reading, we learn how people are supposed to act and what values are important. To illustrate, let's consider the images of two totally different concepts as seen in the media: motherhood and pets. The next time you watch television or thumb through a magazine pay close attention to the way mothers and children are presented. Mass media mommies are usually clean, loving, pretty, and cheerful. Ivory Snow laundry detergent typically adorns the packages of their products with the equivalent of a modern madonna—a wholesome-looking mother and healthy child smile out across grocery aisles (the company was embarrassed a few years ago when one of their clean-scrubbed, all-American types went on to star in X-rated films). The Clairol company sponsored an ad campaign that featured the "Clairol mother," an attractive and glamorous female who never let raising a child interfere with maintaining her hair. Babies, as seen in the media, are usually happy, healthy, content, and cherubic. They seldom cry and never spit up. All of them seem to resemble the bouncing baby that graces the little jars of Gerber's baby food in the supermarket. When they interact with their children, media mothers tend to be positive, warm, and caring. Consider these media mommies drawn from TV. Mrs. Cleaver (Beaver's mother), Mrs. Cunningham (*Happy Days*), Mrs. Partridge, Mrs. Walton, Mrs. Keaton (*Family Ties*), Mrs. Huxtable (*The Cosby Show*), even the sharp-tongued Roseanne (from the show of the same name), to name just a few, are all understanding, reasonable, friendly, and devoted to their children.* Obviously, these examples show that these media portrayals picture motherhood and childrearing as activities that have a positive value for society. Individuals who are exposed to these portrayals are likely to grow up and accept this value. Thus a social value is transmitted from one generation to another.

Pets provide another example in which this transmission of values is readily apparent. Think of some famous media pets: Sandy, Lassie, Rin Tin Tin, Gentle Ben, Flipper, Benji, Boomer, all of the 101 Dalmations, Lady, Tramp, etc.† What do they have in common? They are all pets who are trusted companions, loyal pals, and protectors of the young. Media dogs seldom snarl at baby sister and never soil the carpet. Not surprisingly, as each new generation is exposed to the portrayal of media pets, they are likely to come away with a positive value attached to the idea of owning a pet.

The mass media also teach us about people; they show us how they act and what is expected of them. In other words, the media present us with role models that we may observe and perhaps imitate. A study once indicated that many adolescents learned about dating behavior by watching films and television programs that featured this activity.

Sometimes the media consciously try to instill values and behavior patterns in the audience. In *Happy Days*, the Fonz was always shown wearing a crash helmet when on his motorcycle. More recently, many newspapers have begun reporting if accident victims were wearing seatbelts at the time of the mishap. In 1989, TV writers voluntarily agreed to portray alcohol usage more responsibly in their programs and to include references to "designated drivers" whenever possible. Here's another example. Next time you watch current TV shows, see if you can find anyone smoking a cigarette. The health concerns regarding smoking have prompted it to virtually disappear from prime time TV.

There are probably countless other examples of values and behaviors that are, in part at least, socialized through the media. However, at this point let us examine some of the consequences of having the mass media serve as agents of socialization. At one level, value transmission via the mass media will aid the stability of society. Common

---

* O.K., Peg Bundy of *Married . . . with Children* may be an exception.
† O.K., Cujo may be an exception.

The PBS documentary The Civil War *was the highest-rated program in PBS history. It also demonstrated the "public-making" ability of the media as it created a new interest in the Civil War. The new "public" was kept together by the re-broadcast of the series and by a related show,* The Songs of the Civil War, *promoted by this ad. (Courtesy of General Motors/Everett Collection)*

values and experiences are passed down to all members, thereby creating common bonds between them. On the other hand, the kinds of values and cultural information that are included in mass media content are selected by large organizations that may select values and behaviors that encourage the status quo. For example, the "baby industry" in this country is a multimillion-dollar one. This industry advertises heavily in the media; it is not surprising, then, that motherhood and babyhood are depicted in such an attractive light. To show mothers as harried, exhausted, overworked, and frazzled and babies as colicky, cranky, and drooling would not help maintain this profitable arrangement.

Mass media can also transmit values by enforcing social norms. Media coverage can ensure that the values of the majority society are highlighted and upheld by what they choose to emphasize. For example, in 1991 a man trying out a new home video camera taped several Los Angeles police officers beating a man who was apparently unarmed and not resisting arrest. The videotape of that event was shown numerous times on network TV and on local stations, and stills from the tape were published in newspapers and magazines. The tape prompted an outcry against police brutality and four officers connected with the beating were charged with assault in the case. Despite the tape, a jury acquitted the officers, prompting civil disturbances in Los Angeles and other cities. In another example, the media revealed that the host country club for the 1990 PGA golf championship did not admit blacks and that nearly half of the thirty-nine events on the PGA tour were played at country clubs with no black members. In response, civil rights groups threatened picketing and boycotts. As a response to this unfavorable publicity, the country club accepted a black member and the PGA changed its policy so that it would no longer sponsor tournaments at clubs that had exclusionary membership practices.

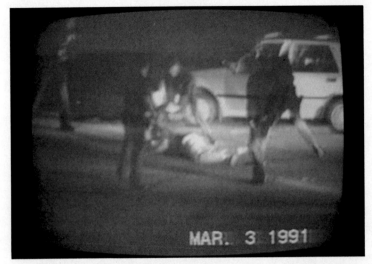

A still from what is probably the most well-known home-video recording in America, the Rodney King tape. Los Angeles erupted in violence when the officers shown in the tape were acquitted of assault charges. (Two of the four were later convicted on civil rights charges.) (Sygma)

Of all the mass media, it is probably television that has the greatest potential for the socialization of young children. By the time an individual has reached eighteen, he or she will have spent more time in watching television than any other single activity except sleep. A prime-time program that is popular with youngsters might draw an audience of 10 million 6- to 11-year-olds. Because of this wide exposure, several writers have warned of possible dysfunctions that might occur if television became the most important channel of socialization. For instance, since so many TV programs contain violence, it has been feared that youngsters who watch many violent programs might be socialized into accepting violence as a legitimate method of problem solving. In one survey among grade school youngsters, heavy TV viewers were more likely than light TV viewers to agree with the statement: "It's almost always all right to hit someone if you are mad at them." Or another possibility might be that the pervasiveness of television violence might encourage attitudes about the "real world" that would reflect the jeopardy found in the television content. One study, for example, found that children who were heavy TV viewers were more fearful of going out at night than were light TV viewers.

Another area that has received detailed attention is the potential negative consequences of mass media presentation of women. To be more specific, surveys about television have indicated that this medium can function as a source of knowledge about occupations. Since TV portrays it own peculiar world, it might present a distorted image of the world of work to its younger viewers. For example, during the 1970s, the two most common occupations held by leading female characters in prime-time TV were those of housewife and law enforcement officer. No other occupation came close to these two in frequency of portrayal. If she had no other sources of countervailing information, a girl growing up in this decade might have been socialized into believing she had two career choices when she grew up: to get married or to become a cop.

The media's function as enforcer of social norms has raised several other questions. When newspaper reporters kept presidential primary candidate Gary Hart under surveillance and revealed a relationship with a young woman, questions were raised about how much of a politician's private life should be open to scrutiny. The same controversy reemerged in 1991–1992 over media reports concerning the private life of Virginia Senator Charles Robb and Democratic presidential hopeful Governor Bill

Clinton. And the videotape of the L.A. beating was displayed so prominently, it raised the specter of a nation of what *Newsweek* called "video vigilantes" (see box below).

Finally, it has been argued that for many years the image of minority groups transmitted from one generation to the next by the mass media reflected the stereotypes held by those who were in power: white, Anglo-Saxon, Protestant males. As a result, American Indians and black Americans endured many years during which Indians were seen as savages who murdered civilized whites and blacks were depicted in menial and subordinate roles. These stereotypes were slow to change, partly because it took a long time for members of these minority groups to influence the workings of large media organizations.

Entertainment

Another obvious media function is that of entertainment. Two of the media examined in this book, motion pictures and sound recording, are devoted primarily to entertainment. Even though most of a newspaper is devoted to covering the events of the day,

Careful, We Might See You

About 15 million Americans now own camcorders and many are using them to chronicle the illegal or questionable activities of friends, neighbors, and police or other government authorities. The most well known of these homemade tapes, of course, is the videotape of Los Angeles police officers beating an unarmed man. Although not as famous, there are many other examples of amateurs catching unsavory activity on tape. A man in California taped a neighbor punching him in the face. Interestingly, the victim didn't tell the police about the tape. Instead, he gave it to a local TV station. In Georgia, a county worker videotaped several dispatchers at the local 911 emergency number sleeping on the job. A biologist went undercover to produce a homemade tape showing dolphins being slaughtered by tuna fishers. This trend toward citizen reporters will doubtlessly continue. CNN gave residents in Eastern Europe and the former Soviet Union low-cost cameras and asked them to be on the lookout for news. Globalvision, an organization in New York, has given cameras to residents on six continents and has asked them to shoot material that could be used in a documentary about human rights. In Italy, a TV show called *The Voice of Conscience* encouraged home viewers to send tapes of cheating office workers, unfaithful neighbors, and anybody else who might be engaged in unsavory activity.

In addition to the above, camcorders are being used in a variety of novel situations. Some patients videotape their own surgical procedures. Demonstrators bring cameras with them to record how police handle the situation. Not to be outdone, police routinely tape demonstrators. New York even has DIVA-TV (Damned Interfering Video Activists) who tote cameras along to potential confrontations. Video cameras are used by insurance companies to document claims, by private detectives looking for spouses who are unfaithful, and by employers looking for employees who might be pilfering. Some criminals have even videotaped their own illegal acts. We may be at the point where everybody in the world may be a TV reporter.

The issues raised by this trend are novel and troubling. Does an amateur video journalist have the same rights as a professional? Do we need laws to regulate where secret cameras can be placed? What about the threat to an individual's right to privacy? Do tapes, such as the one made of the L.A. police, whip up such negative public opinion that a fair trial is impossible? What about the problem of tapes that are faked?

Whatever the answers, a North Carolina TV news executive may have summed up the situation best, "I don't believe there's going to be another event from now to the end of history that won't have a camera pointed at it." Stay tuned. Tape at eleven.

comics, puzzles, horoscopes, games, advice, gossip, humor, and general entertainment features usually account for around 12 percent of the typical content in an American daily paper. (If we considered sports news as entertainment, that would add another 14 percent to this figure.) Television is primarily devoted to entertainment, with about three-quarters of a typical broadcast day falling into this category. The entertainment content of radio varies widely according to station format. Some stations may program 100 percent news, while others may schedule less than 5 percent. In like manner, some magazines may have little entertainment content (*Forbes*), while others may be almost entirely devoted to it (*National Lampoon*). Even those magazines that are concerned primarily with news—*Time* and *Newsweek*, for example—usually mix in some entertaining features with their usual reporting.

The scope of mass media entertainment is awesome. By early 1992 approximately 45 million people had paid money to see *Home Alone*. About 125 million people watched the last episode of *M*A*S*H*. In a typical month, more than 5 million read (or at least look at) *Playboy*. Hammer's *Please Hammer Don't Hurt 'Em* album had sold more than 10 million copies by 1992. The comic strip "Doonesbury" is read by 18 million people. The importance of this entertainment function has grown as Americans have accumulated more leisure time. The work week has decreased from about seventy-two hours at the turn of the century to the current forty hours.

In the past, this entertainment function had been filled by interpersonal communication. Troubadours, storytellers, court jesters, and magicians fulfilled this function in the centuries before the media. What are the consequences of having this task now taken over by mass communication? Clearly, the media can make entertainment available to a large number of people at relatively little cost. This helps make leisure and recreational time more enjoyable. On the other hand, entertainment that is carried by the mass media must, almost by definition, appeal to a mass audience. The ultimate result of this state of affairs is that media content is designed to appeal to the lowest common denominator of taste. More programs that resemble *Murphy Brown* and *The Cosby Show* will find their way to TV than will opera performances. Newsstands are filled with more imitators of *Playboy* than imitators of *Saturday Review*. We are more apt to see sequels such as *Terminator 2*, *Naked Gun 2½*, and *Batman Returns* than we are to see *Romeo and Juliet II* and *More King Lear*. Rock stations outnumber classical stations thirteen to one. Many critics have argued that the media have lowered the level of American culture and have cheapened taste.

One other consequence of the widespread use of media for entertainment is that it is now quite easy to sit back and let others entertain you. Flicking on the TV set, picking up a magazine, and going to a movie require little effort on our part, and some fear that the media do such a good job of entertaining society that they encourage passivity. Instead of playing baseball, people might simply watch it on TV. Instead of learning to play the guitar, an adolescent might decide to listen to a record of someone else playing the guitar. On more than one occasion critics have charged that the mass media will turn Americans into a nation of watchers and listeners instead of doers.

• • • •

HOW PEOPLE USE THE MASS MEDIA

It is probably clear by now that statements made about the functions of mass communication in society could be paralleled by statements about how the media function at the level of the individual. Consequently, we are going to shift from our wide-angle lens to a close-up lens and focus on how the individual uses mass communication (in other words, we are moving from macro- to microanalysis). At the individual level, the functional approach is given the general name of the **uses-and-gratifications model**. In its simplest form, the uses-and-gratifications model posits that audience members have certain needs or drives that are satisfied by using both nonmedia and media sources. This discussion will be concerned more with media-related sources of satisfaction. The actual needs satisfied by the media are called media gratifications. Our knowledge of these uses and gratifications typically comes from surveys that have asked people a large number of questions about how they use the media (much like the questions at the beginning of this chapter). Several researchers have classified the various uses and gratifications into a fourfold category system:

1. cognition
2. diversion
3. social utility
4. withdrawal

We will examine each in turn.

Cognition

Cognition means the act of coming to know something. When a person uses a mass medium to obtain information about something, then he or she is using the medium in a cognitive way. Clearly, the individual's cognitive use of a medium is directly parallel to the surveillance function at the macroanalytical level. At the individual level, however, researchers have noted that there are two different types of cognitive functions that are performed. One has to do with using the media to keep up with information on current events, while the other has to do with using the media to learn about things in general or things that relate to a person's general curiosity. To illustrate, several surveys have found that many people give the following reasons for using the media:

I want to keep up with what the government is doing.
I want to understand what is going on in the world.
I want to know what political leaders are doing.

These reasons constitute the current-events type of cognitive gratification. At the same time, many people also report the following reasons for using mass media:

I want to learn how to do things I've never done before.
I want to satisfy my curiosity.
The media make me want to learn more about things.
The media give me ideas.

These statements illustrate the second type of cognition—using the media to satisfy a desire for general knowledge.

Psychologists and sociologists point out that using the media in this fashion seems to address a person's cognitive needs. These needs are related to strengthening our knowledge and understanding of the world we live in and are based to a certain extent on a desire to explore and master the surrounding environment. Thus the use of the media in this way is linked to the fulfillment of a basic human need.

Diversion

Another basic need of human beings is for diversion. Diversion can take many forms. Some of these forms identified by researchers include (1) stimulation, or seeking relief from boredom or the routine activities of everyday life; (2) relaxation, or escape from the pressures and problems of day-to-day existence; and (3) emotional release of pent-up emotions and energy. Let's look at each of these gratifications in more detail.

Stimulation. One thing that human beings cannot seem to cope with is boredom. In fact, when individuals are deprived of all external stimulation—a situation created by

One of the types of cognition is awareness of current events. Many people use the media to become informed about breaking news, such as the 1991 fire which swept through Oakland, California. (© San Francisco Examiner/SABA)

psychologists in studies dealing with sensory deprivation—the mind begins to hallucinate in order to create its own amusement. In less drastic circumstances, seeking emotional or intellectual stimulation seems an inherent motivation in a human being. Psychologists, in fact, have labeled these activities "ludic behaviors"—play, recreation, and other forms of activity that seem to be performed to maintain a minimum level of intellectual activity. Several surveys have shown that many people report that they watch, read, or listen simply to pass the time. When there is nothing else to do, many individuals fill up their idle time with mass media content simply because it's better than being bored. For example, a good deal of listening to radio and record players occurs when people are alone and are seeking additional stimulation. At the same time, many parties with a lot of people present are characterized by loud music, which also represents an attempt to increase the level of stimulation normally present. The media have taken advantage of this need to avoid boredom in many creative ways. Ted Turner has started an airport TV channel that beams news and commercials to passengers in airline terminals. Some airlines show CNN during long flights. Supermarkets have grocery carts with a video screen that displays the latest bargains. There are now special magazines that are distributed only to doctors' waiting rooms. Advertisements are now found on walls and the backs of stall doors in rest rooms.

Relaxation. Too much stimulation, however, is undesirable. Psychological experiments have indicated that human beings are negatively affected by a condition called "sensory overload" in which too much information and stimulation are present in the environment. When faced with sensory overload, people tend to seek relief. The media are one source of this relief. To illustrate, people read magazines or newspapers or watch TV in an attempt to get away from the cares of the day. Watching *Leave It to Beaver* or reading *People* magazine represents a pleasant diversion from the frustrations of everyday life. The choice of material used for relaxation might not always be apparent from surface content. Some people might relax by reading articles about Civil War history; others might read about astronomy or electronics. Still others might relax by listening to serious classical music. The content is not the defining factor since virtually any media material might be used for relaxation by some audience members. Of all the media, radio or recordings seem to serve the relaxation function most frequently. Many people use clock radios with an automatic shut-off to help them get to sleep at night. "Beautiful music" stations play relaxing music all day long. Even television newcasts are structured in such a way as to help the audience relax. No matter how terrible the events of the day, the newscaster is there with a calm, confident manner, apparently reassuring us that things are under control.

Emotional Release. The last manifestation of the diversion function is the most complex. On the one hand, the use of the media for emotional release is fairly obvious. To illustrate, the horror movie has had a long history of popularity in America. Starting with *Dracula* and *Frankenstein* and continuing through *The Creature from the Black Lagoon, Them,* and *The Thing* right up to *Nightmare on Elm Street, Friday the 13th, Aliens,* and *Silence of the Lambs,* people have sat in dark theaters and screamed their lungs out. Tearjerkers have also drawn crowds. *Broken Blossoms, Since You Went Away, The Best Years of Our Lives, West Side Story, Terms of Endearment, Beaches,* and *Dying Young* have prompted thousands, perhaps millions, to cry their eyes out. Why do audiences cheer when Rocky goes the distance? Probably because people enjoy a certain amount of emotional release. People feel better after a good scream (especially when the monster and bad guy are on the screen where they can't get at you) or a good cry (especially when the troubles are happening to somebody else).

Don't Worry, I'm Not Scared

Teens love to be terrorized—at least at the movies. Eighty percent of the audience for slice and dice films, like the *Nightmare on Elm Street* series, is under twenty-one. In addition, the terror audience is almost always split 50:50 between males and females. This even split is not coincidental; slasher and splatter films are popular date movies. Apparently they serve an important function for their young audience. As one teenager, quoted in a recent issue of *Seventeen*, put it: "Sometimes you feel weird or self-conscious holding onto a guy's hand on the first date but this way you can just grab him." Said another teenage girl: "Guys like to take you to horror movies, hoping you'll be real afraid and need them to comfort you." Said a third: "You can get all rowdy with boys and jump into their lap."

Scientific studies seem to confirm that horror films are performing this social function for teens. In one experiment done at the University of Indiana, female college students were paired with male confederates of the researchers. One male was instructed to remain silent while the couple watched a scene from a horror movie. A second male confederate acted wimpy, saying "Oh my God" at the gory scenes and generally acting afraid. The third male confederate acted macho, showing no signs of fear and shouting "All right!!" during the gory scenes. And males were paired with female confederates who acted the same way.

The results? Males enjoyed the horror film most when they were paired with the females who acted afraid. In contrast, females enjoyed the film most when paired with the macho males. The researchers concluded that horror movies encourage traditional gender-specific ways of behavior for both men and women, a conclusion supported by the preceding quotes from teen moviegoers.

The well-manicured Freddy Krueger and the Nightmare on Elm Street *series provided an outlet for emotional release for thousands of teenagers. The last installment,* Freddy's Dead: The Final Nightmare, *pulled in more than $35 million at the box office. (Photofest)*

On the other hand, emotional release can take more subtle forms. One of the big attractions of soap operas, for example, seems to be that many people in the audiences are comforted by seeing that other people (even fictional people) have troubles greater than their own. Other people identify with media heroes and heroines and participate vicariously in their triumphs. Such a process evidently enables these people to vent some of the frustrations connected with their normal lives.

Before moving on to another topic, we should mention that the notion of emotional release was probably one of the first functions to be attributed to media content. Aristotle, in his *Poetics*, talked about the phenomenon of **catharsis** (a release of pent-up emotion or energy) occurring as a function of viewing tragic plays, In fact, the catharsis theory has surfaced many times since then, usually in connection with the portrayals of television violence. Chapter 22 contains a discussion of research that has dealt expressly with the catharsis notion.

Social Utility

Psychologists have also identified a set of social integrative needs, including our need to strengthen our contact with family, friends, and others in our society. The social integrative need seems to spring from an individual's need to affiliate with others. The media function that addresses this need is called **social utility**, and this usage can take several forms. First, have you ever talked about a TV program with a friend? Have you ever discussed a current movie or the latest record you've heard on the radio? If so, then you are using the media as **conversational currency**. The media provide a common ground for social conversations, and many people use things that they have read, seen, or heard as topics for discussion when talking with others. There is a certain social usefulness in having a large repository of things to talk about so that no matter where you are you can usually strike up a conversation and be fairly sure that the person you are talking to is familiar with the subject. ("What did you think of the Super Bowl?" "How did you like *Jurassic Park*?")

Social utility is apparent in other instances as well. Going to the movies is probably the most common dating behavior among adolescents. The motion picture theater represents a place where it is socially acceptable to sit next to your date in a dark room without parental supervision. In fact, many times the actual film is of secondary importance, and the social event of going out has the most appeal.

Other people report that they use the media, particularly TV and radio, as a means to overcome loneliness. The TV set represents a voice in the house for people who might otherwise be alone. Radio keeps people company in their cars. People who might otherwise be deprived of social relationships find companionship in media content and media personalities. In fact, some viewers might go so far as to develop feelings of kinship and friendship with media characters. Audience members might react to media performers and the characters they portray as if the performers were actual friends. This phenomenon is called a **parasocial relationship**, and there is some evidence that it actually occurs. For example, in one study done during the 1970s that examined parasocial relationships between the audience and TV newscasters, more than half the people surveyed agreed with the statement, "The newscasters are almost like friends you see every day." One person went on to explain, "I grew up watching Walter Cronkite. . . . We've been through a lot together. Men on the moon and things like that."

TV sometimes reinforces the confusion. Many of you have probably seen the ad that starts "I'm not a doctor but I play one on TV." The nondoctor then goes on to endorse a health-related product. Further, one local TV station tried to get closer to its audience by doing an entire newscast from the living room of one of its viewers.

Withdrawal

In our previous discussion we noted that humans occasionally need to escape from certain activities and that, in this connection, they use the media not only for relaxation but also for purposes that are best described as withdrawal uses. At times, people use the mass media to create a barrier between themselves and other people or other activities. For example, the media help people avoid certain chores that should be done. Perhaps many of you have put off your homework and class assignments until after you've finished watching a TV program or reading the newspaper. Children are quick to learn how to use the media in this fashion. This hypothetical exchange might be familiar:

"It's your turn to let the dog out."

"I can't. I want to finish watching this program. You do it."

Or:

"Answer the telephone."

"I can't. I'm reading. You get it."

In both instances, attending to mass media content was defined as a socially appropriate behavior that should not be interrupted. In this manner, other tasks might be put off or avoided entirely.

People also use the media to create a buffer zone between themselves and other people. When you are riding a bus or an airplane or sitting in a public place and don't want to be disturbed, you bury your head in a book, magazine, or newspaper. (The newspaper works best. If you fold it correctly, it can serve as an effective screen. Unfortunately, holding it in this manner makes your arms tired.) If you are on an airplane, you might insert a pair of stethoscopelike earphones in your ears and tune everybody out. Television can perform this same function at home by isolating adults from children ("Don't disturb Daddy. He's watching the game.") or children from adults ("Don't bother me now. Go into the other room and watch *Sesame Street*.").

● ● ● ●

CONTENT AND CONTEXT

In closing, we should emphasize that it is not only media content that determines audience usage, but also the social context within which the media exposure occurs. For example, soap operas, situation comedies, and movie magazines all contain material that audiences can use for escape purposes. People going to a movie, however, might value the opportunity to socialize more than they value any aspect of the film itself. Here the social context is the deciding factor.

It is also important to note that the functional approach makes several assumptions:

1. Audiences take an active role in their interaction with various media. That is, the needs of each individual provide motivation that channels that individual's media use.

2. The mass media compete with other sources of satisfaction. Relaxation, for example, can also be achieved by taking a nap or having a couple of drinks, and social utility needs can be satisfied by joining a club or playing touch football.

3. The uses-and-gratifications approach assumes that people are aware of their own needs and are able to verbalize them. This approach relies heavily on surveys based on the actual responses of audience members. Thus the research technique assumes that people's responses are valid indicators of their motives.

A great deal of additional research needs to be done in connection with the uses-and-gratifications approach. In particular, more work is needed in defining and categorizing media-related needs or drives and in relating these needs to media usage. Nonetheless, the current approach provides a valuable way to examine the complex interaction between the various media and their audiences.

● ● ● ●

SUGGESTIONS FOR FURTHER READING

The sources listed below are good places to go for additional information on this topic.

BLUMLER, JAY, AND ELIHU KATZ, eds., *The Uses of Mass Communication*, Beverly Hills, Calif.: Sage Publications, 1974.

FAUCONNIER, GUIDO, *Mass Media and Society*, Louvain, Belgium: University of Louvain Press, 1975.

KLAPPER, JOSEPH, *The Effects of Mass Communication*, New York: The Free Press, 1960.

MCQUAIL, DENIS, *Towards a Sociology of Mass Communications*, London: Collier-Macmillan, 1969.

RUBIN, ALAN M., "Uses and Gratifications," in Joseph R. Dominick and James Fletcher, eds., *Broadcasting Research Methods*, Boston: Allyn and Bacon, 1985.

———, "Uses, Gratifications, and Media Effects Research," in Jennings Bryant and Dolf Zillmann, eds., *Perspectives on Media Effects*, Hillsdale, N.J.: Lawrence Erlbaum Associates, 1986.

TAN, ALEXIS, *Mass Communication Theories and Research*, New York: Wiley, 1985.

WRIGHT, CHARLES R., *Mass Communication: A Sociological Perspective*, New York: Random House, 1986.

● ●

THE GLOBAL VILLAGE: INTERNATIONAL AND COMPARATIVE MASS MEDIA SYSTEMS

"Я"

"Nyet."

he language is different but the TV show looks familiar: The wheel, the big board displaying some letters in a strange alphabet, the three contestants, an attractive letter-turner, and a congenial host.

"Г"

"Nyet."

A Russian version of *The Wheel of Fortune*? Exactly. And it's not the only familiar thing on Moscow TV. Spend a couple weeks watching TV in the capital of Russia and you would see such shows as *The Love Boat, Dallas, Geraldo, Donahue, Disney Presents*, a U.S.-made soap opera *Santa Barbara*, the hot teen show *Beverly Hills 90210*, and the ubiquitous CNN. Leave the TV set for a moment and you can buy a copy of *USA Today* and the international edition of *Time*. Turn on the radio and you can hear an adult contemporary station run by DJs trained in the U.S. Take a walk down the street and you can see (with subtitles) *Chaplin* and *Die Hard II*. Even *Pravda*, once the official newspaper of the Communist Party, contains that hallmark of capitalism, advertising.

As is obvious, a lot of change has occurred with the Russian media. Moscow, Russia, at least as far as the media are concerned, is beginning to resemble Moscow, Idaho.

Almost thirty years ago, media guru Marshal McLuhan predicted that mass communication would turn the world into a global village. Thanks to modern communications technology, McLuhan's prophecy seems to be coming true. Stocks, currency, and commodities can now be traded throughout the entire day in various markets around the world. Events on the London and Tokyo stock exchanges influence what happens on the New York exchange. Better communications have encouraged global investments and global trade, resulting in a world economy that is complex and interrelated. A company in Minnesota makes chopsticks and exports them to Japan. G.E. light bulbs and Levi's jeans are manufactured in Europe. Chicken processors in Virginia sell chicken feet to restaurants in Hong Kong (they're considered a delicacy there). Mazda, a Japanese company, works with Ford to build the Probe. In rural Calhoun County, Alabama, five manufacturing companies are owned by foreign com-

No, it's not Pat and Vanna. Instead it's Vladislav and Natasha, stars of the Russian version of Wheel of Fortune. *The game show is seen by an annual audience of 150 million people. (SIPA Press)*

panies. It is no longer unusual to find a company with its home office in the U.S. having plants in Mexico, Korea, and Ireland and marketing its products worldwide.

In the entertainment area, residents of the global village are increasingly exposed to common material, much of it produced in the United States. Entertainment is now America's second largest net export, racking up a trade surplus of $8 billion in 1991. As a result, American cultural products are known the world over. Almost everybody has seen *The Cosby Show*. Cable viewers in St. Petersburg (Leningrad) get MTV twenty-four hours a day. *The Arab News*, published in Saudi Arabia and Egypt, carries American baseball scores and the comic strips "Hi and Lois" and "Hagar the Horrible." The Italian paper *Corriere Della Sera* recently devoted twelve column-inches to Elizabeth Taylor's eighth wedding. *Midnight Cowboy*, dubbed in Italian, plays on Rome

What a Blast

When Russian families watch TV they make a point not to sit too near the set. This has nothing to do with eyestrain. Russians don't get too cozy with their TV sets because the TV sets explode. A study of Russian TV audiences done by a Western ad agency found that one of the things Russians dislike most about TV is the fact that their sets might blow up. Russian officials blamed faulty manufacturing for the problem and vowed to improve the quality of their products. Russian families applauded this pledge but still keep a safe distance from the TV.

TV. *Penthouse* publishes twelve foreign editions. Billboards for Wrangler jeans are a common sight in Poland. Time Warner owns 20 percent of a Swedish cable company. Phil Donahue and Russian commentator Vladimir Posner have joined together to host a talk show. The most popular movie ever in Israel is *Pretty Woman*. Because of this common exposure, a teenager in Paris may have more in common with a teenager in Peoria than either does with his or her parents.

Another important indication of the trend toward the global village is in the news area. This was vividly demonstrated during the Gulf War in 1991 when CNN carried live reports from the front into countries all over the world. The size of the audience for this coverage was difficult to judge but one estimate suggested that a billion different people were tuned to CNN at one time or another during the war.

Finally, as noted in Chapter 1, the trend in media ownership in the global village is toward large, multinational corporations. Australia's News Corporation, German-based Bertelsmann, French-owned Hachette, Japanese-based Sony and Matsushita, and U.S.-owned Time Warner control more than a third of the $250 billion or so worldwide information and entertainment industry. It seems likely that those of us who live in the global village will be seeing and hearing content produced by one of these conglomerates.

The above discussion underscores the importance of knowing about mass communication around the globe. In that connection, this chapter has a twofold purpose. First, it will highlight the fact that mass communication doesn't stop at borders and will examine the rapidly changing world of international mass comunication. The second purpose is to illustrate that even within the global village there is variety. The mass media system in the United States is not the only possible system. In fact, there may be differences in media operations within the borders of a single country. Appreciation of the variation that occurs throughout the world is helpful in understanding the nature and function of our own system. Accordingly, the last part of the chapter compares other countries' media systems with our own.

● ● ● ●
INTERNATIONAL MEDIA SYSTEMS

The study of international mass media systems focuses on those media that cross national boundaries. Some media may be deliberately designed for other countries (as is the case with Radio Moscow, the Voice of America, and the international edition of *Newsweek*); other media simply spill over from one country to its neighbors (as happens between the United States and Canada). Let's look first at those media designed for international consumption.

Global Print Media

Many newspapers provide foreign-language or international editions. The popular ones fall into two categories: general newspapers and financial newspapers. As far as U.S.- and British-based publications are concerned, the following were the leaders at the close of 1992:

- The *International Herald Tribune*, published by the *New York Times* and the *Washington Post* and headquartered in France, has a worldwide circulation of about 190,000, most of it in Europe. The paper, which recently celebrated its hundredth anniversary, is printed in ten cities around the world, including Miami, Singapore, and Hong Kong.

- *USA Today International* is a newcomer to the scene with a circulation of about 60,000, again mostly in Europe. The Gannett-owned paper is printed in Switzerland, Singapore, and Hong Kong. Most of its readers are U.S citizens traveling abroad. *USA Today* recently became available in Russia.

- *WorldPaper*, published by the World Times Company in Boston, is distributed as a newspaper supplement primarily in Latin America, Asia, and the Middle East. It's printed in twenty different countries and boasts a circulation of 900,000.

- *The Financial Times of London*, as its name suggests, specializes in economic news and has a circulation of about 300,000.

- *The Economist*, also based in London, carries financial news and analysis. Easily available in the United States, the paper is printed in Virginia, London, and Singapore. It reaches about 400,000 readers.

- *The Wall Street Journal*'s international editions reach about 85,000 people, mainly in Europe and Asia.

Other papers that enjoy international status are the *New York Times, Le Monde* (France), *El País* (Spain), *The Times* (Great Britain), *The Statesman* (India), and *Al Ahram* (Egypt).

The international flow of news is dominated by global news agencies. Reuters, Associated Press, Agence France Presse, United Press International, and ITAR-TASS are the biggest, but in recent years more specialized news organizations such as the New York Times Syndicate and the Los Angeles Times Syndicate have also become important.

As far as magazines are concerned, the *Reader's Digest* publishes 39 international editions in 15 languages that are distributed in nearly 200 countries. The *Digest* has about 10 million readers in foreign countries, making it a formidable vehicle for global advertising. Time Warner Inc., in addition to the international edition of *Time*, which has a circulation of 1.3 million in 190 countries, also publishes *Asiaweek, President* (in Japanese), and *Yazhou Ahoukan*, a newsweekly in Chinese. Many business magazines, including *Business Week, Fortune*, and the *Harvard Business Review*, also have significant foreign readership.

Global Broadcasting

About 150 countries engage in some form of international shortwave radio broadcasting. Most of these services are government run or at least government supervised and seem to have a political purpose: A good deal of the content on many services would be labeled propaganda. Over the last few years, however, private international broadcasting has grown in popularity. In the early 1980s, WRNO, New Orleans, became the first licensed commercially supported station to aim at an international audience. Other stations located in the United States and its island possessions followed suit. Nonetheless, the leading major international services continue to be state supported. Listed below are the five leaders based on broadcast hours in 1991:

- The Voice of America (VOA), now in its fifth decade of operation, broadcasts news, music, editorials, features, and music in more than forty languages. The VOA estimates that about 120 million people, about half of them in Russia and Eastern Europe, are regular listeners. During the aborted Soviet coup of 1991, Russian citizens relied heavily on the VOA to find out what was happening. The United States also operates Radio Free Europe and Radio Liberty, both originally designed to reach communist-controlled Eastern Europe. With the demise of communism, however, the U.S. is reconsidering the future of these two services. The U.S. also operates Radio Marti, a special AM service beamed to Cuba and a TV counterpart, TV Marti.

- Radio Moscow (RM) was the most extensive international radio service in operation. Currently, because of the dissolution of the Soviet Union, its operating hours are being cut back. Its long-range future is unclear.

- The World Service of the British Broadcasting Corporation (BBC) has a world-wide reputation for accurate and impartial newscasts because, in theory at least, it is independent of government ownership. Along with its news, the BBC also carries an impressive lineup of music, drama, comedy, sports, and light features. The BBC pioneered the international radio call-in show in which prominent people, such as Prime Minister John Major, answer calls from listeners around the globe. The BBC broadcasts in 37 languages and has about 120 million worldwide listeners. BBC listenership reached record levels during the Gulf War.

- Radio Beijing (Peking), which is difficult to pick up in the United States, transmits about 1400 hours of programming weekly in 40 foreign languages. Radio Beijing carried strident anti-American propaganda until the early 1970s when improved relations led to a mellowing of their tone. Most of Radio Beijing's programming consists of news, analsysis, commentary, and cultural information about China.

- Deutsche Welle (DW), "German Wave," broadcasts about 800 hours per week in 26 languages. DW's transmitters are located in Germany and in Africa and Asia. It has a large audience, particularly in Africa.

Probably the biggest change in international broadcasting in the 1980s and 1990s has been the increased use of communication satellites to carry TV signals across borders. Ted Turner's Cable News Network (CNN) has been a pioneer in this area. CNN International broadcasts to 65 million households and 1000 hotels in 102 countries. CNN also carries *World Report*, a compilation of uncensored news segments from around the world as reported by local journalists. Japan's NHK is considering an international video service to compete with CNN. International TV news exchanges, such as VISNEWS and Worldwide Television News (WTN), send pictures and audio to stations around the globe. The U.S. Information Agency's Worldnet supplies video to more than fifty countries. It recently added a Spanish-language feed of the *MacNeil-Lehrer Report* to South America in addition to a daily two-hour feed to the Soviet Union and Eastern Europe. Some special programs, such as ABC's *Capital to Capital*, have been transmitted live to both the United States and to Russia. ABC also broadcast a program in which viewers in several American cities were able to question Mikhail Gorbachev and Boris Yeltsin live via satellite. The Fox Television Network recently announced a plan to syndicate its programs worldwide.

In Europe, British Sky Broadcasting, partially owned by Rupert Murdoch, broadcasts five channels to cable systems and home satellite dish owners across the European continent. Two of the channels are free while the others are by subscription only. The European version of MTV is available on cable in more than a dozen European countries, as well as Japan and Australia.

In sum, as one CNN executive put it, it won't be long before "everyone will be looking inside everyone else's electronic window."

Along with the increasing satellite volume, a good deal of global media traffic consists of videocassettes and films that are shipped from one country to another and broadcast on the native country's TV system or played back on VCRs or shown at local movie theaters. The trade imbalance that exists in many areas of the U.S. economy does not exist in TV and film. The United States imports less than 2 percent of its TV shows. In contrast, European and African nations import an average of 30 and 40 percent, respectively. As more people around the world acquire VCRs, the popularity of American movies on cassette will increase dramatically.

American films dominate the box office of many foreign countries. In the early 1990s, for example, American-made movies accounted for about half of all the film revenues in France and Italy. Exporting American films is big business. Film rentals from foreign countries exceeded the $6 billion mark in 1992. More than half of this revenue came from Japan, Canada, France, Germany, and the United Kingdom.

Finally, another aspect of international media is the problem of cross-border spillover. TV signals, of course, know no national boundaries and the programs of one nation can be easily received in another country. The problem has caused some friction between the United States and Canada. Shows on ABC, NBC, and CBS are just as popular in Canada as they are in the United States and they take away audiences from the Canadian channels. Fearful of a cultural invasion of U.S. values and aware of the potential loss of advertising revenue to U.S. stations, the Canadian government has instituted content regulations that specify the minimum amount of Canadian content that must be carried by Canadian stations. Not surprisingly, spillover is also a problem on the crowded European continent. More than a third of TV viewing time in Finland, Ireland, and Belgium is spent watching programs from another country's TV service. In Switzerland, 60 percent of viewing is "out-of-country."

● ● ● ●
ISSUES

The two dominant issues involving international communication in the last few years pertain to two areas: international communication's impact on the changing world political scene and cultural domination. Let's discuss each in turn.

First, many have speculated that mass communication played a part in the movement toward more democratic governments and a free market economy that swept Eastern Europe and the Soviet Union in the late 1980s and early 1990s. Ironically, the push toward more democratization came in countries that generally kept a tight rein on their press systems and controlled the news that their citizens were exposed to. If this was the case, how did the international media have an effect? Steven Ross, Chair of Time Warner Incorporated, argued that the trend toward democracy evident in Red Square, Berlin, Bucharest, Budapest, and Beijing was caused, at least in part, by the exporting of the American Dream overseas. Said Ross, "Media and entertainment . . . have acquired a dramatic level of power and influence that has not been felt since the invention of the printing press . . . [They have] melted away the cold war

Synergy

Synergy means combined action or combined force, and it's the philosophy followed by the world's emerging global media conglomerates. Take Sony. Mariah Carey and Michael Jackson record songs for Sony Music Entertainment. Their CDs can be played on Sony CD players. Sony's Columbia Pictures produces that can be shown in Sony's Loew's theater chain. Sony also releases an 8-millimeter version of the movie that you can watch on your 8-millimeter Sony VCR. Columbia Pictures is also pioneering high-definition television (HDTV). Sony, of course, also manufactures HDTV hardware.

The synergy strategy was also behind Matsushita's purchase of MCA. Matsushita now owns a movie and a record company whose products can be played on Matsushita video and audio equipment. American giant Time Warner is betting on the same approach. Warner Brothers makes movies that play on channels carried by Time Warner's cable systems and distributed in Europe by its home video division. Warner's movies also play in Time Warner movie theaters throughout Europe. To succeed in a big way in the international scene, companies are trying to control both the hardware and the software.

and stood all our presumptions of east versus west on their head." Although the oppressive regimes of Eastern Europe kept a close watch on news, most were quite lenient about the entertainment programs that were imported or spilled over their borders from other countries. (For example, the deposed and executed dictator of Romania, Nicolae Ceausescu, was a big fan of *Kojak* as were many of his subjects.) As a result, their residents were exposed to vivid portrayals of people with lifestyles and possessions that were not available to them, a situation that caused economic and later political unrest. Once the pressure toward democracy was started, the old regimes tried to crack down on the movement by controlling the traditional mass communication channels. In the Baltic republics, Bucharest, and Moscow, it is not surprising that many of the key struggles involved control of the local TV station. The old leaders, however, could not control the newer media of international communication—fax machines, cellular phones, computers, satellite dishes—and these were used to keep the crusade alive. Only in China was the old regime successful in putting down the prodemocracy movement at the cost of a bloodbath. In Eastern Europe, when the democracy movement finally triumphed, the desire for Western mass media products was plainly evident. When East Germans were first allowed into the West, the two things they wanted most were oranges and records.

Will the continuing international reach of the media extend this trend to other countries still under authoritarian regimes such as Cuba, Iraq, and North Korea? That's a hard question to answer but keep in mind that in 1990 the Voice of America's TV Marti started broadcasting music videos into Cuba. Havana, taking no chances, promptly jammed the broadcasts.

Cultural domination refers to the process in which national cultures are over-whelmed by the importing of news and entertainment from other countries, mainly the U.S. and other industrialized nations. Residents of many countries are concerned that their national and local heritage will be replaced by one global culture dominated by U.S. values. Consequently, many countries have placed quotas on the amount of foreign material allowed to be broadcast on their television systems. Canada, for example, concerned about the cultural impact of spillover programming from the U.S., has detailed regulations about the amount of Canadian content that broadcast stations must carry. Europe, which became a unified economic community in 1992, has some quotas in place as well. Spain, for example, requires that its state-run TV stations carry no more than 48 percent foreign-produced shows. Italy has a similar regulation. (Keep in mind that some of this debate over cultural domination has economic implications. A quota that allows no more than 48 percent foreign programming assures that 52 percent of the money spent on programming goes to native production companies.)

The concern over cultural domination has ebbed a bit lately as television and radio programmers have discovered that locally produced series are more popular in their home countries than American-produced shows. U.S. series get respectable audiences but the top-rated shows are almost always locally produced. U.S. movies and records, however, continue to be dominant worldwide.

A somewhat related problem is summed up under the heading of the New World Information Order. The developing nations feel that the existing system of international communication is controlled by the developed countries of the West. As we have seen, much of the media content that is distributed worldwide does indeed originate in the U.S. or in some other Western nation. Under such a system, say the developing countries, news from the Third World is scant, and what news there is reflects unfavorably on the developing nations. Positive news is never carried. (As a class exercise, I ask my students what they know about South America. Invariably, they mention two things: South America has drugs and revolutions. They know little else about the whole continent.) Moreover, critics of the existing system argue that Western countries control the available broadcast spectrum and the technology needed to produce and distribute TV and radio programs. These foreign-produced programs tend to dominate the broadcasting systems of the developing countries, which do not have the resources to produce their own programs. Thus, the cultural values of the West, particularly those of the United States, are replacing the traditional culture of the developing country. In short, the Western media practice a form of media colonialism over many of the Third World nations.

The forum for much of this debate has been the United Nations, and UNESCO (United Nations Education, Scientific and Cultural Organization) has become deeply involved. In 1980, UNESCO adopted a resolution on the topic that substantially reflected the concerns of many Third World nations. The UNESCO resolution endorsed the philosophy that nations should control the news and entertainment that cross their borders. To be specific, each nation would be entitled to monitor all transborder information, monitor and control foreign media and journalists, and require prior consent for direct broadcasting into the country. It went on to suggest that all journalists should submit to a process that resembled a form of licensing.

The response of Western media professionals to this general argument and the UNESCO resolution was predictable. The Western nations sponsored research to show that Third World nations received their fair share of balanced coverage. Further, the Western tradition of freedom of the press sees any type of control as a threat to journalistic freedom and the free flow of information throughout the world. Journalists should not be licensed and countries should not attempt to draw up official codes of conduct for reporters. There should be no censorship and access to news events should be unrestricted.

Critics of the existing system replied that the research that purported to show balanced coverage was ill planned and shortsighted, and that the free flow of information espoused by those in the West simply meant that the West wanted to keep open profitable Third World markets for its media products.

The participants in this debate were able to agree on at least one thing: Third World nations needed help with their communications development. Accordingly, the International Program for the Development of Communications was created in

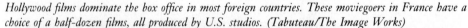

Hollywood films dominate the box office in most foreign countries. These moviegoers in France have a choice of a half-dozen films, all produced by U.S. studios. (Tabuteau/The Image Works)

1980. Its primary function was to gather and exchange information and arrange consultation in order to help communication systems and services in the developing countries. Western nations have given limited financial support to this program and continue to carefully scrutinize its workings.

The debate between developing and developed countries over information flow is not likely to subside in the future. In fact, this conflict was one of the reasons behind the United States' decision in 1984 to withdraw from UNESCO. The essence of this disagreement has to do with philosophy. The West, along with some developing countries, believes in a press free from the state and in the right of the press to criticize government and to publicize all points of view. Other developing countries believe that the press has an obligation to support the government, suppress dissent, and help achieve national goals. As is the case with most philosophical disagreements, this one will be hard to settle.

• • • •
COMPARATIVE MEDIA SYSTEMS

Let's now turn our attention to media systems as they exist in individual nations. Before we start, we should note that the media system that exists in a country is directly related to the political system in that country. The political system determines the exact relationship between the media and the government. Over the years, several theories have developed concerning this relationship. In the sections that follow, there are examples of these theories in operation.

Theories of the Press

Since the sixteenth century, scholars have attempted to describe the relationship between the government and the media and its implications with regard to freedom and control. Over the years, various theories or philosophies of the press, as they have

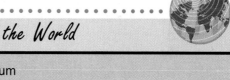

Press Freedom around the World

Freedom House is an organization dedicated to strengthening the notion of a free press. Every year since 1972 it has conducted a Comparative Freedom Survey of countries around the world. Below are listed the countries that have the most and the least press freedom—at least as judged by the Western Concept of the press.

Most Free

Norway
United States
Australia
Italy
Sweden
Denmark
New Zealand

Belgium
Japan
Netherlands
United Kingdom
Costa Rica
Luxembourg
Canada

Least Free

Iraq
South Yemen
Angola
Benin
Equatorial Guinea
Cambodia
North Korea

been labeled, have been developed to articulate and explain this relationship. The most influential of these attempts occurred in 1956 with the publication of a book entitled *Four Theories of the Press*. The main thesis of this book held that there were four main operating philosophies concerning media freedom and control: Authoritarian, Libertarian, Communist, and Social Responsibility. The passage of time and the crush of historical events, however, have overtaken this conceptualization and several recent writers have offered modifications of the original four-part model. Rather than review all of these revisions, this section will offer a simplified model of media-government relations which draws upon the original *Four Theories* arrangement and incorporates some of the newer ideas.

To begin, imagine a continuum ranging from authoritarianism at one end and libertarianism at the other. These two "isms" reflect polar opposites in the amount of control the government exerts over the media, and we shall discuss each in turn. The **authoritarian theory** arose in sixteenth-century England about the same time as the introduction of the printing press to that country. Under the authoritarian system, the prevailing belief held that a ruling elite should guide the masses, whose intellectual ability was held in low esteem. Public dissent and criticism were considered harmful to both government and the people and were not tolerated. Authoritarians used various devices to enforce cooperation of the press including licensing, censorship of material before publication, the granting of exclusive printing rights to favored units of the press, and the swift, harsh punishment of government critics. In fact, in certain societies, not only is the press prohibited from criticizing the government, but it is also required to perform functions for the good of the state. These might include omitting certain news reports that would be embarrassing or harmful to the government and explaining other events in a light favorable to the ruling powers.

The **communist theory** is a variant on the authoritarian theme. The media are "owned" by the people as represented by the state. Their purpose is to support the Marxist system and to achieve the goals of the state as expressed through the Communist party. With the downfall of communism in the U.S.S.R. and Eastern Europe, this philosophy has far fewer proponents today than it had forty years ago.

The **libertarian theory** is directly opposed to the authoritarian theory. Libertarians assume that human beings are rational and are capable of making their own decisions and that governments exist to serve the individual. Unlike the authoritarians, libertarians hold that the common citizen has a right to hear all sides of an issue in order to distinguish truth from falsehood. Since any government restriction on the expression of ideas infringes on the rights of the citizen, the government can best serve the people by not interfering with the media. In short, the press must be free of control. Communications scholar William Hachten, in *The World News Prism*, proposed a modification on the libertarian philosophy which incorporated parts of the original **social responsibility theory** with elements of libertarianism. In his conceptualization, labeled the Western Concept, the press is considered to be privately owned while the broadcasting media may be privately owned or owned by the state (as is the case with the Public Broadcasting Service). The press is to be as free as possible but unlike libertarianism, the freedom is not absolute. The media have a right to criticize government and other institutions but they also incur a responsibility to preserve democracy by properly informing the public and by responding to society's interest and needs. The government may involve itself in media operations by issuing regulations if the public interest is not being adequately served. The regulation of broadcasting by the Federal Communications Commission (see Chapter 17) is a good example of this latter provision. The United States, Britain, Japan, and many Western European countries are examples of countries that subscribe to this philosophy.

Hachten also identified a more recent theory called the Developmental Concept, which is more toward the authoritarian side of the spectrum. In this ideology, the government mobilizes and directs the media to serve national goals in economic and

"The Repeal, or the Funeral Procession, of Miss Americ-Stamp." Colonial newspapers operated under the authoritarian philosophy as practiced by the British government. This English cartoon, published in 1766, satirized the repeal of the Stamp Act, an attempt to suppress hostile opinion by placing a tax on the pages of colonial newspapers. (The Granger Collection)

social development. Some of the goals that the media are expected to help achieve include political integration, literacy, economic self-sufficiency, and the eradication of disease. The notion of developmental journalism, which will be discussed below, was one of the central issues in the debate about the New World Information Order. Many Third World countries exemplify this philosophy. Figure 3-1 displays these various theories and their relationship to one another.

Control and Ownership of the Media

One helpful way of distinguishing among the various media systems throughout the world is to classify them along the dimensions of (1) ownership and (2) control. Finnish Professor Osmo Wiio has developed a useful analysis scheme, presented in Figure 3-2. As can be seen, ownership can range from private to public (public ownership usually means some form of government ownership), while control can range from centralized to decentralized. Note that this typology is an oversimplification. In many countries, there are mixed media systems in which part of the broadcasting system is owned by the government and part by private interests. In some countries, the print media could be placed in one cell of the matrix and the broadcasting system in another. Nonetheless, this model is helpful in displaying some of the major differences among systems.

In the upper-left cell are type A systems. These consist of decentralized control and public ownership, a type best illustrated by the broadcasting systems in European countries such as France, Denmark, and Italy. Some of the broadcasting media are publicly owned, but no single political or special-interest group can control their messages. In Great Britain, for example, the British Broadcasting Corporation is a government-chartered, public owned corporation that is relatively immune to govern-

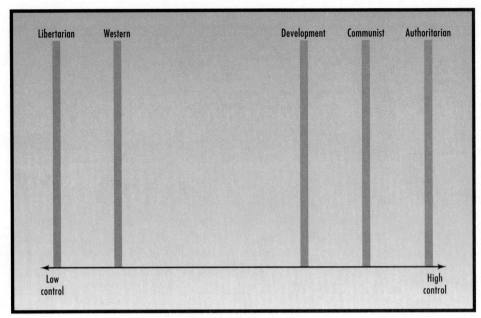

FIGURE 3-1 *Theories of media-government relationships.*

FIGURE 3-2 *Typology of media ownership and control. (From Osmo Wiio, "The Mass Media Role in the Western World," in L. Martin and A. Chaudhary, eds.,* Comparative Mass Media Systems, *copyright 1983 by Longman Inc. Used with permission.)*

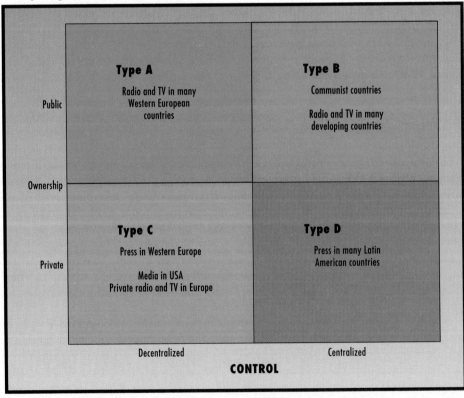

ment censorship and interference. Private broadcasting systems also operate in these countries.

In the upper-right cell are type B systems. This arrangement is typical of communist or socialist countries in which the media are owned publicly and controlled by the dominant political party. China would be an example.

In the lower-left cell is the decentralized control, private ownership model. This is the system that currently operates in the United States and in many European countries. The media are owned by private companies and there is little, if any, centralized control.

The lower-right cell contains the centralized control, privately owned system. In many countries, particularly in the developing countries of Africa and Latin America, the media are owned by private organizations but are firmly controlled by the government.

Far fewer countries would fall into cell B of the matrix today than five years ago. Only a handful of nations still exemplify the communist or socialist media model. (Cuba, China, and North Korea are examples.) In these countries the party exercises control, and freedom of the press belongs to the state, not to the media. Communist countries feel that it is necessary to speak with one voice, and antigovernment or antiparty criticism is forbidden.

Press control is exercised in several ways. First, the government controls the source. Printing and broadcasting equipment are given only to approved organizations. In Cuba, for example, there is a newsprint shortage and only the government newspaper is supplied with it. Next, journalists are state trained and state approved. Finally, news agencies are state owned and news sources state controlled.

Those countries that have abandoned the communist philosophy have generally moved into cells A and C of the matrix. The state-run media organizations have seen much of their control taken away and private media outlets are permitted. Individual media outlets are given much more freedom to criticize the government.

The most significant trend in those countries that fall into cell A of the matrix has been a move toward pluralism in their broadcasting systems. State-owned monopolies in many countries, including France, Italy, Greece, Spain, and some of the Scandinavian countries, have given way to privately owned and commercially sponsored broadcasting systems. In addition, cable promises to bring even more video diversity to these countries.

Role of the Media in Various Countries

The role of a mass media system in a given country will differ according to its place in the above typology. For example, as mentioned above, in many developing countries where there is strong centralized control over the media, the principal role of mass communication is to help develop and build the nation. Not surprisingly, many Third World countries are primarily concerned with economic and political development. This concern is translated into a rather focused definition of the role of mass media. In general, the media are expected to help further modernization or other national goals. In fact, a new term, **developmental journalism**, has been coined to describe this philosophy. In short, developmental journalism means that the role of the media is to support national interests for economic and social development and to support objectives such as national unity, stability, and cultural integrity. On the one hand, developmental journalism entails finding ways to make abstract stories about commodity pricing, agriculture, and educational goals understandable to readers and to highlight the developmental goals achieved by the nation. On the other hand, developmental journalism can also mean that the press refrains totally from any criticism of the government and will print only what the government deems helpful to its cause.

The philosophy of many Asian, Latin American, and African developing nations falls somewhere between these two conceptions of developmental journalism.

In the communist world, the role of the media is clear cut: They are tools of propaganda, persuasion, and education. They function only secondarily as sources of information. This philosophy dates all the way back to Lenin, who decreed that the communist press was to help further the revolution. The political significance of the media is also clearly seen in the high priority that they occupy in the government bureaucracy. Only the Communist party, the party-controlled government, and party-directed organizations, such as trade unions, are permitted to operate media.

As we saw in Chapter 2, Western media inform and entertain, but their content is somewhat different from communist and Third World media. Most of the information carried by the media in the Western democracies is geared to the specific political and economic needs of the audience. An examination of the press in the United States and Canada, for example, would reveal a large amount of news about the local and national government, some of it unfavorable and critical. The role of government watchdog, based on the ideas presented in the Western Concept, is a function that would be unsettling to many of the countries in cells B and D of the matrix in Figure 3-2. Moreover, a great deal of content in the Western media is consumer oriented, consisting of advertising and news about business. On the entertainment side, the content of Western media generally lacks the cultural heritage dimension found in many Third World countries and does not emphasize the national history aspect as heavily as do the communist media. Further, there is, relatively speaking, little regulation of the content of the entertainment media. Aside from some regulations governing pornography and prohibitions against certain content on the broadcasting media, the government takes little interest in entertainment content.

It's the interpretation or editorial function where the biggest differences are found. The United States and other Western countries have a tradition of press freedom that recognizes the right of the media to present ideas to try to persuade the audience to some point of view. The philosophy of the "free marketplace of ideas" is endorsed by most countries in cells A and C of Figure 3-2. All relevant ideas concerning an issue are examined in the media, and a "self-righting" process occurs. Given the autonomous nature of the Western media, it would be difficult for the government to mobilize the media to support some national goal, as is typically done in developing and communist countries. There is a built-in tension and adversary relationship between press and government that makes such efforts rare.

Economic Differences

In the United States, advertising plays a key role in media support (see Chapter 16). Newspapers, magazines, radio, and television all derive a significant amount of their total income from the sale of advertising time or space. Direct government subsidy or support of the media is minimal, limited to the funds given to public broadcasting. (Of course, the government also helps indirectly to support the media by buying a lot of advertising.) In Western Europe, there are several countries that provide indirect subsidies to the media, such as cheaper mailing privileges and tax concessions. Some Scandinavian countries have a system whereby newspapers controlled by various political parties are given direct financial assistance. There are several different systems that are used to support broadcasting. In the United Kingdom, for example, the British Broadcasting Corporation (BBC) is state chartered and gets its operating funds from an annual license fee paid by the owners of TV sets. At the same time, the independent TV networks make their money from the sale of advertising time, in much the same way as do their U.S. counterparts. Many other Western countries follow this same model.

It is difficult to generalize about the means of economic support for media in the Third World. Where the print media are privately owned, money comes from circulation fees and advertising. Publishers are generally free to keep all profits, but in many countries space must be provided free of charge for government announcements. Advertising and license fees are the two major sources of income for broadcasting.

In the communist countries, most economic support for the media comes directly from the government. Since the media are state owned, money for their operation is simply set aside in the government's budget. Newspapers and magazines make a little extra money from circulation, but this is tiny in comparison to their state-derived funds. Because of this subsidy, single-copy costs are quite cheap. In all communist countries, broadcasting derives additional monies from license fees on receivers. There are annual fees for TV sets, home radios, and an extra fee for a car radio. There is also something called "advertising" in all communist media, but it is an insignificant source of revenue and does not resemble Western advertising. Most ads are of a purely informational nature: Such-and-such a product is now available at such-and-such a store. Many newspapers also have small sections devoted to what those in the West would call classified ads, but again, the revenue from these is minimal.

Examples of Other Systems

Let us now take a more detailed look at the mass media in three different countries. One is an industrialized nation, Japan. The second is Mexico, a developing nation, and the third is China, which will serve to illustrate the media system in a communist country.

Japan. More than 120 million people live on this nation of islands. Japan has the highest living standard of all Asian nations and a literacy rate of about 100 percent. Naturally, its media systems are elaborate and pervasive. There are about 125 papers in Japan with a combined daily circulation of about 65 million, a total that exceeds

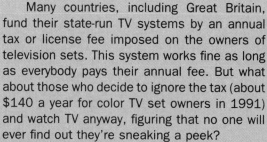

Beware of the Van

Many countries, including Great Britain, fund their state-run TV systems by an annual tax or license fee imposed on the owners of television sets. This system works fine as long as everybody pays their annual fee. But what about those who decide to ignore the tax (about $140 a year for color TV set owners in 1991) and watch TV anyway, figuring that no one will ever find out they're sneaking a peek?

This is where the van comes in.

To catch people illegally receiving signals, the British Licensing Record Office has a fleet of twenty-two TV-detector vans that cruise up and down the streets of the United Kingdom looking for violators. Each van is equipped with a device that can monitor signals to determine whether a house has its TV set on. If it has, the personnel in the van check their records to see if the residents paid the annual fee. If not, the van stops and the homeowner is confronted with the evidence and given a citation. About a quarter of a million Brits a year are prosecuted for nonpayment.

The employees who drive the vans have heard some wondrous excuses. One couple admitted their TV set had been on but argued that they shouldn't have to pay the fee because only their pet monkey watched TV. One man claimed that there was some mistake because his TV set was broken. When the van driver pointed out the top of the TV was still warm, the man said his cat had been sleeping on it. Neither alibi was accepted.

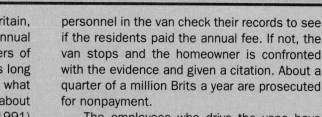

that of U.S. dailies. Japan has fifteen papers with daily circulations over the million mark, whereas the United States has three. Japan's newspaper circulation of 562 copies per 1000 people is the highest in the world. There are five national newspapers, of which the *Yomiuri Shimbun*, *Asahi Shimbun*, and *Mainichi Shimbun* are the largest. (As you may have deduced by now, *Shimbun* is the Japanese word for newspaper.) The *Yomiuri Shimbun* (literally translated as the Read-Sell Newspaper) has a combined morning and evening circulation of more than 13 million, making it the world's largest daily in terms of circulation. (By comparison, *USA Today* has a circulation of about 1.4 million.) Along with the national papers, Japan supports other regional and local dailies and about a dozen sports papers. Tokyo alone has twelve newspapers, three of them in English. By American standards, Japanese papers have circulations and penetrations that are unheard of. *Kyoto Shimbun*, in a city with a population of 1.5 million, has a circulation of 1.5 million. About 98 percent of the households in Japan subscribe to at least one newspaper.

Japan also has two news magazines, a picture-oriented news weekly called *Focus* and an influential business magazine. New leisure magazines are also making their appearance in Japan. One such publication is called *BOX*, which usually has features on clothing, investments, health care, and housing. The Japanese equivalent to *TV Guide* is also popular. In addition, Asian editions of such familiar publications as *Time*, *Newsweek*, and the *Reader's Digest* are widely available. Comic books sell an amazing 1.7 billion copies a year.

Japan has one of the most technologically advanced broadcasting systems in the world. The state-run noncommercial Japan Broadcasting Corporation (*Nippon Hoso Kyokai*, or NHK) is patterned after the BBC and has an annual budget of more than a billion dollars, all of which comes from a license fee imposed on all TV sets in Japan—$50 a year for a color TV and $30 for a black and white set. Competing with the three NHK channels are five commercial TV networks. TV and radio reach virtually 100 percent of the population as 11,000 transmitters blanket the country. Almost all of the programs on Japanese TV are locally produced. American series don't do well in Japan; even *Dallas* flopped. The only popular American show on Japanese TV in the early 1990s was *Bugs Bunny*. About 17 percent of all Japanese homes are equipped for cable. At present, however, cable is used to retransmit regular TV into areas that suffer poor TV reception. About 70 percent of all homes have VCRs, and the video software business is booming.

Because of its mountainous terrain, Japan is developing a direct broadcast satellite system (DBS). In fact, the hottest selling TV sets in Tokyo in 1991 were those equipped with a satellite tuner and a satellite receiving dish about the size of a garbage can lid that can be attached outside a window. NHK has spent about $2 billion in DBS research and now operates two satellite channels that beam programs direct from satellite to living rooms. Programming includes sports, music, specials, movies, and shows imported from other countries. The NHK DBS system carries the newscasts of both Ted Koppel and Peter Jennings (their voices are dubbed into Japanese). High definition television—HDTV—(see Chapter 23) is broadcast by this system but only a few Japanese homes have an HDTV receiving set, primarily because the few that are on the market cost about $18,000 each. Five more DBS and HDTV channels are planned for 1995. Developments in Japan, of course, have more than just local significance because many of that country's leading media companies (Sony, Matsushita) have interests in the United States and throughout the rest of the world. Innovations, products, and services that first appear in Japan are likely to find their way into media systems in many other countries.

Mexico. The media situation in Mexico is typical of many developing countries. It demonstrates some of the many challenges faced by other nations as they strive to form their own indigenous systems. The media system in Mexico has been influenced

The American edition of the Yomiuri Shimbun, *which is transmitted by satellite from Japan and published daily in New York City. The popularity of these satellite editions has increased as more and more Japanese have traveled to the U.S. on business. (Courtesy,* Yomiuri America Inc., *New York, NY.)*

by economics, politics, and geography. A country with 86 million inhabitants and a literacy rate of 75 percent, Mexico has been saddled with massive foreign debt and inflation running at about 20 percent a year. Sharp divisions exist between the rich and the poor segments of society. Many urban areas are characterized by relative prosperity while some rural areas are mired in poverty. Literacy is higher in the cities than in the countryside. Moreover, various governments have taken different attitudes toward the media, vacillating between strict control and relative leniency. Finally, Mexico's media system always operates in the shadow of its neighbor to the north, the United States.

Mexico has 355 daily newspapers and many of them are top flight. The *Excelsior*, of Mexico City, with a daily circulation of 175,000, is the country's newspaper of record, comparable to the *New York Times*. Some provincial newspapers, such as *El Norte* in Monterrey, are also influential. The government publishes its own newspaper, *El Nacional*, which is modeled after *USA Today* and is distributed throughout the country.

Freedom of the press is limited in Mexico. The government and the ruling political party deflect criticism by having the government control the national supply of newsprint. If a magazine or periodical prints things that offend the government, the publication runs the risk of seeing its supply of paper suddenly cut off. The government also controls satellite communication equipment. Moreover, the government and party exert some press control by using the *mordida*, or bribe. Journalists in Mexico are underpaid and are particularly susceptible to offers of money in return for favorable stories. Additionally, some journalists have been threatened with or actually harmed by physical violence. Professional associations of international journalists report that the Mexican government has been indifferent to these incidents of intimidation. A new president took office in the late 1980s, however, and the government was more tolerant toward opposition views.

Radio broadcasting developed in Mexico about the same time as it did in the United States. An official broadcast service signed on in 1923 and the model followed was heavily influenced by the U.S. system. In addition to state-run educational and cultural services, a system of private ownership of stations and commercial support was also instituted. During the 1950s, the state sold most of its stations to private

Scene from the telenovela Mi Pequena Soledad *("My Tiny Solitude"). These Spanish-language equivalents of U.S. soap operas are popular in Mexico and Central and South America. Several are now carried by Spanish-language networks in the United States. (The Photo Works)*

interests. Today, there are more than 800 commercial radio stations and only 50 noncommercial stations, along with a dozen commercial networks.

Television broadcasting was modeled directly on the U.S. system. It began as a commercially supported private enterprise but a 1960 law dictated that TV had to perform certain social functions, such as fulfilling moral principles and preserving human dignity. Government became more involved in TV during the 1970s when an agreement with station owners set aside 12.5 percent of the broadcast day for government-produced programs. The government also acquired a Mexico City station as an outlet for its programs.

The private television sector is dominated by Televisa, an organization that controls about 70 of the 120 TV stations in the country. Televisa is the parent company of Univision, a U.S. Spanish TV network, and Televi.. a produces and exports *telenovelas*, the Spanish version of a U.S. soap opera, which are tremendously popular throughout Latin America. Televisa also has holdings in the print media.

Some U.S. TV programming is popular in Mexico (*MacGyver* was the top-rated U.S. show there in 1991) but the biggest hits tend to be Mexican productions. *Telenovelas* usually dominate the top-ten rated shows.

VCR penetration is about 38 percent, one of the higher figures in Latin America. About 11,000 different video releases are available in video rental stores. Like many developing countries, Mexico has a problem with pirated videos. One authority calculated that about 25 percent of all videos for rent in Mexico were pirated copies.

U.S. films do well in Mexico but the entire film industry has been feeling the effects of inflation and Mexico's foreign debt. The government-subsidized Mexican Film Institute is being restructured and many of its divisions are being sold to private firms. Government-run studios will probably be the first to be sold. Because of the subsidies, movie ticket prices in Mexico are among the cheapest in Latin America, about 50 cents, but this will probably increase as the government gets out of the film business.

The government's use of the media to help modernize and develop the country is vividly demonstrated by several programs. Mexico's *Radioprimaria* project encouraged the growth of literacy and mathematical skills. Its *Telesecundaria* program offered a secondary school curriculum to rural villages and towns without schools. Additionally, the government and Televisa have informal arrangements in which they cooperate to produce educational and cultural programs. Televisa has even agreed to incorporate some high-government-priority social issues into its *telenovelas*.

China. The media system in China is a striking example of how the communist system operates. Several other nations, notably North Korea, Cuba, Iran, and Iraq, have systems similar to that in China. The system in China, however, is the most worthwhile to analyze. The actions of the government and the media following the crackdown on those demonstrating for democracy illustrated quite vividly the workings of the communist system.

Since 1949, the task of the media in this huge country of more than a billion people has been to unite the population behind the advancement of socialism in China. News is looked upon as an instrument for educating the people. The media showed signs of liberalization during the 1980s, and advertising and news stories that pointed out crime and corruption in government began to appear. In 1989, however, after the prodemocracy movement in China reached a climax in the violence at Beijing's Tiananmen Square, the Chinese press demonstrated that it was still firmly under the control of the central government.

First some background. The media in China have been expanding rapidly, particularly in the last ten or fifteen years. The country has about 2200 newspapers, more than half started in the 1980s. Newspaper circulation exceeds 200 million. China has five national newspapers with the *People's Daily* the most influential. Boasting the world's largest readership, probably ten million or so, this paper is the official voice of the party and the government. Other papers in China are careful about what they print and they look to the *People's Daily* for guidance. One English language paper, *China Daily*, was started in 1981. *China Daily* is aimed at foreigners living in China and is also made available to North America and Europe. Its look is Western and it contains far less communist ideology than the *People's Daily* but it is still published under the watchful eye of the government. Much of the news carried in the *People's Daily* and other Chinese newspapers comes from the state-controlled wire service, the Xinhua (New China) News Agency, which has 5000 employees and 82 bureaus in foreign countries. In addition to giving the official government version of news events from across the globe, Xinhua also serves as a link between the people and the Communist party, and much of its content consists of news about party goals and plans.

Radio is the number one mass medium in China and, like the print media, it too functions under the direct leadership of the Communist party. The Central People's Broadcasting Station (CPBS) was started in 1949 and now operates six networks that broadcast news, education, entertainment, and public service content. CPBS is the official mouthpiece of the government and the party. It has been used to popularize national policies and to urge the populace to act in accord with party principles. In addition, there are about 100 regional or provincial networks and numerous local stations. China also makes use of "wire broadcasting" in which loudspeakers are used to broadcast radio programs in public places. All told, radio reaches about 95 percent of the population. China also operates an international service, Radio Beijing.

Television in China showed remarkable growth during the 1980s and early 1990s with the number of TV sets in operation growing by 700 percent, to about 70 million. Chinese Central Television (CCTV) serves all 29 provinces, using a system of satellite transmission. Like CPBS, CCTV is state run by the Ministry of Radio and Television. In addition to CCTV, the larger cities in China also have one or more broadcast stations. CCTV has aired some programming from the West, including *60 Minutes* and National Basketball Association playoff games. The bulk of its content, however, is locally produced news, sports, educational, and entertainment programs. Most of the time, TV functions as more of an entertainment than a political medium.

The events following the Tiananmen Square violence illustrate how powerful the control of the media can be in a communist state. In May, 1989, journalists in Beijing marched through the square carrying banners that read "Don't believe us . . . we print lies." Newspapers carried front page stories sympathetic to the student demonstrators. Beijing TV broadcast a session in which student leaders were shown chastising Premier Li Ping. Amid calls for more press freedom and other reforms, the government ordered a news blackout and cracked down on the demonstrators. Chinese TV stopped carrying live reports from the scene and began broadcasting statements from leaders calling for martial law. Finally, soldiers marched and tanks rumbled through Tiananmen Square and the prodemocracy movement was crushed, temporarily at least.

Thanks to foreign correspondents and local residents with camcorders, scenes of the violence were common on Western TV newscasts and in Western newspapers. Residents of China, however, saw and read something different. The government launched a two-week propaganda campaign that stressed the official version of what happened. Instead of the more than one hundred thousand people who demonstrated in Beijing, the government-controlled media said the demonstrators were a small group of criminals and thugs. Where did they get their ideas? From overseas plotters. The protest lasted so long because the demonstrators threatened to kill anybody who left the square. Violence broke out because the mob became unruly and threatened the soldiers guarding the square. Carefully edited videotape of the scene did not show soldiers firing into the crowd; it showed soldiers firing in the air. There was no tape of civilian dead, only pictures of military casualties. Reporters from foreign countries were forbidden to send satellite reports from the scene. Two American journalists were expelled. Some Chinese did get different versions of the story from the BBC or the Voice of America. Others got faxes from sympathizers in the West who attempted to set the record straight. The government ultimately started posting guards on fax machines and jammed the VOA to quell these channels of information. Copies of foreign newspapers were seized at airports.

After the violence ended, the state-run media continued their propaganda campaign. TV newscasts were filled with scenes of demonstrators, labeled "criminals," who were brought to trial and punished, some of them executed. Some newspapers were shut down. The military propaganda director of the *People's Daily* was named the new editor. Journalism students who supported the protest were arrested and sent to work farms. The continued telling of the government's version of events seemed to be effective. Foreign correspondents in China noted that Chinese citizens outside Beijing were willing to accept the official government story. In sum, the events surrounding the Beijing protest illustrate how potent a force control of the media can be in a volatile situation.

In sum, the media systems in these three countries, although different, illustrate the influence that economics, culture, geography, and politics have on the development of mass communication. Because of these and other influences, each nation will create a media system that is best suited to its needs.

• • • •
SUGGESTIONS FOR FURTHER READING

The following books contain more information about the concepts and topics discussed in this chapter.

AKWULE, RAYMOND, *Global Telecommunications*, Stoneham, Mass.: Focal Press, 1992.

CHANG, WON ITO, *Mass Media in China*, Ames, Iowa: Iowa State University Press, 1989.

DUNNETT, PETER, *The World Newspaper Industry*, London: Croom Helm, 1988.

GERBNER, GEORGE, AND MARSHA SIEFERT, eds., *World Communications: A Handbook*, New York: Longman, 1984.

HACHTEN, WILLIAM, *The World News Prism*, Ames, Iowa: Iowa State University Press, 1981.

MARTIN, JOHN, AND ANJU CHAUDHARY, eds., *Comparative Mass Media Systems*, New York: Longman, 1983.

MARTIN, L. JOHN, AND RAY HIEBERT, *Current Issues in International Communication*, New York: Longman, 1990.

MERRILL, JOHN, ed., *Global Journalism*, New York: Longman, 1991.

MICKIEWICZ, ELLEN, *Media and the Russian Public*, New York: Praeger, 1981.

——, *Split Signals: TV and Politics in the Soviet Union*, New York: Oxford University Press, 1988.

THE PRINT MEDIA

HISTORY OF THE PRINT MEDIA

t had to be true. There it was, printed in black and white in the August 25, 1835, edition of the *New York Sun*. Sir John Herschel, working with a huge telescope at his new observatory in Cape Town, South Africa, had discovered life on the moon!

The August 25 issue quoted Sir John as he described a "moon buffalo":

> Its tail was like that of our *bos gruniens;* but in its semicircular horns, the hump on its shoulders, the depth of its dewlap and the length of its shaggy hair, it closely resembled [the bison]. It had, however, one widely distinctive feature . . . a remarkably fleshy appendage over the eyes.

All of this was pretty hard to believe, but the *Sun* reported that it had taken the story straight from the Edinburgh *Journal of Science*.

Three days later, the *Sun* announced even more fantastic news: Humanlike creatures were flying about the moonscape!

> They averaged four feet in height, were covered, except in the face, with short and glossy copper-colored hair, and had wings composed of a thin membrane, without hair, lying snugly upon their backs, from the top of the shoulders to the calves of the legs. The face, which was a yellowish flesh-color, was a slight improvement upon that of the large orangutan, being more open and intelligent in its expression, and having a much greater expanse of forehead.

The great moon story brought new readers to the *Sun;* its circulation zipped past the 19,000 mark. Suddenly, disaster struck. In an incredible instance of carelessness, Sir John had accidentally left his great telescope facing the sun, and its rays had burned a gaping hole in the lens. No more moon stories.

This last piece of news was too much for some to believe. Scientists demanded to see the original issue of the *Journal of Science* where Herschel's stories had appeared. Letters were on their way to South Africa for confirmation. Finally, a man named Richard Adams Locke had a little too much to drink one night and confessed that he had made up the whole moon story as a gimmick to attract readers to the *Sun*. The *Sun*'s competitors quickly labeled the moon stories as lies, and the *Sun* had to confess to the deception. But it took credit for temporarily diverting the public's attention from the somber cares of the day. The *Sun*'s readers were generally amused and forgiving. The paper never lost its increased circulation.

Newspapers, magazines, and books are in the business of attracting readers. The above example represents an extreme tactic in the process, but it does serve to emphasize a key point. The history of the print media is characterized by political, social, economic, and technological developments that have changed the shape of the newspaper, magazine, and book industries but, in the final analysis, those publications that have succeeded, persisted, and prospered have all been able to attract readers. This short historical sketch will trace the development of newspaper, book, and magazine publishing and briefly illustrate the type of content that managed to get people's attention and interest.

••••
EARLY HISTORY OF PRINTING

The technology necessary to print a newspaper is a simple one—ink is pressed onto paper. The technology necessary to make the newspaper a mass medium is more complicated, and we will begin our brief history with a consideration of the growth of early printing technology. Many historians suggest that the Chinese first invented movable type and also discovered the process for making paper. We do know that Marco Polo described Chinese printing upon his return to Venice in 1295. Nevertheless, prior to the mid-fifteenth century most books and pamphlets available to Europeans were expensive and often inaccurate, handwritten manuscripts. The invention of the printing press and the introduction of movable type to the Western world is usually associated with a German, Johann Gutenberg. Little is known about Gutenberg except that he loved wine, was skilled in metallurgy, had miserable luck as a businessman, and defaulted on several loans (lawsuits filed against Gutenberg provide the only real documentation for naming him father of the printing press). Gutenberg cast his type in soft metal rather than carving it in wood blocks. He borrowed an idea from winemaking and built a crude press that would force the ink onto the paper. Others copied Gutenberg's ideas, and presses spread from Germany throughout Europe during the last half of the fifteenth century. William Caxton, for example, introduced the printing press into Great Britain in 1487 and established a profitable London printing company that published the leading books of the day. Although book publishing was not considered to be a socially important force, Henry VIII recognized its potential in 1530 when he required all printers to obtain a royal approval before setting up shop. This notion of publishing "under authority" from the government would figure prominently in the future of the newspaper.

The idea of a mass-circulated newspaper followed the invention of printing. The bulk of early printed matter consisted of books and religious tracts. As more books went into print, more people were encouraged to learn how to read. As literacy grew, more people turned to education, and universities expanded. As education grew, more people became curious about how they lived, how others lived, and how their government was run. Merchants and businesspeople realized that a knowledge of economic conditions and commercial information from other towns and other countries could be beneficial to their own efforts. It wasn't long before publications sprang up across Europe to meet these needs. In Holland, printers began turning out **corantos**, or currents of news, around 1620. Corantos spread to Britain where news about the Thirty Years War was in great demand. These early forerunners of the newspaper carried mainly foreign and commercial news. The corantos were published on and off for the next twenty years, finally expiring because of circulation and license fee problems. They were replaced by the **diurnals**, daily reports of domestic and local events usually concerned with the doings of the king and parliament. This period also saw the rise of the printing of religious books. The Bible and hymnals were widely distributed, as well as a large number of books detailing the controversy surrounding the Reformation and Counter-Reformation. Along with an increase in book publishing came an increase in book suppression. Censorship was common. Even John Milton, the famous English poet who wrote *Areopagitica*, a defense of freedom to publish, was later a government censor.

Johann Gutenberg, a German, is usually associated with inventing the printing press and introducing movable type to the Western world. (Culver Pictures)

- - - -
JOURNALISM IN EARLY AMERICA

In 1686, Benjamin Harris, who had been pilloried in London for printing anticrown pamphlets, arrived in Boston. Four years later, displaying a certain lack of judgment, he published the first American newspaper, *Publick Occurrences Both Foreign and Domestick,* which again contained material offensive to the ruling powers. (One story alleging an affair between the King of France and his son's wife infuriated Boston's Puritan officials. They were aghast that such an account, impugning the integrity of a Christian king, could have reached the residents of their city.) Because of this and other controversial stories, the paper was suppressed after one issue. The idea of a free press had yet to surface in colonial America, and the majority believed that a paper had to have royal consent to be published. Harris' paper had no such consent, and that alone would have been basis enough for the governor of the colony to halt its publication. Fourteen years would pass before another attempt would surface. In 1704, the *Boston News Letter* was published by John Campbell, the local postmaster. Since he owed his position to the local authorities, Campbell tried hard not to offend them, duly licensing his publication with the colony's government and printing the words "Published by Authority" on the front page. His cautious approach resulted in a paper that was safe from suppression, but one that was also lackluster and dull. No stories of philandering kings were found in the *Boston News Letter* pages. Most of Campbell's news consisted of articles clipped from foreign papers, some stories more than five months old. There were notices of ships arriving and departing, summaries of sermons given by local clergy, and death notices. Campbell's paper was a sideline job for him, and it never turned much of a profit. Circulation was probably around 300 subscribers. In 1719, Campbell lost his job as postmaster and his replacement immediately started a rival paper, the *Boston Gazette.* Campbell did not take kindly to competition. He wrote of the new paper: "I pity [its] readers. Its sheets smell stronger of beer than of midnight oil."

Competition grew as a third newspaper was started in New York and a fourth appeared in Boston. The new arrival in Boston was significant for two reasons. First,

Benjamin Franklin became the publisher of The Pennsylvania Gazette *in 1729 when he was 24 years old. The paper became the most successful colonial newspaper and Franklin became the best-known colonial journalist and publisher. (Culver Pictures)*

it was published by James Franklin (Ben's older brother); and, second, it pioneered a new idea in press philosophy. The elder Franklin correctly noted that other papers carried routine news releases and were careful never to say anything to upset local authorities. Franklin decided that his paper, the *New England Courant*, would be different. He published without the approval of local government. His independence quickly got him into trouble, however, and the colonial magistrates threw him into prison and later forbade him from publishing a newspaper without their prior approval. James neatly got around this latter proscription by naming Ben as the new publisher of the *Courant*. The paper prospered under Ben's tenure as publisher and his writings were highly praised. Sibling rivalry eventually intervened, and Ben moved to Philadelphia where he started the *Pennsylvania Gazette*. Ben Franklin retired from a successful publishing career at the age of forty-two. During this time he started several newspapers, founded the first American foreign-language paper, published one of the first American magazines (see the section on "Magazines of the Colonial Period"), ran the first editorial cartoon, proved that advertising copy could sell merchandise (see the box on page 83) and, perhaps most important, demonstrated that journalism could be an honorable profession.

The Beginnings of Revolution

Tensions between colonies and crown were rising during Franklin's tenure as publisher, and this controversy sparked the development of the early press. One example of this tension was the trial of John Peter Zenger. In 1733, Zenger was persuaded by his influential backers to publish a newspaper that was openly critical of the British-born Royal Governor of New York. The governor promptly jailed Zenger and charged him with criminal libel. Famous lawyer Andrew Hamilton defended Zenger and capitalized upon the growing colonial resentment of Britain to win his case. Hamilton argued that despite precedents in British law to the contrary, truth could be used as a defense against libel and that a jury of Americans ought not feel bound by laws

Early advertising resembled what we today would call classified ads. Ads were set with no display type and were typically found in a column on the last page of the paper. The articles advertised were many and varied. In fact, if you were to read the ads in an early paper, you might not know what was being sold. For example, a 1752 paper advertised the following: durants, duroys, dowlahs, shaloons, camblets, alpoeens, and sagathies.

Ben Franklin was one of the first ad copywriters. The following was the text for one of his ads touting a product called "Super Fine Crown Soap":

It cleanses fine Linens, Muslins, Laces, Chinces, Cambricks, with Ease and Expedition, which often suffer more from the long and hard rubbing of the Washer, through the ill qualities of the soap than the wearing.

(Incidentally, the soap Franklin was describing was made by his brothers John and Peter. A shrewd businessman, Franklin endorsed the idea of keeping the money in the family.)

---

formed in England and not approved in America. The jury agreed and rendered a not-guilty verdict, thus striking a symbolic blow for press freedom.

Newspapers grew in numbers in the period before the Revolutionary War. Most of them were partisan, siding with the colonies or with the crown; others tried to steer a middle ground. In any case, this period marks the establishment of the **political press**, which openly supported a particular party, faction, or cause. The early newspaper editors, divided though they might be over some issues, were united as never before by the passage of the Stamp Act of 1765. The act imposed a penny tax per issue upon each newspaper and was despised by nearly all editors, who saw it as an attempt to put them out of business and as one more example of taxation without representation. The opposition to the act was vehement. Those who went along with the tax risked the wrath of the Sons of Liberty and other colonial action groups. In Boston, a mob hanged the stamp tax collector in effigy and then proceeded to burn down the house of the governor. Some printers were threatened with bodily harm if they stopped publishing simply to avoid the tax. Parliament yielded to the political pressure and repealed the tax the next year. Nevertheless, the Stamp Act accelerated the movement toward colonial independence.

As the revolution commenced, the colonial papers were thoroughly politicized. In addition to news, the papers reprinted excerpts from the many political pamphlets that were circulating at this time. In fact, the Declaration of Independence was published in the *Pennsylvania Evening Post* on July 6, 1776.

As the war intensified, the press became even more polarized, splitting into propatriot and pro-British factions. Most were prorevolution. About thirty-seven papers were published as the war began, and twenty of these survived. Several new papers sprang up during the war, and enough of these managed to stay in business so that by the end of the conflict approximately thirty-five newspapers were published regularly.

Magazines of the Colonial Period

In colonial times, the word "magazine" meant warehouse or depository, a place where various types of provisions were stored under one roof. The first **magazines** printed in America were patterned after this model; they were to be storehouses of varied

A good deal of time and energy was required to publish even a simple newspaper on early colonial presses like the one depicted here. (Culver Pictures)

literary materials gathered from books, pamphlets, and newspapers and bound together under one cover.

It was Ben Franklin who first announced plans to start a magazine in the colonies. Unfortunately for Ben, a competitor named Andrew Bradford got wind of his idea and beat Franklin to the punch. Bradford's *American Magazine* was published a few days before Franklin's *General Magazine* in 1741. The two publications carried political and economic articles aimed at an intelligent audience. Both were ambitious ventures in that they were designed for readers in all thirteen colonies and deliberately tried to influence public opinion; however, both quickly folded because of financial problems. The next significant attempt at magazine publishing occurred in Philadelphia when another Bradford (this one named William) started the *American Magazine and Monthly Chronicle* in 1757. This publication also contained the usual blend of political and economic articles mixed with a little humor; it was well edited and able to support itself for a year.

As America's political relations with England deteriorated, magazines, like newspapers, assumed a more significant political role. Thomas Paine, who, in his rousing pamphlet *Common Sense*, argued for separation from England, became editor of the *Pennsylvania Magazine*. This publication strongly supported the revolution and was a significant political force during the early days of the war. It became an early casualty of the conflict, however, and closed down in 1776. Other magazines appeared during and after the war, but they were seldom profitable and usually ceased publication within a year or two.

To summarize, it is clear that all these early magazines were aimed at a specialized audience—one that was educated, literate, and primarily urban. They contained a variety of articles dealing with the arts, practical science, and politics, and a list of authors who contributed to them would include most of the major poets, essayists, and statesmen of the period. Their overall impact was to encourage literary and artistic expression and to unify the colonies during America's struggle for independence from England.

In 1640, the Puritans in Cambridge, Massachusetts, printed the *Bay Psalm Book*. About 90,000 other titles were to follow it as book publishing took hold in the American colonies. In addition to locally published books, many volumes were imported from England. Among the more popular books printed in the colonies during the second half of the seventeenth century were *The Practice of Piety*, *A Sure Guide to Heaven*, and *Day of Doom*. Reading was a popular pastime of the early settlers and public libraries sprang up to serve their needs. Benjamin Franklin was instrumental in starting a library in Philadelphia. In a short period, other libraries opened in New York, Rhode Island, and South Carolina. During the Revolutionary War, many book printers turned out political pamphlets. Thomas Paine's *Common Sense* sold 100,000 copies in ten weeks.

Content: Topical Items and Partisan Politics

Newspapers and magazines in the colonial period carried a variety of items dealing with politics, crime, commerce, travel, and happenings in Europe. Benjamin Harris' *Publick Occurrences* contained a wide smattering of news items (in addition to the ones that landed him in trouble). Harris informed his early readers about the Indians selecting a day of formal Thanksgiving, an unnamed man committing suicide, the easing of the smallpox epidemic in Boston, and war news. Although the paper made perfect sense to the inhabitants of late-seventeenth-century Boston, some items would be unintelligible for the reader of the 1990s. For example, one item began with the following: "There lately arrived in Piscataqua, one Papoon from Penobscot in a small Shallop. . . ."

The *Pennsylvania Gazette* was notable for several innovations in content and style. Ben Franklin's paper had a cleaner makeup, with rules dividing the various stories and classified ads. The type was easier to read, and Franklin made an attempt to set off what we might call headlines from the rest of the items. He made use of short paragraphs to compress the news into a limited space. Here, for example, is one such news item that illustrates this trend and reveals a little bit about colonial crime and punishment:

> Last Week William Kerr . . . was indicted and convicted at the Mayor's Court of counterfeiting . . . Pieces of Eight . . . for which he received sentence as follows: To stand in the Pillory one Hour To-Morrow, to have his ear nail'd to same, and the part nail'd cut off and on Saturday next to stand another hour in the Pillory and to be Whipt 39 lashes . . . and then to pay a fine of 50 Pounds.

Perhaps the most interesting of Franklin's achievements was his skillful writing of advertising copy. (See the box on page 83.)

During the years of the revolution, news of war and politics dominated the pages of the young nation's newspapers. The most famous of the revolutionary papers was Isaiah Thomas' *Massachusetts Spy*. Although Thomas tried to maintain neutrality during the early years of his publishing career, the pressures for independence in his city were too great and eventually the *Spy* became a revolutionary paper. Thomas has the distinction of being the first war correspondent, and below is a sample of his reporting of the battle of Lexington:

> The [British] troops in the meantime . . . had crossed the river and landed at Phipp's farm. They immediately . . . proceeded to Lexington . . . with great silence. A company of militia, of about eighty men, mustered near the meeting house; the troops came in sight of them just before sunrise. The militia, upon seeing the troops, began to disperse. The troops then set out upon the run . . . and the commanding officer accosted the militia in words to this effect, "Disperse, you damn'd rebels—Damn you, disperse." Upon which . . . one or two officers discharged their pistols, which were instantaneously followed by the firing of four or five of the soldiers; and then there seemed to be a general discharge from the whole body. Eight of our men were killed and nine wounded.

Magazine content in the colonial period was quite varied. An early issue of Franklin's *General Magazine*, for example, carried ten pages of poems, sermons, book reviews, an article on the currency problem in the colonies, and a news section. Later articles would discuss a religious revival in the colonies, an orphanage recently founded in Georgia, and "A New Method of Making Molasses." Franklin's many interests and pursuits were clearly visible in his magazine.

The content of Joseph Dennie's *Port Folio* magazine was of unusually high quality. Its first issue featured an article by John Adams, "Tour through Silesia." Political articles became more numerous in succeeding issues, and in 1804 Dennie devoted an entire issue to an examination of the causes of the Alexander Hamilton–Aaron Burr duel. *Port Folio* was a diverse publication, however, and not all of its contents were somber. Here, for example, is a joke from an 1802 issue: "A gentleman, informed by a bill on a window of a house that apartments were to let, knocked at the door and, attended by a pretty female took a survey of the premises. 'Pray my dear,' said he smiling, 'are you to be let with the lodgings?' 'No,' [she] replied . . . 'I am to be let alone.' " Not exactly *Playboy*'s Party Jokes, but Hugh Hefner was still more than a century away.

Book content during the colonial period was primarily concerned with religion. There were, however, several publications that were more secular in tone. Benjamin Franklin's *Poor Richard's Almanack* sold about 10,000 copies a year. Sentimental novels, many of them imported from England, were also popular.

The Political Press: 1790–1830

The politicization of newspapers did not end with America's victory in the Revolutionary War. Instead, partisan leanings of the press were transferred into another arena—the debate over the powers of the federal government. The lineup of those who were participants in this controversy included some of the best political thinkers of the time: Alexander Hamilton, James Madison, Thomas Jefferson, John Jay. Newspapers were quick to take sides in this debate, and their pages were filled with Federalist or anti-Federalist propaganda. Hamilton and his Federalists used the *Gazette of the United States* as the "official" outlet for their views. The leader of the anti-Federalists, Thomas Jefferson, sought to counteract the influence of the *Gazette* by starting a rival paper in 1791, the *National Gazette*. Heated political debate gave way to name-calling and quarreling between these two groups, and the content of many newspapers became colored by volatile and inflammatory language. A typical example of the rhetoric in these early papers is found in the anti-Federalist *Aurora*, edited by Benjamin Franklin Bache ("Lightning Rod Junior"). Concerning President Washington, Bache wrote, ". . . if ever a nation was debauched by a man, the American nation has been debauched by Washington." Supporters of Washington and Federalism wrecked Bache's office and beat him up (communication scholars would call this an example of negative feedback).

At the vortex of this debate between Federalists and anti-Federalists was the Constitution of the United States. Although the original document made no mention of the right of a free press, a series of ten amendments, popularly called the Bill of Rights, did contain such a provision. The **first amendment** held that "Congress shall make no law . . . abridging the freedom of speech, or of the press. . . ." Thus the idea of a free press, which had grown during the revolutionary period, became part of the law of the new nation when Congress ratified this amendment in 1791.

Unfortunately, even after the amendment had been passed, the notion of a free press was not completely accepted. Press attacks on political leaders continued unabated. Freed from repressive government regulation, early newspapers found it easy to go to extremes. A controversy regarding U.S. relations with France touched off a journalistic battle filled with invective. Here, for example, is what Federalist editor William Cobbett had to say about our friend Benjamin Franklin Bache: ". . . This atrocious wretch . . . is an ill-looking devil. His eyes never get above your knees. He is of sallow complexion, hollow-cheeked, dead-eyed, and [looks] like a fellow who has been about a week or ten days [hanging on a gallows]." Bache seemed to inspire strong feelings. When another angry rival editor, James Fenno, ran into Bache on the street, Fenno beat him with a cane (another example of negative feedback).

In the late 1790s, with Federalist John Adams as president, the government sought to curb press criticism of its policies and check the volatile writings of other irritating journalists by passing the **Sedition Act**. This act made it a crime to write anything about the U.S. government or Congress that might be "false, scandalous or malicious." Public opinion, however, was not on the side of this repressive law and it was allowed to expire in 1801.

Newspapers grew with the country in the first twenty years of the new century. The daily newspaper began in 1783 and grew slowly. By 1800, most large cities had at least one daily paper. By 1820, there were 24 dailies, 66 semi- or tri-weeklies, and 422 weeklies. Circulations were not large, usually around 1500, except for the big-city papers. The number was small because these newspapers were read primarily by the upper socioeconomic classes; early readers had to be literate and possess money to spend on subscriptions (about $10 per year or 6 cents an issue—a large sum when you consider that during these years 5 cents could buy a pint of whiskey). The content was typified by commercial and business news, political and congressional debates, speeches, acts of state legislatures, and official messages. Still, the audience was growing. As the population moved westward, so did the printing presses. A paper was started in St. Louis in 1808. Frontier Detroit had a newspaper, the *Gazette*, in 1817. By 1833, there were approximately 1200 papers printed in the country.

During this period, several newspapers arose in response to the needs and interests of minority groups. *Freedom's Journal*, the first of over forty black newspapers published before 1860, was founded in the late 1820s by the Reverend Samual Cornish and John Russwurm. Written and edited by blacks, the paper championed the cause of black people by dealing with the serious problems arising from slavery and by carrying news of foreign countries such as Haiti and Sierra Leone that appealed to its black audience.

At about the same time, another minority group, the Cherokee Indian nation, was being pressured by the federal government to abandon its tribal lands in Georgia and relocate further west. A Cherokee scholar named Sequoyah became fascinated with the written prose of the whites, for he was convinced that the secret of their superior power lay in their ability to transmit knowledge through a written language. Subsequently, he set out to develop a system of writing for his own people. After experimenting for over a decade, he developed an alphabet, consisting of eighty-six characters, by which the Cherokee language could be set down in written form. His new system enabled his people to learn to read and write. The tribe set up schools where Sequoyah's alphabet was taught and published books in the Cherokee language. Eventually, the first Indian newspaper, the *Cherokee Phoenix*, written in both Cherokee and English, appeared in 1828. The *Phoenix* was edited by Elias Boudinot, a Native American, who had been educated at a northern seminary. The paper was influential among members of the Cherokee nation and even had a large number of European readers. Boudinot resigned in 1832 and the paper ceased publication for two years. A treaty in 1835 evicted the Cherokee nation from their Georgia home. When the Cherokees tried to take their printing press with them, local authorities seized it.

By 1844, a new Native American paper appeared in Oklahoma, the *Cherokee Advocate*. Despite hardships stemming from the Civil War and pressures from settlers to occupy the Oklahoma Territory, the *Advocate* continued to operate until 1906.

FREEDOM'S JOURNAL.

"RIGHTEOUSNESS EXALTETH A NATION."

BY JNO. B. RUSSWURM.   NEW-YORK, FRIDAY, MARCH 14, 1828.   VOL. I.—NO. LI.

THE COLORED AMERICAN.

SAMUEL E. CORNISH, EDITOR.   *New-York, Saturday, May 13, 1837.*   PHILIP A. BELL, PROPRIETOR.

Two early examples of the black press: Freedom's Journal *was started in 1827 by John Russwurm (left), the first black to graduate from a college in the United States, and by Samuel Cornish. Cornish later edited* The Colored American, *a paper that had subscribers from Maine to Michigan. (Schomberg Center for Research in Black Culture, The New York Public Library)*

Magazines After the Revolution

Like the prerevolutionary publications that preceded them, magazines popular during the late eighteenth and early nineteenth centuries contained a mix of political and topical articles directed primarily at an educated elite. The birth of the modern news magazine can also be traced back to this period. *Niles Weekly Register*, which reported current events of the time, was read throughout the country. The *North American Review*, started in 1815, was more parochial in its contents, focusing primarily on New England art and politics.

The influence of the political press was also reflected in magazines of the period. One of the most influential was the *Port Folio*, edited by the colorful nonconformist

Joseph Dennie. Dennie's intended audience was a select one; he wished to reach "Men of Affluence, Men of Liberality, and Men of Letters." Although the major thrust of the paper was political, Dennie interspersed travelogues, theater reviews, satirical essays, and even jokes, some of them mildly suggestive. It was politics, however, that got Dennie into trouble and got the *Port Folio* tremendous visibility. Dennie was an admirer of all things British and despised the new Republic. He once called the Declaration of Independence a "false, flatulent and foolish paper." He declared democracy a mistake. The government indicted him for seditious libel (another form of negative feedback), but Dennie was finally acquitted. *Port Folio* went on publishing until 1827.

● ● ● ●
BIRTH OF THE MASS NEWSPAPER

Benjamin Day was only 22 years old when he developed the idea of a newspaper for the masses. Day probably had no idea that he was starting a revolution in the communications industry when he launched his *New York Sun* in 1833. Nonetheless, journalism would be profoundly altered by his new approach. Several conditions had to exist before a mass press could come into existence:

1. a printing press had to be invented that would produce copies quickly and cheaply

2. enough people had to know how to read in order to support such a press

3. a "mass audience" had to be present

Day would never have been able to launch his newspaper without significant advances in printing technology. Frederick Koenig had perfected a two-cylinder press in 1814 that printed both sides of the paper at once and could turn out copies at the rate of 1100 per hour. The next step was to harness an outside power source to the press to increase its speed. In 1822, Dan Treadwell took this idea literally and harnessed a real horse to his machine, thus creating a true one-horsepower printing press. The horse's career in journalism didn't last long, as the animal was quickly replaced by steam power. In 1830, the U.S. firm of R. Hoe and Company marketed a press that could produce 4000 double impressions an hour. By 1833, the technology had advanced enough to justify the production of an extremely cheap newspaper that almost everybody could afford.

The second element that led to the growth of the mass newspaper was the increased level of literacy in the population. The first statewide public school system was set up during the 1830s and, in addition to a large number of private elementary schools in the major cities, there were also at least fifty colleges scattered about the various states. The increased emphasis on education led to a concomitant growth of literacy as many people in the middle and lower economic groups acquired reading skills.

The third element was more subtle and harder to explain. The mass press appeared during an era that historians call the age of "Jacksonian democracy." It was an age in which ordinary people were first recognized as a political and economic force. Property requirements for voting had died out. Every state but one in 1832 chose presidential electors by popular vote. In addition, this period was marked by the rise of an urban middle class. The shift from homemade goods to factory-made goods encouraged by the Industrial Revolution was plainly evident in the United States at this time. The trend toward "democratization" of business and politics fostered the creation of a mass audience responsive to a mass press. All of these factors made it possible for Day to attract readers to his paper.

Day had seen others fail in their attempts to market a mass-appeal newspaper. Nonetheless, he forged ahead. Day's paper would be a daily and would sell for a penny. This was a significant price reduction when compared to the other New York City, Boston, and Philadelphia dailies, which went for six cents a copy. (The price of six cents was also typical for many weekly papers in other parts of the country. Since they came out less frequently, these papers were cheaper than the *Sun* on an annual basis. Thus although the penny press did not mark a drop in the overall price of American newspapers, it did signal a decrease in the price of urban dailies.) Local happenings, sex, violence, features, and human-interest stories would constitute his content. The first issue contained news of a suicide, police and crime items, shipping information, weddings, obituaries, and feature stories. Conspicuously absent were the stodgy political debates that still characterized many of the six-cent papers. Within six months the *Sun* achieved a circulation of approximately 8000 issues, far ahead of its nearest competitor. Day's gamble had paid off, and the **penny press** was launched.

Others imitated the success of Day's new penny paper. Perhaps the most significant and certainly the most colorful of these individuals was James Gordon Bennett. In 1835, Bennett launched his *New York Herald.* The paper started in humble surroundings—a cellar on Wall Street equipped with two chairs and a desk made by balancing a plank on two flour barrels. Bennett was able to move into more spacious surroundings soon afterward because the *Herald* was even more of a rapid success than the *Sun*. Part of Bennett's success can be attributed to his skillful reporting of crime news, the institution of a financial page, sports reporting, and an aggressive editorial policy. Bennett looked upon himself as a reformer, and in one of his fulsome editorials he wrote: "I go for a general reformation of morals. . . . I mean to begin a new movement in the progress of civilization. . . . Get out of my way ye driveling editors and driveling politicians." This pugnacious attitude was not without risk, and on one occasion one of those rival "driveling editors" cornered Bennett and beat him about the head and shoulders with a cane (more negative feedback).

Another important pioneer of the era was Horace Greeley. His *New York Tribune* appeared in 1841 and would rank third behind the *Sun* and *Herald* in daily circulation, but its weekly edition was circulated nationally and proved to be a great success. Greeley's *Tribune* was not as sensational as its competitors. He used his editorial page for crusades and causes. He opposed capital punishment, alcohol, gambling, and

---

Front page of the New York Sun. *Benjamin Day's reliance on advertising for revenue is illustrated by the several columns of classified ads appearing on the front page. (Courtesy of the New-York Historical Society, New York City)*

tobacco. He favored a high tariff, trade unions, and westward expansion (the famous quotation usually attributed to Greeley, "Go west, young man," was actually first said by an Indiana newspaperman, but Greeley would have agreed with its sentiment). Greeley also favored women's rights. In 1845, he hired Margaret Fuller as literary critic for the *Tribune*. In addition to her commentary on the fine arts, Fuller published articles dealing with the hard lot of prostitutes, women prisoners, and the insane. Her work attracted strong public interest, and today she is regarded as one of the finest critics of her generation. She also became the first woman foreign correspondent. Greeley's decision to hire Fuller is typical of his publishing philosophy: Like Fuller, he never talked down to the mass audience and attracted his readers by appealing to their intellect more than to their emotions.

The last of the major newspapers of the penny-press era that we shall consider began in 1851 and, at this writing, was still publishing. The *New York Times*, edited by Henry Raymond, promised to be less sensational than the *Sun* or the *Herald* and less impassioned than Greeley. The paper soon established a reputation for objective and reasoned journalism. Raymond stressed the gathering of foreign news and served as foreign correspondent himself in 1859. The *Times* circulation reached more than 40,000 before the Civil War.

Finally, all of these publishers had one thing in common. As soon as their penny papers were successful, they doubled the price.

Significance of the Penny Press

At this point, we should consider the major changes in journalism that were prompted by the success of the mass press during the 1833–1860 period. In short, we can identify four such changes. The penny press changed:

1. the basis of economic support for newspapers

2. the pattern of newspaper distribution

3. the definition of what constituted news

4. the techniques of news collection

Before the penny press, most of a newspaper's economic support came from subscription revenue. The large circulation of the penny papers made advertisers realize that they could reach a large segment of potential buyers by purchasing space. Moreover, the readership of the popular papers cut across political party and social class lines, thereby assuring a potential advertiser of a broadly based audience. As a result, advertisers were greatly attracted to this new medium, and the mass newspapers relied significantly more on advertising revenues than did their predecessors.

Older papers were distributed primarily through the mails; the penny press, although relying somewhat on subscriptions, also made use of street sales. Vendors would buy 100 copies for 67 cents and sell them for one cent each. Soon it became common to hear newsboys hawking papers at most corners in the larger cities. Since these papers had to compete with one another in the open marketplace of the street, editors went out of their way to find original and exclusive news that would give their paper an edge. Page makeup and type styles changed in order to attract the attention of the casual passerby.

The penny press also redefined the concept of news. The older papers were passive information collectors; they printed information that others might have sent them or news that might have been published first elsewhere. Thus stories appearing in the foreign press were reprinted, letters from congressmen were reproduced, and official reports from the federal government and presidential speeches were carried verbatim. There was no systematic search for news. The penny press changed that by hiring people to go out and look for news. Reporters were assigned to special "beats": police, financial, sports, and religion, to name a few. Foreign correspondents were popular. Even Karl Marx served as a London correspondent for the *Tribune* (he quit when Greeley forced a salary cut on him). The penny papers created the role of the paid news gatherer. Newspapers changed their emphasis from the affairs of the commercial elite to the social life of the rising middle classes.

This shift meant that news became more of a commodity, something that had value. And, like many commodities, fresh news was more valuable than stale news. The increased competition among the papers of the era further emphasized this fact. Any scheme that would get the news into the paper faster was tried. Stories were sent by carrier pigeon, pony express, railroads, and steamships as the newspapers kept pace with the advances in transportation. (See the box below.) The biggest innovation in news gathering of this time was the invention of the telegraph in 1844. The Mexican War of 1846 made fast news transmission especially desirable, and many newspapers first used the telegraph to carry news about this conflict. All in all, the penny papers increased the importance of speed in news collection.

Magazines in the Penny-Press Era

While the penny press was opening up new markets for newspapers, magazine publishers were also quietly expanding their appeal and coverage. The *Knickerbocker* (as the name suggests, a New York publication), *Graham's Magazine*, and the *Saturday Evening Post* all started between 1820 and 1840 and were written not so much for the intelligentsia as for the generally literate middle classes. By 1842, *Graham's*, under the direction of Edgar Allan Poe, had a circulation of 40,000. The growing social and economic importance of women was illustrated by the birth of *Godey's Lady's Book* in 1830 and *Peterson's* in 1842. These two magazines offered articles on fashion, morals, diets, and health hints and printed elaborate hand-colored engravings in their pages. *Godey's*, under the editorship of Sara Hale, was a pioneer for women's rights and was the first magazine to campaign for wider recognition of women writers. (See the box on page 94.)

Technological improvements in printing and in the reproduction of illustrations also helped to expand the magazine audience. In 1850, *Harper's Monthly* was started

Winging the News

The telegraph didn't get to New York until 1846 but that didn't stop the *New York Sun* from using some imaginative techniques to get the news to its readers more quickly. Most ships from England docked first at Boston Harbor and then went on to New York. The *Sun* realized that they could scoop their competitors with the latest news from England by meeting the incoming ships at Boston and rushing copies of the English papers back to New York. The *Sun* assembled a system that used trains to carry the papers from Boston to Providence, and then fast express boats took them the rest of the way to New York City. By using this arrangement, the *Sun* got foreign news twelve to twenty-four hours ahead of its competition.

The *Sun* also pioneered the use of an unusual kind of air express to speed up news gathering: carrier pigeons. Pigeons had been used for many years in Europe to transmit messages, and several papers in England found them useful in conveying news reports as well. The *Sun* contracted to buy a veteran flock from the London *Morning Chronicle*. These particular birds had flown the Paris-London route and were particularly skilled at navigating across water, a competence that would help them bring news from other port cities to New York. The birds served admirably before the arrival of the telegraph returned them to their roost.

During the late 1800s, magazines and newspapers expanded their audiences by the introduction of elaborate woodcut illustrations. Illustrated articles introduced pictures as a significant element of journalism and opened the door for the acceptance of photographs. Some of the finest woodcuts of the period ran in Harper's Weekly. *This illustration portrays the building of the Statue of Liberty in New York Harbor. (Harper's Weekly)*

as a magazine that would present material that had already appeared in other sources (rather like the *Reader's Digest*, except that the articles were reprinted in full). *Harper's* also included elaborate woodcut illustrations along with its articles in double-sized issues. *Harper's Weekly* was instituted seven years later and was to become famous for its illustrations of the Civil War. In 1863, this magazine began publishing reproductions of Mathew Brady's war photographs.

The sensationalist and crusading approach of the penny press also translated itself into at least two magazines. *Frank Leslie's Illustrated Newspaper* was a sixteen-page weekly that sold for a dime and concentrated on lurid illustrations of murders, morgues, and mayhem. The *New York Ledger*, started in 1855 by Robert Bonner, printed the best work of the period's popular writers and ran melodramatic serials in issue after issue. Bonner promoted his magazine heavily and would occasionally print the first few pages of a detective story in a local newspaper and then break off with "continued in the *New York Ledger*," thus hooking his readers. He would also buy full-page ads

Sara Josepha Buell Hale

Sara Josepha Buell Hale was responsible for having Thanksgiving declared an annual holiday. She was also the author of the popular nursery rhyme, "Mary Had a Little Lamb." She was also one of the women who left a lasting impression on nineteenth-century American journalism.

Sara Josepha Buell married David Hale, a New Hampshire lawyer, who encouraged her to write articles and poems for the local magazines. She was a prolific writer and by the time she was 38 had published seventeen poems, many magazine articles, two short stories, a literary review, and a novel.

Her literary accomplishments brought her to the attention of Louis Godey, publisher of *Godey's Lady's Book*, who offered her the position of editor. She accepted and brought to the magazine an editorial philosophy that emphasized an intimate editor-reader relationship that proved so popular that the magazine had a circulation of 150,000 by 1860, a remarkable figure for the time.

Sara Hale not only edited *Godey's Lady's Book*, but she also wrote about half of every issue. She also found time to advocate women's rights and was influential in persuading Matthew Vassar to start the college that still bears his name.

She spent forty years editing the magazine and finally retired at age 89. Thanks to her efforts, *Godey's Lady's Book* is credited with being the best women's magazine of the period.

in the newspaper that proclaimed "THE NEW YORK LEDGER WILL BE ON SALE TOMORROW MORNING THROUGHOUT THE UNITED STATES AND NEW JERSEY," which probably did little for his popularity in New Jersey.

The crusading spirit was evident in *Leslie's* campaign against contaminated milk in 1858. The magazine took on the power structure of New York City, and the exposé showed that the magazine as well as the newspaper could be used for civic and social reform. The most famous crusade, however, was probably that of *Harper's Weekly* against the corrupt political administration in New York in 1870. Under the control of William "Boss" Tweed, a group of unscrupulous politicians managed to bilk the city out of approximately $200 million. The editorial cartoons of Thomas Nast were credited with helping to bring down this ring.

Books in the Penny-Press Era

The change in printing technology and the growth of literacy also helped the book publishing industry. Many of the publishing companies still active today can trace their roots to this period. Many publishers specialized in professional and educational books, while others addressed their efforts to the general public. Book prices declined and authors such as James Fenimore Cooper and Henry Wadsworth Longfellow were popular, as were the works of English authors. Public education and the penny newspaper created a demand for reading materials. The number of public libraries tripled between 1825 and 1850. Book reading became a symbol of education and knowledge. Paperback books made their debut during the 1830s, but an unfavorable ruling by the postal department ended their popularity by the mid-1840s.

Content: Popular Appeal of the Penny Press

The goal of the print media to reach a mass audience was made possible by advances in printing technology and by a rise in the literacy level of the population. Whereas content of earlier publications had been aimed primarily at an educated elite, newspapers and magazines now hastened to appeal to the interests of new readers in the middle and working classes. The following capsule description of the contents of Ben Day's first issue of the *Sun* on September 3, 1833, will help illustrate the appeal of the penny press. Page size was eight by eleven inches, with three columns to the page, four pages in all. The first column on page one was devoted to news of sailing times for ocean-going vessels. The remainder of page one carried a feature story about "An Irish Captain" who had been in six duels. There was no indication if the story was fact or fiction. On page two was news of a suicide, followed by nine items under the headline "Police Office." Shorter items told of an approaching execution, a murder, a burglary, a fire, an earthquake, a murder trial, cholera in Mexico, and, somewhat out of place, a dinner given for the Postmaster General in Nashville. Page three carried news about another murder, a prison uprising, shipping news, weddings, and death announcements; the rest of the page carried ads. The last page contained a long poem, a table containing the current prices of bank notes (private banks of that period issued their own money), and eight more ads. The political opinion commonly found in the six-cent papers was not present in the *Sun*.

As mentioned earlier, James Gordon Bennett was another prominent figure in the penny-press era. Bennett craved attention and was not averse to using the pages of his *Herald* to brag of his success (he once wrote that his paper would receive $30,000 in revenue for the next two years) and to make plain his lofty goals ("I am determined to make the *Herald* the greatest paper that ever appeared in the world."). Bennett was never one for modesty: "I have infused life, glowing eloquence, philosophy, taste, sentiment, wit and humor into the daily newspaper. . . . Shakespeare is the great genius of the drama . . . and I mean to be the genius of the daily newspaper press." Bennett's desire for self-publicity was perhaps best exemplified by his announcement of his forthcoming marriage, printed in the June 1, 1840, *Herald*:

> I am going to be married in a few days. The weather is so beautiful; times are getting so good . . . that I cannot resist the divine instinct of honest nature any longer; so I am going to be married to one of the most splendid women in intellect, in heart, in soul, in property, in person, in manner, that I have yet seen in the course of my interesting pilgrimage through life. . . . I must give the world a pattern of happy wedded life.

Bennett, of course, was already married in spirit to his newspaper, and he used his upcoming wedding to get in a plug for it: "Association, night and day, in sickness and in health . . . with a woman of the highest order of excellence, must produce some curious results in my heart and feelings, and these results the future will develop in due time in the columns of the *Herald*." Bennett married Henrietta Crean shortly thereafter, took her to Niagara Falls, and continued to send back columns to the *Herald* all during his honeymoon.

The efforts of magazines to appeal to a wider audience are evidenced by a brief examination of the contents of two leaders during this period: *Knickerbocker* and *Graham's*. Washington Irving and James Fenimore Cooper were frequent contributors to *Knickerbocker*, and the work of Nathaniel Hawthorne and Henry Wadsworth Longfellow also appeared in its pages. In 1846, the *Knickerbocker* capitalized on the growing interest in the American West and serialized Francis Parkman's *The Oregon Trail*. *Graham's* content was varied. An 1842 issue contained a love story, a Longfellow poem, and an article by Edgar Allan Poe in which he analyzed the handwriting of some well-known figures of the day. These early magazines succeeded in bringing the work of well-known literary figures to a wider audience.

The novels of Charles Dickens and Walter Scott continued to be best sellers during this period, as were books by Herman Melville and Henry David Thoreau. Specialized books also appeared. In the late 1840s, textbooks were profitable, as were reference, medical, and engineering books. Noah Webster's *Dictionary of the English*

Language appeared in 1828 and the *Encyclopedia Americana* the next year. The first *McGuffey's Reader* was published in 1836. The most significant book of the period, however, was probably Harriet Beecher Stowe's *Uncle Tom's Cabin*, published in 1852. It sold 300,000 copies in its first year and was credited with converting many readers to an antislavery position.

• • • •
A SURGE IN GROWTH

Newspapers Become Big Business

The Civil War, which altered so many things in the United States, also changed American newspaper journalism. A new reporting technique emerged as telegraphic dispatches from the war zones were transformed into "headlines" to give the reader the main points of longer stories that followed. Because telegraph lines were unreliable and often failed, the opening paragraphs of the news story, the "lead," told the most important facts. The rest of the story contained details. If the telegraph line broke during a story, at least the most important part would probably get through. Thus the "inverted-pyramid" style of reporting was developed.

After the war ended, the country underwent major social changes. From 1870 to 1900 the total population doubled, and the urban population tripled. Mass production techniques changed the economic structure. Immigration brought even more people to the cities, especially in the North and East. Newspaper growth was even greater than that of the population. The number of dailies quadrupled from 1870 to the turn of the century; circulation showed a fivefold increase. One trend was clear: Newspapers were becoming big business. As circulation went up, so did operating cost and initial investment. Bennett was able to start the *Herald* for around $500. Greeley invested $44,000 in the *Tribune* in 1841. Ten years later, the *Times* was started on an investment of $50,000. In 1883, the *New York World* was sold for $346,000. Eleven years later, the *New York Morning Journal* was sold for $1 million. But rewards were also high. It was estimated that the *World* made about $1 million a year in profits by the mid-1890s. A second trend also stood out: The newspaper industry was dominated in this period by several powerful and outspoken individuals. We will consider three who had a significant impact on American newspapers—Pulitzer, Scripps, and Hearst.

Joseph Pulitzer came to the United States from Hungary. He was not a promising candidate for the most-likely-to-succeed award. He first tried a career in the military but was turned down by the British Army, the Austrian Army, and the French Foreign Legion. He was finally accepted into the Union Army during the Civil War but was nearly court-martialed for striking a noncommissioned officer. Unable to find work in New York after the war because he could speak little English, he asked his friends where he should go in order to learn his new language. His friends evidently played a practical joke on him and directed him to St. Louis, a city that then had the largest proportion of non–English-speaking immigrants in the country. After working at a string of unsuccessful jobs in St. Louis, Pulitzer became interested in journalism and realized he had found his calling. In 1878, he bought the *St. Louis Post-Dispatch* and quickly turned it into a success. Just five years later, he was ready to try his hand in the high-stakes world of New York City journalism. The *New York World*, a paper in financial trouble, was for sale. Pulitzer bought it. In a little more than a year, circulation increased from 15,000 to 100,000. Two years later it topped the quarter-million mark.

Pulitzer had obviously found a formula for newspaper success, and his innovations are worth considering. First, Pulitzer introduced new practices that appealed to advertisers: He reserved more space for ads and sold his paper on the basis of circulation. Second, Pulitzer used illustrations, clean page makeup, and simple writing to extend his paper's appeal to immigrants with few skills in English. Third, the *World* never

Frederick Douglass

He escaped from slavery when he was 21, published an autobiography at 27, and was publishing his own newspaper before he was 30. So began the remarkable career of Frederick Douglass, one of the most eloquent antislavery speakers and writers of the pre–Civil War era.

After his escape to New York City in 1838, Douglass worked as a carpenter and continued his self-education. His striking speaking style and his insights into the dilemma of slavery brought him a position as a full-time lecturer, giving speeches to abolitionist groups in the North. Douglass also began writing articles for the *Liberator*, the leading abolitionist newspaper. Eventually, he started his own paper, the *North Star*, which continued to publish until the middle of the Civil War.

Douglass lectured all through Britain and Canada, promoting the antislavery cause. During the war, he was instrumental in raising an all-black Massachusetts regiment (the film *Glory* tells the story of this regiment and presents a brief portrayal of Douglass).

Douglass continued his activist career after the war ended. He campaigned for black voting rights, social justice, economic development, and women's rights. In 1878, he published the final volume of his autobiography. Outspoken until the end, Douglass was involved in the fight for voting rights for women when he died in 1895.

---

failed to promote itself in its own pages. Circulation figures were printed on the front page. Stunts were used to promote circulation. Pulitzer sent reporter Nelly Bly on a round-the-world trip to break the time mentioned in Jules Verne's *Around the World in 80 Days*. Ms. Bly spent a night in a haunted house, went down in a diving bell, and worked in the Salvation Army. Her stories on these experiences helped Pulitzer build readership. Fourth, Pulitzer attracted a mass readership by reintroducing the sensationalized news of the penny-press era into his paper. In his first issue, Pulitzer led with a report of a storm that devastated New Jersey and included on his front page an interview with a condemned slayer, an item about a hanging, and a tearjerker about a wronged servant girl. Pulitzer loved headlines with alliteration. If alliteration could be mixed with sex, crime, and violence, so much the better, as these examples indicate: "Little Lotta's Lovers," "Baptized in Blood," "Jim-Jams in the Jury," and "A Preacher's Perfidy." Finally, Pulitzer endorsed the notion that a newspaper should promote the general welfare of its readers, especially the underprivileged. Although Pulitzer did not originate the idea, he went to great lengths to put it into practice. The paper crusaded against the abuses of big business and corrupt politicians. In 1833, a heat wave caused many infant deaths in New York's overcrowded slums. The *World* quickly produced headlines: "How Babies Are Baked," "Little Lines of Hearses." (Alliteration was also mixed in with crusades.) Naturally, the *World*'s support of the working class made it a favorite among the many low-income immigrants then living in New York.

Attempts to reach a working-class audience were not confined to the East. In the Midwest, E. W. Scripps started papers in Cleveland and Cincinnati, both growing industrial cities with large populations of factory workers. The Scripps papers featured concisely edited news, human-interest stories, editorial independence, and frequent crusades for the working class. In 1889, Scripps formed an alliance with his business manager, Milton McRae, allowing McRae to head the day-to-day operations of the paper so that Scripps could fade into the background and concentrate on policy matters. Thus in 1890, Scripps, at age thirty-six, went into "retirement." Scripps and

McRae pioneered the idea of the newspaper chain and expanded their operations into other cities. By 1911, there were eighteen papers under their control. (Scripps was a colorful character in American journalism. Although he championed the cause of the poor, he lived in regal splendor on a huge ranch near San Diego. He bragged that he consumed a gallon of whiskey a day—probably an exaggeration—and smoked cigars incessantly. When he died at age seventy-one, he was worth about $50 million.)

Perhaps the most well known of these three newspaper giants, thanks to the film *Citizen Kane*, which was loosely based on his career, was William Randolph Hearst. While Pulitzer was succeeding in New York and Scripps was acquiring papers in the Midwest, 24-year-old Hearst was given control of the *San Francisco Examiner*, thanks to the generosity of his wealthy father. Hearst went after readers by appealing to their emotions. His first issue carried a story of the mismanagement of a local orphanage with headlines such as "Hapless Babes—Tales of Cowardly Cruelty," "Physicians Who Aid in Murder," and "Infants Purposely Mangled at Birth." Fires, murders, and stories about love and hate were given splashy coverage. Hearst banked heavily on sensationalism to raise his readership level. It worked. The *Examiner* shot to the number-one position.

Yellow Journalism

Hearst, like Pulitzer before him, then invaded the big league—New York City. In 1895, he bought the *New York Journal*. Soon, Pulitzer and Hearst were engaged in a fierce circulation battle as each paper attempted to out-sensationalize the other. As one press critic put it, the duel between these two spread "death, dishonor and disaster" all over page one. Sex, murder, popularized medicine, pseudoscience, self-promotion, and human-interest stories filled the two papers. This type of reporting became known as **yellow journalism** (named after a cartoon character, the Yellow Kid, who wore a bright yellow nightshirt), and whatever its faults, it sold newspapers.

William Randolph Hearst, the successful publisher of the San Francisco Examiner *and later the* New York Journal, *employed sensationalism ("yellow journalism") to win the circulation wars of the late 1800s. He created a major publishing empire consisting of a chain of newspapers, a wire service, and four syndicates. (Culver Pictures)*

Yellow Journalism and the "Bucket of Blood"

New York was not the only hotbed of the new sensational journalism. A brief look at the *Denver Post* in the rip-roaring era around the turn of the century might convince some that this period represents the bad old days of the American newspaper. The *Post* was taken over in 1895 by Harry Tammen and Fred Bonfils, two gentlemen who had questionable credentials in journalism. Bonfils sold insurance and real estate and later operated lotteries. Tammen started out as a pinboy in a bowling alley and went on to be a bartender. The duo met while Tammen was pouring drinks in a Denver bar and immediately went into the newspaper business.

They started by touting the *Post* as a crusader for the citizens of Denver. Slogans such as "The Paper with a Heart and Soul," "Your Big Brother," and "So the People May Know" graced the paper's pages. In addition, the duo attacked everybody in sight. Led by their sports editor, a man with the rather melodious name of Otto Floto, the *Post* went after politicians, corporations, the governor, quack doctors, and ironically enough, given Bonfils' background, lottery operators. Their enthusiasm occasionally exceeded their facts, and "Who's suing the *Post* for libel now?" was a common question among Colorado reporters as the new century opened. The *Post* was a hit with readers, however, and its increased profitability enabled the publishers to afford good lawyers, and none of the charges ever held up in court.

Encouraged by their success, the two moved into a new building and had their office painted red to match the red ink used in the *Post*'s screaming headlines. Bonfils and Tammen called it the "Red Room," but the residents of Denver nicknamed it the "Bucket of Blood." From their new surroundings, the pair carried on their attacks, sometimes with bizarre results, In one instance, the paper's advice-to-the-lovelorn and gossip columnist, Polly Pry, wrote a story in which a man allegedly murdered and ate his business partner during a search for gold. This man's lawyer, naturally enough, resented the story; he showed up in the Red Room one day and fired a volley of shots at the two publishers. His aim was terrible, and he was finally restrained by Polly Pry herself. In another instance, striking transit workers, infuriated by the *Post*'s support of management, broke into the newspaper building and were systematically wrecking the editorial offices until they were restrained by the authorities.

Not all of the *Post*'s efforts had unsavory results. The paper crusaded for child-labor reform and did much to encourage Colorado as a vacation spot. By 1926, the paper was making a million dollars a year and had a daily circulation of more than 150,000. Under more sedate management, the *Post* today is rated as one of the best papers in the West.

The battle between Pulitzer and Hearst reached its climax with the Spanish-American War in 1898. In fact, many historians have argued that the newspapers were an important factor in shaping public opinion in favor of hostilities. When the battleship *Maine* was blown up in Havana Harbor, the *Journal* offered a $50,000 reward for the arrest of the guilty parties. Circulation jumped over the million mark. War was finally declared in April, and the *World* and the *Journal* pulled out all the stops. Hearst chartered a steamer and equipped it with printing presses. He also brought down his yacht and sailed with the U.S. fleet in the battle of Santiago. The *Journal* put out forty extras in a single day.

Yellow journalism tapered off after this episode, although traces would persist for another decade. Pulitzer, in ill health, finally withdrew from the battle with Hearst around 1900. Although the period of yellow journalism cannot be said to have been the proudest moment in the history of the American newspaper, some positive features

The New York Journal, *one of the leading publications of the yellow journalism era, emphasized crime and violence on its front pages. (Newspaper collection, The New York Public Library, Astor, Lenox and Tilden Foundations).*

did emerge from it. In the first place, it brought enthusiasm, energy, and verve to the practice of journalism. Aggressive reporting and investigative stories were emphasized by the *World* and the *Journal*. Second, it brought wide exposure to prominent authors and led to some fine examples of contemporary writing. Stephen Crane, Frank Norris, Dorothy Dix, and Mark Twain all wrote for newspapers during this period (1880–1905). Further, yellow journalism helped popularize the use of layout and display devices—banner headlines, pictures, color printing—that would go on to characterize modern journalism.

The Magazine Boom

In 1860, there were approximately 260 magazines published in the United States; by 1900, there were 1800. Why the surge in growth? The primary factors were more available money, better printing techniques that lowered prices, and especially the Postal Act of 1879, which gave magazines special mailing rates. It was possible to aim for a national market on a mass scale, and several magazines set out to do just that.

The most successful of the magazines seeking a mass market was the *Ladies' Home Journal*, founded by Cyrus Curtis in 1881. The first issue, eight pages long, contained an illustrated short story, an article on growing flowers, fashion notes, childcare advice, needlework hints, and recipes. Curtis was the first to realize the potential for national advertising in the magazine industry. He convincingly demonstrated that a magazine could be sold for less than the cost of producing it and still make a profit by using its large audience as a selling point to attract advertisers. Curtis drew well-known authors to his magazine and promoted it heavily. After 1889, the magazine became even more successful under the editorship of Edward Bok. By 1893, the *Journal* had a circulation of 700,000.

Inspired by Curtis' success, other magazine publishers hastened to try out the same techniques on a more general audience. *McClure's*, *Munsey's*, and *Cosmopolitan* were three inexpensive monthlies (*Munsey's* cost only a dime) that started in 1893. They contained articles designed for widespread popular interest, and advertisers looking for ways to reach a national audience flocked to these newcomers.

The general crusading spirit of the press spilled over onto the pages of leading magazines of the late 1890s and early 1900s. Theodore Roosevelt dubbed the magazines that embraced this reform movement **muckrakers**. Corrupt practices in big business was the first topic to activate the muckrakers' zeal. *McClure's* ran an exposé of the Standard Oil Company by Ida M. Tarbell. Although it carried the innocuous title of "History of the Standard Oil Company," the article was filled with dynamite, for it revealed bribery, fraud, unfair business practices, and violence. Shocking stories on political corruption in big cities and another series on crooked practices in the railroad industry followed Tarbell's initial effort. Other magazines joined in. *Cosmopolitan* published "The Treason of the Senate" in 1906. It followed up with attacks on the International Harvester Company. *Collier's* joined in with a report on the fraudulent patent medicine business, and published articles advocating women's suffrage, pure-food laws, direct election of senators, and an income tax. By 1912, the crusading and exposé trend had spent itself. Many of the problems it uncovered had been remedied. The major investigative writers had turned to other pursuits, but most importantly, the public had grown tired of it and magazines had to search for other ways to attract readers.

Some magazines of this period were geared for more specialized audiences. *St. Nicholas*, for example, was written for the juvenile audience. Under the editorship of Mary Mapes Dodge, the magazine was handsomely printed and lavishly illustrated. It contained articles by leading writers such as Mark Twain and Rudyard Kipling, stories, poems, and games. Some experts regard *St. Nicholas* as the best magazine ever published for youngsters.

The Paperback Boom

During the Civil War, soldiers turned to reading to fill the idle time between campaigns. This created a demand for cheap reading materials, and before long a series of paperbacks priced at ten cents apiece flooded the market. These "dime novels" included the popular Frank Merriwell stories and the Horatio Alger stories. Both series of books stressed a common theme: Virtue, hard work, and pluck were always triumphant. The Alger books were the more commercially successful, selling a total of 250 million copies. The competition between paperback publishers intensified as more companies entered the market. By 1880, about one-third of all the books published in the country were paperbacks, and fifteen different firms were selling the softbound volumes at prices ranging from five to fifteen cents. Many of the best-selling paperbacks were pirated editions of the best sellers in England and other European countries. By the late 1880s, this problem was so bad that a new copyright law was adopted. The effect of this new law combined with years of cutthroat competition and price cutting spelled the end of this era of paperback popularity.

● ● ● ●

TRENDS TOWARD CONSOLIDATION AND SPECIALIZATION

Newspapers in the Early Twentieth Century

In the first two decades of the new century, the economics of mass production would figure heavily in the evolution of the newspaper. Centralization and consolidation were already noticeable in the railroad, grocery, hotel, and department store industries, and it was only a matter of time before the factors operating in those areas would make themselves felt in the newspaper business. Statistics show that there were 2200 daily newspapers in 1910. By 1930, there were 1942. The number of cities with competing daily papers fell from 689 to 288 in the same period. All of this was happening while population showed a 30 percent increase, daily circulation nearly doubled, and newspaper advertising revenue tripled. Why this decline in competition? There were several reasons.

In the first place, innovations in printing—linotype machines, high-speed presses, engraving plants—meant that purchases of new equipment and operating expenses were making newspaper publishing a costly venture. Many marginal papers could no longer compete. Second, advertisers showed a marked preference for the paper with the largest circulation. Large-circulation papers, in turn, were able to afford the latest equipment and turned out a paper at a more efficient per unit price. In many cities, this spelled the end for smaller papers. Third, in their quest for larger readership figures, newspapers turned increasingly to standardized content. The growth of the wire services and syndication companies meant that much of the same news, cartoons, columnists, and features would appear in different papers. Newspaper personality blurred as one daily looked pretty much like another, and a person saw little need of reading more than one. Lastly, many papers went under because of planned business consolidations. Many people who had seen consolidation successfully used in other fields now tried the same tactic with newspapers. In New York, Frank Munsey (mentioned above), who had made a fortune running hotel chains, folded six of the thirteen

Innovations in the early 1900s, such as the high-speed rotary press pictured here, made newspaper publishing easier but more costly. (The Bettmann Archive)

papers he acquired in an attempt to start a profitable chain. In Philadelphia, Cyrus Curtis, the magazine publisher, reduced the number of dailies in that city by folding or merging three existing papers. In Chicago, Herman Kohlsaat, a chain bakery owner, reduced the number of dailies from eight to four. Two large newspaper chains, bearing names we have already mentioned, also led the way toward concentration. The Hearst chain folded sixteen papers between 1918 and 1928; the Scripps-Howard group closed down fifteen in about the same period. Chains grew quickly. By 1933, six chains— Hearst, Scripps-Howard, Patterson-McCormack, Block, Ridder, and Gannett—controlled eighty-one dailies with a combined circulation of 9 million, about one-fourth of all daily circulation.

Jazz Journalism

Appearing with the consolidation trend and enjoying a short but lively reign was **jazz journalism**. At the end of World War I, the United States found itself facing a decade of prosperity: the "Roaring Twenties." The radio, Hollywood, the airplane, Prohibition, and Al Capone were all topics that captured national attention. It was perhaps inevitable that newspapers would reflect the times. The papers that best exemplify jazz journalism all sprang up in New York between 1919 and 1924; all were characterized by two features that were common in jazz journalism: (1) they were **tabloids**, printed on a page that was about one-half the size of a normal newspaper page; and (2) they were all richly illustrated with photographs.

The *New York Daily News* debuted first. After a slow start, by 1924 the *News* had caught on. Its tabloid size was easier for people to handle while reading on buses and subways; it abounded with photos and cartoons; writing style was simple and short. The *News* also blended in large portions of entertainment with its news. Comic strips, gossip columns, advice to the lovelorn, horoscopes, and sports were given large chunks

The New York Tabloids in the Roaring Twenties

In 1927, Judd Gray, a corset salesman, teamed up with his girlfriend, Mrs. Ruth Snyder, and murdered poor, unfortunate Mr. Snyder. After a sensational trial, which was played up by the New York tabloid papers, the duo was sentenced to death. The coverage of their execution was to represent the extreme of this era of jazz journalism. As their January death date neared, one of the tabloids published a full-page drawing of an artist's conception of what the pair would look like as they were strapped into the electric chair. The New York *Graphic*, not surprisingly, was anything but restrained in its coverage. The *Graphic* got an exclusive interview with the condemned Ruth Snyder. It promoted the piece with the following blurb:

> Don't fail to read tomorrow's *Graphic*. An installment that thrills and stuns. A story that fairly pierces the heart and reveals Ruth Snyder's

last thoughts on earth; that pulses the blood as it discloses her final letters. Think of it! A woman's final thoughts just before she is clutched in the deadly snare that sears and burns and FRIES and KILLS! Her very last words! Exclusively in tomorrow's *Graphic!*

The *Daily News*, however, scored a somewhat questionable scoop on this story when one of its reporters smuggled a small camera into the death chamber by strapping it to his ankle and snapped a picture an instant after the current was turned on. The *News* enlarged the picture, and it filled the entire front page of its January 14, 1928, edition. It was captioned, "When Ruth Paid her Debt to the State!" (Exclamation points were used a lot in jazz journalism.) The picture was such a hit that the *News* had to run off an additional 750,000 copies.

of space. And, in a throwback to the 1880s, it emphasized the sensational: crime, sex, gangsters, murder trials, and Hollywood stars. The biggest content innovation of the *News* and the most noticeable was the lavish use of pictures. The entire front page was frequently given over to one or two pictures, and a two-page photo spread was included on the inside. Sports coverage, including detailed racing news, sometimes accounted for 20 percent of the paper's content, but murder trials and love affairs were the areas in which tabloids pulled out all their stops. In 1926, the tabloids discovered the marriage of a wealthy real-estate tycoon to a 15-year-old clerk. The tabloids nicknamed them "Daddy" and "Peaches," and news of their torrid romance filled their pages. In the same year, the *Mirror* unearthed a 4-year-old murder in New Jersey and through its coverage succeeded in having the victim's widow indicted for the crime. The high point (if it can be called that) in the battle of the tabloids occurred during the coverage of the Gray-Snyder murder trial (see the box on page 103).

Success bred imitation; in 1924 Hearst started the tabloid *Daily Mirror*, and Bernarr MacFadden, publisher of *True Story* magazine, started the *Daily Graphic* (called by many the porno-*Graphic*). Hearst's paper tried to copy the *News*, and there were days when it was hard to tell the two apart. The *Graphic*, which did not even bother to subscribe to a wire service, was easy to spot—it was the most sensationalized of the three. News of murder, rape, divorce, scandal, bootlegging, and sex virtually jumped off the pages of this paper. Rather than running photographs, the *Graphic* ran what it called cosmographs, faked composite photos of events that might have happened. After Rudolph Valentino's funeral, one cosmograph showed the actor, dressed in flowing white robes, entering heaven. Neither the *Mirror* nor the *Graphic*, however, was able to match the success of the *News*. Hearst sold his paper in 1928, and the *Graphic* expired in 1932. The Depression effectively marked the end of the jazz journalism era, but before moving on we should note that not all tabloids were like the *Graphic*. Many conventional-appeal papers appeared in this format. Moreover, sensationalism did not end with the passing of the tabloid era. It would crop up again from time to time in the years to come.

The Impact of the Depression

The Depression had great social and economic impact on newspapers and magazines. During the 1930s, total daily newspaper circulation increased by about 2 million; the total population increased by 9 million. The total income of the newspaper industry, however, dropped about 20 percent in this decade. This shortage of revenue meant that marginally profitable papers were unable to stay in business, and approximately sixty-six dailies went under.

Although worsening economic conditions were one cause of the newspaper's decline, more important was the emergence of radio as a competitor for national advertising dollars. In the period from 1935 to 1940, newspapers' share of national advertising revenues dropped from 45 to 39 percent, while radio's share jumped from 6 percent to more than 10 percent. These cuts hurt the print media and, not surprisingly, newspapers saw radio as the villain. Hostility between the two industries grew, ultimately leading to the short but nasty Press–Radio War (see Chapter 8). By 1940, however, thanks to increased revenue from local advertisers, newspaper revenues were back up and hostilities had lessened. Nevertheless, the economic picture was still not rosy, and the number of daily papers declined to 1744 in 1945, an all-time low.

The other significant media trend during the Depression was the press' negative reaction to the excesses of tabloid journalism, a reaction that was transformed into an attempt to respond to the increasingly complex nature of modern life. The 1930s and 1940s were notable for the growth of interpretive reporting. Reporters took on the task of explaining the complicated economic programs of the New Deal in simple terms that the average reader could understand. Foreign correspondents covering international problems and the tense situation in Europe hastened to include the "why" perspective, along with information regarding who, what, and where. Two papers that specialized in interpretive and financial reporting, the *Christian Science Monitor* and the *Wall Street Journal*, gained in popularity during these years, as did magazines such as *Harper's*, *Atlantic*, and *The New Republic*.

Magazine Development

The most striking characteristic of magazine development during the twentieth century was a trend toward specialization. This movement was given impetus by the increasing importance of national advertising to economic success within the industry (magazines received forty-two cents out of every dollar spent on national advertising in the major media in 1929). A magazine not only had to please its readers, but also had to attract an audience that would be valuable to advertisers. And so magazine publishers had to become experts in marketing procedures. Sometimes their audiences were large; other times the audience might consist of a highly specialized group.

Shifting economic conditions and changing lifestyles in the decades following World War I also influenced magazine development. As some of the prewar circulation leaders went into a decline, new publications—many similar to the shorter format, richly illustrated tabloids of the jazz-journalism era—sprang up to take their place. Three distinct types evolved in the years between World War I and World War II: (1) the digest, (2) the news magazine, and (3) the pictorial magazine.

The pioneer digest was the *Literary Digest*, which, although started in the 1880s, became popular after the war, reaching a circulation of 2 million. Hardly literary and seldom a digest, this magazine was one of the few ever written with scissors. Editors clipped stories from the nation's newspapers on current issues and pasted them up side by side. The finest example of this genre, the *Reader's Digest*, appeared in 1922. Although this magazine also reprinted articles that had appeared elsewhere, it first condensed and edited the material so that it would be read by people in a hurry. The busy and booming twenties were very conducive to the success of such a venture, and the *Digest* watched its circulation grow, passing the million mark by 1935.

The idea of a news magazine was not new—examples could be found in the nineteenth century. *Time*, however, borrowed little from its predecessors. From its beginning in 1923, *Time* based its format on an original concept: the distillation and compartmentalization of news under various departments. Other innovations included the use of the narrative style to report news stories; group journalism produced by the pooling of the efforts of reporters, writers, and editors into anonymous articles; the institution of a large research department; and a brash, punchy, jargonish writing style. The magazine prospered slowly, but by 1930 it was turning a substantial profit. Two imitators, *Newsweek* and *U.S. News*, appeared in 1933. These magazines served somewhat as national newspapers, providing information and interpretation to the entire country.

In the mid-thirties, two magazines, *Life* and *Look*, revived the tradition of the pictorial weekly originated by *Harper's* and *Leslie's*. Capitalizing on an increased interest in photography, *Life* was launched in 1936 and had almost a quarter of a million subscribers before the magazine even had a name. The tabloids had shown that people liked to look at pictures; the news magazines had shown that people wanted to learn about current events; the movies had made people "picture conscious." *Life* brought all of these elements together. Photojournalism was given wide coverage, and many of *Life*'s photos of World War II were hung in the Museum of Modern Art in New York. Public figures caught in unguarded moments, photo essays, occasional glamour shots, and articles on the arts all went into the early issues. *Life* itself would live for thirty-six years (it would reappear in the late 1970s in a totally different format). *Look* hit the newsstands in 1937, just two months behind *Life*. *Look* lacked the current-

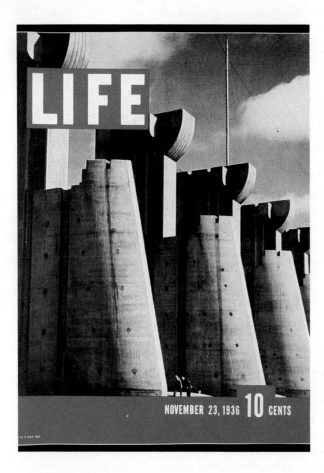

The beginning of life for Life. *The magazine's first cover was shot by famous photographer Margaret Bourke White. (Margaret Bourke White/Time, Inc., 1936)*

affairs emphasis of its forerunner and concentrated more on personalities and features. Over the years, it evolved into a family-oriented magazine. *Look* expired in 1972. The success of these two publications, as you might imagine, inspired copies. *Focus, Peek, Foto, Picture, Click, Pic,* and *See* appeared and disappeared in the years surrounding World War II.

Books in the Early Twentieth Century

The period from 1900 to 1945 saw the commercialization of publishing. Prior to this time, many of the publishing companies were family owned and specialized in publishing one particular kind of book. Publishers were a closely knit group, and their dealings with one another resembled what might take place in a genteel private club. Several events altered this situation. First, a new breed of literary agents, concerned with negotiating the best "bottom line" for their authors, entered the scene. Forced to pay top dollar for their rights to books, the publishing business lost its former "clubby" atmosphere and turned into a business. Second, many publishing houses expanded their publishing efforts into the mass market, publishing popular works of fiction. To compete effectively in the mass marketplace, modern promotion and distribution techniques were introduced to the book industry. Third, a depression in the 1890s and a subsequent sluggish economy meant that the book industry was forced to depend more on banks for finance capital. The banks, of course, insisted that the book companies be run with the utmost efficiency with an eye toward increasing profits. By World War II, all of these factors combined to make the book industry more commercially oriented.

The content of popular books was highly variable during this time period. Outdoor adventures written by such authors as Jack London and Zane Grey were popular at the turn of the century. *Tarzan of the Apes* sold nearly a million copies on the eve of World War I. During the Roaring Twenties, light fiction, such as *The Sheik* and P. G. Wodehouse's *Jeeves* were best sellers, but serious works sold equally well. H. G. Wells' *Outline of History* and Will Durant's *Story of Philosophy* reached the million mark in sales during this period. Detective fiction by Erle Stanley Gardner (Perry Mason was his hero) and Ellery Queen sold well during the Depression. In 1936, two books broke the two million mark in sales, Dale Carnegie's *How to Win Friends and Influence People* and Margaret Mitchell's *Gone With the Wind*.

●●●●
ECONOMIC INFLUENCES: 1945–1969

Postwar Newspapers

After World War II, economic forces continued to shape the American newspaper, magazine, and book industries. Some trends of the postwar period were created by advances in print and electronic technology, but others had begun even before the war. For example, the postwar economy forced the newspaper industry to move even further in the direction of contraction and consolidation. Although newspaper circulation rose from approximately 48 million in 1945 to about 62 million in 1970, the number of dailies stayed about the same. There was actually a circulation loss in cities with populations of more than a million, and several big-city papers went out of business. Moreover, the number of cities with competing dailies dropped from 117 to 37 between 1945 and 1970. This meant that about 98 percent of American cities had no competing papers.

In 1945, sixty newspaper group owners ran sixty chains that controlled about 42 percent of the total daily newspaper circulation. By 1970, there were approximately 157 chains that accounted for 60 percent of total circulation. Why had the number of chains continued to grow? One factor was the sharp rise in costs of paper and labor during the postwar years. Newspapers were becoming more expensive to print. The large chains were in a position to share expenses and to use their presses and labor more efficiently. Under a single owner, several papers could "share" the services of feature writers, columnists, photographers, and compositors, thus holding down costs. This movement toward consolidation resulted in a large number of multiple owners controlling the market, with no single chain dominating circulation. The largest group owner in 1970, for example, accounted for only 6 percent of total circulation. The consolidation trend was also present across media, as several media conglomerates controlled newspapers, magazines, radio, and television stations. Black newspapers were also caught up in the trend toward concentration. In 1956, the Chicago *Defender* changed from a weekly to a daily and its owner, John Sengstacke, started a group of nine black papers, including the Pittsburgh *Courier* and the Michigan *Chronicle*.

Another continuing trend was the competition among media for advertising dollars. Even after inflation had abated, the total amount of advertising revenue spent on all media nearly tripled between 1945 and 1970. Although the total spent on newspapers did not increase at quite this pace, the amount spent on television increased by more than a threefold factor. The rising television industry cut significantly into the print media's national advertising revenue. Although newspapers could take up the slack by increasing local ads, general circulation magazines were not so lucky.

Postwar Magazines

Magazines of the postwar era reflected publishers' firm belief that the one way to become profitable was to specialize. Increased leisure time, made possible by technological advances, created a market for sports magazines such as *Field and Stream*, *Sports Afield*, *Golf Digest*, *Popular Boating*, and *Sports Illustrated*. Scientific advances also generated a resurgence of a popularized version of *Scientific American* and a publication called *Science Illustrated*.

The rapid expansion of urban communities and urban lifestyles gave rise to many specialized publications. Liberalized attitudes toward sex prompted such ventures as *Confidential* (1952) and the trendsetting *Playboy* (1953). During the 1960s, the rebirth of an interest in urban culture encouraged the rise of "city" magazines, of which *New York* is probably the best example. For the black press, the most significant development in the 1950s was the expansion of black magazines. John Johnston had started *Negro Digest* back in 1942 and used his profits to publish *Ebony*, an imitation of the *Life* format in 1945. In the early years of the 1950s he added *Tan*, and *Jet*, a weekly news magazine. These were followed later by *Black World* and *Essence*.

Postwar Books: Paperbacks and Consolidation

Shortly after the end of World War II, new paperbacks published by Bantam, Pocket Books, and New American Library appeared. These books were popular because of their twenty-five-cent price and because new channels of distribution were used to market them. Wire racks filled with paperbacks appeared in train stations, newsstands, drugstores, and tobacco shops. A whole new audience was thus exposed to paperbacks. In 1950, the "quality" paperback appeared. These were serious nonfiction or literary classics that found their prime markets in education.

Speaking of education, the United States received a shock in 1957 when the Soviet Union launched an Earth satellite. In response, the U.S. educational system received a general upgrading and more and more emphasis was placed on schooling. Libraries and classrooms increased their holdings of books. The textbook and educational publishers found themselves in a period of prosperity.

Moreover, expanded leisure time and more disposable income made book reading a popular means of recreation. All in all, the book publishing business looked like a good investment for the future. Consequently, large corporations began acquiring book companies. To name just a few: CBS, Inc., acquired Holt, Rinehart and Winston; Litton Industries acquired Van Nostrand; and ITT purchased Bobbs-Merrill. Between 1958 and 1970, there were 307 mergers or acquisitions of publishing companies. These mergers brought new financial and management resources to the book industry, which helped it stay profitable during the 1970s.

● ● ● ●

MODERN PRINT MEDIA

The Impact of *USA Today*

On September 15, 1982, the nation got a look at a colorful new entrant on the newspaper scene. Delivered by satellite to printing plants across the country, *USA Today* was designed to be a national newspaper. Although the paper lost $233 million in its first five years, it emerged into the black in 1987 but lost money again in each of the next three years. The brainchild of Gannett chairman Allen Neuharth, the paper has had significant impact on the newspaper industry. Some of the innovations introduced by *USA Today* include:

- Splashy graphics and liberal use of color.

- Short, easily digested stories—the longest average about 1000 words.

- Extensive use of graphs, charts, and tables. The sports section in particular is crammed with statistics.

- A full page devoted to weather.

- The use of factoids. (A factoid is a list of boiled-down facts with a little dot in front of them—much like this list.)

Several press observers criticized *USA Today* for superficial coverage and for putting a happy gloss on most of its stories. Nonetheless, the paper was quite popular with its readers.

USA Today has a problem attracting advertisers primarily because many of its sales are from vending machines. Purchasers are anonymous, which doesn't make them appealing to advertisers. In addition, *USA Today* is competing with news magazines (it attracts a similar audience), and news magazines get passed from person to person, giving them more readers per copy. *USA Today* tends to be thrown away more quickly and has only about three readers per copy, whereas news magazines have four or five.

Other areas in the print media in which notable developments have taken place in the last decade are (1) reporting, (2) ownership, and (3) economics.

Reporting

During the mid- to late 1960s, a specialized reporting for a specialized audience developed in the United States—the underground or alternative press. Growing out of the antiestablishment feelings of the time, the **underground press** concentrated on politically liberal news and opinion or on cultural topics such as music, art, and film. Perhaps the most influential papers were the *Village Voice*, the *Los Angeles Free Press*, and *Rolling Stone*. Many alternative papers ran out of steam in the 1970s, and others lost their original flavor. The *Village Voice* and *Rolling Stone*, for example, are now more in line with the mainstream establishment press.

Investigative reporting had roots that could be traced back to the muckrakers, but it enjoyed a rebirth in the 1970s. Best known were the efforts of *Washington Post* reporters Bob Woodward and Carl Bernstein in untangling the Watergate story, which eventually led to the resignation of President Nixon. Their efforts spanned a two-year period from 1972 to 1974 and thoroughly infuriated the White House. At one point, President Nixon, commenting on their coverage of this story, said he had never seen such "outrageous, vicious, distorted . . . frantic, hysterical reporting" (an example from the 1970s of negative feedback).

Ownership

During the mid- to late 1980s, the declining value of the dollar, the lack of rules concerning foreign ownership of American publishing firms, and the general attractiveness of books, magazines, and newspapers lured foreign investors as never before. The Australian-based News Corporation, headed by Rupert Murdoch, led the way when it acquired papers in Chicago and New York, a book publishing company, and several magazines, including *TV Guide*. In 1990, the Tribune Company sold the *New York Daily News*, a paper that was losing money and had been disrupted by a long and sometimes violent strike, to the late British press magnate Robert Maxwell. After Maxwell's death, the *News* was sold to Mortimer Zuckerman, publisher of *U.S. News and World Report*.

In the magazine industry, Hachette, a French company, bought most of the magazines that were formerly published by CBS. The News Corporation of Australia acquired a large number of magazines in the 1980s but sold off several of them in the early 1990s in an effort to reduce its debt. Reed International of Great Britain also acquired several consumer and about fifty trade magazines.

Rupert Murdoch, head of the Australian-based News Corporation. Murdoch's firm owns newspapers, magazines, a book publishing company, a TV network, TV stations, and a movie studio. (Courtesy News Corporation Limited)

In book publishing, Bertelsmann, a German firm, acquired Doubleday, Dell, and Bantam to make it the second largest book publisher in the country. Rupert Murdoch's News Corporation bought Harper & Row and the late Robert Maxwell's British company acquired Macmillan.

All in all, a significant number of companies that produce American literary, cultural, and informational products are now owned by foreign firms. The impact of this arrangement on the content of U.S. publishing has yet to be determined.

Additionally, the ownership pattern of American publishing companies has become more concentrated. In the newspaper area, the independent, family-owned paper is rapidly becoming extinct. More than four out of five Americans read a paper published by a group owner. Magazines are less concentrated than newspapers, but the trend toward centralization is apparent as large companies acquire more publications. The book publishing arena also saw the number of independent companies decline as many were absorbed by large conglomerates. For example, the 1989 merger of Warner Communications and Time, Inc., created Time Warner, a megacompany with annual revenue from book and magazine publishing that topped $2.5 billion in 1990.

Economics

As the 1990s began, all too often newspapers found themselves covering the story of their own hard times. A weakening economy, increasing competition, a poor advertising market, additional expenses incurred during coverage of the Persian Gulf War, and little growth in readership all combined to create one of the worst economic climates for newspapers in recent memory. Several established big-city papers ceased publication; others were kept alive only under joint operating agreements that allowed competing papers to save money by merging their business operations. Those publishers who were bold enough to launch new papers soon found the going too tough. *The National*, a slick sports paper edited by award-winning sports writer Frank Deford, lasted about 15 months. The St. Louis *Sun* lost $30 million in less than a year. The Kansas City *Evening News* lasted only six weeks. Other papers tightened budgets and many laid off personnel in an effort to maintain solvency.

Magazines also faced problems. Increased competition saturated the market, advertising revenues were soft, and single-copy sales continued to decline. Publications were folding at a record rate during the early years of the decade. The book industry, not dependent on advertising, was not hit as hard but it, too, faced competition for the leisure time of readers.

• • • •

RECENT CONTENT TRENDS

Newspapers Standardize; Magazines and Books Diversify: Present Trends

As newspapers moved into the last half of the twentieth century, several trends in their content were apparent. Most obvious was a change in newspaper typography and layout, all with the ultimate goal of making the modern newspaper easier to read. Photography and color were being used more liberally, and many papers showed a willingness to depart from the typical eight-column format that has been traditional. Second, many papers were carrying more of what might be called "feature" stories. Sections entitled "Life," "Lifestyle," "Living," and "Leisure" were becoming more common as papers blended more of this material with their traditional "hard" news. Many big-city papers were attempting to compete with the more localized weeklies by including surburban editions that concentrated on news outside of the core city. The trend toward consolidation also had an impact on newspaper content. The standardization of content and makeup that generally goes along with group ownership prompted critics of this trend to charge that newspaper content had become as uniform as a Big Mac. (*USA Today*, from the Gannett organization, was commonly called McPaper by its critics.)

Trying to describe the content of modern magazines would take far more space than we have available since magazine content is as diversified as magazines themselves. Probably the best way to find out about the content of modern magazines would be to scan a local newsstand and note how many different topics are covered by the publications on sale.

Turning to books, the first big paperback best seller following World War II was Dr. Benjamin Spock's *Baby and Child Care*. Other notable paperbacks followed. Mickey Spillane's Mike Hammer was a hard-boiled private eye who appeared in six novels during the 1950s that sold 17 million copies. *Peyton Place*, a novel famous for its racy parts, sold 10 million in paperback. All in all, from 1940 to 1965, paperback sales were dominated by light fiction and an occasional how-to book.

Hard-cover content during this period is hard to categorize. In nonfiction, cookbooks have enjoyed steady popularity, as have diet books. The late 1960s and early 1970s saw a trend toward self-help and inspirational books such as *I'm OK–You're OK* and *Your Erroneous Zones*. Subsequent years saw physical fitness books become popular, as exemplified by *The Complete Book of Running* and *Jane Fonda's Workout Book*. The early 1980s saw business-oriented books capture surprising sales. *In Search of Excellence* and *The One Minute Manager* both topped best-seller lists. The late 1980s saw a rash of psychological self-help books aimed at women: *Women Who Love Too Much*, *Men Who Hate Women and the Women Who Love Them*, *Women Men Love*, *Women Men Leave*, etc. In the early 1990s, the content of best-selling books showed great diversity.

In nonfiction, exposé biography, such as Kitty Kelley's book on Nancy Reagan, and behind-the-scenes books, such as Bob Woodward's *The Commanders*, topped best-seller lists. Along with these came some surprise hits, such as physicist Stephen Hawking's *A Brief History of Time* and Rush Limbaugh's *The Way Things Ought to Be*.

On the fiction side, books by Danielle Steel, Judith Krantz, and Jackie Collins remained popular, as did techno-thrillers, a genre of books started in the 1980s by Tom Clancy and Larry Bond. Also selling well were books designed to spook and scare by writers such as Stephen King and Dean Koontz. All in all, the varied content of popular books reflected the eclectic tastes of the modern reading audience.

● ● ● ●

SUGGESTIONS FOR FURTHER READING

The books listed below are good sources for additional information about the history of newspapers and magazines.

DAVIS, KENNETH, *Two-Bit Culture: The Paperbacking of America*, Boston: Houghton Mifflin, 1984.

EMERY, EDWIN, AND MICHAEL EMERY, *The Press in America*, 6th ed., Englewood Cliffs, N.J.: Prentice-Hall, 1992.

FOLKERTS, JEAN, AND DWIGHT TEETER, *Voices of a Nation*, New York: Macmillan, 1989.

HYNDS, ERNEST C., *American Newspapers in the 1980s*, New York: Hastings House, 1980.

JONES, ROBERT W., *Journalism in the United States*, New York: E. P. Dutton, 1947.

MOTT, FRANK LUTHER, *American Journalism*, New York: Macmillan, 1962.

PETERSON, THEODORE, *Magazines in the Twentieth Century*, Urbana: University of Illinois Press, 1964.

STEPHENS, MITCHELL, *A History of News*, New York: Penguin, 1989.

TEBBEL, JOHN, *The Compact History of the American Newspaper*, New York: Hawthorn Books, 1969.

———, *The American Magazine: A Compact History*, New York: Hawthorn Books, 1969.

———, *A History of Book Publishing in the United States* (4 vols.), New York: R. R. Bowker, 1981.

WOOD, JAMES PLAYSTED, *Magazines in the United States*, New York: Ronald Press, 1971.

Also, the scholarly publications *Journalism History* and *Journalism Quarterly* frequently carry articles dealing with newspaper and magazine history.

STRUCTURE OF THE NEWSPAPER INDUSTRY

n 1989, an earthquake hit the San Francisco area just before the third game of the World Series was about to be played. Local newspapers used flashlights and emergency power, composed their papers on computers, and dodged piles of rubble to get them on the street.

After the initial shock and trauma wore off, newspapers realized that they would experience some economic aftershocks in the wake of the tremor. The local papers were expecting a bonanza in advertising associated with the Series coming to town. Instead, the Series was postponed and the ads canceled. The papers expected the worst. Then, to almost everybody's surprise, advertising demand increased. Insurance companies took ads detailing their progress; local companies, having survived the quake, ran ads congratulating themselves and praising the mettle of people who lived in the area. Department stores, with bloated inventories caused by people staying home in the weeks after the quake, followed with ads for big sales. When it was all totaled up, advertising had increased by 7 percent over the previous nonquake year.

The 1989 earthquake seems a suitable metaphor for today's newspaper industry. It's been rocked by an economic quake that's left it reeling. Many big-city papers have not survived the shake-up and have folded; papers of all sizes are cutting back and many are laying off workers. Profits are down all over. What caused the upheaval? First, newspapers were victims of the recession and weak economy. Advertising revenue was not as plentiful as it once was. Second, newspapers were faced with increased competition. They competed for readers' time with TV news, video games, fifty-plus channels on cable TV systems, magazines, and rented movies. They competed for advertising dollars with direct mail, TV, magazines, radio, the Yellow Pages, billboards, and even the backs of grocery carts. Finally, newspapers continue to have trouble attracting and holding younger readers, the ones most coveted by advertisers. Despite their best efforts, newspapers continue to lose readers in the under-30 age category.

Nonetheless, as was the case with the local San Francisco papers after the tremor, once the dust settles, things may not be quite as bad as they first looked. The economic downturn is probably cyclical and a stronger economy will doubtlessly improve the newspapers' financial health. Most communities have only one newspaper, and even though that paper must compete with other media, it usually has a solid advertising base and is still the preferred advertising vehicle for many local businesses. Cost-cutting and budget tightening will improve newspapers' efficiency. All in all, they will probably survive the economic tremors but they will emerge as a changed industry, with the most striking changes coming in content, marketing, and distribution. At the center of all this remodeling will be an attempt to make the paper more user-friendly, to give readers more of what they want, and to blend in more harmoniously with the lifestyles of the 1990s.

This chapter will examine the changing philosophy and structure of the newspaper industry and detail how newspapers are endeavoring to meet the challenge of delivering what their readers want and need.

••••

TYPES OF NEWSPAPERS

Ralph Waldo Emerson, who had something to say about virtually everything, once said "the newspaper . . . does its best to make every square acre of land and sea give an account of itself at your breakfast table." If Emerson could see the 1990s version of the newspaper, he might also add that the newspaper does its best to get to your breakfast table before you turn on the *Today* show or *Good Morning America* or leave to drive to work. The newspaper industry is currently examining how well it fits with modern lifestyles and what it must do to keep and attract readers in an age in which competition for their time has become intense.

The newspapers that are published in this country are many and varied. They range from the *Wall Street Journal*, a nationally oriented financial daily, to the *Journal of Commerce*, a small financial paper published in Portland, Oregon; from the *National Enquirer* to the *Daily Lobo*, the college newspaper of the University of New Mexico; from the million-plus-circulation *New York Daily News* to the 6,000 circulation Gallipolis *Daily Tribune* in Gallipolis, Ohio. Obviously, there are many ways to categorize an industry as diverse as this one. For our purposes, we will group papers by frequency of publication (dailies and weeklies), by market size (national, large, medium, small), and, finally, by their appeal to specialized interest groups.

Dailies

To be considered a daily, a newspaper has to appear at least five times a week. In 1992, there were about 1570 dailies, down 3 percent from 1988, and about 7400 weeklies. Whether a daily or a weekly, the chief concern of a newspaper is its **circulation**, the number of copies delivered to newsstands or vending machines and the number delivered to subscribers. Daily newspaper circulation has leveled off at approximately 62.3 million, a figure that has shown little change from 1970 to 1991 (see Figure 5-1). At the same time, the population of the United States has been growing. Consequently, the ratio of newspapers per household has declined. To illustrate, in 1960, 111 newspapers were sold per 100 households; in 1991, about 67 newspapers were sold per 100 households. This circulation crunch has not hit all papers with equal force, and this becomes evident when we divide daily newspapers into market groups.

National Newspapers. Only a handful of papers fall into this category. These are publications whose content is geared not for one particular city or region but for the entire country. These papers typically use satellites to transmit images and information to regional printing plants where the papers are assembled and distributed. The newest addition to this category is the Gannett publication *USA Today*, started in 1982. With a circulation of about 1.5 million, the paper's use of color and graphics and focus on such topics as sports and weather made a significant impact on other newspapers. The *New York Times* started a national edition in 1980. Also printed via satellite, it had a circulation of about 120,000 in 1992. Two other, more specialized papers are also in this category. The *Wall Street Journal*, concentrating mainly on financial news, was published in seventeen printing plants across the country. By 1991, its circulation had topped the 1.8 million mark. The *Christian Science Monitor* concentrates on interpretation of news events and features dealing with literature, music, and art. As of 1991, the *Monitor* had a circulation of about 105,000.

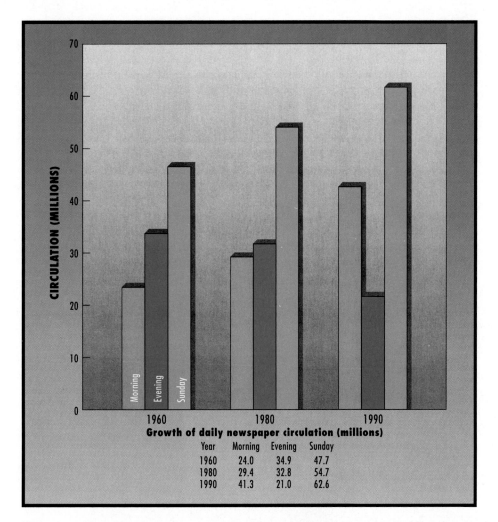

Year	Morning	Evening	Sunday
1960	24.0	34.9	47.7
1980	29.4	32.8	54.7
1990	41.3	21.0	62.6

FIGURE 5-1 *Growth of daily newspaper circulation (1960–1990). (Reprinted by permission from the 1991* Editor & Publisher International Yearbook.)

Large Metropolitan Dailies. The decline in circulation has hit these papers the hardest. Although the total population of the top fifty metropolitan areas increased more than 30 percent from 1960 to 1990, the circulation of newspapers published in these areas dropped about 45 percent. In addition, the last few years have seen the demise of several well-known big-city papers: the Tulsa *Tribune,* the St. Louis *Globe-Democrat,* the Baltimore *News-American,* the Spokane *Chronicle,* the Memphis *Press-Scimitar,* and the Dallas *Times-Herald,* to name just a few. Moreover, both the *New York Post* and the *New York Daily News* were in financial difficulty in 1993. Why the drop in big-city circulation? There are several reasons, including migration from the central city to the suburbs, transient populations, rising costs of distribution, and increased competition from other media, most notably television.

Suburban Dailies. Although suburban communities of between 100,000 and 500,000 residents are home to only 12 percent of total newspapers, they account for about 40 percent of all circulation. Suburban dailies, located in these areas, surrounding the larger cities, are experiencing a period of growth. Circulation of these papers grew by about one-third from 1987 to 1990. One reason for this increase is the growth of suburban shopping centers, which have attracted many merchants formerly located in the central cities. To these merchants, suburban papers represent an efficient way of reaching potential customers. In addition, suburban residents are apparently less inclined to go to the city at night for dinner and entertainment, a factor that has cut down newsstand sales of city papers. Perhaps the best known suburban paper is *Newsday*, aimed at the residents of Long Island. In 1991, *Newsday* had a circulation of about 700,000, thereby making it the eighth largest daily paper in the country.

In a quest to regain readers, large metro dailies have taken on the suburban press on the smaller papers' own turf. Big-city newspapers are putting out more **zoned editions**, sections geared to a particular suburban area. The *Philadelphia Inquirer*, for example, has eight "Neighbors" sections designed to compete with the twenty or so suburban papers that surround metro Philadelphia. The *Los Angeles Times* now runs

Front page from Newsday, *the most successful suburban daily in the United States. This particular page is from the paper's Manhattan edition, an attempt by* Newsday *to compete with the established New York City metro papers. (© 1991, Newsday Inc., New York, Vol. 52, No. 115)*

three daily regional editions and six twice-weekly suburban sections. The metro dailies are also building more suburban printing plants to make delivery easier and cheaper.

This competition has become even more intense because more than 40 percent of suburban papers are owned by large chains and are able to fight back with the financial resources of the parent company. Some successful suburban papers are taking the offensive. *Newsday*, the successful Long Island paper, started an edition aimed at the New York City market. Not all efforts pay off, however. The Gwinnett *Daily News*, in suburban Atlanta, folded in 1992 after a long circulation war with the metro Atlanta papers.

Small-Town Dailies. This category of newspapers has also made circulation gains. From 1979 to 1990, newspaper circulation in towns with 100,000 or fewer inhabitants grew by 19 percent. Recently, circulation among papers in this category has leveled off, although dailies in towns with populations of less than 25,000 have shown modest circulation gains. Surveys have shown that readers of these papers perceive the papers to be sources of local information, for both neighborhood news and advertising.

Weeklies

The number of weekly newspapers in the United States has remained fairly stable at about 7500 over the last 20 years. The circulation of weeklies, however, has nearly doubled for this same period, from 29 million in 1970 to more than 56 million in 1990. Despite this increase in circulation, the rising costs of printing and distribution have made weekly publishers more cost conscious. Most have adopted offset printing while others have sold their presses altogether and made use of central printing plants. Such plants handle the needs of several weeklies located in the same area.

The first weekly papers were published in small towns and in rural areas that did not have a large enough population to support a daily. Although many weeklies are still located in these communities, the last few decades have seen the emergence of weekly papers in local suburban neighborhoods. In the early 1990s, it was estimated that more than one in three weekly papers was published in suburbia. Most weeklies

Newsroom at a medium-sized paper. A substantial part of each reporter's and editor's day is spent at the computer. (Paul Conklin/Monkmeyer)

are purchased by readers who also read a metropolitan or suburban daily. As a result, the weekly is usually in competition with a much larger paper for circulation and advertising. In fact, some weeklies are sandwiched in between substantial neighbors. The Ocean Springs, Mississippi, *Record* (circulation 3700) operates in the backyards of the Biloxi *Sun-Herald* (circulation 50,000) and the Pascagoula *Press* (circulation 30,000). Being a smaller weekly does have its advantages. It can provide readers with a more intimate view of the community in which they live. One 16-page issue of the *Record*, for instance, mentioned the names of 532 local residents. No daily can match that kind of close-up and personal coverage. Weeklies can also offer advertisers more precise local exposure at prices that are more affordable. Daily papers are competing with the weeklies by introducing more zoned editions and special deals for local merchants. It's apparent that the future may bring even more competition.

Recapturing Readers

No matter what their size or frequency of publication, all newspapers are faced with the task of maintaining their local readers while attracting new ones. Newspaper executives are aware that lifestyles have changed and that spending time with the daily paper is no longer the habit it once was. Consequently, in this era of declining advertising revenues and increased competition, newspapers are courting readers and potential readers as never before. A recent trade publication went so far as to say that the 1990s will be the decade of the "reader-driven" newspaper. What are some of the things that newspapers are doing to put readers in the driver's seat?

- They are using more color. Readers generally like color and papers are using it liberally throughout the newspaper. Even the gray and proper *New York Times* introduced color to its pages in 1991.

Top Ten Newspapers by Circulation

Although total newspaper circulation tends to be steady, there are some pronounced variations, as illustrated in the rankings below. Note particularly the changes in the volatile New York metro area (*New York Times*, *New York Daily News*, and *Newsday*).

Paper	1987 Circulation (Millions)	1992 Circulation (Millions)	Percent Change
1. *Wall Street Journal*	1.961	1.795	−8
2. *USA Today*	1.324	1.506	+1
3. *Los Angeles Times*	1.113	1.146	+3
4. *New York Times*	1.022	1.145	+12
5. *Washington Post*	0.761	0.802	+4
6. *New York Daily News*	1.285	0.777	−39
7. *Long Island Newsday*	0.641	0.758	+12
8. *Chicago Tribune*	0.765	0.724	−5
9. *Detroit Free Press*	0.649	0.580	−11
10. *San Francisco Chronicle*	0.568	0.556	−2

- They are changing their makeup. Lots of photos and graphics now show up throughout the paper. Stories no longer "jump" (are continued on another page) as often as before.

- They are changing their writing and editing style. Stories are shorter and written with more punch. Stories are accompanied by summary decks under the headline or have quick story-related information in "channels" on either side of the story. Some papers run highlighted synopses within long stories.

- They are changing the content of the paper. Many papers have become less dependent on lengthy stories dealing with local government. The 20 column-inch story on the city council meeting may be broken up into two or three shorter items. Appearing with more frequency are features dealing with life-styles, fashions, and entertainment, and articles usually described as "news that you can use," e.g., "How to Find the Perfect Babysitter," "Best Open-Late Restaurants," and "Managing Your Money."

- They are closely monitoring audience reaction to their papers. Specially de-signed focus group research sessions and readership surveys are important contributions to editorial and marketing strategy.

Many of the above efforts are specifically intended to attract the audience segment that has been the hardest to recapture: teens and young adults. The difficulty newspapers face in this task is best illustrated by a California paper that put together a special entertainment tabloid directed at teens, covering music, TV, and movies and places to go on dates. A market research study disclosed that almost all teens would gladly pay 50 cents for such a publication. When teens were told that the publication was going to appear inside the regular Friday edition of the local paper and that they could purchase it and the rest of the paper for only 35 cents, only a few said they would buy it. Overcoming this aversion to the newspaper by young adults is a major problem. A 1990 study by the Times Mirror Center found that the current generation of people

Newspapers are trying to recapture readers by looking more "user-friendly." The streamlined makeup and extensive use of color pioneered by USA Today *have been imitated by many dailies. (The Photo Works)*

under 30 knows less, cares less, and reads the newspaper less than any generation in the past 50 years.

Newspapers are trying some novel ideas, however, to regain this demographic group. A St. Louis paper launched a million-dollar television, radio, and billboard advertising campaign trying to attract readers in their twenties. The TV spots were patterned after MTV and showed hip young people buying the paper. A Greensboro, North Carolina, paper hired six teenagers to do movie reviews for their entertainment section. In El Paso, a paper has a monthly high-school roundup written entirely by students and an advice column targeted at teens. Another paper introduced a "Teen Trading Center" and offered teenagers reduced classified advertising rates. A California paper called its teen section "Yo! Info!" The ultimate success of these efforts has yet to be determined but it's clear that the newspapers will be aggressive in their efforts to woo these young readers.

Finally, to close this section on a positive note, the circulation problem discussed above applies mainly to weekday readership. Sunday papers are doing well; their circulation is at an all-time high. Apparently, when Americans have more time to relax, as is the case on Sunday, they still look to the newspaper to fill up some of their leisure time.

Special-Service and Minority Newspapers

As the name suggests, special-service newspapers are those aimed at several well-defined audience segments. These papers may be published daily, weekly, bimonthly, or even monthly and include publications designed for minority groups, students, professionals, and shoppers.

There are, for example, many newspapers published specifically for the black community. The black press in this country has a long history, dating back to 1827. Most early papers were started to oppose discrimination and to help gain equal rights and opportunities. The black press reached its circulation peak in the 1960s when approximately 275 papers had a circulation of about 4 million. Since that time, the black press has seen a significant decline in both numbers of papers and circulation.

In 1991, black papers were publishing in thirty-three states and the District of Columbia. Florida, California, Georgia, and New York were the states with the most black papers. Three black papers are dailies: the *Atlanta Daily World*, the *Chicago Daily Defender*, and the *New York Daily Challenge*; the rest are weeklies. Although some black papers were doing well, others were facing financial problems. In general, the problems faced by the black press stemmed from increasing competition from white-

Unearthing the News

The Greenville, South Carolina, *News* is a paper that really digs for the news. Literally. It all started when the newspaper asked for the records of the University of South Carolina Foundation. The Foundation declined to turn them over. The *News* then filed a request under the Freedom of Information Act. The Foundation said they couldn't produce the records because they had been tossed in the county dump. Undaunted, the *News* procured a bulldozer and proceeded to dig . . . and dig . . . and dig. Their excavating paid off when the records turned up under about a dozen feet of garbage. The records contained incriminating information and led to the indictment of a former university official.

owned papers, decreasing circulation (which made it more difficult to attract advertisers), inflation, and criticism from many in the black community that the papers were too conservative and out of date. In an attempt to recapture readership and advertisers many black papers have changed their format and editorial focus and have begun to concentrate on local news. Additionally, a black press agency, the National Black News Service, was started in order to provide member papers with a steady supply of national and regional news of interest. In the early 1990s it was estimated that the total combined circulation of all black newspapers was about 2 million, down almost 50 percent from the 1960s. In an attempt to gain readers, many black newspapers were trying to appeal to upscale black readers by emphasizing news about education, medicine, and economics. Many papers had added color and updated graphics.

The Spanish-language press dates back to 1835. In the approximately 160 years of its existence, it has grown to include about 100 magazines and periodicals, 7 daily newspapers, and about 48 weeklies. The most prominent daily Spanish-language paper

The best-known member of the Spanish-language press is El Diario, *published in New York City. Note that the front page includes billboards for local and national news as well as stories from Mexico and South America. (Vol. xxxv 131444 Copyright © 1990 El Diario Associates)*

is the New York City tabloid *El Diario-La Prensa*, with a circulation of about 69,000. In Miami, Florida, the *Diario Las Americas* distributes approximately 66,000 copies. Several English-language newspapers have recently begun to turn more attention to their Spanish-speaking readers. The *Miami Herald, Chicago Sun-Times*, and *Arizona Republic* introduced Spanish-language sections.

Another special type of newspaper is exemplified by the college press. Although numbers are hard to pin down, as of 1991 there were about 1200 college papers published at four-year institutions with a total circulation of more than 6 million. College newspapers are big business; consequently, more and more papers are hiring nonstudent professionals to manage their operation. Two of the largest college papers in terms of circulation are the University of Minnesota's *Minnesota Daily* and Michigan State University's *State News*, both with circulations around 35,000. College newspapers get high readership scores. One survey noted that about 96 percent of students read at least part of their campus paper.

Another type of special newspaper is the "shopper" or "pennysaver." As the name suggests, shoppers consist primarily of advertisements with some feature material such as astrology columns or helpful hints mixed in. Most shoppers are distributed free and are delivered weekly, usually on Wednesday or Thursday, in anticipation of weekend shopping trips. Shoppers now have their own professional organization, the Association of Free Community Newspapers, which represents about a thousand publications. Shoppers are big business. They have a combined circulation of about 23 million and have been so profitable that big corporations, such as Harte-Hanks, the Tribune Company, and Capital Cities, are currently publishing them.

● ● ● ●

NEWSPAPER OWNERSHIP

The two most significant facts about newspaper ownership are the following:

1. Concentration of ownership is increasing as large group owners acquire more papers.

2. There has been a decrease in the number of cities with competing papers.

The biggest newspaper group is the Gannett Company with eighty-two dailies and a combined circulation of about 6 million. Knight-Ridder Newspapers Inc. controls twenty-eight dailies with about 3.9 million circulation. Other newspaper chains that own dailies with a combined circulation of more than 2 million are Newhouse Newspapers, the Tribune Company, Dow Jones, and the Times Mirror Company.

The Growth of Newspaper Group Owners

It was pointed out in Chapter 4 that concentration of ownership is not a recent trend in the newspaper business. In 1900, there were eight major group owners in operation. The number of group owners grew steadily over the years until 1970 when there were 157 in operation. By 1992, the number of group owners had decreased by twenty-five, but these 132 groups now controlled about three-fourths of all U.S. dailies and more than 80 percent of circulation.

The feverish pace of newspapers sales that typified the 1980s had slowed to a crawl by the early 1990s, thanks to a weakened economy. The only major sales and acquisitions involved the three New York City papers. The financially troubled and strike plagued *New York Post* was reacquired by Rupert Murdoch's News Corporation. The Tribune Company sold the unprofitable *New York Daily News* to the British company owned by the late Robert Maxwell. After Maxwell's death, the *News* was bought by Mortimer Zuckerman, who also heads *U.S. News and World Report*. Finally, the *New York Times* acquired Affiliated Publications, the owner of the *Boston Globe*.

Deals made in the 1980s, however, were still having repercussions in the 1990s. In many instances, a company acquiring a paper financed the deal through so-called "junk bonds," bonds which promised buyers a rate of return higher than current market values. As long as business was good, companies could meet the interest payment on these bonds but when the economy weakened, some companies found themselves in difficult situations. An illustrative case involved Ingersoll Newspapers Inc. In 1987, the company acquired several papers in New York and Ohio for about $440 million using junk bond financing. A few years later, the company went against tradition and launched a new metropolitan newspaper, the St. Louis *Sun*. By spring of 1990, the *Sun* was losing millions and the company couldn't meet an interest payment on its bonds. As a result, Ingersoll folded the *Sun* and sold his other papers to a New York investment firm.

In a trend similar to that in other media industries, there is a good deal of cross-media ownership among newspaper companies. For example, Affiliated Publications, which publishes the *Boston Globe*, publishes seven magazines. The Gannett Company owns eight TV and fifteen radio stations. The New York Times Company owns twenty-six daily papers, eleven magazines, and radio and TV stations. Advance Publications controls twenty-six papers and several magazines, radio-TV stations, and cable systems. This trend is likely to continue as more newspapers enter the cable television field.

The Decline of Competition

Coupled with the growth of chains is the decline of newspaper competition within single markets. Back in 1923, more than 500 cities had two or more competing daily papers, including 100 that had 3 or more. By 1991, there were only 44 cities where competition existed, and in 22 of these competition was kept alive only through a **joint-operating agreement (JOA)**. A JOA is formed, under approval by the Justice Department, to maintain two newspapers in a city when otherwise one would go out of business. Functions of the two papers—circulation, advertising, and production—are combined to save money. Only the editorial staffs remain separate and competitive. JOAs exist between papers in Nashville, Cincinnati, El Paso, Tucson, and Birmingham to name just a few. JOAs are not without their controversial aspects. In 1987, Gannett and Knight-Ridder requested such an arrangement for their respective papers in Detroit. Opponents argued that a JOA should not be issued since both companies were profitable and could afford to sustain the papers. It was further argued that the papers were losing money because they were offering advertisers and readers price cuts in an effort to lure business away from one another. One paper was selling for only 15 cents and the other for a dime during the height of their competitive battle. Advertisers got similar bargains. Neither paper was losing any circulation. Groups opposed to the merger charged that the JOA would simply allow collusion between two media giants to improve profits and that it went against the underlying philosophies of JOAs. After a legal battle of more that two years that eventually found its way to the Supreme Court, the JOA was granted and began in late 1989.

The Pros and Cons of Group Ownership

The pros and cons of group ownership and decreasing competition are topics that have been widely debated among newspaper executives and press critics. Critics maintain that fewer competing papers means a loss in the diversity of opinions available to the audience. They also claim that top management in group operations places profits above newspaper quality. A newspaper owned by a chain, say these critics, would likely avoid local controversy in its pages in order to avoid offending advertisers. It has also been charged that chain newspapers are usually under the direction of absentee owners who may have little knowledge of or concern for local community interests. Group owners have also been accused of using profits earned in one community to shore up unprofitable operations in another market. A locally owned paper, it is argued, would reinvest those profits back into the community where it earned them.

On the other hand, those who favor newspaper groups argue that group owners can accomplish certain things that smaller owners cannot. For example, a large group owner could afford to improve news coverage by having correspondents and news bureaus in the state capital, Washington, D.C., and foreign cities—an arrangement too expensive for a small owner to maintain. The chains are also better able to afford the latest technical equipment, thereby making newspaper production more efficient. Lastly, chains have the resources to provide for more elaborate training and public-service programs than do individually owned papers. The validity of each of these arguments depends in great measure on the particular group owner involved. Group ownership is not automatically bad, nor is it automatically good. Many group-owned papers are doing excellent jobs. Others may not rate so highly.

••••
PRODUCING THE NEWSPAPER

Departments and Staff

The departmental structure and staffing of a newspaper vary with its size. Obviously, a small-town weekly with only a half-dozen employees will not have the same arrangement as the *New York Times*. All papers, however, have certain common aspects. They have a publisher and are generally divided into three main departments. The publisher is in charge of the entire operation of the paper. He or she sets the paper's editorial policy and is responsible for the tone and overall personality of the newspaper. The three main departments at most newspapers are (1) business, (2) production, and (3) news-editorial. Figure 5-2 is a simplified departmental chart for a typical newspaper. The figure reflects the historical fact that news and opinion are kept separate. The editorial columns contain opinion, while the news columns contain objective reporting.

In the news operation, the central position is that of the managing editor. The managing editor oversees the total day-by-day operation of the news department and coordinates the work of the several departments in the newsroom. The wire editor scans the thousands of words transmitted over the wires of the major news services, Associated Press and United Press International, and selects those stories most relevant to the paper, edits them, and adds headlines. The city editor supervises the newspaper's local coverage. He or she assigns stories to local "beat" reporters or general-assignment reporters. Beat reporters have a specified area to cover: city hall, courts, police station. General-assignment reporters handle a variety of stories, ranging all the way from fires and accidents to the local flower show. Many stories are "enterprisers," and are generated by the reporters themselves. The city editor also assigns photographers to go along with reporters on selected stories. The copy editor usually works inside a special U-shaped desk (called the slot) in the newsroom and supervises the editing, headline writing, and changes in stories submitted by local reporters.

Finally, there are specialized departments in the paper that generally have their own editor and staff. These may vary from paper to paper, but typically they include the sports, business, family, real estate, and entertainment departments.

Publishing the Newspaper

Getting out a newspaper is a twenty-four-hour-a-day job. News happens at all hours, and many stories happen unexpectedly. Not only that, news is perishable; it becomes less valuable as it ages. Trying to cope with the never-ending flow of news and the constant pressure to keep it fresh requires organization and coordination among the

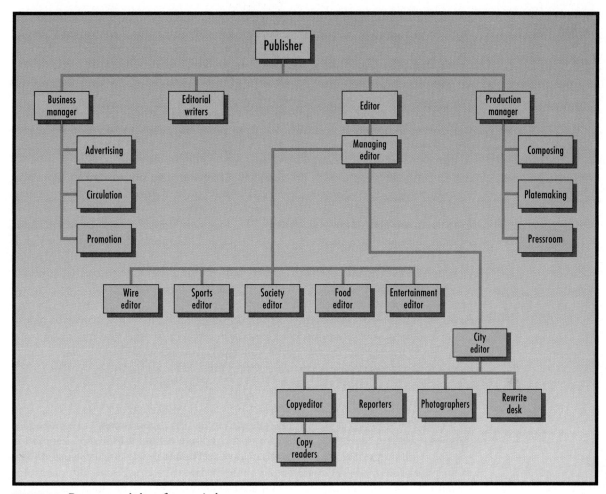

FIGURE 5-2 *Departmental chart for a typical newspaper.*

paper's staff. This section will illustrate the coordination by sketching how a newspaper gets published.

There are two basic sources of news copy: local reporting and the wire services. Early in the day, the wire editor will scan the output from the wire machines and flag possible stories for the day's paper. At the same time, the city editor is checking his or her notes and daily calendar and making story assignments to various reporters. The city editor must also keep track of the location of reporters in case a story breaks unexpectedly during the day and someone has to be pulled off a regular assignment to cover it. While all of this is going on, the managing editor is gauging the available space, called the **newshole**, that can be devoted to news in that day's issue of the paper. This space will change according to the number of ads scheduled to appear on any one day. The more ads, the greater the number of pages that can be printed and the larger the newshole. The editor also checks over available material such as copy that didn't get into the editon of the paper it was meant for or copy that is timeless and can be used to fill space on an inside page.

As the day progresses, reporters return from assignments and write and store their news stories at a personal computer. These stories are "called up" by copy editors, who trim and make changes in the stories and code them for use in the paper. If, upon further reflection, the managing editor decides that the story is not newsworthy enough for inclusion, the story can be purged from the machine. The managing editor can also instruct the computer to store the copy for future use. The newsworthy stories are then processed by the design desk. Decisions about page makeup and the amount of space to be devoted to a story are made as the deadline for publication appears. Other decisions are made about the ratio of wire copy to local and state news. Photographs and other artwork are selected for inclusion; headlines are written; space is cleared for late-breaking stories; updates are inserted in breaking stories.

In the composing room, high-speed computerized **photocomposition machines** take electronic impulses and translate them into images and words. The stories are printed on strips of photographic paper. These strips then go to the makeup room where, along with ads, photos, artwork, and headlines, they are pasted up into full newspaper pages. Computers are now being developed to do this layout task. This pasted-up page looks and reads just like the final printed page. Throughout the day, each page in the paper, including the special sections such as sports, family, classifieds, entertainment, and so on, is pasted up. The paste-ups are taken to the camera room, where a photograph is made of the whole page. This results in a negative, which is sent to the platemaking area. An **offset plate** is made by placing the negative between glass and a sheet of photosensitive metal and exposing the plate to bright light.

As the plates are being readied, huge rolls of newsprint are threaded into the presses. The plates are then attached to the press, and the printing process begins. Finished and folded papers emerge from the press and are sent by conveyor belt to the distribution area. The distribution staff counts and bundles the newspapers and then hands them over to the circulation truck drivers, who then deliver them to newsstands and carriers. Figure 5-3 is a simplified illustration of this process.

Technology in the Newsroom

Newspaper technology is now almost all computer-driven, and most publishers continue to automate their operations as new technology becomes available. Pagination systems, although not quite perfected, made their debut in the late 1980s, and electronic page makeup of display ads with graphics became a reality. Eventually, electronic makeup should eliminate typesetting on photosensitive paper, paste-up of mechanicals, and film used in turning pages into plates. By 1991 about 300 papers were using

Modern printing presses such as this one provide speed, high-quality reproduction, and the ability to print color everywhere in the paper. (Courtesy Rockwell Graphic Systems)

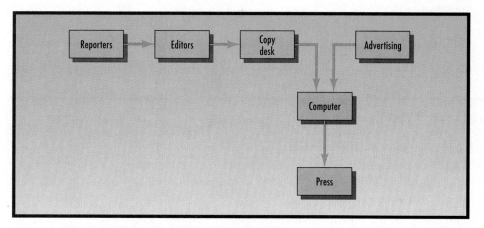

FIGURE 5-3 *Producing the newspaper.*

electronic pagination. This new system should make newspaper composition more flexible and ultimately cheaper.

Technology has also been at work on another messy problem for newspaper publishers—ink rub-off. The tendency of newspaper ink to come off on hands and clothing is one of the principal reasons subscribers cancel. To attack this problem, many companies are experimenting with treated oil inks that adhere strongly to the paper and are less likely to darken fingers.

On the printing side, **flexographic printing**, a system that uses a plastic plate and has a device that controls excess ink, was adopted by several papers. "Flexo," as it's called, has the advantages of better printing quality, less paper waste, and use of a water-based ink that helps the rub-off problem. Flexo now accounts for about 25 percent of the total printing market.

On another front, experts are predicting that newspaper photography as it now exists will be replaced by filmless electronic photography. The next generation of news photographers will record pictures on videotape or with electronic cameras and transmit them via modem to newspaper computers. An editor will view the picture on a computer monitor, crop it to fit available space, and add a caption. The new system means no more silver-based film, darkroom, and traditional photo morgue. Sony and Canon have already developed the prototype for such a system. The Sony still video camera, for example, uses a floppy disk instead of film. Each disk can hold up to 25 images. The resolution is not yet as good as film but the pictures can be sent by phone lines or by satellite from the field to the paper where they are stored until needed. The whole process takes between two and three minutes compared with the hours previously necessary to physically transport the film back to the paper, develop, and print it. Wire services are also starting to use digital technology to transmit photos to their subscribers via satellite. Since each element of a picture is stored using a string of 0s and 1s, it becomes fairly easy to use the computer to edit, change, or modify the photo. Because such modifications would be virtually undetectable, electronic digital photography raises some interesting ethical questions (see the box on page 128).

●●●●

ECONOMICS

Newspapers derive their income from two sources: advertising, which provides 75 to 80 percent of the total, and circulation (revenue from subscriptions and single-copy sales), which accounts for the other 20 to 25 percent. Advertising revenue is closely

Digital Photography and Reality: Is It Real or Is It Manipulated?

A long-standing problem in photojournalism has been intensified by the emergence of electronic digital photography: photo manipulation. Air brushing out details from a photograph, cropping out certain portions of the photo, or using an X-acto knife to put a photo of one person's head on someone else's body or to make it look like two people are standing next to each other have all raised ethical questions. With the advent of digital photography, however, it is now possible to do all of these things—and even more—faster, easier, and undetectably.

Since the images are constructed bit by bit by a computer, a clever programmer can change around the elements that make up a picture and create totally new arrangements. For example, in covering a story about budget allocations for the F-14 fighter plane, *Newsday* took a press release digital photo of an F-14 landing at an airstrip, electronically wiped out the background, cloned the image of the plane many times at various sizes and put the whole thing on a computer-generated blue sky. The finished product looked like a real photo of a squadron of F-14s streaking across the sky.

Several editors criticized the paper for doing this, saying the artificial photo hurt the credibility of photojournalists. Some suggested such a manipulated photo would be acceptable if it accompanied a feature story or some soft news item. Some argued that any and all manipulation was wrong. An editor from Norway pointed out that newspapers in that country require that the word "Montage" be printed with any photo that has been electronically altered.

Some editors, however, felt there might be times when such alteration is not a bad idea. A California paper was going to run a news photo of a young boy. As it turned out, the boy's fly was unzipped. To spare him from ridicule, the paper electronically zippered it for him. The *National Geographic* planned to run a photo of an athlete covered by a towel in a locker room. Upon closer examination, the photo editor discovered the towel had slipped a bit and revealed more than might be thought proper. No problem. The editor simply had the computer raise the towel to a more modest level.

It is obvious that the breakthroughs in digital photography force newspapers to reexamine their standards concerning techniques that compromise photo integrity.

related to circulation since papers with a large circulation are able to charge more for ads that will reach a larger audience.

As mentioned at the beginning of this chapter, the economic news for newspapers in the early 1990s was bleak. Advertising revenues grew by only 4 percent from 1988 to 1989 and then shocked the industry by actually declining 0.3 percent from 1989 to 1990. Much of this advertising slump resulted from a general economic recession that cut into the revenues of big retail department stores (such as Sears and Penney's), which, in turn, tried to cut costs by slashing print advertising budgets. Despite these hard times, newspapers continue to rank first in total ad dollar spending, receiving about 25 percent of all ad revenue compared to TV's 22 percent. This total, however, has been declining since 1980. Despite these figures, newspaper publishers have been in no danger of going on the dole. The average profit margin hovered around 5 to 10 percent in 1991, down from the 20 percent-plus figures of the 1980s, but still formidable.

Advertising Revenue

Advertising revenue comes from four separate sources: (1) national advertising, (2) local advertising, (3) classified advertising, and (4) preprints. Local retail advertising is the most important source of newspaper income, accounting for about 50 percent of all revenue. Classified ads come next with 40 percent, followed by national ads and preprinted inserts. National advertising originates with manufacturers of products that need to reach a national market on a mass basis. The majority of these include cigarette and tobacco products, automobiles, food, and airline services. Local advertising is purchased by retail stores and service establishments. Department stores, supermarkets, auto dealerships, and discount stores are the businesses that buy large amounts of local advertising space. Some national businesses such as Sears, J. C. Penney, and Montgomery Ward do most of their newspaper advertising through their local outlets. Classified advertising, which is bought by local businesses and individuals, is generally run in a special section at the back of the paper. Buyers as well as sellers purchase classified ads. The ads are grouped by content and contain diverse elements. Local governments publish official legal notices in the classifieds; individuals place personal ads to exchange greetings. Preprints are advertising supplements put together by national, regional, and local businesses that are inserted into the copies of the paper. The paper charges the advertiser for the distribution of the preprints.

The newspaper industry, however, has realized that the market for the advertising dollar is becoming more competitive. Consequently, the industry has taken two major steps to maintain its favored position with advertisers. First, the newspaper industry adopted the Standard Advertising Unit (SAU) in 1984. This marked the first time since 1820 that the industry adopted a standardized measure. Before the SAU, advertisers had to cope with different page sizes and column widths in different papers. The use of the SAU made it easier for advertisers to buy standardized space for their ads. Second, in response to advertisers' complaints that not all homes in a market are exposed to a newspaper, many newspapers sent out free weekly papers, containing articles and ads from the daily, to all nonsubscribers, thus helping advertisers achieve more market coverage.

The amount of advertising included in a newspaper has a direct bearing on the amount of news the paper can print. The more advertising that is sold, the more pages that can be printed and the more news that can be included. The ratio of advertising to newscopy has stayed about the same since 1970. A typical paper contains about 65 percent ads. The total number of pages in the typical paper has increased from forty-seven in 1970 to about seventy-five in 1990. As a result, the amount of newscopy has also increased, from about nineteen pages in 1970 to twenty-six pages in 1990.

Circulation Revenue

Circulation revenue includes all the receipts from selling the paper to the consumer. The newspaper, however, does not receive the total price paid by a reader for a copy of the paper because of the many distribution systems that are employed to get the newspaper to the consumer. The most common method is for the paper to sell copies to a juvenile carrier or distributor at wholesale prices, usually about 25 percent less than the retail price. Other methods include hiring full-time employees as carriers and billing subscribers in advance (as do magazines). These methods show promise, but they also increase the cost of distribution.

One closely studied factor important in determining circulation revenue is the effect of increased subscription and single-copy prices. In 1970, 89 percent of newspapers were priced at a dime a copy. In 1991, none cost a dime, less than 1 percent cost 15 cents, and 1 percent cost 20 cents. Around 38 percent cost a quarter, and about 49 percent cost either 30 or 35 cents. Ten percent of dailies had raised their price to 50 cents or more. Sunday papers have shown similar increases. In 1970, the typical price was 25 cents. By 1991, it was one dollar. The rising price of newspapers has probably had some negative impact on circulation revenue. Several papers have noted a decrease in subscriptions among older, fixed-income residents following a price increase.

Faced with decreasing revenues from traditional sources, many newspapers are experimenting with new ways of attracting income:

- *USA Today* has introduced a line of paper goods and clothing bearing the company logo.

- The *New York Times* and the *Los Angeles Times*, among others, have started faxpapers, newspapers sent by fax machines. These are generally short summaries of the day's top stories and a preview of tomorrow's news. Their primary subscribers are businesses that want to get a jump on the headlines.

- Several papers have started audiotex services. These allow callers to dial a number and hear dozens of prerecorded messages on subjects from the stock market to soap operas to traffic reports. Papers sell ten-second advertising messages on these lines.

- About a dozen papers offer videotex, an electronic version of the newspaper delivered over a modem to personal computers for a monthly fee. A few years ago, it was predicted that videotex would revamp the newspaper market. It didn't, and several big companies lost a lot of money experimenting with it. Today, the most common form of newspaper videotex is offered through computer services such as CompuServe and Prodigy.

Income from these services will be small compared with the traditional sources of advertising and circulation, but in a weak economy every bit helps.

General Expenses

The costs of running a newspaper can be viewed in several ways. One common method is to divide the costs by function. This technique shows (1) news and editorial costs; (2) expenses involved in selling local, national, and classified ads; (3) mechanical costs, including typesetting, plate production, camera, and engraving; (4) printing costs such as newsprint (the paper), ink, and the cost of running the press; (5) circulation and distribution costs; and (6) general administrative costs such as secretarial services, clerical services, and soliciting for subscriptions.

Some of these costs are variable. For example, the printing costs will increase as the number of printed copies increases. Distribution costs will also increase with circulation size (more trucks will have to make more stops). Other costs are fixed. The expense of sending a reporter to the airport to cover a visiting dignitary will be about the same for a paper with a circulation of 10,000 and for one with a circulation of 100,000. This means that the cost of running a newspaper will depend somewhat on

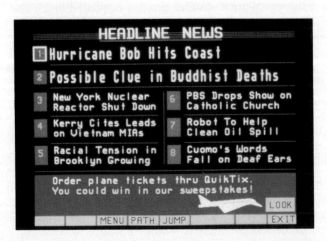

A screen from the Prodigy computer service. Several papers provide electronic editions to companies such as Prodigy and CompuServe. (Courtesy Prodigy ® Interactive Personal Service)

the size of the paper. For a small paper (circulation about 25,000), general administrative costs would rank first, accounting for about one-third of all expenses. The cost of newsprint and ink ranks second, followed by mechanical costs. Total expenses for this size of daily would run about $3 million to $5 million per year. In the case of a big-city daily (circulation 200,000), newsprint and ink costs rank first, followed by administrative expenses and mechanical costs. Newsprint prices rose 5 percent from 1990 to 1991. On the average, newsprint accounts for about 25 cents of every dollar spent by a paper.

In an attempt to cut paper costs, publishers are experimenting with a wood paper substitute called **kenaf**. This soft, fibrous shrub is easier to make into pulp than is wood-based paper and is naturally strong. Kenaf mills are already in operation in Texas and the substance has show itself to work quite well as newsprint. Further refinements should bring the price of kenaf down to where it is competitive with paper.

Another cost-cutting technique involves robots. A Japanese newspaper plant is currently using advanced robotics in its platerooms and pressrooms. Newsprint at the plant is never touched by human hands. Rolls are delivered by automated trucks, spliced and trimmed by robots, and loaded into the press. Although the initial cost of building such a system is expensive, companies are able to save money in the long run because of reduced labor costs.

● ● ● ●

ISSUES

The most controversial issue facing the newspaper business in the early 1990s had to do with striking a balance between what readers want to read and what a good journalist thinks they need to read. The emphasis on the "reader-driven newspaper" means that editors and publishers are depending more and more on what market research tells them the audience wants. In many cases, the audience wants less about local government and more about movies and music. Feature and "fluff" pieces typically score high on audience surveys and interpretation and analysis score low. How far should a newspaper go to entertain its readers at the cost of informing them?

A related issue concerned the amount of influence advertisers have over the paper's content. For example, most papers now have food sections. Did they originate in response to a concern over dietary habits and healthy eating? Not entirely. Most came

Newspaper Rack and Roll?

It's not surprising that the latest innovation in dispensing newspapers from vending racks originated in Nashville, Tennessee, "Music City, USA." Workers at the Nashville *Banner* and *The Tennessean* built a dozen vending racks in the shape of guitars and banjos. The racks are made out of sheet metal and stand about six feet tall. When a customer opens the rack door to buy a paper, the rack plays music, usually some country standard like "Duelling Banjos" or "Rocky Top," but they can be programmed to play any kind of music or to give a straight voice message. Newspaper executives from other cities were looking into plans to customize their own racks. Some possibilities: a rack shaped like a big apple that plays "New York, New York"; one shaped like a cable car that plays "I Left My Heart in San Francisco"; maybe even one shaped like a hot tub that plays "I Love L.A." The possibilities are staggering.

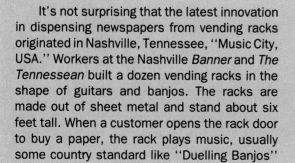

about because big supermarkets account for a healthy portion of a newspaper's local advertising revenue. Big supermarkets wanted content that was compatible with and would encourage readers to see their ads. Hence, the birth of food sections crammed with supermarket ads. The same is true of the "Automotive" sections now appearing in many papers. Does this section actually contain news or is it simply there to please the automobile dealers who spend a lot with the paper? By the same token, the use of color in newspapers was inspired not just by a desire on the part of newspapers to make themselves more easily read and more attractive but also by a desire by advertisers to have their ads appear in color, as they do in magazines and billboards. Faced with increasing competition, newspapers got more colorful.

How far will newspapers go to curry the favor of advertisers? One West Coast newspaper went so far as to get a zip code list of all the affluent neighborhoods in its coverage area. People living in these areas, of course, are highly desirable to advertisers. The newspaper directed its reporters to seek out people living in these areas and write stories about them, hoping that such an approach would drastically increase readership by these people and attract advertising dollars. More traditional thinking prevailed, however, and the plan was dropped.

Nonetheless, there is an old adage that says newspapers ought to comfort the afflicted and afflict the comfortable. If, in their quest for better demographics and bigger numbers, newspapers overlook their historic obligations to inform and to prod, they may do a great disservice to the public.

• • • •

CAREERS IN THE NEWSPAPER INDUSTRY

The newspaper industry is a big employer. In 1990, newspaper employment exceeded 475,000 people. In fact, newspapers now rank among the leaders in the Labor Department's listing of the nation's manufacturing employees. Of these 475,000, about 70,000 are employed in the editorial side of the paper; an additional 50,000 work in promotion and advertising, and another 60,000 in the administrative area. The remainder work in the circulation and production departments. More women are entering careers in journalism. The 1990 work force was about 45 percent female. Competition for jobs at big-city papers can be stiff, but newspapers located in small and medium-sized communities are having trouble attracting skilled employees. In some regions of the country in the early 1990s there were more jobs available than people to fill them. One of the reasons for this shortage was decreasing enrollment of newspaper majors at colleges. Of the 85,000–90,000 students enrolled in journalism schools in 1988, only about 10–15 percent were actually planning careers in newspapers. A second reason was the low salary level. The average starting salary for reporters was about $15,000–$16,000 in 1991. The picture improves somewhat for reporters with experience in big-city markets. The *New York Times* paid veteran reporters an average of $59,000 annually in 1991. At papers in smaller cities—like Portland, Maine, or Indianapolis, Indiana—reporters with a few years' experience made an average of $35,000. Newspapers in smaller cities pay significantly less.

Entry-Level Positions

Students interested in becoming reporters should try to major in journalism. A good course of study includes copyreading, editing, reporting, feature writing, and mass communication law. In addition, a newcomer to the profession should have a well-rounded education in the liberal arts, especially political science, economics, history, literature, and the social sciences. This stress on a well-rounded education is reinforced by the fact that the Accrediting Council on Education in Journalism and Mass Commu-

Poland has more than 35 million people with a 98 percent literacy rate. In 1991, eighteen newspapers served these people and all eighteen were facing formidable challenges during the transition to a noncommunist government. Under the old system RSW, a large government organization, published and controlled virtually every newspaper in Poland. Today RSW is being dismantled and each individual paper is being auctioned off. If no one bids for the paper, it is shut down. The problem with this is that thousands of Polish journalists and newspaper workers will be put out of work if all of the unprofitable papers are shut down.

Another challenge has to do with press philosophy. In Poland, newspapers have been traditionally associated with political organizations. Many Polish citizens believe that each party or faction within a party must have a newspaper as its official mouthpiece and that every newspaper must have an affiliation with some party. The notion of an independent, politically neutral newspaper is a radical concept in Poland. Hence, newspapers are started not because there is a market segment that they can serve but because some new political organization needs an official voice. Thus, the *Electoral Gazette* is the voice of ROAD, a political faction that split off of the Solidarity party, and *Solidarity Weekly* is the voice of Lech Walesa's Center Alliance party. Meanwhile, the *Tribune* is the organ of the Communist Party and the *Republic* is the official government newspaper.

This political orientation to newspapering leads to a reporting style that most Western reporters would find uncomfortable. Polish journalists believe that their job is not merely to report the news but shape it with opinions and viewpoints. Some reporters even consider writing a straight news story a menial task; they would rather be commentators and essayists. Thus, most stories take on a decidedly partisan tone. Indeed, the relationship between politics and journalists is quite intimate. Poland's prime minister is a former newspaper editor and leader of the Solidarity party. The editor of the *Electoral Gazette* is a member of Parliament and a leader of the opposition party.

The newspapers are also having economic problems. The change to a market economy has increased prices for a number of items, newspapers included, and people are apparently cutting back on their reading habits. Readership for many Polish papers has plummeted. *Solidarity Weekly* saw its sales cut in half. The *Tribune* has lost almost all of its former readers. The weak Polish economy has also meant that advertising revenues have decreased. Since advertising accounts for about 70 percent of Polish newspapers' income, the loss of income is significant. A lack of money also prevents the Polish press from modernizing its equipment. Most of it dates from the 1950s or before.

The ultimate solution may be determined by the marketplace. There may be too many papers competing for readers. Unprofitable papers, unless they receive government subsidies, may simply fall by the wayside. Obviously, the change to a more democratic society and a liberated press is not coming easily.

nication, the main organization that accredits journalism schools, recommends that three-fourths of a student's work be taken outside the journalism area. In fact, some editors prefer to hire reporters who have a liberal-arts degree with a minor in journalism.

A person seeking an entry-level job as a reporter has the best chance of landing a job at a small daily paper or weekly. Starting out at a small paper will give a newcomer experience in several areas of newspaper work since the division of labor at these papers is less clear. A reporter might also function as a photographer, edit wire copy, write headlines, and even assist in paste-up work. One possible way to break into the profession is to secure a summer job or an internship at a daily or a weekly. Most newspapers are always on the lookout for new talent, and a good number sponsor their own summer internship programs. The Newspaper Fund sponsors an internship program, and the Journalism Council has a summer internship program for minority students. Additionally, there are other avenues of entry into the news-editorial side. Although the jobs are not glamorous, some people break into the profession as proofreaders, rewrite persons, or researchers. Once inside the newspaper, these people then hope to move up to more responsible positions.

Other entry-level jobs can be found in the business side of the paper. Students who are interested in this type of work should have a background in business, advertising, and economics, along with a knowledge of mass communication. Since advertising is such an important source of newspaper revenue, most newspapers will gladly accept a newcomer who wishes to work in the sales department. Advertising salespeople might work on selling and planning display advertising for local merchants. Or a person might break in with the classified ad department, where he or she would write ads for people who call the paper with items to sell or positions to fill, or would solicit ads for the classified section.

Opportunities also exist in the circulation department for those interested in working with distributors and local carriers. Skills in organization and management are needed for these positions. Since controlling costs has become an important factor in operating a profitable paper, there are also beginning positions for accountants, cost analysts, and market researchers. The production side of the newspaper is staffed by people with technical training and mechanical skills. Most beginners in this department enter it directly from vocational schools or from apprentice programs.

Upward Mobility

In selecting an entry-level position in newspapers and other mass media, it is important to consider where your job might lead and how long it will take you to get there. In short, you should pay attention to the potential for advancement in the particular department you choose. In the case of a reporter, upward mobility can come in one of two ways. A reporter can advance by becoming skilled in editing and move up to the position of copy editor or perhaps state editor, regional editor, or wire editor. The ultimate goal for this person would be the city editor's or managing editor's slot. Other reporters might not wish to take on the additional administrative and desk work that goes with a managerial position. If that is the case, then career advancement for these people consists of moving on to larger circulation papers in big cities or increased specialization in one field of reporting. A beginning reporter, for example, might specialize in covering the business beat. He or she might then advance to become editor of the paper's business section. Eventually, this person might supply a daily business column to the paper. Another reporter might specialize in covering political news. This person might eventually advance to become the paper's Washington correspondent and might even head the paper's Washington bureau.

On the business side the route for advancement in the advertising department usually leads from the classifieds to the national advertising division. This department works with manufacturers of nationally distributed products and services and plans display advertising for these companies. The national ad staff often works hand in hand with the newspaper's national sales representative. The national "reps" have offices in major cities where they solicit ads for local papers. Those who begin in the circulation department can eventually rise to the position of circulation manager, while those who start in the advertising side can advance to advertising director. Ultimately, the top job that can be reached, short of publisher, is that of business manager, the person in charge of the entire business side of the paper.

• • • •
SUGGESTIONS FOR FURTHER READING

The following books contain more information about concepts and topics discussed in this chapter.

BOGART, LEO, *Press and Public*, Hillsdale, N.J.: Lawrence Erlbaum, 1989.
FINK, CONRAD, *Strategic Newspaper Management*, New York: Random House, 1988.
GILMORE, GENE, *Modern Newspaper Editing*, Ames, Iowa: Iowa State University Press, 1990.
HYNDS, ERNEST, *American Newspapers in the 1980s*, New York: Hastings House, 1980.
RANKIN, W. PARKMAN, *The Practice of Newspaper Management*, New York: Praeger, 1986.
SMITH, ANTHONY, *Goodbye Gutenberg*, New York: Oxford University Press, 1980.
WILLIS, JIM, *Surviving in the Newspaper Business*, New York: Praeger, 1988.

STRUCTURE OF THE MAGAZINE INDUSTRY

Savvy magazine, launched back in 1979, is a good metaphor for what's been happening lately to magazines. *Savvy* was aimed, to quote the magazine's own promotional literature, "at today's woman of influence and achievement." It contained profiles of important and successful women and ran articles on money management, fashion, beauty, and travel. With women returning to the work force in larger and larger numbers, a publication aimed at this new audience niche held the promise of great success. *Savvy*, renamed *Savvy Woman* in 1985, did well, attracting more than half a million readers and featuring some upscale advertisers. Over the years, however, the magazine faced increasing competition from publications aimed at the same target audience: *Working Woman*, *New Woman*, *Self*, *Working Mother*, *Executive Females*, *Mirabella*, and *Lear's*. The target market proved to be too small to support all of these magazines, particularly when a weakening economy made advertising revenue harder to come by. In an attempt to save money, *Savvy* dropped from 12 to 10 issues a year. The number of pages was reduced; the editorial budget was slashed. The cutbacks hurt the magazine's quality and readers stopped buying it. More advertising was lost. Eventually, *Savvy* couldn't turn a profit. The publisher pulled the plug on it in early 1991.

Target and "niche" marketing have become the operative concepts as magazines continuously narrow their focus and aim for more specific lifestyle and demographic groups. All of this specialization works pretty well as long as consumers have money to buy magazines and advertisers have money to buy ads in them, and as long as the competition doesn't get too intense. Unfortunately, a weak economy has cut advertising revenue and consumers have fewer dollars to spend on magazines. Moreover, magazine readers have been buried in an avalanche of new publications in recent years. (In the last decade about 3500 new titles hit the newsstands.) The combination of these factors has meant that today's magazine industry is going through a period of shakeout and retrenchment. In addition to *Savvy*, the past several years have seen the demise of such magazines as *Taxi*, *Moxie*, *Southpoint*, *7 Days*, *Cook's*, *Wigwag*, *Egg*, and *Fame*. Others, like *Entertainment Weekly*, which lost an estimated $50 million during its first three years, are still hanging on. The revenue pie is getting smaller and there are more and more magazines out there wanting a piece of it.

Despite the gloomy economic times, magazine reading is still a prominent part of Americans' leisure time. Almost 400 million copies were sold in 1990, up about 20 percent from the mid-1980s. Accordingly, the current downturn is probably not going to spell doom for the industry. Just like the general business world, magazines go through cycles of growth and contraction. Some weaker magazines will not survive the current decline, but the industry will probably emerge leaner and more nimble than before. Indeed, the magazine industry is well-suited to face the future. First, of all the media discussed in this book, magazines are probably the most in tune with social, economic, demographic, and sociological trends. As consumer and business needs and interests change, new magazines appear and existing magazines fine-tune their content to serve them. For example, the American population is getting older. In the mid-1960s, there were no magazines for senior citizens; there were 17 in 1990 with a combined circulation of more than 38 million. The increased popularity of home computing spawned dozens of magazines: *PC World*, *Compute*, *Run*, *Byte*, etc. The recent increased attention given to fitness and health was accompanied by the publication of *Prevention*, *Health*, *American Health*, and about two dozen others.

Moreover, target marketing and the notion of "niche" publishing have been raised to new levels by the use of selective binding and special printing techniques. *Boys' Life* divided its readers into older and younger groupings. Those in the older group got an ad for the Air Force in their issue of the magazine while the younger group got a promotional piece for the magazine in place of the Air Force ad. The American Kennel Club's *Gazette* prints different versions of its magazine for various breed owners. Special printing techniques let publishers and advertisers insert personalized messages into magazines. *Modern Maturity* personalizes the back cover and calls attention to its local pharmacy service. Niche marketing is also the goal of new distribution techniques. Whittle Communications, for example, publishes a magazine that is only delivered to doctors' waiting rooms.

In addition, magazines are permanent. Most magazines are passed along to other readers and many people save at least some copies of magazines for reference. Magazines are convenient. People can take them wherever they want and read them whenever they want. Magazines are attractive vehicles for advertisers. They allow them to reach a narrowly defined target audience spread out over a wide geographic area. Finally, many magazines are printed in color on superior grade paper. This allows advertisers to use high quality graphics and illustrations to make their products attractive. All in all, the industry is built on a stable base that is well-suited for the future. This chapter will examine the structure and organization of the magazine business with a special emphasis on the recent changes in the industry.

● ● ● ●
ORGANIZATION OF THE MAGAZINE INDUSTRY

One of the problems in discussing the magazine industry is deciding what exactly is a magazine. The dictionary defines a magazine as a "periodical publication, usually with a paper cover, containing miscellaneous articles and often with illustrations or photographs." This definition is broad enough to include *TV Guide*, with a circulation of more than 15 million; *Water Scooter*, a magazine for boating enthusiasts; *Sky*, given away to airline passengers by Delta Airlines; *Successful Farmer*, the magazine of farm

Videozines

It's getting harder and harder to tell the mass media apart. Books are on audiotape; TV series, like *The Civil War*, are made into books; movies are on videotape; and now the magazine is no longer confined to the printed page. *Persona*, sort of the video equivalent to *People*, cropped up on supermarket shelves during 1990. The two-hour video, which cost $4.95, contained celebrity interviews and had breaks for sponsors, including Coca-Cola and Perrier. Some of the first to purchase *Persona* figured they couldn't lose much. Even if they didn't like the videozine, they could always erase the tape and use it for something else.

Consumer magazines fall into major general-interest categories such as sports, news, and women's interests, as these examples illustrate. (The Photo Works)

management; *Go*, distributed to Goodyear tire dealers; *The Journal of Social Psychology*; *Gloria Pitzer's National Homemakers Newsletter*; and the *Swine Flu Claim and Litigation Reporter*. As best as we can tell, there are probably around 12,000–14,000 magazines published in the United States. The number and diversity of these publications are staggering. For example, *Standard Rate and Data Service* lists eighty-three automotive magazines, forty-one horse-oriented publications, and four periodicals devoted to snowmobiling. There are more than 2600 magazines sold regularly on newsstands, and the number of new consumer titles continues to go up: almost 600 in 1989. Obviously, classifying the magazine industry into coherent categories is a vexing problem. For our purposes, we will employ two organizational schemes. The first classifies magazines into five main content categories:

1. general consumer magazines

2. business publications

3. literary reviews and academic journals

4. newsletters

5. public relations magazines

The second divides the magazine industry into the three traditional components of manufacturing: production, distribution, and retailing.

Content Categories

General Consumer Magazines. A consumer magazine is one that can be acquired by anyone, through a subscription or a single-copy purchase or by obtaining a free copy. These magazines are generally shelved at the corner newsstand or local bookstore. (Other types of magazines are usually not available to the general public.) These publications are called consumer magazines because readers can buy the products and services that are advertised in their pages. One noticeable trend in the content of consumer magazines is, as we have mentioned, the movement away from broad, general appeal to the more specialized. *Standard Rate and Data Service (SRDS)*, a monthly directory of advertising rates and other pertinent information about magazines, lists approximately fifty content groupings of consumer magazines, ranging from "Antiques," with twenty-five publications, to "Women's," with ninety-two titles. Some of the better known consumer magazines are *People*, *Time*, *Reader's Digest*, *Newsweek*, *Sports Illustrated*, and *Playboy* (see Table 6-1).

Business Publications. Business magazines (also called trade publications) serve a particular business, industry, or profession. They are not sold on newsstands, and their readership is limited to those in the profession or business. The products advertised in these publications are generally those that would be purchased by business organizations or professionals rather than by the general public. *Business Publications Rates and Data*, a companion publication to *SRDS*, lists approximately 4000 different titles of business magazines. Most of these magazines are published by independent publishing companies that are not connected with the fields they serve. For example, McGraw-Hill and Penton are two private publishing companies that publish business magazines in a wide variety of areas. Other business publications are put out by professional organizations, which publish the magazine as a service to their members. The degree of specialization of these magazines is seen in the medical field, which has approximately 375 different publications serving all of the various medical specializations. Some business publications are called vertical, because they cover all aspects of one field. For example, *Pulp and Paper* reports on all segments of the paper mill industry. Other publications are called horizontal because they deal with a certain business function, no matter in what industry it exists. *Human Resource Executive*, for example, would be targeted at personnel managers in general, regardless of their business. Leading business magazines include *Computerworld*, *Oil and Gas Journal*, and *Medical Economics*. Business publishers are also active in supplying data bases and computer bulletin board systems to their clients.

Literary Reviews and Academic Journals. Hundreds of literary reviews and academic journals, generally with circulations under 10,000, are published by nonprofit organizations and funded by universities, foundations, or professional organizations. They may publish four or fewer issues per year, and a large number do not accept advertising. These publications cover the entire range of literary and academic interests, including such journals as *The Kenyon Review*, *Theater Design and Technology*, *European Urology*, *Journalism Quarterly*, *Poultry and Egg Marketing*, and *The Journal of Japanese Botany*.

TABLE 6-1 Top Ten Consumer Magazines (December, 1990)	
TITLE	**CIRCULATION (IN MILLIONS)**
Modern Maturity	22.9
Reader's Digest	16.3
TV Guide	14.5
National Geographic	9.7
Better Homes and Gardens	8.0
Family Circle	5.3
Good Housekeeping	5.1
Ladies' Home Journal	5.0
Woman's Day	4.8
McdCall's	4.7

Source: Advertising Age, June 14, 1993; pp. 5–6.

Sunday Magazines: Heading for Extinction?

The locally produced magazine section that many newspapers sold with their Sunday papers is becoming an endangered species. The Sunday magazine has been around since the early 1900s. It reached its peak in the early 1970s and has been declining steadily since then. There were more than a hundred in operation twenty years ago; now there are around forty. In just the last few years, *Newsday* stopped publication of *The Newsday Magazine*, the *New York Daily News* dropped its magazine, the Portland *Oregonian* dropped its *Northwest Magazine* and the *Omaha World Herald* ceased publishing its *Magazine of the Midlands*.

Why the decline? Expense is one reason. The local magazine was costly and the weakened economic climate hurt the magazine's advertising revenue. Improved technology is another reason. When local Sunday magazines were first published, one of their big attractions was color. Now most newspapers use color in their regular news sections, and advertisers left the magazine for the main sections. A third reason has to do with changes in newspapers themselves. The long feature stories that once typified the local Sunday magazine are now appearing in the regular news sections as newspapers strengthen their content in an attempt to capture more readers.

The bad news for local Sunday magazines is good news for the national Sunday magazines, *Parade* and *USA Weekend*. Many newspapers have replaced their local magazines with one of the nationals. *Parade* appears in 339 Sunday papers, triple the number it was in in the early 1980s. *USA Weekend* is in about the same number, an increase of 30 percent over the last five years.

Newsletters. When some people hear the word *newsletter* they may think of a club, PTA, or church bulletin filled with helpful hints. Although these newsletters are important to their readers, they are not the kind we emphasize here. We are talking about newsletters typically four to eight pages long and usually composed by desktop publishing. They are sold by subscription, and in recent years they have become big

The consumer magazine with the biggest circulation is Modern Maturity. *The aging of the U.S. population assures this magazine of a target market of increasing size. (The Photo Works)*

business. In fact, there is even a *Newsletter on Newsletters*, published for those who edit newsletters. The coverage area of a newsletter may be broad or narrow. It might deal with one particular business or government agency or it might report on a business function that crosses industry lines. The *Federal Budget Report*, for example, reports on just the President's budget and appropriations. On the other hand, the *Daily Labor Report* covers congressional actions that have an impact on many industries.

Most newsletters try to give their readers inside information, news that they couldn't normally get elsewhere. Newsletters try to achieve a personal tone between writer and reader. In fact, a lot of newsletters begin with "Dear Client" or "Dear Reader." Newsletters are extremely specialized with small circulations (typically under 10,000) but with high subscription prices. Typical fees are about $200 to $300 a year, but fees of $600 to $800 are not unheard of and some daily newsletters cost as much as $4000 annually. Some influential newsletters are *Aerospace Daily*, *Oil Spill Intelligence Report*, and *Drug Enforcement Report*. In the mass communication area, the *Gallagher Report* and the *Media Monitor* cover events in the print and broadcast industries, and *Communication Booknotes* reviews new books about the mass media.

Public Relations Magazines. Public relations magazines are published by sponsoring companies and are designed to be circulated among the company's employees, dealers, customers, and stockholders. These publications typically carry little advertising, apart from promotional items for the sponsoring organization. There are thousands of public relations publications, and they have developed their own professional organization, the International Association of Business Communicators.

There are several types of public relations magazines. Perhaps the most common are employee magazines, which contain news of interest to all those who work for the company. A new pension plan, possible layoffs, and safety procedures would be common topics for this sort of publication. Other public relations magazines might be sent to customers, stockholders, and dealers.

Function Categories

A second useful way of structuring the magazine industry is to divide it by function into the production, distribution, and retail segments.

The Production Function. The production phase of the industry, which consists of approximately 2000–3000 publishers, encompasses all the elements necessary to put out a magazine—copy, artwork, photos, titles, layout, printing, and binding. A subsequent section will describe in more detail how a magazine is produced.

The Distribution Function. The distribution phase of the industry handles the job of getting the magazine to the reader. It is not a simple job. In fact, the circulation department at a large magazine may be the most complex in the whole company. As with newspapers, circulation means the total number of copies of the magazine that are delivered through mail subscriptions or bought at the newsstand. There are two main types of circulation. **Paid circulation** means that the readers pay to receive the magazine, either through a subscription or by purchasing it at the newsstand. Paid circulation has two main advantages. First, periodicals that use paid circulation qualify for second-class postal rates, which are lower than other rates. Second, paid circulation provides a revenue source to the publisher in addition to advertising. On the negative side, paid-circulation magazines gain a wide coverage of their area by expensive promotional campaigns designed to increase subscriptions or to sell single copies. Paid-circulation magazines also have the added expense of collecting subscription payments and record keeping. Most consumer magazines use paid circulation.

The alternative to paid circulation is free or **controlled circulation**. Controlled-circulation magazines set specific qualifications for those who are to receive the magazine and send or otherwise distribute the magazine to those who qualify. Magazines that are provided to airline passengers or motel guests are examples of controlled-circulation publications. The advantages of controlled circulation are, first, that publications that use it can reach all of the personnel in a given field and second, that these publications avoid the costs of promoting subscriptions. On the negative side, controlled-circulation magazines gain no revenue from subscriptions and single-copy sales. Further, postage for controlled publication costs more. Controlled circulation has generally been used by business and public relations magazines. No matter what method is chosen, the circulation of a magazine is an important number. Advertising rates are based on circulation figures, and the larger the circulation, the more the magazine can charge for its advertising space.

For a paid-circulation magazine, distributing copies to its subscribers is a relatively simple affair. Address labels are attached to the magazine, and copies are delivered by mail. The complicated (and expensive) part of this process is getting subscribers. There are no fewer than fourteen methods that are used by magazines to build subscription lists. They include employing "cash-field" agencies, which have salespeople make house-to-house calls in order to sell subscriptions directly to consumers; direct-mail agencies such as Publishers Clearing House ("You may have already won $100,000 or other valuable prizes! See inside."), which generates 10 million magazine subscriptions a year; direct-mail campaigns sponsored by the publisher; and, finally, what are called "blow-in" cards, those annoying little cards that fall out of a magazine as soon as you open it.

Single-copy distribution to newsstands and other retailers is a multistep process. The publisher deals with only one party, the national distributor. There are seven national distributors that work with the nation's publishers. The national distributor handles anywhere from a dozen to fifty or more titles. At least once every month, representatives of the magazine sit down with the national distributor and determine the number of magazines to be distributed for an upcoming issue. The national distributor then delivers the magazines to the approximately 500 wholesalers who sell magazines and paperback books within specified areas. In any given month, a whole-

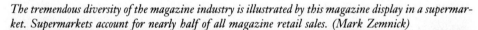

The tremendous diversity of the magazine industry is illustrated by this magazine display in a supermarket. Supermarkets account for nearly half of all magazine retail sales. (Mark Zemnick)

saler might receive 1000 or 2000 magazines to distribute to dealers. The actual distribution is done by route people who drive a truck around to their various retailers on a predetermined schedule, deliver new issues of the magazine, and pick up unsold copies.

The Retail Function. The retailer is the last segment of the industry. Best available figures indicate that there are approximately 140,000 different retail outlets in the United States. Retail outlets may be corner newsstands, drugstores, supermarkets, tobacco shops, convenience stores, and bookshops. Of these, the supermarket accounted for 45 percent of all sales in 1990. Supermarket sales have become so important that publishers pay the stores a premium of about $20 per checkout rack to have their titles prominently displayed. When a dealer receives a magazine, he or she agrees to keep the magazine on the display racks for a predetermined length of time (usually a week or a month). At the end of this period, unsold copies are returned to the wholesaler for credit.

Magazine Ownership

The merger mania of the 1980s has resulted in a magazine industry dominated by large corporations. Many of these conglomerates had extensive holdings in other media as well (such as Time Warner and McGraw-Hill) and some were part of worldwide communication giants (News Corp. and Hachette). Table 6-2 contains a ranking of the top ten consumer magazine publishers by 1990 revenue and lists their most well-known titles.

The increasing involvement of foreign publishers in the U.S. market is also apparent from Table 6-2. Three of the top ten companies have foreign headquarters. Reed Elsevier is based in Europe, the Thomson Corporation in Canada, and the News Corporation in Australia. In addition, had the list been longer, the number-twelve spot would have gone to the Paris-based Hachette, publisher of *Women's Day* and *Elle.*

The last few years have seen a slowdown of merger and acquisitions, but several significant deals have occurred as some companies try to decrease some of the debt incurred under past acquisitions while others try to strengthen their competitive edge. Rupert Murdoch's News Corporation, for example, sold nine magazines to K-III Holdings in an attempt to lessen the News Corporation's $8 billion debt load. In 1993, Conde Nast acquired *Bon Appetit* and *Architectural Digest.* The New York Times

---

Why It Pays to Renew Subscriptions Early (Particularly If You're the Publisher)

Many of you may have had the experience of getting one of those form letters from a magazine publisher informing you that your subscription "expires shortly" and urging you to send a check to renew immediately. Many companies send these notices out some seven months before the expiration date. Why? Simple economics. *People* magazine has about 1.4 million subscribers. Suppose 10 percent of them (140,000) send in their renewals with a check for, say, $50 (let's use round numbers for this hypothetical example). *People* would have $7 million on hand about six months before it was due. The magazine could invest this money at, say, 6 percent annual interest, and collect more than $200,000. The advantages of early renewal are obvious, at least from where the publisher sits.

TABLE 6-2 Top Magazine Publishers

NAME OF COMPANY	1992 REVENUE (BILLIONS)	WELL-KNOWN TITLES
1. Time Warner	$2.02	*People, Time, Sports Illustrated*
2. Hearst Corp.	$1.06	*Good Housekeeping, Redbook, Cosmopolitan*
3. Reed Elsevier	$1.04	*Travel Weekly, Modern Bride, American Baby*
4. Advance Publications	$1.04	*Parade, Glamour, Vogue*
5. Thomson Corp.	$0.82	*Medical Economics, American Banker*
6. Reader's Digest Assoc.	$0.76	*Reader's Digest*
7. International Data Group	$0.72	*Computerworld, PC World*
8. News Corp.	$0.65	*TV Guide, Mirabella*
9. Ziff Communications	$0.50	*PC Magazine, PC Week*
10. Meredith Corp.	$0.46	*Better Homes and Gardens, Ladies' Home Journal*

*In mid-1991, News Corporation sold nine magazines, including *Seventeen* and *Soap Opera Digest*, to the K-III Holding Company.

Company extended its holdings in the women's magazine area by buying *McCall's* for $80 million.

Although the magazine industry is not yet as concentrated as the newspaper industry, major publishers do account for a great deal of the revenue generated. For example, in 1992, the top five publishers accounted for about one-third of the total revenue generated.

The business publication field is dominated by about two dozen publishing companies. Cap Cities/ABC Inc. has more than forty business publications as does Reed Holdings Inc. while Penton Publishing Company has about thirty.

● ● ● ●
PRODUCING THE MAGAZINE

Departments and Staff

A glance at the masthead (the page that lists the magazine's personnel) of a few magazines will show that although there are many variations, a typical magazine is generally headed by a publisher who oversees four main departments: (1) circulation, (2) advertising, (3) production, and (4) editorial. Figure 6-1, page 145, shows a typical arrangement.

The publisher sets the general policy for the publication. He or she is responsible for budgeting, maintaining a healthy advertising position, keeping circulation high, and making sure the magazine has a consistent editorial direction. Strictly speaking, the publisher directs both the business and the editorial side of the publication, but most publishers tend to pay more attention to the financial operations and generally let the editor-in-chief make decisions concerning the content of the publication.

The Circulation Department. This department, under the supervision of the circulation director, is responsible for getting new readers and keeping current readers satisfied. If the magazine is losing readers, the circulation director must find out why. If the publisher thinks the magazine can attract another 50,000 subscribers, the circulation director has to figure out a way to get them. On most magazines, the pressure-filled job of circulation director is an important cog in the magazine's machin-

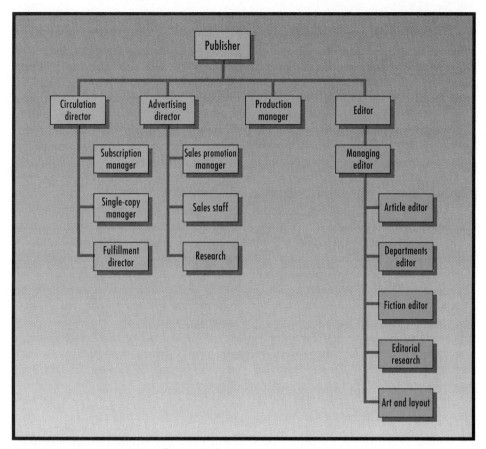

FIGURE 6-1 *Departmental chart for a typical magazine.*

ery. Responsible to the circulation director are the heads of three divisions: (1) the subscription manager, who tries to increase the number of people on the magazine's subscription list; (2) the single-copy sales manager, who works with the national distributors, wholesalers, and retailers; and (3) the subscription-fulfillment director, whose division is in charge of making sure that the magazine gets to subscribers by taking care of address changes, renewals, new subscribers, complaints, and so forth.

One circulation problem that plagues the subscription department of all magazines is late delivery. In 1991, surveys disclosed that 70 percent of monthly magazines and 50 percent of weeklies were delivered late by the postal service.

The Advertising and Sales Division. Under the supervision of an advertising director, the advertising and sales division is responsible for selling space in the magazine to potential advertisers. Also working in this department are the sales promotion manager, who is responsible for putting together new programs to enhance sales; the sales staff, which does the actual selling; and the research director, who studies the audience and compiles data of interest to advertisers.

The Production Department. The production department is concerned with actually printing and binding the publication. In charge of this department is the production manager, who buys paper, handles contracts with printers, orders new typesetting and computer equipment, and makes frequent visits to printing plants to make sure production is going smoothly.

The Editorial Department. The editorial department handles the nonadvertising content of the magazine. The person in charge may be called the executive editor, the editor-in-chief, or simply the editor. On most publications, the job of editor is primarily one of administration, and much of the editor's time is spent in supervising the editorial staff, planning topics that might be used in upcoming issues, informing the advertising department about plans, and taking part in various public relations activities. The day-to-day operation of the magazine falls on the shoulders of the managing editor. Making sure all articles are completed on time, selecting artwork, writing titles, changing layouts, and shortening stories are all functions performed by the managing editor. Helping the managing editor with these tasks are several editors who handle articles, fiction, or other departments that appear regularly within the magazine. Since the managing editor is usually more skilled in the verbal department than in the visual, an art director designs the magazine, selects typefaces for headlines, and supervises the display of photos and other illustrations.

The computer has had an impact on almost all of the departments at a typical magazine. In circulation, computers are used to maintain subscription lists, generate promotional mailing lists, and do accounting. In the advertising department, computerized data bases are used to generate data that are helpful to potential clients. Special computers have been developed for use in editorial work. Along with word processing, these devices have a split-screen feature that allows editors to make marginal comments or rewrite whole paragraphs without altering the original text. Computerized searches of photo files are also possible. Recent advances in computerized composition made it possible to automate typesetting and integrate art and photos into page makeup, thus eliminating manual paste-ups. In the production department, computers are used to track paper flow, maintain schedules, and monitor quality control. In fact, *Folio* magazine publishes ads for thirty different software/hardware systems for publishers.

Publishing the Magazine

Everything moves in cycles. When the first American magazines were published by people such as Bradford and Franklin, the editorial and production functions went hand in hand. Early magazine publishers were printers as well as writers; some even "wrote" at the type case as they picked up the letters of each separate word and fitted them into their composing stick. During the nineteenth century, however, the

Magazine Behind Bars

Magazines spring up to serve groups with common interests or lifestyles. Nowhere is this more vividly illustrated than in the case of *The Angolite*, a prison news magazine published by inmates at the Louisiana State Penitentiary at Angola, Louisiana. The magazine reports on the state's criminal justice system and covers such diverse topics as the soaring suicide rate among prisoners and problems in the system used to distribute clothes to prisoners.

The Angolite has attracted attention beyond the penitentiary gates. In addition to the inmates, it has more than a thousand paid subscribers in all fifty states and a few foreign countries. It has received critical approval from critics as well. *The Angolite* is a four-time finalist in the National Magazine Awards competition. But *The Angolite* has some advantages over its competition. Costs are low, since prison inmates are assigned to the publication as part of their regular duties and are paid the going prison rate of about seven cents an hour. Second, there is little editorial turnover; the coeditors are serving life terms. Finally, as the editors admit, it helps to have a captive audience.

production function was divorced from the editorial function. One set of people wrote and edited the copy while another group set it in type. Many magazines have now gone full circle: Computers allow writers and editors to set their words into type and make up pages, reuniting the production and editorial functions.

Nonetheless, even the computer hasn't changed one thing: Except for weekly news magazines, producing a magazine still requires a great deal of lead time. Most issues are planned several months or at least several weeks in advance. It is not uncommon for an editor to be planning a Christmas issue while sweltering through a late-summer heat wave.

The first step in all magazine production is preliminary planning and the generation of ideas for upcoming issues. Once the overall ideas are set, the next step is to convert the ideas into concrete subjects for articles. It is at this point that preliminary decisions concerning article length, photos, and accompanying artwork are made. Once this step is completed, the managing editor starts assigning certain articles to staff writers or freelancers. It is also at this juncture that the magazine's stockpile of completed manuscripts is checked for any material that might be germane to the scheduled issue. It is possible that some of the magazine's staff may have already completed an article on a relevant topic or that a freelance writer may have submitted a piece that would fit in with the planned issue.

The next step involves putting together a miniature **dummy**. A dummy is simply a plan or blueprint of the pages for the upcoming issue that shows the contents in their proper order. At this stage, the dummy is created by folding and trimming regular-size sheets of blank stationery into the total number of pages that will be published. Even this phase can now be done electronically, thanks to computer programs such as Master Planner which allows editors to view thirty-two pages at a time. The editor takes the miniature dummy and blocks out those pages that will carry advertising, notes those pages that are normally assigned to regular departments, and labels those pages that will be devoted to assigned articles. The editor can then visualize what the completed magazine will look like.

At about this same time, schedules are drawn up that assure that an article will get to the printer in time to be included in the forthcoming issue. A copy deadline is set—this is the day the writer must hand in the story to the editor. Time is set aside for the editing, checking, and verification of all copy. A timetable is also set up for illustrations and artwork. This production schedule represents the master blueprint that brings together all the elements that will make up the finished copy.

Most articles are now written and edited at the computer. Once they are in acceptable form, a computerized typesetter sets the copy in body and display-size type. Photocopies of the pages can be read to catch errors, and changes can be made easily at the keyboard. At the same time, photos and other illustrations are processed by a special camera that fixes them on a special printing plate. After the copy is corrected, the words and illustrations are made up into a mechanical, a page ready to be photographed and transferred to a printing plate. A separate mechanical is required for each color being printed. The mechanicals are photographed and negatives developed. The pages are then positioned in sequence in a special mask, and a press plate is created by shining light through them. The plates then go to the printing press where they are printed.

Many magazines are using satellite transmission to speed up their production process. News weeklies, in particular, are sending copy and illustrations to printing plants located around the country. The new technology allows news magazines to move their deadlines back so that late-breaking news stories can be included. Last-minute insertions and corrections are also much more easily handled.

After the magazine has been printed, it goes to the binding room where it is trimmed and stapled together. Mailing labels containing the names of subscribers are

John Johnson is the founder of the company that publishes Ebony *and* Jet. *(Johnson Publishing Company, Inc.)*

affixed to the magazine and the issues are sorted according to zip codes, bundled, and delivered to the post office. Magazines that will be sold on the newsstand are tied into bundles of fifty to seventy-five each and are shipped to wholesalers.

● ● ● ●
ECONOMICS

There are three basic sources of magazine revenue: subscriptions, single-copy sales, and advertising. At the beginning of 1993, the magazine industry was collecting about $19 billion annually from these sources. It should be pointed out that this $19 billion is not an accurate estimate of the money that was actually received by magazine publishers. For example, a magazine that sells for $3 an issue and sells 500,000 copies generates $1.5 million in revenue; however, the national distributor, wholesaler, and retailer get part of this money. After all of these sectors are paid, the publisher receives about half of the total revenue, or in our example, about $750,000. The $19 billion figure also includes advertising revenue. Most advertising space is purchased through advertising agencies, which collect about a 15 percent commission for their efforts. Thus, if an advertiser purchases $100,000 worth of space, the magazine actually receives $85,000 after the agency deducts its fee.

In general, the magazine industry, as we have noted above, was going through some economic hard times at the beginning of the decade. Expenses were up and although publishers were receiving more revenue from subscriptions, single-copy sales at the newsstand were down significantly. All in all, magazines had a pretax profit ratio of about 6 percent.

For the last six years or so, the magazine industry's share of national advertising has been constant at around 21 percent. The inability of the industry to increase this relative share of the market is the core reason behind some of its difficulties. As more and more magazines battled for a share of the national advertising pie, the market became more competitive and many magazines did not survive. The overall picture is not expected to get any brighter. Experts predict that tobacco and liquor advertisers will respond to public opinion and sharply curtail their ad budgets. A major change in magazine economics that started in the 1980s continued into the 1990s: Consumer spending has become almost as important as advertising revenue in supporting the magazine industry. In 1992, subscriptions accounted for about 30 percent of the typical magazine's revenue and single-copy sales accounted for another 13 percent, for a total of 43 percent. Advertising accounted for the other 57 percent.

Of course, the relative importance of subscriptions, single-copy sales, and advertising varies tremendously from magazine to magazine. *Reader's Digest* gets about 70 percent of its revenue from subscriptions, 22 percent from advertising, and only 8 percent from newsstand sales. On the other hand, *For Women First* gets no revenue from subscriptions, about 20 percent from advertising, and 80 percent from single-copy sales, usually at supermarkets. *Town and Country* displays another pattern: 75 percent of its revenue comes from advertising, 17 percent from subscribers, and 8 percent from single-copy sales. To give some perspective on advertising fees, in 1990 it cost about $100,000 to run a full page, black and white ad in *Reader's Digest*. The same ad in *Playgirl* would cost $3500.

From the point of view of the consumer, one obvious fact is that magazines are getting more expensive. From 1986 to 1992, the average price readers have paid for a subscription has risen 25 percent, from $24 to $30. Cover prices have gone up even more sharply in the same time period, from $1.71 to $3.89, an increase of more than 100 percent. Magazines cost more because they are costing more to produce. From 1970 to 1990 the cost of physically producing the magazine more than doubled. The typical expense dollar for a magazine breaks down as follows:

Advertising expenses	9¢
Circulation costs	31¢
Editorial costs	9¢
Manufacturing and distribution	40¢
Other costs	1¢
Administration	10¢

Two items included in the manufacturing and distribution category have increased at the fastest rate: paper and postage. A postal hike in 1991 increased rates for magazine

An Image to Maintain

You would think that in times of a weak economy and increased competition magazines would be happy to get all the advertising revenue that they can. Not necessarily. Some magazines can be very picky indeed. Upscale magazines, for example, don't want ads that detract from the publication's carefully crafted image. *Conde Nast Traveler* rejected an ad for Keebler Chips Deluxe cookies because the product wasn't prestigious enough. The gourmet magazine *Bon Appetit* will not allow ads for pet foods to sully its pages. Highbrow fashion magazine *Mirabella* rejects ads from such mass appeal products as Avon and K-Mart's Jaclyn Smith clothes. Will such snootiness persist if ad dollars continue to be hard to find? Keep an eye on things. If you start seeing ads for Maybelline in *Mirabella*, then you know times have gotten tough for image-conscious magazines.

companies an average of 20 percent. Some magazines were investigating alternative means of delivery, such as private carrier services, in an attempt to save money. Others were downsizing their magazines, saving postage costs by saving weight.

Still others were considering a new way of billing their subscribers: the **till-forbid subscription.** Many publishers noted that people who subscribe to cable TV don't have to renew every year; the cable company simply keeps billing them until they cancel. The same situation is found in newspaper subscriptions. Some magazine executives think that this system also makes sense for magazines. Instead of spending all that money informing you your subscription is about to expire and coaxing you

International Perspective: Exporting Magazines

American exports dominate the foreign film, television, and sound recording markets. American books are found on the best-seller lists of other countries. So far, however, American magazines have yet to achieve comparable domination of the international scene. Out of all of the thousands of magazines published in the U.S., fewer than 200 titles currently get worldwide distribution. Just a few publish local language editions. *Life, Forbes*, and *Fortune*, for example, publish in German and Italian while *Esquire* has a Japanese edition.

There are several reasons for this lack of international popularity. First, the editorial content of the magazine has to be of interest in other countries. Usually this is a topic where American expertise is tops in the world, such as science, medicine, music, business, etc. *Omni*, for example, sold out in minutes when it first appeared on Russian newsstands, thanks in large measure to the Russians' fascination with science. Second, the magazine must be adapted to the local culture and to local conditions. Some publications, like *Playboy*, might be looked upon with disfavor by many local cultures. Third, many foreign governments are not used to being criticized and sometimes react harshly if a magazine published something unflattering or offensive to their customs. Correspondents have been thrown out of some countries and some single issues of a magazine have been banned entirely or some passages have been blacked out. Other countries make it difficult to get the magazine distributed. Finally, some unexpected problems might arise. *Electronic Business Asia* found that the heat and

humidity in Singapore were so intense that its magazine covers melted.

Trying to generate circulation in other countries has problems all its own. Mailing lists are expensive and difficult to acquire. Translating promotional copy can be tricky. The circulation department for a computer software magazine couldn't figure out why people in Indonesia laughed at the promotional advertising for their magazine until someone told them that the word "software" in the local Indonesian language means ladies' underwear. Getting paid can be challenge, too. The number of potential subscribers in a foreign country drops dramatically when they are required to make payments in U.S. funds. Most magazines in the international market use foreign subscription agents who can collect payment in the local currency. Then, of course, laws and culture differ greatly from country to country. In Germany, for example, privacy protection is highly valued and people must give their approval before their names are placed on any mailing lists. Spain and Italy have no such protection. Finally, old habits die hard. American magazine publishers have a difficult time getting Europeans to subscribe to magazines because people in these countries are used to buying their magazines at the local newsstand and not through the mail.

Despite all these hardships, as the world continues to shrink and barriers to information flow continue to crumble, the demand for U.S. magazines should increase in the future. And if the U.S. economy weakens, publishers will try to compensate by eagerly courting the readers in the expanding international marketplace.

into renewing, some circulation directors want to keep billing consumers until the magazine gets direct orders to cancel. No matter how successful these remedies, most magazines will probably pass increased costs to consumers. If that weren't enough to handle, after holding steady for a year, the average price of paper jumped about 4 percent from 1990 to 1991.

• • • •
ISSUES

One of the most pressing issues facing magazine publishers today has to do with the weak economic position of the industry. In an effort to remain profitable, some magazines are compromising editorial integrity. For example, a poll by *Folio*, the industry magazine, found that 41 percent of consumer magazine editors reported that editorial material had been seriously compromised by a request from an advertiser or publisher. This pressure can take several forms. A magazine might elect not to print a story that puts a major advertiser in a bad light. Or the publication could write glowing articles for advertisers that spent large sums with it. A *Columbia Journalism Review* article criticized *Vanity Fair* for publishing gushy feature articles about fashion designers whose products were prominently advertised in its pages. Or an advertiser might suggest a topic or theme for an upcoming issue to assure that there is a compatible editorial climate for the company's ads.

Poor economic times might also be partly responsible for a second area of concern for the magazine industry—the decline of investigative reporting. Fewer and fewer magazines are engaging in this form of journalism. In fact, only *Mother Jones* and *Common Cause* have won more than three investigative reporting awards in the past decade. In 1989, no magazine was nominated to receive the top award from the Investigative Reporters and Editors Association. Why has the hard-hitting exposé hit hard times? Magazine executives say that it's an expensive proposition. In the current economic doldrums, investigative pieces seem a luxury. In addition, newspapers and CNN have taken over the leadership in this type of journalism. Whatever the reasons, the heritage of the muckrakers seems to have lost its impact on modern magazines.

• • • •
CAREERS IN THE MAGAZINE INDUSTRY

As best anyone can tell, there are only about 113,000 people employed in the magazine industry, thus making it a rather difficult industry to break into. Additionally, the headquarters of large magazine publishing companies tend to be located on the East Coast, especially around New York City. For example, of the top ten magazine group publishers in terms of circulation, eight are located in New York. The Los Angeles area is another region that contains a significant number of magazine publishers. This means that someone serious about a career with a major magazine might consider relocating.

Entry-Level Positions

Most jobs in the magazine industry are found at small publications or at business and trade magazines. In the editorial department, the most common entry-level job is that of editorial assistant. This job is really a training position in which a beginner learns about the actual workings and day-to-day chores that go on in the production of a particular magazine. Editorial assistants do a little bit of everything. Some typical duties might include proofreading, research, replying to authors' letters, coordinating production schedules, filing, indexing, cross-referencing, and answering readers' mail. In specialized publications, editorial assistants might be assigned duties somewhat afield of actual editorial work. During her first days on the job, one editorial assistant at a fashion magazine spent her time carrying around clothing for one of the magazine's photographers. A young man who went to work as an editorial assistant for a motorcycle publication spent his first two weeks repairing motorcycle engines.

Another beginning-level position at some magazines is that of researcher. A researcher spends his or her time pulling together assorted facts and data for staff writers or compiling folders and research notes for articles that are in the planning stage. This particular job requires a person who has a general education, is skilled at using the library, and is familiar with reference books. The researcher might be collecting facts on the storm-door industry one week and compiling data on volcanoes the next. The large news magazines *Time*, *Newsweek*, and *U.S. News and World Report* employ large research staffs.

At other publications, many newcomers start out as readers. When articles or stories arrive at the magazine, they are assigned to a reader who studies them, summarizes them for an editor, and may even make recommendations about what to publish. Some beginners become staff writers. The assignment editor gives the staff writers assignments such as preparing a calendar of upcoming events of interest to the readers or editing a section of helpful household hints. In time, staff writers move on to more challenging assignments.

It should be noted that some beginners attempt to break into magazine work by freelance writing. Magazines give some of their assignments to freelance writers who are paid per story. Other freelancers submit articles or stories on speculation, hoping that the magazine will be impressed enough with their work to buy it. The amount a freelancer gets paid for his or her work varies widely with the particular magazine. Some publications may pay $200 for a typical article; others might go as high as $3000–$5000.

Some larger magazines also prepare small publications that are distributed to their employees. Jobs on these in-house publications represent important entry-level positions for newcomers since they allow their work to be seen almost immediately by magazine executives. An employee who does an outstanding job on one of these in-house publications usually makes a quick transition to the parent magazine's editorial staff.

Newcomers in the circulation department are usually found in the subscription-fulfillment department where they update subscription lists, send out renewal notices, and handle complaints. Other beginning-level positions in this department are subscription salesperson, assistant to the subscription director, or single-copy sales manager. In the advertising department, entry-level positions are typically "assistants to" a staff member. Assistants to an advertising copywriter help prepare copy for leaflets and display cards, compile various reports, and assist in the preparation of direct-mail letters. Assistants to the sales promotion manager spend their time compiling and verifying statistical tables and charts, checking copies of promotional materials, handling routine correspondence, and suggesting new promotional ideas.

Upward Mobility

Career advancement in the editorial department can follow one of two different routes. Editorial assistants move up the ladder to become assistant editors, usually assigned to a specific department of the magazine. The next step up is that of associate editor, a position that carries increased responsibility. Typically, after spending some time as associate editor, the next position is senior editor. From there, if the person has talent and initiative, he or she may go on to be managing editor or perhaps even editor-in-chief. Another possible upward route finds the editorial assistant moving into the assistant copyeditor's slot. In this capacity, the person will spend most of his or her time working with other people's manuscripts and getting them in shape for publication. The assistant copyeditor then progresses to the rank of copyeditor. From this position it is possible, although not probable, that the person can become the managing editor.

In the circulation department, the next step up after an entry-level position is into the subscription director's or single-copy sales manager's slot. Advancement from this position consists of moving into the top management ranks by becoming circulation director. For many, the circulation director's job has led to a position as associate publisher or even publisher. In the advertising department, upward mobility consists of moving into the position the newcomer was formerly assisting. Assistants to copywriters become full-fledged copywriters. Assistants to the sales promotion manager follow a similar course. Another route upward is to join the magazine's sales staff. Ultimately, the top position to aspire to in the advertising department is that of advertising director, a member of the magazine's top management team. The job of advertising director frequently serves as a springboard to the publisher's position.

• • • •

SUGGESTIONS FOR FURTHER READING

The following books contain additional information about the magazine industry.

CLICK, J. W., AND RUSSELL BAIRD, *Magazine Editing and Production*, Dubuque, Iowa: William C. Brown, 1990.

The Handbook of Magazine Publishing, New Canaan, Conn.: Folio Publishing Corp., 1983.

Magazine Industry Marketplace, New York: R. R. Bowker, 1985.

MOGEL, LEONARD, *The Magazine*, Chester, Conn.: Globe Pequot Press, 1988.

RANKIN, W. PARKMAN, AND EUGENE S. WAGGAMAN, *Business Management of General Consumer Magazines*, 2nd ed., New York: Praeger, 1986.

TAFT, WILLIAM, *American Magazines for the 1980s*, New York: Hastings House, 1982.

WOLSELEY, ROLAND, *Understanding Magazines*, Ames: Iowa State University Press, 1972.

———, *The Changing Magazine*, New York: Hastings House, 1973.

STRUCTURE OF THE BOOK INDUSTRY

Best sellers can come from the most unlikely places. In the late 1980s, Patricia Van der Leun, a Connecticut literary agent, found an essay packed in her child's knapsack by the child's schoolteacher. The essay was a brief examination of some of the profound lessons in life that were learned in kindergarten and how these rules had enduring value throughout the rest of life. Some of the simple rules were: "Play fair." "Clean up your own mess." "Flush." and "Share everything."

Intrigued, Van der Leun tried to track down the author of these timeless truisms. It turns out her child's teacher had seen an abbreviated version published in *Reader's Digest*. Further detective work disclosed that earlier renditions had appeared in "Dear Abby" and had been quoted by the Reverend Bob Schuller on his TV show and by Paul Harvey on radio. An even earlier form had been read into the *Congressional Record* by Senator Dan Evans of Washington. Eventually, Van der Leun discovered that the essay was written by Reverend Robert Fulghum, a pastor of a Unitarian church in Seattle. Fulghum had first included the essay as part of a column he wrote for his church's newsletter. The agent contacted Fulghum and asked if he had any more of these insights that might be collected into a book. Fulghum replied that he had been writing these essays for years and literally had boxes of them strewn about his house.

Working together, Fulghum and Van der Leun eventually produced a slender (196 pages) book entitled *All I Really Need to Know I Learned in Kindergarten*. The book was sold to a small publishing company, Villard Books, for a modest (in publishing terms) $60,000. The company had only modest hopes for its success. These hopes weren't bolstered when the book was ignored by most major reviewers and when some of those who did review it did not say very pleasant things about it. Nonetheless, the public loved it and it leaped to the top of the best-seller lists and stayed there for about four months. The paperback rights sold for $2.1 million.

All I Really . . . became one of those books that periodically vaults into the national consciousness by analyzing the meaning of life. In the 1960s, it was *Zen and the Art of Motorcycle Maintenance*; in the '70s, *Jonathan Livingston Seagull*; in the 80's, *When Bad Things Happen to Good People*. Fulghum's books appear to be next in line. *All I Really* . . . and the sequel *It Was on Fire When I Lay Down on It* have sold more than five million copies. Fulghum was offered seven-figure contracts for *Uh-oh*, published in 1991, and for *Maybe (Maybe Not)*, published in 1993. And literary agents all over the country now pay much closer attention to the contents of their children's knapsacks.

This vignette holds several lessons about the publishing industry. In the first place, there's a lot of uncertainty involved. No one knows for sure why some books are popular and some aren't. Second, there are some publishers who will overlook the profit motive and publish a book purely on its artistic, intellectual, or cultural merit. Consequently, books are an important part of the cultural heritage. Third, books are

Books are portable, personal, and can be read whenever and wherever it's convenient. (Margot Granitsas/The Image Works)

read by a relatively small audience. A top-rated TV show will have about 40 million viewers for each of its episodes. It took about forty years to sell 20 million copies of *Gone With the Wind*, but more than 50 million people watched the movie version in a single evening when it came to television. Even a flop TV show might have 15 million–20 million in its audience. These numbers are beyond the wildest imaginings of most authors. A popular hardcover might make the year's best-seller list with 125,000 copies sold. Even a mass-market paperback such as *Zoya* by Danielle Steel might sell only about 4 million copies. Books are the least "mass" of the mass media. Lastly, books can have cultural impact that far outweighs their relatively modest audience size. *All I Really . . .* is simply one of the many books that have influenced our times. *Uncle Tom's Cabin* is credited with helping to change a nation's attitudes toward slavery. Dr. Spock and his *Baby and Child Care* altered the way parents brought up their children and made its author the target of critics who blamed him and his permissive theories for the social unrest of the 1960s.

This chapter examines the book publishing industry. Although we will concentrate primarily on the more practical and concrete aspects of the industry—structure, methods, and economics of publishing—the cultural and social contribution of publishing should not be forgotten.

• • • •

ORGANIZATION OF THE BOOK INDUSTRY

The book publishing industry can be divided into three segments: publishers, distributors, and retailers.

Publishers

The publishing segment consists of the 2000 or so establishments that transform manuscripts submitted by authors into books that are sought by readers. Every year these companies will publish 50,000–55,000 new titles. Book publishing is a highly segmented industry. Publishers have developed a classification system for the industry based upon the market that is served. The following are the twelve major divisions suggested by the Association of American Publishers.

1. *Trade books* are aimed at the general consumer and sold primarily through bookstores. They can be hardbound or softbound and include works for juveniles and adults. Trade books include hardcover fiction, nonfiction, biography, cookbooks, art books, and several other types.

2. *Religious books* include Bibles, hymnals, prayer books, theology, and other literature of a devotional nature.

3. *Professional books* are aimed at doctors, lawyers, scientists, accountants, business managers, architects, engineers, and all others who need a personal reference library in their work.

4. *Book clubs* at first may sound more like a distribution channel than a division of the publishing segment, but some book clubs publish their own books and almost all prepare special editions for their members. Thus, it makes sense to include them here.

5. *Mail order publications* consist of books created for the general public and marketed by direct mail. These are different from book clubs because the books are marketed by the publisher, and customers do not incur any member-

All-Time Best Sellers

The following are the all-time best sellers in hardcover and mass market paperbacks. (Dictionaries and the Bible are not included in this list.)

HARDCOVER

Title	Copies Sold	Date
1. *Betty Crocker's Cookbook*	22 million	1950
2. *Better Homes and Gardens Cookbook*	21 million	1930
3. *The Joy of Cooking*	10 million	1931
4. *Mr. Boston's Bartender's Guide*	9 million	1935
5. *The Tale of Peter Rabbit*	8 million	1902

MASS MARKET PAPERBACKS

Title	Copies Sold	Date
1. *Baby and Child Care*	39.2 million	1946
2. *How to Win Friends and Influence People*	17.4 million	1940
3. *The Hobbit*	14.5 million	1972
4. *1984*	12.8 million	1972
5. *The Exorcist*	12.4 million	1950

ship obligations in an organization. The Time-Life Company, among others, has marketed books dealing with cooking, home repair, the Civil War, Western history, aviation, World War II, and other topics.

6. *Mass market paperbacks* are softbound volumes on all subjects that have their major sale in places other than bookstores. Typically, these are the books sold in wire racks in supermarkets, newsstands, drugstores, airports, chain stores, and so on.

7. *University presses* publish mostly scholarly titles or books that have cultural or artistic merit. University presses are typically run on a nonprofit basis and most of their customers are libraries and scholars.

8. *Elementary and secondary textbooks* are hard- and softcover books, workbooks, manuals, and other printed materials, all intended for use in the classroom. Logically enough, schools are the primary market for these publishers. (This division is also referred to as "elhi" publishers—from *el*ementary and *hi*gh school.)

9. *College text* publishers produce texts and workbooks for the college market.

10. *Standardized tests* comprise a relatively small segment of the industry. These publishers put together tests of ability, aptitude, interest, personality, and other traits. For example, the Educational Testing Service publishes the Scholastic Aptitude Test and the Graduate Record Exam.

11. *Subscription reference books* consist of encyclopedias, dictionaries, atlases, and the like. They are usually marketed in packages to schools, libraries, and individual consumers.

12. *Audiovisual and other media* supply tapes, films, slides, transparencies, games, and other educational material to schools and training companies.

Table 7-1 shows the relative importance of each of these segments to the industry. As can be seen, trade, professional, and textbook publishing are the major divisions, accounting for 74 percent of sales.

Distributors

Only a few kinds of publishers (subscription books, book clubs, mail order) sell their books directly to readers. Most books go to wholesalers and jobbers who, in turn, distribute them to retail and other outlets. There are about fifteen to twenty major

TABLE 7-1 Sales by Publishing Industry Division, 1990

DIVISION	PERCENTAGE OF SALES
Trade	28
Religious	4
Professional	18
Book clubs	4
Mail order	5
Mass market paperback	8
University press	2
Elhi text	12
College text	13
Standardized tests	1
Subscription reference	3
AV and other media	2

wholesalers or jobbers across the country, and these companies usually stock large inventories of trade and/or textbooks. In the mass market paperback field, there are three channels of distribution. National distributors usually distribute both magazines and paperback books. Most national distributors also act as a link between publishers and independent wholesalers (IDs). IDs operate in special geographical areas and are locally owned. There were about 120 independent wholesalers in operation in 1991. The third distribution channel for paperbacks is jobbers. Jobbers service wide geographical areas and differ from independent wholesalers in that jobbers usually do not handle magazines or have their own fleet of delivery trucks. Figure 7-1 illustrates the distribution process.

Retailers

There are more than 20,000 bookstores in the United States, along with about 200,000 drugstores, supermarkets, airports, and specialty shops where books are also sold. Overall, however, there are five main channels through which books get to the consumer. General retailers include bookstores, book sections in department stores, newsstands, book racks in supermarkets and drugstores, specialty stores, and many others. In recent years, large chain bookstores, usually located in shopping malls, have become more prevalent. Waldenbooks has about 1200 stores. BDB Corporation, which owns B. Dalton and Barnes & Noble and recently acquired Doubleday Book Shops, has about 900. Chains sell about 40 percent of all books sold in the U.S. The newest trend in retailing is the "superstore" which stocks an abundance of titles covering a wide range of topics. College bookstores are the principal means of selling books in higher education. Of course, these bookstores also sell many noneducational books as well. The third channel, libraries, includes public, university, and special research libraries. There are approximately 30,000 of these nationwide. Schools and institutions comprise local school systems, book depositories, classrooms, resource centers, and related facilities. The last channel, direct to consumer, includes publishers who directly market to the consumer by mail, telephone, or face to face.

Not surprisingly, the general retail channel accounts for the largest share of the consumer dollar, followed by college bookstores. These two outlets have also shown the most growth since 1972.

FIGURE 7-1 *Channels of book distribution.*

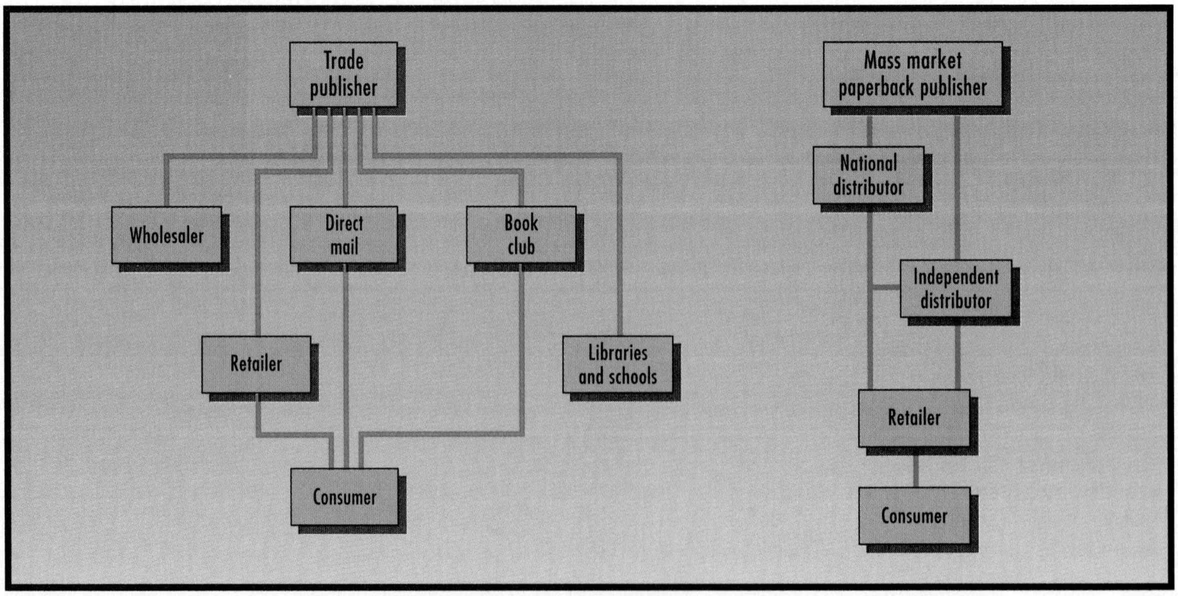

The small, dark, and crowded neighborhood bookstore has given way to the "superstore," which stocks thousands of books along with audiotapes, videotapes, calendars, and other merchandise. (Susan Arnold/Waldenbooks)

Deadly Doings at the Bookstore

The old adage that crime doesn't pay doesn't hold up when it comes to book publishing. In fact, one of the hottest-selling genres of the last few years has been books that describe, sometimes in great detail, real-life crimes. At least thirty publishers are turning out these crime books. They have become so successful that many bookstores now have a special section labeled "True Crime." You can even tell the true crime books by their covers—screaming headlines, lurid photographs, and a smattering of red ink. There are even subcategories of specialization of true crime: drug-related crime, espionage-related crime, Mafia crime, family crime, and perhaps the most successful of all, serial killers.

Why do people read these sometimes grisly volumes? Nobody knows for sure. Some readers probably get interested after watching TV shows like *Cops* or *America's Most Wanted*. Others might want to understand why some of the terrible crimes described in these books happen. Still others might read them to gain a sense of relief because all of the frightful things that are described didn't happen to them. No matter what the reason, these books are flourishing so much that their success is almost . . . criminal.

Reading the Fine Print

Preserving books has traditionally been a perplexing problem. Some books are lost because of paper deterioration; some libraries are running out of shelf space for books. Microfilms and microfiche provide only a temporary solution because they too degenerate over time. A chemist from New York University, however, is working to develop what may be the ultimate solution: the biochip. Based on the molecular structure of the DNA molecule, the genetic blueprint for cell reproduction, the biochip would be so efficient it could save the information now contained in about 30 million average-sized books. How big is this biochip? About the size of a dime.

Ownership

The two major trends that have characterized book publishing in recent years have been (1) increasing foreign ownership and (2) consolidation. The relatively weak dollar and the strength of the publishing industry continue to attract foreign investors. The Bertelsmann Publishing Group, part of the huge Bertelsmann conglomerate of Germany, acquired Doubleday, Dell, the Literary Guild, a textbook company, and several printing plants for more than $475 million. Hachette, a French conglomerate, acquired Grolier. The late Robert Maxwell's British company acquired Macmillan, Inc., and Rupert Murdoch's Australian-based News Corporation acquired Harper & Row and merged it with the U.K.'s Collins to create HarperCollins. Penguin, yet another British Company, bought New American Library and E. P. Dutton. Electronics giant Matsushita of Japan acquired the MCA entertainment conglomerate, parent company of the Putnam Berkley Group, marking the first time an American publishing company was purchased by a non-European group.

On the consolidation front, Harcourt Brace Jovanovich was acquired by the General Cinema Corporation. In 1993, London-based Reed International merged with Elsevier, a Dutch company, to form a multi-billion-dollar international publishing giant. These transactions, along with deals done in the merger-mad 1980s, have resulted in a book industry that is dominated by conglomerates. To illustrate, here are the five companies that dominated the industry in sales at the beginning of the 1990s:

1. *Simon & Schuster*: Owned by Paramount Communications, Inc., a large conglomerate itself, the publishing division includes seven companies in the college text area, seven in the elhi market, three trade press publishers, a paperback publishing company, *Webster's New World Dictionary*, computer software, and a mass market distribution service. Revenues in 1992 exceeded $1.6 billion.

2. *Time Publishing Group*: Part of the world's largest media company, Time Warner, this large communications company owns or holds an interest in sixteen magazines, publishes Time-Life Books, owns two additional publishing companies, the Book of the Month Club, HBO pay cable channel, HBO Movies, and 80 percent of ATC, a multisystem cable operator. In 1992, it had $3.1 billion in revenue.

3. *Harcourt Brace Jovanovich*: This company is the nation's leading publisher of elhi texts; it ranks in the top five of college textbook publishers. In addition to its book publishing ventures, it also publishes elhi standardized tests and scientific journals. In addition, HBJ runs an executive job placement service and owns a

graphics and visual aids company and several insurance companies. Its 1992 publishing revenues were $986 million.

4. *Random House*: Part of Advance Publications, a media conglomerate with extensive print holdings, Random House has branches in Great Britain where it has also dabbled in real estate.

5. *Reader's Digest Association*: This company is best known for magazine publishing, but it is also active in book publishing and mail order book selling (condensed books). It also has holdings in television and computerized data bases, and it even markets insurance to its magazine subscribers. Income for 1992 was $1.7 billion.

● ● ● ●
PRODUCING THE BOOK

Departments and Staff

Figure 7-2 depicts the organizational arrangement at a typical publishing house. The titles may vary at other companies, but the functions will be basically the same. There are four major departments in the publishing company: (1) editorial, (2) production, (3) marketing, and, (4) general administration or business.

The editorial department is in charge of dealing with authors. Essentially, it has a twofold task: the selection of manuscripts to be published and their preparation for publication. It is in the performance of the first task that editors and authors initially meet. Some editors specialize in procurement and visit potential authors to solicit their work. Other editors read manuscripts, write reports on them, and recommend acceptance, rejection, or revision. Once an accepted manuscript is completed, copyeditors sift through it, checking grammar, punctuation, language, internal consistency, and accuracy.

As the name implies, the production department oversees the planning and design of the physical book. Type style, composition, paper, printing, and binding are the responsibilities of this division. Since many books might be entering production at any given time, the production manager and staff must keep track of many tasks, not the least of which is keeping the book on schedule.

FIGURE 7-2 *Organization of a publishing company.*

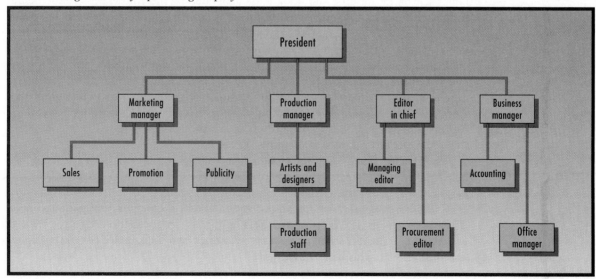

The marketing department supervises several activities, including sales, promotion, and publicity. The actual type of sales activity depends upon the kind of book being marketed. Publishers of elhi textbooks sell mainly to school systems; college text publishers to individuals or committees of professors. Mass market paperbacks must be sold to retailers, who in turn must sell them to the general public. Promoting the book begins long before the book is finished and can take several forms. Advertising in trade magazines, listings in publishing catalogs, and posters are common promotional methods. For trade books, ads in literary magazines and reviews in respected publications can be influential. Publishers wishing to promote mass market books use other techniques. Some examples: *The Day America Told the Truth* was printed with nine different covers designed for separate regions of the U.S. When Kitty Kelley's unauthorized biography of Nancy Reagan appeared, bookstores were provided with a life-size cardboard cutout of Nancy Reagan to stand next to the book display. The publisher of *La Toya*, the biography of La Toya Jackson (who else?), promoted the book with an author tour, a national print and TV advertising budget, excerpts in *Playboy* and *Entertainment Weekly*, and an extensive floor display for bookshop owners.

Promotion is also effective at the retail level. At a Waldenbooks store in California, employees promoted the opening of a new horror book section by dressing up as Dracula, the Wolfman, or a Stephen King character.

The publicity section spreads the news of the book to as many potential customers as possible. There are many tools available to this department: early review copies of the book, press releases, news conferences, publisher's parties, and author appearances on radio and TV talk shows. Getting the book reviewed by a reputable publication is also a tremendous help. This is a challenging task, however. For example, a prestigious publication such as the *New York Times Book Review* might receive anywhere from 12,000 to 15,000 books a year out of which only 10–15 percent might be reviewed.

The business manager at a publishing company is responsible for several functions. One of the most important is accounting. This department oversees processing orders, controls credit, and provides balance sheets on the firm's overall operation. Further, it prepares budgets and makes long-range financial forecasts. The business department's responsibilities include dealing with internal personnel policies and supervising the general day-to-day operational needs of the company.

Publishing the Book

Editors get their books from three main sources: those submitted by agents, unsolicited books sent in by authors, and book ideas generated by the editor. Most trade manuscripts are submitted through literary agents. Editors prefer to receive them this way since agents are known quantities and will not generally submit manuscripts that they know are unacceptable to the editor. Unsolicited manuscripts are given an unflattering name in the business: "slush." As they come in, these manuscripts are put in the slush pile and eventually read, if the author is lucky, by an editorial assistant. Most of the time they are rejected with a form letter, but every once in a while an author gets lucky. *The Office Humor Book*, for example, went from the slush pile into five printings. Editors also generate ideas for books. If an editor has a good idea for a book, he or she will generally talk to one or more agents, who will suggest likely candidates for the assignment. This is another good reason why writers should have agents. In any case, the author typically submits a proposal consisting of a cover letter, a brief description of the planned book, a list of reasons why it should be published, an analysis of the potential market, an outline or a table of contents, and perhaps one or two sample chapters. The proposal usually goes to an acquisitions or procurement editor and is evaluated. If the publishing decision is favorable, then a contract is signed and the author begins work in earnest.

The competitive climate in the book industry has put new emphasis on point-of-purchase displays. Book sellers use innovative techniques, such as a life-size cutout of Nancy Reagan, in order to attract the attention of the casual browser. (Les Stone/Sygma)

Editorial work starts as soon as the author submits chapters to the publisher. Editors look at the overall thrust of the book to make sure it makes sense and achieves its original intent. Moreover, the mechanics of the book are checked to make sure that the general level of writing is acceptable, that all footnotes are in order, that all necessary permissions to reproduce material from other sources have been obtained, and that all artwork is present. Eventually both author and editors will produce a manuscript that is mutually satisfactory.

While all of this editing is going on, other decisions are being made about scheduling, designing the interior "look" of the book, and the cover design. When everything is in order, the production phase—consisting of typesetting, printing, and binding—begins. **Photocomposition** involves taking pictures of pages of print. The film is developed and used to make the forms for offset printing (see Chapter 5). The most recent form of typesetting involves computers and is generally known as electronic publishing. In this system, the author uses a computer with a word processing program and writes the book on floppy disks instead of paper. Using a modem, a device which permits computers to exchange information over phone lines, the manuscript is transmitted electronically to the publisher, where it is edited on another computer. When the editorial process is completed, the publisher can then typeset the manuscript and make up the pages using other computerized equipment. For example, one system contains a graphics scanner (a device that converts photos and line art to digital information), a preview screen that displays page layout, and a laser typesetter. If for some reason the author prefers to produce the traditional paper manuscript instead of an electronic one, optical character readers exist that "read" typed pages electronically and input the material into the publisher's computer.

Once the text has been typeset, the printing process begins. Most books are produced using the photo-offset method since it is usually faster and less expensive. The images to be printed are lightly etched in the surface of a metal plate and ink adheres to these areas. These images are then transferred (or offset) onto another drum covered with a rubber blanket. This rubber-covered drum rolls against and prints onto the paper.

After the sheets of the book are printed, they are fed through a series of machines that fold them into the proper order and trim them to the correct size. The actual binding of the book can be done in a number of ways. The traditional method uses a special sewing machine to thread all of the pages together. This method is still used in some large reference or art books that are expected to receive heavy use. A more common process is "perfect" binding. In this technique, the pages are held tightly in place while a special knife shaves away part of their back edges. Next, a special glue is applied and the cover is wrapped around them and everything is joined together. (You can check the book that you're now reading for an example of perfect binding.) The finished books are then sent to the warehouse to await distribution.

● ● ● ●

ECONOMICS

Despite a weakened economy, the overall book industry enjoys economic health. More than $16.8 billion worth of books were sold in 1992, up 20 percent from 1989, making it the best year in the book business since 1990. Why are books doing so well? First, the population is getting older; the fastest growing age group is thirty-five to forty-nine years old—the age when people buy the most books. Second, people have disposable income to spend on books. Finally, federal and local governments continue to make education a funding priority. Per-pupil expenditures at the elementary and high school levels have increased and are expected to grow in the future, enhancing the market for texts, workbooks, and standardized tests.

At the consumer level, it's obvious that books have gotten more expensive. The average price of a hardcover book in 1992 was $33.38 and the average price of a paperback was up to $5.10. In fact, many paperbacks were selling for $6.95 and some publishers were talking about breaking the $7 mark in the near future.

A publisher has two main sources of income: (1) the money that comes from book sales and (2) money from other sources such as subsidiary rights (money from book clubs, foreign rights, paperback rights, and reprint permissions). Of these two, the income from book sales is the most important. It should be noted, however, that the publisher does not get all the money from the sale of a book. The list price is discounted for wholesalers and booksellers. These discounts might amount to 40 percent for many books.

The costs a publisher incurs are many. First, there is the cost of manufacturing the book itself. This includes the cost of printing, typesetting, and royalties paid to the author. These costs are variable and are tied to the number of books printed. For example, paper costs would be more substantial on a book with a press run of 20,000 than on one with a run of 2,000. There are also operating expenses, including editorial, production, marketing, and general administration expenses. Table 7-2 shows a hypothetical operating statement for an adult trade hardcover book published by a typical publishing company. It is assumed that the book has a list price of $20 (all numbers are rounded off for convenience) and 10,000 copies were printed. After a year, 2000 copies were unsold and were returned to the publisher for a credit. This means that

TABLE 7-2 Profit/Loss Statement of Trade Hardcover with $20 List Price

Press run	10,000 copies		
Returned	2,000 copies		
Gross sales	8,000 copies @ $12	=	$96,000
Returns and allowances		=	19,000
Net sales		=	77,000
Cost of sales			
Manufacturing		=	27,700
Royalties		=	17,700
Total cost of sales		=	45,400
Margin of net sales over cost of sales		=	31,600
Other income		=	6,900
Operating expense			
Editorial		=	4,500
Production		=	1,600
Marketing and fulfillment		=	18,500
Administration		=	10,000
Total operating expense		=	34,600
Net income		=	3,900

8000 copies were sold. Allowing a 40 percent discount from the list price leaves the publisher with revenues of about $12 per book. Multiplying 8000 times $12 gives us the gross sales amount: $96,000. From this is subtracted the costs of returns and allowances, leaving a balance of $77,000 in net sales revenue. Manufacturing costs and author royalties amounted to $45,400. This sum is subtracted from the net sales to find the gross margin on sales (the amount that net sales exceeded the cost of sales), in this case, $31,600. Table 7-2 also assumes that the publisher sold some subsidiary rights (to a book club or a paperback publisher) and received $6900 in return. So far,

Author tours are a common way to publicize and promote a book. Best-selling author Sidney Sheldon has probably been interviewed on hundreds of local talk shows such as the one pictured here. (Donna Zweig/ Gamma Liasion)

the total income from the book is $38,500. From this, however, we must deduct operating expenses of $34,600, leaving the book with a net profit of $3,900 for the year, about 5 percent of its net sales.

These figures, of course, would vary for other publishers and for other segments of the publishing industry. Profit margins typically varied from 2 to 20 percent from 1988 to 1991. Advances and acquisition rights are a couple of the big expenses in publishing. For example, Dell Publishing paid Ken Follett $12.3 million for his next two novels while romance novelist Danielle Steel reportedly received around $60 million for her next five books. Random House paid $3.5 million to actor Marlon Brando to acquire the rights to his autobiography.

Since most of the readers of this book are most closely associated with the economics of the college textbook market, Table 7-3 summarizes what makes up the cost of the average textbook from data provided by the College Stores Research and Educational Foundation.

The audio book has also made great gains in the last ten years. Books on cassette are now available not only in bookstores but have made their appearance in video stores, airport gift shops, truck stops, and supermarkets. California now has two audio-only book stores. As Americans spend more time commuting to work, the audio book should continue to grow.

On the content side, two types of books, light years apart in subject matter, were selling well in the early 1990s. The first is children's books, the fastest growing segment in the publishing industry. Total sales for 1990 were about $990 million, double that of 1985. At the other end of the spectrum was the boom in what's called "trash biography," in which the writer presents a rather unflattering portrait of the subject. Simon & Schuster advanced Kitty Kelley $3.5 million for a biography of Nancy Reagan that became one of the fastest selling books in U.S. publishing history.

• • • •

ISSUES

Despite gloomy predictions about the death of literacy and the dominance of television, book reading continues to be an important part of Americans' leisure time. Perhaps the most notable thing about the impact of today's book publishing industry is the economic symbiosis (see Chapter 1) between books and the rest of the media. The content of books often becomes the content of the other media. In turn, the exposure of this content on the other media helps to sell more books. To illustrate, consider the Hollywood–book connection. In 1990–1991, five films taken from books (*Silence of the Lambs*, *Not Without My Daughter*, *Sleeping with the Enemy*, *Awakenings*, and *Dances with Wolves*) enjoyed major box office success. When *Dances with Wolves* was originally published it sold 57,000 copies, an acceptable but not outstanding performance. One of those copies found its way to Kevin Costner who commissioned the novelist to write the screenplay. The movie, of course, was a big hit and the book was quickly put

TABLE 7-3 Breakdown of Costs for Average College Textbook	
SOURCE	**PERCENTAGE OF TOTAL COST**
Bookstore expenses/profit	25
Publisher profit	16
Production costs	15
Administrative expenses	12
Sales/Marketing	12
Editing	10
Author's Royalty	10

back into print. As of mid-1991, the book had gone through 34 printings and sold about 1.5 million copies. *Awakenings* first appeared in 1973 and got rave critical reviews but didn't sell all that much. After the movie was released, a trade paperback version of the book sold 150,000 copies and made it to the best-seller lists.

The book–TV tie-in has also been apparent. Many of the top nonfiction best sellers in 1990 had some connection with TV. Charles Kuralt's *A Life on the Road* capitalized on his reports for CBS News. Jeff Smith, the Frugal Gourmet, sold a half-million cookbook companions to his TV show. The award-winning PBS series *The Civil War* helped its similarly-named book companion sell more than 600,000 copies at a $50 price tag.

The book industry is frequently the catalyst for debates over significant issues. The trend toward "trash biography" mentioned above sparked a controversy over the proper role of unauthorized and exploitative biographies. Critics charged that writers of some of these books compromised normal journalistic standards in an attempt to be sensational and commercially successful. Some writers worried that these biographies would injure the credibility of other biographers working on more traditional subjects.

Finally, book publishers confronted another censorship issue when Simon & Schuster canceled at the last minute a novel by Bret Easton Ellis called *American*

Censorship or sensitivity? Parts of American Psycho *were so gruesome and hideous that its original publisher refused to print it. Vintage eventually picked it up. (Courtesy Vintage Contemporaries)*

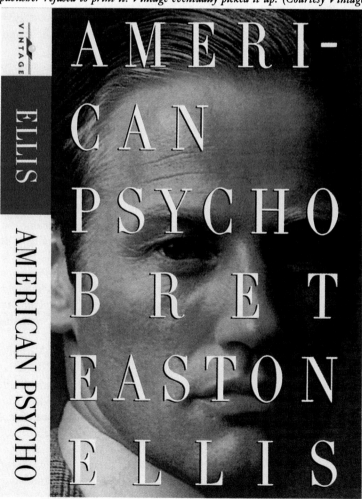

Psycho. The book was extraordinarily violent and contained several passages describing dreadful crimes against women. The publishing company was apparently afraid of the backlash its publication might cause. The book was subsequently picked up by Vintage, the trade paperback division of Random House, and published with only minor changes. Random House became the target of many outraged protesters, among them the National Organization for Women, who argued for a national boycott of Random House books. For his part, Ellis argued that the gruesome passages were only a small part of his book and necessary to make his point. *American Psycho* was just one of many violent media products in the early 1990s and its publication again raised the thorny issue of the social responsibility of a publisher and the free speech rights of authors.

● ● ● ●

CAREERS IN BOOK PUBLISHING

Book publishing is a small industry; there are only 70,000–75,000 jobs nationwide in the entire business. Consequently, there is a lot of competition for many of the jobs, particularly those on the editorial side. Moreover, since most of the large publishing houses are located on the East Coast, it may be necessary for many hopefuls to relocate.

There are two general areas to pursue in book publishing: editorial and business. For someone interested in editorial work, the best training consists of courses in English and composition with a strong emphasis in writing skills. Entry-level positions are competitive, and most newcomers typically join a publishing company as editorial assistants. There are numerous clerical tasks to be performed in publishing: answering authors' letters, reading manuscripts, writing reports about manuscripts, checking facts, proofreading, writing catalog copy, and so on. Editorial assistants do these and countless other tasks.

The next logical step up the career ladder is to become an assistant or associate editor. These individuals work with senior editors in several different areas: manuscript acquisition, copy editing, design and production, artwork, and so on. Eventually, this path leads to a position as an editor. After getting the necessary experience, editors are promoted to senior editors, managing editors, or executive editors, positions which carry a good deal of administrative responsibility.

On the business side there are several career paths open. Many people start as a sales representative and sell their company's books to the appropriate customers. Sales and marketing experience is so vital to the well-being of the industry that the path to top management usually begins in the sales department. At many companies, presidents and vice presidents are almost always former salespeople with extensive experience in marketing. Sales is a challenging profession and top salespeople are usually well rewarded.

Another potential career route that is generally not crowded with new applications is the subsidiary rights department. This job deals with selling the company's books to foreign publishers, translators, book clubs, and paperback publishers. The subsidiary rights department is an excellent place to learn about finances, contracts, and the commercial side of publishing. It can be a path to top management.

Finally, there are usually opportunities for newcomers in the advertising, promotion, and publicity areas of publishing. Copy for print and broadcast ads must be written, author tours must be planned, promotional material must be distributed, press releases written, and special events planned. All of these duties would be the responsibility of people working in this area. The usual career path is to find an entry-level position as an "assistant to" someone and gradually work your way up to the advertising, promotion, or publicity director for the company.

Before closing, it should be mentioned that it is not always necessary to work for a publishing company to find employment in this area. Many people work as freelance

After more than four decades of tight control, the lid has been removed from the publishing industry in Eastern Europe. The results have been both exciting and frustrating.

Under the old system, would-be authors in the Soviet Union, Hungary, Poland, and Czechoslovakia would work within a highly centralized and tightly supervised system. In the Soviet Union, for example, state-chartered publishing houses would submit proposals to the Ministry of Paper, Printing, and Publishing. If the proposals were accepted, each publisher got the necessary allotment of paper and ink. The price of the book was determined by length as was the author's royalty. Since they were being paid by the word, most Soviet authors had a difficult time being brief.

Once the book was in production, a publisher would print a catalog and send it to local bookstores. Potential readers would browse through the descriptions in the catalog and when they found a book of interest, they would fill out a postcard order form. These forms went back to the publishers who used them to determine how many books to print. Each book that was printed was presold—no wasted paper or ink. The printed books went to a centralized distribution agency that delivered the appropriate number to bookstores. In theory, this was a very efficient system. It didn't work in practice because many people found that the catalog description of the book didn't match the final product and declined to buy it. Black market booksellers bought many popular titles before they ever got to the shelves. Books by politically powerful or well-connected authors were given inflated printing figures so as not to offend. Popular titles were hard to find and unsold volumes cluttered the shelves.

Today, under the relaxed rules of a new regime, things are different in Eastern Europe. Anybody who wants to publish can do so as long as they can get paper and ink, which can be a relatively difficult task. Books from the West are no longer banned and can be freely imported. Interestingly, the two book topics that have been most popular under the more permissive regulations are the two that were most repressed under the old regime: sex and politics. In Hungary, books detailing the scandals hidden during the rule of party boss Janos Kadar sold out quickly. At the same time, *Emmanuelle*, a book tie-in with the soft core porn film of the same name, was also selling briskly. In Poland, political books topped the best-seller lists along with the porn classic *Fanny Hill*.

Competing in a free market has also brought problems. Book publishers were without a clue when it came to pricing a volume. Similarly, publishers had little idea about how many copies of a book they should print. Overprinting and underselling were common. Paper became a problem. Paper mills in Russia could make more money by selling paper to Western countries than they could selling it at home or to Eastern European countries. The centralized distribution system that creaked along under a communist regime could not handle the increase in books and publishers resulting from a freer press system. There wasn't enough money to create additional distribution channels. All of these things mean that Eastern European publishing is in a state of change. Western publishers are being asked to visit and offer advice; some governments are encouraging Western companies to invest. Rupert Murdoch's News Corporation has already bought a publishing company in Hungary.

It may take a while for the problems to sort themselves out and there may be some difficulties along the way, but the book publishing industry in Eastern Europe will probably never be the same.

editors, designers, proofreaders, indexers, artists, and photographers. These typically are people who have had some experience and have branched out on their own.

• • • •

SUGGESTIONS FOR FURTHER READING

The following books contain more information about concepts and topics discussed in this chapter.

BALKING, RICHARD, *A Writer's Guide to Book Publishing*, New York: Hawthorn/Dutton Books, 1981.

The Book Publishing Annual, 1986, New York: R. R. Bowker, 1985.

The Business of Publishing, New York: R. R. Bowker, 1976.

DAVIS, KENNETH, *Two-Bit Culture*, Boston: Houghton Mifflin, 1985.

DESSAUER, JOHN, *Book Publishing: What It Is, What It Does*, New York: R. R. Bowker, 1981.

————, *Book Industry Trends, 1987*, New York: Book Industry Study Group, 1987.

GEISER, ELIZABETH, ed., *The Business of Book Publishing*, London: Westview Press, 1985.

SHATZKIN, LEONARD, *In Cold Type*, Boston: Houghton Mifflin, 1982.

Also see *Publishers Weekly*, the leading trade magazine of the industry.

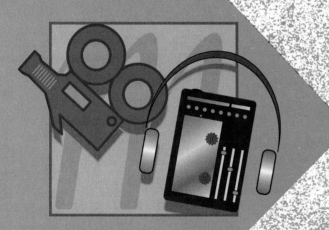

THE ELECTRONIC MEDIA

HISTORY OF RADIO AND RECORDING

How would you like to go home after class one day and listen to the latest CD by REM or U2 on your quadraphonic zonophone? Or maybe you'd rather drop a quarter through the slot in the top of your radio and hear an hour's worth of music brought to you under the watchful eye of the United States Navy? Sound strange? These are just some of the things that might have happened if the recording and radio industries had evolved a bit differently.

A basic knowledge of mass communication is incomplete without examining how media develop and change. Accordingly, this chapter will present a brief history of the sound media industries—recording and radio—and a summary of important content trends. Most discussions of media history generally treat radio and television together and examine sound recording separately (if at all). The current operations of the radio and sound-recording industries are so closely connected, however, that they should be considered together. Further, both media went through similar stages in development: big-business wheelings and dealings, legal fights over patents, technical problems, and formidable competition. Besides, when they both started, no one had a clear idea of what good they were.

EARLY YEARS OF THE SOUND-RECORDING AND RADIO INDUSTRIES

In the last half of the nineteenth century, inventors on both sides of the Atlantic were interested in sound; some tried to capture it, while others tried to make it more elusive by sending it across space without wires. In America, Thomas Edison recorded "Mary Had a Little Lamb," using a hand-cranked device with a cylinder wrapped in tinfoil that preserved the sound. This invention perplexed Edison. He wasn't sure what commercial value his 1877 prototype of the **phonograph** possessed. For many years this "talking machine" was exhibited at lecture halls, vaudeville houses, and exhibition tents as a curiosity. Finally, Edison decided his new invention might best be suited to the business world where it would aid dictation. At that time, the idea of the phonograph as home entertainment was too wild to imagine.

Edison's phonograph faced new competition when Chinchester Bell and Charles Tainter patented a device called the **graphophone**, a machine in which Edison's tinfoil was replaced by a wax cylinder. In 1887, more competition emerged when yet another American, Emile Berliner, patented a system that used a disc instead of a cylinder. He called his new invention a **gramophone**.

Meanwhile, across the ocean, others were caught up in more ethereal pursuits. A Scottish mathematician and physicist, James Clerk Maxwell, published a paper in 1873 that suggested that an electromagnetic signal could be sent through space without using wires. In 1887, a German physicist, Heinrich Hertz, verified the correctness of

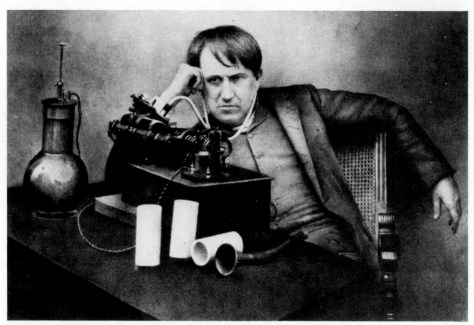

The phonograph is just one of Thomas Edison's many inventions. His 1877 model was hand-cranked, and the sound waves were preserved as scratches in tinfoil. (The Bettmann Archive)

Maxwell's theories in a series of experiments in which Hertz actually sent and detected radio waves. Since Hertz was a theoretical physicist, the practical applications of radio held little interest for him. In fact, he would later argue that radio waves could not be used for communication. Nonetheless, as a tribute to his accomplishment, the basic unit of frequency, the **hertz** (abbreviated **Hz**), is named for him. An Italian, Guglielmo Marconi, refined and improved on Hertz's efforts. In 1896, he could send a wireless signal over a two-mile distance ("wireless" was radio's early name). A businessman as well as inventor, Marconi saw that wireless had promising commercial aspects in maritime communication (ship-to-shore and ship-to-ship messages). At age twenty-three he went to England and established the Marconi Wireless Telegraph and Signal Company, later shortened to British Marconi. By World War I, this company and its U.S. subsidiary, American Marconi, had become a powerful force in maritime and transatlantic communication.

Marconi was sending Morse code—dots and dashes—a system that required special training in order to understand the message. Two Americans, Reginald Fessenden and Lee De Forest, provided the breakthroughs that opened up radio for the general public. Fessenden, building on the work of Nikola Tesla and using a high-speed generator he developed with the help of General Electric, made what might be considered the world's first broadcast in 1906, on Christmas Eve. His audience consisted primarily of ships with wireless receiving sets in New York Harbor. Allegedly, when the shipboard operators heard Fessenden's broadcast of phonograph music, violin solos, and Bible readings, they were so awestruck that many thought they were hearing the voices of angels. Lee De Forest invented the vacuum tube, which made it much easier to receive voice and music transmissions. A lover of classical music, De Forest broadcast a classical phonograph concert from the Eiffel Tower in 1908. Two years later, he would broadcast the voice of Caruso at the New York Metropolitan Opera.

One reason that radio did not progress faster during the first fifteen years of the new decade had to do with the problem of conflicting patents. These early disputes were long and expensive and contributed to the commercial failures of both De Forest and Fessenden. When World War I broke out, the U.S. Navy saw the military advantages of radio and arranged a moratorium on patent suits. In effect, the Navy was able to pull together all available technical skills and knowledge. This led to significant improvements in radio by the end of the war. It also meant that the Navy would be a powerful force in determining radio's future.

By 1890, three machines that recorded and played back sound were on the market: the phonograph, the graphophone, and the gramophone. At about this time, big business entered the picture as Jesse Lippincott, who had made a fortune in the glass-tumbler business, moved from glass to wax and purchased the business rights to both the phonograph and graphophone, thus ending a bitter patent fight between the respective inventors. Lippincott had dreams of controlling the office-dictating market, but stenographers rebelled against the new device and the talking-machine business fell upon hard times. Strangely enough, relief appeared quickly and financial solvency returned—a nickel at a time.

One of Lippincott's local managers hit upon the idea of putting coin-operated phonographs in the many penny arcades and amusement centers that were springing up all over America. For a nickel you could listen through a pair of stethoscopelike earphones to a cylinder whose two-minute recording had a technical quality that could only be described as awful. Still, these **nickelodeons** were immensely popular, and the demand for "entertainment" cylinders grew. Companies quickly scrambled for a share in the new recording production business.

The two decades spanning the turn of the century were a time of intense business rivalry in the recording industry as competitors tried desperately to drive each other under. While the two major companies, the Columbia Phonograph Company and Edison's North American Phonograph Company, fought one another, Berliner's United States Gramophone Company perfected the process of recording on flat discs. These discs had several advantages over the older cylinder in that they had better sound qualities, could not be illegally copied as easily as the cylinder, and were easier to store. Ultimately, Columbia recognized the superiority of the disc and attempted to break into the market by selling the zonophone, its own version of the disc player. As for Berliner, along with machinist Eldridge Johnson, he formed the Victor Talking Machine Company, which had as its trademark the picture of a dog peering into the bell of a gramophone ("His Master's Voice"). Thanks to aggressive marketing, this new company was highly successful and in 1906 introduced the Victrola, the first disc player designed to look like a piece of furniture. By 1912, the supremacy of the disc over the cylinder was established. Even Edison's company, champion of the cylinder for forty years, joined the trend and began marketing discs.

Popular Music Content: Sentiment and Innovation

The nickelodeon established popular records when recording companies discovered that certain artists attracted more nickels than others. Two superstars of this turn-of-the-century era were John Philip Sousa (and the Marine Band) and George H. Diamond (whose big hit was "Have One on the Landlord on Me"). Another popular musical form that developed in the 1890s was ragtime—a musical form characterized by a lively, syncopated rhythm. One of the most distinguished ragtime artists was Scott Joplin, a classically trained black pianist whose "Maple Leaf Rag" (1899) earned him the title of "King of Ragtime."

In general, the songs that were popular during the 1890s were steeped in sentiment. A few representative titles from this period are "Gold Will Buy Most Anything but a True Girl's Heart," "A Bird in a Gilded Cage," "Say *Au Revoir* but Not Goodbye," and "The Fatal Wedding." By the turn of the century sentimentality was still present, but many popular songs were in a lighter vein. On the Hit Parade from 1900 to 1915 were "Fido Is a Hot Dog Now," "Meet Me in St. Louis, Louis," and

A "symphony" orchestra makes a recording before the days of electrical recording. Note how the musicians are crowded close to the large horn and the strange-looking devices that were used to amplify the tones of certain instruments for recording. (Clark Collection of Radioana-Smithsonian Institution Archive Center)

several songs that reflected the continuing popularity of ragtime. A soprano with the interesting name of Alma Gluck became the first recording artist to sell a million records when her old standard "Carry Me Back to Ole Virginny" topped that mark in 1918.

On the eve of World War I, record players were commonplace throughout America. A dance craze in 1913 sent profits soaring, a trend that was to continue throughout the war. Twenty-seven million records were manufactured in 1914; 107 million were produced in 1919 following the end of the war. The record industry had entered a boom period.

The boom continued when the years after the First World War ushered in the Jazz Age, a period named after the spirited, popular music of the Roaring Twenties. **Jazz**, which emerged from the roots of the black experience in America, was spontaneous, individualistic, and sensual. Because of its disdain for convention, jazz was widely denounced as degenerate during its early years (about thirty years later, another spontaneous and sensual musical innovation, rock and roll, would also be denounced). However, the work of great jazz musicians like Louis Armstrong, "Jelly Roll" Morton, and Bix Beiderbecke eventually was recognized all over the world.

Ironically, another source of content for the recording industry during the 1920s came from a new competitor—sound movies. Movie musicals were proving to be very successful, and recording studios rushed to release versions of songs featured in these films. Jeanette MacDonald, Maurice Chevalier, and Rudy Vallee were all performers who signed contracts with RCA Victor during this time.

The good times, however, didn't last. In the beginning, no one in the record industry regarded radio as a serious threat. Record company executives were sure that the static-filled, raucous noise emanating from a radio would never compete with the quality of their recordings. They were wrong.

Recording Pioneer Emile Berliner

The hundredth anniversary of phonograph recording on a flat disc was reached in 1988. This technology was created by Emile Berliner, an immigrant from Germany, who had supported himself working as a stock clerk in a clothing store while investigating on his own the intriguing world of sound amplification and recording. Berliner quickly noted that the cylinders used by Edison had too many disadvantages to be practical. He perfected a way to encode the sound on a flat disc that could be easily duplicated by using a master mold, much like pressing waffles in a waffle iron.

His invention was slow to catch on in the United States, thanks to competition from Edison, but it was a success in Europe. Eventually, Berliner introduced to the American market the phonautograph, which he renamed the gramophone. This eventually replaced the cylinder.

In one area, Berliner clearly saw the future. He predicted that prominent singers and performers would collect royalties from the sale of his discs. He was wrong on another count, however. He thought that musicians and artists who were unable to appear at a concert would simply send a record to be played on stage instead.

Berliner also developed the prototype of the modern microphone and both his inventions, the disc and the microphone, came together when electronic recording was perfected during the 1920s. Even the modern CD owes him a debt. Like his original invention, the CD stores information in a spiral on a flat rotating surface.

THE EVOLUTION OF RADIO AS A MASS MEDIUM

It began modestly enough. A quarter-pound of No. 24 double cotton-covered wire wrapped around an empty Quaker Oats carton, a piece of tinfoil, a lump of galena, a thin piece of wire called a cat's whisker, a pair of headphones and you were in business. You had built a radio. In the years following World War I, all across the country, in attics, garages, on front porches, people were hunched over primitive crystal sets, engaged in the new national craze—listening to radio.

For many people radio seemed to be no more than a toy, a passing fad for hobbyists and those who tinkered with electronics. Early radio broadcasting was crude, amateurish, and thoroughly unpredictable. Occasionally, no one would show up at the local station to perform, and the station would not go on the air. Early microphones overheated, so performers had to be careful not to burn their lips. You could hear far better music on the Victrola. The telephone was a far better way of communicating. Many thought that radio would never amount to much. However, several remarkable events were to change their minds.

Big Business Steps In

While radio development before World War I had been characterized by individual inventions, during the postwar years it would be characterized by corporate maneuvers. Shortly after the war, the Marconi Company started negotiations to acquire rights to Fessenden's generator in an attempt to establish a monopoly in U.S.–European radio communication. The United States, with the lessons of the war still fresh, did not want to give a foreign-owned company access to that much power. Moreover, there were many in the United States who did not want the Navy to maintain the amount of control over radio's development that it had amassed during the war. After much negotiation and bargaining, the Marconi Company agreed to sell its American interests to General Electric. In turn, GE set up a new company, the Radio Corporation of America (RCA), to receive the Marconi assets. Stock in RCA would be held by American Telegraph and Telephone (AT&T), Westinghouse, and GE. All of this happened in 1919, before any of these companies had a clear idea as to what radio's future role would be, and none of them seriously considered broadcasting to the general public as a viable moneymaking activity. Nonetheless, by 1920 it was obvious that radio's future lay in the hands of American private enterprise.

Radio Reaches a Mass Audience

The second element necessary for radio's emergence as a mass medium started in Frank Conrad's garage. Up to this point, radio was looked upon as a competitor to the telephone and telegraph industries. The fact that it was public, that everybody could receive it with the proper equipment, was looked upon as a drawback. No one could quite understand why anybody would want to send messages to a large group of anonymous individuals. Enter Frank Conrad, Horne's Department Store in Pittsburgh, and Westinghouse. Conrad was a Westinghouse engineer who tinkered with radio as a hobby. He had built a radio transmitter in his garage and spent his weekends playing records, reporting sports scores, and even showcasing the musical abilities of his sons in front of the microphone. Other amateurs began to send Conrad postcards requesting certain musical selections. In a short time, he had developed a small but dedicated audience. Horne's Department Store saw an opportunity: The store took out a newspaper ad that highlighted Conrad's broadcasting activities and offered their customers a $10 ready-built wireless set that could be used to listen to the Conrad broadcasts. Westinghouse saw an even bigger opportunity. The company proposed to build a station that would broadcast programs on a more or less regular basis and would, the company hoped, encourage a large audience to listen. Westinghouse would manufacture the radio sets and, in turn, would receive "free" advertising because of its identification with the station. The idea worked. KDKA went on the air November 20, 1920, broadcasting with 100 watts from a shack atop a six-story building. (It is still on the air as of this day, making it the oldest station.)

After a slow start, sales of radio sets reached the half-million mark in 1924. The next year roughly 2 million were sold. Other companies recognized a good thing when they saw it. RCA started broadcasting in 1921; General Electric in 1922. Westinghouse

Broadcasting's Young Pioneers

One of the striking facts about broadcasting is that it was invented and developed by young people. Marconi was only twenty-three when he developed his wireless transmitter. William Paley became president of CBS at the age of twenty-seven. David Sarnoff was twenty-eight when he became chief operating officer of RCA. Heinrich Hertz was thirty when he did his most significant work with radio waves. The alternator was invented by Ernst Alexanderson at age thirty-one. Reginald Fessenden made his first radiophone broadcasts when he was thirty-four. Lee De Forest was the same age when he invented his audion. Frank Conrad was the grand old man of the group; he was forty-two when he started his experimental radio station. Of course, the youngest inventor of them all was Philo Farnsworth, who, at the tender age of sixteen, diagramed an invention called "television."

opened additional stations in Massachusetts, New Jersey, and Illinois. AT&T opened a station in 1922. Radio was on its way. By discovering that an audience existed for broadcast programs *intended* for the general public, radio had found the role it was to play for the foreseeable future.

The Development of Improved Receivers

The third major factor in radio's evolution as a mass medium was due, in part, to Gimbel's Department Store. If you were walking down New York's 33rd Street in May of 1925, you couldn't help but notice. There, in Gimbel's window, was the latest model vacuum tube radio set, which gave far better reception than any of the old crystal sets. For only $15 down, $99 in all (a rather significant amount in 1925), you could buy the new Freed-Eisemann Neutrodyne five-tube receiver with one Prest-O-Lite battery, two 45-volt B batteries, a phone plug, an antenna, and your choice of loudspeakers. Gimbel's entire fifth floor was given over to the sale, and 240 clerks were waiting to serve you. (They sold 5300 receivers the first day.)

Before radio could become a true mass medium, an affordable, easy-to-use, relatively efficient receiving set had to be mass marketed. Westinghouse, Atwater Kent, and Crosley led the way in manufacturing, and Gimbel's and other large department stores helped retail the sets. But radio was still not ready for the living room. By and large, in 1925 receivers were cumbersome affairs. You needed an assortment of bulky batteries (which had an irritating tendency to leak acid all over the floor), and ugly wires led from the set to the condensers and ground (usually a water pipe). Tuning the early sets required a steady hand, patience, and a knowledge of electronics. You couldn't tune the set and sit back and listen since the two batteries needed constant tuning as they supplied current to the receiver's tubes.

Many of the inconveniences associated with the early receivers had been resolved by 1926. Radios that ran on ordinary house current were being marketed in more and more retail stores. Although the new radios were initially expensive (one set sold for $250), they were quickly bought up. Between 1925 and 1930, 17 million radio sets were sold at an average cost of about $80 per set. Furthermore, this later version was

A young boy listens to an early version of the radio. (National Archives)

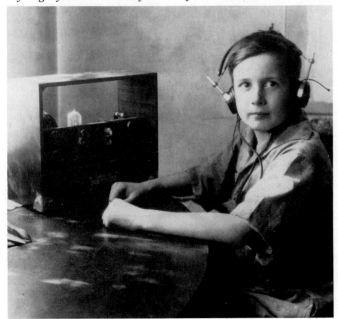

no longer just a curious collection of electronic parts but was designed as a fashionable piece of furniture. Made of mahogany and equipped with built-in speakers, large cathedral-style sets took their place next to the sofa and coffee table. Some of the deluxe models had push-button tuning and a built-in phonograph and even picked up police calls. Families could now gather around the radio set, and listening changed from a solitary to a group activity. The refinement of the radio receiver during the 1920s eased radio's access to the mass audience.

Radio Goes Commercial

One of the curious things about early radio broadcasting was that very little of it was done by broadcasters. The early stations were owned by a polyglot of organizations. WLS in Chicago was owned by Sears, Roebuck (*World's Largest Store*); WGN by the Chicago Tribune (*World's Greatest Newspaper*); WSM in Nashville by the National Life Insurance Company (*We Shelter Millions*); and WHB in Kansas City by the Sweeney Automotive and Electrical School. People went into broadcasting for a variety of reasons. Set manufacturers wanted a service to sell their radios; department stores liked the exposure; universities were convinced that radio would aid education. Some people started radio stations because it was fun. Others started broadcasting for no particular reason at all.

In the beginning money wasn't much of a problem. In 1925, it cost only $3000 to get a station on the air and, once broadcasting, operating expenses weren't high, probably around $2000 per year. It didn't last. Tighter technical standards meant that an engineer was needed; talent started demanding payment; better equipment cost money. The bigger stations felt the squeeze first. In 1927, one large station paid about $350,000 to stay on the air. Even a small station might be faced with annual operating

Early radio sets first appeared in the home but in the 1930s they appeared in cars. The earphone arrangement was replaced by a loudspeaker when it was discovered that drivers using earphones couldn't hear train whistles, sirens, the horns of other cars, and other sounds conducive to safe driving. (Culver Pictures)

costs of about $25,000. Faced with this inflation, stations looked for a method to collect revenue.

Nobody quite knew how to do it. Some felt that listeners should send in voluntary contributions. One station invented an "Invisible Theater" and asked for contributions according to an imaginary floor plan. Another scheme proposed a coin box on top of the receiver in which listeners would deposit quarters; yet another suggested a tax on tubes in the receiver. These ideas, which might have worked, would have taken years to implement. What was needed was a plan that would bring money flowing in immediately. It was the phone company that hit upon the solution.

In the 1920s, AT&T suffered from tunnel vision. It couldn't convince itself that radio was different from the telephone. Consequently, WEAF (AT&T's showcase station in New York) started to broadcast "toll" programs. To the phone company, the arrangement was obvious. If you made a long-distance call, you paid a special toll. Broadcasting was a special instance of making a long-distance call simultaneously to

Radio Commercials: From Queensboro Realty to Things that Glowed, Whistled, Decoded, and Even Looked Around Corners

Early radio commercials were polite and unobtrusive. It was almost as though the companies were embarrassed to invade the privacy of the home with their messages. Commercials were limited to merely mentioning the name of the product or the sponsor. Direct selling or quoting prices over the air was forbidden. Some people argued for a tone to precede the commercial so as to warn listeners of what was to come. There was even a good deal of discussion about the propriety of broadcasting commercials for a product so personal as toothpaste. These attitudes didn't last long.

At first, product names were incorporated into program names as indirect advertising became more accepted. Early listeners were treated to programs such as *The Eveready Battery Hour*, *The Gold Dust Twins*, and the *Balkite Hour*. Other advertisers named performers after their products: the A & P Gypsies, the Clicquot Club Eskimos. From this it was only a short step to direct advertising over radio, and in 1928 Henry Field of KFNF in Shenandoah, Iowa, became one of radio's pioneer salesmen when he invited listeners to buy seeds, bacon, auto tires, fresh hams, prunes, paint, coffee, shoes, and pig meal from his general store. By 1930, the Depression had made most other stations accept direct advertising, and the sixty-second spot announcement became the most widely accepted format. Radio commercials became more ambitious and more elaborate. Dramatic situations were used to sell soap products. Wheaties, Pepsi-Cola, and Barbasol developed the singing commercial. But perhaps the form of advertising that will be best remembered from radio is that of the premium. All it took was a box top and maybe a dime and you could be the proud owner of a Little Orphan Annie Ovaltine Shake-Up Mug, a Tom Mix periscope ring to check around corners, a Captain Midnight Code-o-Graph, a Green Hornet Sign Ring, or a Lone Ranger Special Glow-in-the-Dark Belt. Most premiums were aimed at children, but the adults were not left out. The loyal listeners of *Clara, Lu, 'n' Em* could send in a box top from Super Suds Soap along with a dime and in return they would be sent a package of "Hollywood Flower Garden" seeds. In ten days half a million seed packages were sold. Nonetheless, children were the prime targets for these offers. And no wonder. What kid wouldn't want a Buck Rogers Alien Detector Magic Ring? If you put this ring in the palm of an earthling, it would glow in the dark. If, however, you gave the ring to a Venusian and led him into a darkened room, the ring was guaranteed not to glow. It has not been determined how many Venusians were uncovered by this method.

a large number of people. If you had the money, WEAF had the equipment. The most logical candidates for this new form of conference call were companies that had things to sell. Thus in 1922, the Queensboro Realty Company paid $300 for five radio "talks" that praised the benefits of living in the country. (The company also had country lots they could sell you.) Other companies quickly realized the advertising potential of this system and followed suit. Other stations began to copy WEAF's arrangement, and the problem of financing radio was solved—broadcasting would be supported by advertising.

The Emergence of Networks

The fifth element in radio's evolution also came about because of money. If a station in Philadelphia and a station in New York each had to produce a program to fill one hour's time, each station would wind up paying a bill. It would be cheaper for both to share the costs of a single program and, through a system of interconnection, to broadcast the same show on both stations. This arrangement of interconnecting stations became known as a **network**. Additionally, if enough stations were connected, an advertiser could deal with only one organization and still buy time on the network, thus reaching large audiences by making a single phone call. The economic benefits of a network were apparent to the early broadcasting companies.

The first network was NBC, a wholly owned subsidiary of RCA, set up in 1926. In actuality, NBC instituted two networks. One was formed from the stations that were originally owned by RCA. The second was formed when RCA purchased AT&T's stations and other broadcast assets. (The phone company had decided to end its direct involvement in the broadcasting business. It maintained an indirect involvement by leasing its lines to the networks for station interconnection.) In order to avoid confusion, the two NBC networks were called the Red and the Blue Network.

Shortly after the birth of NBC, a second network, United Independent Broadcasters (UIB), was established. In financial trouble from the start, UIB eventually merged with the Columbia Phonograph Record Company in 1927 to form the Columbia Phonograph Broadcasting System. Eventually, control of this new network, which was subsequently renamed the Columbia Broadcasting System (CBS), was acquired by the Paley family. Among other things, the Paley family owned the Congress Cigar Company, which had been among the first advertisers to sign on with UIB. Sensing the potential of radio, William S. Paley at the age of twenty-seven became the new president of CBS, thus beginning an affiliation that would extend into the 1980s.

In 1927, NBC listed 28 stations as affiliates, while CBS reported 13. Ten years later in 1937, NBC affiliates had grown to 111, while CBS would number 105. National advertising dollars flowed into these young operations. By 1930, advertisers were spending approximately $27 million on network advertising. In this same year, NBC showed a pretax profit of $2.1 million, while CBS reported income of a little less than one million. It was obvious that the network-affiliate arrangement would persist for some time to come.

Government Support and Regulation

The sixth and last element necessary to ensure radio's growth as a mass medium was provided by the federal government. An early attempt at regulation came in 1912 when Congress passed the Radio Act, which empowered the Secretary of Commerce to issue licenses and to specify frequencies of use. Like everyone else, Congress in 1912 did not conceive of radio as a broadcasting medium, and the Radio Act was written with the idea that radio would prove most useful in maritime communications. During the early 1920s, when more and more stations went on the air, it became obvious that the early legislation would not do the job. Interference became a tremendous problem. Stations switched frequency, changed power, and ignored the operation times specified in their licenses. The situation was aggravated when a 1926 court decision effectively stripped the Secretary of Commerce of the little regulatory power he had. Obviously, a new set of regulations was needed to keep the new medium from drowning in a sea of interference and static.

Congress finally acted to resolve this situation by passing the **Radio Act of 1927**. This act set up the Federal Radio Commission (FRC), a regulatory body that would issue licenses and try to clean up the chaos that existed. Eventually, the FRC made some headway. The commission defined the AM broadcast band, standardized channel designations, abolished portable stations, and moved to minimize interference. By 1929 the situation had improved, and the new radio medium was prevented from suffocating in its own growth.

Early Radio Content: Live Music, Variety, and Drama

Music was the main ingredient of the earliest radio programs, and despite the poor reception on the early 1920s–style receiving set, musical programs were quite popular. As early as 1921, remote broadcasts from hotel dining rooms featuring famous bands were common. All in all, before the networks began to dominate broadcast programs, approximately 70 percent of a local station's programs consisted of musical selections. Almost all of this music was performed live. Records were not thought proper content for radio in the 1920s.

Early radio was curiously formal. Announcers had to dress in tuxedos (even though the audience couldn't see them), and studios were decorated with sofas and potted palms. Odder still, announcers didn't give their own names over the air; they used code names instead. (Evidently, early station managers were afraid that announcers would develop personal followings, ask for more money, and generally become hard to handle.)

Radio receivers in the 1930s no longer required a knowledge of electronics to operate. A family could simply sit back and listen. (Brown Brothers)

By 1929, network broadcasting accounted for about fifty-one hours per week of evening programming. Most of this was music (a good portion classical), but variety and dramatic programs were also making their debut. Foremost among the variety programs was a throwback to the days of vaudeville—the comedy variety programs. Eddie Cantor, George Burns and Gracie Allen, Jack Benny, Ed Wynn, and Fred Allen were all early pioneers of this format. In 1928, two comedians working in blackface, Charles Correll and Freeman Gosden, began broadcasting a program for NBC called *Amos 'n' Andy*. By its second season, the show was listened to by half of the people who owned radios. It was a top-rated program for the next five years and literally became a national habit.

● ● ● ●

THE IMPACT OF RADIO ON THE RECORD INDUSTRY

As radio's fortunes were on the rise, the recording industry's were waning. By the end of 1924, the combined sales of players and records had dropped 50 percent from those of the previous year. In the midst of this economic trouble, the recording companies quietly introduced electronic recording, using technology borrowed from their bitter rival, radio. The sound quality of records improved tremendously. But despite this improvement, radio continued to be thought of as the medium for "live" music while records were dismissed as the medium of "canned" music.

In 1926, the record industry joined the radio bandwagon and began to market radio–phonograph combinations, an obvious testament to the belief that the two media would coexist. This attitude was also prevalent at the corporate level. In 1927, rumors were flying that the Victor Company would soon merge with RCA. Frightened by this, Columbia, Victor's biggest rival, tried to get a head start by merging with the new (and financially troubled) radio network, United Independent Broadcasters. All too soon, however, the record company became disillusioned and dissolved the deal. The radio network retained Columbia's name and became CBS. Ironically, in 1938, when CBS was in much better financial shape, it would "reacquire" the phonograph company. The much discussed RCA and Victor merger came about in 1929, with the new company dominated by the radio operation.

Radio and Records

Radio's emergence in the 1920s affected not only the record industry. It also had an impact on popular music itself. Contemplate these titles of popular songs from the 1920s:

- "I Wish There Was a Wireless to Heaven" (Then Mama Would Not Seem So Far Away).

- "Mister Radio Man" (Tell My Mammy to Come Back Home).

- "Tune Your Radio to L-O-V-E."

- "Love Her by Radio."

- "Nettie Is the Nitwit of the Networks."

- "Radio Lady of Mine."

- "Static Strut" (there was a popular dance that went along with this one).

The Great Depression

The Great Depression of the 1930s dealt an economic blow to both radio and sound recording. In the case of radio, the industry was merely stunned; for sound recording, it was nearly a knockout punch.

By most standards, radio was not hit as hard as other industries. For example, the total dollar amount spent on radio advertising grew from 40.5 million in 1930 to 112.6 million in 1935. In fact, the broadcasting economic climate was so favorable that a fourth network (or a third if you count NBC's two nets together) was formed in 1934. The Mutual Broadcasting System (MBS) grew from 4 stations in its initial year to 160 stations in 1940. In addition, the radio audience was expanding. About 12 million homes had radios in 1930, about 46 percent of the U.S. total. By 1940, radio sets were in 81 percent of American homes and had been installed in an additional 7 million cars. New research firms sprang up to tap the needs of radio's growing audience, and broadcasters began to pay attention to the ratings. Although profits were not as high as they might have been in better economic times, the radio industry was able to weather the Depression with relatively little hardship.

The recording industry did not fare nearly as well. Thomas Edison's record manufacturing company went out of business in 1930. Record sales dropped from $46 million in 1930 to $5.5 million in 1933, and several smaller labels also folded. The entire industry was reeling.

In the midst of all this gloom the recording industry was saved once again by the nickel. Coin-operated record players, called juke boxes (the origin of this term is obscure), began popping up in the thousands of bars and cocktail lounges that mushroomed after the repeal of Prohibition in 1933. These juke boxes were immensely popular and quickly spread to diners, drugstores, and restaurants. Starting in 1934, total record sales began to inch upward; by 1939, sales had increased by more than 500 percent.

While records were enjoying a renaissance, radio was experiencing some growing pains. The first problem had to do with the newspapers. Faced with growing radio competition for advertising dollars, newspaper publishers pressured the wire services to cut off the supply of news to radio networks, thus starting the **Press–Radio War**. Eventually, because of economic reasons, the wire services retreated and the flow of news copy resumed. A second skirmish occurred between stations and the American Society of Composers, Authors, and Publishers (ASCAP). When radio went commercial, ASCAP granted licenses to stations to broadcast music for an annual fee. As radio became more profitable, ASCAP raised its fees. In 1937, faced with another increase, the broadcasters rebelled and started their own licensing organization, Broadcast Music Incorporated (BMI). ASCAP also retreated. Taken together, these two events demonstrated that radio was becoming aware of its economic muscle.

The most significant legal development concerning the sound media during the Depression years was the formation of the **Federal Communications Commission (FCC)**. President Roosevelt wanted to create a government agency that would consolidate the regulatory functions of the communications industry in the same way that regulatory powers were consolidated under the Federal Power Commission and the Interstate Commerce Commission. In response to the president's demands, Congress passed the **Communications Act of 1934**, which consolidated responsibilities for broadcast and wire regulation under a new seven-member Federal Communications Commission. Aside from the expanded size of the commission and its increased duties, the fundamental philosophy underlying the original Radio Act of 1927 remained unchanged.

Radio Content: Escapism and Reality

The Depression meant that more and more people turned to radio for free entertainment; thus popular radio programs of this period reflected a need for diversion and escape. In 1933, *The Lone Ranger* started the action-adventure format of radio drama and was soon followed by *Gangbusters*, *The Shadow*, *Dick Tracy*, and *Buck Rogers*. A Chicago station, WGN, carried a program called *Clara, Lu, 'n' Em*, which was to become the first of many soap operas. Following in this program's footsteps were *Helen Trent* (about the plight of a woman over thirty-five), *Our Gal Sunday* (a small-town woman marries into English nobility), and *Backstage Wife* (self-explanatory). By 1940, there were forty different soaps on the air.

One other trend was notable during the 1930s: the growth of network radio news. From a somewhat shaky beginning, the networks by 1930 were providing newscasts five days a week. Special-events coverage was also becoming important. CBS rearranged its entire program schedule to cover the 1932 election. H. V. Kaltenborn reported a battle during the Spanish Civil War while hiding in a haystack. Edward VIII of England abdicated with his famous "The Woman I Love" speech. Coverage of these events drew huge audiences. In September of 1938, with Hitler threatening Europe, CBS and NBC sent more than a thousand foreign broadcasts to the United States from a staff of more than 200 reporters.

Not surprisingly, this trend accelerated during World War II as millions turned to radio for the latest news from the front. Edward R. Murrow gained fame through his reports from London (he once reported during an air raid). George Hicks of CBS recorded the Normandy landings, and in the Pacific, Webley Edwards reported live from a B-29 during an air raid over Japan. The total amount of time spent on news doubled from 1940 to 1944. By 1945, the four radio networks were providing a total of thirty-four hours of scheduled news broadcasts each week. Dramatic programs and

"This . . . is London." Edward R. Murrow's famous opening was familiar to millions of Americans who listened to his reports from the British capital during World War II. Murrow went on to a distinguished career in TV journalism. (Culver Pictures)

music were still popular, however, and some local stations filled about 50 percent of their broadcast day with music, some of it recorded.

World War II

Radio did well during the war. The amount of dollars spent on radio ads nearly doubled from 1940 to 1945. Helped by a newsprint shortage and an excess-profits tax that encouraged companies to advertise, radio broadcasting outpaced the newspapers as a national advertising vehicle in 1943. By war's end, radio was pulling 18 percent of all ad dollars.

Although the number of new stations that went on the air during the war years was relatively small (only thirty-four new AMs from 1942 to 1945) and major alterations to existing stations were frozen by the FCC, the shape of modern broadcasting would be significantly altered by a court ruling that came in the middle of the war. In 1943, the Supreme Court ruled that NBC must divest itself of one of its two networks. NBC chose to sell the weaker Blue network to Edward Noble, who had made his fortune selling Life Savers candy. Noble renamed his network the American Broadcasting Company (ABC) and by the end of the war, ABC had 195 affiliates and was a full-fledged competitor for the older nets.

The record industry did not do as well, primarily for two reasons. The U.S. government declared shellac, a key ingredient of discs, vital to the national defense and supplies available for records dropped drastically. Second, the American Federation of Musicians, fearful of losing jobs because of "canned" music, went on strike. The strike lasted from 1942 to 1944, and, as a result, record sales increased slowly during the war years. It was also during the war that Capitol records embarked on a novel approach to record promotion. The company mailed free records to radio stations, hoping for air play. This marked formal recognition of a new industry attitude: Radio could help sell records.

● ● ● ●

INNOVATION AND CHANGE: 1945-1954

The nine-year period following World War II was marked by great changes in both the radio and recording industries, changes that ultimately drove them closer together. The development of television delayed the growth of FM radio, altered the nature of network radio, and forced the radio industry to rely on records as the most important part of a new programming strategy. For its part, the record industry began to use radio as an important promotional device.

FM

The radio industry was in generally good economic shape as the postwar years started. There was one group of broadcasters, however, who might not have shared this assessment: the owners of FM radio stations. Despite the fact that FM sounded better than AM, was static free, and could reproduce a wider range of sound frequencies than AM, AM broadcasting had started first and FM had to struggle to catch up. Following the war, two events occurred that curtailed the development of this new medium. FM had the misfortune of beginning its development at the same time as TV; in addition, because of technical considerations, both FM radio and TV are suited for about the same place in the electromagnetic spectrum. In 1945, the FCC decided to give the rapidly expanding TV service the space formerly occupied by FM. The commission moved FM "upstairs" to the 88- to 108-MHz band (where it is today), thus rendering obsolete about half a million FM radios. In addition, many AM operators took out FM licenses as insurance and convinced the FCC that it was in the public interest to "simulcast," that is, to duplicate the content of the AM station over the FM channel. As a result, since little new programming was available, the public had little motivation to purchase FM receivers. It took FM more than thirty years to overcome these (and other) handicaps.

TV

Of course, the biggest change in radio's fortunes came about because of the emergence of television. (We will have more to say about the development of TV in another chapter.) For the time being, it is important to note that by 1948 it was apparent that TV would take over the mass entertainment function currently served by network radio. The emergence of TV meant changes in the content, economics, and functions of radio. Although many individuals believe that television cut into the revenues of the radio industry, no such thing happened. In fact, the revenue of the radio industry rose steadily from 1948 to 1952 and, after a brief drop from 1953 to 1956, continued to rise. The part of the industry upon which TV did have a drastic effect was *network* radio. The percentage of local stations with network affiliations dropped from 97 percent in 1947 to only 50 percent by 1955. Network revenue dropped by 60 percent for approximately the same period. Faced with this loss, stations relied more heavily on revenue from ads for local businesses. In short, they redistributed the makeup of their revenue dollar. As TV became the new mass medium, local stations cut back on their budgets, relied more heavily on music, talk, and news, and began searching for a formula that would allow them to exist with television. The recording industry was to figure heavily in radio's future.

Innovations in Recording

While radio was adjusting to the coming of TV, several important events were permanently altering the shape of the record industry. Using techniques and ideas that

During the 1940s, the local record shop was the place to "hang out" with friends and listen to the latest releases. (Nina Leen, Life *magazine, © Time, Inc.)*

were developed in Germany during the war, the 3M Company introduced magnetic recording tape in 1947. The arrival of tape meant improved sound quality, easier editing, reduced cost, and multitrack recording.

The next year Columbia introduced the 33⅓ long-playing record (LP). The new discs could play for twenty-five minutes a side and were virtually unbreakable. Rather than adopt the Columbia system, RCA Victor introduced its own innovation, the 45-rpm extended play record. The next few years were described as the "Battle of the Speeds," as the record-buying public was confronted by a choice among 33⅓, 45, and 78 records. From 1947 to 1949, record sales dropped 25 percent as the audience waited to see which speed would win. In 1950, RCA conceded and began issuing 33⅓ records. Columbia won only a partial victory, however. The 45 would become the preferred disc for single pop recordings while the 33⅓ would dominate album sales. The 78 became obsolete. There were also changes in record players. High-fidelity sets came on the market in 1954, followed four years later by stereophonic record players. Record sales more than doubled during this period.

Two other events were also important: the formation of small, independent recording companies and the emergence of radio as a promotional device. Because the increased importance of tape in record production had cut costs, small companies could now afford to compete with the larger labels. The unbreakable LP could be sent easily through the mail, and profitable mail-order operations were soon thriving. All of these factors favored the formation of new labels. Moreover, the relationship between records and radio became more firmly established. It was recognized that air play was essential to sell a significant amount of records. The emergence of a promotion staff at the record companies signaled this change in marketing technique. In the future, the relationship between the sound recording and the radio industries would be close, sometimes too close, as we shall see.

• • • •
GROWTH AND STABILIZATION: 1955–1970

Faced with a loss of programs from the networks and increasing rivalry from an ever-growing number of competitors on the radio dial (the number of stations on the air increased from 3343 in 1955 to 5569 in 1965), radio looked for a way to build an image and attract an audience that could be sold to advertisers. The answer was format or formula radio. ("Format" radio attempts to appeal to a particular audience segment.) The first format to develop was middle-of-the-road (MOR), followed in some big cities by a rhythm and blues (R&B) format and by a country/western (CW) format by some stations in rural markets. In the mid-1950s, however, a new format called "Top 40" made its debut. This format demanded strict adherence to a set playlist based on record sales, a distinctive announcing style, rapid pace, and special production gimmicks (like an echo chamber). By 1960, literally hundreds of stations had adopted this format. Very quickly, the Top-40 format became identified with a young audience— a young audience that, as it happened, had a good deal of money to spend on the records they heard played by their favorite disc jockey.

Naturally, the record industry was delighted. Sales skyrocketed from $227 million in 1955 to over $1 billion in 1967. Business had never been better. Radio stations, or at least most of them, were also doing well. Radio industry revenues topped the billion-dollar mark in 1968. Because of this new format, a new figure became important in the marketing of records—the local DJ. Since DJs chose what records were to be played on their programs, they were the focus of attention of dozens of promotional representatives from the record companies. Of course, the record companies were willing to do whatever was necessary to get air play. They began plying the DJs with gifts (followed later by outright bribes) to favor their releases over the competition. It got so bad that it was estimated that some DJs in major markets could supplement their salaries by $50,000 to $100,000 a year by accepting **payola,** as it came to be called. The situation ultimately came to the attention of Congress, and after a series of hearings on the subject the Communications Act was amended in an effort to curtail the practice.

Despite the "payola" scandals, both the radio and recording industries continued to grow during this period. By 1970, there were more than 7700 stations on the air, and total revenue exceeded the $1.2 billion mark. The record business also survived the scandal in good economic shape. In 1970, there were more than 5600 singles released along with about 4000 LPs. Total revenue from record sales had reached $1.1 billion by 1970.

In 1959 another technological development that was to spur sales was introduced by the Ampex Company—the four-track tape. This innovation helped to bring the cost of tape within range of the cost of records. Soon afterward, the development of tape cartridges and tape cassettes that eliminated threading from one reel to another further increased the potential of the tape market. By 1970, tape was accounting for over one-fourth of all recording industry receipts.

The trend toward specialization continued in radio during this period and even reached the network level. In 1968, the ABC radio network splintered into four different services—Contemporary, Informational, Entertainment, and FM—with over 1300 affiliates.

Payola

In the 1950s the disc jockey (DJ) became an important figure in radio programming. In fact, many promoted themselves to such an extent that they became stars in their own right. DJs sent out glossy pictures of themselves to their fans; they appeared at supermarket openings and record hops; they were the emcees at personal appearances by rock-and-roll groups. As the DJs became more influential, they also began to program their own shows. They picked the records that they would play during their airshift.

Record promoters also realized the tremendous importance of air play in the marketing of a hit. The more a record was played on the radio, the more it sold. Quite naturally, record promoters and DJs began to develop close ties. In the beginning, it was innocent enough. Promoters would make sure that DJs got the latest releases their companies were offering, and they also put in a good word or two about their companies' products. Competition got intense, however, and by 1959 there were about 250 new records released every week. Some unscrupulous promoters resorted to more than words to advance their records. At first, they might send the DJs an elaborate Christmas gift, a case of Scotch, a set of golf clubs, a hi-fi. If that didn't work, some even "hired" the DJ as "creative consultant" and paid the disc jockey a fee every month. Others would cut the DJ in on the action and offer to pay a penny to the DJ for every record sold in the market. Eventually, most promoters stopped these charades and simply passed the DJ an envelope filled with money in return for air play of their company's songs. In 1958 and 1959, record distributors reportedly spent over a quarter of a million dollars in the larger markets to promote their records artificially.

The news of this illicit business practice did nothing to help the image of rock and roll or of broadcasting. Section 508 was added to the 1934 Communications Act to stop this practice, but it was not altogether successful. New payola scandals broke out in the industry in the early 1970s. At least one record company was accused of offering drugs to station personnel in return for increased air play, and some concert promoters were accused of offering several monetary bribes. Payola resurfaced in 1986 when the U.S. Senate announced plans to investigate illegal practices in record promotion. It's a problem that doesn't seem to disappear.

1970 TO THE PRESENT

The ABC network experiment was successful enough to prompt others to follow suit. As of 1991, there were about twenty-one major radio networks. Consolidation also characterized network radio. Westwood One bought Mutual in 1985 and purchased the NBC network in 1988. United Stations Radio Network bought the RKO network in 1985 and five years later acquired the Transtar network. Existing networks also restructured. ABC went from seven special networks to five and CBS consolidated its RadioRadio service with its CBS Radio Networks. Radio network revenues rose about 12 percent from 1988 to 1989 but a soft advertising market cut the increase to about 1 percent from 1989 to 1990.

The most significant development in the radio industry during the 1970s was the successful emergence of FM. As noted earlier, FM radio faced several hurdles in its development. By the early 1960s, however, conditions had improved enough for more individuals to consider buying FM stations. Licenses for AM stations were becoming harder to get. People who wished to invest in a broadcast station found it easier to procure an FM license. In 1965, the FCC had passed the **nonduplication rule**, which prevented an AM–FM combination from duplicating its AM content on its FM channel for more than 50 percent of the time. Faced with this ruling and the knowledge that specialized formats were becoming successful in radio, FM stations developed their own kind of sound (many stations adopted a rock format) that capitalized on FM's better technical qualities. Between 1960 and 1970, the number of FM stations tripled. The economic picture also brightened. In 1976, FM broadcasting went into the black as the industry as a whole reported earnings of $21.2 million.

Profits continued to increase for FM as it captured more and more of the listening audience. In 1991, FM accounted for about 70 percent of all audience listening time, with AM accounting for 30 percent. The only age group where AM garnered more listening time than FM was among people fifty or over. AM station executives began rethinking programming strategy in an attempt to stop the audience erosion. AM stereo was introduced in the early 1980s, but the general lack of radio sets designed to receive it lessened its impact (see Figure 8-1).

More and more radio stations were competing for the same basic advertising, which accelerated the trend toward more refined formats (*Broadcasting Yearbook* for 1990 listed more than sixty). Country music was the most widely programmed format on radio stations in 1990 followed by adult contemporary. AM radio was becoming a service dominated by news/talk and the oldies format. FM had become nearly all-music. Stations were relying heavily on program consultants and audience research to get the exact sound they needed to keep their operations profitable.

Making a profit was getting to be a harder task, however, as the 1990s opened. Increased competition from other radio stations for an audience and from the local newspaper for advertisers had made it difficult for some stations to stay in business. Figures released in 1991 showed that expenses actually exceeded revenues for the average daytime-only AM station. Somewhat surprisingly, full-time AM stations did better than FM stations and AM/FM combinations, with a profit margin of about 9 percent compared to 5 percent for the latter two types of stations.

On the horizon, digital audio broadcasting (DAB), a technique that would bring the same high quality sound now found on CDs to radio broadcasting, was undergoing tests in 1992. If DAB is eventually adopted it will cause major shifts in the industry, including erasing all the sound performance differences between AM and FM and making it necessary for the consumer to buy a completely new radio receiver (see next chapter for more details).

The fortunes of the sound recording industry resembled a roller coaster during the 1970–1991 period. A boom period from 1974 to 1978 (thanks in large measure to the popularity of disco) was followed by a slide during the early 1980s. In 1983, the industry went back on the upswing (thanks in large measure to Michael Jackson and

FIGURE 8-1 *Division of AM and FM audiences.*

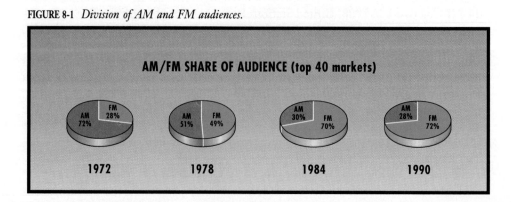

Thriller and a few popular soundtracks from motion pictures). After a couple of stable years in the mid-1980s, industry revenues skyrocketed during the late 1980s thanks to the popularity (and high profit margins) associated with compact discs (CDs). CD sales have grown so much that the vinyl LP is virtually extinct. By the early 1990s, however, there were signs that the CD boom was tapering off and executives were hoping that another down cycle was not in the offing.

Over the last ten years, one factor that had a significant impact on the sound-recording industry was the surprising popularity of music videos and MTV. The videos quickly became an important avenue of exposure for new groups. Radio stations used MTV to pretest additions to the playlists. If a record received heavy play on television, then it was a pretty safe bet that it would be popular on radio as well. In fact, there were many performers who owed their popularity to MTV: Duran Duran, Eurythmics, Prince, Paula Abdul, Madonna, to name a few.

In the realm of technology, the impact of digital audio tape (DAT) was being debated by industry experts. DAT is the tape counterpart to the CD and has equal sound quality. Its big advantage is that, unlike the CD, it can be used for recording. Record companies were afraid that DAT would further exacerbate the problem of pirated CDs and campaigned against DAT. In 1991, however, an agreement was reached between record companies and DAT manufacturers that should pave the way for DAT's eventual entry into the American market.

"I want my MTV." The music-video network started in 1980 and marked the beginning of a whole new avenue for marketing recordings. (Courtesy of MTV Networks, © 1991)

• • • •
CONTENT TRENDS: 1945-PRESENT

Shortly after World War II ended it became apparent that most of radio's biggest stars would soon make the transition to TV. In the beginning, some popular radio programs were simulcast on television, with radio carrying only the audio portion. Soon the simulcast programs abandoned radio altogether, and the radio networks decided to fill the gap with music and quiz programs. By 1956 it was obvious that the networks would no longer be the potent programming source they had been in the past. In that year, radio networks were carrying only about thirty-five hours of sponsored evening programs each week. Finally, by 1960, all the once popular evening programs and daytime serials had come to an end. Radio network service was limited primarily to news and short features, usually amounting to no more than two or three hours of time a day.

Specialized Formats

Local stations soon adapted to this change. Now that they no longer were tied to the networks for the bulk of their programming, the locals were free to develop their own personalities. Most did it by adopting a specialized format, a sound that had distinctive appeal to a certain segment of the audience. In the beginning, most stations resorted to a "middle-of-the-road" format, a throwback to the networks' influence. Others began to experiment. The most successful experiment occurred in the Midwest where a station began monitoring the sales of records and sheet music and playing those tunes that were selling the most. Hence, the Top-40 format was born. A key element in this format was the **clock hour**, which specified every element of programming. The sound had to be continuous, bright, and exciting. No dead air was permitted. The disc jockey had to complement the format. Since one Top-40 station sounded like any other Top-40 station, it was the DJ who gave each station its particular personality. It was not long before DJs became stars in their own right. One of the first was Alan Freed, who left Cleveland and became one of New York's top DJs. Another was Murray the K, who eventually called himself "the fifth Beatle" during the 1960s. Wolfman Jack is another example. The success of this Top-40 sound encouraged radio stations to experiment with other specialized formats. By 1964, at least a dozen different formats had sprung up.

This trend toward specialization continued through the 1970s, 1980s, and 1990s. All-talk and all-news stations have specialized without relying on music. Ethnic stations have become popular along with stations that program a religious format. Recycling is also evident as many stations have turned to a "Golden Oldies" format, and the radio networks have begun to supply original variety programs in the evening.

In the early 1990s, many classical stations were carried on local cable TV systems, broadening their reach. Innovations included one station that went to an all-business news format while another went to all-sports. One in California started an all self-help/inspirational format and there was even one station in Wisconsin that went all-polka. Several stations tried an all-Elvis format but eventually returned to more traditional formats.

Sound Recording

After World War II, the most popular recordings were made by the soloists and featured artists who had performed in front of the big bands. Peggy Lee (featured with Benny Goodman), Frank Sinatra (with Tommy Dorsey), Doris Day (with Les Brown), and Dinah Shore (with Xavier Cugat) all had hit records during the postwar years. This music was designed to appeal to all age groups and was, at times, oversentimentalized. Consider these top songs, popular between 1949 and 1954: "Ghost Riders in the Sky"

The radio audience had no way of differentiating radio performers on the basis of skin color. This fact made it possible for white actors to play black characters as they did in *Amos 'n' Andy*. During the 1930s and 1940s, black performers had only limited opportunities to appear and most had to fight discrimination and prejudice in the radio industry. Nonetheless, blacks made major contributions to the development of American radio programming. Black singer Ethel Waters had her own program; Paul Robeson was the featured singer on a program sponsored by General Electric. Fats Waller, Duke Ellington, and the Mills Brothers frequently appeared on network shows.

Black dramatic actors were not so fortunate. Network advertisers were unwilling to sponsor dramatic programs directed at black audiences. Some ensembles of black actors and actresses produced shows for local stations but all of these series were short-lived. The most successful black actor in a radio series was Eddie Anderson—Rochester, the valet, on the *Jack Benny Program*. Anderson started on the Benny show in 1937 and continued his role in the TV series which ran from 1950 to 1965.

In his early radio days, Rochester was a strong character, always standing up to Benny, his ultrafrugal employer. Nevertheless, since the Benny program had no black writers, his character often displayed the stereotyped behaviors that whites commonly assigned to blacks. Anderson came under frequent criticism for playing Rochester as a stereotype. He defended his actions by saying he was playing the part of one black person, not the part of the entire black race. Rochester's role became a little less stereotyped when the show made the transition to TV.

Other black actors followed in Anderson's path, usually in stereotyped roles. Hattie McDaniel was Beulah, the maid, in the series of the same name. Butterfly McQueen was a secretary on *The Danny Kaye Show* and several black actors were hired for minor roles in *Amos 'n' Andy*.

The status of blacks in radio programming improved slightly after World War II as the networks tried to more fully integrate their programs. In addition, several local stations began to recognize the importance of the black audience and began broadcasting black-oriented programs with black performers. In general, however, radio was still a white performers' medium. Eventually, the coming of television totally changed the content of American radio, and black performers shifted their attention to TV in their quest for equality. Ironically, the coming of rock and roll saved many radio stations from bankruptcy. Rock and roll, of course, had its roots in black culture.

(Vaughn Monroe); "Doggie in the Window" (Patti Page); "Oh My Papa" (Eddie Fisher); and "Three Coins in the Fountain" (The Four Aces). Around 1954, however, music changed. It would never be the same.

The Coming of Rock and Roll

It started with the car. Teenagers had more spending money in these postwar years, and for the first time many of them could afford a car. Pretty soon the car became a symbol of identity; many teenagers customized their cars so that no one would confuse it with the family auto. After the cars came the clothes. By the 1950s, teenage clothes no longer resembled adult clothes. Denim was popular, and leather jackets (à la James Dean and Marlon Brando) were sported by many. Hair styles and makeup became distinctive. After cars and clothes came the movies: *Rebel Without a Cause, The Blackboard Jungle, The Wild One*. Before long sociologists were talking about a "youth culture." One thing this youth culture lacked was a distinctive form of music. Rock and roll would fill that void. The importance of this new form of music to the record industry cannot be minimized. Consequently, our examination of the evolution of popular music content from this point on focuses on the changing trends in rock-and-roll (later shortened to rock) music.

Rock had its roots in black rhythm and blues, commercial white popular music, country and western, and jazz. The first national exposure of rock and roll came in July of 1955 when Bill Haley and the Comets moved into the number-one spot on the charts with "Rock Around the Clock." The song remained there for eight weeks (until replaced by Mitch Miller's version of "The Yellow Rose of Texas"). But Haley was more of a popularizer than a pioneer, for his music sounded a bit like a swing band that had suddenly discovered the big beat. In any event, his popularity quickly faded.

Less than a year later another performer who would enjoy a far more substantial career came on the scene. "Heartbreak Hotel," recorded by a then relatively unknown Elvis Presley, would stay at the number-one position for seven straight weeks. A few months later a second Elvis hit, "Don't Be Cruel," would go to the number-one slot, followed by yet another number-one hit in 1956, a change of pace called "Love Me Tender." It was with Elvis that rock and roll first blossomed. Combining a country and western style with the beat and energy of black R&B music, Elvis' records sold millions. He appeared on Ed Sullivan's network TV show (from the waist up: Sullivan thought Elvis' pelvic gyrations too suggestive). Through Elvis rock and roll gained wide recognition, if not respectability.

Presley's success inspired other performers from the country and western tradition. Jerry Lee Lewis combined Mississippi boogie-woogie with country music to produce a unique and driving style. His "Whole Lotta Shakin' Going On" sold 6 million copies in 1957–1958. At about this time, Buddy Holly and the Crickets made the charts with "That'll Be the Day." Holly's music went back to his Texas roots and combined the warm tone of regional country and western music with inventive arrangements and vocal gymnastics to create a novel sound.

Several rock pioneers came from traditional black rhythm and blues music. Perhaps the most exciting (certainly the most energetic) was Richard Penniman, or, as he

The one and only Elvis. (The Bettmann Archives)

Chuck Berry introduced the Chicago sound—a mixture of blues, guitar chords, and a heavy beat—to early rock and roll. (Charles Stewart/Photo Trends)

called himself, "Little Richard." Except for a period of three months, Little Richard had a record in the Top 100 at all times from 1956 to 1957 (best known are "Long Tall Sally" and "Tutti Frutti"). Both his music and his stage performances boiled over with unrestrained energy. About the same time, on the south side of Chicago, Chuck Berry was singing blues in small nightclubs. Discovered by the owner of a Chicago-based record company, Berry was the first artist who paid more than passing attention to the lyrics of rock and roll. His style would later influence many musical groups, including the Beatles.

Brenda Lee may have been small in stature, but she had a big voice. She placed her first record in the Top-40 charts at the ripe old age of 11. (Photofest)

Rock Goes Commercial

By 1959, through a combination of bizarre events, all the pioneers of rock had disappeared. Elvis went into the Army. Buddy Holly was killed in a plane crash. Jerry Lee Lewis married a thirteen-year-old girl said to be his cousin and dropped from sight. Little Richard was in the seminary. And Chuck Berry, arrested for violating the Mann Act, ultimately entered federal prison. Thus the way was open for a whole new crop of stars. Economics dictated what this new crop would look and sound like.

About this time record companies realized that huge amounts of money could be made from the rock-and-roll phenomenon if it was promoted correctly. Unfortunately, rock and roll had an image problem. In 1959, the record industry was shaken by the payola scandals, which, coming on top of years of bad publicity and criticism that blamed rock and roll for most of society's ills, threatened rock's profitability. Since rock and roll had too much moneymaking potential to be abandoned, the record companies decided to clean up rock's image instead.

As the 1960s opened, the "new look" in rock was characterized by middle-class, white, clean-cut, and more or less wholesome performers. Rock stars were young men and women you wouldn't hesitate to bring home and introduce to your parents. On the male side, Ricky Nelson, Bobby Vee, Bobby Vinton, Fabian, Paul Anka, Frankie Avalon, and The Four Seasons were popular. Although there were fewer examples on the female side, those who had hits included Annette, Connie Francis, Brenda Lee,

Morbidity and Rock and Roll

One of the strangest trends in the evolution of popular rock-and-roll music has been a small but persistent genre of records that can only be classified under the somewhat macabre title of "morbid rock." Although its roots probably go back further, it became especially notable in the 1960s. Among the first songs to become a hit was "Teen Angel," the tale of an unfortunate couple whose car stalled on the railroad tracks. Although the young man of the song is smart enough to run like crazy, the young woman shows a complete lack of judgment and goes back to the car to retrieve her sweetheart's high school ring. The train arrives at the same time. End of romance. Another early example was J. Frank Wilson's "Last Kiss," a tragic tale of a guy and girl out on a date who plow into a disabled car. He survives. She doesn't. End of romance. "Tell Laura I Love Her" told the teary story of a young man who needs money to continue his romance with his lady friend and so resorts to stock car racing to provide extra income. He totals his car and himself. End of romance. "Patches" concerned the romance between a young woman from the wrong side of the tracks and a middle-class young man. Despondent, the young woman drowns herself in the river. At the end of the song, the young man is contemplating the same thing. Even wholesome Pat Boone got into the act with "Moody River," a song that also told the story of two people who throw themselves into the river and drown. The trend was less noticeable in the early seventies, but a song entitled "Billy Don't Be a Hero" enjoyed wide popularity. This effort was about a boy who goes off to war, against the wishes of his girlfriend, and gets killed. End of romance. (For those who are true fans of this genre, Rhino Records has collected ten teen tragedy songs ranging from "Last Kiss" to the little-known but nonetheless moving "The Homecoming Queen's Got a Gun." Incidentally, the back cover of the LP doubles as a tissue dispenser.)

In any event, this trend has not resurfaced during the 1980s and 1990s. Perhaps it's . . . dead.

and Lesley Gore. All fit the new image of rock and roll. Consequently, the early 1960s saw few musical innovations. In 1963, however, the music changed again.

The British Invasion

Their name was inspired by Buddy Holly and the Crickets, but instead of the entomologically correct "Beetles," the group chose the spelling "Beatles" (which, it was later explained, incorporated the word "beat"). In early 1964, they took the United States by storm. Musically, the Beatles were everything that American rock and roll was not. They were innovative, especially in vocal harmony, and introduced the harmonica as a rock instrument. Ultimately, they would change the shape of the music business and American popular culture. The Beatles had seven number-one records in 1964; they held down the top position for twenty of the fifty-two weeks that year. They would have six more chart-toppers over the next two years. When they appeared on the Ed Sullivan show in 1964, it was estimated that 73 million people watched.

Their success paved the way for a veritable British invasion. Most British rock at this time resembled American rock: cheery, happy, commercial, and white. Not surprisingly, some of the first groups that followed the Beatles represented this school (Herman's Hermits, Freddie and the Dreamers, the Dave Clark Five, Peter and Gordon, to name a few). There was another style of British rock, however, far less cheery, as represented by the Rolling Stones and the Animals. This style, which would also enjoy popularity, was blues based, rough hewn, slightly aggressive, and certainly not bouncy and carefree. (One young girl, when asked how she could be a fan of both the Beatles and the Stones, reportedly replied that she liked the Beatles because they were "cute" and sort of liked the Stones because they were "so ugly.")

American artists were not silent during this influx of British talent. Folk music, as performed by Bob Dylan and Joan Baez, was also popular. It was only a matter of time before folk merged with rock to produce "folk rock" ("Mr. Tambourine Man" by the Byrds was one of the first records in this style). Soul music, as recorded on the Motown label, also made its mark during the sixties. The Supremes and the Four Tops had eleven number-one songs between them for this label from 1964 to 1967.

Recent Trends

The late 1960s was a time of cultural transition. Freedom, experimentation, and innovation were encouraged in almost all walks of life, and popular music was no exception. Sparked by the release of the Beatles' *Sgt. Pepper* album, a fractionalization of rock began to take place. Several trends of this period are notable. In 1968, Blood, Sweat and Tears successfully blended jazz, rock, and at times, even classical music. The Band introduced "country rock." The Who recorded a rock opera, *Tommy*. In the midst of all this experimentation, commercial formula music was also healthy. The Monkees, a group put together by ads in the newspaper, sold millions of records. Proponents of "bubble-gum rock," The Archies, kept "Sugar, Sugar" at the top of the charts for a month in 1969 (it replaced, oddly enough, a song by the Rolling Stones, "Honky Tonk Woman").

Still, perhaps the most significant trend in this period was one that changed music again. Toward the end of the sixties and the beginning of the seventies, rock music became part of the counterculture; in many instances, it went out of its way to break with the establishment. Musically, many of the songs of this era were characterized by the **heavy-metal** sound; amplifiers and electronic equipment began to dominate the stage along with the performers. The artists also broke sharply with tradition. The pioneers in this style of rock were all vaguely threatening, a trifle unsavory, and definitely not the type you would bring home and introduce to the family. Consider Janis Joplin, Jimi Hendrix, Sly and the Family Stone, Alice Cooper, Rod Stewart, and David Bowie. They are a far cry from Frankie Avalon and Annette.

Perhaps as a reaction to all this volume, the early 1970s found a softer, more personal style of music gaining popularity. James Taylor, Carole King, Melanie, Carly Simon, and Joni Mitchell were the prime examples of this trend. The most significant development of the early to mid-1970s, however, was the intermingling of rock music with country and western music. During this period and, indeed, even to the present, it is not uncommon to find the top C/W single also high on the pop charts. Many country performers were able to cross over into the pop arena with consistent success. Kris Kristofferson, John Denver, Glen Campbell, Dolly Parton, Anne Murray, Linda Ronstadt, and Olivia Newton-John, among others, have made the distinction between rock and country less clear.

As the 1970s gave way to the 1980s, this trend in crossovers had not diminished; it was not uncommon to find many albums on both the country and the rock best-seller charts. The disco craze faded but gave birth to a new style of heavy-beat dance music. Several other boomlets seemed to have come and gone, among them a phenomenon known as punk rock. The most significant trend in the 1980s was the emergence of "new wave" music, which in a slightly toned-down version became known as simply the "new music" (see Figure 8-2). This style replaced the guitar as the central rock musical instrument with the synthesizer and keyboard and introduced new and innovative rhythm arrangements.

Metal, Rap, Retro Rock, and Folk

In recorded music four big trends characterized the late 1980s and early 1990s: the revival of an established rock style, the mainstreaming of another, the renaissance of many of rock's early stars, and a return to basics. The music that revived itself was heavy metal. Groups such as Bon Jovi, Whitesnake, and Guns 'n' Roses enjoyed their highest popularity ever. Black urban contemporary music and rap increased their base of popularity and were frequently heard on mainstream Contemporary Hit Radio format stations. Ice-T, Hammer, and Run-D.M.C. were performers that got new exposure to a mass audience. The popularity of rap was somewhat surprising. At least

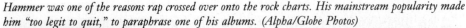

Hammer was one of the reasons rap crossed over onto the rock charts. His mainstream popularity made him "too legit to quit," to paraphrase one of his albums. (Alpha/Globe Photos)

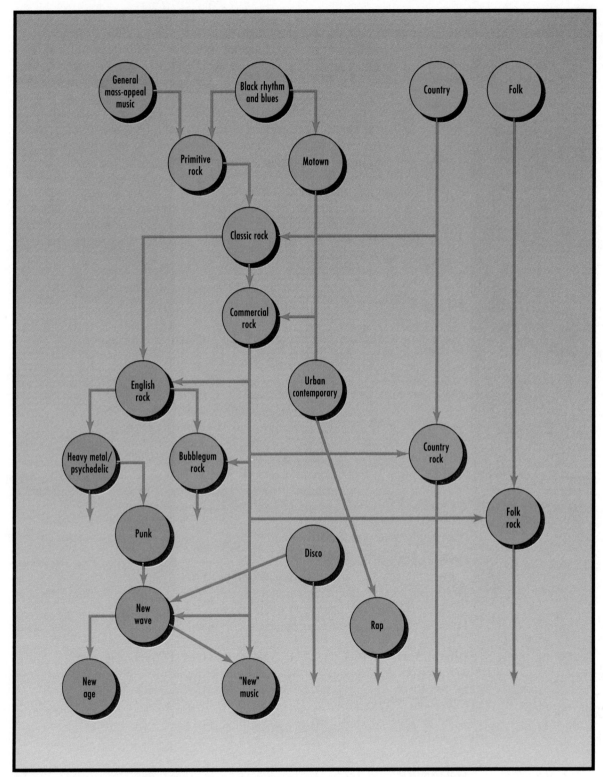

FIGURE 8-2 *The rock-and-roll family tree, circa 1990, greatly simplified and somewhat subjective. If you disagree, draw new arrows and circles.*

two rap groups, 2 Live Crew and N.W.A., released albums with controversial and explicit lyrics but both became best sellers without benefit of radio air play.

Yet a third trend saw the resurgence of some rock performers who had been around since the 1960s and 1970s. The Grateful Dead released a hit album and had their first runaway Top-40 hit in 1987. The Traveling Wilburys brought back Bob Dylan, Roy Orbison, and George Harrison. The Doors were the subject of a big-budget motion picture which helped to revive sales of their records. The Moody Blues, Fleetwod Mac, and Starship (née Jefferson Airplane) all released hit albums. Classic rock and oldies stations were becoming popular on radio. Many people claimed that Elvis was still alive. Rock was obviously a renewable resource.

Finally, politically conscious folk music made a revival during the late 1980s and early 1990s. Folk artists Michelle Shocked and Tracey Chapman sang about social issues. Suzanne Vega decried child abuse in one of her songs. The Indigo Girls, who lobbied for the Coalition for the Homeless, were also attracting attention. Many popular music critics noted that many of these artists were echoing the sound and themes and popular folk music from the 1960s.

• • • •

SUGGESTIONS FOR FURTHER READING

These books represent a good place to go for further information.

The History of Radio

BARNOUW, ERIK, *A Tower in Babel*, New York: Oxford University Press, 1966.
———, *The Golden Web*, New York: Oxford University Press, 1968.
———, *The Image Empire*, New York: Oxford University Press, 1970.
LICHTY, LAWRENCE, AND MAL TOPPING, eds., *American Broadcasting: A Source Book on the History of Radio and Television*, New York: Hastings House, 1975.
MAC DONALD, J. FRED, *Don't Touch That Dial*, Chicago: Nelson-Hall, 1979.
STERLING, CHRISTOPHER, AND JOHN KITTROSS, *Stay Tuned: A Concise History of American Broadcasting*, Belmont, Calif.: Wadsworth, 1990.

The History of Sound Recording and Record Content

CHAPPLE, STEVE, AND REEBEE GAROFOLO, *Rock 'n' Roll Is Here to Pay: The History and Politics of the Music Industry*, Chicago: Nelson-Hall, 1977.
DENISOFF, SERGE, AND WILLIAM L. SCHURK, *Tarnished Gold: The Record Industry Revisited*, New Brunswick, N.J.: Transaction Books, 1986.
JAHN, MIKE, *Rock: From Elvis Presley to the Rolling Stones*, New York: Quadrangle, 1973.
ROXON, LILLIAN, *Rock Encyclopedia*, New York: Grosset & Dunlap, 1969.
SCHICKE, C. A., *Revolution in Sound*, Boston: Little, Brown, 1974.
SKLAR, RICK, *Rocking America*, New York: St. Martin's Press, 1984.
SZATMARY, DAVID, *Rockin' in Time: A Social History of Rock and Roll*, Englewood Cliffs, N.J.: Prentice Hall, 1991.

• • • •

DISCOGRAPHY

A few albums that help illustrate some of the trends in popular music would be the following:

BEATLES, *Sgt. Pepper's Lonely Hearts Club Band*, Capitol MAS 2653.
BOB DYLAN, *Bob Dylan's Greatest Hits*, Columbia KCS 9463.

DEF LEPPARD, *Hysteria*, Mercury 8306751.
MICHAEL JACKSON, *Thriller*, Epic QE 38112.
ELVIS PRESLEY, *Elvis Presley*, RCA LSP 1254.
LITTLE RICHARD, *Little Richard's Grooviest 17 Original Hits*, Specialty SPS 2113.
THE ROLLING STONES, *Let It Bleed*, London NPS-4.
BRUCE SPRINGSTEEN, *Born in the USA*, Columbia QC 38653.
THE WHO, *Tommy*, Decca DXSW 7205.

9

STRUCTURE OF THE RADIO INDUSTRY

hat's a good way to find out about today's radio industry? Take your radio and do a slow scan up and down the AM and FM band. You're likely to hear something like the following:

"Hi. This is Mike from Arlington Heights . . ."

"The hits of the sixties, seventies, eighties, and today . . ."

"No rap . . . no heavy metal . . . just the hits you like best."

"It's 9:03 and the news continues . . ."

"Time for more good fun and great oldies on Eagle 104."

"Soft and bright . . . all day long."

"If you're the nineteenth caller you can win $103.70 from Power 103—your power station."

"Come home to the country on FM 95."

"It's a three-fer Thursday on Z-102, your classic rock station . . ."

Like the magazine industry, radio has concentrated on finding the right target audience, the right demographic niche that will attract listeners. Formats continue to be refined as radio stations contend with a marketplace crowded with stations, a weak economy, changing tastes, and increased competition from other media.

This chapter will examine the ever-changing and highly competitive radio business.

ORGANIZATION OF THE RADIO INDUSTRY

There are more than a half-billion working radio sets in the United States. That works out to about two radios per person. There are about 10,900 radio stations in operation. Radio is ubiquitous. Think for a moment how many working radios are in your house. The typical household has about a half-dozen. When it comes to individual listening time, the average person listens to radio about twenty-five hours per week, just five hours less than are spent watching TV.

Radio is everywhere. Sets are common in the bedroom (where they put people to sleep and wake them up), in kitchens, in cars, in offices, on city streets, on beaches, at ball games, and in a dozen other places. Additionally, in the past twenty years, there has been a tremendous increase in the number of radio stations serving the United States. Thanks in part to an FCC philosophy that encouraged competition, the number of stations grew from about 6900 in 1970 to about 10,900 in 1991, an increase of almost 60 percent. To understand how this rapidly growing business is organized, we will examine it from several perspectives: programming, technology, format, and ownership.

Local Stations, Nets, and Syndicators

Local radio stations operate in cities, towns, and villages across the country. Big cities have many stations. New York City has ninety-five; Los Angeles, sixty. Smaller towns may have only one or two. Whitefish, Montana, for example (population 4000), has two stations. Programming for these stations is provided by networks and by program syndication companies. Technically speaking, the distinction between a net and a syndication service is that all stations on a network carry the net program at the same time while syndicated programming is carried at different times by the stations. In practice, however, much syndicated radio programming is satellite-delivered and carried simultaneously, and many network affiliates tape net programming and broadcast it later. To make it even more complicated, the traditional networks also offer syndicated programs. Consequently, the distinction between the two services may no longer be meaningful.

Historically, networks were important programming sources during the earlier years of radio. After the emergence of TV, the importance of radio networks diminished and they provided only news and public affairs programs to their affiliates. In the mid-1980s, network radio staged a resurgence. By 1991, there were twenty-one networks, each offering a specialized service. ABC, for example, had five different networks, ranging from the news- and features-oriented ABC Prime to the rock-oriented ABC Excel. Westwood One had four networks while Unistar had three. Other prominent networks included the AP and UPI news networks, the National Black Network, and the Business Radio Network. Advertising billing on network radio totaled $435 million in 1991, up 18 percent from 1987. Although this is a solid gain, radio is still a local medium. The $435 million figure amounts to less than 5 percent of total industry revenue.

Program syndication companies offer stations short- or long-form programming of a highly specialized nature. As of 1993, there were more than fifty companies providing syndicated programs. For example, the American Comedy Network offers a library of 640 comedy bits on thirteen CDs. The Motor Racing Network supplies coverage of fifty NASCAR races and NASCAR-related features to about 400 stations.

Radio at War

Radio broadcasting played an important part in the 1991 Persian Gulf War. In order to keep up morale and to make the troops feel at home, Armed Forces Radio set up a radio station to broadcast to the troops. The most listened-to program? *Good Morning Saudi Arabia.*

Radio figured in the propaganda war as well. The United States set up clandestine stations and broadcast news and information to the resistance in Kuwait and to the people in Iraq. The Iraqis also tried propaganda broadcasting but they weren't very good at it. Iraq radio broadcast a program starring a female host the U.S. troops quickly dubbed "Baghdad Betty." In one of her broadcasts, she tried to demoralize the U.S. forces by telling them that while they were in the desert fighting, their wives and girlfriends were back home fooling around with TV and movie stars like Tom Cruise, Arnold Schwarzenegger, and Bart Simpson.

*A DJ at work: Note that everything is in easy reach: mike, sound board, tape players, telephones, etc.
(Paul Conklin/Monkmeyer)*

Musical Starstreams distributes a weekly two-hour program of new age music. Creative Radio Networks provides a six-hour compilation of Elvis Presley songs and the ever-popular "Elvis Hour."

Thanks to networks and syndicators, program directors at local stations can now choose from a diverse menu of music, news, features, and specials.

AM and FM Stations

Radio stations speak in two voices. Stations are either AM or FM. **AM** stands for amplitude modulation, one way of transmitting a radio wave, and **FM** stands for frequency modulation, another form of transmission. As we saw in Chapter 8, since about 1975 the fortunes of FM radio have been increasing while those of AM stations were on the decline. In 1991, almost three-quarters of listenership went to the FM stations. Keep in mind, however, that some AM stations, particularly those in large markets, were doing quite well. In 1991, AMs in Chicago (WGN), San Francisco (KGO), Detroit (WJR), and Boston (WRKO) were the top-rated stations.

All physical factors being equal, radio signals sent by AM travel farther, especially at night, than signals sent by FM. This is because AM radio waves bounce off a layer of the earth's atmosphere called the ionosphere and back to the ground. The AM dial on a typical radio set illustrates the precise frequencies in the electromagnetic spectrum where the AM station operates. AM stations are further classified by channels. There are three possible channels: clear, regional, and local. A clear channel is one with a single dominant station that is designed to provide service over a wide area. Typically, these dominant stations have a strong signal because they broadcast with 50,000 watts of power. For example, the 720 spot on the AM dial is a clear channel with WGN, Chicago, the dominant station, operating at 50,000 watts. The 770 position is also a clear channel with WABC, New York, dominant. A regional channel is one shared by many stations that serve fairly large areas. A local channel is designed to be shared by a large number of stations that broadcast only to their local communities.

FM signals do not travel as far as AM, but FM has the advantage of being able to produce better sound qualities than AM. FM radio is also less likely to be affected by outside interference such as thunderstorms. Similar to AM, FM stations are organized in classes. Class C FM stations are the most powerful, operating at 100,000 watts. Class B and Class A stations are less powerful. A glance at the FM dial of a radio reveals that FM stations operate in a different part of the electromagnetic spectrum than does AM. Figure 9-1 is a simplified diagram of the spectrum showing where AM, FM, and television signals are located. Note that AM radio occupies a portion of the spectrum very close to electrical energy. This is why lightning and electric motors cause interference on AM. FM is a comfortable distance away and is unaffected.

Digital Audio Broadcasting (DAB)

Many radio stations play music from compact discs (CDs). The CD uses high-tech digital technology to achieve a rich, high-fidelity sound. The problem is that the CDs are broadcast on AM and FM radio stations using low-tech transmission methods that were developed back in the early 1900s and some of the quality of the CDs is lost. Now, digital audio broadcasting (DAB) promises to bring radio sound up to CD quality.

Currently, AM and FM stations broadcast an analog signal. The information they transmit causes a range of variation in their carrier waves which is detected by radio receivers and transformed into sound. It's also possible to send sound by first encoding it into digital form—a series of 0s and 1s—with every possible sound corresponding to a long chain of binary numbers. A new improved radio receiving set would decode these numbers and turn them back into sound.

Early tests of DAB were promising. Radio listeners were pleased with the crisp, clean sound quality and the lack of interference. The problem was that DAB took up

FIGURE 9-1 *A simplified diagram of the electromagnetic spectrum.*

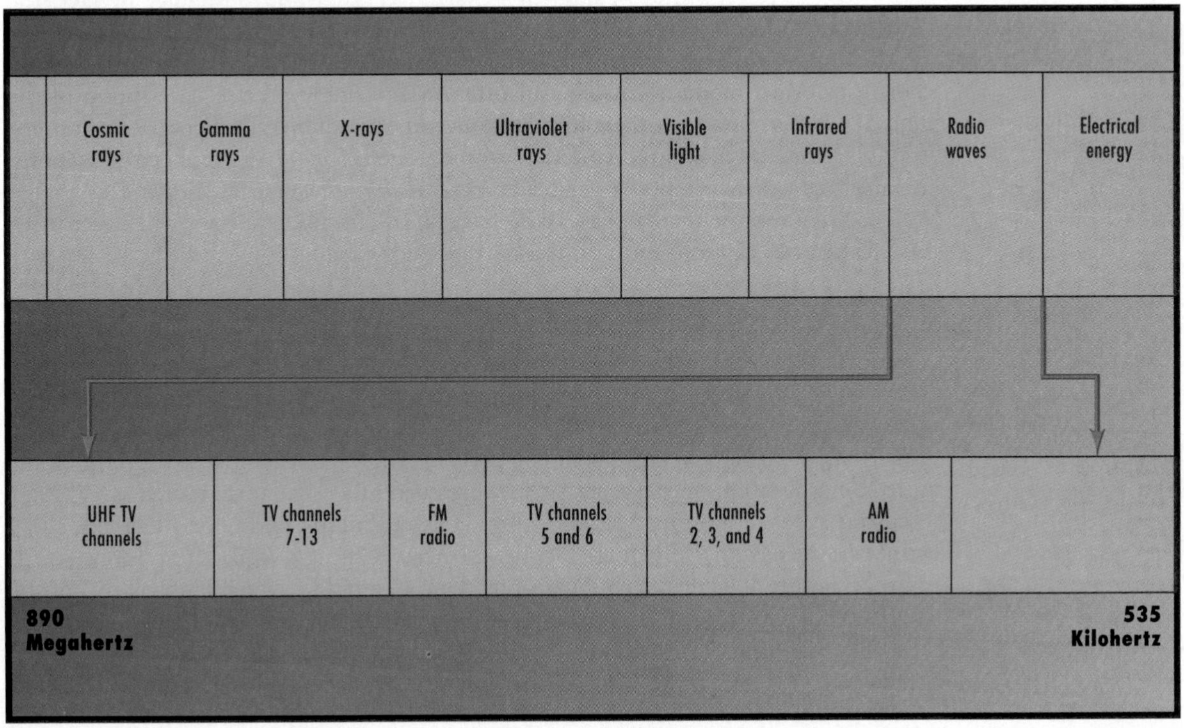

a lot of space in the electromagnetic spectrum. In 1990, however, a system was developed in Europe that would give radio CD-quality sound without hogging up too much of the spectrum. The Eureka DAB process was demonstrated to U.S. broadcasters and most agreed that such a system would eventually be the norm of radio transmission.

The advantages of DAB are many: better quality, cheaper to transmit, easier to maintain. DAB would also allow innovations that are impossible with traditional AM and FM. The radio receiving set would become a small computer with a display screen. Stations could transmit messages that identify their programs and formats. A listener could program his radio set to find a baseball game or a traffic report or heavy metal music. Data might also be transmitted to display weather warnings or station slogans or even ad messages.

The big hang-up, of course, is that DAB signals are incompatible with your current radio set. You would have to purchase a new DAB receiver which right now costs about $200 to $300, but prices are likely to come down.

Broadcasters are uncertain about what DAB means to them. One scenario has radio stations simulcasting both a conventional AM or FM signal and a DAB signal until a convenient spot is found in the spectrum and then switching to exclusively DAB. This would mean that the quality differences between AM and FM would vanish and all stations would have approximately the same coverage areas, erasing differences that now exist because of different power levels. This would obviously restructure traditional radio broadcasting. In any case, American broadcasters will be looking carefully at Canada: A DAB system is scheduled to go into operation there between 1995 and 2000.

Station Formats

Perhaps the most meaningful way we can organize radio stations is according to their **format,** a type of consistent programming designed to appeal to a certain segment of the audience. Formats are important because they give a station a distinctive personality and attract a certain kind of audience that advertisers find desirable. In fact, the development of radio after 1960 is marked by the fine tuning of existing formats and the creation of new ones that appeal to people in distinct demographic and lifestyle categories. Most modern stations can offer an amazingly precise description of the kind of listener they want their format to attract. An adult contemporary station, for example, might set its sights on men and women, aged 25 to 45, with college educations, making more than $40,000 a year, who read *Rolling Stone*, drive either a BMW or Volvo, and go to the mall at least twice a week. In our discussion we will cover three basic categories of radio formats: music, news/talk, and ethnic.

The Music Format. This is the largest category and includes many subdivisions and variations. In the early 1990s, the two most listened to music formats were Adult Contemporary (AC), with about 18 percent of all listening time and Contemporary Hit Radio (Top 40) with about 11 percent. AC is primarily an FM format but a few AMs carry it as well. It consists of a blend of suitable oldies and current soft rock hits, usually about 20 percent current and 80 percent oldies. For example, artists commonly heard on AC stations in the early 1990s were currently popular stars such as Whitney Houston, Michael Bolton, Mariah Carey, Wilson Phillips, and Gloria Estefan, along with past hits from Billy Joel, Fleetwood Mac, Chicago, and Elton John. AC is splintering into four distinct subdivisions. One is soft AC, which emphasizes mostly subdued vocals from the past. Many stations which formerly played the "Beautiful Music" format have switched to soft AC. A second type is oldies-based AC. These stations play few, if any at all, current hits. Instead, their playlist is dominated by softer hits from the sixties, seventies, and eighties. The third type, current AC, takes the opposite strategy. These stations play more contemporary hits and might feature several artists who would also appear on the Top-40 playlists—Madonna, Paula Abdul, Roxette. Finally, there are "full-service" ACs which emphasize news, sports, weather, and DJs who are "personalities."

Contemporary Hit Radio (CHR) is a derivative of what used to be called Top 40. CHR features a small playlist of hit records in a fast rotation. The CHR format has shown a decline in listenership in recent years as part of its audience has been lost to AC and another part to MTV. Additionally, popular music has become more polarized. Many listeners who were formerly CHR listeners have abandoned the format because of an aversion to rap and/or heavy metal. CHR does best with the 12- to 25-year-old age group.

Another popular format was Album-Oriented Rock (AOR). This format was used primarily by FM stations and specialized in playing popular album cuts put out by a particular type of rock artist. Originally, this format was designed to appeal to 18- to 25-year-old males but recently it has shown strong appeal among an older male audience. Some AOR stations try to attract a more mature audience by playing "classic rock" from the sixties, seventies, and eighties.

Country stations, as the name suggests, play hit country and western singles and employ DJs who are down-home, friendly, and knowledgeable about country music. The country format has two main divisions: (1) traditional country stations that play mainstream classic, twangy country music and (2) contemporary country stations that play more current artists who might use synthesizers and other modern sounds. The emergence of country artists such as Randy Travis, George Strait, Trisha Yearwood, Garth Brooks, and Reba McEntire has made country more appealing to a younger demographic, but its main attraction is still an adult audience from 35 to 55.

The Middle of the Road (MOR) format, which is widely used among radio stations, is somewhat hard to describe. As the name implies, this format avoids extremes such as hard rock and semiclassical selections. In their place, the MOR station uses contemporary music and an occasional soft-rock AC hit. Recordings by artists such as John Denver, Neil Diamond, and Barry Manilow are common on MOR stations.

Country singer Clint Black, with his ever-present hat and guitar, is one of the reasons country stations are getting more popular with younger listeners. (Courtesy BMG Music/RCA Records)

Further, MOR stations rely on the personality of their DJs to draw an audience. Particularly important are the morning and evening drive time DJs, who are on the air when the station has its biggest audience. The prime appeal of MOR stations is to 25- to 45-year-olds.

The fastest growing format of the past few years has been Urban Contemporary (UC). Blending together rap, dance music, black, and Hispanic music, UC has strongest appeal among city-dwelling 18- to 35-year-olds. The format features artists such as Bell Biv Devoe, En Vogue, and L. L. Cool J.

Black and Ethnic Formats. These formats aim for special audiences that are defined primarily by race and nationality. There are about 165 stations that program for the black audience and about 260 stations that serve the Hispanic audience. Many of the black and Hispanic stations feature urban contemporary music and run news, features, and special programs of interest to their audiences. In addition, about 60 stations have formats aimed at other ethnic groups: Polish, German, Italian, French, Irish, and Greek.

Format Homogenization

If you've ever taken a long auto trip and listened to the radio stations in the various communities along your route, one of the things you might have noticed is that radio stations sound pretty much alike no matter where you are. Almost all of the major music formats are represented in the large and medium markets and it seems that every market has its morning "zoo crew," an AC station that specializes in "the classic hits" of the sixties, seventies, eighties, and today, a CHR station that calls itself "Power" or "Z" or "Q" something-or-other, an easy listening station with a "warm" format that dedicates love songs at night, and maybe even an AM station that specializes in "golden oldies." Even the DJs sound pretty much the same.

There are several reasons behind this trend toward homogenization. First, many large-market stations are owned by groups and what works for a group owner in one market is likely to work in another. Second, satellite-delivered music services are becoming more common. This means that stations all over the country are playing standardized music. Finally, radio has become so competitive that programming decisions are based on the recommendations of program consultants and audience research firms that compile playlists based on audience surveys and focus groups. There aren't many of these consultants and firms around, and the same records tend to score high from market to market. Consequently, the recommendations tend to be the same from radio station to radio station. Many stations prefer to adopt a "safe" format, one that has worked in similar markets, rather than risking a sizable amount of money on an untested format.

News/Talk Format. This format is becoming more and more popular on the AM band. Some stations emphasize the news part of the news/talk format. National, regional, and local news reports are broadcast periodically throughout the day. Sports, traffic, weather, editorials, public-affairs programs, and an occasional feature would round out the programming day. News stations appeal primarily to a male audience in the 25- to 54-year-old age category.

The talk format attracts listeners in about the same age group. Common types of programs that appear on stations using the talk format features are call-in shows, usually hosted by an opinionated and maybe even abrasive host, interview shows, advice shows, and roundtable discussions. News, weather, traffic reports, and other feature material are blended in with these programs. Unlike the music formats that do not demand their listeners' close attention, the talk format requires that its audience concentrate on the program in order to follow what is said. In addition, talk radio has taken on political implications (see the box on page 212).

Larry King, the dean of talk show hosts, reaches millions of radio listeners. (Courtesy Mutual Broadcasting System/Westwood One Companies)

The news/talk format got a big boost during the 1991 Persian Gulf War as listenership reached its highest levels. The audience declined somewhat after the war ended but news/talk was still attracting about 15 percent of all listening time.

Ownership

The Federal Communications Commission (FCC) ruled in 1992 that no one person or organization can own more than eighteen AM and eighteen FM stations. In addition, the FCC established an ownership cap of four stations in a single large market. This was a big change from the old rules which permitted ownership of twelve AM and twelve FM stations.

The new rules will probably increase the concentration in the industry. As Table 9-1 suggests, large market radio is now dominated by a few big firms. Of the ten group owners listed in the table, seven have stations in both New York and Los Angeles and nine out of ten have a station in Chicago. The next few years will probably see many changes in radio station ownership.

●●●●
PRODUCING RADIO PROGRAMS

Departments and Staff

The departmental structure of a radio station varies according to its size. Obviously, a small station with five or six employees has a different departmental setup than a

No one is quite sure when it started but it got national attention back in 1989 when Congress voted itself a 51 percent pay raise. Coming at a time when the economy was weak and many people were having trouble making ends meet, the pay raise did not go over too well with the general public. The furor might have gone away, however, had it not been for a new political force: talk show radio. Talk show hosts all over the country urged their unhappy listeners to send letters to Congress protesting the pay increase. A Boston talk jockey led a campaign to send members of Congress tea bags to remind them of the Boston Tea Party. The talk show hosts were successful (at least for awhile) in preventing the raise.

When the *Exxon Valdez* spilled oil in Alaskan waters and Exxon was slow to clean it up, talk show hosts mobilized some of the frustration that people felt and collected cut-up Exxon credit cards to send to the company as a form of protest. No topic is too controversial—abortion, gun control, the savings and loan bailout, women's rights—they've all been discussed on talk radio. Even the entertainment world is not exempt. When singer Cat Stevens voiced support for Iran's Ayatollah Khomeini, a talk radio host crushed a pile of his records with a steamroller. When Sinead O'Connor balked at the playing of the U.S. national anthem before one of her concerts, talk show hosts campaigned for a boycott of her records.

Some feel that the amount of power wielded by the gabcasters (as they are called by the trade press) is dangerous. They point out that you need no special training or credentials to be a talk show host and that a lot of politically naive people may be on the air manipulating peoples' emotions. Others think that the trend toward activist talk radio is a sign that free speech is alive and well in the U.S. This topic stirs up some deep-seated feelings, so don't be surprised if you hear it being debated some night on a talk radio show.

large station with a hundred-person staff. Figure 9-2 illustrates the arrangement at a typical medium-sized station.

The two top management positions are the general manager and the program director. The manager has the responsibility for planning and carrying out station policy, maintaining contact with the community, and monitoring program content, audience ratings, and sales information. The program director is responsible for the

FIRM	NUMBER OF STATIONS	POTENTIAL LISTENERS (MILLIONS)
TABLE 9-1 Radio's Top Ten Group Owners—1991		
1. CBS	21	14.3
2. Group W	16	11.7
3. Capcities/ABC	19	11.6
4. Infinity	22	11.4
5. Cox	13	5.9
6. Viacom	13	5.4
7. Bonneville	14	5.4
8. Malrite	10	5.1
9. Gannett	15	4.8
10. Emmis	5	4.3

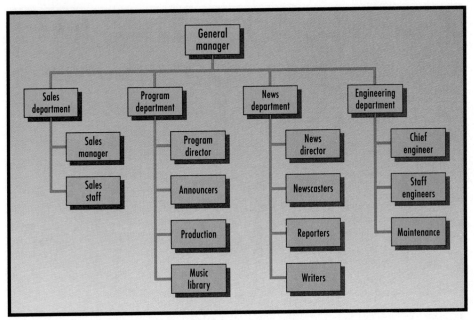

FIGURE 9-2 *Departments and staff at a medium-size radio station.*

station's sound. He or she supervises the music or other program material that the station broadcasts and is also responsible for the hiring and firing of announcers and DJs.

Most stations are divided into the four departments shown in Figure 9-2. The sales department consists of the sales manager and the station's sales force. The news department is responsible for compiling the station's local newscasts and rewriting the wire-service reports of national and regional news. The programming department, under the supervision of the chief engineer, is staffed with technicians responsible for keeping the station on the air and maintaining the equipment.

Putting Together a Program

This section will concentrate on how radio programs are produced for the music, talk, and news formats.

Music Format. Radio programs are put together either by the station's program director and DJs, who receive records from record companies and local retail record outlets, or by an outside programming service, which provides the station with a package of music and voice. For the moment, let us examine how the staff of a local station puts together their program. The first step is generally to lay out a **format wheel** (also called format clock), which is simply a pie chart of an hour divided into segments representing different program elements. Figure 9-3 is a simplified version of a wheel for a contemporary rock station.

Note that the music is structured to flow from one segment to another. Album cuts and hits from the past are spread around the wheel. Additional wheels would be constructed for the various parts of the broadcast day (i.e., one wheel for morning drive time, another for 10 A.M.–4 P.M., another for evening drive time, and another for 7 P.M.–midnight). The 7 P.M.–midnight wheel might contain more hits from the past if the station's rating book showed a greater proportion of 25- to 34-year-olds listening for that period. Morning and evening drive time might contain longer segments for news and weather.

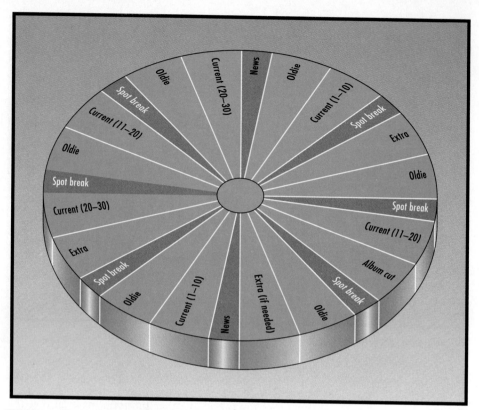

FIGURE 9-3 *Hot clock format rotation for a CHR station.*

Talk Format. Most of the content of the talk format is produced by the local station. As is the case with the music format, the makeup of the audience is taken into account in scheduling the type of show to be broadcast during different parts of the day. During drive time, talk segments should be relatively short and liberally interspersed with news, weather, and traffic reports. The audience for the 10 A.M.–4 P.M. day segment tends to be primarily female and, therefore, topics for discussion should reflect the interests of this group. The early evening audience is generally younger and contains more males. Many talk stations program a sports call-in show during this time period to attract a younger audience.

Producing a talk show requires more equipment than does a simple DJ program. Speaker telephones and extra telephone lines are needed, as well as a delay system.

Blazing Radio

Sometimes owning a radio station can be pure hell . . . especially if you're the number-18 station in your market and your share of the audience is running a minuscule 2 percent. That was the situation facing Chicago radio station WYTZ-FM (Z-95) recently, so they decided to let the station go to hell . . . literally. Station management renamed the station HELL and aired such clever promos as "Want Good Ra-

dio? . . . Go to Hell" and "Think We Should Change Our Name? . . . Go to Hell."

A week later, the station dropped the HELL designation and introduced a new dance-music format on the new Hot 94.7. The whole idea of a Hell Week was simply a promotion to put some distance between the station's old format and its new one. Did the promotion work? Who the hell knows?

The attraction of call-in radio is hard to resist. A convicted murderer broke out of a Minnesota prison. While on the run, he happened to tune in a Minneapolis radio station which was running a trivia contest. The fugitive knew the answer and called in. A sharp-eared listener recognized his voice and alerted police. When he arrived at the station to claim his prize, he was taken back into custody. The police let him keep the prize.

This device gives the talk show moderator a seven- to thirty-second delay period during which he or she can censor what is said by the caller. Another important part of the talk show is the telephone screener, who intercepts phone calls from the audience before they are taken by the host or hostess. The screener ranks the waiting calls for importance, letting the most interesting callers go first, and filters out crank calls or calls from regulars who contact the station too frequently.

All-News Format. The all-news station also works with a programming wheel, similar to that of the music format. Instead of music, however, the news wheel shows the spacing between headlines, weather, news, sports, business reports, and commercials. It also illustrates the **cycle**, the amount of time that elapses before the program order is repeated. By way of illustration, Figure 9-4 shows a simplified news wheel with a thirty-minute cycle.

FIGURE 9-4 *Format wheel at an all-news station.*

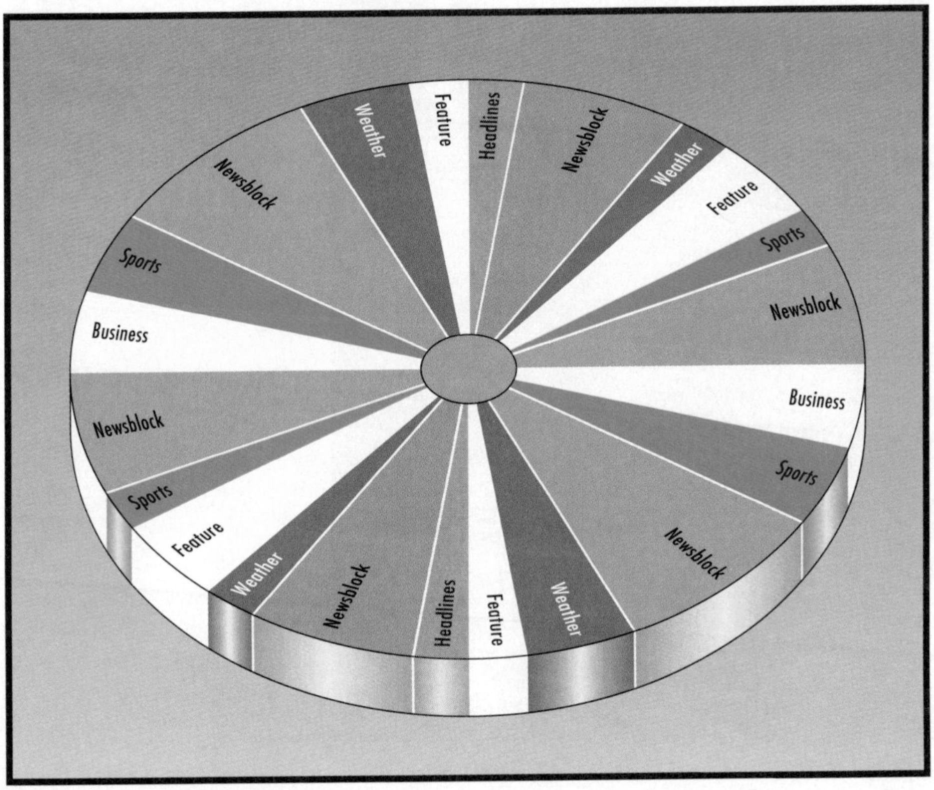

The all-news format is the most difficult to produce. A large staff, consisting of anchor persons, a managing editor, local reporters, editors, rewrite people, a traffic reporter, and stringers (freelance reporters who are paid per story), is needed. The list of necessary facilities is also long: radio wire services, sports wire, weather wire, mobile units, police and fire-frequency scanners, short-wave receiver, and perhaps even a helicopter.

● ● ● ●

ECONOMICS IN THE RADIO INDUSTRY

The profit picture for the radio industry at the beginning of 1992 was not as bright as in previous years. More competition and a recession hurt profit margins at many stations. In 1990, the total industry reported advertising revenues of about $8.8 billion, an increase of about 5 percent over the previous year, but about half of all radio stations actually posted a loss in 1990.

Sources of Revenue

Radio stations earn their money by selling advertising time. The amount that a radio station charges for time is included in its rate card. A typical radio commercial costs several hundred dollars in large cities. The same commercial in a small town might cost only a few dollars.

Like the television industry, the radio industry has three different sources of income from the sale of commercial time. The first comes from the sale of spots on network programs to national advertisers trying to reach a broad market. The second

Nina Totenberg, legal affairs correspondent for National Public Radio, is the reporter who broke the story about Anita Hill's sexual harassment charges against Supreme Court nominee Clarence Thomas. (Diana Walker/ Gamma Liaison)

is the sale of time on local stations to advertisers who wish to reach a specific region (e.g., the Northeast) or a specific type of market (e.g., rural areas). This is called national spot advertising. The third source is advertising purchased by local establishments that want their commercials to be heard only in the immediate community. In 1991, each of these sources represented the following amounts of each dollar of radio revenue:

Network	2¢
National spot	21¢
Local	77¢

Although big-city stations employed large numbers of people and were usually owned by big companies, the radio industry was essentially an assortment of small to medium-sized stations that derived most of its money from local hometown businesses. As the numbers indicate, the overwhelming amount of revenue in radio came from local commercials.

General Expenses

Expenses in radio are divided into six areas: (1) technical, (2) program, (3) selling, (4) general administration, (5) advertising, and (6) news. Technical expenses include the payroll for the engineering staff and the cost of maintaining and replacing technical equipment. Program costs cover salaries paid to talent, cost of tape and records, and music fees paid to the music licensing organizations (see the box below). Sales costs are made up of the salaries of the sales staff and all of the other expenses that go with selling. General administrative expenses include the salaries of all management, secretarial, and clerical personnel, the depreciation of physical facilities, the cost of

Music Licensing: ASCAP and BMI

The Copyright Law of the United States holds that no one may legally perform a musical work for profit without the permission of the copyright holder. The courts have also held that playing a record over a commercial station constitutes such a performance. This law poses a potential problem for radio broadcasters who play dozens of records per day. How do they go about getting permission from the hundreds of copyright owners of the songs they wish to play? How do the copyright holders go about granting permission and collecting payment from the thousands of radio stations that use their material? To solve this dilemma, music licensing organizations were created. They negotiate for permission for the performance of music by stations and secure payment for permission on behalf of the copyright owners. There are two major licensing organizations: the American Society of Composers, Authors and Publishers (AS-CAP) and Broadcast Music Incorporated (BMI).

Radio stations enter into contracts or licenses with these organizations. The stations usually arrange for "blanket" licenses, which allow them to use all the compositions that are listed by the organization for an unlimited number of performances. Both ASCAP and BMI charge fees for this license. These fees amount to about 1 to 2 percent of the station's gross receipts. The copyright holders, in turn, are paid by ASCAP and BMI. The amount that is paid is determined in two ways. First, all network radio and television content is monitored by ASCAP and BMI to discover what songs are played and how often they are performed. Second, frequency of use by local radio and TV stations is determined by sampling a small number of stations and projecting these figures to arrive at a total for all stations. The copyright holders are then paid based on the number of calculated performances.

office supplies, and any interest that is due on loans to the station. As of 1990, the expense dollar was allocated among these six areas as follows:

Technical	4¢
Program	21¢
Sales	19¢
General administration	43¢
Advertising/Promotion	9¢
News	4¢

The low cost of programming reflects the fact that many radio stations pay little or nothing for the records they receive.

Increasing Competition

The proliferation of radio stations has made the industry one of the most competitive in all the media. The overall revenue pie has been sliced into smaller and smaller pieces. In the large markets, which account for the most revenue, the number one station in the market seldom has more than a 10 percent share of the total average listening audience. Further, as Figure 9-5 shows, the gap between the leading station and its competitors has narrowed over the years.

FIGURE 9-5 *Difference in audience share of number one, number five, and number ten rated stations in Top Ten markets 1976–1990.*

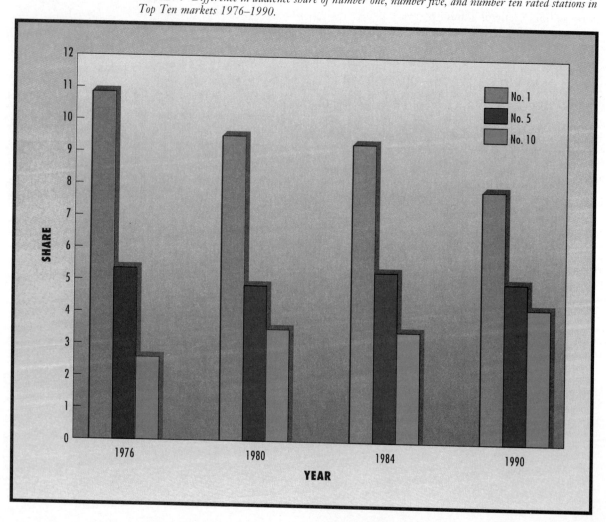

In large markets, listeners generally have several different versions of the same format to choose from. At last count, Los Angeles had nine AC stations; New York had four AOR stations. Increasingly, the same format is competing with itself for listeners. In situations like this, most stations are doing more and more promotions and giveaways to attract listeners (see the box below).

Noncommercial Radio

Many of the early radio stations that went on the air during the 1920s were founded by educational institutions. As the commercial broadcasting system became firmly established, many educational stations were bought by commercial broadcasters, and the fortunes of noncommercial radio dwindled. In 1945, with the coming of FM broadcasting, the FCC was persuaded to set aside several frequencies for educational broadcasting. This action sparked a rebirth of interest in educational broadcasting so that by 1991 there were about 1400 noncommercial radio stations on the air.

Most noncommercial radio stations are owned by colleges, universities, high schools, or other educational institutions. Others are owned by private foundations. Noncommercial radio gets its support from the institutions that own the stations. Ultimately, much of this support comes from tax revenue since taxes support most public educational institutions. Other sources of support are endowments (gifts), grants from foundations or the federal government, and listener donations.

Getting Listeners: Station Promotions

In the highly competitive world of radio, when several stations in the market are programming the same format, the difference between a successful station and a failing station may be the amount of time, money, and effort a station devotes to promotion. The traditional promotion usually involved giving away money to some lucky listeners. Other stations were running promotions that could best be described as unusual. To wit:

- To celebrate Earth Day, a Boston station gave away an environmentally correct lawn mowing service. They sent the winner of this promotion a herd of goats to graze on his lawn.

- A Greenville, South Carolina, station sponsored "An American Dream" promotion in which they awarded a lucky listener a $150,000 home with a pool, $10,000 in furniture, a new car, and a puppy.

- In order to promote Marc Cohen's hit single, "Walking in Memphis," a Memphis station offered an all-expenses paid weekend in Memphis including hotel, dinner, and amusement park tickets. The catch: No transportation was included. They expected the winner to walk in Memphis.

- A Tampa station's promotion for Raid insect spray asked listeners to call in with their worst bug stories. The winners got a thousand dollars and a limo to take them shopping while their house was bug-bombed.

- A Gadsen, Alabama, station celebrated the 100th anniversary of Spam by giving away cans of the stuff to listeners who called and related their worst Spam encounters.

All of the above were radio stations giving away prizes. MTV, however, raised radio promotions to a new height when it actually gave away a radio station as a prize in one of their promotions. Some lucky viewer could win an AM station in Thomasville, Georgia. MTV expected this promotion to draw the most responses ever, suggesting that, even in this age of video, viewers who want their MTV want their radio, too.

Noncommercial stations are served by two networks. National Public Radio (NPR) was founded in 1970. NPR provides program services to about 425 affiliates around the country. Member stations pay a fee ranging from $2000 to $20,000 per year and receive in return about fifty hours of programming per week. Many of these shows are produced at NPR headquarters; others are produced at NPR stations and distributed by NPR. Probably the best known NPR programs are the award-winning *All Things Considered* and *Morning Edition*.

The other noncommercial network is American Public Radio (APR). Serving about 400 affiliates, APR does not produce any of its own programming but does finance program production at member stations. APR broadcasts news, interview, feature, and call-in shows. During the Persian Gulf War, APR carried the BBC's World News Service twenty-four hours a day.

• • • •

ISSUES

Perhaps the most controversial issue facing the radio industry during the early 1990s had to do with how far radio stations should go to attract an audience. In the late 1980s, a significant number of stations went to a "shock jock" format that featured controversial hosts talking about raunchy and formerly taboo topics on the radio. The FCC cracked down on indecency in 1990 and most stations toned down this format. Some, however, still relied on the off-color—and it cost them. Two morning DJs at a Pittsburgh station made jokes about the sexual talents of a newswoman who worked at the station. The woman didn't find the jokes funny. She sued and was awarded almost $700,000. An L.A. station found itself the target of a similar suit.

Some stations went to other extremes to increase their audiences. Morning disc jockeys at a Pasadena, California, station were running a "Confess Your Crime" segment in which people were supposed to call in and confess minor infractions. One morning, however, the DJs got a call from a man who confessed to killing his girlfriend. The call created a good deal of publicity for the station and was even the topic of a 1990 segment of the TV show, *Unsolved Mysteries*. After the TV show aired, some listeners noticed that the caller to the radio station sounded a lot like a new disc jockey who had recently joined the station. An investigation revealed that the whole thing had been a hoax. The call came from a friend of the two DJs who subsequently was hired by the Pasadena station. All of the DJs who participated in the hoax were suspended.

Another station in Arizona claimed one of its DJs had been kidnapped and was in serious danger. The whole thing was a hoax to build listenership, but the station continued with the deception even after the police got involved. The FCC eventually took away the station's license.

During the Persian Gulf crisis in 1991, a St. Louis DJ announced a nuclear attack on the United States. Along with the announcement, the station broadcast the warning tone of the Emergency Broadcasting System and the sound of exploding bombs. The false announcement was apparently an attempt by the morning DJ to dramatize the seriousness of nuclear war in response to listeners who were calling in and urging the use of nuclear weapons against Iraq. Whatever the motive, more than a hundred people called the station and many complained to the FCC.

Several stations have rented billboards that read "I need a job bad. Call _____ ." In reality, the person named on the billboard is a new DJ coming to work for the station.

These examples are the most dramatic but the trend toward stunts and hoaxes has been accelerating in the past few years. Many of these may be harmless, April Fool's Day tricks, but the question remains whether these misleading broadcasts and promotional gimmicks undermine a station's trust and credibility with its audience.

A second issue concerns the trend among radio stations away from serving anybody under 18 or over 55. In the past few years, formats that were historically popular with older and younger listeners have gradually withered away, and these age groups have become demographic undesirables. Why? For one, the 18 to 55 crowd has more money to spend and is more attractive to advertisers. For another, as the baby boomers get older there are more people in the 18 to 55 category and stations interested in drawing big numbers will aim for the largest crowd.

All of this means some formats are getting scarce. Beautiful music stations, a traditional favorite among older listeners, are few and far between as most of them switch to "soft AC" formats to attract the 25–45 crowd. So few stations now play this format that it commands less share of listening time than Spanish-language programming. Middle of the road stations, which also attract the 55-plus demographic, still exist in some big markets but most others have gone to a news/talk format or oldies to attract a younger demographic.

At the other end of the spectrum, Top-40 stations have become less concerned with attracting the teen audience and more eager in their pursuit of 18- to 34-year-olds. The teen-oriented Top 40 of the 1960s and 1970s is hard to find today as programmers have shifted to something called Adult Top 40. In this new format, stations only play mainstream rap which teens don't much like but which some adults can tolerate. They also intersperse some oldies, which have little appeal to teens, among the current hits.

Remember that radio stations are licensed to serve in the public interest. Radio's critics ask whether or not the fascination with demographics has resulted in a system that is underserving large segments of the public.

International Perspective: Commercial Radio in Europe

If you happen to be visiting Europe in the next few years and turn on the radio, you might be surprised at how familiar it sounds. The reason: U.S. radio programmers are investing heavily in European radio. Relaxed government regulation has created a plethora of new commercial radio opportunities. Consider: The United Kingdom, which had only 80 independent commercial stations until 1990 (only one per market), will soon have another 220 on the air. In France, commercial radio became legal only in 1982 and there are already 1400 radio stations operating. Even Russia has announced plans for the private ownership of stations and is looking to purchase programming.

All of these new ventures are depending upon the U.S. and other countries with commercial systems to provide expertise and programming. As a result, a lot of U.S. dollars are going to Europe. In just the last few years, Emmis Broadcasting, a big U.S. group owner of radio stations, has bought 15 percent of Maxximum

FM, a Paris station with transmitters on top of the Eiffel Tower. Group W invested in London Jazz Radio, a new commercial station. Network owner Westwood One is negotiating to provide U.S.–style radio to Russia, and the Satellite Music Network has announced plans to market its programming service all across the European continent.

This foreign venture has its downside. Most countries limit U.S. investment to 20 percent, so American broadcasters will never call the shots. Moreover, advertisers in Europe have become accustomed to a strong public radio service and are not familiar with radio as an advertising medium. Lastly, the economic recession in the U.S. has made investment funds harder to come by. Nevertheless, the overall picture is one of optimism. As the head of Westwood One's international division put it, commercial broadcasting in Europe has nowhere to go but up.

● ● ● ●
CAREERS IN RADIO

There are about 150,000 people employed at radio stations and radio networks. The average station will employ about fourteen full-time people. Competition is tight, but thousands of young people find jobs in radio every year. As in most other industries, radio stations prefer to hire experienced people. How does a newcomer gain experience? One good way is to volunteer to work at your college or university radio station. Try to do as many jobs as possible and learn as much as you can. Another possibility is to arrange for an internship at a local station.

If you intend to look for a job as talent (someone who works in front of the microphone—DJ, announcer, newcaster), you will need to put together an audition tape. This is a five- to fifteen-minute sample of your work. If you're applying for a job at a music format station, the audition tape should include your introduction to appropriate records, some chatter, and a commercial or two. If you're looking for a job as a newscaster, the tape should include your reading of some straight news stories and your integration of some taped interviews into the program. The audition tape allows a potential employer to hear your voice, delivery, style, and general air personality. It constitutes your audition for the job.

Entry-Level Positions

The best place to break into radio is at a small-market station. There are generally more beginning-level jobs in small markets, and the competition is not as fierce as it is in major markets. Another advantage to working at a small-market station is the wide variety of experiences you're likely to have. Small stations hire people who are versatile. A DJ might have to work in sales. A salesperson might have to write commercial copy and produce radio ads. Secretaries and receptionists may cover news stories. It would be virtually impossible to get this sort of experience at a large station.

Most employment counselors recommend that a beginner in radio take any job that is offered to him or her at a station, even if the job is not exactly what the person wants to do. Landing a job is probably more important than starting off in the department that was your first choice. Once inside the organization, it is easier for you to move to your preferred area.

The two areas where most entry-level jobs occur are the programming and sales departments. Of these two, the programming area is the more competitive. Many people who enter the radio field seem to want jobs as announcers or DJs. As a result, there is an oversupply of people in this area. Nonetheless, it is possible to find a job if you are persistent and willing to work unusual hours. Volunteer your services for the midnight to 7 A.M. shift or express a willingness to work weekends or holidays. Tell the program director you're willing to substitute any day any time for a DJ who gets sick. Once you get your own air slot, you can prove yourself as a steady, competent professional and move to better things. Roughly the same sort of advice would apply to those interested in radio news. Make yourself available on the weekends. Offer to work as a stringer. Be persistent.

The best chance of landing a beginning job in radio can be found in the sales department. Radio stations, especially those in smaller markets, are usually in need of competent salespeople with a knowledge of and an interest in radio. If you are able to handle a sales job, it could be the start of a lucrative career in radio.

Upward Mobility

The first job in radio is seldom a lifetime commitment. It usually leads to more challenging positions with more responsibility, more opportunity for creativity, and a larger salary. For talent, there are two distinct avenues of upward mobility. For DJs, it consists of moving up to larger markets and better time slots. The ultimate goal of most DJs is a drive-time air shift in one of the top ten markets. In addition, many DJs progress within a station by moving up to the chief announcer's spot and from there to program director. Radio news reporters also strive to move into the big markets, and those with an interest in administration move into the director's slot. An occasional program director or news director moves up to the general manager's job.

The sales department offers the best route for upward mobility. Competent salespeople are given bigger and more profitable accounts to service. Some will move up to the sales manager position. From sales manager, many will progress to general manager. Salespeople are skilled at making money for the station. They are also used to dealing with people and have many contacts in the community. All of these factors help them move into top management positions. It is an established fact that most radio station managers got their start in the sales department.

Before closing our discussion of radio careers we should point out that radio stations are not the only places of potential employment. Program syndicators such as Drake Chenault hire announcers and those experienced in programming music formats. Companies that produce packaged feature programs need producers, writers, and directors. Radio wire services such as the Associated Press and United Press International need reporters and writers. In short, there are opportunities outside the scope of traditional radio stations.

• • • •

SUGGESTIONS FOR FURTHER READING

The following books contain more information about the concepts and topics discussed in this chapter.

BITTNER, JOHN, *Professional Broadcasting*, Englewood Cliffs, N.J.: Prentice-Hall, 1981.

BUSBY, LINDA, AND DONALD PARKER, *The Art and Science of Radio*, Boston: Allyn and Bacon, 1984.

FORNATALE, PETER, AND JOSHUA MILLS, *Radio in the Television Age*, Woodstock, N.Y.: Overlook Press, 1980.

HILLIARD, ROBERT, *Radio Broadcasting*, New York: Longman, 1985.

KEITH, MICHAEL, *Radio Programming*, Boston: Focal Press, 1987.

KEITH, MICHAEL, AND JOSEPH KRAUSE, *The Radio Station*, Boston: Focal Press, 1989.

MACFARLAND, DAVID, *Contemporary Radio Programming Strategies*, Hillsdale, N.J.: Lawrence Erlbaum, 1990.

SHERMAN, BARRY, *Telecommunications Management: Radio, TV, Cable*, New York: McGraw-Hill, 1987.

SMITH, WES, *The Pied Piper of Rock 'n' Roll*, Marietta, Ga.: Longstreet Press, 1989.

10

STRUCTURE OF THE RECORDING INDUSTRY

When it came to the music business, nobody ever accused David Geffen of bad timing. In 1964, after flunking out of college, he started working in the mail room at the William Morris talent agency. He worked his way up until he was signing rock musicians with the agency. Eventually, he made enough contacts to start his own record company, Asylum Records. He signed some new acts, like the Eagles, and some established stars, like Cher, and his company prospered. In 1972, he sold out to Warners for a cool $7 million.

After a stint in the movie business, Geffen returned to the recording scene by starting Geffen Records in 1980. Again, he signed contracts with some proven stars, like John Lennon and Yoko Ono, but also took a chance on some performers who, at the time, were still up and coming, like Donna Summer. Geffen Records succeeded and by 1990 boasted such acts as Don Henley, Guns 'N' Roses, and Edie Brickell and New Bohemians. And once again, Geffen was swept up in the fast-consolidating world of recorded music. In 1990, Geffen Records was the last major independent record label and was such a hot property that several of the big companies that control the record business wanted to buy it. In mid-1990, Geffen sold to the huge entertainment conglomerate MCA for $550 million. Interestingly, Geffen took most of his money in the form of MCA stock. Less than a year later, MCA itself was acquired by the giant Japanese electronics firm of Matsushita. Geffen sold his stock for about $710 million.

Several facts about today's recording business can be learned from the Geffen saga. First, the trend is toward consolidation. There are no major independents left; six big companies dominate the field. Consequently, the production and distribution of recorded music is a thoroughly corporate affair. Second, American-owned record companies are rare. Five of the big six are owned by international conglomerates headquartered in a foreign country. Third, the recording industry deals with high finance. The risks are substantial but the rewards, as the Geffen case vividly illustrates, can be astronomical, at least for a few shrewd and lucky individuals. Finally, the record business is a unique blend of business and talent. Record companies are continually searching for new artists and new sounds that will succeed in the marketplace. The singers and musicians may become the stars but the record companies are the starmakers. The companies search every place for new talent, no matter how unlikely. The same week the MCA deal was finalized, Geffen Records released "Do the Bartman," recorded by The Simpsons.

ORGANIZATION OF THE RECORD INDUSTRY

The recording industry consists of the various creative talent and business enterprises that originate, produce, and distribute records to consumers. Rock music accounts for about 60 percent of the total sales of the record industry; country and rhythm and blues account for another 10 percent each; gospel, jazz, and classical account for the rest. Although this chapter concentrates on rock music, remember that the other music styles are also part of the industry. For our purposes, we will divide the business into four major segments: (1) talent, (2) production, (3) distribution, and (4) retail.

Talent

The talent segment of the industry consists of all the singers, musicians, songwriters, arrangers, and lyricists who hope to make money by recording and selling their songs. The words "hope to make money" are important because far more performers are laboring in virtual obscurity in and around Detroit, Austin, Nashville, New York, and Los Angeles than are cashing royalty checks from their recordings. Exactly how many people are "out there" hoping to make it big is impossible to pinpoint. We do know that almost $3 billion of musical instruments are sold every year and a great deal of this money is spent by the 30,000–50,000 aspiring performers estimated by industry experts to be looking for a big break.

Performers start out as a beginning act. The initial motivation may be simply personal pleasure. Many begin performing during high school. Bob Dylan (then known as Bob Zimmerman) started out with a high school band in Hibbing, Minnesota. These beginning acts rarely last. Most break up, with some members dropping out of music and others re-forming into new groups. Some group members leave their groups and become single performers; some single performers join groups.

The novice musician or musical group eventually graduates to a "traveling act," which plays anywhere and everywhere to gain experience, a little money, and maybe some recognition. Traveling acts play in bars and clubs where they are little more than human jukeboxes providing accompaniment or background music. INXS got together in high school and toured Australia for eleven years before becoming an international success. The B-52s and REM played college clubs in Athens, Georgia,

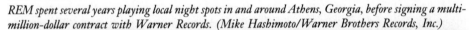

REM spent several years playing local night spots in and around Athens, Georgia, before signing a multi-million-dollar contract with Warner Records. (Mike Hashimoto/Warner Brothers Records, Inc.)

while getting their acts together. Michael Bolton spent almost fifteen years working clubs and giving music lessons before making it big. Even Mariah Carey, who debuted on the charts when she was only 20, spent more than two years waiting tables and trying to sell songs before she was discovered. The income for beginning acts is meager, and the work is exhausting. For most performers, this stage is one in which they learn the trade and pay their dues to the profession. In the early years, the main goal of most acts is to survive.

If the act is talented and lucky, it may be noticed by an A&R (artist and repertoire) scout from a record company, an independent producer, agent, or manager. If things work out right, the act is signed to a contract by a recording company.

Production

The entrance of the recording company marks the transition to the production phase of the industry. The company brings the act to a recording studio where a large number of songs are recorded. Audio engineers and elaborate sound-mixing facilities are used to get exactly the right sound. Eventually, a single or an album is put together. The company also supplies publicity, advertising, merchandising, and packaging expertise. Promotion, which in the recording industry consists primarily of getting the record played on influential radio stations and getting the music video on TV, is also the responsibility of the company. There are dozens of record companies, but six dominate the business. They are Sony, Time Warner, Polygram, EMI/Capitol, Bertelsmann, and MCA (Matsushita).

Distribution

There are four main outlets for record distribution: (1) direct retail, (2) rack jobbers, (3) one-stops, and (4) direct consumer sales. Of these four outlets, the rack jobber is the most important, accounting for approximately 65 percent of all record sales. Retail stores are a distant second, accounting for about 15–20 percent. Direct retail refers to regular record stores that specialize in the sales of records, tapes, and related equipment. Many retail stores are chain operations with several outlets in different parts of the country. Chains having more than 100 retail stores include two that are typically located in shopping malls, Camelot and Record Bar, and several that are "free standing": The Wherehouse, Musicland, and Western Merchandisers.

Rack jobbers service the record racks that are located in variety or large department stores. Such large concerns as Sears, J.C. Penney, and K-mart all have their record departments serviced by rack jobbers. The rack jobber chooses the records that are sold in these locations. The department stores are then relieved of the task of keeping track of what's popular, ordering new releases, reordering, returning unused merchandise, and so on. In some arrangements, the rack jobber makes money by collecting a percentage of the price of each record that is sold. In other cases, the rack jobber simply leases space in the store and owns as well as operates the record department.

One-stops purchase records from record companies and resell them to retail stores and jukebox operators who are not in a position to buy directly from the record company. For example, a small, independently owned retail store might not qualify for credit from the record companies and so might purchase its records from a one-stop.

TV packagers and record clubs sell directly to the consumer. Many of you have probably seen TV ads for collections of music ("The Best of Heavy Metal," Connie Francis' Greatest Hits, Zamfir and the Pan Flute, etc.). Packagers receive licenses from record manufacturers and use large amounts of TV advertising to market their products to the audience. Record clubs depend more on direct mail advertising and usually offer an attractive introductory deal ("6 CDs for 99 cents") with the stipulation that consumers must buy a certain number of offerings in the next year or so.

There are two channels of distributing records to these four outlets: independent distributors and branch distributors. Independent distributors (called "indies") are independently owned companies that contract with various labels to physically distribute their records to their accounts. A branch distributor is linked to one of the big six record companies mentioned above, and the local distribution offices are owned by the record company. Independent distribution accounts for only 5 percent of the business. Independents, however, are still important because they are the ones who usually handle new acts. Rap, for example, would probably have never made it big without the efforts of independent distributors.

During the middle to late 1970s, retail stores were given a 100-percent-return option; that is, they could return to the distributor for credit all of the records that they couldn't sell. When record sales started to decline in 1979 and 1980, this unlimited-return policy was changed and retail outlets were given credit for only 20 percent returns. This prompted retail stores to order small quantities of records—a fact that in turn led record companies to produce fewer copies of a single or album for distribution. Even with the turnaround in record sales in the mid-1980s, record companies were still being conservative in the number of records and tapes shipped to retailers. Figure 10-1 summarizes the distribution process.

Retail

The trend in record retailing has been consolidation; as a result, a few large chain stores now dominate the business. The biggest chain, Musicland, which also operates under the names Sam Goody and Discount Records, has 884 locations. Trans World Music (which includes Record Town, Coconuts, and twenty other store names) has

FIGURE 10-1 *Record distribution channels.*

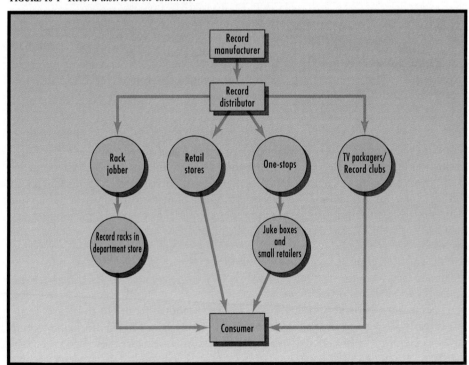

Bright lights, big music: The Sam Goody chain of record stores is owned by Musicland, Inc. (Courtesy The Musicland Group)

485. Target Stores, Inc., has 420. In addition, as mentioned above, consumers purchase tapes and discs at the record departments of various department stores and through phone or mail orders direct to packagers and record clubs.

Ownership

The U.S. record business is now almost entirely foreign-owned. In 1986 the huge German conglomerate Bertelsmann AG paid $300 million to General Electric for RCA/Ariola records. The next year CBS sold its record division to the Sony Corporation of Japan for $2 billion. Not to be outdone, Sony's main Japanese rival, the Matsushita Electrical Industrial Co., acquired the American entertainment conglomerate MCA in late 1991 for a whopping $6.6 billion. Two other recording leaders are owned by European companies: EMI/Capitol is owned by Thorn/EMI of Great Britain, and Polygram is owned by the Phillips Company of the Netherlands. Only one major record company, Time Warner, is U.S. owned. Table 10-1 summarizes the holdings of the six major companies.

This pattern of ownership highlights the international nature of the music business. Nearly 75 percent of the music sold in Germany is in English. In Japan, about half is in English. In fact, along with Great Britain and Canada, these two countries represent the biggest foreign markets for U.S. records. The trade deficit that characterizes most of the United States international dealings does not extend to sound re-

Record buyers in Minneapolis, Minnesota, can buy CDs that are untouched by human hands . . . literally. The Robot Music Store has no employees. Well, at least no human employees. The store, a glass-encased, 140-square-foot kiosk, is staffed by a five-foot-tall, 400-pound robot. A customer selects a CD via computer screen and gives the robot cash or a credit card. The robot gives change, or in the case of a credit card, verifies the transaction using a built-in modem. The robot then moves, slowly but surely, to the racks of CDs, chooses the right one, drops it through a slot to the waiting customer and says, "Thank you."

There's only one problem. A lot of customers will go to a record store and not know the name of the song they want to buy. They hum a few bars to the salesperson who can usually identify it. If you try that at the Robot Music Store, the robot will only stare at you.

cording. In 1990, the U.S. exported about a billion dollars worth of discs and tapes while importing only $250 million.

PRODUCING RECORDS

Departments and Staff

There are seven departments within the typical recording company:

1. artists and repertoire (A&R)

2. sales and distribution

TABLE 10-1 Top Six Record Companies			
COMPANY AND MAJOR LABELS	**1991 REVENUE (BILLIONS)**	**TOP STARS**	**OTHER INTERESTS**
Sony Records: Columbia, Epic	$3.3	George Michael, Billy Joel, Barbra Streisand, New Kids on the Block	Electronics, CD pressing plants, research, batteries
Time Warner Inc.: Reprise, Elektra, Atlantic	2.9	U2, Whitesnake, Anita Baker, Motley Crüe	Home videos, *Mad*, movies, cable TV, book publishing
RCA (owned by Bertelsmann): Ariola, Arista	2.3	Aretha Franklin, Grateful Dead, Bruce Hornsby, The Judds	Printing, book clubs, magazines, film, record clubs, banks, TV
PolyGram (owned by Phillips); Mercury, Deutsche Grammophon, A & M	3.5	Bon Jovi, Def Leppard, Janet Jackson, Vladimir Horowitz	Defense weapons, home appliances, lighting fixtures, data systems, toothbrushes
Thorn/EMI: Capitol, EMI Manhattan	2.1	Hammer, David Bowie, Bob Seger, Roxette	Consumer electronics, appliances, information technology, light bulbs
MCA (Matsushita): Motown, Geffen	2.0	Aerosmith, Tom Petty, Cher	Consumer electronic, movies

3. advertising and merchandising

4. business

5. promotion

6. publicity

7. artist development

Figure 10-2, page 231, shows a common arrangement.

The A&R department consists of talent scouts for the record industry. The title "artist and repertoire" is a throwback to the 1950s when the A&R department actually matched talent with potential songs. In those days the A&R person even signed talent to contracts and provided creative guidance to the performers by arranging their music and supervising their recording sessions. More recently, performers have become more sophisticated in their approach to music and seldom accept advice from the A&R people. Performers now go to independent producers, who assist them in putting together a demonstration record. In fact, many stars, including Stevie Wonder, Ric Ocasek, and Phil Collins, function as both performers and producers. As a result, much of the creative work done by A&R people has been replaced by administrative functions: how much it will cost to sign the act, whether the contract should be for a single or single plus album, what promotional strategies should be used, and so on. Even though the A&R department no longer has the creative clout it once had, it still remains an important part of the industry because the industry depends on new talent and the A&R department is responsible for supplying that talent. A major part of an A&R person's job is to listen to demonstration tapes sent in by hopefuls and to attend auditions. Major companies also send their A&R people out on the road where they move from one club to another, enduring a succession of fourth-rate bands (in the slang of the business, such acts are called "garage bands") in the hope of discovering another Paula Abdul or Wilson Phillips.

The sales and distribution department, as the name suggests, first sells the company's products and then makes sure that the records get to the record stores where consumers can buy them. As mentioned previously, there are four types of accounts that can be sold: retail stores, rack jobbers, one-stops, and TV packagers. The actual selling of the record occurs about a month prior to the record's release. The distribution of the record is usually done through branch distributors.

The advertising and merchandising department aids record sales by planning media ad campaigns and point-of-purchase displays in record outlets. The advertising campaign goes hand in hand with the efforts of the promotion department (see below) to get air play for the record. It includes television and print ads that remind consumers of the record that they have been hearing on the local radio stations. Point-of-purchase displays include posters, mobiles, neon signs, and life-size cutouts that are set up in the record store to help trigger a sale. Market research has indicated that point-of-purchase displays are important in spurring sales, and record companies spend large sums of money for these marketing aids. The advertising and merchandising department also handles other promotional devices such at T-shirts, buttons, and bumper stickers that are used to push the record.

The business department includes lawyers, accountants, market researchers, financial analysts, and secretarial and clerical staffs. It functions in the record business in the same way that such a department would operate in any other business or industry.

In the record business, promotion means getting the record played on radio stations. Since air play is crucial to the success of the record, the promotion department is an important part of all record companies. Since many contemporary stations restrict the records they play to a tightly controlled playlist, the job of the promotion

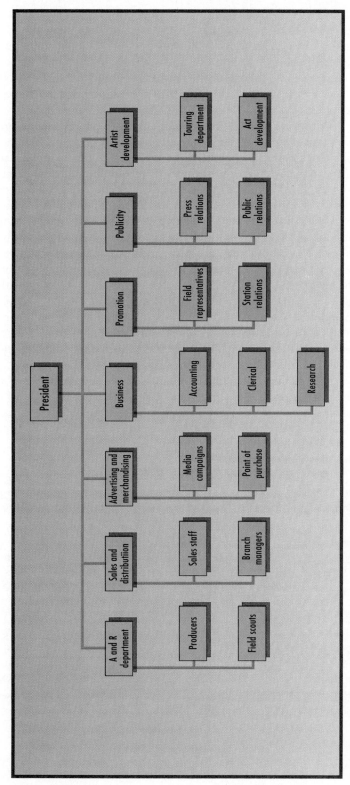

FIGURE 10-2 *Departmental chart for a typical recording company.*

department is a challenging one. Radio stations like to stick with tried and true hits; record company promotion people want to convince the station to play their company's new releases. With about 5000 singles and 2500 albums released in the United States each year and only four or five slots open on a given radio station each week to devote to new records, the job of the promotion department is made all that much harder. The stakes are high. Unless a record gets air play, it has little chance of becoming a hit.

With the advent of music videos, a whole new avenue of promotion opened up. Now it is almost obligatory for a record company to release a video along with an album or single. The popularity of music videos makes it easier to introduce new acts on a national scale. MTV has more than 50 million subscribers and reaches the whole country. In addition, MTV is willing to experiment with new artists and songs. Songs that would usually not break into the playlist of a contemporary hits station are featured on MTV, thus increasing their popularity and making it possible for them to crack through to radio air play. Surveys have shown that MTV has become an important influence in record and tape buying. About half the people in one national survey reported that they had purchased or intended to purchase a recording by a performer they had seen on MTV. On the other side of the coin, music videos are not cheap to produce. Budgets typically range from about $50,000 for a simple performance video to about $250,000 for a complicated concept video. Many record companies tried to get MTV and other stations using music videos to pay a fee for their use. In sum, music videos significantly changed the nature of record promotion, another example of the media symbiosis mentioned in Chapter 1.

The publicity department attempts to get press coverage for its new performers and new releases. This department also has the responsibility of getting new acts and albums reviewed by critics in such publications as *Rolling Stone* and *Billboard*. The publicity department also makes sure that the consumer and trade press is supplied with all the information and photos they need for feature stories and interviews with the label's stars.

The artist development department carries on a wide range of activities. All of this department's efforts are designed to further the career of a group or performer. Some of the duties supervised by this department include coordinating tour dates,

Whose Voice Is it Anyway?

The Grammy for best new artist of 1989 went to Rob Pilatus and Fabrice Morvan, better known as Milli Vanilli, for their multiplatinum debut album *Girl, You Know It's True*. This would not have been remarkable except for one small detail. Rob and Fab didn't sing a note on that album. They were what's called a "front" for a "ghost act," an artist who has a great voice but lacks the appearance, proper image, dynamism, or performance ability to appear in public. Milli Vanilli did dance, prance, and carry on while onstage but they simply lip-synched the lyrics.

Their producer blew the whistle when the pair actually wanted to sing on their next planned album. Caught by surprise, the National Academy of Recording Arts and Science examined stricter procedures for monitoring label credits. Embarrassed, Milli Vanilli had to return their Grammy and endure being the target of thousands of jokes and gibes. As Arsenio Hall sang, "Girl you know it's true . . . oooh, oooh, oooh . . . You are through."

Well, not quite. The duo was signed on to do a commercial spoofing themselves for Carefree gum. It was reported they sang with their own voices.

making sure that the act has a well-produced concert show, and arranging for television appearances.

Making a Record or Tape

In order for a performer or group to win a recording contract, they need to convince someone in a record company that they have a sound that will sell. The first step in the process is to produce a demonstration tape (called a **demo**) that can be sent to the appropriate persons. A demo is usually done in a studio with four-track mixing facilities and does not have to sound as good as the finished product released by the major studios. All the demo has to do is highlight the strengths of the group or performer and capture the attention of record company executives.

The second step is to sell the demo. Sending an unsolicited tape to a record company is probably the worst way to sell it. Although there are some exceptions (the Doobie Brothers were signed by Warner on the strength of an unsolicited tape), most of these tapes are never listened to. A better way is to hire a manager or agent to sell the demo for the act. If the agent is successful, step three entails going to the recording studio and making a master tape.

Resembling something you might see at NASA's mission control center, with banks of modern equipment, blinking lights, and digital readouts, the modern recording studio does multitrack recording. Professional studios have machines capable of recording up to forty-eight different tracks. This means that different instruments and vocals can be recorded on different sections of the same piece of tape. For example, a piano might be recorded on one track, drums on another, bass on another, lead vocal on another, background vocal on yet another, and so on. So that one track does not leak onto another, the studio is set up with careful placement of microphones and wooden baffles—soundproof barriers that keep the sound of one instrument from spilling over into the mikes recording the other instruments. Before the actual recording begins, audio engineers experiment with different microphones, mike placements, and amplifier settings to achieve the right sound. Once the session starts, the producer makes most of the creative decisions. Some groups do their best on the first "take"; others may need to play the same music a dozen times before it's acceptable. The producer decides when the performers take a break, when the tune has to be played over because of a bad note, when the tape should be played back so that the group can hear itself and perhaps make changes in the arrangement, etc.

The advent of multiple-track recording has revamped the music-making process. Currently, it isn't even necessary for a band to record together. The instrumentalists can come in one at a time and "lay down" their tracks, the lead singer or singers can add the vocals later, and everything can be put together at the mixing console. Further, many new recording studios are equipped with satellite uplinks and downlinks, which make it possible for artists in different states to record an album without ever seeing each other. A singer in New York, for example, sings to background music previously recorded on a digital tape recorder and sent via satellite to New York. The solo is sent back to Hollywood where it is taped on another digital machine. The two tracks are then balanced and mixed together.

Modern studios are also equipped with digital sampling synthesizers that are capable of "memorizing" any sound and playing it back on a keyboard over the full musical spectrum. Musician Jan Hammer used a synthesizer to create the sound of horns, drums, woodwinds, guitars, and vibraphones on the "Miami Vice" theme. None of the instruments heard on that piece of music was played by a live musician.

Of course, the biggest change in recording technology has been the move to digital recording. In conventional sound recording, music is represented by a continuous signal. This signal is stored as wiggles and curves in a record groove or as different patterns of magnetic particles on a tape. There are two problems with analog recording.

Backmasking is the technical name for hiding in a record or tape a message that can be heard only by playing the record or tape backward. Controversy has surrounded this technique as many religious and social reform groups claim backmasking is being used to present harmful subliminal messages about Satan and other unsavory topics. Some groups have even burned records and tapes that they claim contained these backward messages.

The first well-known case of backmasking occurred in 1968 on the Beatles' *White Album.* At the time, there was a totally unfounded rumor circulating that Paul McCartney was dead. People who believed this rumor claimed that if the song "Revolution Number Nine" was played backward, you could hear something that sounded like "turn me on, deadm'n," a reference, they claimed, to the departed Paul. Other listeners claimed that it took a powerful imagination and repeated close and careful listening to hear anything resembling an intelligible message.

The other well-known example concerns the group Led Zeppelin and "Stairway to Heaven." The song was written by Jimmy Page and sung by Robert Plant, two performers with an interest in the occult. When played backward, one passage of the song sounds like "so here's to my sweet Satan" or something close to that. Other music scholars have suggested that there are at least a half-dozen references to Satan backmasked in other parts of the song. Did Plant and Page deliberately backmask a message? Probably. The hidden message can be heard only in the studio version of the song and doesn't come across in the concert version, suggesting that it was carefully engineered. Were Plant and Page deliberately trying to plant (no pun intended) satanic visions into the minds of their listeners? Maybe, but it seems more likely that they were merely making an obvious point in a clever way. Proceed backward down the stairway to heaven and you'll wind up with the devil.

In any case, "Stairway" must have started a trend. E.L.O.'s album, aptly entitled *Secret Messages*, contains the message "welcome to the show" when played backward. "Snowblind," by Styx, allegedly contains the backmasked message "ooooh, Satan, move in our voices." Others suggest it sounds more like "ooooh, stakem moota roy hoopskirt." In any case, because of all the publicity, Styx actually did place a backmasked message (the Latin phrase on the dollar bill) in their next album.

Do people unconsciously perceive these messages and sell their souls to Satan? Not likely. Studies have shown that people have enough trouble trying to understand the forward versions of rock lyrics—let alone backward messages.

Nonetheless, the controversy will not stop. Only recently another group of music reformers claimed that after listening countless hours to the backward version of the "Mr. Ed" television theme ("A horse is a horse . . . "), they were able to make out the word "Satan." This, of course, immediately brings up the question of why anyone would spend countless hours listening to the "Mr. Ed" theme being played backward . . . or, for that matter, forward.

First, the process leaves background noise, heard as hiss when there is no signal to drown it out. Second, each time a copy is made from a master the quality decreases. Eventually, the fidelity gets so bad that another master must be produced. Digital recording gets around this by assigning 0s and 1s to each particle of sound and storing this number on tape. This is a big improvement over analog recording since there's no noise. Further, any machine that can read the digital tape can duplicate the sound wave. Since no copy of a copy is made, the ten-thousandth disc or tape made from the master is as crisp as the first.

After the recording session, the next step is called the mix down. This is the technically exacting job of mixing down the multiple tracks onto a two-track stereo master. In the mix down, each track is equalized; echo, overdubbing, or other special effects are added and certain passages are scheduled for rerecording. If an album is being produced, each track has to be precisely placed on the stereo spectrum. A track can be placed in the left or right speaker or in the center, where it is heard as equal in both speakers. Mixing a sixteen- or twenty-four-track tape down to two tracks can take several days. The job has been made somewhat easier in recent years thanks to computerized mixing boards, which quickly re-create a previous mix that can then be modified. After the mix is completed, the master is reproduced on tape and disc for manufacture. At the same time, the promotion department is given a preview of the new release, and the advertising and publicity departments begin their efforts.

• • • •

ECONOMICS OF THE RECORDING INDUSTRY

We will approach the topic of economics at two levels. First we'll examine the economic structure of the industry as a whole. Next we'll focus on a more personal level and investigate the financial ups and downs of a typical musical group trying to make it in the recording business.

Economic Trends in the Industry

The record industry has always been a roller-coaster kind of business. Growth years are inevitably followed by lean years. The early 1990s saw the industry still on the growth curve, but how long this prosperity will last is anybody's guess. The only sure thing is that the record business will remain unpredictable and exciting.

Revenue from the sales of recorded music reached an all-time high in 1992, more than $9.0 billion, up 38 percent from 1989. Worldwide revenues were also at a record $28.7 billion. The continued popularity of the CD still accounted for much of this boom.

The big six companies that dominated the market had reason to feel pleased. Bertelsmann, for example, paid a pricey $330 million for RCA/Arista in 1985 but, thanks to such stars as Whitney Houston and Bruce Hornsby, the company earned back the entire purchase price in less than four years. Sony paid a lot more—$2 billion, to be precise—for CBS Records but earned back a big chunk of that thanks to New Kids on the Block (see box on page 236) and George Michael. Time Warner became the most profitable company thanks to the likes of Madonna, Paula Abdul, Phil Collins, and the B-52s. Profit margins for these companies were averaging a healthy 15 percent.

Nonetheless, there were signs that this prosperity might not last. In the first place, consumers were beginning to rebel at the high cost of CDs. As of 1991, the suggested retail price of a CD by a major artist was hovering between $15.98 and $17.98. This may be part of the reason that growth in sales fell from 93 percent in 1988 to 38 percent in 1989 and 35 percent in 1990. Even cassettes are edging up in price: Madonna and New Kids on the Block retail for $10.95. Record company executives are paying close attention to the price issue, hoping they have yet to reach the numbers where consumers tune out.

Secondly, record companies are gambling big money by handing out huge contracts to performers. Janet Jackson recently signed a deal estimated at $40 million for three albums. At the same time, brother Michael negotiated a $50 million contract with Sony that eclipsed his sister's. Steve Winwood signed a three-album deal for about $13 million. Warner's concluded a multimillion-dollar deal with REM, and Robert Palmer signed a $12 million deal with EMI. Record companies are gambling that these performers can match their previous track records and produce more

It all started back in 1984 when a Boston song producer-promoter named Maurice Starr was treated to a rap song at an impromptu audition by a teenager from nearby Dorchester, Massachusetts, named Donnie Wahlberg. Impressed, Starr selected Wahlberg as the first member of a new group he was forming. Wahlberg next introduced Starr to several of his pals from school, The group was originally called Nynuk and played a few clubs in the Boston area. They were eventually signed by Columbia Records with one condition—the name had to go. In its place, the group chose "New Kids on the Block" and released their first album of the same name in 1986. It flopped.

But the Kids, Donnie, Danny, Jonathan, Jordan, and Joseph, did not get discouraged. Neither did Columbia. A second album, *Hangin' Tough*, was released in 1988. One of the tracks from that album, "Please Don't Go Girl," began to get radio air play. The song's success led to an offer to open for teen star Tiffany on her summer tour. This led to the most phenomenal success a popular group has ever had, eclipsing the Beatles, Elvis, and Michael Jackson. In just thirty months, the New Kids sold 8.5 million copies of *Hangin' Tough* in the U.S. Their follow-up, *Step by Step*, sold 3.5 million. A Christmas album, *Merry, Merry Christmas*, sold 2 million. Even their initial dud, *New Kids on the Block*, was resuscitated and sold 3 million copies. These are just the domestic figures, of course; these albums sold more than 10 million copies internationally. Total revenue from albums and singles both here and abroad: about $175 million. But wait . . . there's more.

The number one, number two, and number three top-selling music videos of all time belong to New Kids on the Block. Their total sales amount to more than 3.5 million copies in the U.S., not to mention another million or so abroad. Total revenue from videos: about $140 million. But wait . . . there's more.

The group attracts huge crowds to their concerts. A sixty-show tour in 1990 attracted 1.85 million fans. Total tour revenue: about $150 million. But wait . . . there's more.

The New Kids on the Block get most of their income from merchandising. At their concerts and at retail stores everywhere fans can buy New Kids buttons, T-shirts, posters, sheets, towels, keychains, dolls, tape players, and dozens of other items. The Kids get a percentage from each sale. Total estimated revenue: about $450 million. But wait . . . there's more.

The Kids also have a 900-number that fans can call. More than two million did at an average of $4 per call. The Kids also have a fan club whose members pay $20 a year. The Kids also have a Saturday morning cartoon show, do commercial endorsements, and make personal appearances. And that's not all. A motion picture is in the works. About $2 million worth of books about the group have been sold. Total for these miscellaneous activities: about $80 million. Add everything up and the total is right around a billion dollars.

The Kids have only one problem: their name. Since all of them are in their early twenties, they're hardly kids. And, since they've been around for a few years, they're hardly new. Perhaps a more descriptive name might be "Rich Guys Who Own the Block."

chartbusters. If they don't, an awful lot of money can be lost. So far, some of these bets haven't paid off. Steve Winwood's follow-up to his *Roll with It* was a commercial failure. Palmer's first album for EMI sold a little more than a million copies but his second one failed to make the Top 100. Even superstars like Madonna and Whitney Houston are not selling as well as before. Madonna's *Like a Virgin* sold seven million in 1984; her more recent releases have sold about two million. Houston sold nine million copies of her debut album; her follow-up, *I'm Your Baby Tonight*, had sold a little more than three million by the end of 1991. All of this has some record companies a little uneasy.

Further, the record industry knows that music sells records. The Beatles and the English sound sparked sales during the 1960s. Disco helped pull the industry of a slump in the 1970s and Michael Jackson single-handedly did the same thing with *Thriller* in the 1980s. Record executives note that there doesn't appear to be a new compelling sound on the horizon to spark record sales in the early 1990s. In fact, some critics charge that the domination of the industry by big conservative conglomerates has discouraged innovation and change as the big companies stick with formulaic proven styles.

Finally, the introduction of a new technology makes things harder to predict. Digital audio tape (DAT) cassettes are the tape equivalent of CDs. They are smaller than ordinary cassettes but hold more music. What is most significant about them, however, is the fact that, unlike the CD, you can record, erase, and record again on DAT. This fact had many in the record industry worried about piracy if CDs were copied to DAT and sold illegally. As a result, the record industry opposed the introduction of DAT players into the United States. In 1991, however, a tentative agreement was reached that would place a surcharge on DAT players and DAT blank tapes. The money from this surcharge would be distributed among the singers, musicians, producers, and songwriters to help offset some of the lost revenue from DAT piracy and copying. Further, DAT cassettes would be manufactured so that you could copy a recording only once. For instance, you would be able to make a copy of a CD on a DAT tape but you couldn't use the DAT copy to make another tape copy. The DAT players currently available for purchase are rather expensive, however, as are the DAT cassettes, and it is unclear what their fate will be once they enter the marketplace. Few expect them to be as big a revenue producer as the CD.

Revenues from Record Sales

The CD has virtually caused the extinction of the vinyl record. In 1992, about 39 percent of all revenue came from the sale of tapes, about 60 percent from CDs, and

Music recorded on DAT (digital audio tape) sounds just as good as music on a CD and, unlike CDs, you can record on DAT. DAT players such as these came on the market in the early 1990s. (David Berkwitz/ Newsweek)

only one percent from LPs and EPs. Many stores had phased out vinyl records entirely. Table 10-2 breaks down the typical costs associated with producing and marketing a CD at a list price of $12.98. Keep in mind these figures are approximations and subject to change.

Rock Performers: The Bottom Line

Now let's turn our attention to the finances connected with an individual or group involved in making records. There are many stories about the fantastic sums of money earned by pop music stars. Well, some stars do make a lot of money. Others, however, are not quite as lucky. Let's look at some numbers. A new artist or group will receive a royalty rate of about 7–9 percent of the suggested retail price of a CD or cassette. A more established act might negotiate a rate that's a little higher, maybe 10–12 percent. Really successful performers might get around 15 percent. Royalty rates on singles run about 6–9 percent. For simplicity, let's say a hypothetical group of four performers is getting a 10 percent royalty rate. This works out to about $1 for each tape or CD sold and about 15 cents per single. It doesn't take a genius to see that the sale of a million albums will generate about $1 million in royalties plus whatever a hit single would sell. Even split among a group of four, it still comes out to a healthy sum for a few months' work. Sounds pretty good so far . . . but it's not that simple.

There are two main sources of income for recording artists—record royalties, mentioned above, and personal appearances. If an individual or a group is well known and consistently able to put out hits, then it is true that they will earn large sums of money. Unfortunately, not all groups and performers are able to do this. In fact, only relatively few are able to command huge incomes. The rest do their utmost to survive. The riches are disproportionately divided, with a small number at the top earning most of the money. Moreover, the odds on any newcomer's making it big in the recording industry are slim. Although the figures are rough estimates, about 30,000 young and not-so-young hopefuls try to break into the business in any given year. Perhaps twenty or so will crack the hit lists, putting the odds of success at about 1500 to 1.

Furthermore, the fact that an act is lucky enough to put out one hit album is no immediate guarantee of riches. Getting started in the recording business takes money. Usually, this money is lent to a new group or single by the recording company as an advance against future royalty income. In some cases, a group that brings in a million seller finds itself barely breaking even once all advances and expenses are paid back. To illustrate, let's pretend that you're a member of a four-person rock group that is lucky enough to land a recording contract. The first thing your group will probably

TABLE 10-2 Costs and Profits of a Typical CD

Manufacturer's costs	
Recording expense	$ 0.48
Manufacturing cost	0.80
Packaging	1.00
Advertising and promotion	1.00
Artist's royalty	1.10
Freight	0.07
Payment to musicians' trust fund	0.50
Manufacturer's profit	4.00
Distributor's expenses and profit	1.75
Retailer profit	2.36
TOTAL	$12.98

A sophisticated mixing board such as this one handles as many as forty-eight separate sound tracks that contain recordings of many different instruments and vocals. These boards now contain computer memory devices that retain previous mixing setups, making the process easier and faster. (Alan Carey/The Image Works)

need is top-of-the-line instruments and equipment. (Your competition will surely have them.) These do not come cheap. A good guitar goes for about $1000. A five-piece set of drums costs about $2000, and amps retail for about the same price. Then, of course, your group will need some money to live on while you're making your records. The record company will also advance you this sum from your future royalties. Then there is the cost of producing the album. This expense is also charged against your royalties. Some record companies might even subtract another 10 percent or so for the packaging of the record. For purposes of illustration, let's say that the record company advances your group about $25,000 for new equipment and living expenses and $200,000 for the cost of recording your album. So far your group is in the hole for $225,000.

Now let's pretend that the group hits it big and sells 400,000 copies of the album and 800,000 copies of a single from the album (a rather optimistic assumption). This nets the group about $400,000 in royalties from the CD and about $120,000 in royalties from the single, for a total of $520,000. Before you can go out and buy a Porsche 944, you learn that the record company will deduct 15 percent for "free goods," records and tapes given away to customers to promote sales. Fifteen percent of $520,000 equals $78,000, so your earnings now total $442,000. Paying back the advance and recording session costs still leaves the group $217,000. (We're assuming the company cheerfully picked up the $50,000 tab for your music video.) Sounds good so far. Unfortunately, we've left out some key expenses. Every group has a manager and the manager's fee is 15 percent (sometimes more) of royalty income, or in our example $78,000. Most groups also hire on a part-time basis a publicity agent, an accountant, and a lawyer. Your group will need a lawyer because most record company contracts are about thirty-five to sixty single-spaced pages long. Legal fees can run from $2000 to $8000 for a recording agreement. Let's say these combined costs total $20,000. Left for the group, $119,000.

The other major revenue source for a group is a tour. Tours are important because they help promote the album. Most record companies insist that a new group go on tour. Let's pretend that your manager has booked the group on a forty-night tour playing various clubs and arenas across the country. Let's also pretend that the group collects $6000 per night as a fee. Working the road is not a pleasant experience for most groups, and many acts split up because of it. But, assuming your group stays together, forty nights at $6,000 per night yields $240,000. Again, things look good. The road, however, has its own special expenses. Airline fees, hotel bills, meals, costumes, transporting equipment, roadies, insurance, and so on, all must be paid for. Touring has become so expensive that many recording artists are linking up with a commercial sponsor who picks up part of the costs. In recent years, Reebok underwrote a Bruce Springsteen tour and Miller, Coca-Cola, and Sun Country Wine Coolers have sponsored tours in return for a little advertising during the concert. Returning to our example, let's say that expenses run $3500 per night. To complete a forty-night engagement tour might require fifty nights on the road (probably more). This amounts to a total tour expense of at least $175,000. Fifteen percent of your gross income goes to the manager ($36,000) and another 20 percent to your road manager and booking agents ($48,000). Then there's the cost of replacing broken gear and equipment and miscellaneous expenses such as extra musicians. As a rough figure, let's say $10,000 goes to miscellaneous expenses. Total tour expenses: $269,000. Total tour income: $240,000. Net loss for the tour: $29,000.

So the bottom line is this: royalty income, $119,000; touring losses, $29,000; total income for the group, $90,000. Divided four ways, this yields $22,500 per member (before taxes). Not bad, but a little out of the Porsche range. Maybe a Ford Taurus would do instead.

Of course, if you personally write some of the songs on the album, you would receive more royalties as the songwriter. You would also make some money from TV appearances, record sales overseas, and merchandising deals. Most artists, however, don't see much money until they've had a couple of hits back to back. After two years, the Grateful Dead were about $180,000 in debt to their record company. Northeastern rock group Rubber Rodeo wound up owing $500,000 to their company even after four years of recording and touring. The only group to stay out of this debt situation in recent years was 'til tuesday. This group took only a modest advance and cut recording and touring costs. Also, keep in mind that we optimistically assumed that our hypothetical group's first single and album did well. Most groups usually don't sell that many copies. Remember that all the advances and costs of making a flop album would be recouped against the earnings of future successful records, another reason why most groups start off in debt. Finally, we would also have to take into account the potential earning power of a group over time. There is no guarantee that a group's subsequent albums would do well. You can probably generate a long list of groups that had one hit and then faded into obscurity. All in all, big money can be made in the record industry, but few are lucky enough to cash in.

● ● ● ●
ISSUES

The sound recording industry functions as a socialization agency for many young people. Indeed, knowing a person's favorite kind of music can often allow others to predict that person's attitudes and behavior in other areas. One research study asked adolescent girls to rate potential dates based on a written description of them. The

On the Road

Below is the schedule followed by heavy metal groups Kingdom Come and Silent Rage during a recent tour.

5/31	Poughkeepsie, NY	6/23	St. Louis, MO
6/1	Portland, ME	6/24	Memphis, TN
6/2	Springfield, MA	6/25	Huntsville, AL
6/3	Boston, MA	6/27	Atlanta, GA
6/4	Washington, DC	6/28	Daytona, FL
6/6	Pittsburgh, PA	6/29	Ft. Lauderdale, FL
6/7	Wilkes Barre, PA	6/30	Tampa, FL
6/8	Clifton Park, NY	7/2	Biloxi, MS
6/9	Philadelphia, PA	7/3	Houston, TX
6/10	New York, NY	7/4	McAllen, TX
6/12	Toronto, ONT	7/6	Corpus Christi, TX
6/13	Cincinnati, OH	7/7	San Antonio, TX
6/14	Cleveland, OH	7/8	Dallas, TX
6/15	Detroit, MI	7/11	Phoenix, AZ
6/16	Dayton, OH	7/12	San Diego, CA
6/17	Chicago, IL	7/13	Anaheim, CA
6/18	Milwaukee, WI	7/14	Los Angeles, CA
6/20	Minneapolis, MN	7/15	Oakland, CA
6/22	Kansas City, KS	7/16	Sacramento, CA

East Coast to West Coast. Thirty-eight different cities in forty-seven days. Thirty-eight hotel rooms that all look the same. Is it any wonder that most groups don't like to tour?

descriptions were the same except for the kind of music the guys liked. The girls rated guys who liked heavy metal music as more likely to be more fun on a date and a little more dangerous than guys who liked Top 40.

For some young people, the type of music defines the "in-group" and the "out-group." People who buy an Amy Grant record generally talk, dress, and act differently from people who buy Guns 'N' Roses or 2 Live Crew who, in turn, should be different from those who like the Trash Can Sinatras.

Further, the sound recording industry has probably made many young people more socially and politically aware. Rock stars give frequent concerts for some political or social cause, such as saving the rain forest, helping the homeless, fighting famine, ending apartheid. The destruction of the Berlin Wall prompted a concert starring

Pink Floyd. Some stars have made announcements that urged political participation. Madonna, for example, in a spot on MTV, wrapped herself in the American flag and urged viewers to get out and vote. Bill Clinton appeared on MTV during the 1992 presidential campaign. All in all, popular music has become a political force.

Some of the consequences of listening to recorded music have prompted concerns among parents. There is a fear that many impressionable young people might be adversely affected by the messages some parents think are contained in rock songs. The record industry has gone so far as to adopt its own uniform warning sticker. In a related area, Judas Priest and Ozzy Osbourne were sued because it was claimed that listening to their records caused some teens to commit suicide. In Osbourne's case, the alleged suicide message was straightforward; he had recorded a song entitled "Suicide Solution." The Judas Priest case was more involved. Parents of the deceased youths claimed that a suicide message had been backmasked (see box on page 234) in the song and had had a subliminal effect on their children. Both suits were unsuccessful. The courts ruled that Osbourne's song couldn't be proven as the cause of the suicide and that the supposed backmask on the Judas Priest song was an accidental combination of sounds and not deliberately placed there. The courts, however, did not rule out the possibility of other claims based on subliminal messages. These legal proceedings raise the issue of the social responsibility of the artist. Should rock performers, who are addressing a young and impressionable audience, have a special obligation to safeguard the mental and emotional well-being of their listeners? Or should they, as artists laboring under the protection of the First Amendment, be free to record anything they want? It's a question that crops up with regard to other industries as well and one that is not easily answered.

Finally, popular music represents an area where cultures meet and mix and sometimes clash. During the 1950s, rock and roll first introduced middle-class whites to the black rhythm and blues sounds. More recently, rap music, originating in the black urban folk culture, has become widely popular among both blacks and whites.

Obscenity or political commentary? After 2 Live Crew was arrested in Florida for giving an obscene performance, their lawyer argued that their lyrics, raunchy though they might be, were really a form of protest and dissent. The jury agreed and the group was acquitted. (Newton/Sygma)

International Perspective: Popular Music in Scandinavia

Artists from Scandinavia have enjoyed a substantial amount of success on the U.S. popular music charts. Starting with Abba and continuing through a-ha, TNT, and up to the most recent success, Roxette, performers from Denmark, Finland, and Norway rank behind only the United Kingdom and Canada in achieving popularity in the U.S.

This fact is not surprising since rock music enjoys great popularity in these countries and the U.S. acts that dominate their record charts are widely imitated by local talent. Scandinavia, however, contends with some unique problems in record making and record selling. First, there's the language barrier. Finnish has nothing in common with Swedish, Danish, or Norwegian and even though the latter three are derived from common roots, most Scandinavian record buyers prefer recordings in their native tongue. As a result, most sales are generally limited to the country of origin, making it difficult to make any money with anything less than a blockbuster hit.

In addition, buying music in Scandinavia is more expensive than in the U.S. Although CD players sell for as little as $300, the discs themselves cost anywhere between $20 and $30. CD growth has also been hampered by poor marketing. Many consumers erroneously believed that CDs were not compatible with existing sound systems. Recent advertising efforts were directed toward erasing that misconception. Last, the Scandinavian recording business is usually submerged by U.S. exports. American acts account for around 65 percent of all sales in some Scandinavian countries. Some acts sell better in these countries than they do in America. Elvis Presley is still a superstar when it comes to selling records in Denmark. Two Presley CDs of old hits sold more in Denmark than in any other country in the world. The Danes are also big fans of the Carpenters, a 1960s duo, whose records sell only anemically in the U.S. In Finland, the U.S. influence is apparent as native Finnish rap music is the hottest selling format. Although they may not be in the same league as Hammer, some Finnish rappers you might want to look out for are Rapteri, MC Nikki T, and Hausmylly.

Sometimes, however, the cultural blending does not go smoothly. The release of 2 Live Crew's album *As Nasty as They Wanna Be* illustrates this. The rap album contains some strong and sexually explicit language, so explicit that the album was declared obscene in Florida and a record store owner was convicted of selling obscene materials when he sold a copy of the album to an undercover police officer. 2 Live Crew itself was arrested and charged with giving an obscene performance after an appearance at an adults-only Florida nightclub. The performers argued that their language was a form of black political dissent, designed to cast derision on racial stereotypes. A jury agreed and 2 Live Crew was acquitted. Similar situations are likely to develop as rap becomes more mainstream. Aware of this possibility, rap groups have formed their own legal defense fund.

• • • •

CAREERS IN THE RECORDING INDUSTRY

Of all the mass media, the recording industry employs the fewest employees. Not counting performers, there are only about 15,000–18,000 people in the entire industry. This section will emphasize careers in the nonperformance side of the business. Those of you interested in pursuing careers as performers, writers, and arrangers obviously should concentrate on developing musical skills.

Entry-Level Positions

Basically, there are at least three distinct career paths within the recording business: (1) engineering, (2) creative, and (3) business. We will examine each of these in turn.

Over the past two decades, the technical aspects of sound recording have become tremendously complex. The control room of a twenty-four-track studio resembles something like the bridge of the starship *Enterprise*. Sometimes it takes two engineers to operate the giant control panel—one to run the tape machines and the other to do the actual recording. If the engineering side of the industry is of interest to you, it would be of some advantage to study at a college that has its own recording studio so that you may become familiar with the equipment. Failing that, the Recording Institute of America (RIA) offers courses in multitrack engineering and sound production. Alternatively, you might volunteer your services as an apprentice at a local recording studio and learn the skills by watching others. There are recording studios all across the United States. Although many of them are located in New York, Nashville, and Los Angeles, there are others in Atlanta, Memphis, Philadelphia, Orlando, Miami, Toronto, Cincinnati, Seattle, Minneapolis, Chicago, Detroit, Ogden (Utah), and Bogalusa (Louisiana).

If your interests lie more in the creative area and you wish to become a record producer, college courses in mass media, business administration, and music are relevant. Some colleges offer courses in the music industry, and a few even offer a bachelor's degree in the music business. You will also need some practical experience in directing a recording session. This can be done by working at a college that has a recording studio or, as suggested above, by volunteering your services at a local commercial studio. Another possible route is to start out at a record company in a low-level position, perhaps in the warehouse or mailroom, and work your way into the A&R department and try to gain experience as a demo producer. From there, you might advance to a regular staff producer. In every case, you should try to learn as much as possible about the record business. Producers also must have some knowledge about sales, accounting, and the legal aspects of production.

If the business side of the profession appeals to you, a college background in business administration and mass media would be most helpful. Those interested in promotion and sales should start out by checking to see if there's a branch office of a major label or independent distributor located nearby. The big-six companies have about twenty branches in various cities across the country. Send a résumé, telephone, appear in person, or do whatever else is necessary to meet the local manager. Your goal should be an entry-level position as a local promotion person or a sales representative in a particular market.

The same advice holds for someone interested in advertising and merchandising. A branch office might be able to start you off at a beginning position from which you can move up to the parent company. An alternative route would be to gain some experience at an advertising agency, preferably one that has a record label as an account, and then move to the record company. Those seeking careers in publicity usually have a college background in journalism or public relations. Many entry-level positions in this area can be found at small record companies. Other publicists work as independents and are hired by an artist's manager or agent.

It is a little more difficult to provide advice on how to get started in the A&R department. Many A&R people come from the promotion department. Others start off at the bottom as secretaries or clerks and work their way up within the division. A good ear and a knowledge of what will sell and how to sell it are essential for a career in this area.

There are several paths that lead toward advancement in the recording industry. Again, the precise nature of job advancement will depend upon the particular starting place. Beginning audio engineers progress to staff engineers and ultimately to senior supervising engineer. Some engineers do cross over and become record producers, but this is generally rare. Once you've committed yourself to a technical career in the control room, you'll generally stay there.

People who start out as producers advance by becoming staff producers with major labels. The next step up would be the position of executive producer. At major companies, executive producers are basically administrators. They approve budgets, settle disputes among artists, producers, and studio personnel, and oversee the efforts of the A&R department. The executive producer in the record business is analogous to the excutive producer in motion pictures or TV. Another upward path sometimes followed by producers is to start off with an established label and then go into independent production. Independent producers freelance from one label to another, taking on projects that interest them and that promise to make money. Independent producers make money by receiving royalties from the records they produce. Many independent producers go on to form their own labels.

Those who start off in one of the business departments at a record company advance by moving up the corporate ladder. Salespeople move up to regional manager and then to sales director. Promotion people progress from smaller to larger markets. Advertising department employees advance first by taking on more important and lucrative accounts and later by moving up into management and administration. The most common route to top management has been through either the production or sales and distribution department.

In closing, it should be mentioned that we have discussed only the most common types of careers in the recording industry. There are related careers such as agent, or personal manager, or positions in the areas of concert promotion, music publishing, retailing, and marketing. Furthermore, although the record business is hard to break into, the rewards come fast. Since most popular music is performed and purchased by young people, many top managers and producers are also young. Many people become top executives in their late twenties and early thirties. Similarly, many successful producers are in this same age range. Although this can be an advantage, it also means that a person has to make a mark early in his or her career. If a person is not on the way up by his or her middle thirties, the road to advancement becomes harder.

● ● ● ●

SUGGESTIONS FOR FURTHER READING

The following books contain more information about the concepts and topics discussed in this chapter.

BASKERVILLE, DAVID, *Music Business Handbook*, Los Angeles: Sherwood Co., 1985.

SCHEMEL, SIDNEY, AND WILLIAM KRASILOVSKY, *This Business of Music*, New York: Billboard Publications, 1990.

SIEGEL, ALAN, *Breakin' in to the Music Business*, Port Chester, N.Y.: Cherry Lane Books, 1986.

ZALKIND, RONALD, ed., *Contemporary Music Almanac*, New York: Schirmer Books, 1980.

Also, *Billboard* and *Rolling Stone* are two publications that provide extensive coverage of the recording industry.

11

HISTORY OF FILM AND TELEVISION

S tanding in line was nothing new to the crowd of New Yorkers congregated in front of Koster and Bial's Music Hall that mild spring evening. Many of them had stood in line to see a vaudeville show before. But tonight, April 23, 1896, was different. The crowds walking up Broadway and across Herald Square were coming to see the first public exhibition of Thomas Edison's latest invention, the **Vitascope**, a machine that actually projected moving pictures onto a screen large enough for everybody in the theater to view them at once. The first half of the program consisted of skits and songs by the European singer Albert Chevalier. But the real star of the evening was hidden under blue brocade in the second balcony of the theater. Resembling the gun turret on a destroyer, the projection booth housed two Vitascopes (one was a spare), loaded with film and ready to run. When the vaudeville stopped, attention was focused on a twenty-by-twelve-foot screen in the middle of the stage. The projectors started whirring, sending forty-six frames of film past the lens every second, and immediately the audience was enthralled. Two young dancers in pink and blue dresses (each frame of film had been tinted by hand) performed an umbrella dance. Next, scenes of surf breaking on the beach amazed the spectators. A comic boxing match, a vaudeville skit, and another dance routine quickly followed. The audience cheered and cheered. A reviewer for the *New York Times* called the presentation "wonderfully real and singularly exhilarating." The movies had arrived.

Koster and Bial's Music Hall is gone now, replaced by Macy's Department Store. But even today, if you walk the streets of New York or any town across the country on a balmy spring evening, you are likely to see people standing in line, waiting to see moving pictures on a screen.

Motion pictures and television both integrate sight and sound in their presentations. Their histories at first seem to be separate, but on closer examination the two media have much in common. Both depend on the same perceptual mechanism to achieve the illusion of motion; their economics are intertwined; directors and stars from one medium cross over into the other; and, in the future, new technologies will further erase the differences between them. Thus this chapter treats the evolution of motion pictures and television simultaneously. We will, of course, have more to say about film, because it developed earlier than TV.

• • • •

EARLY HISTORY OF THE MOTION PICTURE

Motion pictures and television are possible because of two quirks of the human perceptual system: the **phi phenomenon** and **persistence of vision**. The phi phenomenon refers to what happens when a person sees one light source go out while another one close to the original is illuminated. To our eyes, it looks like the light is actually moving from one place to another. In persistence of vision, our eyes continue to see an image for a split second after the image has actually disappeared from view. First observed by the ancient Greeks, persistence of vision became more widely known in 1824 when Peter Roget (who also developed the *Thesaurus*) read a paper about it before the British Royal Society of Surgeons. Roget demonstrated that human beings retain an image of an object for about one-tenth of a second after the object is taken from view. Following Roget's pronouncements, a host of toys that depended on this principle sprang up in Europe. Bearing fanciful names (the Thaumatrope, the Zoetrope), these devices made a series of still pictures appear to move. In the Zoetrope, for example, a strip of pictures, each differing slightly from the others, was placed inside a topless revolving drum. As the drum spun around, the viewer looked through vertical slits to see hand-drawn acrobats, clowns, and horses appear to come alive. These primitive playthings, of course, were illustrating the technique we now use to produce cartoons—animation. In fact, if Mickey Mouse were ever to trace his roots, he would find that they led back to a Frenchman, Emile Reynaud, and his magical device, the Praxinoscope. By combining the Zoetrope with a primitive slide projector, Reynaud became the first person to project his drawings onto a large screen. In the late 1880s, Reynaud added a frame and tiny settings and began to charge admission to a small room he dubbed the Théâtre Optique.

Unfortunately, Reynaud and his imitators had to draw each of their pictures by hand—a long, painstaking, and arduous task. The development of the motion picture would have taken far longer if this method had been the only one available. Luckily, at about this same time, tremendous advances were being made in the field of still photography. Louis Daguerre invented a photographic process that used burnished metal as a base and produced splendidly clear and detailed photographs. Never one for modesty, Daguerre called the picture produced by this process the daguerreotype. Nevertheless, despite their fine quality, daguerreotypes sometimes took thirty minutes to expose and the subject had to remain rigid and motionless throughout. (This is the reason many of our ancestors appear to be somewhat stiff.) Moreover, the daguerreo-

An early version of Emile Reynaud's Praxinoscope. Later models would be able to project a moving image onto a large screen for many people to view at once. (The Bettmann Archive)

type could not be used to make copies. Eventually, flexible celluloid film replaced the metal, exposure times were shortened, and photography became more practical.

Before long, several people realized that a series of still photographs could be used instead of hand drawings in variations of the Zoetrope and Praxinoscope. In the 1860s, an American, Henry Heyl, mounted a series of still photos on a glass disc and by spinning this disc in front of a bright light that was masked periodically by a shutter device, he projected the images onto a screen. In 1878, a colorful Englishman later turned American, Edward Muybridge, attempted to settle a $25,000 bet over whether the four feet of a galloping horse were ever simultaneously off the ground. He arranged a series of twenty-four cameras alongside a race track in order to photograph a running horse. Rapidly viewing the series of pictures produced an effect much like that of a motion picture. Muybridge's technique not only settled the bet (they were) but also demonstrated, in a backward way, the idea behind motion picture photography. Instead of twenty-four cameras taking one picture each, what was needed was one camera that would take twenty-four pictures in rapid order. It was Thomas Edison and his assistant, William Dickson, who finally developed what might have been the first practical motion picture camera and viewing device. Edison was apparently trying to provide a visual counterpart to his recently invented phonograph (see Chapter 8). When his early efforts did not work out, he turned the project over to his assistant. Using flexible film, Dickson solved the vexing problem of how to move the film rapidly through the camera by perforating its edge with tiny holes and pulling it along by means of sprockets. In 1889, Dickson had perfected a machine called the **Kinetoscope** and even starred in a brief film demonstrating how it worked.

These early efforts in the Edison lab were not directed at projecting movies to large crowds. Still influenced by the success of his phonograph, Edison thought a similar device could make money by showing brief films to one person at a time for a penny a look. The Kinetoscope reflected this idea; it was much like a modern-day peep-show machine. Edison built a special studio to produce films for this new invention, and by 1894 Kinetoscope parlors were springing up in major cities. The long-range commercial potential of this invention was lost on Edison. He was dead set against developing motion picture projection equipment. He reasoned that the real money would be made by selling his peep-show machine. If a large number of people were shown the film at the same time, fewer machines would be needed. Edison once argued that only ten projectors would be needed to show films to everyone in the entire country. His estimate was a little off. Furthermore, when Edison took out patents for his devices, he neglected to pay an additional $150 to secure international patent rights, an oversight that would return to haunt him.

In Europe, other inventors quickly seized upon Edison's ideas. Since they could use his equipment without paying royalties, several Europeans borrowed freely from Edison's ideas and improved upon them. The most noteworthy of these entrepreneurs were the Lumière brothers. In 1894 they had developed a device that not only took motion pictures but projected them as well. By the next year, they were showing films to paying customers in the basement of a Paris café. Other projection devices were developed in both Europe and the United States. In 1895, audiences in several major American cities were able to attend demonstrations of this new equipment. In the face of all this competition, Edison finally changed his mind. His Vitascope, a projection version of the Kinetoscope, premiered at Koster and Bial's in 1896.

Vaudeville theaters across the country were soon showing films as part of their programs. These early films were simply bits of action—acrobats tumbling, horses running, a man sneezing, prizefighters, jugglers, and so on. The novelty of seeing things in motion was sufficient to impress and even awe early moviegoers. When the film portrayed a locomotive roaring down the track toward the camera, many in the audience actually jumped out of the way. The novelty effect quickly wore off, however, and before long films were used as "chasers"—appearing at the end of the vaudeville

Hale's Tours and Scenes of the World

George C. Hale, ex-fire chief of Kansas City, Missouri, was one of the first people to make a million dollars in the film industry. Hale mounted a camera on the rear platform of a speeding train and shot film of the landscape as it whizzed by. He then took an old railroad car and converted it into a motion picture theater. When customers paid their money to the ticket collector, dressed as a train conductor, they were ushered in to one of the train's seats. Then, when the ''train'' was full, the conductor would yell ''All Aboard,'' bells would clang, and the whole car would be rocked back and forth, simulating the motion of a moving train. Finally, the lights would darken and the motion pictures that Hale had taken earlier were projected onto a screen, thus re-creating the illusion of travel for the delighted ''passengers.''

Hale's Tours were introduced at the 1903 St. Louis Exposition and were an instant hit. During the next two years, Hale's Tours sprang up around the country and became something of a national fad. Hale himself was reported to have made two million dollars from this idea.

shows to clear the theater for the next performance. Once the newness was gone, the attraction of the motion picture began to wane.

Public interest was soon rekindled when early filmmakers discovered that movies could be used to tell a story. In France, Alice Guy Blache produced *The Cabbage Fairy*, a one-minute film about a fairy who produces children in a cabbage patch, and exhibited it at the Paris International Exhibition in 1886. Although not widely recognized, some argue that Blache's achievement qualifies her as the first director to bring a narrative film to the screen. Blache went on to found her own studio in America. Better known is the work of a fellow French filmmaker and magician, Georges Méliès. In 1902, Méliès produced a science fiction film that was the great-great-grandfather of *Star Wars* and *Star Trek*. Called *A Trip to the Moon*, it can be appreciated by modern film fans for its technical sophistication. Méliès, however, did not fully explore the freedom in storytelling that film was capable of. His films were basically extravagant stage plays photographed by a stationary camera. It was an American, Edwin S. Porter, who in his *Great Train Robbery* (the ancestor of dozens of John Wayne westerns) first discovered the artistic potential of editing and camera placement. These new narrative films were extraordinarily popular with audiences and proved to be financially successful. Almost overnight, fifty- to ninety-seat theaters, called nickelettes or nickelodeons because of the five-cent admission price, were springing up in converted stores thoughout the country. In Pittsburgh, the projectors of the Harris and David Nickelodeon ground away from eight in the morning until midnight. Soon the theater was averaging about 20,000 nickels ($1000) a week in 1905. The growth of these nickelodeons was fantastic; over a hundred more were to open in Pittsburgh within the next year. In New York, licenses were being issued to new establishments at the rate of one a day.

Nickelodeons depended on audience turnover for their profits. To keep the audience returning, films had to be changed often—sometimes daily—to attract repeat customers. This policy created a tremendous demand for motion pictures, and new production companies were quickly formed. (In these early days, films were regarded as just another mass-produced product; hence, early film studios were called "film factories.") New York and New Jersey served as the bases for these early film companies.

Birth of the MPPC

Events in moviemaking during the decade 1908–1918 had far-reaching effects on the future shape of the film industry. As the basic economic structure of the film industry developed, the center of filmmaking moved to the West Coast, and independent film producers, having survived attempts by the major studios to stamp them out, became an important force in the industry. The tremendous demand for new pictures brought enormous competition into the field. Small film companies cut corners by using bootlegged equipment (for which they paid no royalty fees) and started making films. Competition quickly reached the cutthroat level; lawsuits were filed with alarming frequency. In an effort to bring order to the business (and to cut down legal expenses), the leading manufacturers of films and film equipment banded together, pooled their patents, and formed the **Motion Picture Patents Company (MPPC)**. It was the intent of this organization to restrict moviemaking to the nine companies that made up the MPPC. Film exhibitors were brought into line by a two-dollar-per-week tax, which entitled the theaters to use projection equipment patented by the MPPC. Failure to pay this tax meant that the theater owners would no longer be supplied with MPPC-approved films. Eventually, in order to accommodate the growing industry, a new role, that of film distributor, was created. The film distributor served the function of a wholesaler, acquiring films from the manufacturers and renting them to exhibitors. This three-level structure—production, distribution, and exhibition—is still with us today. The MPPC was quick to take control of film distribution also.

To call the MPPC conservative would be an understatement. The organization refused to identify actors and actresses appearing in their films, for they were afraid that if some of their performers were identified and became popular, they might demand more money. They didn't want to pay some actors more than others because they sold film by the foot, and film was priced the same per foot no matter who was in it. In addition, they were convinced that audiences would not sit through movies that ran longer than one reel in length (about ten minutes). The MPPC also refused to use close-ups in their films, arguing that no one would pay to see half an actor.

Instead of squelching competition, the MPPC actually encouraged it. Annoyed by the repressive regulations, independent producers began offering films to exhibitors at cheaper rates than MPPC members. Full-length feature films, several reels in length, were imported from Europe. The MPPC declared war. "Outlaw" studios were raided and equipment smashed. Violence broke out on more than one occasion. In an effort to escape the harassment of the MPPC, independent producers fled New York and New Jersey. They were looking for a location with good weather, interesting geography, low business costs, and proximity to a national border so that the independents could avoid the MPPC's subpoenas. Several areas were tried. Florida proved to be too humid (the studios, see below, have recently returned to Florida, thanks to air-conditioning); Cuba was too inconvenient; Texas was too flat. Finally, they found the perfect environment—a rather sleepy suburb of Los Angeles called Hollywood. By 1913, this new home had so encouraged independent filmmaking that the MPPC could no longer contain its growth. By 1917, for all practical purposes, the patents organization had lost its power.

The Star System

The street is a little tawdry now, but the stretch of Hollywood Boulevard between La Brea and Vine is still called the Walk of Fame. Bronze medallions bearing the names of stars dating from the days of the nickelodeon to the present have been inserted in the sidewalk. Moving west along the boulevard toward Beverly Hills, one comes to the Chinese Theater, originally conceived by master Hollywood showman Sid Grauman. In the forecourt of this ornate movie theater are slabs of concrete bearing the footprints and handprints of the stars.

This aura of glamour surrounding Hollywood and its stars might not have arisen if the MPPC had not been so stubborn. Whereas the patents company refused to publicize its performers, the independents quickly recognized that fan interest in film actors and actresses could be used to draw crowds away from the movies offered by the MPPC. Thus it was that Carl Laemmle, an independent producer, shrewdly publicized one of his actresses who possessed a poetic name—Florence Lawrence—until she became what we might call the first movie star. As Florence's fame grew, her pictures brought in more money, spurring other independents to create their own "stars" to maintain pace. Theda Bara (the original vamp), Lillian Gish (who was still appearing in movies over seventy years later), and William S. Hart were among other early performers to gain celebrity status. The two artists who best exemplified the growth of the star system, however, were Mary Pickford and Charlie Chaplin. In 1913, Chaplin was working in movies for $150 a week, a good salary in those days. Just four years later he was paid a million dollars for making eight pictures. Mary Pickford, nicknamed "America's Sweetheart," was paid $1000 per week in 1913. By 1918, she was making $15,000–$20,000 per week in addition to a cut of up to 50 percent of her films' profits. In 1919, the star system reached its natural conclusion. Both Chaplin and Pickford joined with other actors, actresses, and filmmakers to start their own production company—United Artists. The employees now owned the shop.

The star system had other more subtle effects. Once stars became popular, their public demanded to see them in longer movies. However, feature-length films that ran one to two hours were more expensive to make. Furthermore, audiences couldn't be expected to sit for two hours on the wooden benches found in many of the nickelodeons. A need had been created for large, comfortable theaters that could accommodate thousands of patrons and, at the same time, justify higher admission costs. These new motion picture palaces were not long in coming. In 1914, the Strand

Charlie Chaplin, one of the first movie superstars created by the Hollywood star system, delighted film audiences throughout the world. This scene is from the 1925 comedy The Gold Rush. *(The International Museum of Photography at the George Eastman House. © United Artists)*

opened in New York. With seats for more than 3000 people, it occupied a whole city block and had space for an entire symphony orchestra. The Rialto, which opened down the block in 1916, featured deep pile carpeting and an interior done in ivory. On the West Coast, Sid Grauman opened his Egyptian Theater (across from the Chinese Theater) in 1922 at a cost of almost a million dollars. His usherettes were dressed in Cleopatra costumes. Clearly, the nickel was no longer the symbol of the movies.

● ● ● ●
CONSOLIDATION AND GROWTH

The increased cost of filmmaking made it imperative for the producer to make sure that the company's movies were booked into enough of these new theaters to turn a profit. Under this economic pressure, the film industry moved in the direction of consolidation. Adolph Zukor, whose company would ultimately become Paramount Pictures, combined the production and distribution of films into one corporate structure. It was only a matter of time before the big studios had extended their influence into the exhibition end of the business as well. Paramount and its chief rival, Fox, began building their own theaters. The trend toward consolidation was also picked up by theater owners. Marcus Loew, owner of a large chain of theaters, purchased his own studio (later to become MGM). Studio owners could exert control over independent exhibitors by another policy known as **block booking**. In order to receive two or three top-flight films from a studio, the theater owner had to agree to show five or six other films of lower quality. Although this policy was not very advantageous to exhibitors, it assured the production companies of steady revenue for their films. Of course, all of this was taking place while World War I was devastating Europe. When the war ended in 1918, the American film industry was the dominant force in the world, accounting for upwards of 80 percent of the worldwide market. By the beginning of the twenties, the major production companies were comfortable and prosperous and enjoyed as firm a lock on the film business as had the old MPPC, which, ironically, they had replaced only a few years earlier.

The Roaring Twenties

In the early years of the Roaring Twenties, the film industry continued its move toward consolidation and growth. The prosperity boom that followed the war exploded in Hollywood with more force than in other business sectors. Profits were up, and extravagance was the watchword as filmmakers endorsed the principle that the only way to make money was to spend money. Before long, film costs were soaring. Between 1914 and 1924, there was a 1500 percent increase in the cost of a feature film. Salaries, sets, costumes, props, rights to best-sellers all contributed to the mushrooming costs of films. Even the lawyer for United Artists was paid $100,000 a year. By 1927, the average film cost about $200,000, and many films easily topped that. *Ben Hur* (1925) was made for a reported $6 million.

Huge salaries created a boomtown atmosphere in Hollywood, and many people— some still quite young—were unprepared to deal with the temptations that came with sudden wealth. It wasn't long before newspapers were reporting stories about orgiastic parties, prostitution, studio call girls, bootleg whiskey, and drugs. Hollywood was dubbed "Sin City." Scandals were inevitable. In 1922, within a few short months, comedian Fatty Arbuckle was involved in a rape case, two female stars were implicated in the murder of a prominent director, and popular actor Wallace Reid died while trying to kick his drug addiction. Public reaction to these revelations was predictable: indignation and outrage. By the end of 1922, politicians in thirty-six states had introduced bills to set up censorship boards for films. The motion picture companies hired a well-respected former Postmaster General, Will Hays, to head a new self-regulatory body for the industry. Called the Motion Picture Producers and Distributors Association, this organization was successful in heading off government control, and the basic standards it laid down would be in force for almost four decades.

By the mid-1920s theater expansion had peaked, and it was obvious that lavish, expensive films would not always bring in enough profits to cover their costs. Hollywood embraced the techniques of budget control and cost accounting that had helped other industries cut expenses. Consequently, a new title was introduced to filmmaking—the production supervisor. These individuals, typified by MGM's Irving Thalberg, decided how studio money should best be spent. They planned what stories to film, what director to hire, how much should be spent on props, and how to organize filming to minimize costs. Although these people brought financial stability to the business, they sometimes went to excess (one production supervisor decided that his studio could save money by straightening out and reusing bent nails) and many creative people were forced out of the business. The increased power of the production supervisor also meant that studios wanted pictures that would sell. The easiest thing to sell was a picture that imitated a recent success (notice how this philosophy is still with us: *Rambo II, Rocky II, Terminator 2*, etc.). As a result, the mid-1920s saw the birth of the "formula" picture with proven ingredients for success—big stars, successful and familiar stories, expensive-looking sets. Hollywood films had adopted commercial and industrial practices that would last for the next few decades.

Telling Stories with Film: Content Trends to 1927

Trends and directions in film and television content are best illustrated by examples. Consequently, this and subsequent sections examining content contain the titles of many films or television programs. Of course, if you've never seen the particular film or program that's mentioned, the example may not be entirely effective. Nonetheless, the titles are listed here in the hope that those who have not seen them will make an effort to view these examples, perhaps at film revivals, media history courses, on videocassettes or discs, or on late-night TV. This section will become more meaningful the more you view the films and TV shows that are mentioned.

Horses jumping hurdles, trains rushing by the camera, acrobats tumbling—the earliest films simply recorded motion. As photographic techniques improved, it became possible to take the camera to news events and record them on film. Prizefights, inaugurations, and battle scenes (many of them faked) were popular film subjects at the turn of the century.

After the narrative films of Georges Méliès and Edwin Porter proved that movies could tell a story, film topics became more varied. Still, the majority of these early films ran for only one reel and were aimed at a mass audience composed primarily of working-class immigrants, recently arrived in America. Despite some innovative film techniques such as special effects, sequences of scenes, and crosscutting, the camera remained a stationary spectator to theaterlike productions.

The decade between 1906 and 1916 proved to be an important period for the development of film as a unique means of artistic expression. In 1912, film producer Adolph Zukor decided to copy European filmmakers who were making longer, more expensive films aimed at a middle-class audience. He acquired the four-reel French film *Queen Elizabeth*, starring Sarah Bernhardt, the most famous actress of the period, and distributed it in the United States at the then unbelievable price of a dollar a ticket. His experiment was successful, proving that American audiences would pay more and sit still for longer films. Nevertheless, *Queen Elizabeth* remained essentially the filming of a stage play.

It was an American, D. W. Griffith, who eventually took full advantage of the film medium and established film as its own art form. His brilliant Civil War drama,

Birth of a Nation, was released in 1915 and became the most expensive American film produced to that date ($110,000). The three-hour movie, which was shot without a script, introduced history as a film topic. It also was a milestone in cinematography. Griffith explored the potential of the camera for visually enhancing story line as well as capturing and communicating the intense emotions of his actors. In addition, through masterful editing, he showed how to control both time and space, to prolong suspense, and to emphasize central themes. He went on to top *Nation*'s figures with an even bigger epic, *Intolerance*, a piece composed of four scenarios dealing with life's injustices. The movie was completed in 1916 at a cost of about $2 million (the same film made in the 1990s would easily cost $40 million to $50 million). Griffith's later productions still demonstrated his skills in set design, editing, and cinematography, but his stories were oversentimentalized, ponderous, and preachy. He was unable to sense the changing tastes of the filmgoers of the 1920s and never mastered the technology of sound as he had the eye of the camera.

While Griffith was producing lavish and highly serious spectacles, other Americans were developing a totally different form of film—the comedy. The pioneer in this area was a former coworker of Griffith's named Mack Sennett. The slapstick antics of his wondrously incompetent Keystone Cops entertained audiences throughout World War I. It was Sennett's protégé—a former comic in English music halls named Charlie Chaplin—who, dressed in oversized pants and a too-small coat and twirling a cane, created a character known as "The Tramp," probably the most successful comic

Intolerance, completed in 1916 for the then unbelievable cost of $2 million, included lavish sets such as this one. Despite the large investment in production, the film did poorly at the box office. (Culver Pictures)

character in film history. Chaplin's films were popular throughout the entire world. The film that showed him at his best was the 1925 production *The Gold Rush.* Second only to Chaplin in popularity were the films of Buster Keaton, sometimes called the "Great Stone Face" because of the deadpan expression his character maintained even in the most chaotic situations. He is best remembered for his 1926 classic, *The General.*

Two other film forms—the western and the nonfiction film—also gained prominence during the 1920s. After Porter's *The Great Train Robbery*, cowboys, Indians, covered wagons, outlaws, and cattle drives became popular subjects with filmmakers. In fact, the western film (along with radio soap operas) was one of the few uniquely American entertainment forms to be developed in the twentieth century. The foremost director of western thrillers was Thomas Ince, whose films were characterized by strong plots and lots of shoot-'em-up action. Ince also made famous the strong, silent cowboy hero. "Bronco Billy" (G. M. Anderson) was the first cowboy star, but he was soon followed by a whole posse of others: William S. Hart, Tom Mix, Buck Jones, Hoot Gibson, and Ken Maynard, to name a few. The early 1920s also saw the birth of the epic western, in which the sprawling, wild American West itself became a star in the film, a genre that would reappear in the films of the 1960s (*How the West Was Won,*) the 1970s (*Jeremiah Johnson*), the 1980s (*Silverado* and *Pale Rider*), and the 1990s (*Dances with Wolves*).

Many films of the postwar decade focused on a topic popular during the Roaring Twenties—sex. Exotic (and erotic) red-hot romances offered an escape to the 1920s moviegoer. This type of film got off to a flying start when a 1921 desert romance, *The Sheik*, starring a smoldering Rudolph Valentino, enjoyed phenomenal box-office success. This led to a whole caravan of sun-scorched romances: *Arabian Love, Tents of Allah, When the Desert Calls, Burning Sands*, and many more. When the desert theme wore out, other action-adventure films starring such leading men as Ramon Navarro and Douglas Fairbanks took its place. The heroes of all these films were passionate and aggressive lovers (had the word been popular during the 1920s, they would have been called "macho"), who literally swept a woman off her feet and rode off into the sunset. Speaking of women, several leading ladies of the period portrayed liberated, sexually aware, and sophisticated characters. Greta Garbo, Joan Crawford, Norma Shearer, and Gloria Swanson were among the actresses who specialized in playing these more daring roles. All in all, many movies of this period, especially those of director Cecil B. DeMille (see box on page 256), demonstrated a new attitude toward sexual themes.

The Coming of Sound

Silent films, of course, were never silent. Full orchestras, big Wurlitzer organs, sound effects, and narrators had all brought sound to the early screen. As far back as the 1880s, there had been experiments to synchronize a disc recording to the picture. Advances in radio technology, especially those by Lee De Forest, led to a primitive sound system for movies in 1922. Since optical recording of sound on film had been feasible since 1918, why did Hollywood wait until the late 1920s to introduce sound films? Money.

Business was good during the 1920s, and the major studios did not want to get into costly experimentation with new techniques. Warner Brothers, however, was not as financially sound as the other studios. Since Warner did not own theaters in the big cities and could not exhibit all its pictures in the most lucrative markets, the company was willing to try anything to get its films into movie theaters. Primarily as a novelty, in 1926 Warner released *Don Juan*, a silent film starring John Barrymore, which played with synchronized musical accompaniment. The program included music by the New York Philharmonic Orchestra, singers backed by the Metropolitan Opera Chorus, and solo violinists. Neither the industry not the audience was overly im-

A Cecil B. DeMille Production

As America progressed through the early part of the 1920s, probably the best known Hollywood director was the master showman Cecil B. DeMille. Among the first to realize that the moral climate of the nation following World War I was becoming more permissive, DeMille turned out a string of sophisticated comedies that dealt with mature topics: infidelity, sexual adventures, eroticism, and immorality. "See your favorite stars commit your favorite sins" was a line in one of the ads for a DeMille film.

His films also glorified the bathroom. When one of DeMille's stars took a bath, it was not in your basic tub. Sumptuous and opulent bathrooms, filled with ornate decorations and big as living rooms, were a characteristic of his films. A bath was a ceremony, not some sanitary necessity. (It was also a marvelous excuse to show his leading ladies in various forms of undress.)

When the industry became more strict about depictions of immorality, DeMille found an ingenious way to get around their guidelines. He put his erotic adventures into biblical films such as *The Ten Commandments* (1923) and *The King of Kings* (1927). Showing sin was okay, as long as it was ultimately punished. Furthermore, how could anyone be against a film that featured Moses and God in leading roles?

Of course, DeMille's great contribution to film was his emphasis on production values. His films were visually ornate with meticulous attention paid to details—costumes, sets, props, makeup, scenery. A "Cecil B. DeMille Production" was a film that had a certain style or class all its own. He knew how to please his audiences. None of his films ever lost money.

pressed. However, in 1926 Warner followed up *Don Juan* with *The Jazz Singer*, in which Al Jolson not only sang but spoke from the screen. There were only 354 words in the entire film, but the movie was a huge success, and within two years the silent film, for all practical purposes, was dead.

The coming of sound ended many promising film careers. Big, brawny heroes of action-adventure films who had squeaky, high-pitched voices could not make the transition to the new era; neither could beautiful leading ladies with accents too thick for the audience to understand. Directors were suddenly faced with learning how to direct for the microphone as well as for the camera; some didn't learn quickly enough. In addition, mobile camera techniques, so painstakingly developed by directors such as Griffith, suffered a setback, because cameras had to be immobilized in soundproof booths to keep microphones from picking up their whirring sound.

The production of sound films cost Hollywood industries millions of dollars in investments in new equipment, new technicians, and new creative talent. A significant percentage of this cash came from banks, insurance companies, and investment firms, all of which wanted a say on how their funds were to be spent. As a result, production-line filmmaking that encouraged certain conventions of acting, directing, and writing was favored over creative innovations. The early talkies became highly stylized. Nevertheless, in a remarkably short time, the creative side of the industry adjusted to the new demands of sound, and good movies continued to be produced.

By 1930, the industry had improved its technical resources for reproducing sound; the camera and microphone could be moved together, and a more effective balance between picture and sound emerged. The novelty of sound gave a boost to the film industry, despite the economic effects of the Depression. In 1929, average weekly movie attendance was 80 million; by 1930 it had reached 90 million—a fact that led many to regard filmmaking as a Depression-proof industry. They were quickly proven wrong as attendance dropped in 1931 and again in 1932. New innovations were needed

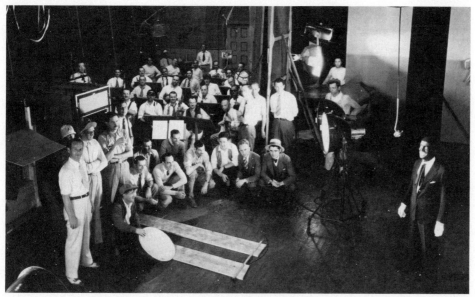

Al Jolson sings into the mike in The Jazz Singer *(1927). This film convinced the public that talkies were possible, thus ushering in a new era in Hollywood. (Culver Pictures)*

to attract audiences. *Becky Sharp* was filmed in the new Technicolor process in 1935. Theaters also began the practice of showing **double features**, two feature films on the same bill. Animated cartoons were also emerging as a force to be reckoned with in the film industry. All this new activity called for Hollywood to produce even more films—almost 400 per year during the 1930s—in order to meet the demands of the market. This high production volume was a boon to major studios since they could churn out large numbers of films more economically. Moreover, the tremendous amount of money needed to convert to sound and the poor financial conditions created by the Depression forced many small companies out of business and left eight major studios with a lock on the film industry.

The Studio Years

The twenty years from 1930 to 1950 were the studio years, with MGM, 20th Century Fox, RKO, Warner Brothers, Paramount, Universal, Columbia, and United Artists dominating the industry. The corporate office of Hollywood's film moguls controlled the key personnel of the major studios. These studios created hundreds of acres of back-lot movie sets, constructed elaborate sound stages, and built up showy stables of creative talent, carefully groomed for stardom. Audiences adored and emulated their favorite screen idols, who were presented as larger-than-life gods and goddesses inhabiting a glamorous fantasyland.

Different studios left their imprint on the films of the period as certain studio products took on a distinct personality. For example, during this period, Warner Brothers became best known for its gangster films; 20th Century Fox for its historical and adventure films; and MGM for its lavish, star-studded musicals. Let's take a closer look at the content of films in the studio era. The successful premiere of *The Jazz Singer* and the arrival of sound drastically altered the content of films. One new film form—the musical—was created immediately; a well-established film genre—physical and slapstick comedy—virtually ceased to exist; and another established form—the western—suffered a temporary setback.

Since music was easier and cheaper to put on film than dialogue, musical films quickly became popular among Hollywood producers and directors. At first, Broadway shows popular in New York were simply transported to Hollywood and filmed. *Rio Rita* (1929), *Showboat* (1929), and *Gold Diggers of Broadway* (1929) were among the first to appear. Because early sound cameras were awkward and cumbersome, these first efforts were primarily filmed versions of stage plays, photographed by a single, stationary camera. Then in 1930, a New York dance director named Busby Berkeley came to Hollywood and invented the musical extravaganza. Taking advantage of technical advances that made the sound camera more mobile, Berkeley filmed dance numbers that were totally different from stage numbers. Berkeley had his camera shoot straight down on the dance floor where dancers performed kaleidoscope routines; props were animated so that they seemed to glide by themselves across the stage. Although his dance numbers were usually inserted into clichéd backstage musicals, Berkeley's productions (perhaps best exemplified by the film *Gold Diggers of 1933*) still remain the purest blends of sight and sound ever to show up on film.

The physical and visual comedy practiced by Chaplin and Keaton did not make an entirely successful transition to sound. Only the silent-film comedy team of Laurel and Hardy was able to maintain its popularity in sound film, probably because of a sense of timing that carried over from slapstick comedy into dialogue. The new comedy stars, such as W. C. Fields and the Marx Brothers, relied on snappy one-liners, amusing delivery, wisecracks, and outrageous puns.

The western was also hampered initially by ungainly sound cameras, which were so clumsy that they could not be taken out for location shooting. The visual appeal of wide open spaces and panoramic views of mountains and deserts, however, had been an important factor in the popularity of silent westerns. As a result, not a single western was filmed in the two-year period following the arrival of sound. Eventually, when portable cameras reopened the potential of this genre, moviemakers discovered that sound provided a new, dramatic dimension to traditional cowboy-and-Indian films.

A variety of film genres flourished during the 1930s. Adventure and romance were common themes, popularized by swashbuckling heroes like Errol Flynn and Douglas Fairbanks and tragic beauties like Garbo in *Camille*. There was also a smattering of exotic fantasies, from Johnny Weismuller's jungle series, *Tarzan* and its sequels, to *Frankenstein* (1931) and *King Kong* (1933), a film distinguished by its fine miniature creations and its special effects. After 1935 several literary classics and best-selling novels were adapted to the large screen, among them *Lost Horizon* (1937), *The Good Earth* (1937), *Pygmalion* (1938), and *A Christmas Carol* (1938).

As the 1930s wore on, films blending romance with light banter and comedy arising from the situation became increasingly popular. Director Frank Capra was responsible for several of these, including *It Happened One Night* (1934), *Mr. Deeds Goes to Town* (1936), and *Mr. Smith Goes to Washington* (1937). Generally, Capra's films follow the adventures of a naive and sincere "ordinary guy" who goes up against rigid convention or corrupt social forces and eventually emerges victorious. Clark Gable, Gary Cooper, and Jimmy Stewart were all leading men who played the honest but shrewd protagonist.

In the field of drama, the 1930s saw a rise in popularity of the gangster film, a genre that introduced the American public to yet another character type: the world-weary tough guy. Jimmy Cagney, Humphrey Bogart, and Edward G. Robinson personified these hard-boiled leading men in such films at *Little Caesar* (1930), *The Public Enemy* (1931), and *The Petrified Forest* (1936).

The potential of suspense and mystery dramas was explored by a notable British director, Alfred Hitchcock. Hitchcock became well known in the United States during the pre-World War II period for films such as the *The 39 Steps* (1935), *The Lady Vanishes* (1938), and *Suspicion* (1941). Another foreign-born director, Josef von Sternberg, teamed up with the most famous and glamorous female star of this period, Marlene Dietrich, to produce several sophisticated romances. Usually playing a

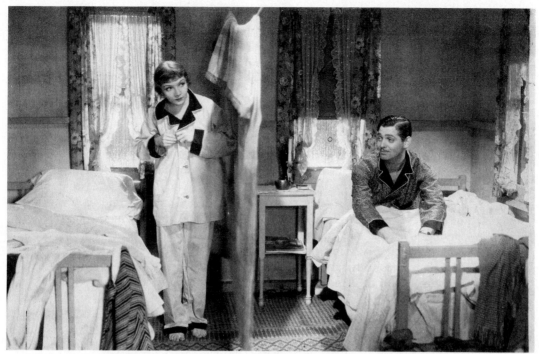

Clark Gable and Claudette Colbert share a unique sleeping arrangement in Frank Capra's comedy It Happened One Night. *(Culver Pictures)*

worldly, somewhat cynical seductress, Dietrich was at her sultry best in *The Blue Angel* (1930), *Shanghai Express* (1932), and *Blonde Venus* (1934).

Perhaps the most significant period for motion picture achievement during the early sound era were the years 1939–1941. In 1939, David O. Selznick produced the monumental Civil War epic *Gone With the Wind*, which proved to be an effective showcase for the newly developed Technicolor process (*Gone With the Wind* was rereleased in 1989 with its original color restored). Another film that used color effectively was released that same year, the perennially popular fantasy *The Wizard of Oz*. Yet a third classic was to premiere during 1939, the western epic *Stagecoach*, starring John Wayne in his first major role. Two years later, a young Orson Welles revolutionized filmmaking techniques with his controversial first film, *Citizen Kane*. Loosely based on the life of William Randolph Hearst, Sr., the movie failed at the box office but became a favorite of critics and students of film. Making use of deep focus, innovative camera angles, special lighting techniques, and dissolves from scene to scene, Welles created a work that some critics have hailed as America's single best film.

When World War II broke out, it did not take Hollywood long to turn out a number of patriotic films. Although several focused on the fighting overseas (*Wake Island*, 1942; *Bataan*, 1943) the most successful films were those portraying the lifestyle and cultural values that the United States was trying to preserve. Consider the most popular films during the war years: *Yankee Doodle Dandy* (1942), *Meet Me in St. Louis* (1944), *Bells of St. Mary's* (1945), and *Spellbound* (1945). The first two are escapist musicals, the third is a celebration of old-fashioned values, and the fourth is a mystery thriller. Very few popular movies of the day depicted the actual combat.

To summarize, the financial backing and diverse holdings of the studio system helped the film industry survive the Depression. Attendance and profits began climbing in 1934 and held steady throughout World War II. During the 1940s, going to a movie was just as much a part of American life as looking at television is today. In fact, the all-time peak for filmgoing was 1946, when average weekly attendance reached over 90 million. By 1947, however, all of this was to change.

● ● ● ●

COMPETITION AND CHANGE: TELEVISION

During the late 1920s, while the film industry was experimenting with the addition of sound to pictures, some enterprising inventors were busy working on ways to add pictures to sound. The product of their endeavors would drastically change the economics and the content of motion pictures. The two people associated with the early development of electrical television, Philo Farnsworth and Vladimir Zworykin, could not have been two more different individuals. Zworykin was the organization man, working first with Westinghouse and later with RCA. He made full use of these companies' large labs and research money and by 1928 had perfected a primitive television camera tube, the iconoscope (from the Greek, "image" and "to see"). At the other end of the spectrum was Farnsworth, the prototype of the individualistic, lone-wolf, and somewhat eccentric inventor. In 1922, at the age of sixteen, when most teenagers were worrying about the prom, Farnsworth diagramed his idea for a televison system on the chalkboard before his somewhat stunned high school science teacher. Because he carried out most of his later research in apartment laboratories behind closed blinds, Farnsworth's work aroused curiosity and suspicion. (In fact, his laboratory was once raided by police, who thought that only someone manufacturing illegal drugs and/or alcohol could be using all those glass tubes.) Farnsworth's hard work paid off in 1930 when he got a patent for his TV system. Television might have gotten off to a faster start, but the Depression slowed down its growth as well as that of the film industry.

Picture quality on the early television systems was poor, but technical developments during the 1930s indicated that improvements were possible. With the help of Zworykin and under a patent arrangement worked out with Farnsworth in 1939, RCA set out to develop the commercial potential of the new medium. NBC, owned by RCA, gave a public demonstration of television at the 1939 New York World's Fair with regular two-hour broadcasts. After the fair opened, RCA had TV sets with five-inch picture tubes on display in department stores. Filmmakers did not take the new invention seriously. Like radio in its infancy, early TV was looked upon as a toy, something that would never amount to much. Consider the following: In the early days of TV, performers had to wear thick green makeup to appear "normal" to the TV camera. Lights were incredibly hot and made the green makeup melt and run down the actors' faces. The heat was so intense that performers had to swallow salt tablets. Who could have had the foresight to predict that one day this bizarre, amusing, new toy could challenge and change the film industry?

Government Intervention

Back in 1938, the Justice Department had filed suit against Paramount and the other major film companies, charging that the industry's vertical control of production, distribution, and exhibition constituted restraint of trade and monopolistic practices. The case had been set aside during the war, but by 1948 the courts had ordered the major studios to get rid of at least one of their holdings in these three areas. Most chose to divest themselves of their theater chains. The court also eliminated the block booking system and thus deprived the studios of guaranteed exhibition for all their films. As a result, the studios had to cut back on film production and reduce costs as foreign films and movies made by independent producers cut into the major studios' revenues.

Television itself faced some uncertain times. During World War II, the FCC put a freeze on new TV stations, and most efforts were redirected away from TV to radar. When peace returned in 1945, however, new technology developed during the war was soon applied to the television industry. New picture tubes required drastically less light to perform; microwaves and coaxial cable were used to link stations into networks. Big-screen TV sets were being manufactured in large quantities. All of the signs pointed to big things ahead for TV. There were eight stations on the air in 1945; there were ninety-eight by 1950. Only 8000 homes had TV in 1946. Ten years later, almost 35 million households had TV sets.

TV's rapid success caught the industry and the FCC off guard. Unless technical standards were worked out, the TV spectrum was in danger of becoming overcrowded and riddled with interference. To guard against this possibility, the FCC imposed a freeze on all new applications for TV stations. The freeze, which went into effect in 1948, would last for four years, while the FCC gathered information from engineers and technical experts. When the freeze was lifted in 1952, the FCC had established that twelve VHF and seventy UHF channels (see page 306) were to be devoted to TV. In addition, the commission drew up a list that allocated television channels to the various communities in the United States and specified other rules to minimize interference. Also, thanks largely to the efforts of Frieda Hennock, the first woman to serve on the commission, TV channels were set aside for educational use.

The Structure of Early Television

The structure of early television was modeled after that of radio. Local stations provided a service for their communities and in turn might be affiliated with networks. There were four early TV nets: CBS, NBC, ABC, and DuMont, a smaller network that went out of business in 1956. The Mutual radio network did not make the transition into television.

One of the big problems in early TV was the difficulty in "storing" programs. In the 1950s, most shows were either broadcast live from the networks' New York studios or filmed on the West Coast using conventional Hollywood techniques. Live programs, of course, lacked the potential to be run again, and often they had to be repeated for the West Coast audiences. These programs could not be recorded on film for later showing since film was too expensive to use and took too long to process and edit. Kinescopes (films of the TV screen) were of poor quality but were used because they were the only means available. What was needed was an electronic medium for storing television pictures much in the same way audiotape stores sound. In 1956, the Ampex company solved the storage problem with the invention of videotape. With the new tape, programs could be prerecorded, edited, and polished before broadcast. Tape was much cheaper than film, could be played back at once, and, best of all, could be reused. By the beginning of the 1960s, most of TV's live programming had switched to tape.

UHF, Color, and Network Dominance

After the freeze, both new TV stations and new TV sets rapidly multiplied. Total advertising revenue passed the billion-dollar mark in 1955, and by the close of the 1950s there were 559 stations on the air and almost 90 percent of all American homes had TV. On the negative side, broadcasters and the FCC began to notice that the high hopes expressed in 1952 for the future of UHF television had been too optimistic. Few sets equipped with UHF receivers were made in the 1950s. If you wanted to receive these signals, you spent an additional $25–$50 for a converter. UHF stations also had a smaller coverage area than VHF operations, and most network affiliations and advertising dollars went to the more powerful VHF stations. As a result, UHF TV, much like FM radio, started off at a major disadvantage.

Another technological breakthrough took place in the 1950s with the introduction of color television. Led by NBC (RCA, the parent company, was manufacturing color sets), the networks were broadcasting about two to three hours of color programming per day in 1960.

The 1950s also saw the networks rise to primary importance as programming sources for their local affiliates. NBC and CBS were the two networks that usually dominated television ratings while ABC trailed behind. In the early days of TV, most network prime-time programs were produced by advertising agencies that retained control over their content. After the scandal that followed the discovery that some quiz shows were "fixed" in 1959, the networks began to assert their own control over programming. This trend away from advertiser control of programs has continued. The networks now allow independent producers to supply most of their evening programming (the networks, however, still share in the cost of producing the shows).

Live . . . From New York

Much of early television was done live. You saw it as it actually happened in a studio in New York or Chicago. There were no opportunities to stop the videotape and do it over. It was an exciting time because you knew that if you watched long enough, if you watched closely enough, and if you watched carefully enough, you would see something go wrong. For example, in one live show actor Lee Marvin had to make a quick move to get out of one scene set in an apartment and into another that took place in a phone booth. The idea was that the camera would tilt down from Marvin to a cigarette smoldering in an ashtray and stay on it until Marvin dashed across the set and into a mock phone booth in the wings. In dress rehearsals, no matter how fast Marvin ran, the camera still spent twenty to thirty seconds on that smoking cigarette, waiting for Marvin to get into the booth. That was too long and everybody looked for a way to shorten Marvin's run. Just before air time, the director had a brainstorm. He put the phone booth on wheels and moved it just off the edge of the apartment set. Marvin should make it easily.

Unfortunately, the director forgot that the studio was built on a slight incline and the phone booth was now at the top of it. He also forgot the rush of adrenalin that actors get when they perform live before the cameras. Anyway, the show went on the air and Marvin must have been running about twenty miles an hour when he jumped in the phone booth. He hit it so hard that the thing began to roll down the incline and across the studio. Astonished, the studio camera operators had no choice but to follow the booth. Viewers at home were surprised to see a traveling phone booth pass in front of the lighting crew, in front of bare studio walls, and even in front of a half-naked actress changing for the next scene, thinking she was comfortably out of camera range. The phone booth eventually thudded against the wall at the far end of the studio in total darkness. The director finally regained his composure and cut to a commercial while the technical crew ran to guide Marvin back to the set.

On another occasion, a live TV drama had a scene in which one man supposedly shot another. In early TV this had to be handled carefully so as not to injure the sensitive microphones with a loud sound. What was usually done was to have the actor point the gun and pull the trigger, while an offstage technician, far enough from the microphone not to cause harm, would fire a blank. When the show was being telecast live and the time for the shooting scene arrived, the first actor pointed the gun and squeezed the trigger. Nothing happened. The first actor again pointed and pulled the trigger. Again, no sound, nothing. The second actor, the supposed victim of the shooting, quickly grasped his chest and cried out, ''My God! Where did you get that silencer?'' as he crumpled to the floor.

It was an exciting time to be in the TV audience.

CHANGING CONTENT TRENDS IN TV

The changing content of television programs can be accounted for both economically and socially. When TV service first started in the late 1940s, it was in a period of experimentation. Most of the early programs were based on formats developed during radio's era of great popularity. In fact, some of the early TV shows were actually simulcasts of radio programs. Typical low-cost formats included game shows such as *Face the Music* and *Charade Quiz* and interview shows such as *Meet the Press* and *America's Town Meeting of the Air*, as well as a variety of westerns, soap operas, and comedies, all directly transposed to television. Another popular feature was the sports program. In a typical week in 1948, fully twenty-five hours in prime time were devoted to sports.

The Golden Age of Television

The 1950s are known as the "golden age" of television. This was a period marked by tremendous growth and innovation. Every program was a pioneer. The show that best typified early TV, however, was the variety show. In a way, this format marked the return of an entertainment style not seen since the motion picture spelled the end of vaudeville. *Ted Mack's Original Amateur Hour* premiered in 1948, as did *Arthur Godfrey's Talent Scouts*, Ed Sullivan's *Toast of the Town*, and the long-running *Texaco Star Theater*, starring ex-vaudevillian Milton Berle. When the definitive history of early TV is written, several pages will have to be devoted to this pioneering comedian, whose incredible popularity soon won him the title of "Mr. Television." Berle probably sold more TV sets than any other human being as people bought the new invention just to see what wacky costume "Uncle Miltie" would show up in next.

The first demonstrable trend in television programming was due in large measure to economic factors. Many buyers of early TV sets were people of above-average income and education who tended to live in urban areas, especially the New York City

Mr. Television, Milton Berle, dressed in one of the outrageous costumes that became his trademark on the Texaco Star Theater. *(Personality Press)*

region. This audience had long enjoyed live theater, and it was only natural that popular shows during the late 1940s and early 1950s should feature "live" dramas that would appeal to these sophisticated viewers. *Studio One* (1948–1958) featured plays by Rod Serling, Gore Vidal, and Reginald Rose. *The U.S. Steel Hour* (1953–1963) featured Broadway stars such as Tallulah Bankhead, Rex Harrison, and Gary Merrill. In the mid-fifties, U.S. Steel presented Cliff Robertson in a play called *The Two Worlds of Charley Gordon*. In 1968, Robertson re-created this role in the film *Charly* and won an Academy Award. Other programs that featured prestige drama were *Robert Montgomery Presents* (1950–1957), *Armstrong Circle Theater* (1950–1963), and *Kraft Television Theater* (1947–1958).

A second trend—the rise of the "adult western"—was also the result of monetary factors. In 1953, ABC merged with Paramount Theaters, which had recently been severed from Paramount Pictures because of the Justice Department's decree. ABC was looking for a program format that was guaranteed to be popular yet relatively inexpensive to produce, and Paramount had experience in producing westerns, a format that had enjoyed steady popularity since 1903. As it happened, ABC could not afford the tremendously expensive location shooting associated with the traditional western, so they modified the genre into something more affordable—the "adult western," in which character and motivation took precedence over huge battles between wagon trains and Indians. Two such programs premiered in 1955: *The Life and Legend of Wyatt Earp* (1955–1961) and *Gunsmoke* (1955–1975). These shows started a trend that spawned many imitators: *Cheyenne*, *Wagon Train*, *Rawhide*, *Have Gun Will Travel*, and *Maverick*. By 1959, the high-water mark for the western, there were twenty-six westerns in prime time. Networks had long since discovered that it paid to copy each other's successful programs.

Economics lay behind a third programming trend of the late fifties. After about 1958, TV became less exclusively an urban medium. As set prices dropped, television set ownership became more widespread. Stations sprang up in small towns, and TV antennas sprouted in rural areas. Soon, television programmers, in their quest for higher ratings, began providing shows that catered to this new audience. One early forerunner was the *Tennessee Ernie Ford Show* (1956–1961), which was followed by *The Andy Griffith Show* (1960–1968) and *The Real McCoys* (1957–1963). The quintessential show of this genre was the highly popular *The Beverly Hillbillies* (1962–1971), which attracted as many as 60 million viewers every week. Other shows, mainly from CBS (*Green Acres*, *Petticoat Junction*, *Gomer Pyle*, *Mayberry RFD*), were quick to imitate this series' success.

The Reaction of the Film Industry

When television began building a sizable audience during the late 1940s, it cut into the motion picture industry's profits. The first reaction of the film industry was to fight back. Studios stubbornly refused to advertise their films on TV, and they would not release old films for showing on the newer medium. Many studios wrote clauses into the contracts of their major stars forbidding them to appear on TV. None of their efforts had an appreciable effect on television's growing popularity—more and more Americans bought TV sets, while film attendance slipped even further.

Hollywood looked for ways to recapture some of its audience from TV. By the early 1950s, the film industry thought it had found the answer—technical wizardry. The first technical gimmick was 3-D (three-dimensional film). The audience wore special polarized glasses to perceive the effect and were treated to the illusion of spears, trains, arrows, knives, birds, and Jane Russell jumping out at them from the film screen. Unfortunately, the glasses gave some people headaches, and the equipment was too expensive for most theater owners to install. Audiences quickly became bored

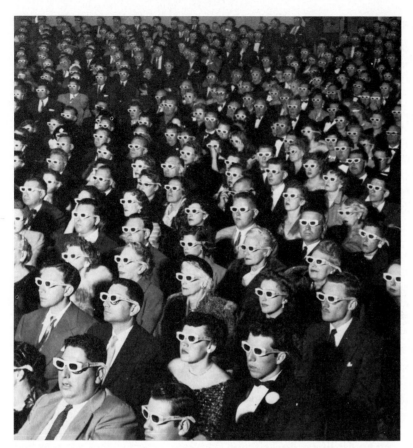

One of the problems with 3-D movies was the uncomfortable plastic glasses that audience members had to wear in order to appreciate the three-dimensional effects. (F. R. Eyerman, © Time, Inc.)

with the novelty. It soon became apparent that 3-D was not the answer. The second technical gimmick concerned screen size. Cinerama, which involved the use of three projectors and curved screens, surrounded the audience with film. It was too costly to achieve widespread use. Less expensive techniques that enlarged screen size, such as Cinemascope, Panavision, and Vistavision, were ultimately adopted by the industry but did little to stem Hollywood's loss of money.

The attitude of the movie companies toward TV during these early years was a clear example of shortsightedness. The film studios were still closely allied with their theater outlets. TV was hurting the neighborhood theater; therefore, TV was the enemy. What the film companies failed to see was that they could have played a dominant role in TV's evolution. Because major networks were not eager to supply early television programs, film companies would have been logical sources for television shows. However, the studios held so much animosity toward the new medium that production of early television series went to the advertising agencies, which assumed the role almost by default. Somewhat belatedly, Hollywood recognized that it was in its best interests to cooperate with television. In the late 1950s, the studios began to release their pre-1948 films to TV and also began to supply programs to the networks. In 1960, post-1948 theatrical films were made available to the smaller TV screens.

Recapturing an Audience: Film in the TV Age

During the postwar period, Hollywood produced several films that were more realistic in content and focused on social problems. By the 1950s, however, when it became clear that TV would be a formidable competitor, the film industry hastily cast about for new and unusual gimmicks to draw audiences back to the theaters. First it tried spectacle, complete with big budgets, lavish sets, and a cast of thousands: *Ben Hur* (1959), a remake of *The Ten Commandments* (1956), *El Cid* (1960), *Spartacus* (1960), and the highly touted production of *Cleopatra* (1962), starring Elizabeth Taylor and Richard Burton, that failed to recoup its $44 million price tag. Ironically enough, another trend was taking place during this same period at the other end of the financial spectrum—the cheap film. Movies like *I Was a Teenage Werewolf* (1953), *I Was a Teenage Frankenstein* (1954), and *Hercules* (1956) were all made for less than $300,000, a sum the studios could make back after playing for several weeks at local theaters.

With the relaxation of content restrictions, films began addressing subject matter that could not be shown on TV. *Peyton Place* (1957), *From Here to Eternity* (1953), and *Advise and Consent* (1962) dealt respectively with promiscuity, adultery, and homosexuality. In addition to controversial themes, another film genre that came across more effectively on the big screen than on TV was the musical. Subsequently, wholesome and light musicals that made use of vivid color, expensive props, and elaborate costumes and settings (items that could not be matched in a small TV studio) made an appearance. *An American in Paris* (1951), *Singin' in the Rain* (1952), and *The Bandwagon* (1953) were perhaps the best examples.

Although difficult to categorize, the films of the late fifties and early sixties generally continued to rely on subject matter or production techniques that were ill-suited for television. For example, big-budget spectaculars were successful: *West Side Story* (1961), *The Sound of Music* (1965), *Doctor Zhivago* (1965). Additional hit films were drawn from popular literature, as action-adventure capers, spiced with sex and

Hollywood vs. TV: Dollars and Scents

As the motion picture industry tried to cope with the rising competition of television, it tried many technical gimmicks to get the audience away from the tube and into the theater. Increased screen size and 3-D were, as has been pointed out, the techniques that got most attention. Lesser known but no less imaginative was another piece of gimmickry that TV could never hope to imitate—Smell-O-Vision.

Smell-O-Vision, also known by the more genteel name of "Aromarama," was first developed in 1959. The following year, producer Mike Todd backed a film called *The Scent of Mystery*, which was accompanied by odors. The smells came from little pipes built into the backs of the theater seats. It worked like this: An early scene in the film showed a rose garden next to a monastery in Spain. While this scene was projected,

the faint scent of roses was piped into the theater. Scenes at the seashore were accompanied by the appropriate sea smells. The clue to unraveling the mystery had to do with a certain brand of pipe tobacco that had a distinctive aroma. Unfortunately, it was difficult for the theater's air-conditioning system to eliminate one odor before the next was piped in. As a result, some smells hung in the air and mixed with the next odors that came wafting out from behind the seats. Toward the end of the film, many odors were floating about the theater, and their combination caused an overall disagreeable smell that many audience members complained about. The technique was never tried again, although John Waters tried something similar in his *Polyester*. It wasn't very successful either.

featuring indestructible heroes like James Bond (*Goldfinger*, 1964; *Thunderball*, 1965), became audience favorites. In 1967, the release of Arthur Penn's *Bonnie and Clyde* marked a pivotal point in the evolution of film content. Capitalizing on the newly emerged "youth culture," the picture reflected the changing concerns of its audience: dissatisfaction with traditional values, a desire to protest, and a preoccupation with individuality and an unencumbered lifestyle. Other films exploring the conflict between nonconformists and the establishment quickly followed: *The Graduate* (1967) and *Cool Hand Luke* (1967). The youth cycle reached its peak during the late sixties with *Easy Rider*, *Alice's Restaurant*, and *Medium Cool*.

• • • •

MODERN TRENDS IN FILM AND TV

Waning Power: The 1960s Film Industry

In the film industry, the 1960s were marked by the waning power of the major studios and by a closer affiliation with their old competitor, television. The continued rise of the independent producer led to a concomitant loss of power by the studios. As major production houses cut back, they released many actors, writers, and directors who, naturally enough, formed small, independent production companies. Using the big studios for financing and distribution, these independents and the artists they employed frequently took small salaries in exchange for a percentage of the film's profits. By the mid-1960s, roughly 80 percent of all American films were independent productions.

The poor economic climate brought about other changes. Large studios, faced with ever-worsening financial conditions, were absorbed by larger conglomerates. United Artists became part of the TransAmerica Corporation (it would later be absorbed by MGM, and MGM itself would later be acquired by Turner Broadcasting); Paramount, a division of Gulf + Western; and Warner Brothers, a part of Kinney National. The twilight of the studios extended into the next decade. In the early 1970s, both the MGM and 20th Century Fox studios were sold to make room for real estate developers. Universal, the only studio to remain more or less unchanged, has done so by supporting itself through TV production and by becoming a major tourist attraction for visitors to southern California.

The late 1960s also saw a change in the regulatory climate that surrounded films. The Supreme Court issued several decisions during this time that loosened controls on content, and filmmakers were quick to take advantage of their new freedom. In 1968, the Motion Picture Association of America liberalized its attitudes toward self-regulation. Whereas the old Production Code attempted to regulate content, the new system attempted to regulate audiences by instituting a G-PG-R-X labeling system.

The relationship between film and television became even closer in the 1960s, as movies made expressly for TV appeared in the middle of the decade. By 1974 about 180 of these "TV movies" were shown on network television. In that same year, the major film companies distributed only 109 films to theaters. In addition, many directors like Sidney Lumet and Sam Peckinpah, who started in television, went on to successful careers as film directors.

Coming of Age: Television in the 1960s

By the early 1960s, television's ecstatic trial period had come to an end. TV by then had lost much of its novelty and had become just another part of everyday life. During this decade, the number of TV stations increased by 54 percent, and by 1970, 95 percent of all American households owned a least one working television. Advertisers, lured by the potential profits to be reaped from this vast audience, increased their advertising 120 percent. As the influence of television became more apparent, critics of television programming became more outspoken. Parents were joined by educators,

A salesman taking an order in a 1950s television and radio store. (The Bettmann Archive)

politicans, psychologists, and minority leaders in expressing their concern over the new medium's social and political impact on its viewers. In response to these economic and social pressures, television development during the 1960s moved in the direction of expansion, diversification, and sensitivity to the growing potential of television journalism.

In 1960, the Kennedy–Nixon debates were telecast to an audience of 65 million. Three years later, NBC and CBS expanded their nightly newscasts to thirty minutes (ABC followed suit shortly thereafter), and the heated competition between Walter Cronkite on CBS and the team of Chet Huntley and David Brinkley on NBC began. In November of 1963, TV journalism demonstrated the highest degree of professionalism during its coverage of the assassination and funeral of President John F. Kennedy. The networks also covered the growing civil rights movement during the sixties as well as the social unrest on campus and in the cities. Perhaps the most exciting moment for television news came in 1969 with its live coverage of Neil Armstrong's historic walk on the moon.

Noncommercial broadcasting was also evolving during the 1960s. Educational stations, as they were called then, got off to a rather shaky start since the choice VHF frequencies in the large markets had been snapped up by commercial stations. Despite this drawback, the number of educational stations grew during the fifties and sixties so that by 1965, ninety-nine were on the air. It was obvious, however, that some stable source of financial support was needed to keep many of them from going dark. A report issued by the Carnegie Commission proposed that Congress establish a Corporation for Public Broadcasting. The commission's recommendations were incorporated into the **Public Broadcasting Act of 1967**, which set up the Public

Live TV coverage of the first moon landing in 1969 reached hundreds of millions of viewers. (Ed Carlin/ The Picture Cube)

Broadcasting Service. Unfortunately, the act did not provide for secure, long-term financing of the new service, an omission that later led to political problems with the executive branch of the government and prompted yet another study by a new Carnegie Commission in the late 1970s.

Another segment of the broadcasting industry was also experiencing growth in this decade—the cable television (CATV) industry. CATV originated as an attempt to bring TV signals to hard-to-reach mountainous areas (in fact, CATV first stood for "Community Antenna Television"), but operators soon began to import signals from distant stations to communities in nonmountainous areas that were without full three-network service. By 1960, CATV systems were capable of providing twelve different channels to their subscribers, including specialized news and information channels, movie channels, and even several audio services. Faced with increased pressures from over-the-air broadcasters, the FCC, which initially did not want to get involved in the regulation of CATV, did an about-face in 1966 and issued a set of regulations for CATV that would slow down its growth for the next half-dozen years. Related to the fortunes of CATV were those of the emerging pay-TV industry. The FCC had okayed an experimental over-the-air pay-TV operation in Hartford, Connecticut, in 1960, and in 1968 the commission issued rules governing the new pay operations. By this time, however, pay-TV companies were turning to CATV systems rather than pursuing over-the-air pay TV. Cable operators were also eager to add one or more pay channels to increase the attractiveness of their service. As the 1970s began, the future of these two industries would become more closely entwined.

Years of Turmoil: TV Content in the 1960s

The 1960s were years marked by growing social turmoil—dissent over the Vietnam War and civil rights and concern over outbursts of violence and the economic recession. These volatile social conditions appear to have been the impetus for two major

Although still outnumbered by their male counterparts, women directors in television and film are becoming more common. Joan Tewkesbury (*Cold Sassy Tree*), Joan Micklin Silver (*Crossing Delancey*), Martha Coolidge (*Valley Girl*), Susan Seidelman (*Desperately Seeking Susan*), Elaine May (*Ishtar*), Barbra Streisand (*Prince of Tides*), and Penny Marshall (*Awakenings*) are all established Hollywood directors. All of them, however, owe a debt to Ida Lupino, the most prolific female director of the modern era and a pioneer in elevating the status of women behind the camera.

An actress who starred in several hit movies in the 1940s, Ida Lupino turned to directing in 1949. At the time there were no women working as directors in male-dominated Hollywood. Lupino and her husband founded a small studio, Filmakers, and turned out high-quality, low-budget films that made a comment on life in America. Between 1949 and 1954, Ida Lupino wrote and directed six feature films for her company, with topics ranging from unwed mothers to bigamy. Perhaps her best is *The Hitchhiker*, a tense psychological thriller released in 1953. These films established her as a no-nonsense, competent director with a particular flair for action scenes.

With television taking away the audience from motion pictures, Lupino's production company was forced out of business. Undaunted, she moved to the new medium and directed episodes of thirty TV series, from westerns like *Have Gun, Will Travel*, to the sci-fi *Thriller*. During her career, which spanned the better part of two decades, she directed more than a hundred TV episodes. She retired from the industry in the 1970s, leaving behind a legacy that few, male or female, have matched.

Ida Lupino at work behind the camera. (Photofest)

content trends of this period. Having learned that audiences would tolerate a high level of violence, network programmers produced a steady stream of action-adventure shows. Two of the most successful of these were *The Untouchables*, based on the exploits of G-man Eliot Ness, and *Naked City*, a cops-and-robbers show set in New York. After the Kennedy assassination in 1963, however, public protest against televised violence resulted in a modification of program content. To satisfy viewers who wished to avoid the harsh realities of life, prime-time television presented shows that can best be categorized as fantasy and escapist situation comedies. In the fall of 1964, for example, the following shows were on the networks' schedules: *My Living Doll* (about a glamorous robot), *My Favorite Martian* (about a Martian), *The Munsters* (a family of monsters making a go of it in suburbia), *Bewitched* (about a friendly witch), *I Dream of Jeannie* (about a friendly genie), and *My Mother the Car* (self-explanatory). Other shows featuring escapist fantasy that appeared during this period were *Batman*, *The Wild Wild West*, *The Man From U.N.C.L.E.*, and *Get Smart*.

By the late sixties, however, there was another shift in programming. Growing concern over social conditions was reflected in the watchwords of television content during this period: youth and relevance. In 1969 and 1970, the following shows premiered: *The Young Rebels*, *The Young Lawyers*, *The Interns* (about young doctors), *Storefront Lawyers* (more young lawyers), *The Headmaster* (about young teachers and young students), and *Matt Lincoln* (about young social workers). None of these shows survived into a second season, thus making this the shortest trend on record.

Upward Trends: The 1970s Film Industry

Film history since the early seventies has been marked by several apparent trends: Revenue went up, as did the budgets of many feature films, and several motion pictures racked up astonishing gross receipts. Foremost among these trends was a reversal of the slump in box-office receipts that began in 1946 and finally bottomed out in 1971. With the exception of temporary declines in 1973 and 1976, the general trend has been upward. In 1977, total box-office gross was about $2.4 billion; by 1981 it had risen to nearly $3 billion, although some of this increase could be attributed to inflation.

Portrayals of Blacks and Women

During the early years of television, leading female and black performers were restricted to stereotypical roles. Women were either scatterbrained wives (as in *I Love Lucy*) or model housewives and mothers (*Leave It to Beaver*). Blacks were practically nonexistent.

In 1965, however, a young Bill Cosby co-starred with Robert Culp in *I Spy* and created a new role for blacks in TV—the assistant to the hero. By the 1970s, several shows featuring black casts appeared in prime time; most were situation comedies, such as *Good Times* and *The Jeffersons*. By the 1990s, blacks were more numerous in the prime-time schedules, more in situation comedies (nine sitcoms featured a primarily black cast in 1991) than drama (only five dramatic series had blacks cast in major roles).

Women appeared sparingly in lead roles during the 1960s. *Honey West*, the first female private eye in a leading role in a TV series, lasted one season (1965). Marlo Thomas starred in *That Girl* for six seasons as a somewhat kooky but modern-thinking woman. Other shows portraying women a little more realistically premiered in the 1970s: *The Mary Tyler Moore Show*, *Maude*, and *One Day at a Time*. In the late 1970s, however, producers seemed to select female leads more for their looks, and series such as *Charlie's Angels* and *Three's Company* were on the schedules. By the 1990s, the portrayal of females had become more diverse, as evidenced by *Designing Women*, *The Golden Girls*, *Murphy Brown*, *The Trials of Rosie O'Neill*, and *Murder, She Wrote*. Nonetheless, throwbacks to the old female-as-sex-object formula still appear (*Married . . . with Children*).

With more cash flowing into the box office, more money became available for the budgets of feature films. In fact, films of the late 1970s and early 1980s were reminiscent of the extravaganzas of the 1920s. For example, *Dune* (1984) and *Cotton Club* (1984) each cost about $40 million to make; *Superman II* (1983) and *Raise the Titanic* (1980) each cost about $36 million. Although the expense of making such films seems astronomical, the final movie product offers a chance at fabulous financial rewards. Perhaps the most interesting film phenomenon of the era has been the rise of the super box-office blockbuster. From 1900 to 1970, only two films (*The Sound of Music* and *Gone With the Wind*) managed to surpass $50 million in film rentals; between 1970 and 1980, seventeen films surpassed this mark (Table 11-1). The science-fiction epic *Star Wars*, which cost approximately $10 million to make, had grossed $400 million worldwide by 1979. Interestingly enough, it was not just the big-budget films that were earning big profits. Several small-budget films also returned revenues far in excess of their costs. For example, *Easy Rider*, released in 1969, cost only $370,000 to make but earned more than $40 million. *Rocky* (1976) was made for about $1 million and took in $55 million. Even when the effects of inflation are taken into account, it is apparent that a small group of films has dominated revenues in recent years.

One important factor behind the industry's renewed success at the box office was an increased use of market-research data as part of the filmmaking process. During this time period, motion pictures discovered their own well-defined audience. A survey done in the early 1970s confirmed what most in the industry had suspected: The majority of filmgoers were under thirty, well educated, and primarily urban. Hollywood, with few exceptions, takes great care to satisfy this audience. This trend toward appealing to a specialized audience was manifested in the construction of movie theaters as well. Lavish motion picture palaces were no longer being built. Modern theaters were small and often conveniently set in clusters of three or four within suburban shopping centers.

The trend toward closer cooperation between the TV and film industries was reflected by the production of more movies aimed at a television audience. In 1978, Hollywood produced around 180 films expressly for the small screen; only two dozen more were made for release in motion picture theaters. This move toward cooperation

---

TABLE 11-1 All-Time Top Money-Making Films

The figures below are based on film rentals, that is, money received by the film distributors from motion picture theaters. This figure is not the same as total box-office gross receipts. Also, the table includes only rentals from the U.S. and Canadian markets.

FILM	YEAR	RENTALS (MILLIONS)
1. *ET*	1982	$229
2. *Star Wars*	1977	194
3. *Return of the Jedi*	1983	168
4. *Batman*	1989	150
5. *The Empire Strikes Back*	1980	142
6. *Home Alone*	1990	140*
7. *Ghostbusters*	1984	133
8. *Jaws*	1975	129
9. *Raiders of the Lost Ark*	1981	116
10. *Indiana Jones and the Last Crusade*	1989	115

*Estimate

Source: *Variety*, January 6, 1992, p. 86.

was reflected in another way when, at the end of the 1970s, two television networks, ABC and CBS, reversed tradition and began producing films that were to be released to movie theaters. NBC followed suit in 1986.

On another front, after receiving considerable criticism for giving a PG rating to films such as *Indiana Jones and the Temple of Doom* and *Gremlins*, which contained graphic violence, the Motion Picture Association of America instituted a new category—PG-13. This category was designed for those films where parental guidance for children under 13 was recommended. Yet another new category, NC-17, replaced the X rating in 1990.

Increasing Fortunes: Film in the 1980s and 1990s

The last decade or so has been generally favorable for the film industry. Although theater attendance increased only slightly, higher admission costs pushed box-office revenues to all-time highs. The $5 billion mark was passed in 1989 and again in 1990 but revenues slumped to $4.87 billion in 1992. Pay cable and videocassettes have eclipsed the theatrical box office as the most important revenue source for film. Making movies however, is still a risky business. Despite its success with *Dances with Wolves*, Orion Pictures filed for bankruptcy in 1991. The number of movie screens was also at an all-time high, about 23,700. Movie budgets continued to soar with 1991's *Terminator 2* topping the $90 million mark.

Foreign ownership of movie studios also increased as the Japanese electronics conglomerate Sony acquired Columbia Pictures and its chief rival, the Matsushita Corporation, bought MCA, the parent company of Universal. A European company, Pathe, bought MGM/UA. Add these to 20th Century Fox, owned by the News Corporation of Australia, and more than half of the major U.S. movie studios were foreign-owned.

In the past few years, however, U.S.-owned studios have led the others in box-office share of the market. The Disney Company's Buena Vista organization and Warner Brothers were the top two studios in 1990, 1991, and 1992.

Disney was a leader in another way as well. It opened studio facilities in Orlando, Florida, and was soon followed by Universal. Florida was rapidly becoming Hollywood East.

Vertical Integration II

Hollywood is fond of sequels so it's not surprising that the end of the 1980s saw the major studios get back into the business of owning motion picture theaters. In 1948, Paramount decision barred motion picture producer-distributors from the exhibition business because the Justice Department thought it was restraint of trade. In the 1980s, with a more deregulation-minded administration in power, movie studios were given the green light to return to the exhibition business provided they didn't discriminate against the films released by other distributors or engage in any other monopolistic practice.

Studios "reverticalized" in a grand way. Cannon, Paramount, Tri-Star, United Artists, and Universal all acquired chains of movie theaters. In addition, theater owner Cineplex Odeon announced a partnership with MCA that would allow Cineplex to produce the films that its theaters would show. By the time the buying spree was over, about one-third of North America's theaters had changed hands. Consequently, the large studios are once again firmly entrenched in the production, distribution, and exhibition of motion pictures.

By mid-1991, however, the trade press reported that some big studios had cooled on the idea of theater ownership and were looking to sell their holdings.

Florida is rapidly becoming Hollywood East as, first, Disney and then Universal opened studios in the Orlando area. (Karen Kuehn/Matrix)

Film Content: 1970–Present

The 1970s saw the reemergence of the director as a major creative force. Francis Ford Coppola, the first major filmmaker to graduate from a college film program, became the first of several talented film students to burst on the scene during the early 1970s. Coppola made three blockbuster films in that decade: *The Godfather* (1972), *Godfather II* (1974), and *Apocalypse Now* (1979). Another film student, Steven Spielberg, directed the hugely popular *Jaws* (1975), the visually attractive but abstruse *Close Encounters of the Third Kind* (1979), the action-packed *Raiders of the Lost Ark* (1981), and the record-breaking *ET* (1982). Yet another film graduate, George Lucas, directed two of the all-time biggest box-office attractions, *American Graffiti* (1973) and *Star Wars* (1977). This last film marked a noticeable trend in film content of the late 1970s—big-budget science fiction films tht relied heavily on special effects. In 1979–1980, for example, these films were all released: *Superman, Alien, Star Trek: The Movie, The Black Hole,* and *The Empire Strikes Back.*

Probably the most notable film trend of recent years has been the steady popularity of the sequel—a movie that continues a story started in an earlier film. *Godfather II,* which began this recent trend, was quickly followed by *Rocky II, III, IV,* and *V, Star Trek II, III, IV,* and *V, Superman II, III,* and *IV,* and a host of others. In fact, in 1983 a record sixteen sequels were released. Fourteen more followed in 1984. Some sequels were threatening to go on forever. In 1991, *Star Trek VI* was released. The motivating factor behind this large number of sequels is an economic one. As films cost more to produce, Hollywood financiers believe it is less risky to finance a story and a cast of characters that already have proven box-office appeal.

The other type of film that was popular in the first half of the 1980s was the comedy. *Ghostbusters, Mr. Mom, Trading Places,* and *Splash* were all big box-office hits from 1983 to 1985. Another type of comedy was also produced in great quantities by Hollywood studios. This was tabbed the "teenage exploitation" film and featured

Spike Lee

The early 1990s saw a number of films by young black directors about the black experience in America. Mario Van Peebles was in charge of the controversial *New Jack City*. *Straight Out of Brooklyn* was directed by 19-year-old Matty Rich. John Singleton, 23, directed the critically acclaimed *Boyz N the Hood*. The most well-known of all black directors, however, is the 34-year-old Spike Lee. In fact, it was Lee's success that helped pave the way for other black directors. Lee showed that there was an audience for black films that took an unflinching look at contemporary black life.

Lee got interested in films while a student at Atlanta's Morehouse College. After graduation, he enrolled in New York University's Tisch School of the Arts. After completing the program, he put together his first film in 1986, *She's Gotta Have It*, on a microscopic budget of $175,000, raised mainly from friends and family. The film made about $8 million at the box office and brought Lee to the attention of the major studios. It also demonstrated that

Lee was a director who did things his own way and did not flinch from criticism. His next film, *School Daze*, was a satire of social climbing at a black university. It got lukewarm reviews and angered some blacks because of its unflattering portrayals of some black characters.

It was Lee's next film, *Do the Right Thing*, that catapulted him into the national spotlight. Lee played the part of a pizza delivery man who sparks racial violence. The film got excellent reviews but was strongly criticized as being inflammatory. Lee did not shrink from controversy. His next effort, *Mo Better Blues*, prompted protests from the Jewish community because of its sardonic portrayals of Jewish businessmen. Lee's next film, *Jungle Fever*, was even more controversial, dealing with interracial romance. In late 1991, he was working on a biography of black leader Malcolm X. Not surprisingly, he was taking a lot of heat, this time from leaders in the black community who were afraid he was going to dishonor Malcolm X's image. Predictably, Lee stood his ground.

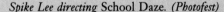

Spike Lee directing School Daze. *(Photofest)*

young stars in sexy and/or raunchy situations. Some examples of this genre include *Hot Dog, The Movie, Porky's, Porky's II,* and *Weird Science.* These films were obvious attempts to appeal to the prime moviegoing audience—teenagers.

In contrast, the last half of the decade and the early part of the 1990s saw the motion picture studios releasing films that appealed to audience segments other than teenagers. This is partly because the film audience is getting older and partly because the teen audience is renting movies and watching them at home. A glance at some of the big hits of the last few years bears out this trend. *Rainman, The Hunt for Red October,* and *Driving Miss Daisy* were aimed at more mature audiences. At the same time, Hollywood was releasing more films with a broad, general appeal, designed to attract both young and old. *Pretty Woman, Ghost, Batman* (I and II), *Home Alone* (I and II), and *Jurassic Park* had fans from every age group. Perhaps the most disturbing content trend from the past few years has been the number of big-budget films that contained graphic violence such as *Terminator 2, Total Recall, Die Hard 2, Goodfellas,* and *Freddy's Dead.*

Growing Public Concern: Television in the 1970s

On the television side, as the 1970s began, public concern over the impact of television programming and over local station practices was steadily growing. A scientific advisory panel composed of mass communication researchers was set up by the Surgeon General's office to investigate the impact of exposure to TV violence (see Chapter 22). The report that was released by this group, although it did contain some controversial elements, indicated that TV violence was related in a modest way to aggressive behavior, especially in young children. Following the publication of this report, the three networks issued statements that said, in effect, that they were reducing the amount of TV violence in their shows. Additionally, the FCC exerted informal pressure on broadcasters to come up with a more formal plan to address this continuing concern. In 1975, the networks agreed to the idea of a "family viewing hour," in which programs suitable for the entire family would be aired. A Los Angeles court ruled late in 1976 that this agreement was unconstitutional and came about as a result of unfair government pressure. This 1976 decision was itself overturned in 1979. In late 1984, the case was settled out of court and the family viewing hour quietly faded into history.

The early 1970s were also characterized by the growth of citizen-group involvement in FCC decisions concerning station licensing and station programming policy. Groups such as Action for Children's Television, the Office of Communication of the United Church of Christ, the Citizens Communications Center, and coalitions of minority groups have become more influential in the regulatory process. One other action by the FCC also had important consequences for the TV industry. In 1970, the **Prime Time Access Rule** was issued. The idea behind this rule was to expand program diversity by requiring stations in the larger cities to schedule programs that were not produced or licensed by the three networks. In effect, this rule took the 7:30–8:00 P.M. (EST) time slot away from the nets and gave it back to the locals. Although many would argue over the efficacy of this rule in producing more diversity, it did have one somewhat unanticipated effect on the economic situation of the networks. ABC, which had been a perennial third-place finisher in the ratings race among the three nets, saved money because of this ruling since it no longer had to program (and lose money on) the 7:30–8:00 P.M. time period. Partly because of this fact, the network was able to stage a resurgence, and in the late 1970s, ABC was usually in the top position among the three nets in their quest for the prime-time audience. ABC's dominance didn't last long, however, as CBS took over the top spot and NBC moved up to second. During the late 1980s and early 1990s, NBC was usually the top network but the margin separating the top network from the bottom became narrower as the competition got more intense.

The biggest trend in the TV industry in the 1980s and 1990s was the continuing erosion of network audiences. In the early 1970s, the three networks routinely pulled down about 90 percent of the prime-time audience. In 1991, thanks to competition from independent stations, cable, video games, and VCRs, their share had slipped to about 60 percent. In addition, a fourth network, the Fox Broadcasting Company, started operations in 1987 and after a couple of rough years began to turn a profit. Fox's programming was designed to appeal to a younger audience and by 1991, Fox was making a further dent in the ratings of the three older networks. This loss of audience and a weak economy translated into decreased network advertising profits and resulted in significant cost cutting and layoffs at all three nets.

Unlike the turbulent times of the mid-1980s, when all of the networks changed ownership, the late 1980s and early 1990s saw no network bought or sold. How long this situation will remain stable, however, is difficult to tell. In late 1991, there were reports, for example, that at least one and maybe two networks might be acquired by a major Hollywood studio. Stay tuned.

Cable's Continued Growth

Cable continued to grow, reaching about 60 percent of the population by 1992. As cable systems increased their capacity, new cable programming services rushed to fill the new channels. By 1992, there were six national pay-per-view services, six premium services including HBO and Showtime, and approximately sixty superstations and cable networks with another sixteen planned for launch in the next year, including the Sci-Fi channel, the Auto Channel, and the Cowboy Channel. This proliferation of

Although it rarely appeared in the top 30-rated TV shows, Beverly Hills 90210 *was a big hit among teenagers and helped the Fox network attract the young consumers that advertisers want to reach. (Andrew Semel)*

channels, however, can't go on forever. As audiences are divided into smaller and smaller fragments, it becomes difficult for a channel to sustain the critical mass necessary to stay profitable.

Advertising revenue also grew, topping the $2 billion mark in 1990 as some big advertisers such as Procter & Gamble and Phillip Morris moved significant portions of their ad budgets to cable. The regulatory situation, however, changed drastically in 1992. In response to many consumer complaints, Congress passed the 1992 Cable Act. Among other provisions, this act gave the FCC the power to regulate cable rates, obliged cable companies to make programming in which the company has an interest available to competitors, and gave TV stations the right to demand compensation from cable systems that carry their signals. Cable companies appealed this new law and in late 1993 the Supreme Court announced that it would consider their appeal.

Zipping, Zapping, and Grazing

A development that had significant impact on both traditional TV and the cable industry was the spectacular growth of VCRs. Fewer than 5 percent of households had VCRs in 1982. By 1991, that figure was 70 percent. In fact, the VCR has been adopted faster than any other appliance except television. The effects of the VCR are many. First, the renting of movies on cassettes has become a multibillion-dollar business, with motion picture studios depending on cassettes for a large part of their revenue. VCRs sparked the growth of the prerecorded videocassette industry. As of 1991, there were about 30,000 home video rental shops in the United States.

Second, the VCR encourages **timeshifting**, playing back programs at times other than when they were aired. Although this has helped traditional television since it increased the total audience by allowing people who might not otherwise view a program to do so, it has caused some new problems for advertisers. Some viewers have special machines that "zap" commercials: The VCR pauses while the commercial is aired and then starts up again when the program is on. Also, when viewers play back programs, many will fast forward, or "zip," their way through the ads, diluting their effectiveness.

Finally, the proliferation of the hand-held remote-control device has also caused problems for advertisers and programmers. Remote units are in almost two-thirds of all households and have encouraged the tendency toward "grazing," rapidly scanning all the channels during a commercial or dull spot in a program in search of greener pastures. Advertisers and producers both tried to make their messages so interesting that grazing was discouraged. Nonetheless, it was still a widespread practice.

In other developments, many of the highly touted new technologies failed to catch on. Videotex and teletext (see Chapter 5) cost many media companies a lot of money and most were out of the business by 1991. Some still thought the technique had promise, however, and Sears and IBM launched Prodigy. **Low-power television (LPTV)**, which would allow a new class of TV stations with a small service area, grew slowly, hampered in part by an unexpected avalanche of applications for stations reaching the FCC. As of 1991, most LPTV stations were marginal operations at best. **Direct broadcasting by satellite (DBS)**, while available in other countries, still had trouble getting off the drawing board. Although a couple of companies launched limited services in the U.S. and a major consortium announced plans for a system called SkyCable, DBS is still not a major player in the television arena.

On the legal side, the deregulation philosophy of the 1980s was not so prevalent, but the major decisions of the earlier decade had not been overturned. The Fairness Doctrine, abolished in the late 1980s, had not reappeared nor had new rules reemerged concerning how long stations must be held before sold. In fact, the FCC was considering even more liberal rules regarding the number of broadcast stations one organization or individual could own. Congress did pass a new law with regard to children's television and TV violence regulation (Chapter 17) but there was no widespread return to stricter regulation.

CHAPTER 11 279
HISTORY OF FILM
AND TELEVISION

or individual could own. Congress did pass a new law with regard to children's television and TV violence regulation (Chapter 17) but there was no widespread return to stricter regulation.

In sum, the traditional television industry had been significantly altered by developments in the 1980s and 1990s. Audiences were able to choose among several alternatives to network television. New and expanded uses of the medium were possible and viewers were quick to take advantage of most of them. This trend toward expanded choices will likely continue as the decade progresses.

TV Content: 1970s to the Present

The early 1970s were the law-and-order years. In 1971, seventeen and a half hours of prime time were devoted to cops-and-robbers programs as the networks introduced viewers to a country cop (*Cade's County*), young cops (*Mod Squad*), Hawaiian cops (*Hawaii 5-0*), handicapped cops (*Ironside*), uniformed cops (*Adam 12*), and federal cops (*The FBI*), not to mention a fat private eye (*Cannon*), a blind private eye (*Longstreet*), and a tough private eye (*Mannix*). This trend remained popular until the mid-seventies when it was replaced by one of television's most significant programming developments—the more sophisticated, "adult" version of the old situation comedy. The trend began in 1970 with the controversial sitcom *All in the Family*. The adult comedies that followed, including *M*A*S*H*, *Soap*, *Sanford and Son*, and *Barney Miller*, all dealt with previously taboo topics (for television) such as premarital sex, racial prejudice, and abortion. True to the belief that imitation of success breeds more success, networks did not hesitate to "spin off" characters from well-established shows. Leaders in this movement were the highly popular *Mary Tyler Moore Show*, which spawned *Rhoda*, *Phyllis*, and *Lou Grant*, and *All in the Family*, which led to *Maude* and *The Jeffersons*.

During the late seventies and early eighties, prime-time series began to imitate daytime soap operas as programs that continued a story line from week to week went to the top of the ratings. These shows were typically about a rich and powerful family and featured at least one nasty villain or villainess that the audience evidently enjoyed hating. First show of this genre was the extremely popular *Dallas*, which was followed by *Dynasty*, *Flamingo Road*, and *Falcon Crest*. These shows seemed to demonstrate the fact that audiences love to see that money and power do not necessarily guarantee happiness. This trend had declined by decade's end.

The mid-1980s marked the comeback of comedies, particularly warm, family-oriented comedies. These shows, dubbed "warmedies" by the trade press, included *Family Ties*, *The Cosby Show*, *Growing Pains*, *Our House*, and *Who's the Boss?* One big reason for the popularity of this genre was economic. Family-oriented sitcoms did well in the syndication aftermarket. The warmedies were replaced by "dramadies," shows that were still warm but more reality-oriented and shot without the traditional laugh track. Shows falling in this category were *Slap Maxwell*, *Frank's Place*, and *The Days and Nights of Molly Dodd*. Although these shows were generally praised by critics, audience reaction was lukewarm at best, and these shows generally were not around very long. The last, and perhaps most significant, programming trend was the introduction of series with "targeted" demographics. These were shows carefully constructed to appeal to a narrow but desirable segment of the mass audience. The most obvious example is *thirtysomething*, a program about and designed to appeal to the upwardly mobile thirty-to-forty crowd, the "yuppies." *Beauty and the Beast* also fits in this category with its female-oriented stories. By the early 1990s, these "targeted" shows were no longer in vogue, as both *thirtysomething* and *Beauty and the Beast* bit the dust. The limited audience they attracted was not sufficient to justify their cost. The early 1990s also saw the networks try to recapture audiences by presenting some innovative, quirky, and rather offbeat programming. *Twin Peaks* became quite popular during its early episodes and inspired a cult following. The novelty quickly wore off, however, and the show was canceled in its next season. *Cop Rock*, a musical about police work, didn't last a season. More successful were *China Beach*, a gritty drama about the Vietnam War that was on for three seasons before being canceled, and *Northern Exposure*, which was still on the air as of the 1993–1994 season.

Speaking of the 1993–1994 season, "reality" programs such as *60 Minutes, Dateline NBC*, and *America's Most Wanted* dominated the prime-time schedule, accounting for thirteen hours on ABC, NBC, CBS, and Fox. Much of this trend is explained by the fact that these shows are cheaper to produce than traditional sitcoms and action-adventure series.

● ● ● ●

SUGGESTIONS FOR FURTHER READING

The books listed below represent some of those available that cover the history of television and film.

ACKER, ALLY, *Reel Women*, New York: Continuum, 1991.

AULETTA, KEN, *Three Blind Mice*, New York: Random House, 1991.

BARNOUW, ERIK, *A Tower in Babel*, New York: Oxford University Press, 1966.

———, *The Golden Web*, New York: Oxford University Press, 1968.

———, *The Image Empire*, New York: Oxford University Press, 1970.

———, *Tube of Plenty*, New York: Oxford University Press, 1990.

BOHN, THOMAS, AND RICHARD STROMGEN, *Light and Shadows*, Palo Alto, Calif.: Mayfield, 1987.

BROOKS, TIM, AND EARLE MARSH, *The Complete Directory of Prime Time Network TV Shows, 1946–Present*, New York: Ballantine Books, 1988.

BROWNLOW, KEVIN, *The Parade's Gone By*, New York: Alfred Knopf, 1968.

ELLIS, JACK, *A History of Film*, Englewood Cliffs, N.J.: Prentice-Hall, 1990.

JACOBS, LEWIS, *The Rise of the American Film*, New York: Teachers College Press, 1968.

KNIGHT, ARTHUR, *The Liveliest Art*, New York: Macmillan, 1978.

LICHTY, LAWRENCE, AND MALACHI TOPPING, *American Broadcasting: A Source Book on the History of Radio and Television*, New York: Hastings House, 1975.

MAST, GERALD, *A Short History of the Movies*, New York: Macmillan, 1986.

MONACO, JAMES, *American Film Now*, New York: New American Library, 1984.

SKLAR, ROBERT, *Movie-Made America*, New York: Random House, 1975.

STERLING, CHRISTOPHER, AND JOHN KITTROSS, *Stay Tuned: A Concise History of American Broadcasting*, Belmont, Calif.: Wadsworth, 1990.

UDELSON, JOSEPH, *The Great Television Race*, University: University of Alabama Press, 1982.

WILK, MAX, *The Golden Age of Television*, New York: Dell Publishing Company, 1976.

STRUCTURE OF THE MOTION PICTURE INDUSTRY

erhaps screenwriter William Goldman (*Butch Cassidy and the Sundance Kid*, *Marathon Man*, *Princess Bride*) said it best in his book *Adventures in the Screen Trade*: The single most important fact of the entire movie industry is "Nobody knows anything." As Goldman elaborates, not one person in the entire industry knows for certain what will work and what won't. Every time a picture opens, it's a roll of the dice.

Consider, for example, what happened in 1990. Warner Brothers had taken a look at a script about an 8-year-old kid who mistakenly gets left behind when his family flies to Paris. Not enough appeal for teens, decided Warners and rejected the script. About the same time, Warners was putting the finishing touches on a film starring three established stars, Tom Hanks, Bruce Willis, and Melanie Griffith, based on a best-selling book by Tom Wolfe and directed by a Hollywood veteran, Brian De Palma. Warners thought the combination couldn't miss and spent $45 million producing *Bonfire of the Vanities*.

What about that other script that Warners turned down? 20th Century Fox picked it up, assigned it a modest budget of $18 million, filled the cast with competent but relatively unknown actors and actresses, and gave it to a new director to film. When it opened during Thanksgiving week of 1990, *Home Alone* was up against strong competition: *Three Men and a Little Lady*, *Kindergarten Cop*, and *Look Who's Talking Too*. Given the circumstances, Fox did not have high expectations for *Home Alone*.

What happened? *Bonfire of the Vanities* was a colossal flop, picking up just $9 million before beating a hasty retreat to the video store. So much for big stars and big budgets. *Home Alone*, as everybody is probably well aware, went on to become the biggest moneymaking comedy in film history, raking in more than $280 million at the box office. The *Home Alone* video was also poised to become the number-one seller as well. As William Goldman might say, go figure.

This chapter will examine the structure of this unpredictable, precarious, and risky business.

ORGANIZATION OF THE FILM INDUSTRY

The film industry is a business whose ultimate goal is to make money. This statement may seem crass to many people who believe that film is an art form produced by creative and imaginative people whose primary goal is to achieve aesthetic excellence. Although it may be true that film is an art form, the film industry is in business to make a profit. If an occasional moneymaking film also turns out to have artistic merit, so much the better, but the artistic merit is usually a by-product rather than the main

Despite being left home alone, 8-year-old Kevin (Macauley Culkin) proved more than a match for the bad guys. Home Alone *ranks number 4 on the all-time list of moneymakers for its studio, 20th Century Fox, trailing only the films of the* Star Wars *trilogy. (Everett Collection)*

focus. In our analysis of the film industry, we will divide its structure into three levels: (1) production, (2) distribution, and (3) exhibition.

Production

The production side of the industry will be discussed at some length later in this chapter. For now, we will mention only some of the basics.

Films are produced by a variety of organizations and individuals. For many years, the major studios controlled virtually all production, but independent producers have recently become prevalent. In 1992, independents produced more than two-thirds of all feature films. The major studios now finance and distribute many films made by independent companies.

Probably the biggest change in production in the late eighties has been the increased number of films that are released each year. Prompted in part by the additional revenues from home video and the theatrical box office, a total of 414 films were released in 1992, an increase of 25 percent since 1982. The major film production companies (Columbia, Paramount, 20th Century Fox, MGM/United Artists, Disney, TriStar, Warner Brothers, Universal) will each produce twelve to twenty films a year. Table 12-1 shows the share of the domestic box office for each major studio in 1992.

Distribution

The distribution arm of the industry is responsible for supplying prints of films to the thousands of theaters and drive-ins located across the United States and to cinemas across the entire globe. In recent years, distribution companies have also supplied films to TV networks and to makers of videocassettes and videodiscs. Distribution companies maintain close contact with theater owners all over the world and also provide a transportation and delivery system that ensures that a film will arrive at a theater before its scheduled play date. In addition to booking the film at local movie

TABLE 12-1 Domestic Box-Office Market Shares—1991

COMPANY	SHARE (%)
Warner's	19
Disney	19
20th Century Fox	14
Universal	13
Columbia	12
Paramount	11
TriStar	7
MGM/UA	1
Others	4

houses, the distribution company is responsible for making the multiple prints of a film that are necessary when the film goes into general release. They also take care of advertising and promotion for the film. Most of the distribution of motion pictures is handled by the large studios listed above. These companies are firmly entrenched in both the production and distribution aspects of the business.

The distribution picture has changed in the last few years. A record number of motion picture screens (see page 284) has created a demand that the majors cannot fulfill. Consequently, independent distributors have carved out a specialty niche for themselves. New Line Cinema, for example, concentrated on films aimed at a young

Little-Known Hollywood Jobs—Part 1

The script supervisor on a movie has the job of maintaining continuity. Since films are shot out of sequence and some scenes may be shot days or weeks apart, someone has to make sure that the actors are wearing the exact same thing from one shot to another, that the furniture and props are in exactly the same place, that the hair length and style of the actors are the same, and that there are no extraneous or out-of-place objects in the scene. Given the tremendous complexity of motion picture production, these continuity supervisors do an outstanding job. Nonetheless, an occasional mistake slips by:

- In *Die Hard 2*, Bruce Willis makes a call from a Washington, D.C., airport. The phone he is using bears the logo of the Pacific Telephone Company.

- In the classic *Gone With the Wind*, as Scarlett runs through the streets of 1860s' Atlanta, she passes an electric street light. Electric street lights were still a couple of decades away.

- In the classic car chase from the thriller *Bullitt*, the car that Steve McQueen is chasing loses *six* hubcaps.

- The horror classic *Halloween* is set in Illinois but all the cars have California license plates.

- In *Spartacus*, set in biblical times, some of the soldiers are wearing wristwatches and tennis shoes.

- In *Goodfellas*, actor Ray Liotta is with his mistress when he is visited by two of his Mafia cohorts. In the beginning of the scene Liotta is wearing a Star of David around his neck. A minute or so later he is seen wearing a cross.

Watch closely. You'll probably see more.

market, such as *Teenage Mutant Ninja Turtles* and its sequel. Another independent, Miramax, focused on quality films such as the Oscar-winning *My Left Foot* and *Mr. and Mrs. Bridge*.

The nature of film distribution, however, assures that the large companies will always control a large portion of the business. First, it's too expensive for an independent producer or a small distribution company to contact theaters and theater chains spread out all over the globe. The big studios already have this communication network set up and can afford to maintain it. Second, the large studios can offer theater owners a steady stream of films that consistently feature big-name stars. A small company could not withstand that competition for long.

Distribution companies also serve as a source of financing for independent producers. These companies lend money to the film's producer to cover all or most of the estimated cost of the film. In this way, the major studios acquire an interest in films that they did not directly produce. This arrangement will be discussed further in the section of this chapter that deals with film economics.

Exhibition

Perhaps the biggest surprise of recent years has been the tremendous expansion of the exhibition side of the industry. In an era when experts believed that movie channels on cable, VCRs, and movies on cassette would keep people away from the theater, the number of theatrical motion picture screens in this country hit an all-time high, about 23,690 in 1991, an increase of almost 17 percent since 1984. Most industry executives agree, however, that the buildup of screens is slowing down. Some are even fearful that America has become "overscreened," with too many screens competing in major markets, making it hard to make a profit.

Multiplex theaters, featuring four, six, or eight screens clustered around a central concession stand, are still the rule. Most new theaters seat about 200–400 patrons. The massive movie palaces of the 1920s and 1930s have not reemerged, but there are noticeable changes inside the motion picture theater as exhibitors go after a slightly older market. Soundproofing to prevent spill from adjoining theaters is now common, and concession stands are putting real butter on popcorn, with a few even offering mineral water and cappuccino to their customers.

One other trend: Drive-in movies are rapidly becoming extinct. There were only about 1000 left in 1990 as most operators found that they could make far more money by selling the real estate on which the drive-in was located than by keeping it in operation.

The exhibition segment is controlled by large chain owners. Very few independent operators are left in the large markets. Screens owned by the top seven chains account for about 80 percent of all box-office revenue. In addition, motion picture distributors are back into the exhibition segment as several studios have acquired theater chains (see Chapter 11). Consequently, as of 1991, the biggest theater chain was United Artists Theater Circuit with about 2500 screens, followed by American MultiCinema and Cineplex Odeon, 50 percent of which is owned by Universal. The studios, however, seem to have cooled a bit on the exhibition side of the business. There have been no major acquisitions of theaters since 1988 and there have been reports that several of the studios have been trying to sell their theater holdings.

Ownership

The biggest ownership development in the motion picture industry has been the entrance of foreign companies. In late 1989, the Sony Corporation of Japan paid $3.4 billion for Columbia Pictures Entertainment, acquiring a 2700-film library and 260 television properties along with the movie studio. Sony is a global conglomerate with

Although the total number of motion picture seats has increased slightly over the last fifty years, the total number of screens has increased dramatically thanks to the advent of the multiplex which features several smaller theaters under one roof. (Mark Zemnick)

interests in audio and video electronics. A year later, not to be outdone, Sony's main Japanese rival, the Matsushita Corporation, acquired U.S. entertainment conglomerate MCA, parent of Universal, for $6.6 billion. Finally, after a deal with an Australian company fell through at the last minute, MGM-UA was acquired by a European Company, Pathe, which controls about 1000 movie screens in five countries, has a movie production company, and owns an extensive library of newsreels and feature films. MGM/Pathe, as it was called, ran into financial difficulties and barely avoided bankruptcy in 1991. Pathe executives were discussing spinning off United Artists as a separate company, along with other plans to give the new company some stability. As of this writing, the long-term outlook for this company was unclear. Finally, 20th Century Fox is owned by the News Corporation of Australia.

Thus, of the eight major U.S. movie companies, four are now controlled by large foreign conglomerates. Conglomerate ownership is also apparent in the remaining four companies that are U.S. owned.

1. Warner Brothers: part of Time Warner, a multi-billion-dollar conglomerate with interests in book and magazine publishing, recorded music, motion picture theaters, and cable TV, to name a few.

2. Paramount: owned by Paramount Communications Inc., a large international company with interests in dozens of industries. In late 1993, both Viacom (a company with major holdings in broadcasting and cable) and QVC (the Home Shopping Network) were trying to acquire Paramount.

3. Disney: the Walt Disney Company has two movie enterprises, Touchstone, for mature films, and Buena Vista, for general films. It also owns hotels, amusement parks, a record label, golf courses, and real estate and makes a tremendous amount of money licensing the Disney characters for use by other companies.

4. Orion: the least diversified of these companies, Orion controls a TV production company, a home video operation, and motion picture production and distribution facilities. A string of box-office flops forced Orion to begin bankruptcy proceedings in 1991.

The economics of the motion picture business have made conglomerate ownership almost inevitable. The parent conglomerate, a large and diversified company, provides a reservoir of money and if the film organization has a bad year, losses can be covered by another division in the conglomerate that had a better year.

● ● ● ●
PRODUCING MOTION PICTURES

Departments

Film studios differ in the way they are structured but Figure 12-1 displays a conventional departmental chart. There are three main departments illustrated. The distribution department handles sales and contracts for domestic and worldwide distribution. The production division is in charge of all those elements that actually go into the making of a film. Also illustrated is the TV production division, which would handle

FIGURE 12-1 *Departmental chart for a typical motion picture company.*

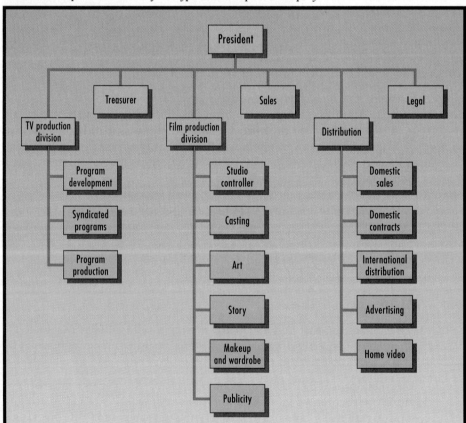

all the studio's work in the development and production of series and made-for-TV motion pictures.

Behind the Scenes

How does a film get to be a film? There are three distinct phases in moviemaking: (1) preproduction, (2) production, and (3) postproduction. Similar to television, all films begin with an idea. The idea can be sketchy, such as a two-paragraph outline of the plot, or detailed, such as a novel or a Broadway play. When an idea is submitted to a producer, it is referred to as a **property**. If the producer is interested in the property, the producer may draw up an **option contract**. As the name suggests, an option contract is an exclusive right to put into effect for a fixed period of time an agreement for rights or services. For example, the producer might want an option on the property for six months. During these months, the producer will try to interest talent and financial backers in the project. If no one is interested, at the end of six months the option is dropped and full ownership of the property reverts to the original author. On the other hand, if there is potential, the producer will exercise his or her option and purchase the rights to the property.

Many of today's motion picture deals are put together by agents. In fact, many industry experts suggest that big agencies such as William Morris and International Creative Management are the most powerful forces in the motion picture business. Agents put together packages—a star or stars, a director, a producer, and other creative talent—that are sold to studios. In return for their services, agents collect hefty packaging fees.

Once the rights have been secured, the preproduction process continues to the next step—writing the screenplay. In general, the route to a finished motion picture script consists of several steps:

Director Robert Townsend prepares to shoot a scene. Townsend, Spike Lee, Matty Rich, and John Singleton are four black directors whose films won critical praise and garnered box-office success during the early 1990s. (Photfest)

1. Step one is called a treatment. This is a narrative statement of the plot and descriptions of the main characters and locations; it might even contain sample dialogue.

2. Step two is a first-draft script. This version contains all the dialogue and camera setups and a description of action sequences.

3. The third step is a revised script incorporating changes suggested by the producer, director, stars, and others.

4. Finally, step four is a script polish. This includes adding or subtracting scenes, revising dialogue, and other minor changes.

The latest trend in Hollywood is somewhat encouraging for anybody who wants to be a screenwriter. In years past, screenwriters have traditionally been the lowest paid of all the creative people who put together a movie. A script by an established writer seldom sold for more than $300,000. Scripts by newcomers and less-established writers brought far less. In 1990, the prices for scripts skyrocketed, thanks to a record year at the box office which gave studios more money to spend and an increased number of films in production. Writer Shane Black (*Lethal Weapon*) got $1.75 million for *The Last Boy Scout*. The script for *Robin Hood* went for $1.2 million, and Joe Eszterhas (*Flashdance*) got a record $3 million for *Basic Instinct*. The recession and tighter budgets have driven prices down since then, but screenwriters are still better off than they were five years ago.

While all this is going on, the producer tries to find actors and actresses (talent) who will appear in the film. The contracts and deals that are worked out with the talent vary from the astronomical to the modest. One common arrangement is for the star to receive a flat fee or salary for his or her services. Sometimes this can be a substantial amount. Meryl Streep gets about $5 million per film. Warren Beatty got $9 million to direct and to star in *Dick Tracy*. Tom Cruise got $10 million for *Days of Thunder*. Arnold Schwarzenegger got about $15 million for *Terminator 2* (he took most of this in the form of a Gulfstream jet). Some stars prefer a smaller salary and

Mega-Budget

As of 1992, *Terminator 2* was the most expensive American movie ever made, at a cost of about $94 million. How can anyone spend $94 million on a movie? Here's a rough breakdown of where the money went.

- Star salaries—about $22 million. Schwarzenegger got about $15 million. James Cameron, the director, got $6 million. Linda Hamilton was a bargain at $1 million.

- Production costs and special effects—about $50 million

- Rights for the sequel—$10 million

- Interest and overhead—$10 million

- Other salaries—$2 million

Interestingly enough, the film was able to cover these costs even before it was released. *T2* had advances or guarantees of $61 million from overseas theatrical and TV rights, about $10 million in domestic video rights, $7 million in domestic TV rights, and a potential $20 million from merchandising rights.

Finally, at the risk of stretching the point of cost accounting, Schwarzenegger spoke a total of 700 words in the entire movie. With his $15 million paycheck, that works out to about $21,400 per word. Enough said.

a percentage of the film's profit. Jack Nicholson, for example, made a deal that gave him a share of the profits from *Batman* and a share in all the merchandising revenue. He has probably made about $50 million from this arrangement. At the other end of the scale, the Screen Actors Guild has a contract that spells out the minimum salary that must be paid to actors in minor roles and walk-on parts.

Meanwhile, the producer is also trying to secure financial backing for the picture. We will have much more to say about the monetary arrangements in film in the section on economics. For now, it is important to remember that the financial arrangements have to be worked out early in the preproduction process.

At the same time, the producer is also busy lining up skilled personnel to work behind the camera. Of these people, the film's director is most central. When all the elements have been put together, it will be the director's job to actually make the movie. He or she will determine what scenes get photographed from what angle and how they will be assembled in the final product. Working closely with the director is the cinematographer (the person responsible for the actual lighting and filming of the scenes) and the film editor (the person who will actually cut the film and assemble the scenes in the proper order). In addition to these individuals, a movie crew also contains dozens of other skilled people: set designers, makeup specialists, electricians, audio engineers, crane operators, painters, plumbers, carpenters, property masters, set dressers, caterers, first-aid people, and many others.

Shortly after the director has been signed for the project, he or she and the producer scout possible locations for shooting the film. Some sequences may be shot in the sound studio, while others may need the authenticity that only location shooting can provide. As soon as the locations have been chosen, the producer makes the necessary arrangements to secure these sites for filming. Sometimes this entails renting the studios of a major motion picture production company or obtaining permits to shoot in city streets or other places. The producer must also draw up plans to make sure that the filming equipment, talent, and technical crew are all at the same place at the same time.

Once all these items have been attended to, the film moves into the actual production phase. Cast and crew assemble on the chosen location, and each scene is shot and reshot until the director is satisfied with what has been filmed. The actors and crew then move to another location, and the process starts all over again. Overriding the entire production is the knowledge that all of this is costing a great deal of money. Shooting even a moderate-budget film can cost $300,000 to $350,000 *per day*. Therefore, the director tries to plan everything so that each dollar is used efficiently. To give you an example of how expensive and labor-intensive filmmaking can be, take the case of a five-minute sequence in the Michael Keaton-James Woods film, *The Hard Way*. The sequence which shows Woods and Keaton chasing a killer through a crowded movie theater took nine twelve-hour days to film and cost about $2 million to complete.

Most films make use of a production schedule that lists the order in which the scenes are shot, the location, the needed crew, the talent involved, special equipment, props, and transportation. This schedule sets up the most efficient sequence of filming. The first step is to group all scenes according to location. Next, all scenes at one location are divided into interior or exterior shots. To illustrate, suppose the script calls for scenes one and three to be shot inside a bank and scenes two and four to be shot outside in the bank's parking lot. It is more efficient to film scenes one and three first so that the same lighting setup can be used before moving outside. Because of this scheduling, film scenes are generally shot in a sequence different from the order in which they appear in the story. For example, let's suppose a film script calls for a helicopter shot of Yankee Stadium to open the film and a similar shot at the close. Rather than filming those scenes on the first and last day of shooting, it makes more sense to film them on the same day. Thus the helicopter would be rented for only one day, permission to use the stadium would be needed only once, and so on. After the scenes are shot, they can be spliced into their proper place.

The average shooting schedule for the typical film is about fifty days. Each day's shooting (and some days can be twelve to sixteen hours long) results in an average of two minutes of usable film. Exhibitors prefer feature films that are about 100 minutes in length. This means the movie can be shown every two hours with a 20-minute break in between for people to visit the concession stand.

At the end of each day's shooting, the film is sent to the laboratory where it is developed overnight. Also, the film of the previous day's shooting is projected for the director and cast. This is called viewing the "dailies" and lets the director see how the film is coming along. Recently, many directors have been using TV cameras to videotape the scenes as they are being filmed. Since tape can be played back immediately, there is no delay in seeing the dailies.

The postproduction phase begins after the filming has been completed. A film editor arranges the various scenes into a coherent and aesthetically pleasing order. Working with the director, the editor decides where close-ups should be placed, the angle from which the scene is shown, and how long each scene should last. The elaborate optical special effects that some films require are also added during postproduction. Once the scenes have been edited into an acceptable form, postproduction sound can be added. This might include narration, music, sound effects, and original dialogue that, for one reason or another, has to be redone. (About 10 to 15 percent of outside dialogue has to be rerecorded because of interfering noises.) Finally, the edited film, complete with final sound track and special effects, is sent to the laboratory where a release print of the film is made. In the case of some films, the final version is shown to special preview audiences. These audiences fill out special preview cards that indicate their reactions to the film. If the reaction is overwhelmingly negative, the film may be returned to the editing room for more work. If the reaction is favorable, the film is made ready for distribution.

One of the tasks that must be accomplished during postproduction is synchronizing the sound track with the film. (David H. Wells/The Image Works)

Since 1970, the box-office receipts of the movie industry have shown more or less steady growth. In 1992, the movie industry posted $4.87 billion in revenue, down from the record $5.03 billion of 1989. (To keep this figure in perspective, note that the total revenue from the rental and sale of videocassettes during the same period was almost $15 billion.) Theater admissions dropped by about 10 percent, but higher admission prices offset the audience decline.

Movies are an expensive medium. In 1992, the average movie cost $29 million to produce—up 61 percent since 1988—and another $8 to $10 million to advertise and market. Some films cost much more (see box on this page). Financial success for most films is a function of U.S. and foreign box-office revenue, cassette sales, cable fees, and broadcast TV rights. Once the only source of income for the movie business, the domestic box office now accounts for less than one-fourth of a film's total revenue. The consistent growth in nontheatrical and foreign revenues has meant that the percentage of studio films that break even or make a profit has risen from about 20 percent in 1980 to more than 60 percent in 1990. If a film can recoup its production costs from the money it earns while playing in U.S. theaters, it is well on its way to making a profit. Increased marketing costs and a general leveling off in the growth of videocassette sales and foreign box office, however, indicate that the road to profits might not be so smooth in the future. Table 12-2 contains a cost-revenue analysis of a typical big-budget film.

The Ten Most Expensive Films

Although the average movie cost about $23 million to produce in the early 1990s, many films cost much more. In fact, some cost much, much more. The table lists the ten most expensive films of all time. Please note that the figures are approximate and that the table contains only films from Western nations. The most expensive film of all time is probably *War and Peace* produced by the government of the Soviet Union. The Soviets apparently failed to keep a budget for the film, but some industry experts report it must have cost at least $100 million.

Film	Year	Cost (millions)
1. *Terminator 2*	1991	$94
2. *Batman Returns*	1992	80
3. *Die Hard 2*	1990	70
4. *Godfather Part III*	1990	66
5. *Total Recall*	1990	65
6. *Rambo III*	1988	60
7. *Days of Thunder*	1990	55
8. *Tango and Cash*	1989	54
9. *Superman II*	1980	53
10. *Who Framed Roger Rabbit?*	1988	52

TABLE 12-2 Cost and Revenue Estimates for Disney's *The Rocketeer* (all dollars are in millions)

COSTS	
Production	$40.00
Interest and Overhead	10.00
Worldwide Distribution	23.00
Video Marketing	3.50
TOTAL COSTS	$76.50

REVENUES	
Domestic Box-Office Rentals	$22.00
Foreign Box-Office Rentals	14.00
Pay and Network TV	10.00
Foreign TV	3.00
Domestic and Foreign Video	24.50
Broadcast TV and Other Sources	3.00
TOTAL REVENUE	$76.50
TOTAL PROFIT	$ 0.00

Source: Variety, September 23, 1991, p. 95—used with permission. Data are current up to September 1991. *The Rocketeer* may yet show a profit as more video dollars trickle in.

Financing Films

Where do producers get the enormous sums of money necessary to make a film? Let's take a look at some common financing methods. If a producer has a good track record and the film looks promising, the distributor might loan the producer the entire amount needed to make the film. In return, the distributor gains distribution rights to the film. Moreover, if the distributor also has studio facilities, the producer might agree to rent those facilities from the distributor.

A second method is to arrange for a **pickup**. Under this arrangement, a distributor guarantees a producer that the distributor will pick up a finished picture at a later date for an agreed-upon price. For example, a distributor might agree to pay a producer $10 million eighteen months in the future provided that the producer delivers a finished picture by that date. Although this money helps, it does not do the producer any immediate good since the money won't appear for a year and a half. Armed with this agreement, however, the producer can arrange for a bank loan to secure the money needed immediately. If the bank is satisfied with the financial status of the distributor and feels that the producer can bring in the picture for $10 million or less, the bank grants the loan. But what happens if the bank feels that the producer won't be able to finish the film in eighteen months or that the movie will go over budget? In this case, a third party, called a completion guarantor, is brought in to make sure that the loan will be repaid.

A third method is to finance the picture through outside investors, most frequently through a **limited partnership**. Under this arrangement, a number of investors put up a specific amount to pay for the film. Their personal liability is limited to the amount they invest; that is, they can't lose any more than what they put up, even if the picture goes over budget. The limited partners have no artistic control over the picture. They simply invest their money and hope to make a profit. Limited partnerships have recently declined in popularity primarily because studios have found that they can get cheaper forms of financing overseas. In fact, Japanese banks have become a primary source of film financing for many American companies.

A fourth method is a **joint venture**. Under this arrangement, several companies involved in film production and distribution pool their resources and agree to finance one or more films. (There are also some uncommon methods of financing. Robert Townsend, producer of *Hollywood Shuffle*, charged the $40,000 he needed to finish the film on his personal credit cards.)

No matter how films are financed, movie studios are becoming more cost conscious. Many are distributing more movies made by independents, who can make films at lower cost; others are moving their productions to Canada or to states other than California to cut labor costs. Disney, for example, built an elaborate studio in Florida.

The producer and distributor also agree on how to divide the distributor's gross receipts from the film (the money the distributor gets from the theater owners, TV networks, pay-TV operations, and videocassette and videodisc operations that show the film). Since the distributor takes the greatest risk in the venture, the distributor is the first to be paid from the receipts of the film. Distribution companies charge a distribution fee for their efforts. In addition, there are distribution expenses (cost of making multiple prints of the film, advertising, necessary taxes, insurance), which must also be paid. Lastly, the actual production cost of the film must be repaid. If the distributor or a bank loaned the producer $10 million to make the film, that loan has to be paid off (plus interest). Because of all these expenses, it is estimated that a film must earn two and a half to three times its production cost before it starts to show a profit for the producers. Hollywood accounting tends to be complicated, however, and sometimes it's hard to determine when a film is profitable (see box on page 294).

Dealing with the Exhibitor

The distributor is also involved in other financial dealings—this time with the exhibitors. An exhibition license sets the terms under which the showing of the film will occur. The license specifies the run of the film (the number of weeks the theater must agree to play the picture), holdover rights, the date the picture will be available for showing, and the clearance (the amount of time that must elapse before the film can be shown at a competing theater).

The license also contains the financial terms for the film's showing. There are several common arrangements. The simplest involves a specified percentage split of the money that is taken in at the box office. The exhibitor agrees to split the money with the distributor according to an agreed-upon formula, perhaps fifty–fifty the first week, sixty–forty the second, seventy–thirty the third, and so on, with the exhibitor keeping more money the longer the run of the film. Another alternative is the **sliding scale**. Under this setup, as the box-office revenue increases, so does the amount of money that the exhibitor must pay the distributor. For example, if a week's revenue was more than $30,000, the exhibitor would pay the distributor 60 percent; if the revenue was $25,000–$29,999, the distributor would receive 50 percent, and so on. Another common approach is the ninety–ten deal. Under this method, the movie theater owner first deducts the house allowance (called the "nut") from the box-office take. The house allowance includes all the operating expenses of the theater (heating, cooling, water, lights, salaries, maintenance, etc.), plus a sum that is pure profit for the theater (this sum is called "air"). From the revenues (if any) that remain, the distributor gets 90 percent and the house 10 percent.

A less commonly used practice is called **four-walling**. In this system, the distributor actually rents the theater for a specified fee for a predetermined length of time and keeps all of the box-office receipts. Four-walling has been used most often by small distribution companies that handle low-budget films such as *The Wilderness Family*. Four-walling has some appeal for exhibitors since they are guaranteed a profit no

Sometimes the most imaginative writing in Hollywood is not done by screenwriters but by accountants. In 1990 a judge ruled that the script for the Eddie Murphy hit picture *Coming to America* was based in part on an idea submitted to Paramount by humorist Art Buchwald. As compensation Buchwald was awarded $250,000 plus 19 percent of the film's profits. Buchwald had run up about a million dollars in legal fees so the $250,000 didn't completely solve his problems. But since the film had grossed $350 million worldwide and was the third most successful film of 1988, it looked like Buchwald would receive a hefty chunk of change. Then Paramount's accountants entered the scene. They pointed out some additional expenses that had to be deducted from the film's income. In the first place, not all of that $350 million went to Paramount. After the exhibitors and various other intermediaries took their cut, Paramount reported it took in only $125 million. (Not included in that $125 million was about $35 million for fees paid to Paramount's own home video subsidiary—money that, in effect, Paramount was paying itself.) From the remaining $125 million, the studio subtracted the $48 million it cost to make the film. Next, the studio deducted a $42 million distribution fee (which again Paramount paid to itself), $36 million in distribution expenses, $11 million in participation payments (these were bonuses paid to Murphy and John Landis, the film's director, based on a percentage of the gross income), and $6 million in interest (included in this figure was interest on production facilities which Paramount paid to itself). Add all these things up and the total is $143 million. So actually the film was $18 million in the hole and Buchwald was entitled to nothing.

Buchwald's attorneys were not impressed with Paramount's accounting and pursued the matter in court. They argued that Paramount had made more than $50 million from the picture and was still claiming it was in the red. A judge ultimately sided with Buchwald and ruled that Paramount's accounting procedure was designed to avoid making payments to those who had contractual rights to a percentage of the profits. In 1992, the judge ruled that Buchwald was entitled to $150,000 as his share of the profits.

There is a lesson to be learned from all of this: When discussing a film's profit, it is important to specify to whom the profit applies.

matter how poorly the picture draws. If the picture draws well, the exhibitor will make money from the sale of popcorn, candy, and soft drinks at the concession stand.

Speaking of concession sales, it should not be overlooked that this is a source of significant income for movie-theater owners. According to industry figures, the average moviegoer spends about a buck and a quarter on popcorn, soda, candy, and other concession munchies. Since an average of slightly more than a billion tickets has been sold for the last decade or so, this translates to about $1.25 billion taken in at the concession stand. At some theaters, 90 percent of the profits come from concessions. (And no wonder. That $2.50 soft drink costs the theater owner less than 50 cents.) Consequently, it should come as no surprise that theater owners were worried when 1990 concession sales were down by $80 million from the year before.

Higher ticket prices coupled with large markups at the concession stand mean that a trip to the movies can be an expensive proposition. For example, consider the costs for two at a theater in New York City: admission for two, $15.00; two small boxes of popcorn, $4.50; one package of Twizzlers and one box of Milk Duds, total $3.50; two large Cokes, $4.50. Total tab: $27.50.

• • • •
CABLE AND HOME VIDEO: THE HOLLYWOOD CONNECTION

Hollywood has seen a drastic shift in the revenue mix for motion pictures in the last few years. Theatrical revenue now takes a back seat to cable and home video. In 1991, an estimated 40 percent of film revenue came from cassettes, 15 percent from pay cable services, and 5 percent from network and syndicated TV, making a total of 60 percent from video. Theater box office and other nonvideo sources now account for only 40 percent of revenue.

The cassette rental business boomed during the late 1980s but has recently showed signs of leveling off. Cassette rentals and sales brought in about $16 billion in 1992 with about $11 billion coming from rentals and the remainder from sales. More than 4 billion rental transactions took place in 1992. About 6 million Americans rent a video on an average day, about twice as many as go to a movie.

Studios have an interesting pricing strategy when it comes to videocassettes. Some films that did not do well at the box office are priced higher than films that were box-office winners. Thus, a film like *The Babe*, which did little business in theaters, was priced at $92.95, while the smash hit *Home Alone II* was priced at $19.95. At first glance this seems to run counter to the laws of supply and demand (films that had a high demand like *Home Alone II* should cost more than films nobody wants to see) but consider the situation from the point of view of the studio. The studios figure that the relatively small group of people who might want to see *The Babe* would probably prefer to rent it rather than own it. Conversely, *Home Alone II* was so popular that a lot of people would want to see it over and over again, so they would prefer to own rather than rent. Consequently, films that had an average or below average theatrical run are priced higher with the expectation that mostly video rental stores will buy them. Hit movies make up what studios call the "sell-through" market and are usually priced under $30 to make them affordable to the average consumer. Classifying tapes as sell-through or rental is a tough marketing decision for most companies. Those that choose wisely can reap a large financial reward. *Batman*, for example, took in about $250 million in cassette sales. To further capitalize on the home video market, some companies are putting commercials on their cassettes. *Home Alone II* was preceded by spots for American Airlines and Pepsi.

The home video market is driven by big hits, just like the theatrical box office. Movies that were popular on the big screen are almost always popular on the smaller screen. Some movies that were box-office duds do quite well on videocassette. *Medicine Man* and *Final Analysis*, for example, were more popular as rentals than as theatrical releases. Home video has been a plus to films with smaller budgets as well. First, home video has opened up a whole new market for small-budget (about $3 million–$4 million) films. Some of these films cover their production costs with up-front money from cable and videocassette rights even before release to local theaters. It appears that many people are unwilling to spend $25 to take a family of four to a marginal movie but are willing to spend $2 to rent a cassette. As one video rental customer put it, "If it's lousy, I just do a fast forward and say goodbye."

In the long run, movie studios are betting on pay-per-view (PPV). In this system the studios feed movies to cable systems at certain hours when subscribers can view them for a fee of usually $3–$4—sort of like an electronic rental system with no late fees or charges for rewinding. Nearly 18 million U.S. homes are equipped with PPV and the number is increasing rapidly. New technology will allow cable operators to greatly expand the number of channels available and many of these will be dedicated to PPV. Experts suggest that the industry could generate $1 billion in gross income in the next five years. The biggest moneymaking events on PPV for the last few years have been championship fights (the 1991 Holyfield-Foreman fight brought in $55 million). Consumer interest in movies, however, is still lukewarm. PPV movies gener-

International Perspective: Movies Overseas

American films are popular the world over. Consider this list of box-office leaders in various countries as of late 1991:

Amsterdam, Netherlands

1 *Terminator 2*

2 *Delicatessen* (local production)

3 *Robin Hood*

Tokyo, Japan

1 *Terminator 2*

2 *Doc Hollywood*

3 *Hudson Hawk*

Sydney, Australia

1 *Terminator 2*

2 *Doc Hollywood*

3 *City Slickers*

Rome, Italy

1 *The Doors*

2 *The Naked Gun 2 1/2*

3 *Thelma and Louise*

Paris, France

1 *The Fisher King*

2 *Backdraft*

3 *Robin Hood*

Stockholm, Sweden

1 *Backdraft*

2 *Terminator 2*

3 *The Fisher King*

ated only $103 million for all of 1990. Some reasons for this underperformance include inadequate marketing of the PPV channels and a release pattern which puts the movie on the shelves of the video-rental store before it appears on PPV.

ISSUES

Movie violence was the issue on most people's minds in the early part of the decade. Never before in recent memory had so much graphic violence made its way to the big screen. Even more troubling to some was the fact that the violence was shown in such a lighthearted fashion. In *Lethal Weapon II*, one of the heroes kills two villains by shooting them in the head with a nail gun. When asked how it went, he replies, "I nailed 'em both." Audiences predictably giggled at the line. In *Goodfellas*, a mobster kills a young man over a tiny affront and tells his shocked friends not to make a big deal of it. In *Another 48 Hours*, Eddie Murphy shoots a rabble-rouser in the knee and then asks if anybody else wants a limp. Audiences laughed at this scene. In the little-seen *Hudson Hawk*, a criminal is decapitated and Bruce Willis quips that the villain won't be attending an upcoming hat convention. And, of course, there's Arnold Schwarzenegger's memorable "Hasta la vista, baby" as he blows the bad guys away.

Also to be considered is the fact that violent films keep trying to top themselves with more and more violence. The original *Robocop* portrayed 32 killings; the 1990 sequel had 81. *Die Hard* had a body count of 18; *Die Hard 2* killed off 264.

As discussed in Chapter 22, much of the research about the harmful effects of mass communication concerns the potential harmful effects of exposure to media

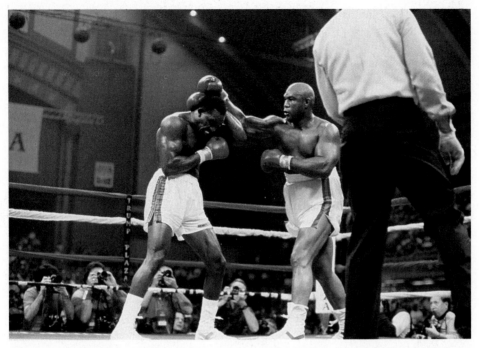

Pay-per-view operators are banking on movies and special events, like the Evander Holyfield-George Foreman championship fight, to make their industry profitable. People were charged an average price of about $35 per household to view this fight. (Tony Triolo)

violence. The research suggests that there is a small, but persistent, link between watching media mayhem and violent behavior in real life. Most of the criticism about violence, however, has been directed at TV because of the medium's pervasiveness. Film violence, although more lifelike, has not come in for as much criticism. Today, however, with movie special effects reaching new heights of realism, violent films are more and more a cause for concern. One apprehension is that all of this violence and high-tech killing, particularly when it is presented in a comic or amusing way, might numb us to the pain and suffering that accompany real-life violence. Some psychologists point out that growing insensitivity is a common human response to repeated exposure to violence.

Moviemakers argue that movies simply reflect the world. If the world has turned insensitive, then movies will mirror that fact. Martin Scorcese, director of *Goodfellas*, suggests that movies serve as a cathartic release, sort of like the Roman circus. Screenwriter John McNaughton contends that violence is part of an accepted dramatic formula that dictates that the bad guys must get blown away in the end—the more villainous they are, the more brutal their deaths. But perhaps the most common argument holds that all of this media brutality has little impact. Only the rare, already disturbed audience member will be negatively affected by screen violence. The ordinary film viewer will come away unfazed.

Critics are not satisfied by these arguments. They maintain that although adults might understand the dramatic conventions and fictitious nature of screen violence, children might not, and the increasing availability of violent films on cable TV and on videocassette has made them more accessible to impressionable youngsters. One survey of 5-year-olds found that about 20 percent had seen the R-rated *Friday the 13th* on cable. Finally, concerning the contention of little impact, critics note that this argument relegates the arts to a role of total passivity and rules out any potential for influence, a circumstance that runs counter to the experience of most audience members.

This argument is not likely to be resolved any time soon. Violence on the screen attracts an audience and that means big bucks. The ultraviolent *Terminator 2* earned $170 million in its first seven weeks. What kind of violence will *Terminator 3* contain?

• • • •
CAREERS IN FILM

Finding a job in the film industry is difficult but not impossible. Film is a young person's medium; many of Hollywood's top directors are not too many years removed from their college-student days. As a result, motion picture companies are always looking for bright, young talent. Unfortunately, the industry is not large enough to accommodate all of the newcomers who are seeking jobs, and competition is formidable.

A young person who has actual experience in films and filmmaking will probably enjoy more success in finding a job. How do you get this experience? In general, there are two ways: (1) taking college courses that deal with film and (2) making your own films. About 750 colleges and universities now offer courses in film, 227 offer bachelor's degrees, and many offer graduate degrees. The advantages of a university major in film are substantial. In the first place, the university or college provides the

Little-Known Hollywood Jobs—Part II

In Hollywood, the word "coverage" doesn't mean what you read in a newspaper or how a football team defends against the pass. Coverage is a technical term that describes a short summary and evaluation of a movie script.

The system of coverage was invented because a typical movie script is about 120 pages long and the Writer's Guild of America registered about 25,000 scripts and treatments in 1990. If movie executives took time to read every script that was submitted to them, they would have time to do nothing else. Enter the script reader who provides coverage.

Coverage has taken a standard five-part form in Hollywood. The first part pigeonholes the script by genre—coming-of-age film, courtroom drama—while the second part is the "log line," a one- or two-sentence summary of the story that resembles what you might see in a TV log listing, like *TV Guide*. "An army officer mistakenly becomes a Civil War hero and as a reward is assigned an isolated command in the Great Plains. There he makes friends with Indians and wolves, and leads an idyllic existence until ruined by the appearance of whites." This section

may be the most important since it's the easiest to read. Section three allows the reader to give an evaluation of the script. This is followed by a one- or two-page summary and a final section for the reader to mark with boxes labeled "Recommend," "Consider," and "Pass."

Bad coverage can sink an otherwise good script. *Field of Dreams*, for example, almost never got made because the story was too complicated and unusual to summarize easily. *Risky Business* was produced in spite of coverage that called it "sophomoric and repellent."

The script readers who provide coverage are generally recent college grads who are looking to become screenwriters or movie executives and take the reader job temporarily to make ends meet. Freelance readers make $50 per script while those belonging to the Story Analysts Union in Hollywood make $700 per week.

The crowning irony in all of this is that veteran movie executives who make $20,000 a week often depend upon the advice of an entry-level employee making $700 a week about what movies should get made.

student with an opportunity to practice with technical equipment: lights, meters, editing machines, cameras, and so forth. Most students cannot afford to buy this equipment or rent it for long periods of time, and film production companies usually cannot afford to set aside equipment for on-the-job training. Second, students can take courses in film aesthetics and film history and learn by observing how others have made films. Third, students can take courses in other areas that relate to film, such as art, literature, history, music, and photography. Knowledge of these areas can be valuable for filmmakers. Finally, during the course of his or her studies, the student may have the opportunity to make a film as a final classroom project. This finished film can be shown to potential employers as a sample of the student's capability.

The other approach to gaining experience is to become an independent filmmaker. This method is valuable because it allows a person to gain knowledge of every aspect of filmmaking. By necessity, the independent filmmaker must learn about financing, writing, producing, editing, directing, accounting, and marketing. A potential employer knows that a person who successfully produces an independent film is dedicated to the film profession and is competent in the mechanics of filmmaking. Of course, this approach requires that the individual have some money to invest in basic film equipment and the time necessary to devote to the film. A person looking to go this route should be prepared for some financial hardships while the film is being made.

Entry-Level Positions

Once a person has some experience, the next step is to find an entry-level job. This requires securing a job interview—not an easy task. The common technique of mailing a résumé to a potential employer seldom works in the film industry. Because of the competition, most unsolicited résumés rarely generate a positive response, and no small number are immediately discarded.

There are three ways to overcome this hurdle. The first is to know somebody. As is the case in most industries, if you have a friend or a friend of a friend in the industry, getting a job interview is less difficult. Unfortunately, most people don't fall into this category.

The second way is to get yourself noticed. A newcomer accomplishes this by seeking out internships or training programs with production companies. The American Film Institute's *Guide to College Courses in Film and Television* lists such opportunities. Many times help in finding out about and applying for internships can be secured from teachers or placement offices. Once you've gotten yourself into an organization, you will have better success in arranging an interview. Another way to get yourself noticed is to enter the many student film festivals. These events are excellent ways for students to gain public exposure and professional recognition for their work. A newcomer who wins one or more awards at these festivals may find getting through the door into the film industry a little easier.

The third way is to be persistent. This is also the hardest way. Make a list of those companies where you wish to work and call on them personally. Since most film production companies are located in southern California and New York, this means that the job seeker might have to relocate. (Most experts agree that you would probably have to make this move eventually if you are serious about a career with the major feature film companies. Hiring takes place in these two areas, and it is necessary to be there to be hired.) Once you've got your list together, start calling on the companies. Bring along a one-page summary of your education and special skills. If you have a completed film that is available for viewing, indicate it in your summary. Don't be discouraged if your first visit is fruitless. Keep checking back. Even companies with immediate openings may suggest others that are hiring. As is the case with television, a newcomer should be prepared to take practically any job as a starter. Once inside the company, the path to more creative and challenging positions is easier to follow.

A new employee should try to select his or her first job with an eye toward future advancement. Some routes are better chosen if the person's ultimate goal is producing and directing. Other avenues suggest themselves if top management is the ultimate goal. One early choice an aspiring filmmaker must deal with is the choice between editing and directing. Although there are some exceptions, most people who start in the editing room tend to stay there, advancing ultimately to the post of supervising film editor. Those interested in producing and directing are better advised to begin as production assistants and progress to assistant directors, director, and perhaps producer. To reach high-level management, a person might consider breaking in with the distribution or sales division.

Two last points should be considered. First, what most students think of when they say they are interested in the film industry is a career in Hollywood feature films. This is understandable because this is the most visible part of the industry. It should be kept in mind, however, that there are opportunities in the educational and industrial film areas as well. Many organizations produce their own training or promotional films. There are also several companies that specialize in producing educational films for high schools and colleges. These organizations are potential places of employment. Second, when many students consider film careers, they tend to think only about careers as producers, writers, or directors. Although these jobs are perhaps the most glamorous, it should be remembered that the film industry also needs publicists, advertising experts, promotion directors, business managers, accountants, salespeople, and market researchers. In short, there are opportunities for more than production people.

● ● ● ●

SUGGESTIONS FOR FURTHER READING

The following books contain additional information about film.

AMERICAN FILM INSTITUTE, *Guide to College Courses in Film and Television*, Princeton, N.J.: Peterson's Guides, 1990.

BLUEM, A. WILLIAM, AND JASON SQUIRE, eds., *The Movie Business: American Film Industry Practice*, New York: Hastings House, 1972.

BOBKER, LEE, *Making Movies: From Script to Screen*, New York: Harcourt Brace Jovanovich, 1973.

FINLER, JOEL, *The Hollywood Story*, New York: Crown, 1988.

GOLDMAN, WILLIAM, *Adventures in the Screen Trade*, New York: Warner Books, 1983.

GOODELL, GREGORY, *Independent Feature Film Production*, New York: St. Martin's Press, 1982.

JOWETT, GARTH, AND JAMES LINTON, *Movies as Mass Communication*, Newberry Park, Calif.: Sage Publications, 1989.

KERR, PAUL, *The Hollywood Film Industry*, London: Routledge and Kegan, 1986.

LITWAK, MARK, *Reel Power*, New York: Morrow, 1986.

MONACO, JAMES, *American Film Now*, New York: Zoetrope, 1984.

13

STRUCTURE OF THE TELEVISION INDUSTRY

Television is now in its second half-century of existence and one thing is certain: the next fifty years will be totally different from the first fifty.

In the first place, the word itself has changed in meaning. It wasn't so long ago that "television" meant the few program choices that were available on a rather bulky piece of furniture that sat in the corner of the living room. These days, the television set has become smaller, more mobile, and is likely to be in several rooms of the house. Furthermore, the television set might not even be hooked up to what used to be called "television." Instead, the wires from the back of the set might lead to a computer keyboard, video game, VCR, or video camera.

The change in television programming has been equally dramatic. Instead of having to choose among shows offered by the three networks and maybe one or two independent or public broadcasting stations, today's TV viewer is faced with a plethora of choices: four networks and several independent stations, public stations, cable systems that provide sixty or more channels of TV, pay services that provide recently released theatrical movies and other special events, prerecorded cassettes whose content ranges from exercise instruction to sports highlights to Hollywood movies, home-made video tapes, video games, and special interactive programs that allow the viewer to become part of the action.

Even the act of watching television has been fundamentally changed. In the past, viewers generally watched shows from start to finish, overcoming inertia to get up and change channels only when intolerably bored or offended. Today, almost everybody has a remote control that allows them to "graze"—rapidly change channels until some small segment of a program catches their interest for a while before the boredom level rises to the point where they go on another quest for something better. Some TV sets and VCRs even have a feature that lets people watch two or more shows at the same time via a split screen.

Not surprisingly, this new world of television has changed the structure of the television industry. For about thirty years, the three major television networks, ABC, NBC, and CBS, dominated the industry, supplying programs to their affiliated stations that consistently attracted about 90 percent of the viewing audience, and raking in profits in the hundreds of millions of dollars. Now, with the increased number of choices available, some experts are speculating whether all the networks will be able to survive to the turn of the century in their present form.

This chapter will examine the rapidly metamorphosing world of TV. We will first examine the structure of the traditional TV industry and then discuss some of the newer TV services: cable, home video, and satellite broadcasting.

• • • •
ORGANIZATION OF THE TRADITIONAL TELEVISION INDUSTRY

Before we begin, it is necessary to define some of the key concepts and discuss the arrangements between major elements of the industry. The **commercial television system** consists of all those local stations whose income is derived from selling time on their facilities to advertisers. The **noncommercial system** consists of those stations whose income is derived from sources other than the sale of advertising time.

A local TV station is licensed by the Federal Communications Commission to provide TV service to a particular community. In the industry, these communities are customarily referred to as markets. There are 211 markets in the United States, ranging from the number-one market, New York City, with about 6.6 million homes, to number 211, Miles City, Montana, with about 6000 homes. Some of these local TV stations enter into contractual agreements with TV networks. As in the radio industry, a television network is a group of local stations linked electronically so that programs supplied by a single source can be broadcast simultaneously. Four commercial networks in the United States supply programs to local stations: the American Broadcasting Company (ABC), the Columbia Broadcasting System (CBS), the National Broadcasting Company (NBC), and the Fox Broadcasting Company (FBC). The Public Broadcasting Service (PBS) serves as a network for noncommercial stations. The electronic part of the program distribution is done through microwave and satellite facilities. A local station that signs a contract with one of the networks is an affiliate. Each of the three major commercial networks has about 200 affiliates scattered across the country; Fox has slightly fewer. Local stations that do not have network affiliation are independents. With this background in contractual arrangements, let us now turn to an examination of how the industry is organized.

Much like the film industry, the TV industry is divided into three segments: (1) production, (2) distribution, and (3) exhibition. The production element is responsible for providing the programming that is ultimately viewed by the TV audience. The distribution function is handled by the TV networks and syndication companies. The exhibition of television programs—the element in the system that most people are most familiar with—is the responsibility of local TV stations. It should be kept in mind that there is some overlap in the performance of these various functions. Networks produce and distribute programs; local stations also produce programs as well as exhibit them. Let's take a more detailed look at each of these three divisions.

Production

Pretend for a moment that you are the manager of a local TV station in your hometown. Your station signs on at 6 A.M. and signs off at 2 A.M. That means your station must provide twenty hours of programming every day, or approximately 7000 hours of programming each year. Where do you get all this programming? There are basically three sources:

1. local production

2. syndicated programming

3. for some stations, network programs

Local production consists of those programs that are produced in the local station's own studio or on location with the use of the station's equipment. The most common local productions are the station's daily newscasts, typically broadcast at noon, in the early evening, and late in the evening. Stations have found that these newscasts attract large audiences, which in turn attract advertisers. As a result, the local news accounts for a major proportion of the ad revenue that is generated by a local station. Not surprisingly, local stations devote a major share of their production budgets to their news shows. Many stations are equipped with portable TV cameras, mobile units, satellite news-gathering vans, and even helicopters. Other locally produced programming might consist of local sports events, early morning interview programs, and public affairs discussion shows. It would be difficult, however, for a local station to fill its entire schedule with locally produced programming. As a result, most stations turn to programming produced by other sources.

If the station is affiliated with a network, much of its programming problem is solved. Networks typically supply about 65–70 percent of the programming carried by their affiliates. Not all of this programming is actually produced by the networks. In fact, only network news, documentaries, sports events, talk shows (such as *Today* and *Good Morning America*), some soap operas, and an occasional prime-time series are network productions. The other programs carried by the networks are actually produced by independent production companies or the television divisions of film production companies. Even though the network does not produce the program, it still has a stake in its performance since the network and the production company combine to finance it. If the program is a hit, both the network and the production company will make a profit. In the case of a motion picture, the network buys the rights to show the film one or more times on TV. Table 13-1 lists some programs produced by independent production companies and TV divisions of major film studios.

Many independent production companies sell their shows to syndication firms. Tribune Entertainment syndicates *Geraldo* and *Now It Can Be Told*. King World Productions handles *Wheel of Fortune*, *Jeopardy*, and *Oprah*. Programs that have already played on the network schedules (*Cheers*, *Full House*, *Who's the Boss?*) are also distributed by syndication companies. In addition, packages of movies, made up from some of the 23,000 films that have been released for television, can be leased from syndication companies. Obviously, an independent station would rely more heavily on syndicated material than would a network affiliate.

Distribution

As we have mentioned, the two main elements in the distribution segment of television are the networks and the syndication companies. The network distributes programs to its affiliates by transmitting them by satellite. The station then transmits them to its viewers as they are received, or it videotapes them and presents them at a later time period or different day. The affiliation contract between a local station and the network is a complicated document. In simplified terms, the station agrees to carry the network's programs, and in return the network agrees to pay the station a certain amount of

TABLE 13-1 Examples of Production Companies and their Programs for the 1991–92 Season	
PRODUCTION COMPANY	**PROGRAMS**
Independents	
Witt-Thomas	*Blossom, Empty Nest, Nurses*
Carsey-Werner	*Roseanne, Grace Under Fire*
Spelling Productions	*Beverly Hills 90210, Melrose Place*
TV Divisions of Film Companies	
Disney	*Home Improvement, Boy Meets World*
Paramount	*Frasier, Mommies*
Universal	*Coach, Murder, She Wrote*
20th Century Fox	*Picket Fences, LA Law*

Behind the scenes of The Oprah Winfrey Show. *(Kevin Horan/Picture Cube)*

money for clearing its time so that the network programs can be seen. (Although it may seem contradictory that the network actually pays the station to carry the network's programming, remember that the network is using the local station's facilities to show the network's commercials.) The amount of money paid by the network varies by market size. For example, in the late 1980s, in Anchorage, Alaska, the local NBC affiliate received about $300 per hour. NBC compensated its local station in Dallas about $2,500 per hour, while it paid its New York affiliate $10,000 an hour. The

Anchors Steve Fiorina and Lisa Kim prepare for the morning news on KGTV, San Diego. News is the most common form of productions at local stations and also produces the most revenue. (Thom Vollenveider/KGTV, A McGraw-Hill Company)

network then sells time in its programs to advertisers seeking a national audience. Decreasing network revenues have lowered the compensation rates that are now paid to affiliates. The Fox Network has even instituted a plan in which compensation is tied to the performance of its shows. The better the net shows do in the ratings, the more compensation given to affiliates.

Syndication companies provide another kind of program distribution. These organizations lease taped or filmed programs to local television stations. Sometimes, as mentioned above, the syndication company also produces the program, but more often it distributes programs produced by other firms. Local stations that purchase a syndicated program receive exclusive rights to show that program in their market (a situation complicated by cable TV systems that bring in distant stations; see below). Usually a station buys a package of programs—perhaps as many as 120 episodes or more—and the contract specifies how many times each program can be repeated.

Contractual arrangements take different forms. In a **straight cash** deal, the stations pay a fee for the right to show the program a specified number of times and retain the rights to sell all of the commercial spots available in the program. In a **cash plus barter** deal, the station pays a reduced fee for the program but gives up some commercial spots to the syndication company, which, in turn, sells the spots to national advertisers. In a straight **barter arrangement**, no money changes hands but the syndicator keeps more commercial minutes to sell nationally, leaving fewer spots for the local station to sell. For example, in 1991, Viacom was offering sixty-nine episodes of *A Different World* to local stations for a straight cash deal. The stations would be able to repeat each episode eight times during the course of the deal. In contrast, the *Jenny Jones Show* (a talk show) was being offered as a straight barter deal with the distributor, Warner Brothers Television, keeping seven minutes of commercial time.

Inside a TV control room. The director is the man with glasses toward the upper part of the picture. It's his job to scan the monitors and choose the most appropriate shot. To his left in front of the large control panel, called the switcher, is the technical director, who actually pushes the buttons that put the cameras on the air. (Shelly Gazin/The Image Works)

Syndication companies try to sell their shows in as many TV markets as possible. The greater the coverage of the show, the more appealing it is to national advertisers. Shows that have less than 50 percent market coverage usually have a tough time being successful. Top-rated syndicated shows, like *Wheel of Fortune* and *Jeopardy*, are seen in nearly all TV markets.

Traditionally, tapes of syndicated programs were placed in containers and sent to stations by air or rail express. Recently, however, many syndication companies have distributed their shows electronically by satellite, allowing some programs to treat current topics. *Entertainment Tonight*, for example, is distributed the same day it's produced.

Syndication functions as an important "aftermarket" for prime-time TV shows. In fact, most prime-time series are produced at a deficit, sometimes $200,000 or more for each one-hour episode. Production companies gamble that they can make back this money in the syndication market. It's a risk, but if an off-net show hits it big in syndication, like *Cosby*, it might earn half a billion dollars or more. To be attractive in the syndication market, however, a prime-time show must have enough back episodes stockpiled so that stations can run episodes for a long time without repeats becoming a problem. One hundred seems to be the magic number, and most series usually have a big party to commemorate the production of their hundredth episode. Since only twenty-two or twenty-four new shows are produced each season, it's obvious that those series that last four or five years are the best bets for syndication success.

Exhibition

At the start of 1992 there were approximately 1125 commercial TV stations and 350 noncommercial stations in the United States. One important difference between TV stations is a technical one. Some TV stations are licensed to broadcast in the very high frequency (**VHF**) band of the electromagnetic spectrum; these stations occupy channels 2–13 on the TV set. Other stations broadcast in the ultra-high frequency (**UHF**) part of the spectrum; these stations are found on channels 14–69. VHF stations have a signal that covers greater distances than UHF stations. Consequently, VHF stations tend to be more desirable to own and operate.

As we suggested earlier, another important difference between stations concerns their affiliation with national networks. As of 1991, more than 80 percent of all commercial stations were affiliated with CBS, NBC, ABC, or Fox. Each of the networks owns and operates stations (called **O and Os**) in the largest markets in the United States. These stations tend to be very profitable and contribute a great deal to the overall revenues of their parent network.

Those stations not affiliated with networks are called **independents**. For many years, independents were hampered because most were UHF stations and had less coverage area than VHFs. The emergence of cable, however, gave UHF independents more of a competitive advantage, since both UHF and VHF stations have the same audience reach on the cable. The growth of independent stations (their number tripled in the 1980s) and changing viewing patterns over the last decade or so have given independent stations a more powerful position in the TV industry. The combined share of the prime-time audience that views independent stations is about the same as views a TV network, making the independent stations a rival for advertising dollars. In addition, the share of the audience for independent stations has risen 29 percent in the last six years while the share for network affiliates has dropped by more than 10 percent. From 1980 to 1990, the annual revenue of independent stations more than doubled. In the last few years, increased competition and skyrocketing program costs have slowed down the growth of independent stations, but they continue to be a formidable force in the market.

Ted Danson and Kirstie Alley at the bar where everybody knows your name. More than 42 million homes tuned in Cheers' *final episode in 1993. (Paramount Pictures)*

Ownership

American broadcasting saw an unprecedented restructuring in the late eighties. Due in part to their economic situation and the increased competition facing the networks, the following changes occurred. Capital Cities Broadcasting assumed control of ABC. Long known for its emphasis on the bottom line, Capcities immediately instituted drastic cost-cutting measures to stem the company's flow of red ink. In an example of history repeating itself, NBC was taken over by General Electric, one of its original owners back in 1927. Although NBC's ratings were best of all the networks, its new owners also cut back on the budget. Technically, CBS did not change hands, but it came under the control of Laurence Tisch, head of the Loews Corporation. Tisch assumed control of the network with the backing of its founder, William Paley, who came out of retirement to ease the transition (another example of history come full circle). The cost-cutting at CBS received the most publicity as numerous news personnel were laid off. Tisch also sold several CBS properties in order to improve the company's solvency.

As of 1993, then, two networks were under the control of large conglomerates, another was controlled by a parent company with interests in publishing and cable, and a fourth had become almost completely broadcasting oriented. To be specific:

- NBC is under the control of RCA, which is in turn owned by General Electric. In addition to its holdings in nonmedia areas such as aerospace, aircraft engines, consumer products, and financial services, G.E./RCA has interests in home video, owns and operates seven TV stations, has a production company and a corporate video production firm. RCA/NBC recently sold off its record company, the NBC Radio Network, and some of its radio stations. (Every now and again, rumors circulate that G.E. is looking to sell the network. G.E. has always denied the rumors.)

- Capcities/ABC has interests in magazine publishing and owns seven daily newspapers, Chilton Books, part interest in three cable channels, a video production company, eight TV stations, and twenty-one radio stations.

- CBS Inc. has a video production company, a home video distribution firm, a radio network, and five TV and eighteen radio stations. In its move toward streamlining, CBS sold off its book publishing, magazine publishing, and recording divisions.

- Fox Broadcasting Corporation is part of 20th Century Fox, a major film and TV production company, which, in turn, is owned by Rupert Murdoch's News Corporation, a multinational conglomerate with holdings both in the print and electronic media.

At the station level, a 1984 FCC ruling that raised the number of TV stations a person or organization could own from seven to twelve (provided that the twelve stations reached no more than 25 percent of the country's TV households after allowing for a 50 percent UHF "discount") sparked a massive trend toward consolidation in the industry. A change in tax law also accelerated the process, so that in 1985 and 1986 a record 227 TV stations changed hands. When all the dealing was done, it was evident that group ownership was the major defining characteristic of TV broadcasting. As of 1991, about 190 groups owned about 77 percent of all the stations in the top 100 markets. Table 13-2 lists the top five group owners.

● ● ● ●

PRODUCING TELEVISION PROGRAMS

Departments and Staff

There are many different staffing arrangements in television stations. Some big-city stations employ 300–400 people and may be divided into a dozen different departments. Small-town stations may have twenty to thirty employees and only a few departments. Staffing arrangements are diverse. However, Figure 13-1, page 309, represents one possible staffing structure.

At the top of the chart is the general manager, the person ultimately responsible for all station activities. The rest of the staff is divided into five different departments. The sales department is responsible for selling time to local and national advertisers, scheduling ads, and sending bills to customers. Maintaining all the technical equipment is the responsibility of the engineering department. The production department puts together locally produced programming. Producers, directors, camerapersons, artists, and announcers are part of this department. At many stations the programming function is also handled by this department. Those involved in programming decide what programs should be broadcast and at what times they should be presented. The function of the news department is self-evident. It includes the news director,

TABLE 13-2 Top Five Owners of TV Stations		
COMPANY	NUMBER OF STATIONS	PERCENTAGE OF COVERAGE
Capcities/ABC	8	23.8
CBS	7	22.1
NBC	6	20.4
Tribune Co.	7	19.6
Fox	8	19.4

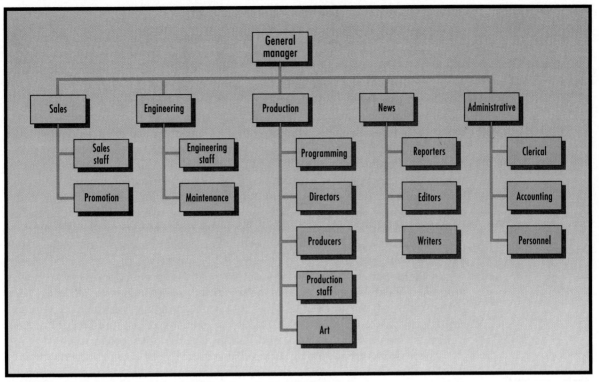

FIGURE 13-1 *Departmental chart for a medium-size television station.*

anchorpeople, reporters, and writers responsible for the station's newscasts. The administrative department aids the station manager in running the station. Under this umbrella are included legal counsel, secretarial help, and the personnel, accounting, and bookkeeping departments.

At the network level, the divisions are somewhat more complicated. Although the major networks differ in their setups, all seem to have departments that perform the following functions:

1. Sales: handles sale of network commercials and works with advertising agencies.

2. Entertainment: works with producers to develop new programs for the network.

3. Owned and operated stations: administers those stations owned by the networks.

4. Affiliate relations: supervises all contracts with stations affiliated with the network (and generally tries to keep the affiliates happy).

5. News: responsible for all network news and public affairs programs.

6. Sports: responsible for all sports programming.

7. Standards: checks all network programs to make sure they don't violate the law or the network's own internal standards. All nets have recently cut back on this department.

8. Operations: handles the technical aspects of actually sending programs to affiliates.

Producing television programs ranges from the incredibly simple—two chairs and a potted palm placed in front of a camera for an interview show—to the incredibly complex—the millions of dollars and hundreds of people who produced the miniseries *Lonesome Dove*. At the local level the biggest effort at a TV station goes into the newscast. Every station has a studio that contains a set for one or two anchorpeople, a weather forecaster, and a sportscaster. The station's news director assigns stories to reporters and camera crews, who travel to the scene of a story and videotape a report. Back at the station, the newscast producer and news director are planning what stories to air and allotting time to each. In the meantime, the camera crews and reporters return; the reporters write copy and editors prepare videotape segments. When the final script is finished (this may be only a few minutes before airtime), it is given to a director, who is responsible for pulling everything together and putting it on the air. In some markets, the production of the local news also includes live reports by correspondents at the scenes of news events. These reports are sent back to the station by microwaves.

In addition to the news, the local station might also produce one or two interview programs. These are usually done in the studio and taped for later broadcasting. Some stations are involved in producing a "magazine" program consisting of segments videotaped on location by portable equipment and later edited into final form. Aside from these kinds of shows, most local stations do little other production.

The networks are the organizations that are heavily involved in program development and production. Because they are responsible for filling the hours when the biggest audience is watching (called prime time, 8–11 P.M., Eastern Standard Time), the networks must pay special attention to cultivating new shows. For the moment, let's concentrate on how a prime-time series is produced.

Everything starts with an idea. Network executives receive hundreds of ideas every year; some come from independent producers, some from TV departments of motion picture companies, some from network employees, and a good many from amateurs hoping for a break. From this mass of ideas, the networks select perhaps fifty to seventy-five, usually submitted by established producers or companies, for further attention. After examining plot outlines and background sketches of the leading characters for these fifty to seventy-five potential series, the networks trim the list once again. For those ideas that survive, the networks request a sample script and a list of possible stories that could be turned into scripts. If the idea still looks promising, the network and producer enter into a contract for a **pilot**, the first episode of a series. In a typical year, perhaps twenty-five pilots are ordered by each net. Pilots are expensive. The networks spent more than $110 million on 125 pilots for the 1991–1992 season; few of them made it into sustained production. If the pilot show gains a respectable audience, the network may order five or six episodes to be produced and may place the program on its fall schedule. From the hundreds of ideas that are sent to the network, only a few ever make it to prime time.

The process does not stop with the fall season. If a program does well in the ratings (see Chapter 20), the network will order enough episodes for the rest of the season. If the show does not do well, it will be canceled and another show will replace it. Meanwhile, network executives are sifting through the hundreds of program ideas for the next season, and the cycle begins once again.

The actual production of these series is done by independent or movie-affiliated production companies. Many of these companies own their own studios and production facilities; others rent or lease the space and equipment they need. There are two basic types of production: film and tape. Film programs are produced through the traditional techniques of motion pictures. There is typically one film camera, and each

Sitcom Uber Alles?

Premises for situation comedies can be pretty far out. *Mork and Mindy*, for example, was based on an alien who came to Earth in an egg and settled in Colorado. *Doogie Howser* is a teenage doctor. *The Flying Nun* was based on . . . a flying nun. The British, however, may have come up with the wildest premise yet.

Heil Honey, I'm Home was premiered in 1991 on the British Satellite Broadcasting system. The show, which can be picked up only by those with satellite dishes or on cable, is a situation comedy which features Adolf Hitler as a suburban husband married to Eva Braun.

Their next-door neighbors are a Jewish couple named the Goldsteins. In the pilot episode, Neville Chamberlain (the prime minister of Britain at the outbreak of World War II) stops by for tea and a chat with the Hitlers. In another episode, Benito Mussolini (dictator of Italy during the war) pays a visit.

Some Jewish groups raised concerns that the show would be offensive, but the producers assured them that the show would not affront anybody. As a spokesperson put it, "Hitler is always outwitted. The only people this series will offend are Nazis."

scene is shot several times from different angles until the director is satisfied. The scenes are shot out of sequence and later spliced into their proper order.

Other programs are shot on videotape with three or more TV cameras. The director selects the best shot from the three cameras to be recorded. In some cases, each episode is taped twice (typically, the dress rehearsal and final performance are recorded), and the director and tape editor select the best scenes from each and assemble them into the final version.

Of course, not all network programs are put together in this manner. Newscasts are usually done live with film and tape segments inserted in them. Shows such as *Good Morning America* and *Today* are done live. Soap operas and game shows are typically done with multiple cameras and recorded on tape and, after minor editing, saved for future broadcast.

Once the shows have been produced, where and when to place them in the schedule must be decided. This task, known as **programming**, is a crucial one. A bad programming decision might mean failure for a good show while a shrewd decision might make a mediocre show a hit. Programmers at both the network and local levels use certain principles to help them in their decisions. For example, one important consideration is **audience flow**. Ideally, the audience from one program should flow to the program that follows it. Mindful of this, programmers tend to schedule similar programs back to back so as to not interrupt the flow. For example, on Thursday nights during the fall 1993–1994 season, NBC scheduled four situation comedies in a row: *Mad About You, Wings, Seinfeld*, and *Frasier*. On that same night ABC ran three adult shows back to back: *Missing Persons, Matlock*, and *Prime Time Live*.

Another principle is **counterprogramming**, airing a program designed to appeal to a different segment of the audience than those on competing stations. To illustrate, during the 1993–1994 season, CBS scheduled *Murphy Brown* and *Love and War*, shows with a lot of appeal to women, against ABC's *Monday Night Football*, which drew a large number of male viewers.

Of course, the increasing use of VCRs to timeshift programs further complicates programming decisions.

● ● ● ●

ECONOMICS

Overall, the television industry has been profitable since 1950, and its total income has increased every year since 1971. In 1990, television advertising revenue amounted to $28.6 billion, more than double the 1980 figure. The changing structure of the television industry, however, has had a significant economic impact on both local stations and the networks. More about this after we look at the traditional sources of television advertising revenue.

Commercial Time

Where did the $28.6 billion in revenue come from? It came from the sale of commercial time by networks and local stations to advertisers. A station or a network makes available a specified number of minutes per hour that will be offered for sale to advertisers. There are three different types of advertisers who buy time on TV stations:

1. national advertisers

2. national spot advertisers

3. local advertisers

National advertisers are those who sell general-consumption items: soda pop, automobiles, deodorant, hair spray, and so on. These advertisers try to reach the biggest possible audience for their messages and usually purchase commercial time on network programs.

In contrast, other advertisers have products that are mainly used in one region or locale. For these advertisers, buying time on a network show would not be the most efficient way to spend their money since many people who are not potential customers would be exposed to their messages. For example, a manufacturer of snowmobiles would gain little by having his or her ad seen in Miami or New Orleans. Likewise, a manufacturer of farm equipment would probably not find many customers in New York City. These companies turn to national spot buying. This method affords the advertiser flexibility since ads can be placed in precisely those markets that have the most sales potential. The snowmobile manufacturer would buy spots in several northern markets such as Minneapolis, Minnesota; Fargo, North Dakota; and Butte, Montana. The farm equipment company would place ads in primarily rural markets.

Finally, there are many local businesses that buy advertising time from TV stations. They need to reach only the area from which they get most of their customers. Consequently, they purchase time on one or more TV stations located in a single market. The industrywide figures for 1990 showed the relative importance of these three types of advertising. Network spots accounted for 38 percent of the total amount of advertising dollars, while the remainder was divided about equally between national spot and local advertising.

At the local station level, revenues depend upon the amount of money a station charges for its commercial time. The larger the audience, the more money a station can charge. The prices for thirty- and sixty-second commercials are listed on the station's rate card. The cost of an ad will vary tremendously from station to station. A thirty-second ad might cost only $100–$200 in a small market, while the same time would cost thousands in a major market. The same general pricing principles apply at the network level. Shows with high ratings have higher advertising charges than shows with low ratings. For example, in 1990, the average network thirty-second spot in prime time cost about $100,000. On top-rated shows, spots were going for about $300,000; on lower-rated shows the cost was about $80,000. To give some perspective on how expensive it can get, on the 1992 Superbowl a thirty-second spot was going for $850,000.

The Bottom Line

Ever wonder why it costs around $700,000 to produce one half hour of TV? The salaries of the stars, of course, represent a large part of the budget but a recent *TV Guide* article detailed some other reasons why costs add up. For example:

Weekly wardrobe costs for *Designing Women*:	$12,000
Airfare for guests on *Geraldo*:	$2 million per year
Cost of necktie worn by Elliot on *thirtysomething*:	$52
Sally Jesse Raphael's red-framed glasses:	$5000 per year
Conference table used in *LA Law*:	$5000
Suspenders worn by Bill Cosby in *The Cosby Show*:	$37–$70 per pair
Doughnuts on the now defunct *Twin Peaks*:	$150 per week

Where Did the Money Go?

At the network level, one of the biggest expenses is programming. To give you some examples, *Roseanne* costs about $675,000 per episode to produce, *Rescue 911* costs $650,000. *The Simpsons* runs about $600,000 for each show. An hour show such as *Knots Landing* has a price tag of about $1.3 million per episode. ABC spends about $2.5 million for each *Monday Night Football* telecast. Twenty-two episodes (about the usual number produced in a season) of the average hour-show cost almost $30 million.

Murphy Brown (Candice Bergen) and Miles Silverberg (Grant Shaud) argue about getting Murphy a secretary. Murphy Brown *cost about $650,000 an episode in 1992. (© CBS Inc.)*

At the local station level, the costs are broken down somewhat differently but the heavy cost of programming is evident there as well. A report by the Broadcast Cable Financial Management Association broke down 1991 local station expenses as follows:

Advertising/promotion	5¢
Technical	7¢
Program	35¢
Selling	9¢
Administration	30¢
News	15¢

It is obvious that the pattern of costs in television is quite different from that of radio (see Chapter 9).

The Networks and the Case of the Vanishing Viewer

As recently as 1979, the three major TV networks commanded about 90 percent of the prime-time audience. By 1985, that figure had dropped to 73 percent and by 1991, it was down around 60 percent. To put it another way, the networks had lost one-third of their audience in a dozen years. Where did they go? Well, during this same time period, VCR penetration increased from 1 percent of all households to about 70 percent. The number of independent TV stations tripled and cable TV penetration increased nearly as much. A new competitor, Fox, came on the scene in 1987. This proliferation of choices has fragmented viewers and stolen away much of the network audience.

Throughout the 1980s, much of the economic fallout of this trend was offset by rising prices charged for network commercial time. The economy of the early 1990s, however, resulted in a gloomier picture for network profits. After years of steadily increasing advertising income, network ad revenues actually dropped from 1988 to 1989. Revenues increased slightly from 1989 to 1990 but network profits fell by roughly one-third. In fact two of the three major networks (CBS and NBC) lost about $500 million between them in 1991. Accordingly, the networks were trimming costs and laying off employees in an effort to improve their profit picture.

Fin-Syn

In addition to their cost cutting, the nets were also searching about to find new sources of revenue. One area the networks have concentrated on involves the syndication market. Way back in 1970, the Federal Communications Commission (FCC), worried about too much domination by the networks, passed the financial interest and syndication rules (fin-syn) which effectively limited the number of shows the nets could produce themselves and limited their share in the lucrative syndication aftermarket. This ruling stimulated the creation of TV series by independent producers (many of them Hollywood studios) and encouraged the growth of many syndication companies.

During the 1980s, when network shares started to decline, the FCC attempted to repeal the rules but its action was met by a flurry of lobbying from the motion picture industry (which had a lot to lose if the rules were repealed). After several years of futile negotiations between regulators, the TV networks, and the movie studios, the fin-syn rules were finally replaced in 1991. The new rules appeared to favor the networks by giving them the right to syndicate shows in the foreign markets and to syndicate shows produced in-house so long as the amount of in-house programming didn't exceed 40 percent of the prime-time schedule. The FCC also defined a network as an organization that delivers more than fifteen hours of programming a week to its affiliates. (This was a boon to Fox, which could expand its offerings to every night of the week.) The FCC was somewhat surprised when its new rules didn't appear to satisfy anybody.

The movie studios thought the new regulations went too far; the three networks thought they didn't go far enough. Plans were announced to ask the FCC to reconsider, and chances are good that the whole thing will be appealed to the federal courts.

Although the situation for network TV seems foreboding, let's not be too quick to write its obituary. The major nets still command a healthy chunk of the audience. In this age of media fragmentation, a 55 to 60 percent share of the audience is pretty good. No motion picture, magazine, cable channel, newspaper, or billboard gets anywhere near that figure. Advertisers who want to reach a general audience in a hurry are still drawn to network TV. Although the number and function of the nets might change over the next few years, it is a good bet that some form of network TV will survive.

At the local station level, there was also a feeling of pessimism. Although some individual stations were doing well, many stations, particularly in smaller markets, were struggling to stay profitable. The situation didn't improve when a 1991 report issued by the FCC's Office of Plans and Policy concluded that broadcast TV "has suffered an irreversible long-term decline in audience and revenue shares, which will continue during the current decade." As a result of this report, the FCC and the industry are looking for ways to make broadcast TV more viable in the future.

Out-Fox-ing the Three Networks

When the Fox Broadcasting Company started operations, few in the TV industry gave it much of a chance. After all, others had tried to start a fourth network before and had failed. Plus, the Fox network had fewer affiliates than the three major nets and most of its stations were UHF with limited signal range. (Fox was referred to as "the coat hanger network," a reference to the special antennas many people had to have to receive its affiliates' UHF signals.) Many of those carried by local cable systems also had an unfavorable channel position. Undaunted, Fox launched its prime-time schedule in 1987 and found instant failure. A talk show starring Joan Rivers bombed. Sitcoms like *Mr. President* and *Karen's Song* that mimicked those on ABC, CBS, and NBC attracted few viewers. By the end of its first year, Fox was averaging a paltry 2 percent share of the audience and its shows were always bunched at the bottom of the Nielsen ratings. Losses for the first year came to $95 million and most in the industry were saying "I told you so."

Then things changed. A writers' strike in 1988 forced the three established networks to show reruns and more reruns. Restless viewers reached for the remote control and found shows like the irreverent *Married . . . with Children* and

the hip *21 Jump Street*. Fox also concentrated on attracting a young audience. Shows such as *Beverly Hills 90210*, *In Living Color*, and the irrepressible *The Simpsons* have given Fox programs the demographics that advertisers like. Almost half of the viewers of Fox programs are 12 to 34; the three other networks have a much older audience. Thanks to its youthful appeal, Fox ended 1989 with a small profit.

By 1990 Fox was flexing its muscles. It started programming fifteen hours per week, premiered its series before ABC, NBC, and CBS, and stole some of their viewers. In a move designed to get publicity, Fox scheduled *The Simpsons* up against the perennial ratings powerhouse, *The Cosby Show*. Bart and his family did OK against the Huxtables, usually finishing a strong second for the time period and often ending up in the top twenty shows for the week, along with *Married . . . with Children*. Other Fox shows did well enough to bring Fox a $70-million profit for 1990–1991.

The future looks equally bright. Thanks to the financial-syndication ruling by the FCC, unlike the three major networks, Fox can produce and syndicate all its shows. *Married . . . with Children* was the number-one show for the first week in September of 1991, the first time a Fox show ever hit the top spot. In 1992, Fox reported higher profits than both CBS and NBC. The coat hanger is no longer the appropriate symbol for Fox.

"Don't have a cow" networks. Bart and the Simpson clan helped Fox become a contender in the prime-time TV arena. (Photofest)

• • • •
PUBLIC BROADCASTING

A Short History

In 1992, the act that established the Public Broadcasting Service reached its twenty-fifth anniversary. During those two plus decades, public broadcasting's achievements were considerable but its evolution was hampered by political infighting, a lack of a clear purpose, and most of all, an insufficient amount of money. Let's quickly review some of the history of noncommercial television in the United States.

Until 1967, noncommercial TV was known as educational television. Most of the programs were instructional and were criticized for being dull. In 1967, following the recommendations of the Carnegie Commission, Congress passed the Public Broadcasting Act, which authorized money for the construction of new facilities and established the Corporation for Public Broadcasting (CPB), an organization that was to oversee noncommercial TV and distribute funds for programs. The government also created the Public Broadcasting Service (PBS), an organization whose duties resemble those performed by commercial networks, that is, promotion and distribution of programming among member stations. Although this arrangement seemed to work well at first, internal disputes soon surfaced concerning which of these two organizations had final control over programming. Another squabble developed in 1974 between public television and the Nixon administration when the White House felt that

PBS programs were antiadministration. President Nixon eventually vetoed a CPB funding bill. Organizational problems continued to plague public broadcasting into the 1990s.

In addition, several cable channels began to offer programs that competed for public TV's audience. CBS Cable, with all the formidable resources of its parent company at its disposal, led the way in this area of cultural programming, with a schedule that included drama, ballet, opera, and concerts. Many experts felt that much of the traditional programming on public TV would eventually move to cable or to videocassette. On top of this came further reductions in federal funds for public broadcasting. In fact, the National Telecommunications and Information Administration, which recommends broadcasting policy to the White House, announced in 1983 that it was considering a suggestion that would end *all* federal funding of public TV. The future did not look promising.

Then things started to change. CBS Cable went out of business after losing $30 million. Other "arts" cable networks were struggling along in the red. There was little competition from videocassettes. Somewhat surprisingly, cable turned out to be more of a friend than foe to public TV. Those same must-carry rules that aided independent TV stations also helped public stations. Since two-thirds of all public stations are in the UHF band, carriage by local cable systems increased their coverage area and helped public TV double its audience from 1980 to 1984. The end result was that public TV wound up as the primary cultural channel in the nation with 90 million viewers every week.

In the mid-1980s, however, the must-carry rules were declared unconstitutional and the future of cable-carried public stations became uncertain. Although most cable systems continued to carry local-market public stations, there is now no guarantee that they must continue to do so.

Things were not bright on the monetary front either. The Reagan administration cut funds for public broadcasting and proposed to freeze future funding at current levels. Congress restored some of the cuts, but in 1987 the system was struggling to get along on about the same amount of money it had in 1982. Faced with this uncertainty, public TV looked to other sources for funding: corporate underwriting, auctions, viewer donations, and sales of program guides. Some noncommercial stations even briefly experimented with commercials.

Shots of classical paintings such as this were used to illustrate Columbus and the Age of Discovery, *the showcase series of the 1991–1992 PBS season. (Giraudon/Art Resource)*

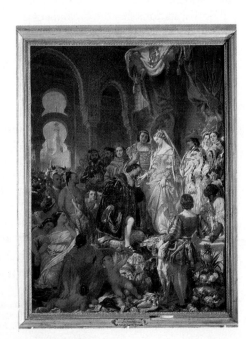

Moreover, the goal of public broadcasting was becoming less clear. Cable channels, such as the Arts & Entertainment Network and the Discovery Channel, carry programs once identified with public broadcasting. Public TV stations themselves further blurred their identity by rerunning shows that were once popular on the commercial networks, such as *The Avengers, Leave It To Beaver*, and *The Lawrence Welk Show*. The problems became so severe that a major restructuring of the programming function of public TV was accomplished in 1990. Faced with dwindling funding from government and private sources, PBS centralized much of its programming decision making in the hope that the new system would save money and be more efficient. The first season under this new system proved to be a success (see below) but the future of PBS was still somewhat uncertain.

Programming and Financing

In 1990, the Public Broadcasting Service (PBS) presented an 11-hour documentary entitled *The Civil War* which became the highest rated program in the history of PBS. Although it might be a bit of an exaggeration, much of the history of PBS programming can be described as a civil war between the local public stations and the centralized PBS organization. Each side has scored significant victories in this fray over the years, but most recently the tide has turned in favor of the centralized authority. Let's quickly review how the system used to work and how it has changed.

Before 1990, PBS used a mechanism called the Station Program Cooperative (SPC) to determine what programs were carried by its member stations. The SPC system was unique to PBS and represented a decentralized decision-making process in which the local stations carried a great deal of clout. In short, member stations were given a ballot which contained the descriptions of possible programs and voted for those they wished to broadcast. After several rounds the initial list was pared down and stations voted again, but this time each station had to promise that it would help pay for the programs it voted for.

This system encouraged the broadcast of programs that already had some previous funding or series that could be acquired cheaply (series purchased from BBC were relatively inexpensive and have been a longtime favorite of PBS partly because of this SPC system). Innovative or daring series that were expensive and had no prior funding commitments were seldom produced. The system also leaned heavily on a few big public TV stations that did the bulk of the production work. Much of the time, smaller PBS stations simply chose from a menu constructed by the larger stations. Finally, PBS had no cohesive national scheduling system. The local PBS stations were free to schedule programs whenever and wherever they chose, making it difficult to coordinate and promote national programming.

In 1990, faced with declining funds and viewers, PBS suspended the SPC and moved toward more centralized programming. An executive vice president for national programming was appointed with the power to develop and schedule new programs. The first person to hold this position was Jennifer Lawson, and she made an auspicious debut. It was her decision to lead off the 1990–1991 season with the *The Civil War* and to concentrate the program into five nights rather than running only one episode per week. In addition, Lawson spent about $2 million for ads on commercial and cable stations to promote "Showcase Week," a sampling of PBS's favorite programs, an event that gave PBS a fall premiere week much like the commercial networks. By any measure, the first PBS season under the new centralized system was a success. The 1991–1992 season did not have the equivalent of *The Civil War* but it did include the big ticket *Columbus and the Age of Discovery*, a seven-hour series aired on four consecutive nights.

PBS programs have earned numerous awards and substantial praise from critics. *Sesame Street* revolutionized children's TV by presenting educational content in an entertaining format. Millions of avid fans gave up other activities to watch the latest episode of *Jewel in the Crown*. *Nova* and *Cosmos* introduced millions to the wonders of science.

Like commercial stations, public TV stations receive licenses from the FCC. As of 1992, there were about 350 public stations operated by about 175 different license holders. Of these 350 stations, about 35 percent are licensed to states or municipalities and many of these are organized into state-operated networks. About 30 percent of public stations are licensed to colleges and universities; another 27 percent are owned by community organizations and the remainder by public school systems.

Unlike commercial TV, public TV gets much of its support from the government. About 40 percent of public TV's revenue comes from the federal, state, or local government. Local residents who subscribe to public TV stations by paying a yearly fee to the local station account for about 20 percent. Support of programs by business accounts for another 15 percent. The remaining support comes from foundations, private colleges, and auctions held by some stations. To provide some comparison between the economics of commercial and noncommercial TV, recall that *one week* of commercial TV cost about $70 million. For 1990, the *entire budget* of the Corporation for Public Broadcasting was about $168 million, less than the cost of a month of network programs.

• • • •

CABLE TELEVISION

The best word to describe cable television (CATV) is growth. The number of households subscribing to cable continues to grow (about 60 percent at this writing), the amount of advertising dollars spent with cable is up, its prestige is flourishing (thanks in large measure to CNN's performance during the Gulf War), and the number of specialized cable channels has hit an all-time high (close to 70 as of 1992).

Problems, however, have accompanied the progress. As of 1992 CATV operators were facing potential formidable competition from telephone companies, serious government examination concerning CATV's regulatory status, a host of complaints from subscribers, and growing difficulty in attracting and maintaining an audience thanks to competition from other cable services.

History: From Puny Weakling to Bully?

Cable TV began modestly in the 1950s as a device used to bring conventional television signals to areas that could not otherwise receive them. Communities in mountainous areas or communities too small to support their own stations were the first to be wired for CATV. As cable grew, some systems imported signals from distant stations into markets that were already served by one or two local stations. The local stations, as you might imagine, were not pleased since their audiences were being siphoned off by the imported signals. This situation caused some political maneuverings as stations affected by CATV appealed to the FCC and to Congress for help. The FCC vacillated over the question of cable regulation before issuing in 1965 a set of rules that had the effect of retarding the growth of CATV in large markets. In 1972 the FCC enacted a new set of less restrictive rules for cable. These new rules helped spur the growth of CATV systems during the 1970s. By 1980, in a move toward deregulation, the FCC dropped virtually all rules governing CATV.

This deregulation move helped systems grow as various cable companies scrambled to acquire exclusive cable franchises in communities across the nation (see Figure 13-2). Some companies made extravagant promises to win these contracts: 100 plus channels, local-access channels, community channels, shopping and banking at home, two-way services—and all at bargain prices. After the smoke cleared, the industry

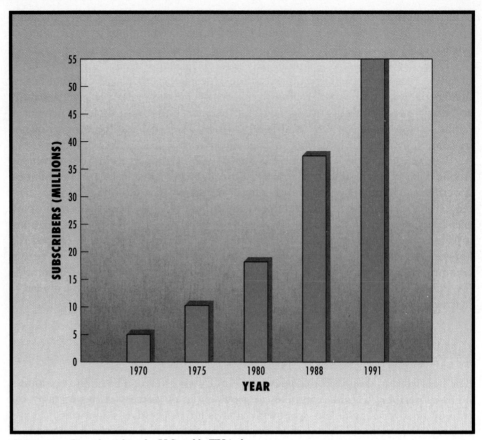

FIGURE 13-2 *Growth within the U.S. cable TV industry.*

quickly realized that economic reality dictated that its performance would fall short of promises.

Cable quickly recovered from these setbacks and continued to grow. As of 1991, there were 7500 cable systems serving about 55 million households. Keep in mind that this growth occurred despite the fact that cable companies generally avoided expensive urban installations.

By 1989, cable had begun to flex its newfound muscles. On the political front, the industry was able to steer the 1984 Cable Communications Policy Act through the Congress. This legislation took the lid off cable rates, allowing many systems to increase profits. On the legal front, the court system struck down the must-carry rules, which had required cable systems to carry all local broadcast stations. Now, pending congressional action, cable systems can carry whatever services they want to. Many broadcasters feared that it was only a matter of time before cable systems charged some stations a fee to carry them on the cable. Others voiced concern that cable systems were moving some independent stations from the lower numbered cable channels (2–16) into cable "Siberia" (channels 16 and up), where there are fewer viewers and where independents are less competitive with other cable channels in which the local system has an ownership interest.

On the economic side, cable advertising revenues exceeded $2 billion in 1990. Although still small in comparison to the ad revenues generated by traditional television, this figure represents an increase of more than 100 percent over 1988, enough to get the attention of traditional broadcasting.

Cable scored several recent programming coups that made traditional broadcasting take notice. ESPN signed a three-year deal with the National Football League to carry prime-time pro football games, breaking the network monopoly on that sport. As more sports programming traditionally carried by over-the-air broadcasters, such as New York Yankees baseball, went to cable, many feared it was only a matter of time before the Superbowl and the World Series moved to the wire. Other big-ticket network series were bypassing the traditional syndication route and premiering first on cable. *LA Law* and *Murder She Wrote* were the first to make the leap to cable. These shows will offer increased competition to traditional broadcast stations.

Perhaps the one thing that worried traditional broadcasters and programming suppliers most was the increasing vertical integration of the cable industry. Lack of regulation allowed cable operators to become more and more involved with programming, thus controlling both the hardware and the software side of the business. TCI, the biggest cable system operator, owns part of Turner Broadcasting System, which includes superstation WTBS, CNN, and the TNT cable network. TCI also owns half of the American Movie Classics Channel and parts of the Discovery Channel, Black Entertainment Television, and The Fashion Channel. ATC, another large operator, is owned by Time Warner Inc., which also owns HBO and Cinemax. Viacom, which operates systems in seven states, owns Showtime, The Movie Channel, and MTV.

All of these developments have cable's chief rivals, the motion picture and broadcasting industries, charging that cable systems are unregulated monopolies and asking for some kind of reregulation. One network executive likened cable to a "toll bridge into the home," controlling to a large extent what programs Americans got to see on their TV sets. Critics charge that cable is cornering the market on information and entertainment and is putting itself into such a strong position that it can bully its rivals into submission. The cable industry, of course, denied this charge. Nonetheless, some regulators and lawmakers are concerned about the growing power of cable. In 1988, the FCC reenacted the syndication exclusivity rules that protect the programming of local stations against duplication from distant stations brought in by cable. In addition, in mid-1991, a federal judge cleared the way for regional telephone companies to com-

---

The Discovery Channel specializes in educational and informative programming such as People of the Forest: The Chimps of Gombe. *(John Hyde, Courtesy of the Discovery Channel)*

pete with cable by offering information services, including electronic classified ads, catalogs, or even newspapers, to consumers over their TV sets or personal computers. Further, the ruling appeared to clear the way for the regional phone companies to acquire or to build cable TV systems outside their service area. Moreover, a 1993 court ruling declared unconstitutional parts of the 1984 Cable Act that barred common ownership of telephone and cable systems in the same market area. The ruling allowed Bell Atlantic and perhaps other telephone companies to provide video services to their telephone customers.

Cable was also facing potential competition from other sources. Two services using direct satellite broadcasting (see Chapter 23), SkyPix and Primestar, were planning to offer subscribers up to 80 channels of programming. (A third service, Sky Cable, a consortium of NBC, Hughes Communication, Rupert Murdoch's News Corporation, and Cablevision Systems, was announced with great fanfare in 1990 but a year later a weak economy had put the proposed service in limbo.) At the same time, the FCC appeared to favor the concept of duopolies, two cable systems covering the same area as opposed to one company having an exclusive franchise, as a way to promote better service and lower prices. In any event, it seems clear that cable TV will be facing a more competitive environment in the future.

International Perspective: The Global TV Marketplace

As we have seen in Chapter 3, commercially supported broadcasting systems are proliferating throughout Europe. Since American TV programs have long been popular favorites throughout Europe and the rest of the world, it should be boom times for the companies that sell American programming overseas. Well, not quite.

Although American programs are still the most pervasive worldwide, they are seldom scheduled during prime time. Television has become so deeply embedded in a nation's culture that viewers demand something familiar and indigenous in prime time.

Added to this is the fact that a lot of recent American TV programming has become offbeat and quirky and may not appeal to viewers everywhere. Unlike *Dallas* and *Dynasty*, two prime-time soap operas with easily understandable themes that became popular in virtually every country where they were shown, shows like *Twin Peaks*, *Northern Exposure*, and *In Living Color* may be baffling to viewers in another country. Some American comedies, such as *The Cosby Show* and *Cheers*, do well overseas but shows like *Roseanne* and *Married . . . with Children* are too abrasive for foreign audiences. As a result, some countries are buying old and familiar programs like *The Waltons* and *The Dukes of Hazzard* to fill marginal time slots.

Sometimes the actual show may not be exported but its concept is adapted to the local culture. *Wheel of Fortune*, for instance, has, among others, a French version, *La Roue de la Fortune*, and a Spanish version, *La Rouletta de la Fortuna*. *America's Funniest Home Videos*, which, incidentally, was inspired by a show on Japanese television, has been licensed in Germany, France, Spain, and the Netherlands.

Occasionally, a show that was rather marginal in the U.S. will hit it big overseas. *Baywatch*, an NBC series about lifeguards which got mediocre ratings in the U.S., was the most popular American show on British TV in 1990. The soap opera *Santa Barbara* is shown in the evenings on French TV and captures almost half of the available audience. *Moonlighting* is still doing well on Greek TV and the long-canceled *Knight Rider* is remarkably popular in Germany. In any case, selling American TV shows overseas is a lot harder than it used to be.

On the regulatory front, Congress passed the 1992 Cable Act. The major provisions of this law are: (1) broadcasters can choose between "must carry" (the cable system has to carry the station's signal) or retransmission consent (broadcasters have the right to negotiate compensation for the retransmission of their signals); (2) the FCC can regulate cable rates (in late 1993, the FCC was still developing a formula for calculating allowable rates); (3) exclusive contracts between cable program suppliers and cable operators have been eliminated, opening up competition from MMDS and SMATV systems (see page 325).

One interesting result of this law was that it prompted many broadcasters to enter the cable business. As part of their retransmission consent agreement, many big broadcasting companies opted to start new cable channels which were guaranteed space on local systems rather than ask for a cash payment for retransmission.

Lastly, cable is becoming a victim of the same fragmentation process that is hurting the traditional television networks. As more and more services are offered on the cable channels, the audience is divided into smaller and smaller segments. In 1992, cable had reached the point where cable channels were drawing viewers not only from traditional TV but from each other as well. Ratings for cable channels were flat or even decreased during 1991. The number of basic subscribers for the top 100 cable systems failed to grow in the first quarter of 1991 and the number of people subscribing to pay-TV services actually dropped about 3 percent in the same time period. This suggests that cable may be seeing an end to its growth period and entering maturity.

Ownership

The trend in the cable industry, like that in other media, is toward consolidation. In late 1993, Bell Atlantic, a regional phone company, announced plans to acquire TCI, Inc. This $33 billion megamerger will combine the capabilities of both phone and cable networks and will pave the way for an "information highway" into every home. The five largest cable systems are listed in Table 13-3.

Structure of CATV Systems

CATV systems are structured differently from those of conventional TV. There are three main components in a CATV system (see Figure 13-3, p. 324):

1. the head end

2. the distribution system

3. the house drop

The **head end** consists of the antenna and related equipment that receives signals from distant TV stations or other programming services and processes these signals

TABLE 13-3 Five Largest Cable System Operators	
SYSTEM	**NUMBER OF SUBSCRIBERS (MILLIONS)**
TCI, Inc.	10.2
Time Warner	6.8
Continental Cablevision	2.9
Comcast	2.8
Cablevision Systems	2.1

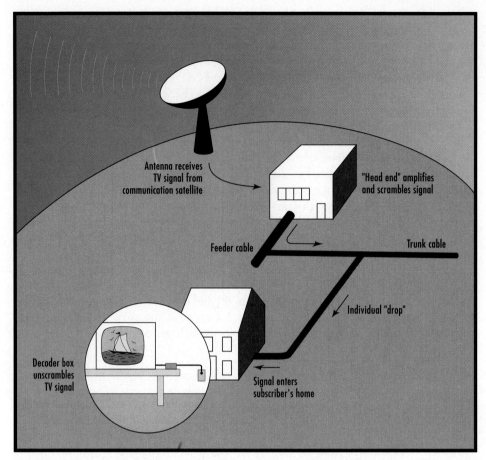

FIGURE 13-3 *Diagram of the transmission of HBO programming from videotape studios, via satellite, to the pay subscriber's television set. At the head end, the signal is assigned to a cable TV channel before being sent on its way to the subscriber's home.*

so that they may be sent to subscribers' homes. Some CATV systems also originate their own programming, ranging from local newscasts to weather dials, and their studios may also be located at the head end.

The **distribution system** consists of the actual cables that deliver the signals to subscribers. The cables can be buried or hung on telephone poles. In most systems, the main cable (called the trunk) has several feeder cables, which travel down side streets or to other outlying areas. Finally, there are special amplifiers installed along the distribution system, which boost the strength of the signal as it comes from the head end.

The **house drop** is that section of the cable that connects the feeder cable to the subscriber's TV set. Drops can be one way (the signal travels in only one direction—from the head end to the house) or two way (the signal can also be sent back to the head end by the subscriber). Most cable systems built before 1972 provided twelve channels for their subscribers; those built afterward have at least twenty. In some communities, there are fifty-four channels. Advanced two-way systems offer shopping-at-home and banking-at-home services.

Programming and Financing

We will examine these topics from two perspectives: (1) from that of a local cable system operator and (2) from that of a national cable network.

The sources of programming for a local system consist of:

1. Local origination—This might range from a fixed camera scanning temperature dials to local news, high school football, and discussions. Other local origination programs include a government channel, which carries city council meetings or zoning board hearings. Some systems have set aside public-access channels available for anyone to use for a modest fee.

2. Local broadcast television stations—Until recently, cable systems were required by law to carry the signals of all local TV stations. As we have already seen, this law has been overturned, but most systems continue to carry the local channels. In addition to local channels, some cable systems carry signals from nearby cities.

3. Superstations—These are independent stations whose signals are carried by many systems nationwide. There are five main superstations: WTBS, Atlanta; WGN, Chicago; WWOR and WPIX, New York, and KTVT, Dallas. Superstations primarily broadcast sports, movies, and syndicated shows.

4. Special cable networks—These are services distributed by satellite to cable systems. Most of these networks are advertiser supported. Examples include MTV, The Weather Channel, the USA Network, Black Entertainment Television, and the noncommercial C-SPAN (which covers Congress).

5. Pay services—These are commercial-free channels that typically provide theatrical movies and original programming: HBO, Showtime, The Movie Channel, Cinemax, The Disney Channel.

A local cable system has two basic sources of income, subscription fees from consumers and local advertising. Most systems charge a basic fee for local stations, superstations, and special cable networks. In addition, consumers might pay an additional fee to receive one or more pay channels. Looking at expenses, cable is a capital-intensive industry (this means it takes a lot of money to start a system). The cost of stringing the cable, hardware, maintenance, installations, disconnects, and franchise fees makes it expensive. Once in place, the operating costs of a typical system become more reasonable. A good part of the basic cable monthly subscription fee goes to cover construction and maintenance costs. Cable systems must also pay for their

SMATV and MMDS

Two services that are connected to the cable industry are MMDS (Multipoint Multichannel Distribution Service) and SMATV (Satellite Master Antenna Television).

An MMDS transmitter sends microwaves to special antennas and receivers. MMDS is an ideal means to transmit pay programming (such as movies) to apartments and hotels. Sometimes called "wireless cable," MMDS has also been sold to homes where cable was not available.

SMATV offers a small-scale version of cable. It is particularly attractive to urban areas where cable is not yet available. Most big apartment buildings have a rooftop master antenna that picks up traditional TV signals. Tenants can plug into this system for better reception. In the SMATV system, a satellite receiving dish is installed that picks up the signals from the national cable networks. Tenants pay a subscription fee and in effect belong to a miniature cable system. Of course, the fortunes of SMATV may change radically when the big cities are wired for cable.

programming. Some national cable channels supplement their advertising revenue by charging cable systems a small fee per subscriber (called a **carriage fee**), which is often passed on to the consumer. In the case of pay services, the consumer fee is split between the cable system and the cable network. For example, if a pay channel costs the consumer $8 a month, $5 might go to the cable network while $3 is retained by the cable operator. Local advertising on cable represents the other source of income for operators. This sum is growing, but it still represents less than 10 percent of total income for local systems.

Turning to the national level, cable networks draw upon three major sources for their programming: (1) original production, (2) movies, and (3) syndicated programs. The all-news channel, CNN, relies upon original production for virtually all of its content. Most of ESPN's programming is original as is C-SPAN's. Movies make up most of the content on HBO and Showtime, although both channels have recently relied more on original productions. Superstations program a mix of all three sources, while channels such as the USA Network and the CBN Cable Network depend heavily upon syndicated programs. Many of the programs on cable are reruns of network series from the 1950s and 1960s and recent shows from the networks, giving these shows a second life.

There are three main revenue sources for national cable services: advertising, carriage fees, and subscription fees. Pay-TV channels such as Showtime and HBO make their money from subscription fees paid by the consumer. Some cable networks, such as MTV and ESPN, will charge local operators a carriage fee (also called an affiliation fee) that ranges from about 5 to 30 cents per subscriber. Some channels, such as C-SPAN, support themselves entirely from this money. Other networks will sell advertising in addition to the carriage fee while still others, such as The Nashville Network, support themselves entirely through ads. As mentioned earlier, advertising revenues for cable are growing, but cable still accounts for only a small percentage of the total TV ad dollars. Table 13-4 lists the top cable channels.

Three recent trends will have a significant impact on the near future of cable TV programming. First, the lines between cable and traditional broadcasters are blurring. Nickelodeon produced a sitcom called *Hi Honey, I'm Home* that was carried both on Nickelodeon and ABC. HBO produced the sitcom *Roc* for the Fox Network. A made-for-cable movie, *Stop at Nothing*, was also aired on ABC. In more than 2 million

TABLE 13-4 Top Cable Services	
Top Five Pay Channels	
CHANNEL	**SUBSCRIBERS (MILLIONS)**
1. HBO	17.3
2. Showtime	7.4
3. Cinemax	6.4
4. Disney Channel	5.6
Top Five Basic Services	
CHANNEL	**SUBSCRIBERS (MILLIONS)**
1. CNN	58.8
2. ESPN	57.2
3. WTBS	56.6
4. Nickelodeon	55.4
5. MTV	55.0

households, local television stations do a five-minute news summary that runs on CNN. In New Orleans, a cable channel ran live and taped newscasts from a local broadcast TV station around the clock. Apparently, broadcasters and cablecasters, at odds for many years, are finding advantages in cooperation.

Secondly, a new method of transmitting cable signals, called compression technology, will drastically increase the number of channels a cable system can carry. Using this new technology, cable systems with 500 channels will be possible. Looking toward this multiple channel universe, existing cable services are planning to expand their own services. HBO planned to test a system that would offer HBO movies and programs on three channels instead of one. This way viewers could have three different starting times for a film. ESPN is considering a plan to divide into three separate channels, one for sports news, one for major sports, and one for lesser-known sports. C-SPAN is considering four or five different services.

This cornucopia of channels will also help the emergence of pay-per-view (PPV), an arrangement we have already discussed in Chapter 12 with regard to movies. As of 1993, about 20 million households were equipped for PPV and the number is expected to grow to 25 million by 1995. Experts estimate that future cable systems may have as many as forty or fifty channels devoted to pay-per-view offerings, including concerts, sports, special events, and movies. Although, as we have mentioned, movies over PPV have yet to become a big moneymaker, special events have done somewhat better. For example, while revenues from PPV movies rose by about 25 percent from 1990 to 1991, PPV revenues from special events (championship fights, Wrestlemania, rock concerts) more than doubled in the same period. The biggest moneymaker in PPV history was the Evander Holyfield-George Foreman championship fight in 1991 which grossed $55 million. About 9 percent of all cable TV subscribers with access to PPV paid $35.95 to see the fight. A big test for PPV came during the 1992 Summer

---

Special events, such as the Judds' farewell concert, are becoming more common on pay-per-view. (Ken Stills Co., Inc.)

Olympics when NBC presented about 600 hours over PPV in addition to broadcasting another 160 hours. Unfortunately, few subscribers signed up. Nonetheless, one expert estimates that PPV could easily generate $1 billion in revenue in just five years.

• • • •

HOME VIDEO

We've already mentioned the connection between Hollywood and the home video business in Chapter 12. This section will take a broader look at the industry.

The home video industry came into existence because of the tremendous growth of VCR sales. In 1982, only 2 million VCRs were sold. The number doubled in 1983 and doubled again in 1984. Obviously, such a swift pace could not sustain itself forever, and VCR sales plateaued from 1985 to 1987. Nonetheless, 78 percent of U.S. homes were equipped with the device by 1993 and experts predicted that figure would ultimately rise to about 85 percent. The average VCR household spent about $169 renting and buying cassettes in 1991. In any given week, about 35 million households will play tapes during prime time.

VCR owners use their machines to timeshift, that is, to record TV shows for playback at a more convenient time. As of 1993, the shows that were timeshifted the most were soap operas, movies, and *Late Night with David Letterman*. VCRs are also used for playing back prerecorded tapes bought or rented at video counters and video stores. There are more than 25,000 prerecorded cassette titles on the market and an estimated 400 new titles are introduced every month. This pace will probably slacken in the future as all of the most desirable tapes of years past are transferred to cassette, leaving only current releases.

Like most other businesses, home video can be divided into three segments: production, distribution, and retail. The production side of the industry consists of those companies that produce prerecorded cassettes. Since much of the home video market consists of movies, many of the large motion picture studios also dominate the cassette business. In 1993, for example, about two-thirds of videocassette sales went to the ten largest motion picture studios, with 20th Century Fox and Columbia leading the pack. In fact, as we discussed in Chapter 12, the home video market has become the most important source of revenue for the motion picture industry.

Few of these companies sell directly to dealers. Instead, they sell to distributors, who form the bridge between production and retail. Currently some ninety distributors in the United States handle videocassettes. Major companies include HBO Video,

How Do You Stop the 12:00 from Blinking????

Many people are overwhelmed by all the little buttons on their remote control units and VCRs. In fact, a lot of people don't know how to program their machines to record when they are not at home, nor do they know how to record a program off one channel while watching another, nor can they stop that 12:00 from blinking on and off.

Fret no more. Help is on the way. Panasonic has developed a new VCR that uses voice recognition technology. No buttons to push. No hard instructions to follow. All that's necessary is to speak to the unit in your normal voice and tell it what you want it to do. There's only one catch. So far, the machine only understands Japanese.

CBS/Fox Video, RCA/Columbia Home Pictures, Vestron, Tri-Star, and Orion. Moreover, the cassette distribution business now resembles record distribution as a new breed of rack jobber is making it easy for many retail and department stores to get into the video renting business. Companies such as Stars-To-Go and CEVAXS install and operate video rental counters in convenience stores and grocery stores, usually paying rent to the store and collecting a percentage of the video rental business in return. Most of the 60,000 or so convenience stores in the United States have or plan to install a video rental area.

The retail side of the industry is the most volatile. Precise figures are hard to come by because of rapid change, but it was estimated that in 1991 there were about 30,000 video rental/sales stores in the United States in addition to the thousands of tape counters at grocery and convenience stores. The typical large retail store carries a library of about 3000–5000 different titles, representing a balance of current hits with other titles that have a longer shelf life. In contrast, convenience stores and other outlets stock only 200–500 titles, most of them current hits. Competition has grown so much that video stores now resemble fast-food franchises since most of them serve customers in about a three-mile radius.

The video rental business is dominated by large chains, with Blockbuster Video the most prominent. In late 1990, Blockbuster acquired Erol's Inc., the third biggest video retail chain. This gave Blockbuster more than 2000 stores. West Coast Video is the second largest with about 500 stores. Blockbuster alone accounts for about 12 percent of all tape rentals and sales.

Independently owned stores find it tough to compete with the big chains, and hundreds went under from 1985 to 1990. Those that did survive became more specialized, building up an inventory of foreign films, 1940s movies, art films, or films in some other area. Small video stores frequently have a cash flow problem. Suppose a store bought five copies of twenty-five new cassettes a month at an average cost of $50. This amounts to $6250 a month spent for new product. At an average cost of $2.25 a rental, almost 2800 rental transactions would be required just to pay the bill for new releases. Most small stores can't generate that amount of volume.

On the other hand, videocassette sales and rental constitute big business. In 1992, consumers spent about $16 billion on cassettes, with about 70 percent of that sum going to tape rentals and the remainder to tape sales. The industry has shown recent signs of leveling off and revenues are expected to grow more slowly in the future. Competition brought down rental fees. The overall industry average mentioned above was $2.25 per tape, but lower fees—sometimes below $1—are common. A tape has to be rented about thirty times before a retailer can show a profit.

Traditional broadcasters reacted to the increased competition from home video. The networks began offering more shows that attract an older audience (such as *The Golden Girls* and *Murder, She Wrote*), since older viewers were less likely to own VCRs. Further, the networks were scheduling some of their strongest shows on the weekends, when VCR usage is highest, to counterprogram the machine. Some local stations are running promotions that urge viewers to watch their channel while taping the competition's. And if all of this fails, the three major networks have released some of their programs to the home video market.

●●●●
SATELLITE DISHES

The satellite dish collects faint microwave signals from an orbiting satellite and amplifies them about a million times. A cable carries these signals to a converter where they are changed so that they can be received over a normal TV set. Most satellite dishes (also called TVROs—for TV Receive Only) also have a remote-control device that permits the viewer to aim the dish at the appropriate orbiting satellite. A TVRO

Modern video stores stock thousands of tapes ranging from current movies to more specialized content, such as old TV shows. (Louie Psihoyos/Matrix)

can receive not only all the regular TV channels but also "raw feeds," signals sent by networks and cable channels to local stations and cable systems and not intended for public viewing. A good backyard dish can pick up 75 to 100 channels.

In the early 1980s, owners of TVROs were able to pick up free programming off the satellites and the TVRO business was booming. Then the pay movie services and other cable channels scrambled their signals and the bottom dropped out of the TVRO business. To illustrate, in 1985, before widespread scrambling, about 90,000 dishes a month were being sold. After scrambling, the average dropped to about 14,000. About 3 percent of all U.S. homes have a TVRO.

Currently, most dish owners and potential buyers have accepted scrambling as a given. Consumers are now required to buy a descrambling device, which costs several hundred dollars, and pay a monthly fee to receive the now-scrambled channels. Despite the increased costs, sales have been picking up lately, particularly among people living in rural areas unlikely to receive cable.

A whole new program distribution industry has been springing up to serve TVRO owners. Companies such as the Satellite Broadcast Networks (SBN) uplink stations' signals and sell subscriptions to the service to dish owners. The pay-TV channels (Showtime, HBO, etc.) also offer dish owners subscriptions to their programming for a monthly fee.

Future developments in technology will drastically change this industry. High-power satellites can be received on smaller and cheaper dishes. In fact, one new type of antenna developed by the Japanese is not even a dish. The Matsushita Corporation recently unveiled a flat-plate antenna that is only 15 inches square and can be installed on an outside wall instead of on an ugly concrete slab in the backyard. In the future, these new dishes might be receiving signals from direct broadcast satellites (see Chapter 23 for a description of DBS) providing original programming.

• • • •
ISSUES

The television industry is so vast and touches so much of our lives that it difficult to summarize briefly the many issues that it has raised. TV has had profound impact on American culture, politics, family life, education, and institutions. Chapters 21 and 22 discuss some of the specific concerns in these areas. For the moment, however, perhaps the best way to proceed is to rely on the perceptions of someone who has closely followed the evolution of American television over the last thirty years.

In 1961, President John Kennedy appointed Newton Minow the chair of the Federal Communications Commission. In May of that same year, Minow gave his first major speech to a convention of the National Association of Broadcasters. In that speech he criticized broadcasting as a "vast wasteland" characterized by a procession of game shows, murder, sadism, violence, and cartoons. Minow questioned whether or not the broadcasters were actually serving the public interest as they were required to do. The broadcasting industry was incensed and outraged. Nonetheless, Minow's "vast wasteland" speech became one of the most famous in the history of American mass communication and has been reprinted hundreds of times.

Thirty years later Minow was invited to take another look at the television industry and see what, if anything, had changed. Minow's 1991 speech, "How Vast the Wasteland Now?" is an excellent summary of the main issues facing today's television industry. To begin, Minow gave TV an A+ for technological advancement but only a C for serving the needs of society. One of the biggest weaknesses he saw was that TV had not fulfilled its potential for the child audience. It was still a "dim light" in education and despite some recent improvement, had a long way to go.

Minow also voiced disappointment that public television was still cast in the role of a "perpetual beggar" and suggested new ways to help improve its financial situation. He also thought television could improve the electoral process by giving candidates free air time so that they would not be in debt to special interest groups who donate the money used for TV commercials.

The most troubling change over the last thirty years? The increase in the amount of violence. R and PG-13 rated movies did not exist thirty years ago. Today any child can watch them over cable. Minow said in 1961 he worried that his children would not benefit from television; in 1991, he worried that his grandchildren might actually be harmed by it.

The increased channel capacity brought about by cable was a mixed blessing. Viewers have far more choices now, but they must pay more for them and some low income individuals might be priced out of the information marketplace. In addition, said Minow, increased channel capacity might create information overload without any increase in information substance, or as he put it, ". . . more media, fewer messages. Tiny sound bites without large thoughts."

Minow closed his 1991 speech by urging broadcasters and cablecasters to put the vision back into television, "to travel from the wasteland to the promised land." It will be interesting to see what the next thirty years bring.

• • • •
CAREERS IN THE TELEVISION INDUSTRY

How does a young person get started in a career in television? Where should you look for that first job? Someone hunting for a job in TV quickly discovers that it's a relatively small industry. According to recent figures provided by the FCC, about 110,000 people are employed in commercial TV; 100,000 in CATV; 10,000 in non-commercial television; and about 16,000 at TV networks. This means that there are about 236,000 employees in the entire industry. (To give you some perspective on this figure, General Motors employs 775,000 and IBM, 383,000.)

In any given year, probably 5,000 to 10,000 people are hired by the TV industry. Many of these people are replacing employees who have retired or gone on to other careers, while others are filling newly created positions. Also, in any given year, about 15,000 to 20,000 people are looking for TV jobs. Speaking conservatively, we can say that there are at least two people looking for each available position. In some areas of television, especially for the so-called glamour jobs (TV reporter, network page, on-camera host for an interview show, series writer), the competition will be much more intense.

Entry-Level Positions

Despite this competition, individuals who are skilled, intelligent, and persistent are likely to be successful in finding jobs. Here are some general hints on job hunting in TV.

1. Think small. As in radio, small-market TV stations offer more employment potential than larger-market stations. True, the big markets pay more and have more employees than small markets, but the competition and the number of people looking for jobs will also be greater. Moreover, at a small station, you have a chance to do more and learn more than you might at a larger station.

2. Don't be afraid to start at the bottom. Most industry professionals and employment counselors advise job-seekers to take any type of job that will get them into a TV organization. Once you get in, it is easier to move upward into a position that might be more to your liking. Many successful people in TV started in the mailroom, secretarial pool, or shipping department.

3. Be prepared to move. Your first job will probably not be a lifetime commitment. Most people in TV change jobs several times in their careers. Frequently, the road to advancement in TV consists of moving about and up—from a small station to a large station, from an independent station to a network affiliate, from the station to the network. Most newcomers to TV spend about twelve to eighteen months at their first job.

Upward Mobility

Those interested in producing TV shows might consider looking for jobs as a camera operator, floor manager (the person who gives cues to the talent and makes sure everything in the studio goes smoothly during the telecast), or production assistant (a person who handles all the odd jobs that need to be done during a show). From there you might progress upward to become an assistant director or assistant producer or perhaps a writer. Eventually, you would hope to become a full-fledged director or producer.

Those thinking about a career in TV journalism have to make an early decision. If you are interested in being an on-camera news reporter, your best bet might be to find a general reporting job at a smaller station. If your interests lie behind the camera, your possibilities are varied. You can start out as a news writer or news researcher or even a cameraperson or tape editor. Most people interested in performing before the camera generally stay in that capacity. Upward mobility for general-assignment reporters consists of moving into the anchor position. For anchors, it consists of moving to bigger and more lucrative markets. For those behind the scenes, the first move up will probably be to the assistant news director slot and then on to the news director position.

Sales is the one division that offers the most upward mobility. Unlike radio sales, TV sales usually is harder to break into. Most stations prefer people who have had some experience in selling (many move from radio sales to TV sales). Once a salesperson is established, however, the monetary rewards can be substantial. Salespeople advance their careers by moving to larger markets or by moving up to the sales manager position.

The highest level a person can reach at the local level is the general manager's position. In the past, most general managers have come from the sales department. This trend is likely to continue, but it is also probable that more people who started off in the news departments move into management, since news is becoming more of a moneymaker. Historically, only a few people from the programming side enter top management.

Other Opportunities

A television station is not the only place to look for employment. The cable TV industry is expanding and needs people skilled in every facet of TV—production, sales, programming, and management. As cable provides more local programming and adds more channels, the industry will need more people in promotion, publicity, performance, marketing, and community relations. Allied with cable are the pay-TV services (HBO, Showtime, etc.). These organizations will also need skilled personnel. CATV and pay TV should not be overlooked as potential job sources.

Another emerging employment source is the home video area. The production of prerecorded cassettes and videodiscs represents another area where there are expanding opportunities for those interested in the creative and business sides of TV. Finally, many large companies, such as IBM and Xerox, have in-house production facilities. In fact, some companies have studios that are on a par with many large TV stations. These companies use TV to produce employee training programs and to fill other internal communication needs. Although not as visible as some other parts of the industry, this is an important source of employment for a large number of people.

● ● ● ●

SUGGESTIONS FOR FURTHER READING

The following books contain more information about the concepts and topics discussed in this chapter.

BALDWIN, THOMAS, AND D. S. McVOY, *Cable Communication*, Englewood Cliffs, N.J.: Prentice-Hall, 1988.

DOMINICK, JOSEPH, BARRY SHERMAN, AND GARY COPELAND, *Broadcasting/Cable and Beyond*, New York: McGraw-Hill, 1990.

HEAD, SYDNEY, AND CHRISTOPHER STERLING, *Broadcasting in America*, 6th ed., Boston: Houghton Mifflin, 1990.

HICKMAN, HAROLD, *Television Directing*, New York: McGraw-Hill, 1991.

SMITH, LESLIE, *Perspectives on Radio and Television*, New York: Harper & Row, 1990.

STEINBERG, COBBETT, *TV Facts*, New York: Facts on File, 1985.

SPECIAL
MASS MEDIA
PROFESSIONS

NEWS GATHERING AND REPORTING

The biggest story of the decade was breaking all around him and John Holliman couldn't find his pants. As was his custom, the CNN reporter had carefully laid out a fresh change of clothes so that if anything happened overnight, he would waste little time getting dressed. Now, when every minute counted, he couldn't find his pants.

Holliman had returned to his ninth-floor room at Baghdad's Al Rasheed hotel early on the night of January 16, 1991, to get some much needed sleep. He and his colleagues, Peter Arnett and Bernard Shaw, were covering the continuing crisis in the Persian Gulf and were the only CNN reporters in the Iraqi capital. The deadline for Iraq to pull out of Kuwait had passed and everybody expected something to happen.

Exhausted, Holliman had no trouble falling asleep but he was awakened about 2:30 A.M. by air raid sirens. This had been a fairly common occurrence the last few nights and Holliman was not alarmed. Suddenly, he heard a new sound—the poom-poom-poom of antiaircraft guns. Within a split second, there was a deafening "whump" sound as the explosion of a nearby bomb literally shook the bed loose from its frame. Holliman knew exactly what was happening—the air assault against Iraq had begun.

After a minute or so of confused scrambling, Holliman located his pants and ran down the hall to the room that CNN was using as an office. Arnett and Shaw were already there and Shaw was on a special phone hookup to CNN headquarters in Atlanta urging them to put him on the air as soon as possible. At that moment, both Arnett and Holliman realized that they would probably soon lose all electric power. It dawned on Holliman that without electric power, they would not be able to open the safe in the hotel room. The CNN reporters had stored a large amount of cash in the safe in case they had to make their escape quickly from Baghdad and needed money to smooth the way. While Shaw and Arnett were on the air, Holliman worked away at the safe. He got it open only minutes before the electricity went out.

The CNN trio, dubbed "The Boys in Baghdad," broadcast live the opening air attack on the Iraqi capital, sometimes holding the microphone out the hotel window to pick up the sound of exploding bombs and antiaircraft fire. CNN had scooped the other networks. CNN's special phone hookup bypassed the Iraqi phone system; the other networks' communication system did not. When bombs destroyed the Iraqi phone network, the three network correspondents were off the air.

The trio broadcast for sixteen hours before being shut down by Iraqi authorities. (It turns out that they were able to stay on the air for such a long time because the head of Iraqi security, a man weighing about 300 pounds, was in the hotel's basement bomb shelter. When the electricity went out, the elevators and local phones no longer functioned. Having no desire to walk up ten flights of stairs, the Iraqi simply permitted the broadcast to go on until he was directly ordered to stop it by his superiors.)

*After a harrowing night ride through Iraq to Jordan, John Holliman and Bernard Shaw, two of CNN's
"Boys in Bagdhad," told of their experiences in a CNN interview. (© CNN, Inc.)*

The CNN coverage brought home the immediacy and the impact that broadcast
news can have. Indeed, during the next six weeks, the American public watched TV
news, listened to radio newscasts, and read newspapers and magazines to a far greater
degree than they normally would. The Gulf War demonstrated how important news
is to Americans.

Before anything becomes news, however, it must be reported. An air raid, a city
council meeting, an accident, all must be filtered through the eyes and ears of a
professional news gatherer. A reporter must be aware of the qualities that characterize
a news story, the types of news that exist, and the differences in the way the various
news media covers news. This chapter examines these topics and looks at the career
possibilities of news gathering and reporting.

●●●●

DECIDING WHAT IS NEWS

Out of the millions of things that happen every day, print and electronic journalists
decide what few things are worth reporting. Deciding what is newsworthy is not an
exact science. News values are formed by tradition, technology, organizational policy,
and increasingly by economics. Nonetheless, most journalists agree that there are
common elements that characterize newsworthy events. Below are listed the five
qualities of news about which there is the most agreement.

1. Timeliness. To put it glibly, news is new. Yesterday's news is old news. A
   consumer who picks up the evening paper or turns on the afternoon news
   expects to be told what happened earlier that same day. News is perishable and
   stale news is not interesting.

2. Proximity. News happens close by. Readers and viewers want to learn about their neighborhood, town, or country. All other things being equal, news from close to home is more newsworthy than news from a foreign country. A train derailment in France, for example, is less likely to be reported than a similar derailment in the local trainyard. Proximity, however, means more than a simple measure of distance. Psychological proximity is also important. Subway riders in San Francisco might show interest in a story about rising vigilantism on the New York subways, even though the story is happening 3000 miles away.

3. Prominence. The more important a person, the more valuable he or she is as a news source. Thus, activities of the president and other heads of state attract tremendous media attention. In addition to political leaders, the activities of sports and entertainment figures are also deemed newsworthy. Even the prominence of the infamous has news value. The past lives and recent exploits of many criminals are frequently given media coverage.

4. Consequence. Events that have an impact on a great many people have built-in news value. A tax increase, the decision to lay off thousands of workers, a drought, inflation, an economic downturn—all of these events have consequence. Note that the audience for a particular news item is a big factor in determining its consequence. The closing of a large factory in Kankakee, Illinois, might be page one news there, but it probably wouldn't be mentioned in Keokuk, Iowa.

5. Human Interest. These are stories that arouse some emotion in the audience; stories that are ironic, bizarre, uplifting, or dramatic. Typically, these items concern ordinary people who find themselves in circumstances with which the audience can identify. Thus, when the winner of the state lottery gives half of his winnings to the elderly man who sold him the ticket, it becomes newsworthy. When a ninety-year-old brickmaker from North Carolina volunteers to go to Guyana to help the local construction industry, it becomes news.

In addition to these five traditional elements of news value, there are other things that influence what information gets published or broadcast. Most journalists agree that economics plays a large role. First, some stories cost more to cover than others. It is cheaper to send a reporter or a camera crew to the city council meeting than to assign a team of reporters to investigate city council corruption. The latter would require a long time, extra resources, extra personnel, and patience. All of which cost money. Some news operations might not be willing to pay the price for such a story. Or, conversely, after spending a large sum of money pursuing a story, the news organization might run it, even if it had little traditional news value, simply to justify its cost to management. By the same token, the cost of new technology is reflected in the types of stories that are covered. When TV stations went to electronic news gathering (ENG), stories that could be covered live became more important. In fact, many organizations, conscious of the scheduling of TV news programs, planned their meetings and/or demonstrations during the newscast to enhance their chances for TV coverage. Further, after helicopters became an expensive investment at many large TV stations, traffic jams, fires, beautiful sunsets, and other stories that lent themselves to airborne journalism suddenly became newsworthy.

The relationship between economics and network TV news was vividly demonstrated in 1987 when the three networks, reacting to declining profits, sharply reduced the budgets of their news departments. The cutbacks triggered a round of controversy between news staffs and management that ultimately led to unprecedented hearings called by the House Telecommunication Subcommittee to examine how corporate economics has affected news coverage.

A news reporter in action: Light-weight cameras and videotape recorders as well as electronic news-gathering (ENG) technology make it easy to broadcast from the scene of a news event. (John Coletti/Stock Boston)

When the controversy finally settled down, the networks accepted the reality that declining revenue would mean changes in the way they gathered and reported the news. In fact, continuing economic hard times at the networks and the huge costs of covering the Gulf War have prompted more cuts in personnel and services. NBC shut down bureaus in Miami and New York, and ABC closed its St. Louis and Rome operations. The networks have also relegated more of their routine news gathering to outside services. ABC, for example, relies on World Television News (which it partially owns) for footage from abroad. NBC has a similar arrangement with Visnews. CBS has recently discussed plans for a news-gathering arrangement with CNN.

Newspapers are not immune from the pervasive influence of the bottom line. As more corporations and large newspaper chains dominate the business, more MBAs than journalists are becoming newspaper executives. The topics of greatest interest to this new breed of manager are marketing surveys, budget plans, organizational goals, and strategic planning—not the news-gathering process. This new orientation usually shows up in the newspaper's pages. The paper's "look" improves: more color, better graphics, an appealing design; there are more features: food sections, personal finance columns, entertainment guides, and reviews. In all, the paper becomes a slickly packaged product. At the same time, however, the amount of space devoted to local news decreases, reporters are discouraged from going after expensive investigative stories, and aggressive pieces about the local business community tend to disappear. Many experienced editors fear that the new corporate breed of managers will change the traditional news values of American journalism.

Economics alters news values in other, more subtle, ways. Ben Bagdikian, in *The Media Monopoly*, noted that the rise of media conglomerates (big companies that own newspapers, broadcasting stations, and other properties) poses a problem for journalism. Can a newspaper or TV station adequately cover the actions of its parent company? For example, could NBC news objectively report the activities if G.E. was involved in some alleged wrongdoing? (Such a situation occurred in 1989. A report on defective airplane bolts done by WMAQ-TV in Chicago criticized the General Electric Company. When a summary of the report aired on NBC's *Today* program the reference to G.E. was edited out. After receiving some harsh publicity for the action, the *Today* show aired a follow-up story that did mention G.E.'s involvement.) Or could a Gannett-owned paper adequately cover events at *USA Today*, another Gannett property? Economics plays a part in local markets as well. Newspapers make their money from circulation figures, and it has been charged that some publishers pander to public taste to inflate circulation figures. Media baron Rupert Murdoch was criticized for this when he took over the *New York Post*. He was chastised for placing great emphasis on sensationalism in an attempt to attract new readers. (He eventually sold the *Post* and its new owner has toned it down.) A similar situation exists in local TV news. The local newscast is an extremely profitable item for most TV stations, and competition is fierce. During special ratings weeks—called "sweeps" (see Chapter 20)—when viewing in every market is measured, a whole new set of news values comes into play at many TV stations. All of a sudden, special programs on teenage prostitution, UFOs, pornography, the singles scene, and similar reports appear on the news. The quest for higher ratings (and revenues) at the expense of traditional news values is evident.

● ● ● ●
CATEGORIES OF NEWS AND REPORTING

Generally, news can be broken down into three broad categories: (1) hard news, (2) features or soft news, and (3) investigative reports.

Hard News

Hard news stories make up the bulk of news reporting. They typically embody the first four of the five traditional news values discussed above. Hard news consists of basic facts: who, what, when, where, how. It is news of important public events, such as government actions, international happenings, social conditions, the economy, crime, environment, and science. Hard news has significance for large numbers of people. The front sections of a newspaper or magazine and the lead stories of a radio or TV newscast are usually filled with hard news.

There is a standard technique used to report hard news. In the print media, it is the traditional inverted pyramid form. The main facts of the story are delivered in the first sentence (called the lead) in an unvarnished, no-nonsense style. Less important facts come next, with the least important and most expendable facts at the end. This structure aids the reporter (who uses it to compose facts quickly), the editor (who can lop off the last few paragraphs of a story to make it fit the page without doing wholesale damage to the sense of the story), and the reader (who can tell at a glance if he or she is interested in all, some, or none of the story). This format has been criticized for being predictable and old-fashioned. More literary writing styles have been suggested as alternatives, but the inverted pyramid has survived and will probably be around far into the future.

In the broadcast media, with the added considerations of limited time, sound, and video, the inverted pyramid format is not used. Instead, broadcast reporting follows a square format. The information level stays about the same throughout the story. There's usually no time for the less important facts that would come in the last paragraphs of a newspaper story. TV and radio news stories use either a "hard" or a "soft" lead. A hard lead contains the most important information, the basic facts of the story. For example, "The city council has rejected a plan to build the Fifth Street overpass." A soft lead is used to get the viewers' attention; it may not convey much information. For example, "That proposed Fifth Street overpass is in the news again." The lead is then supported by the body of the story, which introduces new information and amplifies what was mentioned in the lead. The summation, the final few sentences in the report, can be used to personalize the main point ("This means that the price you pay for gasoline is likely to go up"), introduce another fact, or discuss future developments.

Of course, the writing style of broadcast news is completely different. The writing is more informal, conversational, and simple. In addition, it's designed to complement sound bites (the sound of the newsmaker) or videotape segments.

Soft News

Soft, or **feature**, **news** covers a wide territory. Features may not be very timely or have much importance to the lives of the audience. The one thing that all soft news has in common is that it interests the audience. Features typically rely on human interest for their news value. They appeal to people's curiosity, sympathy, skepticism, or amazement. They can be about places, people, animals, topics, events, or products. Some stories that would be classified as soft or feature news might include the birth of a kangaroo at the local zoo, a personality sketch of a local resident who has a small part in an upcoming movie, a cook who moonlights as a stand-up comedian, a teenager who mistakenly gets a tax refund check for $400,000 instead of $40, and so forth.

Features are entertaining and the audience likes them. Indeed, one of the trends of the mid-1980s was the growing popularity of television and print vehicles based primarily on soft content, for example, *Entertainment Tonight*, *E!*, the cable entertainment network, *Showbiz Tonight*, *People*, *Life Styles of the Rich and Famous*, *Us* magazine, the *Life* section of *USA Today*. Even the prime-time news magazines *60 Minutes* and *20/20* have substantial amounts of soft news. Likewise, the fiercely competitive early morning network TV shows are turning more to soft news.

The techniques for reporting features are as varied as the features themselves. In the print media, features seldom follow the inverted pyramid pattern. The main point of the feature is often withheld to the end, much like the punch line to a joke. Other features might be written in chronological order; others might start with a shocking statement such as "Your secrets just might kill you" and then go on with an explanation, "If you have a medical problem, you should wear a Medic-Alert bracelet." Still other features can be structured in the question-and-answer format. In short, reporters are free to adopt whatever structure they think is suitable.

TV features are more common than radio features. In some large TV markets, one or more reporters may be assigned to cover nothing but features. Almost all stations have a feature file where story ideas are catalogued. If a local station does not have the resources to produce local features, there are syndication companies that will provide general-interest features for a fee. Broadcast features also use a variety of formats. Humorous leads and delaying the main point until the end sometimes work well, a technique often used by Andy Rooney in his features for *60 Minutes*. Other times a simple narrative structure, used in everyday storytelling, will be quite effective, as evidenced by the award winning *On the Road with Charles Kuralt*. The interview format is also popular, particularly when the feature is about a well-known personality.

Investigative Reports

As the name implies, **investigative reports** are those that unearth significant information about matters of public importance through the use of nonroutine information-gathering methods. Most day-to-day reporting involves investigation, but the true investigative piece requires an extraordinary expenditure of time and energy. Since the Watergate affair was uncovered by a pair of Washington newspaper reporters, investigative reporting has also been looked upon as primarily concerned with exposing corruption in high places. This connotation is somewhat unfortunate for at least two reasons. In the first place, it encouraged a few short-sighted reporters to look upon themselves as self-appointed guardians of the public good and to indiscriminately pursue all public officials, sometimes using questionable techniques in the hope of uncovering some indiscretion. Much of this investigative journalism turned out to be insignificant. In the second place, this emphasis on exposing political corruption distracted attention from the fact that investigative reporting can concentrate on other topics and perform a valuable public service.

Investigative reports require a good deal of time and money. Because of this heavy investment, they are generally longer than the typical print or broadcast news item. Broadcast investigative reports are usually packaged in thirty- or sixty-minute documentaries, in a series of short reports spread through the week on the nightly newscast (called "minidocs"), or in a ten- to fifteen-minute segment of a news magazine program (such as *60 Minutes* or *20/20*). Print investigative pieces are usually run as a series of articles. Sometimes magazines will print a special issue devoted to a single report, as did *Time* in 1991 when it published a special volume on "Women in the '90s."

Interestingly, the mechanics of investigative reporting are similar in the print and broadcasting media. First, a reporter gets a tip or a lead on a story from one of his or her sources. The next phase consists of fact gathering and cultivating news sources. Eventually, a thick file of information on the topic is developed. These facts are then organized into a coherent piece that is easily digestible by the audience. Here the differences between print and broadcast reporting techniques become apparent. The print journalist can spend a good deal of time providing background and relating past

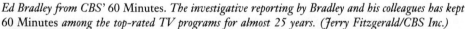

Ed Bradley from CBS' 60 Minutes. *The investigative reporting by Bradley and his colleagues has kept* 60 Minutes *among the top-rated TV programs for almost 25 years. (Jerry Fitzgerald/CBS Inc.)*

events to the topic. Additionally, the print investigative reporter can draw heavily upon published documents and public records. (The Pentagon Papers story, for example, depended primarily on official government documents.) In television and radio, the investigative report usually has less time to explore background issues. Documents and records are hard to portray on TV, and less emphasis is placed on them. In their place, the TV reporter must come up with interviews and other visual aspects that will illustrate the story. Moreover, the format of the TV report will sometimes dictate its form. As noted above, one of the most popular formats on TV is the minidoc. Minidocs run for a brief period each day for several days. At the beginning of each, the story has to be summarized or updated. Toward the end of the week, the summary might take up the first half of the report.

Some noteworthy examples of recent investigative efforts include these from 1989–1991. The San Jose *Mercury-News* published an exposé of the self-help organization "est." The Associated Press won an award for its lengthy coverage of how the savings and loan scandal affected the average citizen. Twelve *Newsday* reporters spent eight months preparing a ten-part series on segregation on Long Island. Television station WBRZ in Baton Rouge, Louisiana, aired an hour-long documentary on irregularities in the state's insurance industry. KCTS-TV in Seattle and the *MacNeil/Lehrer NewsHour* received a Peabody award for the investigation of illegal practices in the trucking industry.

● ● ● ●

THE NEWS FLOW

As mentioned in Chapter 1, one of the characteristics of mass communication is the presence of a large number of gatekeepers. This fact is easily seen in the gathering and reporting of news. Reporting is a team effort, and quite a few members of the team serve as gatekeepers.

Proximity and Disaster

In late 1989, two plane crashes happened at about the same time. In one crash, a USAir jet slid into the East River while attempting to take off from New York's LaGuardia Airport. Two people died. In the African nation of Chad, a French plane exploded, apparently the victim of a terrorist bomb. One hundred and seventy-one people died. Despite the difference in casualties, the *Los Angeles Times* ran ten stories about the New York crash and six about the Chad tragedy. The *New York Times* ran twelve stories about the LaGuardia mishap and six about the one in Chad. ABC's *Nightline* devoted an entire show to the LaGuardia accident but didn't mention the Chad crash.

This is not an isolated case. In most incidents, the severity of a disaster has little to do with how much coverage it gets. To elaborate,

in a study reported in the *Journal of Communication*, researcher William Adams compared TV news coverage of natural disasters that occurred around the world. An earthquake in Italy that killed a thousand people got about seven and a half minutes of air time. Another earthquake in Indonesia that killed nine times as many got twenty seconds. Psychological proximity was evident in the factor that was most closely connected to coverage time: the number of U.S. tourists likely to visit the region. In fact, based on his data, Adams was able to work out an illustrative if somewhat callous table of equivalencies between deaths and news coverage: One Western European death equaled three Eastern European deaths, nine Latin American deaths, eleven Middle Eastern deaths, and twelve Asian deaths.

Print Media

Figure 14-1 illustrates the typical organization in a newspaper newsroom. Looking first at the newspaper, there are two main sources of news: staff reports and the wire services. Other, less important sources include feature syndicates and handouts and releases from various sources. Let's first examine how news is gathered by newspaper personnel. The city editor is the captain of the news-reporting team. He or she assigns stories to reporters and supervises their work. There are two types of reporters: general assignment and beat. A beat reporter covers some topics on a regular basis such as the police beat or the city hall beat. A general-assignment reporter covers whatever assignments come up. A typical day for the general-assignment reporter might consist of covering an auto accident, a speech by a visiting politician, and a rock concert. Stories from the reporters are passed along to the city editor, where they are okayed and sent to the copy desk for further editing. The managing editor and assistant managing editor are also part of the news team. They are responsible for the overall daily preparation of the paper. Let's review the news flow and the various gatekeepers in the process. The city editor can decide not to cover a story in the first place or not to run a story if the event is covered. The reporter has a wide latitude of judgment over what he or she chooses to include in the story. The copy editor can change the story as needed, and the managing editor has the power to emphasize or deemphasize the story to fit the day's needs.

Broadcast Media

The sources of news for the broadcast media are similar to those for the newspaper. Special wire services cater to television and radio stations, and local reporters are assigned to cover nearby events. In addition, many broadcast newsrooms subscribe to syndicated news services or, if affiliated with a network, have access to the net's news feeds.

The broadcast newsroom, as seen in Figure 14-2, is organized along different lines from its print counterpart. At the local station, the news director is in charge of the overall news operation. In large stations, most news directors spend their time on administrative work—personnel, budgets, equipment, and so on. In smaller stations, most news directors might perform other functions (such as being the anchorperson) as well. Next in command is the executive producer. This person supervises the work of all the producers in the newsroom. Typically, there are producers assigned to the

FIGURE 14-1 *Organization of a newspaper newsroom.*

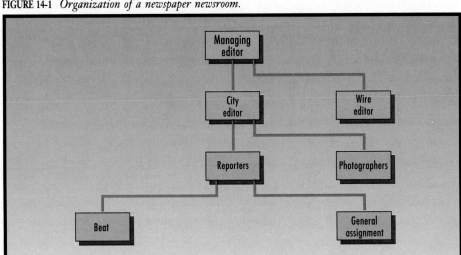

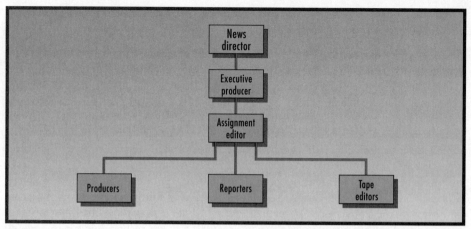

FIGURE 14-2 *Organization of a TV newsroom.*

early morning, noon, evening, and late night newscasts. In addition to looking after the other producers, the executive producer might also produce the evening news, typically the station's most important. As is probably clear by now, producers are important people in TV news. Their actual duties, however, are not well known. In capsule form, here are some of the things that a news producer does:

1. decides what stories are covered, who covers them, and how they are covered

2. decides the order in which stories appear in the newscast

3. determines the amount of time each story is given

4. writes copy for some stories

5. integrates live reports into the newscasts

The assignment editor works closely with the news producer. The assignment editor is in charge of coverage planning and execution. He or she assigns and monitors the activities of reporters, camera crews, and other people in the field. Since speed is

Hyperlocal News

There may come a time when every neighborhood cable system has its own version of CNN. Since local TV news shows can't possibly cover all of the communities that make up their market, cable systems are filling in the gaps. Probably the most successful is News 12, a twenty-four-hour cable service operated by the Cablevision system on Long Island. News 12, as you might imagine, spends a great deal of time on local traffic and commuting news but it also covers more traditional stories. Its reporting on a 1990 plane crash near Kennedy Airport won it a local Emmy.

A similar channel recently started operating in Orange County, California. This channel even sent a news crew to Saudi Arabia to interview Orange County soldiers stationed there during the Persian Gulf War. Other local cable news channels are scheduled for Chicago, Washington, D.C., and New York City.

So far neighborhood news has not been profitable. All of the existing systems are still operating in the red. Despite this, they all have high hopes that the local-local news will bring in enough viewers to attract advertising dollars.

important in most broadcast news operations, there is great pressure on the assignment editor to get the crews to the story in the shortest amount of time.

Then, of course, there are the "glamour" jobs—on-air reporters and anchors. Most reporters in broadcast news function as general-assignment reporters, although the large-market stations might have one or two regularly assigned to a beat, such as the entertainment scene. In many stations, anchors will occasionally do field reports, but most of the time they perform their work in the studio, preparing for the upcoming newscast. In addition to the people seen on camera, there are quite a few workers that no one ever sees or hears. Photographers usually accompany reporters to shoot the video. Tape editors trim the footage into segments that fit with the time allotted to the story. Big stations also have news writers and production assistants who pull slides and arrange other visuals needed during the newscast.

Obviously, the chain of gatekeepers in broadcast news is a long and complicated one. Starting with the assignment editor and ending with the anchor, usually more than a half-dozen people have some say-so over the final shape of the newscast. Sometimes, the way a story ends up might be drastically different from the way it started at the beginning of the gatekeeper chain. It is not unusual for a reporter to work all day on a story and then be told by a producer that the story will get only forty seconds of air time.

• • • •

THE WIRE SERVICES

The next time you read your local newspaper, you will probably notice that many stories have the initials AP or UPI in the datelines. The AP stands for Associated Press and the UPI for United Press International. These two organizations are called wire services, and together they provide you with most of the news about what's going on outside your local community.

The Associated Press can trace its roots back to 1848 when several New York newspapers chipped in to cover the cost of sending small boats out to meet incoming ships from Europe to obtain the latest news. This news-gathering service was expanded during the 1850s when it started providing news to member papers via the telegraph (hence the name "wire" service). This new organization was called the New York Associated Press. In 1892, a regional press service called the Western Associated Press established a rival wire service, called simply the Associated Press, and began to provide news service to member papers. The New York organization folded soon after the debut of this new service. Eventually, the Associated Press moved its headquarters to New York, where it is currently located.

United Press was formed in 1907 by newspaper-chain owner E. W. Scripps. Scripps was dissatisfied with the service his papers had been receiving from the AP and started his own news-gathering organization. In 1958, the United Press absorbed the International News Service, a competitor that was founded in 1909 by William Randolph Hearst, and changed its name to United Press International.

In simplified form, here's how the wire services work. A correspondent covers a local news event; for the sake of illustration, let's say it's a fire. He or she reports the event to the bureau chief of the local wire service. If the bureau chief thinks the story is newsworthy enough, the chief will send it on to the state bureau to go out on the state or regional wire. The state bureau chief then decides whether to send it on for inclusion on the national wire. All in all, the wire services are the eyes and ears for local papers and broadcasting stations that can't afford to have people stationed all over the country.

The AP has about a hundred regional bureaus in the United States and about sixty foreign bureaus. Members of the association pay for this service according to their size and circulation. A large paper, such as the *New York Times*, will pay more

Local papers and broadest stations rely on the wire services for national and international stories to which they would otherwise not have access. Shown here is the newsroom at UPI headquarters in New York City. (Robert McElroy/Woodfin Camp)

than a small-town paper. Approximately 1200 papers use AP's service. United Press International also has about a hundred domestic bureaus and a large number of foreign offices. As with the AP, member payment is based on the subscriber's size and audience.

Together, the two wire services churn out about 8 million words every day. The news is transmitted in about a dozen different languages. AP and UPI also have facilities to transmit news photos electronically. In addition, both agencies offer a wide range of services to their clients. AP, for example, has a weather wire, a sports wire, and a financial wire. Both agencies also provide a broadcast wire that is used by radio and TV stations in preparing their newscasts. An audio service is also available to radio stations as well as a video service that displays written news summaries electronically on the TV screen and is used by cable TV systems. In the early 1990s, AP had 10,000 customers worldwide, including about 1300 daily papers. It also served about 4000 domestic radio and TV stations plus another 400 or so cable systems. UPI had about 7000 customers, including approximately 900 newspapers, about 3000 radio and TV stations, and several hundred cable systems. As of this writing, UPI was in continuing financial difficulty, a situation that dates back several years. Its parent company, Infotechnology Inc., filed for bankruptcy in 1991 and started a search to find a potential buyer. UPI was acquired in 1992 by the London-based Middle East Broadcasting Centre. Even with the new owner, UPI's long-term future is uncertain.

AP and UPI are not without competition. The New York Times News Service and the Los Angeles Times–Washington Post News Service are rivals that also offer supplemental news stories, not generally covered by the major wire services, to their subscribers. Some newspaper groups also have their own special news services. For example, the Gannett News Service sends material to all the Gannett-owned local papers and to *USA Today*. There's competition overseas as well. The British-based Reuters agency now has ten bureaus in the United States. Reuters gained prominence and praise as a result of its coverage of the Persian Gulf War. Agence-France-Press is also a formidable worldwide competitor.

• • • •

MEDIA DIFFERENCES IN NEWS COVERAGE

It doesn't take a genius to see that broadcast journalism is different from print journalism. Over the years these differences have led many to argue which is "better": print or broadcast journalism. Proponents of print journalism correctly point out that the script of a typical network evening newscast would fill up less than one page of a typical newspaper. They argue that the print media have the potential for depth reporting and lengthy analysis, elements that are usually missing from broadcast news because of time pressure. Moreover, some critics have taken to looking down on broadcast journalism, labeling it "show biz" and commenting on its shallowness. The supporters of broadcast news answer that measuring a network newscast by comparing its word count to that of a newspaper is using the wrong yardstick. They suggest it is more appropriate to ask how many pages of a newspaper it would take to print the thousands of different visuals that regularly accompany a TV newscast. The emergence of twenty-four-hour news channels and late-night newscasts, say these proponents, now makes it possible to cover news in depth. Print journalism is criticized for being slow, old-fashioned, and dull.

And so the debate goes. Unfortunately, the argument covers up the essential fact: Both print and broadcast news have their own unique strengths and weaknesses. One should not be considered better than the other. Both play important roles in informing the public.

Words and Pictures

Having said that, however, it is also important to add that the inherent characteristics of both media have an impact on what news gets covered and how it gets covered. In the first place, the physical structure of each medium means that there will be some obvious differences. Print journalism is organized in space; TV journalism in time. Hence, the newspaper can contain far more stories than the typical TV newscast. Moreover, there can be more details provided about any one story. Within the limited time constraints of broadcasting (even including the all-news stations), it is hard for radio and television to provide much more than a headline service and in-brief look at a few stories. If a topic is treated in depth, the amount of information and detail included is typically far less than what is contained in its newspaper counterpart. Some observers have said that TV is better at transmitting experience or impressions, while the newspaper is better at facts and information. In any case, stories dealing with lengthy analysis and complicated interpretation tend to be better suited to the print medium.

Second, print news has permanence. A reader can go back and reread difficult and complicated parts as many times as necessary for understanding. An idea missed the first time can be reexamined. Broadcast news does not have this luxury. Radio and TV newscasts are written for a single exposure. This means that complicated and complex stories are sometimes difficult to cover in the electronic media. Newspapers and magazines have a built-in advantage when it comes to reporting these types of stories. Of course, television news has the advantage of the visual dimension. TV news directors ask if a story has action, visual appeal, something that can be seen. Faced with a choice

Video News Releases

You may recall seeing news coverage of the first McDonald's to open in the Soviet Union—long lines of people waiting patiently for their turn to pass beneath the golden arches. It might surprise you to know that this coverage may have actually been provided by a firm working for McDonald's. A Toronto-based PR firm supplied the footage as part of a video news release (VNR) to local TV stations and the major networks. The PR firm estimated that about 22 million people saw the pictures. Or maybe you saw a report on the 16th Annual International Rotten Sneaker contest. You might have thought this was a clever feature story. The truth is that the story was a VNR distributed by Odor Eaters. Or maybe you saw a cute feature about a cow in Maine that had spots on its side that were shaped like Mickey Mouse's head. This was actually a VNR distributed by the Walt Disney Company.

A video news release is the electronic equivalent to the traditional paper press release so well-known in the newspaper business. The potential problem with VNRs is that they have become so carefully crafted that it is often hard to tell them apart from a regular news report put together by the station.

VNRs have grown in popularity lately since news time at most stations has increased and the news budget has shrunk. Consequently, stations are scrambling for an inexpensive way to fill air time. VNRs fill the bill. They are timely, slickly produced, and free. One major distributor estimates that as many as 5000 VNRs were circulated to TV news operations in 1991. Many stations run the VNRs in their original form; others just take the video and do their own voice-overs.

However they are used, VNRs have sparked controversy in the newsroom. Some experts think they undermine the integrity of TV news and mislead the viewer. Others suggest that all VNRs that are shown should be identified as coming from an outside source.

Next time you watch TV news, see if you can spot any stories that might be VNRs. Usually, a product logo or a product name will be plainly visible or at least mentioned. If nothing else, VNRs may make us more alert to the content of TV news.

between two events that are of equal importance, the television news organization will most likely choose the one that has better pictures available. Sometimes the visual dimension of a story may be further enhanced by studio graphics, as happens when a smoking gun or the word "murder" is inserted over the anchorperson's shoulder. Obviously, the visual dimension is important and represents a powerful weapon in the arsenal of TV reporting. Some of the visuals carried by TV news are deeply ingrained in the national memory: Boris Yeltsin atop a tank during the attempted coup, the hostages in the Middle East, the Chinese students in Beijing, antiaircraft fire over Baghdad. Nonetheless, it is easy for television news to needlessly cater to the visual and run items that have little news value other than their potential for dramatic pictures. There have been many instances of a small, relatively insignificant fire leading a local newscast simply because good pictures were available. Murders and violent events that have occurred half a world away show up on American TV not because of their intrinsic news value but because the pictures are dramatic.

This is not to say that print reporters don't like a visual story. Quite the opposite. The advent of good color reproduction in newspapers and magazines means that a good photo to accompany a story is a real plus. Recall that *Life* magazine brought the news in pictures to eager readers for decades. It is fair to say, however, that the print media are less likely to be influenced by only the visual impact of a story.

In October of 1988, three California gray whales stayed too long at their feeding grounds north of Point Barrow, Alaska, and were trapped by ice. Normally, this would not draw attention; every year several whales get caught beneath the ice and perish. In the spring their carcasses wash ashore and serve as food for polar bears and other animals. Their deaths are lamentable, but they are a necessary part of the food chain that sustains the fragile Arctic ecosystem. These three whales, however, were luckier than most. They got trapped just twenty miles from a satellite uplink earth station. The story of their rescue reveals a lot about how news, particularly TV news, works.

Eskimos first discovered the trapped whales and reported their plight to two biologists working for the Department of Wildlife Management. The two biologists brought along a two-person camera crew from the local TV station and shot a powerful video of the whales struggling to breathe.

News of the video reached TV stations in the lower 48 and a Seattle TV station alerted NBC News, which used the footage to close Tom Brokaw's nightly newscast. Once the story broke, Point Barrow, Alaska, became the focal point of one of the biggest media events of the late 1980s. During the next two weeks, 150 journalists from four continents would descend on Barrow (that's about one journalist for every seventeen residents). In addition, representatives from the U.S. Coast Guard, the big oil companies, Greenpeace, and the American and Soviet governments turned Barrow into a boomtown. Motel rooms (what few there were) went for $300 a night. Eskimos charged $400 each way for dog sled rides to the whales; a five-minute shower went for $50. Ultimately, about $6 million was spent covering the saga of the whales.

Why all the commotion? The story was perfect for television. It had great visuals. The video of the whales rising to breathe was compelling and forceful. It even overshadowed the less photogenic upcoming U.S. presidential elections. Just three weeks before the national elections, the whales led all of the three network newscasts; the Bush-Dukakis race took a back seat.

The story was simple and required little analysis. It was a race for freedom; the whales would either make it or they wouldn't. TV has trouble covering more complicated stories. For example, alcohol and drug abuse are higher among the Eskimo population in Barrow than among any other ethnic group in the rest of the U.S. The complicated reasons for this were not explored by the national news agencies.

Third, the story had tremendous human interest value. Whales were a hot topic and efforts to save them made for a great emotional appeal that seemed to involve everybody. (After NBC first aired the story, their switchboards were jammed with people calling up and offering to help. Less involving stories are less likely to make a national newscast.) For example, the government of Iceland nearly fell as a result of the publicity given the whales. Iceland, which has a whaling industry which killed seventy-five whales in 1988, became the target of West German activists who seized upon the whale publicity to urge a boycott of all Icelandic fish products. The government finally enacted a two-year moratorium on whaling. Ironically, the Soviet Union, which slaughtered more than 150 whales that same year, was praised because one of its icebreakers helped save the trapped whales. Also not making much of a splash on the network news was the fact that Japan, which supposedly signed an agreement in 1986 to outlaw commercial whaling for five years, was still very much in the business. A loophole in the 1986 agreement gave Japan the right to hunt whales for scientific purposes. By the late 1980s, the Japanese were killing more than a thousand whales every year for "scientific" reasons, about the same number that were harvested when commercial whaling was allowed.

Finally, the story eventually took on a life of its own. There was so much media attention that the story became important simply because of the media attention. TV crews from Japan and Australia traveled thousands of miles to Alaska to cover not so much the event itself but the

(Continued)

media attention surrounding the event. The story got so big it eclipsed other potentially newsworthy happenings in the area. During the height of the efforts to save the whales, three children perished in a fire that occurred right across the street from the Barrow Fire Statiion. The firefighters had gone home early to get some sleep. They were exhausted from working long hours to help save the trapped whales. Few news agencies even mentioned this tragedy.

The media event finally ended when two of the three whales survived and made it to open water. Biologists considered tagging the whales with an electronic device so that their ultimate fate might be monitored. This was not done, in part because of fear of the backlash that might occur if both whales subsequently perished before making it back to their feeding grounds off California—that would have ruined the story.

Print and Broadcast Journalists

A second key difference has to do with the fact that in TV news, the appearance and personality of the reporter are an important part of the process. This situation is in direct contrast with print journalism, where the reporter stays relatively anonymous with perhaps only a byline for identification. Very few newspaper reporters become nationally known figures (Bob Woodward and Carl Bernstein, the Watergate reporters, are an obvious exception). In TV, the person reading or reporting the news is part of the story. TV news is not anonymous; each story has a face to go with it. Repeated exposure of newcasters on the local and the network levels has turned many of them into celebrities or "stars" in their own right. One of the explanations for this is that some viewers evidently develop what amounts to a personal relationship or a sense of empathy with reporters and anchors. There are many stories that illustrate this peculiar audience-reporter relationship. When Dan Rather replaced Walter Cronkite at CBS, news executives tried all sorts of things to make him look appealing to the audience. Finally, one winter night in 1982, Rather wore a sweater under his jacket. Few people remember anything about what stories Rather reported that night, but almost everyone remembered his sweater. During her first years on the *Today* show, correspondent Jane Pauley received more comments about the way she wore her hair than about any of the stories she covered. Examples abound at the local level as well. The late Fahey Flynn, longtime anchor at WLS-TV in Chicago, wore a bow tie as his trademark. One year a new management team came to the station and in an attempt to make him look younger replaced his bow tie with the traditional long necktie. The extremely negative response of the audience caught the station's management by surprise, and Flynn quickly reverted to his familiar bow tie. Apparently, audience involvement with reporters is much more prevalent in TV than in print.

As personalities in TV news became more popular with the audience, they were able to command higher salaries. Annual salaries for the three network anchors range from about $1.8 million (Peter Jennings) to $2.5 million (Dan Rather). Even at the local level, salaries between $250,000 and $750,000 are common in large markets. Not surprisingly, with all this money at stake, many well-known broadcast journalists are being represented by agents. The entrance of the agent into the news arena has given TV journalism some problems all its own. Some journalists have negotiated contracts that safeguard them from general-assignment reporting and other less glamorous tasks; others have a contractual clause that guarantees them so much air time per week; still others have been granted total editorial control over their reports. The situation has become so widespread that a session at a recent convention of radio–TV news directors was entitled "The Most Important People in TV News Are Not in TV and Not in News." The session had to do with how to deal with agents representing TV newscasters.

Yet another difference between print and broadcast journalists is the amount of control that outside news consultants have on the news itself. Market research consultants are employed by both newspaper and broadcasting organizations, but their activities are most noticeable at local TV stations. Consultants introduced the audience survey to local stations; they made recommendations to management based on what the public said they wanted to see in local news, not on what journalists thought should be in the newscast—a fundamental shift in the traditional definition of news. The heyday for the consultants was the 1970s, exactly the same time that local TV newscasts were becoming extremely profitable. Station management soon realized that increased news ratings meant increased revenues, and increased ratings were what the consultants promised to deliver.

Recently, local TV newscasts have returned to a more traditional approach to covering the news. This doesn't mean that consultants have disappeared; they are still a strong force in local TV news. (It's easy to see their influence, particularly if you travel across the country. The local TV news in Anchorage looks very much like the local TV news in Atlanta. Newscast formats, styles, and even the anchorpeople all seem quite familiar—a direct result of stations all over the country using the same consultants.)

Technology and TV News

The last difference we shall discuss concerns two sets of initials that have had tremendous impact on TV news—**electronic news gathering (ENG)** and **satellite news gathering (SNG)**. We'll look at ENG first.

Back in the 1950s and 1960s, television cameras were clumsy, heavy, and needed a lot of light. Consequently, they were studio-bound equipment. If news was to be

The 1991 Gulf War was the first to carry live broadcasts from the front; consequently, interviews such as this were monitored carefully by the military to make sure no sensitive information was transmitted. (D. Hudson/Sygma)

covered in the field, it had to be done on film. Film cameras were portable but had one major disadvantage: The film had to be developed before it could be shown on the news. Getting pictures of an event that happened thousands of miles away might take hours since the film had to be shot, sent back by airplane, developed, edited, and broadcast. The ENG revolution in the mid-1970s changed all of that. At the heart of the revolution was technology. Small, lightweight cameras and videotape recorders meant that pictures of news events could get on the air much quicker. Videotape is ready to edit immediately after it is shot. Second, with advances in helicopter, microwave, and satellite technology, ENG made it possible to broadcast live from the scenes of major stories. News could be shown as it was happening. With ENG, TV can cover a war, an attempted assassination, or a disaster in real time, or very close to it. The story may not be as complete as it might be in the next issue of *Time* or *Newsweek*, but it is much more immediate.

This benefit, however, was not without its risks. When ENG first came on the scene, there was a tendency for news directors to use it simply because it was there, without regard for the newsworthiness of the event itself. There were times when reporters did live reports from places where news had happened hours earlier or was about to happen or did live interviews with people where a taped interview might have sufficed. Things that could be covered live suddenly possessed elevated news value. It took a while to learn that immediacy was not an automatic virtue in news reporting.

By the same token, a live interview is an unedited interview. Vulgarity, obscenity, and demagoguery have all been included in many live ENG interviews. The reporter in the live situation has special responsibilities and problems to face (see box below). A live broadcast attracts a crowd. Sometimes the crowd is friendly; other times it is nasty or tries to make the reporter's life miserable. More than a few correspondents have been showered with water, beer, or worse while doing a live report.

The Dangers of Live ENG

News reporters are well aware of the many things that can go wrong during a live report from the field. It takes an agile mind to cope with all the complications. For example, a reporter in a northeastern city was assigned to do a story on an increase in bus fares. A perfect spot, thought her news director, for a live interview with some disgruntled bus riders.

The reporter was sent to a metropolitan bus stop where she found three typical bus riders waiting for the 6:10 bus that would take them to their homes far away in the suburbs. This seemed to work out fine because the reporter was scheduled to go on the air live at 6:02 and do a three-minute interview segment. She lined up her three interviewees and waited for her cue. By this time, she only had about five minutes to wait before the news show went on the air.

Then things started to go wrong. A gang of teens rode by on their bicycles and started shouting obscenities at the reporter. Luckily, she and her camera operator managed to chase them away before six o'clock. At one minute after six, the reporter heard through her earpiece that her report was going to be delayed a bit. She and her three bus-riding interviewees waited patiently. At exactly ten minutes after six, the reporter heard the director say that they would be coming to her for her three-minute report in a matter of seconds. She breathed a sigh of relief. Suddenly, the 6:10 bus pulled up and the three riders, not willing to wait another hour for the next bus, got on. The bus doors closed and the bus drove off, leaving the reporter completely alone with not another person in sight. At that very moment, the ENG camera went live and the reporter faced the longest three minutes of her career.

Live reports also run the additional risk of violating standards of good taste or ethics. There is no eraser in live TV news; the reporter can't go back and do it over. Going live to the scene of an accident carries with it the chance of televising scenes of extreme gore or gruesomeness. ENG offers new opportunities for a reporter to invade someone's privacy. A hostage or terrorist situation presents special problems. In these instances the news value of a live report must be closely examined.

The experiences of live news coverage during the Persian Gulf War demonstrated once again the hazards of instantaneous reporting. During a live transmission from Tel Aviv, Israel, a CBS correspondent reported that seven missiles had just hit Jerusalem. He later had to admit that the report was in error. CBS also had to retract a report which stated that Israeli planes had retaliated against Iraq for its missile attacks. CNN erroneously reported that Iraq had launched a chemical weapons attack. The problem of obtaining dependable and reliable information is greatest when going live.

SNG is a relatively recent trend but its effects on the traditional affiliate—network news relationship could be far-reaching. About 200 TV stations, most of them in the large markets, have specially equipped vans or trucks that enable them to cover and transmit live stories from any location. The SNG vehicle uplinks the story to a communication satellite, which in turn sends it to the local station. SNG allows local stations to be on the scene of national and international news stories, a service that only the networks previously provided. For example, the local station's anchors could travel to Saudi Arabia in 1991 and report live on the impact that the war had on Portland, Austin, Jacksonville, or wherever they came from. Most local station news directors prefer their correspondents over network reporters when it comes to covering some big stories. The directors like the local angle and the additional prestige that go along with the coverage.

Moreover, the networks and independent companies, such as Conus Communications, provide satellite feeds (pictures and words) of breaking spot news. CBS News, for example, sends out about 150 stories every weekday to its stations. Affiliates put

A clustering of satellite news gathering vehicles. Sights like this are common at many news events. (J. L. Atlan/Sygma)

their own local audio over the pictures and use them in their newscasts. Viewers are increasingly seeing the same video coverage on their local and network newscasts. Further, both independent and affiliate stations belong to regional and national satellite services. At Conus, for example, if there's a plane crash in Milwaukee or an earthquake in Palo Alto, a local Conus member covers it and sends the report to Conus, which, in turn, puts it on the satellite for all of its other member stations to use. CNN has a similar service called Newsource, which has seven scheduled feeds a day.

Given these advances, local stations are asking if they still need the network newscast. Many local stations think they can do the job of covering local and international news for their market better than the nets. Even the networks themselves are seriously examining the future of their newscasts. As mentioned earlier, the net newscast is expensive and networks are looking for ways to cut back. Network news ratings are down about 15–20 percent from 1981. Most large market stations now run sixty or ninety minutes (or more) of local news before going to the network and many people are "newsed out" by then. The nets have already cut back on coverage of live events. Only CNN was on the air when the space shuttle exploded, and CNN provided the only on-scene live coverage of the start of the Gulf War. Some network executives envision the day when the networks provide merely a video feed and a "correspondents service" for their stations. In any case, the shape of network news may have already been changed unalterably by the new technologies.

Similarities in the News Media

Before closing, it should be mentioned that although there are significant differences between print and electronic journalism, there are actually many similarities as well. To keep the topic in perspective, these should also be mentioned. To begin, both print and electronic journalists share the same basic values and journalistic principles. Honesty in news reporting is crucial for both television and newspaper reporters. Stories must be as truthful as humanly possible. The print journalist should not invent fictional characters or make up quotations and attribute them to newsmakers. Electronic journalists should not stage news events or rearrange the questions and answers in a taped interview. High standards of honesty are important no matter what the medium. Another shared value is accuracy. Checking facts takes time, but it's something that a professional reporter must do with every story. Misspelling a name in a newspaper is analogous to mispronouncing it during a news broadcast. Details, big and small, should be checked. A third common value is balance. Every story has two or more sides. The print or broadcast journalist must make sure that he or she does not publicize or promote just one of them. Information should be offered on all sides of a story. Finally, both print and broadcast reporters share the value of objectivity. Objectivity is a difficult concept to define; in fact, the concept includes many of the shared values that we have already discussed. Briefly summarized, objectivity means that the reporter tries to transmit the news untainted by conscious bias and without personal comment or coloration. Of course, complete and total objectivity is not possible because the process of reporting itself requires countless judgments, each influenced in some way by the reporter's value system. Nonetheless, journalists have traditionally respected the truth, refused to distort facts deliberately, and consciously detached themselves as much as possible from what they were reporting.

Second, both print and broadcast reporters must maintain credibility with their audiences. The news media periodically undergo crises of confidence when many people begin to doubt that their newspapers and broadcast stations are telling them the complete and honest truth. Sometimes these crises appear when some journalistically unacceptable reporting is disclosed, as in the 1980s when the *Washington Post* had to give back a Pulitzer Prize because one of its reporters had fictionalized a story and passed it off as fact. Sometimes they occur when the news media seem to be exploited by some self-serving group, as occurred in 1985 during the coverage of an airplane hijacking and subsequent hostage taking by Middle Eastern terrorists. Other times credibility is called into question by legal events, such as libel suits brought by Ariel Sharon and William Westmoreland in the mid-1980s that revealed some questionable reporting practices. Whenever public opinion polls reveal that the news media have slipped another notch or two in credibility, both print and electronic journalists try to regain the lost confidence. After much soul searching, the crisis usually passes. Credibility, however, is not something that should be examined only during journalistic crises. It is important no matter what the medium. If a reader or a viewer loses trust or stops believing what is being reported, the fundamental contract between audience and reporter is undermined and the news organization cannot survive. It matters little if the news organization is a newspaper, magazine, radio, or TV station; credibility is paramount.

● ● ● ●
ISSUES

Not surprisingly, coverage of the recent war in the Persian Gulf renewed questions about a potential conflict between the public's right to know and national security (see Chapter 17). News from the war was tightly controlled by the Pentagon. Unlike Vietnam, where reporters generally had free rein over the battlefield, reporters in the Gulf War were shepherded around by military public information officers and were limited in what they could show and whom they could interview. The Pentagon issued a six-page list of "don'ts" that spelled out what couldn't be done: No photos of wounded soldiers, no interviews without a military escort present, no submission of stories without military review.

Throughout most of the war, TV and newspaper reporters relied upon "pool" coverage—a small group of reporters who filed stories that everyone could use. These

Peter Arnett's reports from Baghdad for CNN were cleared by Iraqi censors and criticized by many in the U.S. (© CNN, Inc.)

restrictions prompted criticism from reporters who claimed that the Pentagon was managing the news. Some reporters, like CBS correspondent Bob McKeon and ABC's Forrest Sawyer, eventually broke away from the pool and provided independent accounts. For its part, the military argued that such restrictions were necessary from a security standpoint. The American public apparently sided with the Pentagon. Public opinion polls showed that sentiment generally was on the side of the military and few people complained about a lack of coverage from the media. Indeed, many wondered if there was enough censorship being used.

The second major issue from the war concerned CNN's Peter Arnett who, for a time, was the only Western reporter in Baghdad. This was an unprecedented event—a reporter working for an American organization relating the news from the enemy's backyard. There were no guidelines to cover this event. Arnett's heavily censored

International Perspective: Covering Social Revolutions

As far as media coverage was concerned, the biggest story of 1989 was the social revolution that swept across Eastern Europe and brought democratic reforms to the people of a half-dozen different countries. It may surprise you to learn that another and perhaps equally significant social revolution was underway about the same time in South America. The media, however, basically ignored this story.

In December, 1989, Brazil and Chile held their first free presidential elections in two decades, marking the end of oppressive regimes in both countries. Brazil is the sixth most populous nation on earth with about 150 million people. Chile has about ten million. The population of all the countries of Eastern Europe combined is 140 million. Population, of course, is not the only way to judge what is newsworthy, but it is also interesting to note that both Brazil and Chile are experiencing the same kinds of economic problems that the countries of Eastern Europe are likely to face as they move toward a more capitalistic economy. Despite these similarities, compared to Eastern Europe, coverage of the South American countries was paltry. *Newsweek* devoted ninety pages to the events in Europe but less than a page to Brazil and Chile. *Time* did a little better: ninety-eight pages on Europe, about six on South America. The *New York Times* gave Europe thirteen times more space than South America. The situation on network television was even more lopsided. The nets spent an enormous amount of time on

the developments in Eastern Europe, with some anchors even reporting from the scene. In contrast, the elections in Brazil and Chile got about a minute of coverage on NBC and ABC and weren't even mentioned on CBS.

All of this is not to say that the changes in Eastern Europe were insignificant. They were indeed momentous and deserving of the large amount of coverage they received. What is interesting is the lopsided imbalance of the reporting. Why were events involving more people and occurring closer to home not given more attention?

One reason had to do with the nature of the story. Eastern Europe had the great visual symbol—the Berlin Wall. It was a natural rallying point for crowds and media alike. When the Germans started literally to tear down the Wall, it was symbolism that couldn't be resisted by TV news crews. Chile and Brazil had no comparable evocative symbol. A second reason had to do with economics. The media couldn't afford to send correspondents and crews to both places. They opted to cover the more familiar territory of Eastern Europe. A final reason has to do with stereotypes in the way news is defined. Much of the past coverage from South America has been confined to natural disasters (earthquakes, floods, etc.), military coups, and drug trafficking. Sometimes it is difficult for the media to break these past formulas of news gathering and broaden their definition of what constitutes important events in foreign nations.

reports from Iraq prompted critics to claim that he was giving aid and comfort to the enemy, that he was being manipulated, that he was broadcasting enemy propaganda, and many other charges. The citizens' group, Accuracy in Media, asked its members to threaten CNN with a boycott of its advertised products.

Another issue that received attention during the early 1990s was news rigging. A report on *Dateline NBC* investigating potential fire hazards in General Motors trucks contained a segment that showed a GM pickup exploding into flames after being struck by a car. Subsequent investigation disclosed that the truck had been equipped with the wrong cap for its gas tank, the tank had been overfilled, and incendiary devices had been attached to the trunk to assure that a fire would take place. In the wake of these disclosures, NBC aired a four-minute segment on the program admitting its mistakes. The resulting furor also prompted the resignation of the president of NBC News. Critics charged that this episode was an example of how news gathering ethics might be compromised under the pressure for high ratings.

CAREERS IN NEWS GATHERING AND REPORTING

The career prospects for a young person interested in the news profession vary with the type of job desired. The job market for newspaper reporters and editors in the early 1990s was competitive. Copy editors were in more demand than general-assignment reporters, and persons skilled in specialized reporting areas, such as business and financial news, were also in demand. On the other hand, jobs for sports writers were scarce. As a general rule, a person with good writing and reporting skills will have a good chance at landing an entry-level job at a newspaper. In fact, some better journalism students are hired right off the campus by big-city newspapers.

Jobs in magazine journalism are harder to come by, primarily because there are so few of them. Most news magazines look for experienced people. Some even recommend that a prospective employee have a specialty in some area, such as law, finance, or science, along with journalism training.

Things are a bit tighter in broadcast journalism. Deregulation has meant that many radio stations have decided not to increase their news-reporting efforts. Consequently, the job market in radio journalism is sluggish. In television news, the glamour jobs of anchor and on-camera reporter continue to have far more applicants than there are available positions. There is some good news, however. The emergence of two-hour newscasts at large-market stations, the growth of the Cable News Network, and the increased prominence given to news at local stations have meant that there has been some expansion of the job market in news. Getting that first job, however, is still difficult and the market is highly competitive. Most newcomers are content to start in a small market and work their way up.

The outlook is a little brighter in the other positions. ENG camerapersons are in some demand, as are tape editors. The news producer position is another one where prospects for employment are favorable. The Cable News Network offers entry-level positions called "video journalists" for people interested in the writing and producing end of TV news. Again, most experts in this area suggest that a newcomer start in smaller markets, gain valuable experience, and then progress to larger cities.

To give you some perspective on TV news salaries, in 1990 anchors in the top twenty-five TV markets were averaging about $100,000 annually. In the top three or four markets, salaries were much higher. Top anchors in Chicago, Los Angeles, or New York might be close to the $1 million mark. Anchors in medium market stations had salaries that ranged from $60,000 to $100,000 while their small market counterparts were in the $25,000 to $35,000 range. A general-assignment reporter, who reports from the scene of a news event, averaged about $50,000 to $70,000 in big markets, $30,000 to $50,000 in medium markets, and $20,000 to $30,000 in small markets. A news producer averaged about $40,000 in large markets and about $25,000 in smaller markets.

••••

SUGGESTIONS FOR FURTHER READING

The following books contain more information about the concepts and topics discussed in this chapter.

BAGDIKIAN, BEN, *The Media Monopoly*, Boston: Beacon Press, 1990.

BLAIR, GWENDA, *Almost Golden*, New York: Simon & Schuster, 1988.

GOEDKOOP, RICHARD, *Inside Local Television News*, Salem, Wisc.: Sheffield Publishing, 1989.

LEWIS, CAROLYN, *Reporting for Television*, New York: Columbia University Press, 1984.

NEWSOM, DOUG, AND JAMES WOLLERT, *Media Writing: News for the Mass Media*, Belmont, Calif.: Wadsworth, 1985.

ROSE, TOM, *Freeing the Whales*, New York: Birch Lane Press, 1989.

STOVALL, JAMES, *Writing for the Mass Media*, Englewood Cliffs, N.J.: Prentice-Hall, 1990.

YOAKAM, RICHARD, AND CHARLES CREMER, *ENG: Television News and the New Technology*, New York: McGraw-Hill, 1989.

15

THE STRUCTURE OF THE PUBLIC RELATIONS INDUSTRY

hen they first saw the results, the county water testers thought it was a mistake. Somebody must have gotten the samples mixed up. Perrier mineral water had such a good reputation for purity that these government workers in North Carolina had routinely used it to calibrate their equipment before they tested local water supplies. A recheck showed that there was no mistake. A sample of bottled Perrier water contained traces of the cancer-causing chemical benzene. (Granted the amount found in the bottles was minuscule; a person would have to guzzle about 26,000 bottles of Perrier before raising the odds of getting cancer by one in a million, but even this is enough to cause problems for a company which prides itself on purity.) The news media quickly latched onto the story, and thus began a public relations nightmare that almost took all the fizz out of Perrier.

Perrier, it goes without saying, was initially caught off guard. The company was one of the huge success stories of the 1980s. Capitalizing on the decade's fitness fad and the growing yuppie predilection for something with a European cachet, Perrier sales jumped 190 percent in seven years, selling about $120 million in the U.S. The sparkling water in the green bottles, which costs several times more per gallon than gasoline, had become the drink of choice of a whole generation. No one had imagined that the roof would collapse so quickly.

To begin with, Perrier violated several cardinal rules of public relations. Rule number one: Don't speculate without having all the facts. When pressed by French reporters, a company spokesman speculated that the whole thing was a minor event, caused by a worker using a dirty rag to clean some bottling equipment. A few contaminated bottles had gotten out and that was that. But the press quickly reported that workers don't use benzene around the bottling equipment precisely because they are afraid of contamination. It was also discovered that traces of benzene had cropped up in Perrier bottles in the Netherlands, Denmark, and the United Kingdom. Embarrassed, Perrier withdrew the careless worker explanation.

Rule number two: Don't stonewall. When faced with persistent reporters asking about the extent of the problem, Perrier evaded the questions. Not surprisingly, rumors fly when information is not forthcoming: Perrier was the target of industrial sabotage; terrorists had poisoned Perrier. The company also was reluctant to disclose how it gets and bottles its water in the first place, leading to even more speculation. Perrier's stock dropped 15 percent.

With bad publicity mounting quickly, Perrier was forced into drastic action. It recalled all Perrier bottles (about 160 million of them) from all global markets, something that hadn't been done since Johnson and Johnson recalled Tylenol after tampering had caused some consumers to die from tainted capsules. The bottled water would be pulled off the shelves (at a cost of about $30 million) until the cause of the contamination was found and corrected.

While all of this was going on, the company hired the big public relations firm of Burson-Marsteller to handle its media relations. Not coincidentally, Burson-Marsteller was the PR firm that gained much praise for its handling of the Tylenol crisis mentioned above.

Perrier's fortunes started to rebound. News media were informed that the cause of the impurity was traced to a gas filter that was supposed to trap contaminants before they were mixed with the spring water. The filter had become supersaturated and had leaked some benzene into the water. It was replaced and the problem cleared up.

Burson-Marsteller designed a campaign to relaunch the product into the world market. The new Perrier had a label indicating the date of production and a certification that it had been approved for purity. A $25-million ad campaign was launched around the theme "Perrier is back." After an eight-week absence, Perrier started to appear on grocery shelves and on restaurant menus.

Surprisingly, Perrier's rivals were unable to capitalize on its hiatus. They, too, were caught by surprise and couldn't increase production quickly enough to capture market share. In addition, other bottled water companies were reluctant to knock Perrier, which had become almost synonymous with the industry, for fear of giving themselves a bad name.

Perrier Group President Ronald Davis personally demonstrates his confidence in his product as the new, benzene-free Perrier is reintroduced to the market. (Anthony Barboza/Ken Barboza Associates)

Within a year, thanks in part to better public relations, Perrier had recaptured its sparkle and sales were back to normal.

Perrier's problems are not typical of those faced by PR agencies and corporate PR departments, but they do indicate the tremendous importance that favorable PR plays in the corporate and consumer setting. The rest of this chapter examines the role of public relations in contemporary society.

• • • •

DEFINING PUBLIC RELATIONS

Before trying to explain what public relations is, it may first be helpful to differentiate it from other concepts. There are, for example, several similarities between advertising and public relations. Both are attempts at persuasion and both involve using the mass media. Public relations, however, is a management function; advertising is a marketing function. Second, advertising uses the mass media and machine-assisted communication settings; it does not involve interpersonal communications. A third difference is seen in the fact that advertising is normally sponsored. Public relations messages appear as features, news stories, or editorials, and the space or time involved is not paid for. In many instances, advertising, particularly corporate advertising, is used to help further the public relations program.

Another concept that is sometimes confused with public relations is **publicity**, the placing of stories in the mass media. Publicity is a tool in the public relations process but it is not equivalent to PR. For example, it is perfectly possible for a firm to have extensive publicity and bad public relations. Further, publicity is primarily one-way communication; public relations is two way.

Having examined what public relations is not, we now turn to look at what it is. The term *public relations* has many interpretations and meanings. One PR veteran has compiled 500 different ones ranging from the concise, "PR is doing good and getting credit for it," to the one-hundred-word definition in the *Encyclopaedia Britannica.* Most of the leading textbooks on PR usually lead off with a chapter that attempts to define exactly what public relations is or isn't. Rather than catalog these many definitions, it seems more useful to define PR by examining what PR people do.

First, almost everyone in the PR industry would agree that public relations involves working with public opinion. On the one hand, PR professionals attempt to influence public opinion in a way that is positive to the organization. For example, in the Perrier episode, the company wanted to persuade consumers that it was doing everything it could to protect their safety. In short, the public relations effort was designed to restore a favorable public opinion. On the other hand, it is also the function of the PR department to gather information from the public and interpret that information for top management as it relates to management decisions. Again, referring back to the Perrier case, the company commissioned several surveys during the crisis to find out how the public viewed the product in the wake of the problems. Strategic management decisions were made with the results of these surveys in mind.

Second, public relations is concerned with communication. Most people are interested in what an organization is doing to meet their concerns and interests. It is the function of the public relations professional to explain the organization's actions to various publics involved with the organization. Public relations communications is two-way communication. The PR professional also pays close attention to the thoughts and feelings of the organization's publics. Some experts refer to public relations as a two-way conduit between an organization and its publics.

Note that the word "publics" in the preceding section is plural. This is because the organization typically deals with many different publics in its day-to-day operations. Several PR scholars divide these groups into internal and external publics.

The World's Toughest PR Job?

This is going to sound like the plot of a bad comedy movie. The Committee for State Security of the U.S.S.R. (better known as the KGB) was looking for a PR agency to help improve its image. This was obviously a big challenge but at least one firm, BBDO Worldwide, was willing to take it on. In 1991, BBDO said that it wanted to help the KGB "disassociate itself from its embarrassing history" of repression and lawlessness and to give it a more positive image. What might such a campaign look like? "We will grill no spy before his time." "KGB. The Right Choice . . . and you'd better make it." "Sometimes you gotta break the rules . . . and we do." The possibilities are endless.

The makeover got put on hold, however, after the aborted 1991 coup against Mikhail Gorbachev, the dissolution of the Soviet Union, and the restructuring of the KGB itself. According to an official of the new KGB: "We tend to think the best advertisement is our own work." No quarrel here.

Internal publics include employees, managers, labor unions, and stockholders. External publics consist of consumers, government, dealers, suppliers, members of the community, and the mass media. Public relations serves as the link for all these various publics.

Third, public relations is a management function. It is designed to help a company set its goals and adapt to a changing environment. Public relations practitioners regularly counsel top management. Inherent in the specification of public relations is a planned activity. It is organized and directed toward specific goals and objectives.

Of course, public relations involves much more than just the three functions mentioned above. Perhaps it would be easier, for our purposes, to summarize them in the following definition approved by the World Assembly of Public Relations:

> Public relations is the art and social science of analyzing trends, predicting their consequences, counseling organization leaders and implementing planned programs of action which serve both the organization's and the public's interest.

SHORT HISTORY OF PUBLIC RELATIONS

If the term is interpreted broadly enough, the practice of public relations can be traced back to ancient times. The military reports and commentaries prepared by Julius Caesar can be viewed as triumph in personal and political public relations. During medieval times, both the Church and the guilds practiced rudimentary forms of public relations.

It was not until the American Revolution that more recognizable public relations activities became evident. The early patriots were aware that public opinion would play an important role in the war with England and planned their activities accordingly. For example, they staged events, such as the Boston Tea Party, to gain public attention. They also used symbols, such as the Liberty Tree and the Minutemen, that were easily recognized and helped portray their cause in a positive light. Skillful writers such as Samuel Adams, Thomas Paine, Abigail Adams, and Benjamin Franklin used political propaganda to swing public opinion to their side. As a case in point, note that the altercation between an angry mob and British soldiers became known as "the Boston Massacre," an interpretation well suited to the rebel cause.

Later, the presidency of Andrew Jackson marked the beginning of political public relations. Jackson, born on the frontier, was not a skilled communicator and needed help to get his ideas across to the people. Jackson relied on Amos Kendall, a former newspaperman, to handle his public relations. Kendall wrote speeches, served as press secretary, and arranged public events to help Jackson's cause.

The Industrial Revolution and the resulting growth of mass production and mass consumption led to the growth of big business. Giant monopolies were formed in the railroad, steel, and oil businesses. Many big corporations tended to disregard the interests of the consumer in their quest for more profits. In fact, many executives felt that the less the public knew about their practices and operations, the better. Around the turn of the century, however, public hostility was aroused against unscrupulous business practices. Led by the muckrakers (see Chapter 4), exposés of industrial corruption and ruthless business tactics filled the nation's magazines. Faced with these attacks, many corporations hired communications experts, many of them former newspaper writers, to counteract the effect of these stories. These specialists tried to combat this negative publicity by making sure that the industry's side of the issue was also presented. These practitioners were the prototypes of what we might call press agents or publicists.

The debut of modern public relations techniques dates back to the first decade of the 1900s. Most historians agree that the first real public relations pioneer was a man named Ivy Lee. In 1903, Lee and George Parker opened a publicity office. A few years later, Lee became the press representative for the anthracite coal operators and the Pennsylvania Railroad. When confronted with a strike in the coal industry, Lee issued a "Declaration of Principles." This statement endorsed the concepts of openness and honesty in dealing with the public; it also marked the shift from nineteenth-century press agentry to twentieth-century public relations. Lee went on to have a successful career counseling people such as John D. Rockefeller, Jr. Among other achievements, Lee is credited with humanizing business and demonstrating that public relations is most effective when it affects employees, customers, and members of the community.

Public relations pioneer Ivy Lee. (The Bettmann Archive)

Moreover, Lee would not carry out a public relations program unless it was endorsed and supported by top management.

Following World War I, two more public relations pioneers, Carl Byoir and Edward L. Bernays, appeared on the scene. Bernays is credited with writing the first book on public relations, *Crystallizing Public Opinion*, published in 1923. In 1930, Byoir organized a public relations firm that is still one of the world's largest.

The Depression caused many Americans to look toward business with suspicion and distrust. In an attempt to regain public favor, many large corporations established their own public relations departments. The federal government, in its attempt to cope with the bad economic climate, also used good public relations practices to its advantage. Franklin Roosevelt introduced his New Deal reform program complete with promotional campaigns to win public acceptance. Roosevelt also recognized the tremendous potential of radio in shaping public opinion, and his fireside chats were memorable examples of personal public relations. The government intensified its public relations efforts during World War II with the creation of the Office of War Information.

Since the end of the war, changes in American society have created an atmosphere in which public relations has shown tremendous growth. What are some of the reasons behind the recent surge in this area?

1. Many corporations have recognized that they have a social responsibility to serve the public. Finding the means of fulfilling this responsibility is the task of the public relations department.

2. A growing tide of consumerism has caused many corporations and government agencies to be more responsive and communicative to their customers or clients, a function served by the public relations department.

3. The growing complexity of modern corporations and government agencies has made it difficult for them to get their messages to the public without a department that is specifically assigned to that task.

4. Increasing population growth along with more specialization and job mobility have made it necessary for companies to have communication specialists whose task it is to interpret the needs of the audience for the organization.

All of the above have combined to make the last thirty years or so the "era of public relations." The profession has grown from about 19,000 members in 1950 to more than 200,000 people in 1991. More than 80 percent of the top 300 companies in the United States have some kind of public relations department. Along with this growth has come increased professionalization among public relations practitioners. A professional organization, the Public Relations Society of America, was founded in 1947 and adopted a code of standards in 1954. Public relations education has also made great strides. Recent estimates suggest that about 400 colleges across the country offer courses in public relations. In 1967, the Public Relations Student Society of America was founded. It now has 150 chapters and 5000 members.

The last few years have seen public relations assume even greater importance. Mergers, acquisitions, and a 1987 collapse of the stock market meant that corporations had additional responsibilities in communicating with their publics. A weak economy has prompted many organizations into downsizing. This typically creates an intense need for internal company communications programs to explain the exact nature and impact of the reductions. On the global front, the success of Mikhail Gorbachev's perestroika policy and the improved image that the Soviet Union enjoyed, at least temporarily, among Western nations have been attributed in part to Gorbachev's skill at international public relations. Whether Boris Yeltsin and the new Russian Commonwealth continue to enjoy the benefits of this improvement is yet to be seen.

Perhaps the most telling moment in the struggle for public opinion during the recent Persian Gulf War came not on the battlefield nor in the Oval Office nor in the press briefing rooms in Saudi Arabia. Instead, it came on *Saturday Night Live*. An opening bit designed to look like one of the military briefings that had become familiar to all Americans satirized not the military but the press. The reporters in the skit were portrayed as short-sighted and insensitive, asking patently inappropriate questions: "What's the one piece of bad news you can give us that would most demoralize our troops?" President George Bush later reported that the *Saturday Night Live* skit fully convinced him that public opinion was on his side.

Throughout the war, the military public relations operation went almost as smoothly as the war itself. The military briefings were filled with facts and figures and delivered by officers who were candid and skilled at performing on TV. Restrictions on what could be covered galled journalists but resulted in stories that showed the American efforts in a positive light. Military moves were also conducted with a nod to PR. The first aerial ace of the war was a Saudi who shot down two Iraqi jets. It was later revealed that American pilots were closer to the Iraqi planes but the Saudi pilot was vectored to their location so that he could receive the "Top Gun" coverage.

The military also used the press to strategic advantage. Coverage of massive rehearsals for an amphibious invasion was used as a diversion. No amphibious landings ever occurred. Before the ground offensive started, reporters were taken to see troops near the Kuwaiti border in an effort to distract Iraqi attention from the main thrust which was taking shape miles to the west. Perhaps the most memorable PR event took place after hostilities were over when General Norman Schwarzkopf gave a 57-minute briefing on the allied strategy that won the war. His performance was so memorable that videocassettes of it were made available for sale to the general public.

The most vibrant example of modern public relations at work occurred during the 1991 Persian Gulf War. The military received high marks for its media performance during this conflict (see box above).

ORGANIZATION OF THE PUBLIC RELATIONS INDUSTRY

Public relations activities are generally handled in two ways. Many organizations have their own public relations departments that work with the managers of all other departments. About 85 percent of the 1500 largest U.S. companies have such a department. These departments are part of top management, and the PR director is responsible to the president of the company. For example, General Motors and AT&T both have about 200 people in their PR departments. Other organizations hire an external public relations counsel to give advice on press, government, and consumer relations. In business and industry, about one-third of the PR activity is handled by outside counseling firms. Many major corporations retain an outside agency in addition to their own internal public relations department.

Each of these arrangements has its particular advantages and disadvantages. An in-house department can be at work on short notice; an internal department has more in-depth knowledge about the company, and its operations tend to be less costly. On the other hand, it's hard for a corporate PR team to take an objective view of the company. Further, internal PR departments tend to "go stale" and have trouble coming up with fresh ideas unless new personnel are frequently added. An outside agency offers more services to its clients than does an internal department. Additionally, external counselors have the advantage of being objective observers, and many firms like the prestige associated with being a client of a respected PR firm. On the other side of the coin, outside agencies are expensive, it takes time for them to learn the inner workings of their client's operations, and their involvement might cause resentment and morale problems among the staff of the client's organization.

Internal or external, public relations professionals perform a wide range of services. These include counseling management, preparing annual reports, handling news releases and other forms of media coverage, supervising employee and other internal communications, managing promotions and special events, fund-raising, lobbying, community relations, and speech writing, to name just a few.

Public relations is practiced in a variety of settings. Although the general principles are the same, the actual duties of the PR practitioner will vary according to the setting. Below is a brief description of the major areas where public relations is practiced.

1. Business. Public relations helps the marketing process by instilling in the consumer a positive attitude toward the company. Public relations also helps promote healthy employee management relations and serves as a major liaison between the firm and government regulators. Lastly, all businesses have to be located somewhere, and the PR department markets sure the company is a good citizen in its community.

2. Government and politics. Many government agencies hire public relations specialists to help them explain their activities to citizens and to assist the news media in their coverage of the different agencies. These same specialists also communicate the opinions of the public back to the agency. Government PR is big business; its total expenditures on public information rival the budgets of the three TV networks. The Department of Defense, for instance, produces thousands of films and TV programs every year. The Department of Agriculture sends out thousands of news releases annually. Political public relations is another growing field. A growing number of candidates for public office hire a PR expert to help them get their message across to voters.

A PR effort from the Council of Energy Awareness, a trade association for the nuclear energy industry. (Courtesy U.S. Council for Energy Awareness)

3. Education. PR personnel work in both elementary and higher education. The most visible area of practice in elementary and high school concerns facilitating communication between educators and parents. Other tasks, however, are no less important. In many school systems, the PR person also handles relations with the school board, local and state legislative bodies, and the news media. Public relations at the college and university level, although less concerned with parental relations, has its own agenda of problems. For example, fund-raising, legislative relations, community relations, and internal relations with faculty and students would be concerns of most college PR departments.

4. Hospitals. The rising cost of health care and greater public expectations from the medical profession have given increased visibility to the public relations departments in our nation's hospitals. Some of the publics that hospital PR staffs have to deal with are patients, patients' families, consumers, state insurance commissions, physicians, nurses, and other staff members. Despite the increasing importance of hospital public relations, many hospitals do not have a full-time PR staff. Consequently, this is one area that will see significant growth in the future.

5. Nonprofit organizations. The United Way, Girl Scouts, the Red Cross, and the Salvation Army are just a few of the organizations that need PR professionals. Probably the biggest PR goal in organizations such as these is fund-raising. Other objectives would include encouraging volunteer participation, informing contributors how their money is spent, and working with the individuals served by the organization.

6. Professional associations. Organizations such as the American Medical Association, the American Dairy Association, and the American Bar Association employ PR practitioners. In addition to providing news and information to the association's members, other duties of the PR staff would include recruiting new members, planning national conferences, influencing government decisions, and working with the news media.

7. Entertainment and sports. A significant number of PR experts work for established and would-be celebrities in the entertainment and sports worlds. A practitioner handling this type of client has two major responsibilities: Get the client favorable media coverage and protect the client from bad publicity. Additionally, many sports and entertainment events (e.g., the Superbowl, a motion picture premiere) have PR campaigns associated with them.

From the above, it appears that the profession requires PR specialists as well as generalists.

● ● ● ●
DEPARTMENTS AND STAFF

This section discusses the structure of both internal public relations departments and external public relations agencies. The internal department setup will be discussed first. At the outset, it should be remembered that no two company departmental charts are alike, so the precise makeup of the PR department will vary. In any case, Figure 15-1 displays a common organizational arrangement. Note that the PR director is directly responsible to the president (or the chief executive officer). Since PR affects every department, it makes sense for it to be supervised by the person who runs the entire organization. The figure also illustrates that the department is designed to handle communication with both internal and external publics.

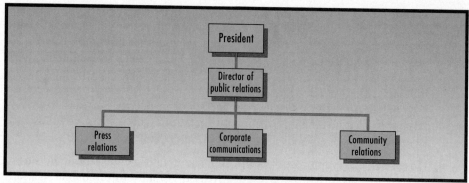

FIGURE 15-1 *Arrangement of a corporate public relations office.*

The organization of a public relations agency is more complex. Figure 15-2 shows one possible departmental arrangement. As is apparent, the structure is somewhat similar to that of an advertising agency. Also, note that the range of services provided by the agency is more extensive than that of the internal corporate PR department.

THE PUBLIC RELATIONS PROGRAM

Pretend you're the public relations director for a leading auto company. The company is entering into an agreement with a foreign car manufacturer to produce the foreign model in the United States. Unfortunately, in order to increase efficiency and centralize its operations, the company will have to close one of its plants located in a Midwestern city. About a thousand employees will have to be transferred or find new jobs, and the community will face a significant economic blow. It will be the job of the public relations department to determine how best to communicate this decision to the community.

The thorny problem outlined above is not an atypical one of the public relations professional. To handle it adequately, however, requires a planned, organized, and efficient public relations program. This section will trace the main steps involved in developing a typical PR campaign.

FIGURE 15-2 *Arrangement of a public relations counseling agency.*

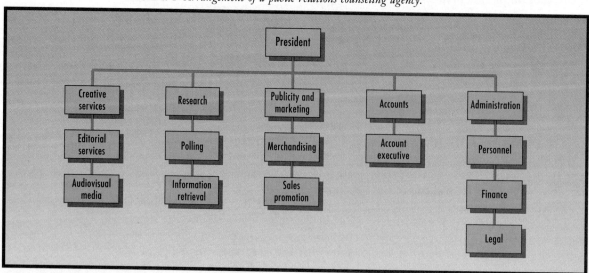

People spend $5 billion a year on dolls; they consistently outsell every other toy and are among the top ten most popular items to collect. Nonetheless, the industry still likes to promote itself. A PR firm offered one suggestion: Hold an international awards program. The doll industry liked the idea and instituted the "Doll of the Year" awards (the DOTYs). Plans call for more than 300 manufacturers to submit photos of their entries in twelve categories including fashion doll, baby doll, action doll, and limited edition doll. The preliminary judging will be done by the International Doll Academy, which will narrow the lists to five dolls in each category. The general public will then vote on the twelve dolls of the year. Ballots will be available at toy and department stores and in magazines.

One contender in this competition will surely be the Barbie doll. Barbie is past thirty and after countless parties, costume changes, and dates with Ken, Barbie's PR firm has come up with a fresh, new look for her. Barbie is going to be an executive. Her career apparel includes a pink business suit, matching hat, pumps, and an attaché case containing a calculator, credit cards, and her business cards. Her office play set contains fold-out desk, personal computer, phone, and file folder. At last report, Ken was still unemployed.

An effective public relations effort is the result of a four-step process:

1. information gathering
2. planning
3. communication
4. evaluation

Information Gathering

The information-gathering stage is an important one because what is learned from it will influence the remaining stages. Information gathering can be achieved through several means. Organizational records, trade journals, public records, and reference books serve as valuable sources for existing data. Personal contacts, mail to the company, advisory committees, and personnel reports represent other sources of information. If more formal research methods are required, they might be carried out by the PR department or by an outside agency that specializes in public opinion polling or survey research. To return to our example, the PR director at the auto company will need to gather a great deal of information. How much will the company save by its reorganization? Exactly how many workers will be transferred? Will the company help to find new jobs for the workers who will be unemployed? What will be the precise economic impact on the community? What will become of the empty buildings that will be left behind? Will the employees believe what the company tells them? What do people expect from the company? Will the company's image be hurt in other areas of the United States?

Planning

Phase two is the planning stage. There are two general types of planning: **strategic** and **tactical.** Strategic plans involve long-range general goals that the organization wishes to achieve. Top management usually formulates an organization's strategic plans. Tactical plans are more specific. They detail the tasks that must be accomplished by every department in the organization to achieve the strategic goals. Plans might be drawn up that can be used only once or they might be standing plans that set general organizational policy.

Planning is a vital part of the PR program. Some of the items involved in a PR campaign involve framing the objectives, considering the alternatives, assessing the risks and benefits involved in each, deciding on a course of action, figuring up the budget, and securing the necessary approvals from within the organization. In recent years, many PR practitioners have endorsed a technique known as **management by objectives (MBO)**. Simply put, MBO means that the organization sets observable and measurable goals for itself and allocates its resources to meet those objectives. For example, a corporation might set as a goal increasing sales by 25 percent over the next two years. When the time elapsed, it would be easy to see if the goal had been achieved. This approach is becoming more popular in PR because top management typically thinks in these terms, and it allows PR practitioners to speak the same language as chief executives. Second, it keeps the department on target in solving PR problems; and, finally, it provides concrete feedback about the efficiency of the PR process. In our hypothetical example, some possible objectives might be informing more than 50 percent of the community about the reasons to move or to make sure that community and national attitudes about the company are not adversely affected.

Communication

Phase three is the communication phase. After gathering facts and making plans, the organization assumes the role of the source of communication. Several key decisions are made at this stage concerning the nature of the messages and the types of media to be used. Because mass communication media are usually important channels in a PR program, it is necessary for public relations practitioners to have a thorough knowledge of the various media and their strengths and weaknesses. Moreover, PR professionals should know the various production techniques for the print and broadcast media. Some common ways of publicizing a message through the mass media include press releases, video news releases, press kits, photographs, paid advertising, films, videotapes, press conferences, and interviews.

Public relations also makes use of other channels to get messages to its publics. These might include both the interpersonal and the machine-assisted settings. House publications, brochures, letters, bulletins, posters, billboards, and bulletin boards are possible communication channels used by a company to reach its own employees. On a more personal level, public meetings, speeches, demonstrations, staged events, open houses, and tours are other possibilities.

In the hypothetical example, our PR director would probably use a variety of messages and media. News conferences, ads, news releases, and public meetings would seem appropriate vehicles for explaining the company's position to its external public. Meanwhile, house publications, bulletin boards, speeches, and letters could be used to reach its internal public.

Evaluation

The last phase concerns evaluation of the PR program. How well did it work? The importance of evaluation in public relations is becoming greater because of the development of the MBO techniques discussed above. If a measurable goal was proposed for the PR program, then an evaluation technique should be able to measure the success in reaching that goal. There are several different things that might be measured. One easy method is simply to gauge the volume of coverage that the campaign generated. The number of press releases sent out, the number of letters mailed, speeches made, and so on, is simple to compute. In like manner, press clippings and mentions in TV and radio news can also be tabulated. It's important to remember, however, that volume does not equal results. A million press clippings mean nothing if they are not read by the audience. To measure the impact of a campaign on the audience requires more sophisticated techniques of analysis. Some common techniques would include questionnaires distributed to random samples of the audience, telephone surveys, panels, reader-interest studies, and the use of experimental campaigns. It is likely that many of the above techniques would be used by our hypothetical PR director.

Before closing, it should be pointed out that the above discussion talks about these four steps as though they are distinct stages. In actuality, the PR program is a continuous process, and one phase blends into the next. The results learned in the evaluation stage, for example, are also part of the information-gathering phase of the next cycle of the PR program.

● ● ● ●
ECONOMICS

Large sums of money are spent on public relations. The total amount spent on corporate PR activities is extremely hard to measure but there is some information about the revenues of PR agencies. In 1992, the top fifty firms with major PR operations in the United States earned more than $1.1 billion dollars in fee income, up by more than 50 percent since 1987. The industry is dominated by three giants. Burson-Marsteller led the way in 1992 with more than $200 million in net fees.

London-based Shandwick and an American firm, Hill and Knowlton, followed, both with fees exceeding $145 million. The PR business can be volatile, especially for smaller agencies. Fee income might vary anywhere from 40 to 80 percent in a year. Consolidation is evident in the industry. Nine of the top fifteen PR agencies are also connected with ad agencies.

PR agencies earn their money in a number of ways. Some will perform a specific project for a fixed fee. An annual report, for instance, might cost $5000. Some charge their clients a retainer every month which might range from a few hundred dollars to the thousands. Hill and Knowlton, for example, has a minimum monthly fee of $7500. Other firms will keep track of the time spent on various projects and will charge clients an hourly rate. Still others might bill for time plus special fees for extra services and materials.

● ● ● ●

ISSUES

The central concern about public relations has to do with its persuasive dimension. As mentioned above, one of the goals of PR is to influence public opinion. There are questions, however, about how far PR can go in achieving this goal without manipulating or otherwise beguiling the public. For example, how much of a role did PR play in the U.S. decision to go to war with Iraq in order to liberate Kuwait? Few people were aware that the exiled Kuwaiti government hired the big PR firm of Hill and Knowlton in an attempt to influence American and world public opinion. Hill and Knowlton, for example, arranged press conferences to show evidence of torture and other atrocities committed by the Iraqis. The PR firm also distributed thousands of "Free Kuwait" T-shirts and bumper stickers at colleges across the country. A "National Free Kuwait Day" was orchestrated by Hill and Knowlton, as was a "National Prayer

The United Nations Security Council hears testimony from Kuwaiti victims of Iraqi atrocities. Unknown to many Americans, much of this presentation was put together by Hill and Knowlton, a PR firm hired by the Kuwaitis to shape U.S. public opinion. (Haviv/SABA)

Day" for Kuwait. Twenty video news releases were distributed to local TV stations. A special photograph and videotape presentation was put together for the United Nations Security Council before its vote on actions to be taken against Iraq. All in all, the PR firm spent about $3 million in its attempts to shape American attitudes in favor of the Kuwaiti cause.

As in most PR campaigns, Hill and Knowlton was careful about the image it portrayed of Kuwait. In a workshop held for public relations practitioners, the managing director of the company stressed that the goal of the campaign was to help the American people better understand Kuwait. He contended that Kuwait was a free, tolerant, and open society with a constitution that guaranteed freedom of the press, freedom of worship, and due process. The executive did not point out that only 85,000 of about 825,000 Kuwaitis have the right to vote (none of them women), that the Kuwaiti parliament was suspended in 1986, and that Amnesty International had put Kuwait on its list of human rights violators. Some members of Congress blasted Hill and Knowlton's efforts as "warmongering" and called its activities dangerous. These criticisms, however, faded into the background as hostilities commenced and American public opinion was overwhelmingly in support of the effort to liberate Kuwait. How much the PR effort had to do with this public support will probably never be known.

The essential problem with this kind of activity is that policy makers may never be sure how much of public sentiment is legitimate and how much is orchestrated. As PR firms become connected to other controversial issues, such as abortion or gun control, it will become difficult to detect earnest and serious public convictions from PR efforts designed to achieve a particular goal. The same techniques used to promote Madonna and basketball shoes will be employed to promote far more serious causes. The news media, in particular, face a dilemma in reporting these activities. Few media publicized the Hill and Knowlton activities for Kuwait. Do they have an obligation to inform the public about the behind-the-scenes maneuvers or do they simply cover the results of these efforts as though they were genuine news events?

● ● ● ●
CAREERS IN PUBLIC RELATIONS

Newcomers to the public relations field typically begin their work in the corporate area, with most people starting off in the public relations department of a medium to large organization. A smaller number go directly into PR counseling firms. Others follow a different career path into the profession by first working at a newspaper or broadcasting station and then moving into public relations. In any case, those in the PR industry recommend that prospective job seekers have excellent communications skills, particularly in writing, since many entry-level jobs entail writing and editing news releases, reports, employee publications, and speeches. Other qualifications that are desirable are a knowledge of public opinion research techniques, business practices, law, and the social sciences. Because of the importance of writing skills, many professionals recommend that young people major in journalism—many journalism schools now offer emphasis in PR. In other colleges, public relations courses might be found in the business school or in the department of speech.

New employees in the PR department are expected to perform a wide range of duties. A recent survey of the field found that media relations, advising top management, publicity, and community relations were the activities carried out most often by PR practitioners. More specifically, a newcomer would be expected to write news releases, update mailing lists, research materials for speeches, edit company publications, arrange special events, produce special reports, films, and tapes, and give public speeches.

The job market in public relations is expanding, but competition for entry-level positions will remain keen. One way that is helpful in gaining initial entry into the profession is to secure an internship with a public relations firm while still in college. A survey of recent graduates now working in public relations revealed that undergraduate internships turned into full-time jobs for about one-fifth of all those surveyed. These internships might carry a modest salary or they may involve no pay at all; some internships carry college credit, others do not. In any event, all internships can be valuable training experience.

Salary data are hard to summarize because of the varied nature of the field, but here are some 1990 figures. Note that the jobs for which information is available are those that require some experience. Entry-level positions would be somewhat less. Account executives at PR counseling firms averaged about $29,000 annually while vice presidents averaged about $68,000. For PR specialists in organizations other than counseling firms, the median salary for account execs was about $30,000 and for manager/supervisors, about $51,000.

As with the advertising area, those considering a career in public relations should develop a portfolio to show prospective employers. This portfolio should consist of news stories, brochures, magazine articles, photos, and scripts that exemplify your work. Applicants having a strong portfolio enjoy a definite advantage in the job hunt. In addition, membership in the Public Relations Student Society of America is also a good way to make valuable contacts.

A note of caution is also appropriate here. Many advertised jobs that are labeled "public relations" sometimes turn out to be something else. It's not unusual for sales jobs, receptionist positions, and even bartending slots to be called "PR positions." The newcomer should check each position carefully before applying.

In closing, as in other media-related work, the job applicant should not be too choosy about his or her first job. Most counselors recommend taking any job that is available, even if it lacks the glamour and the salary that the applicant was hoping for. Once inside the firm, it is much easier to move to those positions that are more attractive.

● ● ● ●

SUGGESTIONS FOR FURTHER READING

The following books contain more information about concepts and topics discussed in this chapter.

BOTAN, CARL, AND VINCENT HAZELTON, *Public Relations Theory*, Hillsdale, N.J.: Lawrence Erlbaum, 1989.

CUTLIP, SCOTT, AND ALLEN CENTER, *Effective Public Relations*, Englewood Cliffs, N.J.: Prentice-Hall, 1985.

HABERMAN, DAVID, AND HARRY DOLPHIN, *Public Relations: The Necessary Art*, Ames: Iowa State University Press, 1988.

LESLY, PHILIP, *Lesly's Handbook of Public Relations and Communications*, Chicago: Probus Publishing, 1991.

REILLY, ROBERT, *Public Relations in Action*, Englewood Cliffs, N.J.: Prentice-Hall, 1988.

SIMON, RAYMOND, *Public Relations: Concepts and Practices*, Columbus, Ohio: Grid Publishing, 1980.

WILCOX, DENNIS, PHILLIP AULT, AND WARREN AGEE, *Public Relations: Strategies and Tactics*, New York: Harper & Row, 1992.

16

THE STRUCTURE OF THE ADVERTISING INDUSTRY

L et's start this chapter with a pop quiz. Below are some slogans. What products are they associated with?

1. The ultimate driving machine.

2. Make a run for the border.

3. Just do it.

4. They keep going and going and going. . . .

5. The choice of a new generation.

The fact that most of us could readily name the products (BMW, Taco Bell, Nike, Energizer, Pepsi) is a testament to the advertising industry. This chapter will examine its history, structure, and career opportunities.

DEFINING ADVERTISING

Simply defined, advertising is any form of nonpersonal presentation and promotion of ideas, goods, and services usually paid for by an identified sponsor. Note three key words in the above definition. Advertising is nonpersonal; it is directed toward a large group of anonymous people. Even direct-mail advertising, which may be addressed to a specific person, is prepared by a computer and is signed by a machine. Second, advertising typically is paid for. This fact differentiates advertising from publicity, which is not usually purchased. Sponsors such as Coke and Delta pay for the time and the space they use to get their message across. (Some organizations such as the Red Cross or the United Way advertise but do not pay for time or space. Broadcast stations, newspapers, and magazines run these ads free as a public service.) Third, for obvious reasons, the sponsor of the ad is identified. In fact, in most instances identifying the sponsor is the prime purpose behind the ad—otherwise, why advertise? Perhaps the only situation in which the identity of the advertiser may not be self-evident is political advertising. Because of this, broadcasters and publishers will not accept a political ad unless there is a statement identifying those responsible for it.

Advertising fulfills four basic functions in society. First, it serves a marketing function by helping companies that provide products or services sell their products. Personal selling, sales promotions, and advertising blend together to help market the product. Second, advertising is educational. People learn about new products and services or improvements in existing ones through advertising. Third, advertising plays an economic role. The ability to advertise allows new competitors to enter the business arena. Competition, in turn, encourages product improvements and can lead to lower prices. Moreover, advertising reaches a mass audience, thus greatly reducing the cost of personal selling and distribution. Finally, advertising performs a definite social function. By vividly displaying the material and cultural opportunities available in a free-enterprise society, advertising helps increase productivity and raises the standard of living.

Keep in mind that advertising is directed at a **target audience**, a specific segment of the population for whom the product or service has a definite appeal. There are many target audiences that could be defined. The most general are consumers and business. Consequently, **consumer advertising**, as the name suggests, is targeted at the people who buy goods and services for personal use. Most of the advertising that most people are exposed to falls into this category. **Business-to-business advertising** is aimed at people who buy products for business use. Industrial, professional, trade, and agricultural advertising are all part of this category. Consumer advertising is the focus of most of this chapter but we will also take a brief look at business-to-business advertising.

● ● ● ●

CAPSULE HISTORY OF ADVERTISING

Advertising has been around ever since people have been around. Its earliest beginnings, of course, are impossible to pinpoint, but there are several examples dating back thousands of years. Clay tablets traced to ancient Babylon have been found with messages that touted an ointment dealer and a shoemaker. Ancestors of modern-day billboards were found in the ruins of Pompeii. Later, the town crier was an important advertising medium throughout Europe and England during the medieval period. In short, advertising was a well-established part of the social environment of early civilization.

In more recent times, the history of advertising is inextricably entwined with changing social conditions and advances in media technology. To illustrate, Gutenberg's invention of printing using movable type made possible several new advertising media: posters, handbills, and newspaper ads. In fact, the first printed advertisement in English was produced in about 1480 and was a handbill that announced a prayerbook for sale. Its author, evidently wise in the ways of outdoor advertising, tacked his ad to church doors all over England. By the late 1600s, ads were common sights in London newspapers.

Advertising made its way to the colonies along with the early settlers from England. The *Boston Newsletter* (see Chapter 4) became the first American newspaper to publish advertising. Ben Franklin, a pioneer of early advertising, made his ads more attractive by using large headlines and considerable white space. From Franklin's time up to the early nineteenth century, newspaper ads greatly resembled what today are called classified ads.

The Industrial Revolution caused major changes in American society and in American advertising. Manufacturers, with the aid of newly invented machines, were able to mass produce their products. Mass production, however, also required mass consumption and a mass market. Advertising was a tremendous aid in reaching this new mass audience.

The impact of increasing industrialization was most apparent in the period following the end of the Civil War (1865) to the beginning of the twentieth century. In little more than three decades, the following occurred:

1. The railroad linked all parts of the country, making it possible for Eastern manufacturers to distribute their goods to the growing Western markets.

2. Thanks in large measure to an influx of immigrants, the population of the United States grew quickly, doubling between 1870 and 1900. More people meant larger markets for manufacturers.

3. The invention of new communication media—the telephone, typewriter, high-speed printing press, phonograph, motion pictures, photography, rural mail delivery—made it easier for people to communicate with one another.

4. Economic production increased dramatically, and people had more disposable income to spend on new products.

This improved economic and communication climate helped advertising thrive. Magazines were distributed from coast to coast and made possible truly national advertising. The development of the halftone method for reproducing photographs meant that magazine advertisers could portray their products more vividly. By 1900, it was not unusual for the leading magazines of the period (*Harper's*, *Cosmopolitan*, *McClure's*) to run 75–100 pages of ads in a typical issue.

Not surprisingly, the increased importance of advertising in the marketing process led to the birth of the **advertising agency**, an organization that specializes in providing advertising services to its clients. The roots of the modern-day agency can be traced to Volney B. Palmer of Philadelphia. In 1842, Palmer bought large amounts of space in various newspapers at a discount and then resold the space at higher rates to advertisers. The actual ad—the copy, layout, and artwork—was still prepared by the company wishing to advertise; in effect, Palmer was a space broker. That situation changed in the late nineteenth century when the advertising agency of N. W. Ayer & Son was founded. Ayer & Son offered to plan, create, and execute a complete advertising campaign for their customers. By 1900, the advertising agency became the focal point of creative planning, and advertising was firmly established as a profession.

This new profession, however, was not without its problems. Around the turn of the century, patent medicine ads that made extravagant claims of curing every known disease were found in many publications. The wild and unsubstantiated claims for these products sparked a consumer revolt, and in 1906 Congress passed the Pure Food and Drug Act, the first federal law to control advertising. Several years later, Congress

An ad from the 1900s for Coca-Cola. Included at the bottom is a coupon for a free Coke. (Culver Pictures)

also created the Federal Trade Commission (FTC), an agency designed to protect businesses from unfair competitive practices. At about this same time, efforts aimed at wiping out fraudulent advertising also began within the advertising profession (Chapters 17 and 18).

The 1920s saw the beginning of radio as an advertising medium (see Chapter 8). The rise of network broadcasting made radio an attractive vehicle for national advertisers. By 1930 about $27 million was spent on network advertising, and many of the most popular shows of the day were produced by advertising agencies. The stock market crash of 1929 had a disastrous effect on the U.S. economy. Total dollars spent on advertising dropped from $2.8 billion in 1929 to $1.7 billion in 1935. It would take a decade for the industry to recover. World War II meant that many civilian firms cut back on their advertising budgets. Others simply changed the content of their ads and instead of selling their products instructed consumers on how to make their products last until after the war.

The growth of advertising from the end of the war in 1945 to the early 1990s can only be described as spectacular. The changeover from a war economy to a consumer economy prompted a spurt in advertising as manufacturers hurried to meet the demand for all the goods and services that people had put off buying because of the war. From 1950 to 1975, the amount of money spent on advertising increased an incredible 490 percent. Also during this period several significant developments took place. The most important was probably television's rise as a national advertising medium. TV's growth had an impact on both radio and magazines. Radio became a medium used primarily by local advertisers. Magazines that aimed at specialized audiences attracted more advertisers, but general-interest publications (such as *Collier's* and *Look*) could not compete with TV and eventually went under. Second, the consumer became a more powerful force in the marketplace. Responding to increased consumer pressure, the FTC introduced corrective advertising during the 1970s (see Chapter 17). Third, direct advertising (much of it done through the mail) increased by more than 800 percent from 1950 to 1980. This increase was due to the growth of computerized mailing lists, the emergence of the telephone as a marketing tool, and the expanded use of credit card shopping.

The 1980s and 1990s saw the media environment for advertising change drastically. Cable television opened up dozens of new and specialized channels that siphoned advertising dollars away from the major TV networks. Videocassettes and computer-

This Space for Sale

Advertising messages can be found in some pretty unusual places these days:

- One company sells space at the bottom of golf holes.

- Another company will reproduce your logo or trademark as a removable tattoo that you can wear on your arm or some other part of your anatomy.

- Many restaurants sell the space on restroom walls or stall doors.

- In Canada, cows grazing near a highway were painted with advertising messages.

But perhaps the most innovative is a Chicago company called Viskase that has developed a process that places edible-ink messages on the outside of hot dogs—now that's an idea to relish.

ized data services such as Prodigy have opened up new avenues for advertising. Moreover, improved transportation and communication gave birth to the mega-ad agency with branches throughout the world. Political changes in Europe have created new opportunities for global marketing. In sum, contemporary advertising must cope with a multitude of social, governmental, economic, and technological factors to adapt to the modern world.

• • • •

ORGANIZATION OF THE CONSUMER ADVERTISING INDUSTRY

There are three main components of the advertising industry:

1. the advertisers

2. advertising agencies

3. the media

Each of these will be discussed in turn.

Advertisers

Advertising is an important part of the overall marketing plan of almost every organization that provides a product or a service to the public. Advertisers can range from the small bicycle shop on the corner that spends $4 on an ad in the local weekly paper to huge international corporations such as Procter & Gamble, which spends more than $2.1 billion annually for ads.

At a basic level, we can distinguish two different types of advertisers: national and retail. **National advertisers** sell their product or service to customers all across the country. The emphasis in national advertising is on the product or service and not so much on the place where the product or service is sold. For example, the Coca-Cola Company is interested in selling soft drinks. It doesn't matter to the company if you buy their product at the local supermarket, a small convenience store, or from a vending machine; as long as you buy their products, the company will be happy. **Retail advertisers** (also called local advertisers) are companies such as local restaurants, car dealerships, TV repair shops, and other merchants and service organizations that have customers in only one city or trading area. The retail advertiser wants to attract customers to a specific store or place of business. Some companies are both national and local advertisers. Sears and K mart, for example, advertise all over the country, but their individual stores use local advertising to highlight their specific sales and promotions. Franchises, such as McDonald's and Burger King, keep up their national image by advertising on network TV, while their local outlets put ads in the paper to attract customers from the local community.

Naturally, the way organizations handle their advertising depends on their size. Some companies have their own advertising departments; a small retail store might have one person who is responsible for advertising and marketing and who may also have other job functions. Large or small, there are several basic functions that must be attended to by all advertisers. These include planning the ads and deciding where they will appear, setting aside a certain amount of money for the advertising budget, coordinating the advertising with other departments in the organization, and, if necessary, supervising the work of an outside agency or company that produces the ad. In addition, some large advertisers have departments that can create and prepare all the advertising materials, purchase the space and airtime for the ads, and check to see if the ads were effective in achieving their goals.

No matter how the advertising is handled, it is likely that quite a few people in the organization are really part of the advertising business. In some companies, the

The familiar face of Victor Kiam, president and chief spokesperson for Remington. (Remington Products, Inc.)

president or chief executive becomes actively involved (for example, Dave Thomas of Wendy's, Victor Kiam of Remington—he liked the razor so much he bought the company—Frank Perdue of Perdue Chickens). Moreover, sales and marketing personnel keep a close watch on the type of advertising that is planned and where the advertising is to appear. Even the people in the design and production departments are often asked to contribute ideas to the company's ads. In short, it could be said that almost everyone in the company feels that he or she is involved with the company's ads because the advertising represents them in some way.

Agencies

According to the American Association of Advertising Agencies, an agency is an independent business organization composed of creative and business people who develop, prepare, and place advertising in advertising media for sellers seeking to find customers for their goods and services. The big advertising agencies tend to be located in the big cities, particularly New York, Los Angeles, and Chicago. Smaller agencies, however, are located all across the country. In fact, most cities with more than 100,000 people usually have at least one advertising agency. When it comes to income, however, the bigger agencies dominate.

The last few years in the agency business have seen the spawning of superagencies, or "mega-agencies," resulting from the merger and consolidation of several large ad agencies. In addition, the business has been "globalized," since these new mega-agencies have branches all over the world. The half-dozen mega-agencies listed in Table 16-1 dominated the industry at the close of 1990.

The impact of foreign ownership is apparent in the agency business as in many other media. Three of the megagroups in Table 16-1 are foreign-owned.

Agencies can be classified by the range of services that they offer. In general terms, there are three main types: (1) full-service agencies, (2) media buying services, and (3) creative boutiques.

As the name implies, a **full-service agency** is one that handles all phases of the advertising process for its clients; it plans, creates, produces, and places ads for its clients. In addition, it might also provide other marketing services such as sales promotions, trade show exhibits, newsletters, and annual reports. In theory, at least,

TABLE 16-1 Mega-Agencies Ranked by Worldwide Income, 1990

AGENCY	HEADQUARTERS	GROSS INCOME (MILLIONS)
WPP Group	London	$2813
Interpublic Group	New York	1989
Omnicom Group	New York	1807
Saatchi & Saatchi	London	1696
Dentsu	Tokyo	1387
Young and Rubicam	New York	1072

there is no need for the client to deal with any other company for help on promoting their product.

A **media buying service** is an organization that specializes in buying radio and television time and reselling it to advertisers and advertising agencies. The service sells the time to the advertiser, orders the spots on the various stations involved, and monitors the stations to see if the ads actually run.

A **creative boutique** (the name was coined during the 1960s and has hung on to the present) is an organization that specializes in the actual creation of ads. In general, boutiques create imaginative and distinctive advertising themes and produce innovative and original ads. A company that uses a creative boutique would have to employ another agency to perform the planning, buying, and administrative functions connected with advertising.

Not surprisingly, full-service agencies saw media buying services and boutiques as competitors. Consequently, the full-service agencies improved their own creative and media buying departments. It wasn't long before the services and boutiques began to feel the effects of the agencies' efforts. As it stands now, only a few services and a few boutiques still handle large national advertisers.

What does a full-service ad agency do for a client? To begin with, the agency studies the product or service and determines its marketable characteristics and how it relates to the competition. At the same time the agency studies the potential market, possible distribution plans, and likely advertising media. Following this the agency makes a formal presentation to the client detailing its findings about the product and its recommendations for an advertising strategy. If the client agrees, the agency then launches the execution phase. This phase entails writing and producing the ads, buying space and time in various media, delivering the ads to the appropriate media, and verifying that all ads actually appeared. Finally, the agency will work closely with the client's salespeople to make sure that they get the greatest possible benefit from the ads.

Media

The last part of the advertising industry consists of the mass media. The media serve as the connection between the company that has a service or product to sell and the customers who wish to buy it. The media that are available for advertising include the obvious ones—radio, television, newspapers, magazines—and others that are not so obvious, such as direct mail, billboards, transit cards (bus and car cards), stadium scoreboard ads, and point-of-purchase displays. Chapters 5, 6, 8, 9, and 13 presented a general overview of newspapers, magazines, radio, and television and also discussed their dependence on various kinds of advertising. This section examines them from the perspective of an advertiser and also discusses direct-mail and other out-of-home advertising media.

Even the slickest and most imaginative advertising message will fail if it is delivered to the wrong people. To make sure that this catastrophe doesn't happen, advertisers employ highly skilled media planners to help them place and schedule their ads. With the numerous mass media that are available to deliver the message and the hundreds (even thousands) of individual media outlets to choose from, it is necessary to study closely what each of the various media can offer.

When advertising specialists look at the various media, they tend to evaluate them along four dimensions:

1. Reach—how many people can get the message?

2. Frequency—how often will the message be received?

3. Selectivity—does the medium actually reach potential customers?

4. Efficiency—how much does it cost to reach a certain number of people? (this is usually expressed as cost per thousand people)

Newspapers have good reach; they can go to every geographic location in the country and are read by millions of people. Many newspapers are published daily, which means that advertisers can present their messages to the audience with a high degree of frequency. The newspaper, unless it is a specialized publication aimed at a certain ethnic group, does not score high on the selectivity dimension. Although it gives an advertiser geographic selectivity by being distributed in a certain area of the market, within that area its readership is not specific. It would be inefficient, for example, to use the newspaper alone to reach eighteen- to twenty-five-year-old females since the paper is not specifically targeted to that group. In terms of cost, it is hard to generalize because there are so many newspapers to consider. In general terms, the absolute cost of advertising in many papers is inexpensive, but the standardized cost of reaching a thousand people tends to be relatively high.

Magazines tend to have a more limited reach than newspapers. Further, most magazines come out once per month, which means that the potential for frequent presentations of an ad is not high. On the other hand, magazines offer a tremendous degree of selectivity for advertisers. If an advertiser wanted to reach teenage girls, he or she could choose among several publications designed for that audience segment. The cost of magazine advertising tends to be relatively high, but this cost must be evaluated against its efficiency in reaching a target group.

Radio has excellent reach and allows advertisers to present their messages with great frequency. In addition, radio stations aim for specialized audience groups, allowing advertisers to pinpoint a specific group with their messages. The cost of radio advertising is low and represents a good value to advertisers. The problem with radio advertising is that there are so many stations competing for basically the same audience—a situation that makes it difficult for an advertiser to select the most efficient mix of stations.

Television has almost universal reach and allows for frequent repetition of messages. Television is not very selective in the audience it reaches, but the advertiser does have some flexibility. For example, certain programs tend to draw a certain kind of audience. The network news, for example, draws an older audience; soap operas still tend to attract primarily a female following. The potential of selectivity for TV will increase with the widespread growth of cable TV channels. MTV, for example, attracts an audience composed mainly of fifteen- to twenty-five-year-olds. On the cost dimension, television's situation is almost the opposite of newspapers. In absolute terms, the cost of advertising on TV, especially network TV, is high because it reaches so many people. It's so expensive that many smaller companies simply cannot afford it. If the cost for reaching a thousand viewers is calculated, however, it is relatively low.

Billboards and other outdoor advertising media score high in terms of reach and frequency dimensions. With proper positioning and lighting, outdoor advertising can be seen twenty-four hours a day all year long. Its selectivity is limited, however, since its audience will be composed of all people who happen to pass a certain point. Outdoor advertising also tends to be a relatively expensive way to advertise.

Direct advertising, especially direct mail, has the potential for widespread reach. Virtually everybody has a mailbox. It also has the potential for frequent delivery of the message. Direct advertising is probably the most selective of all advertising media. Special mailing lists allow the advertiser to focus on his or her particular target audience. One disadvantage of direct advertising is its high cost. Direct mail in particular has become rather expensive with the recent increases in postal rates.

Finally, of course, in addition to the above considerations, advertisers have to take into account many other factors before deciding on what medium to use. An important part of any decision involves considering the creative limitations imposed by the physical properties of each medium. Television, for example, allows the advertiser to show the product in action. On the other hand, TV ads are short and cannot be used to present a great deal of technical information. A magazine ad can be in full color and can present a large amount of data, but it might not have the same impact as a TV ad. All in all, choosing what media to use in the final advertising mix is a difficult decision.

●●●●
PRODUCING ADVERTISING

Departments and Staff

Figure 16-1 shows the departmental chart for a typical advertising agency. Remember also that many large companies have their own advertising departments in the overall corporate organization, and their arrangement would be similar to the one presented here. As can be seen, there are four major departments:

1. creative

2. account services

FIGURE 16-1 *Structure of a typical advertising agency.*

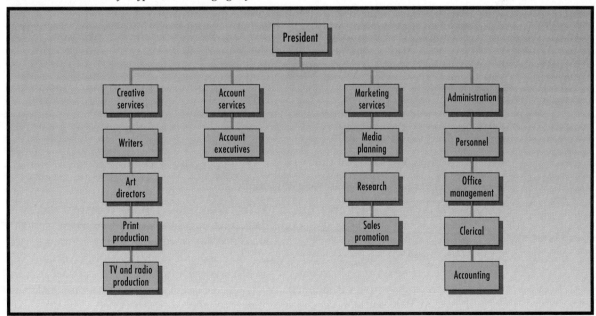

3. marketing

4. administration

The creative department, as the name implies, actually produces the ad. The people in this department write the advertising **copy** (the headline and message of the ad), choose the illustrations, prepare artwork, and/or supervise the scripting and production of radio and TV commercials.

The account services department is responsible for the relationship between the agency and the client. Because the advertising agency is an organization outside the firm doing the advertising, it is necessary to appoint someone, usually called an account executive (AE), to promote communication and understanding between client and agency. The AE must represent the viewpoint of the agency to the client but at the same time must keep abreast of the needs of the advertiser. Needless to say, since the AE tends to be the person in the middle, his or her job is an important one in the agency.

The marketing services department is responsible for advising the client as to what media to use for his or her messages. Typically this department makes extensive use of the data collected by the Audit Bureau of Circulations, Arbitron, Nielsen, and the other audience research services mentioned in Chapter 20. This department is also in charge of any sales promotions that are done in connection with the advertising. These may include such things as coupons, premiums, and other aids to dealers.

Finally, like any other business, the advertising agency needs a department to take care of the day-to-day administration of the agency. This department is in charge of office management, clerical functions, accounting, personnel, and training of new employees.

The Advertising Campaign

Advertising appears in a variety of media, and the production techniques vary with each. In addition, much of the actual creative work involved in putting together the ads takes place before the production process and reflects strategic decisions made during the initial planning process. Consequently, perhaps the best way to illustrate how ads get produced is to present a general discussion of an advertising campaign for a national product. A **campaign** consists of a large number of advertisements all stressing the same major theme or appeal that appear in a number of media over a specified time. Greatly simplified, there are at least six different phases of a typical campaign:

1. choosing the marketing strategy

2. selecting the main appeal or theme

3. translating the theme into the various media

4. producing the ads

5. buying space and time

6. executing and evaluating the campaign

In the first phase, a great deal of research is done to determine the target audience, the marketing objective, the appropriate price for the product or service, and the advertising budget. It is during this phase that the word **positioning** is often heard. Positioning has many interpretations, but in general it means fitting a product or service to one or more segments of the broad market in such a way as to set it apart from the competition without making any change in the product. For example, during 1989 and 1990 oat bran cereals and other products were positioned as health foods since it was thought they might lower the risk of heart attack. (Subsequent research

Sometimes ideas that look good at first glance may not turn out that way. Take Reebok's famous bungee jumper ad. Two people jump off a bridge with bungee cords tied to their feet. One is wearing Reeboks, the other Nikes. They fall until they reach the end of the cords. The jumper wearing the Reeboks dangles safely at the end of the cord. The other cord is attached only to an empty pair of shoes. The jumper, we assume, has perished. The voice-over says that Reeboks "fit a little better than your ordinary athletic shoe." Consumers didn't exactly warm to the notion of watching someone fall to their death, even in a "humorous" commercial. Hit by bad publicity, Reebok pulled the ad.

Then there was the mix-up with Premier, the "smokeless" cigarette, and *TV Guide*. The cigarette was being test marketed in Phoenix, Tucson, and St. Louis. Ads were supposed to appear in *TV Guide* in those markets and nowhere else. Somebody slipped up, however, and the ads appeared in all issues of *TV Guide* except those in Phoenix, Tucson, and St. Louis.

Then there was the print ad for Marriott's Residence Inn that dramatized the difference between the average stay at a Residence Inn versus the stay at most hotels, using jockey-type shorts. Above the words "most hotels" were two pairs of shorts while above "Residence Inn" were ten pairs. Many consumers were offended by having to look at what they thought was dirty underwear. Women especially objected to the ad. In an era when more and more women are traveling on business, it's hard to understand why Marriott associated their inn with men's shorts.

Some ads surprise their creators by stirring up unexpected resentment on the part of some consumers. An ad for Coors Extra Gold offered a humorous solution for how to order at a crowded bar. The star of the ad played a polka on the jukebox and the place emptied out. Polish-Americans in general and the polka industry in particular were offended by the ad and circulated leaflets suggesting Polish beer drinkers stay away from the brand. Coors pulled the ad and was even considering running a "pro-polka" spot to make up for it.

Similarly, Continental Air Lines faced threats of a boycott from Asian-Americans who objected to an ad showing a samurai warrior slashing an airline seat in half to demonstrate reduced airfares. A Black Flag insecticide commercial offended veterans' groups because it played "Taps" to mark the death of the bugs it killed. These days you can't be too careful.

disclosed their benefits were overrated and the products abandoned this approach.) Jergens Advanced Therapy Lotion attempted to position itself as an upscale skin lotion, much like the ones that are sold at department store counters, by emphasizing the product's ability to heal damaged skin cells with a special blend of moisturizing ingredients. Kellogg's Big Mixx cereal was positioned as a healthy presweetened cereal for kids. It was designed to appeal to parents who want to buy something they feel is wholesome for their kids. Pert Plus positioned itself as the product for men and women on the go who find it more convenient to use a combination shampoo-conditioner than two separate products.

Sometimes positioning doesn't work, as was the case with Uptown cigarettes, which tried to position itself as the brand for urban blacks but had to be withdrawn after protests by black antismoking groups. Stouffer's low-fat, low-sodium Right Course entrees failed in part bcause they weren't positioned differently enough from the same company's low-calorie Lean Cuisine meals. Minute Maid orange juice failed in its attempt to reposition its product from simply a breakfast drink to an all-purpose beverage. Despite an $18 million campaign featuring the message "Not just for breakfast anymore," sales of orange juice remained flat as consumers didn't respond to the switch.

After the product or service has been positioned, an overall theme for the campaign is developed. Once again, considerable research is done to find the proper themes. For example, Glidden, the paint company, found that most paint is bought by people between 35 and 55 who are rehabilitating homes they already own. As a result, a $10 million campaign stressed the durability of the product. Pontiac discovered a significant jump in consumer concern about safety and subsequently redesigned the ads for its Bonneville model to stress its antilock brakes, air bag, and traction control as opposed to its power and styling. When it introduced its new Saturn, General Motors was aware of the poor image that U.S. auto manufacturers had developed among many consumers. As a result, Saturn ads were careful not to make a connection between GM and the new company. The theme was "A different kind of company. A different kind of car."

The next phase consists of translating the theme into print and broadcast ads. Advertisers try to achieve variety in their various ads but with a consistency of approach that will help consumers remember and recognize their product. The recent "It's a good time for the good taste of McDonald's" campaign is a case in point. McDonald's advertising agency created 1000 variations on that theme in a single year. Competitor Burger King scored so big with their 1970 theme "Have it your way" that they reintroduced a variation of it into their 1990 ads, "Your way. Right away." The U.S. Army has used its "Be all that you can be" theme for nine years in its print and broadcast ads and has only recently introduced variations.

The actual production of the ad is done much in the same way as other media content is produced. In the print media, the copy, the headline, subheads, any accompanying illustrations, and the layout are first prepared in rough form. The initial step is usually just a thumbnail sketch that can be used to experiment with different arrangements within the ad. The headline might be moved down, the copy moved from right

An ad for Saturn. The car is made by General Motors, but the ad is careful not to mention that fact. (Reprinted by permission of Saturn Corporation. © 1991, Saturn Corp.)

Subliminal persuasion consists of sending persuasive messages just below the threshold of perception. (In psychology, the perceptual threshold is called a "limen," hence the term "subliminal.") Whether or not subliminal persuasion really works in ads has been an advertising controversy for about thirty years. It all started back in the 1950s with an experiment in a movie theater. While the movie was playing, messages were flashed on the screen for about 1/3000 of a second, too fast for the conscious mind to perceive them. The messages said "Drink Coca-Cola" and "Eat Popcorn." The experimenters claimed that sales figures jumped 57 percent for popcorn and 18 percent for Coke in the six weeks of the study. Was subliminal persuasion at work? Probably not. All subsequent attempts to replicate this finding failed. Quite probably the increased sales were the result of the particular film that was shown—*Picnic*. This movie had plenty of scenes of people eating and drinking in hot summer weather, which probably inspired the audience to imitate the actors. Other experiments have indicated that subliminal persuasion is unlikely. Perceptual thresholds vary tremendously among people. Even if the message was perceived, it would probably be distorted. "Eat Popcorn" might come out "Cheat Your Horn."

The subliminal controversy erupted again in 1972 with the publication of *Subliminal Seduction* by Wilson Bryan Key. The author claimed that advertisers manipulated consumers by deliberately embedding sexual symbols and words within the artwork of their ads. Key's book contained illustrations of this alleged subliminal persuasion. These examples ranged from supposed phallic symbols hidden in the ice cubes in the illustration for a liquor ad to a four-letter word allegedly hidden in an ad for dolls. Most people who saw Key's examples were hard pressed to find the images he described without a huge dose of imagination and poetic license. It turned out, however, there was at least a tiny particle of truth to Key's charges. Several photographers and photo touch-up artists confessed that they had indeed introduced carefully disguised sexual references to ads as a private practical joke. These instances were few in number, and it hardly constituted a conscious manipulation by the advertising industry.

In any case, there is no proof that ads with camouflaged sexual content sell better than the tamer versions. Subliminal persuasion is fun to talk about but there is little evidence that it exists.

to left, and so on. Next a **rough layout**, a drawing that is the actual size of the ad, is constructed. There are usually several of these rough layouts prepared, and the best of these are used to produce the **comprehensive layout**, the one that will actually be used to produce the ad. Many agencies use outside art studios and printers to help them put together print ads and billboards.

Radio commercials are written and created much in the same way that early radio drama shows were produced. A script is prepared in which dialogue, sound effects, and music are combined to produce whatever effect is desired. The commercial is then either produced in the sound studio or recorded live on location. In either case, postproduction editing adds any desired special effects, and eventually a master tape is prepared for duplication and distribution.

The beginning step in the preparation of a television commercial is the preparation of a **storyboard**, a series of drawings depicting the key scenes of the planned ad. Storyboards are usually shown to the client before production begins. If the client has any objections or suggestions, they can be incorporated into the script before the expensive production begins. Once the storyboards are approved, the commercial is ready to go into production. Most TV commercials are shot on film (although some

Great Advertising Ideas that Failed (Part II)

Everybody thought it was a great idea. Pepsi Cola had signed the hottest star around, Madonna, to star in a commercial for their soft drink. Madonna did not come cheap. Her fee for the commercial was $5 million. When they saw the finished product, Pepsi execs thought it was worth it. In the slick and well-produced spot, Madonna, sipping a Pepsi, watches a home movie of her eighth birthday party, travels back to her childhood, dances, sings, and frolics with teens in a street scene, all to the tune of "Like a Prayer." At the end, the seductively-clad songstress issues her own version of an updated Pepsi challenge: "Go ahead. Make a wish."

What Pepsi didn't know was that Madonna was also releasing a music video of "Like a Prayer." The video was sexy, suggestive, and many thought it portrayed religion in an unfavorable light. Numerous viewers associated the Pepsi spot with the music video and complained to the soft drink company. Faced with the threat of a consumer boycott, Pepsi withdrew the ad after running it only twice.

Pepsi, however, learned a lesson from this affair. In the future, the company will insist on the right to review any music videos with which its spots are associated. Further, when it came time to pick a celebrity to launch a new cherry cola, Pepsi selected the un-Madonna-like puppet, Howdy Doody. As far as we know, Mr. Doody has not made a music video.

are now switching to videotape) and the production process is similar to that described in Chapter 12. Television commercials are the most expensive ads to produce. A thirty-second commercial can easily cost $200,000. Special effects, particularly animation, can drive the costs even higher. In order to keep costs down, much of the time spent producing TV commercials consists of planning and rehearsal. As with the print media, many agencies hire outside production specialists to produce their commercials.

While the creative department is putting together the print and broadcast ads, the marketing department is busy buying time in those media judged to be appropriate for the campaign. If the product is seasonal (e.g., suntan lotion, snowmobiles), the ads are scheduled to reflect the calendar, appearing slightly before and during the time people begin buying such items. Other products and services might call for a program of steady advertising throughout the year.

The last phase of the campaign consists of the ads actually appearing. Testing is done during and after this phase to see if consumers actually saw and remembered the ads. In addition, sales data are carefully monitored to determine if the campaign had the desired effect on sales.

● ● ● ●
ECONOMICS

This section will examine the economics of advertising on two levels. First, we will look at the total industry and trace expenditures in the various mass media. Second, we will narrow our focus and examine how an ad agency makes money.

Advertising Volume in Various Media

About $130 billion was spent on advertising in the United States in 1990. Newspapers accounted for the biggest share of advertising volume—about 25 percent. TV ranked second, accounting for 22 percent, followed by direct mail, radio, magazines, and outdoor advertising. To give some idea of the dollar amounts involved, in 1990 approx-

The medium of outdoor advertising has grown rapidly over the last decade. Modern billboards use striking new designs and graphics. (Institute of Outdoor Advertising)

imately $31 billion was spent on newspaper ads compared to $29 billion spent on TV. About $25 billion was spent on direct mail. Since 1960, newspapers have shown a slight decrease in their relative share of advertising volume, as have direct mail and magazines. Television has shown a significant increase while radio and outdoor advertising have shown modest growth from 1960 to 1990. The weak economy of the early 1990s forced many businesses to cut back on advertising expenditures. Consequently, growth rates in the near future may not be as substantial.

Agency Compensation

How an advertising agency makes money is not well known outside the agency and media community. This section will discuss two common methods; (1) media commissions and (2) retainers.

Historically, the major mass media have allowed advertising agencies a 15 percent commission on the time and space that they purchase. This practice came about because the media recognized that agencies saved them a great deal of expense in making sales and collecting fees. In simplified form, here's how the commission system works. Let's assume you have a new product and have enlisted the services of an agency to help you market it. You wish to run an ad in a particular magazine that will cost $1000. Your agency places the order, prepares the ad, and sends it to the magazine. After the ad appears, the magazine sends the agency a bill for $1000. The agency passes this bill on to you. You send $1000 to the agency, which then deducts its 15 percent commission ($150 in this case) and sends the remainder ($850) to the magazine. If the total ad charges were $10,000, the agency would retain $1500 in commission. Recently, however, the traditional 15 percent commission fee has come under fire. Some advertisers feel the figure is too high and negotiate for a lower percentage. The big three automakers, for example, pay about a 12 percent commission. Other advertisers are putting agencies on a sliding scale that's tied to the performance of the advertised product. If sales go up, the agency gets more money. If they go down, compensation is reduced. The Campbell Soup Company, for example, sets sales goals with the ad agency before the campaign starts. If the goals are met, the agency gets 15 percent. If they are exceeded, the commission goes to 16 percent. If the goals are not met, compensation is reduced to 14 percent. Nabisco has a system in which agency compensation is set between 10 and 15 percent with bonuses ranging from 5 to 20 percent if sales goals are met. Other companies are opting for a fixed fee plus reduced commission arrangement. In fact, by the early 1990s, less than half of all advertisers were using the straight commission arrangement.

The retainer or fixed fee system is somewhat similar to the retainers paid to lawyers or accountants. The agency and the advertiser agree on a minimum monthly or annual fee that the agency is to receive for its services. Sometimes any commissions earned by the agency during this period are charged against this fee. In other instances, the services performed by the agency for the client may not produce commission income (e.g., research, annual report preparation), in which case the flat fee is charged.

● ● ● ●

BUSINESS-TO-BUSINESS ADVERTISING

As its name suggests, business-to-business advertising is designed to sell products and services not to general consumers but to other businesses. This type of advertising is not as visible as consumer advertising since business advertising is typically confined to specialized trade publications, direct mail, professional journals, and special display advertising planned for trade shows. Recently, however, some business-to-business ads have turned up in the mass media.

Although its visibility might not be high, business-to-business advertising is big business, ringing up more than $100 billion in revenue in 1990. Some students ignore a career in business-to-business advertising because they feel it's not as glamorous as consumer advertising. There may be some truth to this: Selling a chemical solvent, bench-top fermenter, or blast furnace is not as flashy as designing a campaign for a sleek new sports car. It its own way, though, business advertising poses greater creative challenges. Coming up with a theme to sell the sports car is probably a lot easier than coming up with a winning idea for the chemical solvent.

Consumer vs. Business-to-Business Advertising

There are some obvious differences between advertising directed at consumers and business advertising. This section will list four.

First, the target audience in business advertising is much smaller. In some industries, the audience may number in the hundreds. Companies that manufacture storage tanks for petroleum products have determined that there are only 400 people in the United States authorized to purchase their product. In other areas, it may be in the thousands. This means, of course, that the media used to reach the target market must be selected carefully. In the nuclear reactor business, perhaps one or two publications are read by everyone in the market.

Second, most of the products that are advertised tend to be technical, complicated, and high priced. For the advertiser, this means that the ads will probably contain a great deal of technical information and will stress accuracy.

Third, the buyers will be professionals. Unlike the consumer market where anybody can buy the product, the targets in business-to-business advertising are usually purchasing agents whose only job is to acquire products and services for their company. Generally speaking, the decisions of the purchasing agent are based on reason and research. An error of a penny or two on a large purchase might cost the company thousands of dollars. Consequently, business advertising typically uses the rational approach. Additionally, it's important for the advertisers to know exactly who makes the buying decision, since most purchases in large business are generally made in consultation with others in the company.

Fourth, personal selling plays a greater role in the business arena and advertising is frequently seen as supporting the sales staff in the field. As a result, ad budgets in the business sector may not be as high as their consumer counterparts.

The media mix for business advertising is also different from consumer advertising. Since the target audience tends to be small, personalized media are best. Business publications tend to be the mainstay of a lot of campaigns. One study suggested that about 60 percent of industrial advertising dollars went to business and trade publications. Trade publications can be horizontal, dealing with a job function without regard to industry (such as *Purchasing Agent*), or vertical, covering all job types in an entire industry, such as *LP/Gas*.

Direct mail is also a valuable business advertising tool. Highly differentiated mailing lists can be prepared and ads sent to the most likely prospects. Research has shown that direct mail is perhaps better accepted among business people than among consumers. Whereas a large percentage of direct mail material is thrown out unopened by the general public, about three-quarters of all business people, according to a survey done in the early 1980s, read or at least scan their direct mail ads.

Advertising in trade catalogs is particularly important to those companies that sell through distributors rather than their own sales staff. Since a catalog is a direct reflection of the company, extra care is taken to make sure it is up-to-date, accurate, and visually appealing.

Business-to-business advertising in the mass media used to be rare, but some large companies, such as Federal Express, IBM, and Xerox, have used it to great effect. Federal Express, for example, found that its business increased more than 40 percent after it started to advertise in consumer media. Purchasing time and space in the mass media must be done skillfully because of the expense and the chance of wasted coverage if the right decision makers are not in the audience. Consequently, those firms that do use the mass media buy time on TV shows that draw an older demographic mix, such as *60 Minutes*, or buy space in business magazines or general news magazines. *Business Week*, *Fortune*, and *Forbes* are obvious choices. Some publications, such as *Time* and *Newsweek*, have special editions that go to the business community.

An example of business-to-business advertising. This ad for industrial equipment ties in with Operation Desert Storm. (Courtesy Clark ® Material Handling Company)

Close attention is paid to the copy in business-to-business advertising. A lot of consumer ads depend on impression and style to carry their message. The copy tends to be brief and can cater to the emotions. Business copy tends to be longer, more detailed, and more factual. A premium is placed on accuracy and completeness. If the ad contains technical inaccuracy or unsubstantiated exaggeration, the credibility of the product is compromised. Some of the most used formats in business advertising are testimonials, case histories, new product news, and demonstrations.

This is not to say, however, that all industrial ads should be stodgy and dull. In recent years, several ad agencies specializing in business ads have introduced warmth, humor, and creativity into their messages. The philosophy behind this movement is that business people are also consumers and that they respond as consumers to business and trade ads. For example, the headline in an ad for New Zealand Kiwifruit promised to tell grocers "how to rid your store of these ugly little brown things." The body copy stressed the importance of displaying the kiwis next to traditional fruit such as strawberries and peaches, which would encourage shoppers to snap them up. Federal Express ran a print ad that featured a Federal Express Overnight Letter Package next to a plain brown envelope that might be sent through the postal system. Under the Federal Express envelope was "V.I.P."; under the brown envelope, "R.I.P." It's likely that this trend will continue.

● ● ● ●
ISSUES

One of the most controversial and long-standing issues concerning advertising has to do with its effects on children. This matter is discussed in detail in Chapter 21. This section will concentrate on more general issues that are of more recent origin.

The first involves appropriate environments for ads. This worry was ignited by the formation of "Channel One" by the Whittle Communications Company. In the fall of 1990, the company began producing and distributing by satellite a twelve-minute news and information program that was designed to be seen in the classroom. What was controversial about this proposal was the inclusion of two minutes of commercials in the newscast. In return for carrying the newscast, each school that participated would receive about $50,000 in video equipment including monitors, VCRs, and a satellite dish. Whittle's plans called for eventually reaching about 8000 schools and 6.5 million to 12- to 17-year-olds. Advertisers that signed up for the "Channel One" spots included Levi Strauss, the U.S. Army, Wrigley's gum, and Gillette.

The program met with controversy as soon as it was announced. Several educators felt it was inappropriate to bring commercials into the classroom and to show them to a captive audience. Some felt the forced viewing of commercials was not an educational activity and should not be permitted. Critics felt it was as if the school system was telling kids what they should go out and buy. Officials in California and New York felt so strongly about the project, they vowed to keep it out of the school systems there.

Other educators, however, were pleased. They argued that young people are exposed to so many commercials in everyday life that the impact of in-school viewing of ads would be infinitesimal. In addition, other forms of advertising, such as posters, vending machines, notebooks, and designer-label clothing are common in middle schools and high schools. Many school systems, hard pressed for cash, were particularly appreciative of the video equipment that came with the program. Most of the teachers who saw the program thought that it was well done and did improve students' current events knowledge. Nonetheless, the debate continued. Should the sanctity of the

High school students watching Channel One from Whittle Communications. The inclusion of commercials in Channel One's programming prompted controversy among educators. (Courtesy Whittle Communications)

classroom be defiled by the presence of advertising? Would you be willing to pay $10 less for this textbook if there were twenty pages of ads serving as chapter dividers and a full color spread for Pepsi on the back cover? Would you be willing to pay $200 less for tuition if your professor wore a Coke blazer and had a Coke logo on the lectern? The idea does have some interesting implications.

The second current issue that was receiving significant attention as the 1990s opened was the social responsibility of advertisers toward minority groups. The controversy was sparked by groups of black citizens who objected to the presence of billboards in black neighborhoods that advertised alcohol and tobacco products. These groups argued that lung cancer and alcoholism were severe problems in the black community and that advertising simply made them worse. Some groups even took to whitewashing or otherwise obliterating the billboards. In a related development, Health and Human Services Secretary Dr. Louis Sullivan joined with other black groups to stop the R. J. Reynolds Company from marketing and advertising Uptown cigarettes, a brand aimed at urban blacks. The Nike Company was heavily criticized for targeting young black youths in their commercials (directed by Spike Lee) for their $125 basketball shoes, a price that most urban blacks could not afford. Operation PUSH went so far as to organize a boycott against Nike products.

The advertising industry responded to this situation in various ways. Several liquor advertisers discontinued their billboard ads in inner-city neighborhoods. Hennessy Cognac and Canadian Mist, for example, redirected their ads from billboard to black consumer magazines. Seagrams, on the other hand, did not change its outdoor advertising strategy. For its part, Nike hired a minority-owned advertising agency to help it

Changes in Europe have made advertising there a new challenge. Europe becomes a single market in 1992 and the members of the European Community (EC) are proposing strict regulations concerning advertising that would cover everything from beer to bananas. Some of the directives under consideration included a total ban on tobacco advertising; a prohibition of advertising alcoholic beverages that promise sexual or social success; and careful scrutiny of all health and nutrition claims in food advertising.

The increasing acceptance of the free-market philosophy has meant that Eastern Europe may be the scene of the next advertising explosion. Things are changing so fast, however, it's difficult for advertisers to keep track of the changing status of East European media. Almost all newspapers, for example, accept advertising. Magazines in Czechoslovakia and Hungary resemble American magazines and accept ads. In Poland, however, slick magazines printed on coated paper don't exist. The state-owned TV network in Hungary is called MTV; it broadcasts ads throughout the day. In Czechoslovakia, however, commercials can be run only in two ten-minute blocks, one in

(Courtesy Stolichnaya ® Vodka)

Sometimes the best relationships start on the rocks.

Tomorrow, the superpowers begin yet another historic summit. Stolichnaya®—the import that broke the ice in 1972— hopes their discussions go as smoothly as their toasts.

Stoli.

the afternoon and one in the evening. Poland groups commercials together in blocks of up to four minutes. There are no commercial breaks within programs.

The one country that has seen the biggest shift in its attitude toward advertising has been Russia. Advertising used to be looked upon as a symbol of capitalistic decadence but as the country moves to a free-market system, Russian leaders are trying to learn as much as they can about the technique. In a recent seminar in Moscow organized by *Advertising Age*, participants wanted to know about writing slogans, how to name products, how to attract advertising, and how to use emotional appeals in ads.

Advertisers in the U.S. have also been quick to capitalize on the thaw in Russian-U.S. relations. A flurry of specially prepared ads greeted former Soviet leader Mikhail Gorbachev's 1990 visit to the U.S. An ad for Stolichnaya vodka showed two glasses with swizzle sticks that were miniature U.S. and Soviet flags. The copy read, "Sometimes the best relationships start on the rocks." Another ad for a rug company promised to solve all of Gorbachev's border problems with bordered rugs. Perhaps the most memorable was an ad by DOC Optique that showed Gorbachev wearing a pair of designer shades. The copy simply said "Sunglassnost."

with ethnic media planning. One of the tasks the agency was to supervise was a $7 million antidrug campaign and a series of proeducation spots with Bo Jackson. All of this has served to remind the industry of the importance of the social environment within which advertising must function.

CAREERS IN ADVERTISING

Although exact figures are hard to determine, there are more than 200,000 people working in the advertising business, with approximately 85,000 of those employed at advertising agencies. Job prospects appear bright for the future. The increasing amount of consumer goods being produced along with more intense competition among existing companies will create a sustained need for advertising specialists in the years ahead. Many experts think that opportunities will be the greatest in the advertising departments of large to medium size companies. No matter where a person intends to work, there are certain guidelines that are helpful in providing an overall view of the field.

Entry-Level Positions

Most advertising departments or advertising agencies rarely hire generalists; they prefer people with some degree of specialization. Consequently, a job applicant must make some basic decisions early in his or her professional training. Probably the first decision is whether to concentrate on the creative or the business side of the industry.

The creative side, as mentioned earlier, consists of the copywriters, art directors, graphic artists, photographers, and broadcast production specialists that put the ads together. Entry-level jobs would include junior copywriter, creative trainee, junior art director, and production assistants. In most of these positions, a college degree in advertising or the visual arts is helpful, with a secondary concentration in marketing, English, sociology, or psychology also a benefit. For those preferring to work in the creative area, you need to develop a **portfolio**, a collection of the best examples of your professional work. This work might have been done while you were still in school or on the job. Most employers expect to see such a sampling of your work during the job interview.

Working on the business side of the industry refers to choosing a career as an account executive, a media planner, market researcher, traffic manager, or business manager. Proper preparation for this career includes extensive course work in both advertising and business with particular emphasis on marketing. Common entry-level positions in these fields are assistant media buyer, research assistant, junior account executive, account service trainee, or a position in the traffic department. One of the most common entry-level jobs is that of traffic coordinator, the person who makes sure that all production work gets to the proper place at the proper time. Since this job provides a good experience with all the various departments in the firm, it is a good place for a newcomer to gain valuable experience. Some advertising agencies have training programs (although these are becoming harder to find), and others sponsor internships that make the initial jump into the business a little easier for the newcomer to master. The American Association of Advertising Agencies also has a free pamphlet, *A Guide to Careers in Advertising*, which can be requested from its New York office.

Finally, agency and advertising departments in private companies are not the only places to look for potential employment. There are a significant number of opportunities available in companies that supply their goods and services to advertisers. For example, freelance artists, photographers, jingle writers, film and videotape producers, sound recording specialists, and casting specialists are just some of the people needed by media suppliers. And, as has been pointed out in previous chapters, many people work for the various media in their advertising departments. These include copywriters at radio stations, people who sell newspaper and magazine space or radio and TV time, market researchers, sales promotion experts, and many others.

Upward Mobility

Opportunities for advancement in advertising are excellent. Outstanding performance is rewarded quickly, and many young people progress swiftly through the ranks. Beginning creative people typically become senior copywriters or senior art directors. Eventually, some may progress to become creative director, the person in charge of all creative services. On the business side, research assistants and assistant buyers can hope to become research directors and media directors. Account trainees, if they perform according to expectations, move up to account executives and later may become management supervisors. The climb to success can occur rapidly; many agencies are run by people who achieved top status before they reached forty.

● ● ● ●

SUGGESTIONS FOR FURTHER READING

The following books contain information about the concepts and topics discussed in this chapter.

ARLEN, MICHAEL, *Thirty Seconds*, New York: Penguin Books, 1979.

BOVEE, COURTLAND, AND WILLIAM ARENS, *Contemporary Advertising*, Homewood, Ill.: Richard D. Irwin, 1982.

DUNN, S. WATSON, ARNOLD BARBAN, DEAN KRUGMAN, AND LEONARD REID, *Advertising: Its Role in Modern Marketing*, Hinsdale, Ill.: Dryden, 1990.

RUSSELL, THOMAS, AND RON LANE, *Kleppner's Advertising Procedures*, 11th ed., Englewood Cliffs, N.J.: Prentice-Hall, 1990.

SEIDEN, HANK, *Advertising Pure and Simple*, New York: Amacom, 1990.

REGULATION OF THE MASS MEDIA

17

FORMAL CONTROLS: LAWS, RULES, REGULATIONS

ormal controls over the mass media include laws, court decisions that refine those laws, and rules and regulations administered by government agencies. In this chapter we will discuss five different areas where these formal controls are important: (1) the controversy over a free system of mass communication, (2) copyright, (3) restrictions on obscenity and pornography, (4) the regulation of radio and television, and (5) the regulation of advertising. Unfortunately, many students have the idea that the field of mass communication law and regulations is dull and boring. Nothing could be further from the truth. In what other textbook could you read about raunchy magazines, the CIA, soldiers of fortune, mass murderers, women in men's locker rooms, juicy divorces, and a man who owned a submarine?

THE PRESS, THE LAW, AND THE COURTS

A Free Press

As noted in Chapter 4, the idea of a free press did not catch on at first in America. The early colonial papers had problems if they were not "published by authority," that is, open to censorship by the Crown. Through the Stamp Act, the British government attempted to suppress hostile opinion by taxation. Recognizing these dangers to a free press, the framers of the Constitution added an amendment to that document. This amendment (the **First Amendment**) stated in part that "Congress shall make no law . . . abridging the freedom of speech, or of the press." The precise meaning and interpretation of these words, however, have been open to some debate. Let's examine some key instances in which press and government have come into conflict.

Prior Restraint

When the government attempts to censor the press by restraining it from publishing or broadcasting material, it is called **prior restraint**. Such attempts have been relatively rare. Nonetheless, this area does serve to illustrate that the provisions in the First Amendment are not absolute. The Supreme Court has ruled that under certain circumstances, prior restraint or censorship of the press is permitted, but the government faces a difficult task in proving that the restraint is justified. There are some obvious examples of legal censorship. During wartime a newspaper could be prevented from publishing the sailing schedules of troop transports; a radio station could be prohibited from broadcasting the location and numbers of soldiers on the front lines. Other attempts at prior restraint have not been particularly successful; the Supreme Court has generally upheld the right of the press. There are two specific cases in this area that are beneficial for us to examine. One is not widely known; the other made the front pages.

Near Case. During the 1920s, the Minnesota legislature passed a law under which newspapers that were considered public nuisances could be curtailed by means of an **injunction** (an order from a court that requires somebody to do something or refrain from doing something). The motives behind this law may have been praiseworthy because it appears to have been designed to prevent abusive attacks on minority groups. Using this law, a county attorney sought an injunction against the *Saturday Press* and the paper's manager, J. M. Near, on the grounds that the paper had printed malicious statements about city officials in connection with gangland activities allegedly controlled by minority groups. In 1931, the Supreme Court ruled that the Minnesota law was unconstitutional. Said the Court:

> The fact that for approximately 150 years there has been almost an entire absence of attempts to impose previous restraints upon publications relating to the malfeasance of public officers is significant of the deep-seated conviction that such restraints would violate constitutional rights.

It would be forty years before this issue was raised again.

The Pentagon Papers. U.S. Attorney General John Mitchell was anxious to see the Sunday, June 13, 1971, edition of the *New York Times*. Mitchell had attended the wedding of President Richard Nixon's daughter Tricia the day before, and he wanted to see how the *Times* had covered it. On the left side of page one, Mitchell saw a

---

The first installment of the Pentagon Papers appeared in the New York Times. *Attempts by the government to halt further publication ended when the Supreme Court ruled in favor of the* Times. *(© 1971 by the New York Times Company.)*

flattering picture of the president with his daughter on his arm. Next to the wedding picture, another story caught Mitchell's eyes: "Vietnam Archive: Pentagon Study Traces 3 Decades of Growing U.S. Involvement." As Mitchell read further he realized that the *Times* article was sure to cause problems.

The basis for the story in the *Times* began three years earlier when then Secretary of Defense Robert McNamara became disillusioned with the Vietnam War and ordered a massive study of its origins. This study, known eventually as the Pentagon Papers, was put together by thirty-six different people and ran for more than 7000 pages. The final report was classified "Top Secret—Sensitive." During April of 1971 one of those Pentagon staff members who compiled the report leaked a copy to a reporter for the *New York Times*. After much study and secrecy (the *Times* rented a suite at a New York hotel for staff members working on the story, furnished it with a safe, and put guards outside), the paper was ready to publish the story in nine different installments. The U.S. Justice Department, under John Mitchell's direction, asked a U.S. District Court judge to halt publication of the stories on the grounds that they would "cause irreparable injury to the defense interests of the United States." The order was granted, and for the first time in history a U.S. paper was ordered by the courts to suppress a specific story. By then, however, other newspapers had obtained copies of some or all of the Pentagon documents and started publishing them. The Justice Department sought more restraining orders, but as soon as one paper was ordered to stop publishing another newspaper in another part of the country would pick up the series. It was obvious that the Supreme Court would eventually have to intervene.

The Court did intervene and with uncharacteristic haste. On June 30, 1971, only seventeen days after the papers first appeared and only four days after hearing oral arguments on the case, the Court decided in favor of the newspapers' right to publish the information. Naturally, the staff at the *New York Times* was delighted. The paper called the decision a "ringing victory for freedom under law." Upon closer examination, however, the victory was not quite as ringing as it was made out to be. The Court did not state that prior restraint could never be invoked against the press. Instead, it pointed out that the government "carries a heavy burden of showing justification" for imposing restraint. The government, in the opinion of the Court, had not shown sufficient grounds for doing this. The government was free, if it wished, to bring other prior-restraint cases to the courts to establish exactly how much justification it needed to stifle publication. In addition, each of the nine judges wrote a separate opinion that highlighted the ambiguities and complexities surrounding this topic. Perhaps the best summary of the case was put forward by the Twentieth Century Fund's Task Force on Government and the Press: "While basic issues were posed, basic issues were not resolved." The Task Force went on to say: "The fact remains that there is as yet no authoritative concept of whether publication boundaries exist."

After the release of the Pentagon Papers, the prior restraint problem cropped up several times in cases involving former CIA agents. In one instance, the CIA was successful in having portions of a book deleted because they revealed classified information. In another, the government successfully sued a former agent who was the author of a book about the CIA, because the book was not submitted for prepublication review as required by the employment agreement with the intelligence agency. In 1982, Congress passed the Intelligence Identities Protection Act which made it a federal crime for people to publish anything that they have reason to know will disclose the identity of U.S. intelligence agents.

Covering the Military. The most recent cases involving prior restraint have involved reporting activities of the military. Much to the chagrin of the press, the Reagan administration was able to keep all civilian reporters and photographers from early coverage of the invasion of Grenada in 1983. Partly because of this problem, the press

Prior Restraint and the High School Press

A 1988 Supreme Court decision left little doubt that there was one area where authorities could exercise prior restraint—the high school newsroom. The case began in 1983 when a principal in Hazelwood, Missouri, deleted from the high school paper two articles, one on teenage pregnancy and one about divorce, on the grounds that they were inappropriate.

Three students, with the help of the American Civil Liberties Union, filed suit in district court, arguing that their First Amendment rights were being violated. The district court found in favor of the school system. The students appealed this decision and were delighted when the appeals court reversed the district court. Ultimately, however, the case wound up at the Supreme Court, which sided with the district court's decision in favor of the school system.

In its decision, the Court ruled that the paper was an integral part of the school's educational function. The paper was part of the regular journalism curriculum and produced using school supplies and personnel. The staff was restricted to journalism students. As such, it was not a "public forum" and not entitled to First Amendment protection.

Campus Crime Records

Traci Bauer was the editor of the *Southwest Standard*, the student newspaper at Southwest Missouri State University. After hearing a report that a rape had happened on campus, she went to the campus police department and asked to see the official report. School officials turned down her request, citing a law passed in the 1970s, the Family Education Rights and Privacy Act (also called the Buckley Act), that protected the privacy rights of students by prohibiting the release of students' records without their permission. The university argued that the act also protected students named in crime reports and that release of these reports could cause the federal government to withdraw its support from the university.

Southwest Missouri State was not the only college that interpreted the rule in this way. The Department of Education had informed schools that the Buckley Act prohibited the release of campus crime information. At Kansas State University, reporters for the daily newspaper found that campus police kept two logs, one for themselves and one for the newspaper that omitted reports of serious crime. The University of Toledo and James Madison University, among others, did not release the names of students mentioned in their crime reports. Other universities offered only the barest of summaries, mentioning the number of crimes in a category but not the location or seriousness involved.

Traci Bauer sued her own university for the full release of information. With some help from the local paper, the case went before a district court judge who ruled in favor of Bauer and her newspaper. The Buckley Act, wrote the judge, did not extend to campus law enforcement records nor should the mere fact of enrollment at a college or university entitle an individual to more privacy rights in the criminal investigation and incident report realm than members of the general public. As a result of the decision, many colleges changed their policies.

and the military established guidelines for a National Media Pool. This arrangement worked satisfactorily during 1988 when the U.S. escorted Kuwaiti tankers through the Persian Gulf. Two years later, however, when the Gulf War broke out, the Defense Department issued restrictive rules on how the press could cover military activities (see Chapter 14). Reporters were assigned to press pools whose members were under strict military control, and all pool reports were subject to review. Two news agencies challenged the constitutionality of these reports but shortly after the war ended, a federal district court ruled the suits were no longer relevant. Nonetheless, executives from seventeen news organizations sent a proposal to the Defense Department containing a list of principles for the coverage of future military actions. The principles were described as a balance between military security and the public's right to know. No official change of Defense Department policy was announced.

Restraint by Taxation? Owners of media properties have long feared that a government could exert power over what was reported about its activities by levying discriminatory taxes on them. Newspapers that strongly criticized the government, for example, might be put out of business by special taxes aimed specifically at their operations. Over the years, the courts have struck down many attempts at discriminatory taxation. In 1936, for example, the state of Louisiana attempted to squelch criticism of Governor Huey Long by enacting a tax that applied only to large circulation newspapers (the governor's loudest critics). The Supreme Court ruled that the tax was unconstitutional. In 1987, an Arkansas sales tax that applied only to general circulation magazines was ruled discriminatory.

In April of 1991, however, the Supreme Court ruled that it was constitutional for a state to impose a general business tax on one medium while exempting others. At issue was an Arkansas law that allowed taxation of cable TV and satellite systems but exempted the print media. The Court viewed the tax as nondiscriminatory because it applied to all cable and satellite systems throughout the state and to other services including telephone, electricity, water, and even tickets to amusement parks. As such, it was not directed at suppressing ideas or the expression of views. Cable TV operators feared that the ruling would open the door to similar taxation by other states and ultimately result in increased monthly bills for consumers.

To sum up, there is a strong constitutional case against prior restraint of the press but gray areas exist where censorship might be legal. These areas will probably remain ambiguous until further court cases help define the limits of government authority in this area. It is likely, however, that the barriers against prior restraint will remain formidable.

• • • •

PROTECTING NEWS SOURCES

Before we begin an examination of this topic, we should point out that the issues are fairly complicated. Conflicting interests are involved. Reporters argue that if they are forced to disclose confidential sources, those sources will dry up and the public's right to know will be adversely affected. The government arguments cite the need for the administration of justice and the rights of an individual to a fair trial.

Perhaps a hypothetical example will help bring these issues into focus. Suppose you are a reporter for a campus newspaper. One of your sources calls you late one night and informs you that several students have started a drug ring that has monopolized the sale of illegal drugs on campus. To check the accuracy of this report, you call another one of your sources, one who in the past has given you reliable information on campus drug dealing. This second source confirms what your caller told you and adds more details. For obvious reason, both of your sources ask not to be identified and you agree. Based on these reports and some additional research on your part, you publish a lengthy article in the campus newspaper about the drug ring. A few days later you are summoned before a grand jury that is investigating criminal drug dealings. You are asked to reveal your sources. If you refuse, you will be charged with contempt and possibly fined or sent to jail. What do you do?

The Reporter's Privilege

Other reporters have found themselves in the same fix. One was Paul Branzburg. In 1969, Branzburg wrote a story for the *Louisville Courier-Journal* in which he described how two local residents were synthesizing hashish from marijuana. His article stated that he had promised not to reveal their identities. Shortly thereafter, Branzburg was subpoenaed (ordered to appear) by the county grand jury. He refused to answer questions about his sources, claiming, in part, that to do so would violate the First Amendment provision for freedom of the press. The case ultimately reached the Supreme Court, which ruled that the First Amendment did not protect reporters from the obligation of testifying before grand juries to answer questions concerning a criminal investigation. Initially, this ruling was viewed as a setback for reporters' rights. Upon closer examination, however, the Court did suggest some situations in which the reporter's claim to privilege would be valid. These included harassment of news reporters, instances in which grand juries do not operate in good faith, and situations in which there is only a remote connection between the investigation and the information sought. Additionally, the Court suggested that Congress and the states could further define the rights of a reporter to protect sources by enacting legislation (called **shield laws**) to that effect. Twenty-eight states now have such laws.

After the Branzburg decision, state courts were somewhat inconsistent in their rulings. On the one hand, several cases have ended with the courts upholding the reporter's right to keep his or her sources secret. In Florida, Lucy Ware Morgan, a reporter for the *St. Petersburg Times*, refused to disclose her source for a story about a grand jury report that discussed corruption in city government. She was promptly convicted of contempt of court and received a ninety-day jail sentence. In 1976, however, the Florida Supreme Court overturned the conviction and ruled in Ms. Morgan's favor. Using the Branzburg decision as a guideline, the court concluded that the name of her source was not relevant to the investigation of a crime and that the contempt charge was designed to harass her. Other decisions have narrowly defined the test of relevancy between the case at hand and the reporter's sources. In Virginia, a newspaper reporter refused to identify a source during testimony at a murder trial. The lawyer for the accused argued that the source's name was needed to question the credibility of a prosecution witness. The Virginia Supreme Court ruled in favor of the reporter and stated that a reporter's privilege must yield only when the defendant's need for the information is essential. To be essential, said the court, the information had to (1) relate directly to the defendant's guilt or innocence, (2) bear on the reduction of an offense, or (3) concern the mitigation of a sentence.

Nevertheless, there are other decisions that, from the point of view of working journalists, appear less reassuring. For example, consider the somewhat complicated case of William Farr. In 1971, Farr was a reporter for the *Los Angeles Herald-Examiner*, covering the Charles Manson murder trial. Farr discovered that a potential witness was going to reveal a bizarre plot in which the Manson "family" was going to slay several movie stars. Farr's story made page one and angered the trial judge. (The judge had ordered all participants in the trial not to talk to the press. Someone evidently had violated that order.) The judge subsequently ordered the reporter to reveal his sources. Farr cited California's shield law and refused to divulge his sources, and the judge did not press the issue at the time. After the trial ended, however, Farr left journalism and took a different job. The Manson trial judge once again ordered Farr to reveal his sources, now claiming that Farr was no longer covered by California's shield law. Farr again refused and was given an open-ended jail sentence for contempt. After serving forty-six days, Farr was released pending the outcome of an appeal. In a related action, he was ordered to serve another five days and pay a $500 fine. In 1974, Farr was almost forced to go through the whole ordeal again when he was called before a grand jury investigating perjury charges; once again, he refused to reveal his sources. Farr was initially found in contempt of court, but this action was reversed within a week. To make matters even more complicated, Farr became involved in a libel suit connected with this case and once again refused to answer questions about his sources. Farr's ordeal finally came to an end when the statute of limitations ran out before those bringing the libel suit were ready for trial.

Just because these examples are from the 1970s, don't get the idea that reporters no longer go to jail. In 1990, a reporter for KMOL-TV in San Antonio who refused to disclose the name of a confidential source in connection with a murder case was sentenced to six months for contempt of court. The reporter spent eleven days in jail before his source released him from his promise of confidentiality.

As the 1990s began, journalists regarded shield laws as helpful, but most realized they were not the powerful protectors of the press that many had hoped for. In addition, the laws themselves represent a bewildering collection of provisions, qualifications, and exceptions. Some state laws protect only confidential material; some protect the reporter from revealing the name of a source but do not protect the information obtained from sources. Other state laws confer less protection if the reporter is involved in a libel case. In some states, shield laws don't apply to reporters subpoenaed by a grand jury.

Further, many state courts are interpreting the shield laws on a case-by-case basis and ignoring or limiting the interpretation of some of the broad protections contained in the law. For example, in New York, which has a strong shield law, the court ruled that its protection did not extend to TV station outtakes (tape or film segments not shown on the air). A Pennsylvania court recently ruled that its state shield law doesn't apply to some libel cases.

Overall, about a third of the shield law rulings by state courts since the mid-1970s have been against the press. On the positive side, however, is the fact that even in those states that have no shield laws, many have recognized a reporter's privilege to resist a subpoena. It's obvious that this is an area where reporters should tread carefully (see box on page 408).

Search and Seizure

Finally, there is the troublesome question of protecting notes and other records that might disclose sources. In this regard, the courts have offered little protection. Three particular cases have disturbed the news media. In 1971, four police officers entered the offices of the *Stanford Daily*, the campus newspaper of Stanford University, and produced a search warrant authorizing them to search for photographs of a clash between demonstrators and police that the *Daily* had covered the day before. The newspaper brought suit against the authorities, charging that its First Amendment rights had been violated. In 1978, the Supreme Court ruled that the search was legal. (In 1980, however, Congress extended some protection to newsrooms by passing a bill that would require the government to secure a subpoena in order to obtain records held by reporters. The scope of a subpoena is somewhat more limited than that of a search warrant. In addition a subpoena can be challenged.)

In the second case, the U.S. Court of Appeals in the District of Columbia decided another case that further eroded reporters' rights to protect sources. In 1974, the Reporters Committee for Freedom of the Press filed suit against the American Telephone and Telegraph Company (AT&T) because the company would not pledge to keep records of reporters' toll calls safe from government scrutiny. (An analysis of

During the 1982 election for governor in Minnesota, a public relations consultant named Dan Cohen was working for the Republican candidate. Cohen offered reporters a tip about the Democratic candidate on the condition that Cohen's identity would not be disclosed. The reporters promised to protect his confidentiality. Cohen then revealed that the opposing candidate had been convicted of shoplifting some twelve years before. Two newspapers used the story and named Cohen as the source despite the promise he had received from the reporters.

As a result Cohen lost his job and sued the newspapers. Part of his suit relied on Minnesota common law that required that a promise be legally enforced if breaking it would cause an injustice. A jury initially agreed with Cohen and awarded him $700,000. An appeals court, however, reversed the decision and suggested that the First Amendment rights of the press outweighed the common law provisions of keeping a promise.

The case was appealed to the Supreme Court which ruled in 1991 that the First Amendment does not excuse the press from following laws that apply to everyone. The Court noted that members of the press cannot break into a residence to gather news, nor should they be excused from a law that says people must keep their promises. The case was sent back to the state court to decide if indeed an injustice was done when the confidentiality promise was broken.

This case demonstrates once again why promises of confidentiality should not be given lightly nor breached without due consideration.

these calls might help to locate a reporter's source of information.) The Court of Appeals ruled that it was legal for the government to examine such records without the reporter's knowledge or consent.

The last case involved *New York Times* reporter Myron Farber. During 1976, Farber had been reporting the investigation into mysterious deaths at a New Jersey hospital. The stories led to the indictment of a prominent physician on charges of poisoning five patients. Defense lawyers ultimately subpoenaed notes and documents pertaining to the case that were held by Farber and the *Times*. Both Farber and the paper refused, and both were convicted of contempt of court. Farber was sentenced to six months in jail and a $1000 fine; the *Times* was slapped with a $100,000 fine and was ordered to pay $5000 every day until it complied with the court's order. The *Times* ultimately turned over its files, but a judge ruled that the paper had "sanitized" them by removing some relevant material and reinstated the fine. Farber, meanwhile, had spent twenty-seven days in jail. (The case was complicated somewhat when it was disclosed that Farber had agreed to write a book on the case for a major publishing company. Some felt that Farber was holding out in order to make revelations in his book and thus increase its sales.) Eventually, Farber wound up spending forty days in jail, and the *Times* paid $285,000 in fines. All penalties finally ended with the jury's verdict that the physician was innocent.

Judging from the above, perhaps the safest conclusion that we can draw is that a reporter's privilege in protecting sources and notes is unlikely to be absolute. Even those decisions that have favored journalists have been qualified. It also appears that further developments in this area will be put together on a piece-by-piece basis by lower courts unless the Supreme Court generates a precise decision or the legislature passes a comprehensive law. As for reporters, they must carefully consider these issues when they promise confidentiality to a news source.

● ● ● ●
COVERING THE COURTS

The conflict of competing interests has repeatedly cropped up when news media attempt to cover the courts. On the one hand, the Sixth Amendment guarantees a trial before an impartial jury; on the other, the First Amendment guarantees the freedom of the press. Trial judges are responsible for the administration of justice; reporters are responsible for informing the public about the legal system. Sometimes the responsibilities clash.

Publicity Before and During a Trial

If a potential jury member has read, seen, or heard stories in the news media about a defendant that appear to indicate that person's guilt, it is possible that the defendant will not receive a fair trial. Although research has not produced definitive evidence linking pretrial publicity to prejudice, this concern has been at the heart of several court decisions that have castigated the news media for trying cases in the newspaper or on television instead of in the courtroom.

The 1960s saw a flurry of cases that suggested that the Supreme Court was taking a close look at pretrial publicity. In 1961, the Court for the first time reversed a state's criminal conviction entirely because pretrial publicity had made it impossible to select an impartial jury. The case concerned Leslie Irvin, a rather unsavory character who was arrested and charged with six murders. Newspapers carried police-issued press releases that said "Mad Dog" Irvin had confessed to all six killings. The local media seized upon this story with a vengeance, and many stories referred to Irvin as the "confessed slayer of six." Of the 430 potential jurors examined by attorneys, 90 percent had formed opinions about Irvin's guilt—opinions that ranged from suspicion to

The murder conviction of Dr. Sam Sheppard (shown here at his first trial) was overturned by the Supreme Court because of the extremely prejudicial publicity surrounding his arrest and trial. In a second trial, Sheppard was found not guilty. (UPI/Bettmann Newsphotos)

absolute certainty that he was guilty. Irvin was convicted—hardly a surprise—and sentenced to death. After six years of complicated legal maneuvers, made even more complicated because Irvin managed to escape from prison, the case went before the Supreme Court. The Court ruled that the pretrial publicity had ruined the defendant's chances for a fair trial and sent the case back to be retried. (Irvin, who had been recaptured, was again found guilty but this time was sentenced to life imprisonment.)

Perhaps the most famous case of pretrial publicity concerned an Ohio physician. On July 4, 1954, the wife of Cleveland-area osteopath Dr. Sam Sheppard was found slain in the couple's home. Sheppard became a prime suspect, and the news media, especially the Cleveland newspapers, were impatient for his arrest. "Why Isn't Sam Sheppard in Jail?" and "Why Don't Police Quiz Top Suspect?" were headlines that appeared over page-one editorials. News reports carried the results of alleged scientific tests that cast doubt on Sheppard's version of the crime (these tests were never brought up at the trial). Articles stressed Sheppard's extramarital affairs as a possible motive for the crime. After his arrest, the news stories and editorials continued. There were enough of them with headlines such as "Dr. Sam Faces Quiz at Jail on Marilyn's Fear of Him" and "Blood Is Found in Garage" to fill five scrapbooks. Every juror but one admitted reading about the story in the newspapers. The sensationalized coverage continued during the trial itself, which produced a guilty verdict. Twelve years later the Supreme Court reversed Sheppard's conviction because of the extremely prejudicial publicity. This case assumed added importance because the Court listed six safeguards that judges might invoke to prevent undue influence from publicity. These safeguards included sequestering the jury (i.e., moving them into seclusion), moving the case to another county, and placing restrictions on statements made by lawyers, witnesses, or others who might divulge damaging information.

In 1990, a federal court ordered CNN not to broadcast tapes of conversations between deposed Panamanian dictator Manuel Noriega and his lawyer until the court could review them. CNN appealed the decision on First Amendment grounds and aired part of the tape before the appeal was heard. A federal court upheld the restraining order and the Supreme Court declined to review the case. CNN eventually turned the tapes over to a federal judge who, after reviewing them, decided they contained nothing that would damage Noriega's right to a fair trial. The possibility remained, however, that CNN might be charged with contempt for broadcasting the tapes in violation of the restraining order.

These cases and others like them have prompted efforts to develop guidelines to prevent this problem from recurring. The U.S. Justice Department issued a set of rules that would restrict what information could be released to the press when a person was arrested for a federal crime. The American Bar Association adopted a similar but more stringent set of guidelines covering information release. In many states, voluntary agreements between the press and the legal profession have been drawn up.

Gag Rules

Despite these efforts, however, the controversy has persisted. Some judges have announced restrictive orders, or **gag rules,** that restrain the participants in a trial (attorneys, witnesses, defendants) from giving information to the media or that actually restrain media coverage of events that occur in court. For example, a Superior Court judge in a Washington murder trial ordered reporters to report only on events that occurred in front of a jury. Two reporters violated this rule by writing about events that took place in the courtroom while the jury was not present; they were subsequently charged with contempt. The Washington Supreme Court refused to review this ruling. In other cases, the news media have won what might be called hollow victories. To illustrate, in New York in 1971 a judge closed a trial to both public and press. News organizations appealed, and the judge's ruling was ultimately declared incorrect.

Although the press may have won a victory in principle, it lost one in fact—by the time the closure rule had been judged invalid, the trial had already been conducted behind closed doors. Two Louisiana reporters also won but lost when they violated a gag order and reported testimony given in open court. They were found guilty of contempt and fined $300. A higher court ruled that the gag order was unconstitutional, but the contempt fine was nonetheless upheld. The gag order, said the court, could not be ignored even though it might be invalid. Reporters must obey judicial orders until they are reversed, or reporters will suffer the consequences.

The whole question of gag orders reached the Supreme Court in 1976. A Nebraska judge had prohibited reporters from revealing certain information about a mass murder case. The Nebraska Press Association appealed the order to the Supreme Court. The Court ruled on the side of the press association and held that reporting of judicial proceedings in open court cannot be prohibited. Once again, upon first examination, this rule appeared to be a significant victory for the press. As time passed, however, it became apparent that the Nebraska decision had left the way open for court-ordered restrictions on what the trial participants could say to the press. The decision also seemed to indicate that some legal proceedings, primarily those that take place before the actual trial begins, might be legitimately closed to the public. By the early 1980s, this was exactly what was happening. Although the press was left free to report what it chose, its news sources were muzzled by judicial order. During the late 1970s, judges began holding pretrial hearings in private in order to limit pretrial publicity. A 1979 Supreme Court decision held this practice to be constitutional. In 1980, the Court did go on record as stating that the press did, in fact, have a constitutional right to attend criminal trials. *Pretrial* events, however, such as those stated above, might still be closed. Because many criminal cases are settled out of court, these pretrial hearings are often the only public hearings held.

In the last decade, the press has gained wider access to court proceedings. In 1984, the Supreme Court ruled that the jury selection process should be open to the press except in extreme circumstances. In a second case that same year, the Court established standards that judges must meet before they can close a pretrial hearing. A 1986 Supreme Court decision, however, gave the press a major victory in its efforts to secure access to pretrial proceedings. The Court held that preliminary trial proceedings must be open to the press unless the judge could demonstrate a "substantial probability that the defendant's right to a fair trial would be violated." Additionally, lower courts have held that the First Amendment right of access to trials also extends to documents used as evidence. Also in 1986, the Supreme Court ruled that the jury selection process, as well as the trial itself, must ordinarily be open to the public. The Court also provided a set of strict guidelines that would justify a private selection of a jury.

These decisions, however, do not give the press an absolute right of access to all court proceedings. Some parts of trials and pretrial hearings may still be closed if the judge can fulfill the court's guidelines regarding closure. Further, the recent court decisions have not changed the legal status surrounding the privacy of grand jury hearings—they continue to have the right to secrecy. All in all, it might be safe to conclude that the press has been given a green light to report matters that occur in open court with little fear of reprisal. But gag orders on news sources and the closing of various legal proceedings threaten to be an area of tension between the press and the judiciary for some time to come.

Cameras and Microphones in the Courtroom

For many years the legal profession looked with disfavor on the idea of cameras and microphones in the courtroom. There was a time when this attitude may have been entirely justified. The whole problem seems to have begun in 1935 when Bruno Hauptmann was put on trial for the kidnaping and murder of the son of national hero

Charles Lindbergh. Remember that news photography and radio journalism were still young in 1935, and this fact may have contributed to some of the abuses that occurred during this trial (see box below). After the trial, the American Bar Association adopted Canon 35 of its Canons of Professional Ethics. This provision stated that the taking of photographs in the courtroom and the broadcasting (later amended to include telecasting) of court proceedings ". . . detract from the essential dignity of the proceedings, distract the participants and witnesses in giving testimony" and should not be permitted. Although Canon 35 was not law, its language or some variation of it was adopted as law by every state except Colorado and Texas.

In 1965 the Supreme Court entered the picture when it ruled on the Billie Sol Estes case. Estes was on trial in Texas for allegedly swindling several farmers. The trial judge, over Estes' objections, had allowed the televising of the trial. Estes was found guilty, but he soon appealed that decision to the Supreme Court on the grounds

Canon 35 and the Hauptmann Trial

In 1935, nearly three years after the crime, Bruno Hauptmann was tried for the kidnaping and murder of the nineteen-month-old son of national hero Charles Lindbergh. The trial was held in the small, rural town of Flemington, New Jersey. When it opened, more than 150 reporters were packed into a small area reserved for the press. During the trial, this number swelled to about 700 as members of the press corps prowled the corridors and surrounding rooms of the courthouse in an attempt to cover every aspect of the trial. The wire services transmitted more than 11 million words of trial coverage—a million on the first day. About one hundred telegraph technicians had to be on the premises to operate this system, further adding to the crowd. Photography during the trial was forbidden, but photographers were allowed in the courthouse and some were even allowed in the courtroom itself to take pictures when the trial was not in session.

As the trial progressed, the overcrowding got worse and it became obvious that the trial had turned into a media event. The ban against photography during court sessions was broken, but nothing was done about it. A newsreel motion picture camera was placed in the balcony of the courtroom and, despite a promise from the newsreel people that they would not take films during the trial, footage was taken of the testimony of Lindbergh, Hauptmann, and oth-

ers. The film was shown in movie theaters throughout the country. Photographers, many of them freelancers, became more aggressive as the trial progressed and contributed to a general lack of courtroom decorum. The crush of reporters also aggravated the already severe overcrowding in the courtroom. The crowds got so bad that the attorneys for both sides actually subpoenaed their friends in order to make sure that they got into the courtroom. One radio reporter, Gabriel Heatter, had no problem getting a seat. The judge's wife enjoyed his broadcasts so much that she prevailed on the judge to give Heatter a place in the front row. In an attempt to scoop the opposition, an Associated Press employee rigged a secret radio transmitter inside the courtroom. On February 13, 1935, the jury brought in a guilty verdict. (Unfortunately, the Associated Press employee got confused and incorrectly sent out the word that Hauptmann was innocent. Embarrassed, the Associated Press had to send out a correction ten minutes later; the employee was subsequently fired.) Out of all this confusion and carnival-like atmosphere came Canon 35, a rule adopted by the American Bar Association that would limit courtroom reporting by photographers and radio and television reporters. Controversies that started in that overcrowded courtroom in Flemington are still debated today.

that the presence of television had deprived him of a fair trial. The high court agreed with Estes and argued for the prohibition of television cameras from the courtroom. The decision said that broadcasting a trial would have a prejudicial impact on jurors, would distract witnesses, and would burden the trial judge with new responsibilities. But, the Court went on, there might come a day when broadcast technology would become portable and unobtrusive and television coverage so commonplace that trials might be broadcast. Thus the decision in the Estes case was not a blanket provision against the televising of trials.

Since 1965, the trend has been toward a general relaxation of the tension between the legal profession and the electronic press. In 1972, the American Bar Association adopted a new code of professional responsibility. Canon 3A(7) of this document superseded the old Canon 35. Canon 3A(7) still maintained the ban against taking photographs and broadcasting in the courtroom, but it did allow the judge the discretion to permit televising a trial to a pressroom or to another courtroom to accommodate an overflow crowd. In 1981, the Supreme Court ruled that broadcast coverage of a criminal trial is not inherently prejudicial, thereby clearing the way for the presence of radio and TV in the courtroom. At the same time, however, the Court left it up to the states to devise their own system for implementing such coverage.

As of 1991, several different systems had evolved in the various states. Some states require the consent of all parties involved before electronic coverage of a case is allowed; other states simply require the consent of the prosecution and the defense. Six states allow no coverage at all. Thirty-five states have set up permanent rules regarding coverage; the remainder have experimental rules in effect. In addition, a limited experiment was begun in 1991 that allowed TV into a few federal courtrooms. TV and radio are still barred from the Supreme Court.

Scenes like these from inside the courtroom are becoming more common as most states permit some kind of TV coverage. This scene is from Court TV, a cable network devoted to courtroom coverage. (Courtesy Courtroom Television Network)

• • • •
REPORTERS' ACCESS TO INFORMATION

Government Information

Reporting the doings of the government can be a frustrating task if the government insists that information about its activities be kept secret. After World War II, many members of the press complained that government secrecy was becoming a major problem. Reporters were being restricted from meetings, and access to many government documents was difficult to obtain. In the midst of continuing pressure from journalists and consumer groups, Congress passed the **Freedom of Information Act (FOIA)** in 1966. This law gave the public the right to discover what the federal government was up to—with certain exceptions. The law states that every federal executive-branch agency must publish instructions on what methods a member of the public should follow to get information. If information is improperly withheld, a court can force the agency to disclose what is sought. There are nine areas of "exemption" that do not have to be made public. Some of these exemptions are trade secrets, files of law-enforcement investigations, and oil-well maps.

Journalists, however, have not made extensive use of this law. The primary reason seems to be the length of time necessary to secure the actual information. Reporters usually need information in a hurry, and the long time lag associated with the proceedings under the Freedom of Information Act generally makes it less attractive in the eyes of a reporter. Nonetheless, the act has helped in the development of several major stories. The *Seattle Times* used Department of Energy reports obtained under the FOIA to put together an award-winning story on safety problems at a nuclear weapons plant. KRON-TV in San Francisco used the FOIA to get Federal Aviation Administration records for a story on air safety.

A "Sunshine Act" also ensures that regular meetings of approximately fifty federal government agencies will be open to the public. There are, however, ten different situations that might permit the agency to meet behind closed doors, so the right of access to these meetings is far from absolute. In addition, many states have similar laws to ensure open records and open meetings.

Access to News Scenes

We have already mentioned this issue in our discussion of the right of the press to attend certain judicial proceedings. But what about the reporters' right of access to news settings outside the courtroom? The law here appears to be in the developmental stage. In the few decisions that have been handed down, the courts have given little support to the notion that the First Amendment guarantees a right of access. In separate rulings, the courts declared that journalists could be sued for invasion of privacy, for trespassing on private property, and for disobeying a police officer's legitimate command to clear the way at the scene of a serious automobile accident. Three of the most relevant Supreme Court opinions have focused on the question of access to prisons and prisoners. In these cases, the courts have ruled that reporters do not have the right to visit specific parts of a prison, to speak to specific prisoners, or to bring cameras inside. In general, the Court seems to be saying that the access rights of the press are not different from the access rights of the general public. When the public is not admitted, neither is the press.

There have been some rulings, however, that have recognized a limited right of access. A Florida decision found that journalists who are customarily invited by police onto private property to view a news scene cannot be prosecuted for trespassing.

On the other hand, another decision in Florida held that local police could not invite the press along on a raid conducted on private property. In another case, a

Wisconsin court found that a TV photojournalist who had entered private property with permission from a police officer responding to a call was guilty of trespass. Other recent cases have also questioned the legality of government officials inviting journalists onto private property. In another case, reporters who followed antinuclear demonstrators through a fence onto the property of a utility company were found guilty of trespass. It is becoming difficult for journalists to rely on the argument that common custom and practice serve as a defense against trespass. Probably the safest thing for a journalist to do is to obtain the consent from the owner before entering private property. This is often difficult, of course, since the owner may not be available during a breaking news event.

The courts have also denied requests by TV stations to film or tape executions. A Texas court ruled that the First Amendment right to gather news did not extend to filmed coverage of executions. More recently, a federal judge in California upheld that state's ban on cameras at executions because of security concerns.

The courts have allowed access to news settings in order to halt discrimination among journalists. For example, in one case it was ruled that a female journalist could not be barred from entering a baseball team's locker room if male reporters had been admitted. And it was also ruled that the Tennessee State Senate could not bar the reporters of a particular Nashville newspaper from the Senate floor if it allowed reporters from other organizations to be admitted. In sum, the final words on this topic have yet to be written by the courts. A case as influential as the Branzburg or Estes decision has yet to be adjudicated in the area of press access. It is a good bet, however, that such a test will not be long in surfacing.

● ● ● ●
DEFAMATION

From the above, it is clear that in its news-gathering activities, the press often collides with the government. In addition, the right of free speech and the rights of a free press sometimes come into conflict with the right of an individual to protect his or her reputation. Protection for a person's reputation is found under the laws that deal with defamation.

In order to understand this somewhat complicated area, let's start with some general definitions:

Libel: written defamation that tends to injure a person's reputation or good name or that diminishes the esteem, respect, or goodwill due a person.

Slander: spoken defamation. (In many states, if a defamatory statement is broadcast, it is considered to be libel even though technically the words are not written. Libel is considered more harmful and usually carries more serious penalties.)

Libel per se: Some words are always libelous. Falsely written accusations, such as labeling a person a "thief" or a "swindler," automatically constitute libel.

Libel per quod: Words that seem perfectly innocent in themselves can become libelous under certain circumstances. Erroneously reporting that Mr. Smith was seen eating a steak dinner last night may seem harmless unless Mr. Smith happens to be the president of the Worldwide Vegetarian Society.

In order for someone to win a libel suit brought against the media, that person must prove five things: (1) that he or she has actually been defamed and harmed by the statements; (2) that he or she has been identified (although not necessarily by name); (3) that the defamatory statements have been published; (4) that the media were at fault; and (5) in most instances, that what was published or broadcast was false.

Not every mistake that finds it way into publication is libelous. To report that James Arthur will lead the Fourth of July Parade when in fact Arthur James will lead it is probably not libelous because it is improbable that leading a parade will cause harm to a person's reputation. (Courts have even ruled that it is not necessarily libelous to report incorrectly that a person died. Death, said the courts, is no disgrace.) Actual harm might be substantiated by showing the defamatory remarks led to physical discomfort (such as sleepless nights), or loss of income, or increased difficulty in performing a job.

Identification need not be by name. If a paper erroneously reports that the professor who teaches Psych 101 at 10 A.M. in Quadrangle Hall is taking bribes from his students, that would be sufficient.

Publication, for our purposes, pertains to a statement's appearance in a mass medium and is self-explanatory.

Fault is a little more complicated. To win a libel suit, some degree of fault or carelessness on the part of the media organization must be shown. As we shall see, the degree of fault that must be established depends on several things: (1) who's suing; (2) what the suit is about; and (3) the particular state's laws that are being applied.

A 1986 Supreme Court decision held that private persons (as opposed to public figures) suing for libel must prove that the statements at issue are false, at least when the statements involve matters of public concern. For all practical purposes, however, proving that the media were at fault also involves proving the falsity of what was broadcast or published, so that virtually everyone who brings a libel suit must show the wrongness of what was published.

It should be emphasized that a mass medium is responsible for what it carries. It usually cannot hide behind the fact that it only repeated what someone else said. In most situations, a magazine could not defend itself against a libel suit by claiming that it simply quoted a hospital worker who said a colleague was stealing drugs. If, in fact, the hospital worker's colleague was not stealing drugs, the magazine would have to look to some other defense against libel.

Handle With Care

Below are listed some red-flag words and expressions that are typical of those that may be libelous per se. Extreme care should be exercised in using these words in news reports:

bankrupt	corrupt	blockhead
intemperate	dishonest	rascal
unprofessional	amoral	scoundrel
communistic	disreputable	sneak
incompetent	illegitimate	deadhead
morally delinquent	hypocritical	fool
smooth and tricky	dishonorable	slacker
profiteering	cheating	skunk
sharp-dealing	unprincipled	poltroon
unethical	sneaky	ignoramus

(This list is also a handy reference guide for insults. Simply choose one word from the left list, one from the center, and one from the right, e.g., "You profiteering, amoral poltroon," or "You incompetent, corrupt deadhead." Just make sure that you don't put it in writing and that no third party is listening. Otherwise, you may get hit with a defamation suit.)

What are some of the defenses that can be used? There are three. The first is truth. If what was reported is proven to be true, there is no libel. This defense, however, is rarely used since it is extremely difficult to prove the truth of a statement. In addition, since the Supreme Court's decision placed the burden of proving the falsity of a statement on the person bringing the libel suit, the defense of truth has become even less attractive. A second defense is privilege. There are certain situations in which the courts have held that the public's right to know comes before a person's right to preserve a reputation. Judicial proceedings, arrest warrants, grand-jury indictments, legislative proceedings, and public city-council sessions are examples of situations that are generally acknowledged to be privileged. If a reporter gives a fair and accurate report of these events, no lawsuits can result, even if what is reported contains a libelous statement. The third defense is fair comment and criticism. Any person who thrusts himself or herself into the public eye or is at the center of public attention is open to fair criticism. This means that public officials, professional sports figures, cartoonists, artists, columnists, playwrights, and all those who invite public attention are fair game for comment. This defense applies only to opinion and criticism, not to misrepresentations of fact. You can report that a certain director's new movie stank to high heaven without fear of a lawsuit, but you could not report falsely that the director embezzled funds from the company and expect protection under fair criticism. However, criticism can be quite severe and caustic and still be protected from lawsuit. (In 1990, the Supreme Court ruled that expressions of opinion are not automatically exempt from charges of libel. Opinions that contain an assertion of fact that can be proven false might trigger a defamation suit.)

In 1964, the Supreme Court significantly expanded the opportunity for comment on the actions of public officials. In a case involving the *New York Times* and an official of the Montgomery, Alabama, police department, the Court ruled that a public official must prove that false and defamatory statements were made with actual malice before a libel suit can be won. The Court also clarified what is meant by actual malice—publishing a statement with the knowledge that it was false or publishing a statement in "reckless disregard" of whether it was false or not. A few years later, the Court expanded this protection to include statements made about public figures as well as public officials. In 1971, it appeared that the Supreme Court would even require private individuals who become involved in events of public concern to prove actual malice before collecting for a libel suit. Three years later, the Court seemed to retreat a little from this position when it held that a lawyer involved in a civil lawsuit was not a public figure, that he was not involved in an event of public interest, and that he did not have to prove actual malice. Even more protection was extended to the private citizen in 1976 in a case concerning the divorce of Mary Alice Firestone from her husband, tire heir Russell Firestone, Jr. The trial lasted seventeen months and received large amounts of media coverage. Ms. Firestone even called several press conferences while the trial was taking place. When *Time* magazine erroneously reported that the divorce had been granted on the grounds of extreme cruelty and adultery, Ms. Firestone sued for libel. (Her husband had charged her with adultery, but adultery was not cited as grounds for the divorce.) *Time* argued that she was a public figure and contended that Ms. Firestone had to show not only that the magazine was inaccurate but also that it acted with malice. The Supreme Court ruled that she was not a public figure, despite all the attendant press coverage, and drew a distinction between legitimate public controversies and those controversies that merely interest the public. The latter, said the Court, are not protected, and actual malice need not be proved.

The Court affirmed this distinction in 1979 by noting that the fact that someone is involved in a "newsworthy" event doesn't make the person a public figure. When a U.S. senator presented a scientist with a satirical award used to denote wasteful spending of government funds, the scientist sued for defamation. The Court ruled that even though the scientist became the subject of media attention, his public prominence before receiving the satirical award did not merit labeling him a public figure. Therefore, he did not have to meet the actual malice standard. Private citizens, however, do have to show some degree of fault or negligence by the media. In many states, this means showing that the media did not exercise ordinary care in publishing a story. Establishing this will allow a private citizen to collect compensation for any actual damages that stemmed from the libel. The big bucks, however, come from punitive damages assessed against the media. These awards are designed to punish the media for their past transgressions and serve as a reminder not to misbehave again. To collect punitive damages, even private citizens must show actual malice.

The mid- to late 1980s were characterized by a large increase in the size of the dollar awards made by jurors to the winners of libel cases. To illustrate, from 1980 to 1982, only 17 percent of the awards were over $1 million. In 1983–1984, some 75 percent exceeded that figure. By 1986, more than 40 percent of the awards were half a million or more. The amounts awarded declined in the late 1980s but in 1990 and 1991, six multimillion dollar verdicts were decided against the news media. A jury in Texas awarded a former district attorney who claimed he was libeled by a TV station $58 million, the most money ever awarded at a libel trial. The *Philadelphia Inquirer* lost a $34 million suit. Wayne Newton was awarded a $20 million judgment against NBC. Even the prestigious *Wall Street Journal* was hit with a $2.5 million decision.

On the other hand, 70 to 75 percent of these awards were reduced on appeal and some were reversed. (In the Wayne Newton case, the original award of $20 million was first reduced to $5.2 million and then in 1990, an appeals court threw the case out altogether). Some recent awards, however, have been sustained on appeal (see box on page 419).

Additionally, juries do not always return with verdicts against the media, particularly when public figures are involved. Former Israeli Defense Minister Ariel Sharon sued *Time* magazine for $50 million over a paragraph in a 1983 cover story that linked him to a massacre of Palestinian civilians. The jury found that the paragraph in question was indeed false and defamatory and that certain *Time* employees had acted negligently and carelessly. But the jury also found that *Time* had not published the material with actual malice (*Time* did not know the material was false when it was published), something that Sharon had to prove since he was a public figure. Consequently, no cash award was made.

As of 1992, the libel scene had quieted down a bit. The number of newly filed lawsuits against the press was down. Part of this was due to several court rulings that favored the press. After nearly ten years of litigation, a libel suit brought by a former Mobil Oil president was dismissed by an appeals court and was refused hearing by the Supreme Court. The Supreme Court also threw out a libel suit brought by the Liberty Lobby against columnist Jack Anderson and upheld a lower court's decision that a particularly offensive ad parody in *Hustler* magazine involving TV evangelist Jerry Falwell was not libelous. In short, for a while at least, the libel crunch had let up, but had not vanished.

In the early 1990s, these two little symbols, " ", were at the center of the most significant libel litigation. A psychiatrist sued the *New Yorker* for allegedly attributing false quotations to him that damaged his reputation. The Supreme Court ruled that fabricated quotations can indeed be harmful to a person's reputation. The Court, however, went on to reject the psychiatrist's argument that any modifications of a speaker's remarks enclosed in quotation marks is automatic evidence of actual malice. The Court concluded that material enclosed in quotes does not always reproduce exactly what a speaker said and that the quote would have to be changed substantially in a defamatory way to constitute a knowing falsehood.

To summarize, although the laws vary from state to state, it appears that to win a defamation suit a private citizen must show that published material identifying the citizen was false and harmful and that the media bear some degree of fault. Public

Many people are confused by the meaning of the phrase "actual malice" as it applies to defamation. Some individuals mistakenly think that a person who is defamed has to prove evil motives, spite, or ill will on the part of the person or medium that allegedly committed the defamation. Not so. In the famous *New York Times* v. *Sullivan* case, the Supreme Court defined actual malice as (1) publishing something that is known to be false ("I know what I'm publishing is not true but I'm still going to publish it anyway."); or (2) publishing something with reckless disregard for whether it's true or not ("I have good reason to doubt that what I'm publishing is true, but I'm still going to publish it anyway.").

A recent libel case involving CBS, Inc., and Walter Jacobson, a news anchor and commentator at WBBM-TV (the CBS affiliate) in Chicago, illustrates this definition. The Brown & Williamson Tobacco Corporation (maker of Viceroy cigarettes) claimed that Jacobson libeled their company when he charged during a TV commentary that Viceroy was using an ad campaign to persuade children to smoke. Viceroy, said Jacobson, was equating cigarette smoking with "wine, beer, shaving or wearing a bra . . . a declaration of independence and striving for self identity . . . a basic symbol of the growing up process." The commentary cited as evidence a Federal Trade Commission report that claimed the company had been advised by its advertising agency to launch such a campaign. Brown & Williamson, forced to prove actual malice on the part of Jacobson because of the company's position as a public figure, denied ever having launched such a campaign. In fact, company lawyers argued that Brown & Williamson was so outraged by its ad agency's advice that it fired the advertising firm. Further, Brown & Williamson argued that Jacobson knew this fact before he broadcast his commentary. In court, one of the officials for the tobacco company testified that a researcher for Jacobson had been told that the ad agency had been fired and that the campaign was not used. During the trial, Jacobson said that he had rejected a suggestion from this researcher that a disclaimer should be included in the commentary stating that Brown & Williamson had not used the campaign. Evidently, this fact was enough to convince the jury that Jacobson knew that what he was saying was false—thus establishing actual malice. The jury found in favor of the tobacco company and awarded Brown & Williamson more than $5 million in damages.

For their part, Jacobson and CBS still maintain that the commentary was an accurate summary of the Federal Trade Commission report and that Brown & Williamson had a strategy directed toward children, even if the company didn't fully implement it. In late 1985, CBS announced plans to appeal the decision. The appeal was decided in 1988 in favor of the tobacco company. CBS was ordered to pay $3.05 million in damages.

officials, public figures, and private citizens seeking awards for punitive damages have a harder task. They must also show that the media acted with actual malice—something that is usually difficult to prove.

●●●●
INVASION OF PRIVACY

Closely related to libel is the right of privacy. In fact, a single publication will often prompt both types of suits. The big difference between the two is that while libel protects a person's reputation, the right of privacy protects a person's peace of mind and feelings. A second difference is that libel involves the publication of false information; invasion of privacy might be triggered by disclosing the truth.

There are four different ways that the mass media can invade someone's right of privacy. The first is intruding upon a person's solitude or seclusion. This generally occurs when reporters wrongfully use microphones, surveillance cameras, and other forms of eavesdropping to record someone's private activities. A TV news crew that hid in a van outside your room and secretly taped your activities while you were inside would probably constitute a situation of intrusion.

The second occasion is the unauthorized release of private information. A newspaper publishing private medical records that reveal that a person has a dread disease might be an example in this area. The courts allowed a suit claiming invasion of privacy to be filed when a newspaper published information about a person's sex change operation without the person's consent.

A third method is publicizing people in a false light or creating a false impression of them. This invasion is most closely related to libel because falsity is also involved. Some TV stations get into trouble in this area through the practice of putting new narration over some stock tape footage which creates a false impression. For example, a Chicago TV station was sued when it ran stock footage taken three years earlier of a doctor performing a gynecological exam with a story describing how another doctor allegedly used an AIDS-infected swab during a similar exam. The face of the doctor in the stock footage was readily identifiable and she sued the station, claiming the story made it appear that she performed the allegedly negligent procedure.

The last means of invading privacy is through appropriation of a person's name or likeness for commercial purposes. This commonly involves stars and celebrities who find their names or images used without their permission in some business or promotional activity. Model Christy Brinkley, for example, successfully filed suit to stop poster stores from selling her picture without her permission. The not-so-famous are also protected against appropriation. One man sued because he found that a camera company had used his picture without permission in their instruction manual.

The privacy area was in the news in the 1990s because of a lawsuit alleging rape that was filed in Florida against William Kennedy Smith. In the course of reporting the facts surrounding this case, several media revealed the name of the young woman who claimed she was raped. Publicizing the name violated a Florida statute and a lawsuit was filed against national tabloid. (NBC and the *New York Times* also reported the name of the woman but were not charged in the suit.) This revelation prompted an intense reexamination of the legal and ethical guidelines followed by the media when reporting a rape case. It also highlighted the continuing tension between an individual's right to solitude and the public's right to know.

● ● ● ●

COPYRIGHT

Copyright provides the author with protection against unfair appropriation of his or her work. Although its roots go back to English common law, the basic copyright law of the United States was first enacted in 1909. In 1976, faced with copyright problems raised by the new communications technologies, Congress passed new legislation. The current copyright statute is found in Title 17 of the United States Code. The new law covers literary, dramatic, and musical works, as well as motion pictures, television programs, and sound recordings. The law also states what is not covered. For example, an idea cannot be copyrighted, nor can a news event or a discovery or a procedure.

Copyright protection lasts for the life of the author plus fifty years. In order to obtain full copyright protection, it is necessary to send a special form, copies of the work, and a small fee to the Register of Copyrights. The owner of a copyrighted work can then reproduce, sell, display, or perform the property.

It is important to note that copyright protection extends only to copying the work in question. If a person independently creates a similar work, there is no copyright violation. As a result, one of the things that a person who brings a copyright suit must prove is that the other person had access to the work under consideration. Thus, if you contend that a hit Hollywood movie was actually based on a pirated script that you submitted to the company, you must show that the people responsible for the movie had access to your work. (To guard against copyright suits, most production companies won't open the envelopes of what look like unsolicited scripts.) Note, however, that you don't have to prove that someone intentionally or even consciously copied your work.

In addition, the law provides that people can make "fair use" of copyrighted materials without violating the provisions of the Copyright Act. Fair use means that copies of the protected work can be made for such legitimate activities as teaching, research, news reporting, and criticism, without penalty. In determining fair use, these factors are taken into consideration:

1. the purpose of the use (whether for profit or for nonprofit education)

2. the nature of the copyrighted work

3. the amount reproduced in proportion to the copyrighted work as a whole

4. the effect of the use on the potential market value of the copyrighted work

Thus, a teacher who reproduces a passage from a long novel to illustrate writing style to an English class will probably not have to worry about copyright. On the other hand, if a commercial magazine reproduces verbatim a series of articles published in a not-for-profit magazine, it is likely that the copyright statute has been violated.

Recent cases involving copyright law have dealt with the new communication media. In what was popularly known as the "Betamax" case, the Supreme Court ruled in 1984 that viewers who own videocassette recorders could copy programs off the air for later personal viewing without violating the copyright act. Such taping, said the Court, represented fair use of the material. A second area that has copyright implications has to do with the rebroadcasting of the signals of local and distant stations by cable systems without permission or payment of fee. Under the new copyright law, cable systems are free to retransmit distant signals containing copyrighted materials without obtaining permission of the copyright holder, but the system must pay a compulsory license fee, determined by the size of the cable system and whether the distant signal is commercial or educational. The money goes to a Copyright Royalty Tribunal, which distributes the money to program producers, syndicators, and TV broadcasters. As of 1991, this system of payment was being closely studied, and it is likely that some modifications may be forthcoming.

In a copyright case that has relevance for college students, a federal court ruled in 1991 that commercial photocopying companies, like Kinko's, violate the publishers' copyrights when they copy and sell collections of articles and book excerpts used for college courses. The court said that such activity did not constitute fair use of the material and that Kinko's and other companies like it must get permission from the publishers before copying and selling their material.

• • • •

OBSCENITY AND PORNOGRAPHY

Our previous discussion has generally referred to the problems of the working press in their efforts to gather and publish timely and important news and information. The complicated and confusing area of law that surrounds obscenity seldom touches the press; instead, it concerns films, magazines, and books, which function more as entertainment media. Nonetheless, the rights of free speech under the First Amendment can come into conflict with the right of society to protect itself from what it considers harmful messages.

Obscenity is not protected by the First Amendment; that much is clear. Unfortunately, nobody has yet come up with a definition of obscenity that seems to satisfy everybody. Let's take a brief look at how the definition of this term has changed over the years. (If, when we are done, you are a litle confused about this whole issue, don't feel bad. You are not alone.)

For many years, the test of whether something was obscene was the **Hicklin rule**, a standard that judged a book (or any other item) by whether isolated passages had a tendency to deprave or corrupt the mind of the most susceptible person. If one paragraph of a 500-page book tended to deprave or corrupt the mind of the most susceptible person (a twelve-year-old child, the village idiot, a dirty old man, etc.), then the entire book was obscene. The standard was written in the 1860s and would be widely used for the next eighty years.

In a 1957 case, *Roth* v. *United States*, the Supreme Court tried its hand at writing a new definition. The new test for detecting obscenity would be the following: whether to the average person, applying contemporary standards, the dominant theme of the material taken as a whole appeals to prurient interests. ("Prurient" means "lewd" or "tending to incite lust.") The Roth test differed from the earlier rule in two significant ways. Not only did the entire work, rather than a single passage, have to be taken into consideration, but the material had to offend the average person, not anyone who saw it. Obviously, this standard was less restrictive than the Hicklin rule, but fuzzy spots remained. Should the community standards be local or national? How exactly would prurient interest be measured?

To give you some idea as to the difficulties in this area, here is one example of how someone tried to use the strict language of this test to beat an obscenity charge. In 1966, the case of Edward Mishkin came before the Supreme Court. Mishkin, who was appealing his sentence, operated a bookstore near New York's Times Square. The books he sold emphasized sadism and masochism. In his defense, Mishkin argued that his books were not obscene since under the literal interpretation of the Roth test the books he sold would have to incite prurient interests in the average person. Since Mishkin's books appealed to a somewhat deviant crowd, the average person, he argued, would not find them lewd. In fact, the average person would be disgusted and sickened by them. Therefore, they were not obscene. Wrong, said the Court, and let his sentence stand.

The next few years produced more obscenity cases to plague the high court. Other decisions added that the material had to be "patently offensive" and "utterly without redeeming social value" to be obscene. During the 1960s, the Supreme Court began considering the conduct of the seller or distributor in addition to the character of the material in question. For example, even if material were not considered hard-core pornography, it could be banned if sold to minors, thrust upon an unwilling audience, or advertised as erotic in order to titillate customers. A 1969 ruling intoduced the concept of "variable obscenity" when it stated that certain magazines were obscene when sold to minors but not obscene when sold to adults.

By 1973, so many legal problems were cropping up under the *Roth* guidelines that something had to be done. Consequently, the Supreme Court attempted to close up loopholes in the case of *Miller* v. *California*. This decision did away with the "utterly without redeeming social value" test and stated that the "community standards" used in defining obscenity could be local standards, which, presumably, would be determined by local juries. The new test of obscenity would include these principles:

1. whether the average person, applying contemporary community standards, would find that the work as a whole appeals to prurient interest

2. whether the work depicts or describes in a patently offensive way certain sexual conduct that is specifically spelled out by a state law

3. whether the whole work lacks serious literary, artistic, political, or scientific value

Despite this new attempt, problems weren't long in coming. The language of the decision appeared to permit a certain amount of local discretion in determining what was obscene. The question of how far a local community can go in setting standards continues to be troublesome. The Supreme Court has since ruled that the motion picture *Carnal Knowledge* was not obscene, even though a state court said that it was. The Court has also said that *Screw* magazine and the *Illustrated Presidential Report of the Commission on Obscenity and Pornography* were obscene no matter what community's standards were invoked. The Court further clarified the third of the Miller guidelines in a 1987 case when it ruled that judges and juries must assess the literary, artistic, political, or scientific value of allegedly obscene material from the viewpoint of a "reasonable person" rather than applying community standards. The first two guidelines, however, will still be decided with reference to contemporary community standards.

In 1982, the Court ruled that laws banning the distribution of pornographic materials involving children were not violations of the First Amendment. The Court ruled that a state's interest in safeguarding the physical and psychological well-being of children took precedence over any right of free expression. If it strikes you as somewhat bizarre that the members of the highest court of the United States have spent considerable time plowing through publications like *Screw* magazine and looking at such movies as *Deep Throat*, you are not alone. Obscenity is one problem that the Court would probably like to disappear, but it seems that this is highly unlikely to happen.

After a federal judge ruled that 2 Live Crew's As Nasty as They Wanna Be *album was obscene, record-store owner Charles Freeman sold a copy to an undercover detective and was promptly arrested. Freeman was ultimately convicted of selling obscene material. (Wide World Photos)*

Over the years it has become apparent that the Court has taken a somewhat more lenient view as to what constitutes obscenity. The Miller case suggests that the Court is encouraging the states to enact laws to deal with the problem at the local level. Given the long history of controversy that surrounds this topic, however, it is unlikely that this predicament will end soon. In fact, the whole issue surfaced again in 1986 when the Justice Department released a report on pornography. The report, which had strong political overtones, called for more stringent laws concerning pornography. One such law, the Child Protection and Obscenity Enforcement Act, took effect in 1988.

More recently, the main focus in obscenity litigation has been music lyrics. A Florida record store owner was convicted under the state's obscenity law for selling copies of rap group 2 Live Crew's *As Nasty as They Wanna Be*. The group itself was arrested on obscenity charges after an adults-only concert at a Florida nightclub but was later acquitted. Another rap group was arrested in New York for performing some of the songs from the album. Appeals stemming from these cases are currently working their way through the court system.

● ● ● ●

REGULATING BROADCASTING

The formal controls surrounding broadcasting represent a special case. Not only are broadcasters affected by the laws and rulings discussed above but they are also subject to additional controls because of broadcasting's unique position and character. When broadcasting was first developed in the early twentieth century, it became clear that more people wanted to operate a broadcasting station than there were suitable frequencies available. An overcrowded spectrum led to problems of interference that threatened the future of the entire industry. As a result, the early broadcasters asked the U.S. Congress to step into the picture. Congress did exactly that when it passed the Radio Act of 1927. This law held that the airwaves belonged to the public and that broadcasters who wished to use this resource had to be licensed to serve in the public interest. A regulatory body, called the Federal Radio Commission (later known as the Federal Communications Commission), was set up to determine who should get a license and whether or not those who had a license should keep it. Because of this licensing provision, radio and television are subject to more regulations than are newspapers, magazines, films, and sound recording.

The Federal Communications Commission (FCC) uses the 1934 Federal Communications Act (an update of the 1927 Radio Act) as the basis for its regulatory power. The FCC does not make law; it interprets the law. One of its big jobs is to interpret the meaning of the phrase "public interest." For example, the FCC may write rules and regulations to implement the Communications Act if these rules serve the public interest. Moreover, the FCC awards and renews licenses if the award or renewal is in the public interest. Over the years, several significant FCC rulings have shed some light on this rather ambiguous concept. One of the first things the commission established was that it would examine programming and determine if the public interest was being served. It was not enough for a station to adhere to the technical operating requirements of its license. It would also have to provide a "well-rounded" program structure. In its 1929 Great Lakes decision, the commission also put broadcasters on notice that the broadcasting of programs that tended to injure the public—fraudulent advertising, attacks on ethnic groups, attacks on religions—would not be in the public interest.

Another facet of the public interest as interpreted by the FCC appears to be diversity. The underlying philosophy of the commission seems to be that the public is better served if it has a large number of competing stations from which to choose. Consequently, during the 1940s, the commission adopted the **duopoly rule**, which prohibited the ownership of more than one AM, one FM, or one TV station in a single community. Another FCC rule limited ownership to twelve AM, twelve FM, and twelve TV stations. These rules were relaxed in 1992 when the FCC raised the ownership limits to eighteen AM and eighteen FM radio stations. The duopoly rule was modified to allow one company to own up to four radio stations in a large market. The cap on TV station ownership was under review. The commission has also moved to limit the cross-ownership of newspapers and broadcasting stations. The Prime Time Access Rules during the 1970s (see Chapter 11) were another reaffirmation of this emphasis on diversity.

Localism is another important component of the public interest as it has been defined by the FCC. In a 1960 policy statement, the commission stated that programs featuring local talent and aimed at local self-expression were necessary elements in serving the public interest.

What can the FCC do to stations that do not operate in the public interest? It can take several official actions. At the mildest level, it can fine a station up to $250,000. The next level of severity is to renew a station's license only for a probationary period (usually a year). This action typically puts the station on notice that it has to improve its performance or face even more serious consequences. The most severe form of official action is revoking or nonrenewal of a license. This is tantamount to the death sentence for a station. Revocation/nonrenewal is more of a threat, however, than a reality. From 1934 to 1978 the FCC took away the licenses of 142 stations. This figure should be weighed against the thousands of renewals that the commission granted each of these years. In fact, it has been calculated that 99.8 percent of all licenses are renewed. Nonetheless, the threat of revocation is a potent one that is universally feared among broadcasters. Despite the fact that it is prohibited from censoring programs, the FCC is able to regulate broadcasters by what is called the "raised-eyebrow technique." This means that the commission will make known its attitude and opinion on a certain questionable practice outside of formal rulemaking; stations generally take the hint and respond accordingly. For example, during the 1970s the FCC issued a notice that radio stations might not be serving the public interest by playing what the commission considered drug-oriented music. Stations that did play such songs would be subject to extra scrutiny at license-renewal time. Radio stations all over the country took the hint.

During the 1980s, as was the case in many industries, the prevailing regulatory philosophy that governed broadcasting was one of deregulation. The FCC and Congress had eliminated literally dozens of rules and regulations, including the controversial Fairness Doctrine (see below). The rush to deregulation slowed during the early 1990s as the FCC and Congress established new rules and regulations for broadcasting and cable.

Congress passed the Children's Television Act which required that TV stations present programs designed to meet the educational and informational needs of young persons through the age of 16. The bill also created a $2 million endowment to fund children's educational programs. Additionally, the act limits the amount of commercial time during children's programming to 10 1/2 minutes an hour on weekends and 12 minutes per hour on weekdays, a limit that applied to both broadcasters and cable operators. Stations and systems that violate these standards could be subject to a fine.

Under the leadership of Senator Paul Simon of Illinois, Congress became interested in the problem of TV violence. Seven different measures were under consideration in late 1993, ranging from a plan to set up an 800-number for viewer complaints to a proposal that would require TV sets to be manufactured with a special device that would allow parents to censor violent programs. Feeling the heat, the major TV networks announced plans to place warning announcements before shows of a violent nature.

The Equal Opportunities Rule

The **Equal Opportunities rule** is contained in Section 315 of the Communications Act and is thus federal law. Section 315 deals with the ability of bona fide candidates for public office to gain access to a broadcast medium during political campaigns. Stated in simple terms, this section says that if a station permits one candidate for a specific office to appear on the air, it must offer the same opportunity to all other candidates for that office. If a station gives a free minute to one candidate, all other legally qualified candidates for that office are also entitled to a free minute. If a station sells a candidate a minute for a hundred dollars, it must make the same offer to all candidates. Congress has made some exceptions to this law, the most notable of which are legitimate newscasts and on-the-scene coverage of authentic news events. This last exception provided the loophole by which the networks were able to broadcast the recent presidential debates. They were simply covering a news event that was under the sponsorship of another organization.

The Fairness Doctrine

As of 1992, the **Fairness Doctrine** no longer existed. The FCC repealed it in 1987. This doesn't mean, however, that it's dead and buried. There were several proposals in Congress to revive it, the most recent attempt in 1993. In fact, by the time you read this it might be back on the books or it might still be dormant.

When it was still in force, the Fairness Doctrine provided that broadcasters had to seek out and present contrasting viewpoints on controversial matters of public importance. On any issue, broadcasters had to make a good-faith effort to cover all the opposing viewpoints. This didn't have to take place in one program, but the broadcaster was expected to achieve balance over time. Note that the Fairness Doctrine never said that opposing views were entitled to equal time. It simply mandated that some reasonable amount of time be granted.

• • • •

REGULATING CABLE TV

The regulatory philosophy of the FCC toward cable TV has shown wide variation over the years. In the 1950s, the FCC ruled that it had no jurisdiction over cable. This notion changed in the 1960s when the commission exerted control over the new medium and wrote a series of regulations governing its growth. By 1972, a comprehensive set of rules governing cable was on the FCC's books. The growth of cable during the 1970s led to successful lobbying efforts by the industry to ease many of these restrictions. In the 1980s, in line with the general deregulation philosophy, almost all of the FCC's rules over cable were dropped. That the FCC has gotten out of the picture does not mean, however, that there are no regulations governing cable. Other organizations have gotten into the act. On the federal level, Congress passed the Cable Communications Policy Act in 1984. Among other things, the new law sets out specific guidelines for the renewal of a cable system's franchise (a **franchise** is an exclusive right to operate in a given territory), gives state and local governments the right to grant franchises, allows cable operators greater freedom in setting rates, provides criminal penalties for the theft of cable services, frees cable systems from most programming regulations, and legalizes backyard satellite dishes but also requires owners to pay to receive programming that has been descrambled. At the state level, cable franchising is regulated by five states, and others have enacted laws governing ownership and public access channels. Although many of the provisions of the 1984 Cable Act are still in force, the early 1990s saw a major change in regulatory attitude toward cable.

As mentioned in Chapter 13, the Cable Act of 1992 imposed new regulations on the cable industry. In addition to capping cable rates and eliminating exclusive programming deals between cable program suppliers and cable systems, the bill mandated that all cable systems must carry all the broadcast signals that were significantly viewed in their market area. Cable companies argued that this was a violation of their First Amendment rights. The Supreme Court will have the final say on this issue.

• • • •

REGULATING ADVERTISING

Deceptive Advertising

"Rapid Shave outshaves them all!" At least that's what a 1959 commercial for that shaving cream claimed. In order to drive that point home, a demonstration was included in the ad. As an announcer extolled the benefits of the product, Rapid Shave was applied to a substance that looked like sandpaper. A razor then shaved the paper clean, whisking away every grain of sand. Unfortunately, the substance wasn't sandpaper. It was really sand applied to a sheet of plexiglass. The Federal Trade Commission (FTC) claimed that the commercial was deceptive. The FTC's investigations discovered that Rapid Shave could not shave actual sandpaper unless the sandpaper was first soaked with the stuff for about eighty minutes. The advertising agency that put together the commercial appealed the commission's ruling all the way to the Supreme Court. The Court sided with the FTC.

The problem of deceptive and potentially harmful advertising has been around a long time. The philosophy of *caveat emptor* (let the buyer beware) was dominant until the early 1900s. Exaggerated claims and outright deception characterized many of the early advertisements, especially those for patent medicines. Spurred on by the muckrakers (see Chapter 4), the government took steps to deal with the problem when it created the Federal Trade Commission in 1914. In the early years of its existence, the commission was concerned with encouraging competition through the regulation of questionable business practices such as bribery, false advertising, and mislabeling of products; protecting the consumer was not the main focus. Thus an ad that identified underwear as "wool" when it actually contained only 10 percent wool was deemed unlawful because it hurt the business of those manufacturers who actually produced 100 percent wool underwear and truthfully labeled their product. The consumer started to receive some protection in 1938 with the Wheeler–Lea Act, which gave the FTC the power to prevent deceptive advertising that harmed the public, whether or not the advertising had any bad effects on the competition.

Like the Federal Communications Commission, the Federal Trade Commission has several enforcement techniques available to it. First of all, it can issue trade regulations that suggest guidelines for the industry to follow. In 1965, for example, it ruled that auto ads must contain both the city and highway estimates of gas mileage. The FTC also uses **consent orders**. In a consent order, the advertiser agrees to halt a certain advertising practice but, at the same time, the advertiser does not admit any violation of the law; there is only an agreement not to continue. Somewhat stronger is a **cease-and-desist order**. This order follows a hearing by the commission that determines that a certain advertising practice does indeed violate the law. Violation of a consent order and failure to comply with a cease-and-desist order can result in fines being levied against the advertiser.

In the late 1960s and the 1970s, the FTC took a more active role in the regulation of advertising. The rising tide of interest in the rights of the consumer and the presence of consumer activist groups (such as Ralph Nader's Raiders) were probably behind this new direction. A flurry of activity took place. First, the FTC wanted documentation for claims. If Excedrin claimed to be more effective in relieving pain than Brand X, the advertiser was now required to have proof for that statement. The FTC also ordered "corrective advertising" in which some advertisers were required to clarify some of their past claims. Profile Bread, for example, had been advertised as a weight-reducing aid, with fewer calories per slice than normal bread. (This was literally true. Profile Bread had seven fewer calories per slice, but only because it was sliced thinner.) The company agreed to run corrective ads with copy that included the following:

> I'd like to clear up any misunderstanding you may have about Profile Bread. Does Profile have fewer calories than other bread? No, Profile has about the same per ounce as other breads. To be exact, Profile has seven fewer calories per slice. That's because it is sliced thinner. But eating Profile will not cause you to lose weight. . . .

(Interestingly enough, the corrective ads were so well received by the audience that the company wanted to present them more often than the ruling required.) Ocean Spray Cranberry Drink and Listerine were other products that were subjected to corrective advertising. At about the same time, the FTC also came out for the notion of counteradvertising. This idea would have required TV stations to provide free time to consumer groups in order to reply to TV commercials. If a station ran an auto company's ads for a compact car, it would also have to run ads from a public interest group that pointed out possible safety problems with that car. This proposal was not greeted with widespread support and eventually was abandoned.

The other area of FTC concern during the 1970s was advertising directed toward children. A 1978 study by the FTC recommended that *all* TV advertising directed at young children be prohibited. In 1980, a new administration took office and the FTC quietly dropped its inquiry into this area. The new chairman of the FTC endorsed less federal control over advertising and was in favor of deregulating much of the industry. This philosophy persisted into the 1990s.

Commercial Speech Under the First Amendment

The 1970s also marked a change in judicial thinking toward the amount of protection that advertising, or commercial speech, as it is called, receives under the First Amendment. Before the 1970s, advertising had little claim to free-speech protection. In the 1940s, F. J. Chrestensen found this out the hard way. Chrestensen owned a former U.S. submarine. There is not much that a private individual can do with a submarine, aside from making a few dollars by charging admission to view it. This was Chrestensen's idea, and he wanted to distribute handbills advertising the sub. No way, said the New York City police commissioner. The city's sanitation code did not allow the distribution of advertising matter in the streets. Chrestensen did discover that handbills of information or of public protest were allowed. Inspired, Chrestensen put his submarine advertising message on one side of the handbill, while the other side was printed with a protest against the City Dock Department. Sorry, said the city, the protest message could be handed out, but the advertising on the other side would have to go. Chrestensen, still stuck with his submarine, appealed and two years later the Supreme Court ruled against him and agreed with the City of New York that advertising merited no First Amendment protection.

Since that time, however, the Supreme Court has retreated from this view. In 1964, it extended First Amendment protection to ads that dealt with important social matters. Seven years later, the Court further extended this protection when a Virginia newspaper editor ran an ad for an abortion clinic located in New York and thus violated a Virginia law against such advertising. The Supreme Court ruled in favor of the editor and stated that the ad contained material in the public interest and merited constitutional protection. Virginia was also involved in the next significant court ruling. A state law made it illegal to advertise the price of a prescription drug. Because of the importance of this information to the public, the Court ruled that the Virginia law was invalid. More recent cases suggest that in many instances commercial speech will fall under the protection of the First Amendment.

In a 1980 ruling concerning advertising by an electric utility company, the Supreme Court enunciated a four-part test for determining the constitutional protection for commercial speech. First, commercial speech that involves an unlawful activity or advertising that is false or misleading is not protected. Second, the government must have a substantial interest in regulating the commercial speech. Part three asks if the state's regulation actually advances the government interest involved. Finally, the state's regulations may be only broad as necessary to promote the state's interest. A 1984 ruling illustrated the use of these principles when the Court upheld a prohibition against posting signs on city property. The Court first noted that although the advertising was for a lawful activity and not misleading, the government has a substantial interest in reducing "visual blight" and that the ordinance directly advanced that interest and was not overly broad. Further, the Court affirmed that corporations also have the right of free speech and granted lawyers, doctors, and professionals the right to advertise their prices. Although not all of the questions surrounding this issue have been answered, it seems safe to conclude that at least some commercial speech is entitled to First Amendment protection. Its status, however, is less than that given to

The Soldier of Fortune Case

A simple ad started it all;

Ex-Marine—67–69 'Nam vet—Ex-DI, weapons specialist—jungle warfare, pilot. M.E., high risk assignments, U.S. or overseas.

This ad was placed in *Soldier of Fortune* magazine by John Hearn. Robert Black saw the ad and contacted Hearn. Four months later, Black arranged to have Hearn murder Black's wife. The wife's parents sued the magazine, claiming that the publication should have foreseen that running the ad would result in a crime, perhaps murder.

At the trial, evidence introduced by the murdered woman's parents established that the magazine had previously run "hired-gun ads" that strongly implied that some illegal conduct was contemplated. The editor of the magazine was also aware that at least one such ad, seeking an expert in poisons, had resulted in a solicitation to a murder. These and other facts apparently convinced the jury that *Soldier of Fortune* should have known that the ad might lead to foul play and was negligent in running it.

This verdict raises some knotty problems.

What about ads for radar detectors, illegal in many states? Suppose a car equipped with such a device gets into an accident because of excessive speed. Should the publication that advertised the detector be held liable? What about a woman who answers an ad in the personals column of a newspaper and is raped on the first date? Is the newspaper at fault? Must a publisher investigate any and all ads for hidden meanings?

Publishers were relieved when an appeals court reversed the $9.4 million award that was originally returned by the jury and decreed that the magazine was not responsible for ads with ambiguously worded content. The Supreme Court declined to review this verdict. In 1991, however, *Soldier of Fortune* was the subject of a similar lawsuit in another state. At issue was another personal ad describing a "gun for hire." It was alleged that the man who placed the ad was subsequently hired to kill someone. A motion to dismiss the case was denied and the whole issue must now go to trial. For its part, *Soldier of Fortune* no longer accepts these personal ads.

In the 1940s and 1950s, much cigarette advertising promoted the health benefits of smoking. This ad for Camels suggests that doctors endorse not only this brand of cigarette but smoking in general. (PAR Archive)

political and other forms of noncommercial expression. In the future, it's likely that more and more advertising will fall into the category of protected speech.

Three other cases had repercussions for advertisers. In the first, a tobacco company was found partially liable for the death of a smoker from lung cancer, in part because early ads for cigarettes stressed their health benefits for smokers. Although it seems hard to believe, during the 1940s and 1950s many cigarettes were advertised as "just what the doctor ordered," even after information linking smoking to lung cancer and other diseases came to light. This case may have limited impact since it dealt primarily with pre-1966 claims, before health warnings appeared on packs. On the other hand, it raises the broader question of whether advertising contains an implied warranty for the product.

In the early 1990s, the advertising industry won one and lost one before the Supreme Court. In one case, the Court appeared to strengthen the legal protection for commercial speech when it struck down a Cincinnati ordinance that banned newsracks of advertising brochures from city streets but allowed newspaper vending racks. In another case, however, the Court upheld federal regulations that prohibited a state from broadcasting ads for lotteries in adjoining states if lottery advertising was prohibited in the state where the station was located.

Can You Spot the Rigged Ad?

It was a powerful commercial. A "monster" truck named "Bear Foot" rolled over the roofs of several cars, smashing them in like tinfoil. But after the truck had rolled out of the frame, in the middle of the lineup there was one car whose roof was still intact, a Volvo station wagon. The announcer then said, "Apparently not everyone appreciates the strength of a Volvo." Magazine ads used a picture of the scene with the tag line, "Can you spot the Volvo?"

The only problem with this highly memorable ad was that it was rigged. As photos taken at the scene conclusively demonstrated, steel beams were welded inside the Volvo wagon to reinforce the roof (a nonreinforced Volvo had been crushed during an earlier rehearsal). In addition, the B-pillars which serve as roof supports on some of the other cars in the ad were sawed through so that their roofs would collapse more easily and more dramatically. The attorney general of the state of Texas (where the commercial was filmed) was alerted to the situation. After the ads ran, the attorney general filed a lawsuit against Volvo for deceptive advertising, and the Federal Trade Commission threatened its own investigation.

Volvo maintained that it didn't know about the rigging until after the ads were completed. The company explained that the ad was really a re-creation or dramatization of something that actually happened earlier during a monster truck demonstration in Vermont. To help ensure the safety of the crew and to make sure the Volvo withstood the multiple runs of the monster truck necessary to film a completed commercial, the production company that actually produced the ad had the car's roof reinforced.

Volvo moved quickly to settle the suit. It ran corrective ads in nineteen Texas newspapers, *USA Today*, and the *Wall Street Journal* and paid about $300,000 to the Texas attorney general's office for legal fees. Volvo also began its own investigation to determine why industry standards about deception had been breached.

Volvo's controversial ad got the car company some unwanted publicity. Here the commercial is discussed on the CNBC cable network. (The Photo Works)

• • • •
CONCLUDING STATEMENT

The term "half-life" is a useful concept in physics. It refers to the length of time in which one-half of the radioactive atoms present in a substance will decay. We might borrow this term and reshape its meaning so that it is relevant to this book. The half-life of a chapter in this text is the time it takes for half of the information contained in the chapter to become obsolete. With that in mind, it is likely that the half-life of this chapter may be among the shortest of any in this book. Laws are constantly changing; new court decisions are frequently handed down and new rules and regulations are written all the time. All of this activity means that what is written in this chapter will need frequent updating. In addition, it means that mass media professionals must continually refresh their understanding of the law. Of course, this also means that there will be a continuing stream of colorful characters, intriguing stories, and high drama as the courts and regulatory agencies further wrestle with the issues and problems involved in mass communication regulation.

• • • •
SUGGESTIONS FOR FURTHER READING

The following books contain more information about the concepts and topics discussed in this chapter.

CARTER, BARTON, MARC FRANKLIN, AND JAY WRIGHT, *The First Amendment and the Fourth Estate*, Mineola, N.Y.: Foundation Press, 1988.

GILLMOR, DONALD, AND JEROME BARRON, *Mass Communication Law*, St. Paul, Minn.: West Publishing Company, 1990.

HOLSINGER, RALPH, *Media Law*, New York: McGraw-Hill, 1991.

LIVELY, DONALD, *Modern Communications Law*, Westport, Conn.: Greenwood, 1991.

MIDDLETON, KENT, AND BILL CHAMBERLIN, *The Law of Public Communication*, New York: Longman, 1991.

NELSON, HAROLD, DWIGHT TEETER, AND DON R. LEDUC, *Law of Mass Communications*, Mineola, N.Y.: Foundation Press, 1989.

INFORMAL CONTROLS: ETHICS, CODES, SELF-REGULATIONS, AND EXTERNAL PRESSURES

aws and regulations are not the only controls on the mass media. Informal controls, stemming from within the media themselves or shaped by the workings of external forces such as pressure groups, consumers, and advertisers, are also important. The following hypothetical examples illustrate some situations in which these controls might spring up.

1. You're the program director for the campus radio station. You get a call one morning from the promotion department of a major record company offering you a free trip to California, a tour of the record company's studios, a ticket to a concert featuring all the company's biggest stars, and an invitation to an exclusive party where you'll get to meet all the performers. The company representative explains that this is simply a courtesy to you so that you'll better appreciate the quality of his company's products. Do you accept?

2. You're a reporter for the local campus newspaper. The star of the football team, who also happens to be the president of the Campus Crusade for Morality, has been involved in a minor traffic accident, and you have been assigned to cover the story. When you get to the accident scene, you examine the football player's car and find a half-dozen pornographic magazines strewn across the back seat. You have a deadline in thirty minutes; what details do you include?

3. You're the editor of the campus newspaper. One of your reporters has just written a series of articles describing apparent health-code violations in a popular off-campus restaurant. This particular restaurant regularly buys full-page ads in your paper. After you run the first story in the series, the restaurant owner calls and threatens to cancel all of his ads unless you stop printing the series. What do you do?

4. You're doing your first story for the campus paper. A local businessman has promised to donate $5 million to your university so that it can buy new equipment for its mass communication and journalism programs. While putting together a background story on this benefactor, you discover that he was convicted of armed robbery at age eighteen and avoided prison only by volunteering for military duty during the closing months of World War II. Since then, his record has been spotless. He refuses to talk about the incident, claims his wife and his closest friends do not know about it, and threatens to withdraw his donation if you print the story. Naturally, university officials are concerned and urge you not to mention this fact. Do you go ahead and write

the story as one element in your overall profile? Do you take the position that the arrest information is not pertinent and not use it? Do you wait until the university has the money and then print the story?

We could go on listing examples, but by now the point is probably clear. There are many situations in the everyday operation of the mass media where thorny questions about what to do or not to do have to be faced. Most of these situations do not involve laws, regulations, legalities, or illegalities but instead deal with the tougher questions of what's right or what's proper. Informal controls over the media usually assert themselves in these circumstances. This chapter will discuss the following examples of informal controls: personal ethics, performance codes, internal controls such as organizational policies, self-criticism, and professional self-regulation and outside pressures.

● ● ● ●

PERSONAL ETHICS

Ethics are rules of conduct or principles of morality that point us toward the right or best way to act in a situation Over the years, philosophers have developed a number of general ethical principles that serve as guidelines for evaluating our behavior. We will briefly summarize five principles that have particular relevance to those working in the mass media professions. Before we begin, however, we should emphasize that these principles do not contain magic answers to every ethical dilemma. In fact, different ethical principles often suggest different and conflicting courses of action. There is no "perfect" answer to every problem. Also, these ethical principles are based on Western thought. Other cultures may have developed totally different systems. Nonetheless, these principles can provide a framework for analyzing what is proper for examining choices and for justifying our actions.

Ethical Principles

The Principle of the Golden Mean. Moral virtue lies between two extremes. This philosophical position is typically associated with Aristotle, who, as a biologist, noted that too much food as well as too little food spoils health. Moderation was the key. Likewise, in ethical dilemmas, the proper way of behaving lies between doing too much and doing too little. For instance, in the restaurant example mentioned above, one extreme would be to cancel the story as requested by the restaurant owner. The other extreme would be to run the series as is. Perhaps a compromise between the two would be to run the series but also give the restaurant owner a chance to reply. Or perhaps the story might contain information about how the restaurant has improved conditions or other tempering remarks.

Examples of the Golden Mean are often found in media practices. For example, when news organizations cover civil disorders, they try to exercise moderation. They balance the necessity of informing the public with the need to preserve public safety by not inflaming the audience.

The Categorical Imperative. What is right for one is right for all. German philosopher Immanuel Kant is identified with this ethical guideline. To measure the correctness of our behavior, Kant suggests that we act according to rules that we would want to see universally applied. In Kant's formulation, categorical means unconditional—no extenuating circumstances, no exceptions. Right is right and should be done, no matter what the consequences. The individual's conscience plays a large part in Kant's thinking. The categorical imperatives are discovered by an examination of conscience; the conscience informs us what is right. If, after performing an act, we feel uneasy or guilty, we have probably violated our conscience. Applied to mass communication, a categorical imperative might be that all forms of deception in news gathering are wrong and must be avoided. No one wants deception to become a universal practice. Therefore, a reporter should not represent himself or herself as anything other than a reporter when gathering information for a story.

The Principle of Utility. The greatest benefit for the greatest number. Modern utilitarian thinking originated with the nineteenth-century philosophers Jeremy Bentham and John Stuart Mill. The basic tenet in their formulations holds that we are to determine what is right or wrong by considering what will yield the best ratio of good to bad for the general society. Utilitarians ask how much good is promoted and how much evil is restrained by different courses of behavior. Utilitarianism provides a clear method for evaluating ethical choices: (1) calculate all the consequences, both good and bad, that would result from each of our options; then (2) choose the alternative that maximizes value or minimizes loss. Looking at the mass communication area, we can easily see several examples of utilitarian philosophy. In 1971, the *New York Times* and other papers printed stolen government documents, the Pentagon Papers. Obviously, the newspapers involved thought that the good that would be achieved by printing these papers far outweighed the harm that would be done. (Note that the Kantian perspective would suggest a different course of action. Theft is bad. Newspapers do not want the government stealing their property so they should not condone or promote the theft of government property.) Or take the case of a small Midwestern paper that chose to report the death of a local teenager who had gone East, turned to prostitution and drugs, and was murdered while plying her trade. The paper decided that the potential benefits of this story as a warning to other parents outweighed the grief it would cause the murder victim's family.

The Veil of Ignorance. Justice is blind. Philosopher John Rawls argued that justice emerges when everyone is treated without social differentiations. In one sense, the veil of ignorance is related to fairness. Everybody doing the same job equally well should receive equal pay. Everybody who got an eighty on the test should get the same grade. Rawls advocated that all parties concerned in a problem situation should be placed behind a barrier where roles and social differentiations are gone and each participant is treated as an equal member of society as a whole. Often Rawls' veil of ignorance suggests that we should structure our actions to protect the most vulnerable members of society. It is easy to see the relevance of this principle to the workings of the mass media. If we applied the veil of ignorance to the problem of hammering out the proper relationship between politicians and journalists, Rawls would argue that the blatant adversarial relationship so often found between the groups should disappear. Behind the veil, all newsmakers would be the same. Inherent cynicism and abrasiveness on the part of the press should disappear as well as mistrust and suspicion on the part of the politicians. On a more specific level, consider the case of someone working in the financial department of a major newspaper who frequently gets tips and inside information on deals and mergers that affect the price of stock and passes these tips on to personal friends who use this information for their own profit. The veil of ignorance suggests that the reporter must treat all audience members the same. Personal friends should not benefit from inside information.

Principle of Self-Determination. Do not treat people as means to an end. This principle, closely associated with the Judeo-Christian ethic and also discussed by Kant, might be summarized as "Love your neighbor as yourself." Human beings have unconditional value apart from any and all circumstances. Their basic right to self-determination should not be violated by using them as simply a means to accomplish a goal. A corollary to this is that no one should allow himself or herself to be treated as a means to someone else's ends. For example, sources inside a government investigation on political corruption leak the names of some people suspected of taking bribes to the press, which, in turn, publishes the allegations and the names of the suspects. The principle of self-determination suggests that the press is being used by those who leaked the story as a means to accomplish their goal. Perhaps those involved in the investigation wanted to turn public opinion against those named or simply to earn some favorable publicity for their efforts. In any case, the press should resist being used in these circumstances. The rights, values, and decisions of others must always be respected.

A Model for Individual Ethical Decisions

There are numerous instances where personal ethical decisions have to be made about what is or is not included in media content or what should or should not be done. These decisions have to be made every day by reporters, editors, station managers, and other media professionals. Too often, however, these decisions are made haphazardly and without proper analysis of the ethical dimensions involved. This section presents a model that media professionals can use to evaluate and examine their decisions. This model is adapted from the work of Ralph Potter.*

DEFINITIONS → VALUES → PRINCIPLES → LOYALTIES → ACTION

In short, the model asks the individual to consider four aspects of the situation before taking action. First define the situation. What are the pertinent facts involved? What are the possible actions? Second, what values are involved? Which values are more relevant to deciding a course of action? Third, what ethical principles apply? We have discussed five that might be involved. There may be others. Lastly, where do our loyalties lie? To whom do we owe a moral duty? It is possible that we might owe a duty to ourselves, clients, business organizations, the profession, or to society in general. To whom is our obligation most important?

Let's examine how this model would apply to a real situation. In 1987, the State Treasurer of Pennsylvania held a press conference just hours before he was to be sentenced for his conviction in a kickback scandal. After 30 minutes of proclaiming his innocence, he pulled a .357 Magnum from a brown envelope, displayed it to the crowd, placed the gun barrel in his mouth, and, in full view of news photographers and TV cameras, pulled the trigger. Available news photos and tapes showed the entire event, and several angles showed the particularly grim aftermath of the gunshot wound. How should a situation like this be handled?

First, we need to specify the key facts. A public figure has committed suicide. Some photos and tapes are available that show blood and gore. We could opt to show all the graphic details, show only a part of them, or not show them at all. What values are involved? Obviously, as journalists we value freedom of expression and the right of society to be informed of all events, no matter how unpleasant. At the same time, we value the right to privacy and the right of people to be spared unnecessary grief. We also value our own sensibilities and those of our readers. Do they need to be shocked by seeing graphic portrayals of the effects of violence?

What principles are involved? Obviously, Aristotle's principle of moderation is relevant. At one extreme, we could publish the goriest of the pictures. At the other, we could publish no pictures at all. The principle of the mean suggests that we look for a middle ground between these two poles. Further, the principle of self-determination applies. If we show these pictures merely to use sensationalism to spur our newspaper's circulation or TV rating, then we are treating the victim and his family as a means toward fulfilling our end goal of selling papers or getting ratings. Further thought indicates that the principle of utility is also germane. The potential

---

*Ralph Potter, "The Logic of Moral Argument," in *Toward a Discipline of Social Ethics*, P. Deats (ed.), Boston: Boston University Press, 1972.

harm caused to readers' sensibilities and the victim's family must be weighed against the good that might result from society seeing how abhorrent violence really is. A graphic photo might deter some readers from resorting to violence in the future. As for the loyalty dimension, there are conflicting obligations. As an employee of the media, we have an obligation to the business to make a profit. Sensational photographs will probably sell more papers and get higher ratings. We also have a duty to the profession to report the news as it happens and a duty to society to keep it informed. We also have a duty to ourselves not to exploit sensational events and to maintain standards of our personal conscience. Which takes precedence? Will the journalism profession and society in general suffer from not seeing the violent photos? Must the media depend on violence to keep them solvent?

In this particular instance, different editors at TV stations and newspapers made different decisions. An ABC station in Harrisburg, Pennsylvania, interrupted a rerun of the sitcom *Webster* and ran the entire tape. A station in Pittsburgh did the same. A suburban Philadelphia newspaper ran a series of photos of the suicide, including one snapped an instant after the trigger was pulled, clearly showing blood and gore. These stations and this newspaper justified their decision based on their duty to inform the public about news, no matter how unpleasant. Other stations and papers apparently endorsed the principle of moderation and declined to show the violence. Many stations cut the tape at the point when the man raised the gun to his mouth. Two of the three networks did not show the tape and one cut it just after the gun was revealed. Most newspapers used a photo of the victim with the gun placed in his mouth, a picture that was disturbing enough but did not show the actual suicide.

Consider a more recent example. In 1991, a young woman accused William Kennedy Smith, a member of the prominent Kennedy family, of rape. The case and its resultant publicity raised ethical questions about the reporting of the name and personal life of a rape victim. (The case raised some legal questions as well but for now let's just focus on the ethical ones.) Most papers and broadcast stations have a

Handling of sensational cases involving famous people, such as the trial of William Kennedy Smith, poses special ethical problems for the media. (Les Stone/Sygma)

policy against naming the victim in a rape case. In this instance, however, several media sources—including the reserved *New York Times*, NBC News, and the supermarket tabloid, the *Globe*—chose to reveal the woman's name. The *Times* even revealed details of her personal life. From an ethical point of view, there are several conflicting values at issue here. In the first place, the privacy of the woman involved in this episode needs to be considered. Her right to privacy ought not be violated lightly. On the other hand, journalists support the value of a free flow of information under the First Amendment. The more people know, the better informed they will be when making up their minds. The ethical principles involved give some guidance. Kant's Categorical Imperative might suggest that the task of a journalist is to disseminate news, not suppress it. No matter how unpleasant or inconvenient or stigmatizing a report might be to a person, it should be published. Stifling the flow of news is unacceptable in all cases. The principle of the Golden Mean would recommend that some middle course be followed. Some general information about the alleged victim might be reported short of identifying her by name. One interpretation of the Veil of Ignorance might point out that if journalists for the print and electronic media routinely withhold the names of rape victims, the same policy should be followed in this situation. The fact that the person accused of the crime came from a prominent family ought not change the situation. A utilitarian would argue that the benefit of revealing the name should be weighed against the harm to the individual involved. Perhaps more exposure might help erase the stigma of rape and eventually outweigh the additional suffering brought on the victim. The principle of Self Determination would caution against using the sensationalistic content of the story to promote readership or viewership. People have a right not to be exploited for the personal gain of others.

The reasons given by the media for naming the woman involved and for revealing her personal life varied widely. The tabloid *Globe* seemed to endorse the Categorical Imperative when it argued that the public's right to know had to be served in this case because it involved the nephew of a prominent and powerful politician. The *New York Times* seemed to justify its decision on considerations unrelated to ethics. The newspaper argued that since the woman's name had already been revealed by NBC and the tabloid press, she had little privacy left to violate. (The *Times* later published an apology for the tone of its article.) NBC, on the other hand, embraced the Veil of Ignorance. In a memo written to staffers, the head of NBC News maintained that since the organization had named the man involved in the case, even though at the time he was still a suspect and had not even been charged, fairness suggested that the woman receive comparable journalistic treatment.

Let's look at one further example of applying ethical analysis to a real-life situation. In this case, a Pennsylvania newspaper chose to run a dramatic photo of a paramedic giving mouth-to-mouth resuscitation to an infant victim of a car wreck. (The baby later died.) In his analysis of the situation, the paper's editor clearly relied on the utilitarian principle. He decided that the social good that might result from running this photo outweighed any offense to readers' sensibilities or additional suffering to the victim's family. He wrote:

> In running the photograph we hope it caused everyone to take another look at auto safety and how their family is protected. Are little children sufficiently buckled up? . . . We hope (the photo) gave everyone a new appreciation for the volunteer rescue teams in the region. Perhaps now we won't be so quick to refuse a contribution next time they seek funds for better life-saving equipment.

In addition to matters of taste and exploitation, reporters and editors frequently face instances where they must weigh the public's right or need to know against possible repercussions on individual lives. To illustrate, a man suspected of a robbery has a perfect alibi because several witnesses testify that at the time of the crime he was sharing a motel room with a woman who was not his wife. How much of this story needs to be reported? Is the apparent infidelity a necessary element? Or what of the reporter who gets crucial information "off the record"? Are there circumstances in which this confidence can be violated?

Individual ethical judgments are made in the entertainment area as well. The principle of moderation is often apparent as filmmakers have been known to delete certain scenes in their movies or soften dialogue in order to receive a PG rating instead of an NC-17 or an R. Television station managers frequently decide if a network program is suitable for their market. For example, when the network broadcast the Charles Bronson film *Death Wish*, many local stations were faced with a problem. The film, even in its edited-for-TV version, was extraordinarily violent and advocated violence as a means to solve personal problems. The value underlying the situation appeared to be a belief that freedom of expression should be preserved even in the case of violent content. Not showing the movie would be a blow against artistic expression. On the other hand, many station executives valued the right of the audience to be free from undue risk. The possibility certainly existed that some people who saw the film might go out and commit copycat violence. There were several ethical principles involved in this situation. The veil of ignorance suggests that the most vulnerable of the audience should be protected against copycat violence. Many managers might have endorsed the categorical imperative that violence is wrong and should not be condoned or encouraged under any circumstances. Other managers felt that there was some balancing point between the extremes of showing the film as planned or not showing it. Still others felt that the harm to freedom of expression caused by not carrying the film was far worse than what might happen if it were broadcast. The loyalties in this situation are not complicated. Station managers have a duty to preserve the safety of their community. They also have a duty to their employees and shareholders to make a profit and keep their station in business (*Death Wish* promised to get good ratings, which would translate into increased profits). Finally, the managers had a duty to other professionals to preserve freedom of expression.

Situational Ethics

A more recent ethical philosophy was articulated by American theologian Joseph Fletcher. In 1966, Fletcher published *Situation Ethics: The New Morality* in which he argued that the most important aspect of morally correct behavior was not blind adherence to prefabricated rules or ethical principles but an appreciation that the moral quality of an action varies from one situation to another. Traditional ethical guidelines may be compromised or even set aside if a particular situation calls for it. Fletcher suggested that individuals trust their own intuitive sense of justice and their instinctive love of their neighbor to show them the right thing to do. Thus, there may be situations where a reporter might be justified in lying to a source if his or her motives were perceived as morally right and if the lie resulted in the maximization of beneficial consequences to all concerned. (Note how Fletcher's viewpoint shares some of the philosophy of utilitarianism.)

Many critics of situational ethics argue that Fletcher's conceptions depend too much on a person's prior moral training and ethical experience. If a person lacks the insight to recognize that his or her behavior is unjust or morally wrong, situational ethics might be used to justify any kind of behavior, no matter how reprehensible. Nonetheless, situational ethics help us to appreciate that ethical behavior is not static or mechanical but is influenced by the changing and dynamic context of modern life.

The decisions made by station managers in this case were varied. Some showed the film as scheduled. Others placed warning announcements at the beginning and in the body of the program to alert viewers to the violent content. Other managers taped the program and showed it late in the evening when fewer impressionable children were in the audience. Still others declined to show it at all.

Most of the time, ethical decisions are made in good faith with a sincere desire to serve the public and reflect positively on the profession. Sometimes, however, ethical judgments may be adversely affected by other influences.

One of the factors that influences the judgment of some reporters is a phenomenon known as **acculturation**. Simply defined, acculturation in a media context means the tendency of reporters or other media professionals to accept the ideas, attitudes, and opinions of the group that they cover or with whom they have a great deal of contact. Many political reporters, for instance, come to share the views of the politicians they cover. So do many police-beat reporters. Publishers and station managers who spend a great deal of time with business leaders might come to adopt the point of view of industry. A 1977 study of reporters and legislators in Colorado revealed that political reporters and politicians held quite similar views. The investigation also revealed that many reporters actually identified with capitol legislators, felt a sense of kinship with them, and actually considered that they, the reporters, were part of the legislative process. In the Potter model, these individuals have confused their loyalties. They see their duty to the group they are covering as more important than their duty to the profession of journalism.

Acculturation is not necessarily bad; it can cause concern, however, when it begins to affect judgment. Recently, a California newspaper learned that several off-duty police officers had terrorized a bar and had gotten into fistfights with some of its patrons. The disturbance was so serious that the chief of police recommended that three of the officers be dismissed. The paper, however, sat on the story for almost six weeks. It turned out that in the past the police and the paper had developed an easy sense of cooperation. Police officers had been given the OK to look at the paper's files; in turn, the officers would give the paper "mug shots" if the paper needed a picture of a suspect. It is possible that this close and cooperative atmosphere led some journalists to identify with the police officers and affected their news judgment in handling this story.

● ● ● ●

PERFORMANCE CODES

Many ethical decisions have to be made within minutes or hours, without the luxury of lengthy philosophical reflection. In this regard, the media professional is not very different from other professionals such as doctors and lawyers, who also face complicated decisions. In these professions, codes of conduct or of ethics have been standardized in order to help individuals in their decisions. If a doctor or a lawyer violates one of the tenets of these codes, it is possible that he or she might be barred from practice by a decision of a panel of colleagues who "police" the profession. Here the similarity with the mass media ends. Media professionals, thoroughly committed to the notion of free speech, have no professional review boards that grant and revoke licenses. Media codes of performance and methods of self-regulation are less precise and less stringent than those of other organizations. But many of the ethical principles discussed above are incorporated into these codes.

The Print Media

During the colorful and turbulent age of jazz journalism (see Chapter 4), several journalists, apparently reacting against the excesses of some tabloids, founded the

American Society of Newspaper Editors. This group voluntarily adopted the Canons of Journalism in 1923 without any public or governmental pressure. There were seven canons: responsibility, freedom of the press, independence, accuracy, impartiality, fair play, and decency. By and large, the canons are prescriptive (telling what ought to be done) rather than proscriptive (telling what should be avoided). Some of the canons tend to be general and vague, with a great deal of room for individual interpretation. Under responsibility, for example, it is stated that "the use a newspaper makes of the share of public attention it gains serves to determine its sense of responsibility, which it shares with every member of its staff." This is a noble thought, but it is of little guidance when it comes to deciding if a newspaper should include the detail about the pornographic magazines in the football player's car. Other statements seem simplistic. Under accuracy, for example, one learns that "headlines should be fully warranted by

Early Codes of Performance and Ethics in the Newspaper Business

One of the first books to consider ethics and performance codes in journalism was *The Ethics of Journalism*, published by Nelson Crawford in 1924. Below are excerpts of performance codes written by press associations and newspapers that Crawford cataloged.

From the Kansas Code of Ethics, adopted by the Kansas Editorial Association:

Reporters should not enter the domain of law in the apprehension of criminals. They should not become a detective or sweating agency for the purpose of furnishing excitement to the readers.

However prominent the principles, offenses against private morality should never receive first-page position. . . .

From the Brooklyn *Eagle*:

Beware of seekers of free publicity. Remember that space in *The Eagle* sells for 25¢ a line. . . . Don't help press agents cheat the advertising department.

Don't emphasize locality in fire or burglary stories or in news reports which give a special section an unsavory reputation.

From the Springfield *Union*:

The Union does not publish the names of persons arrested for drunkenness, nor of "drunks" who are fined nominal amounts by the court. . . . Give them a chance to reform.

In automobile accidents do not give the name of the car, nor in shooting accidents the make of the weapon used.

Don't help publicity agents to cheat the advertising department.

From the Seattle *Times*:

Remember that young girls read *The Times*.

When it is necessary to refer to improper relations between the sexes, the limit permitted in *The Times* is some such statement as "The couple were divorced," or "The couple separated," or "Various charges were made not considered fit for publication in the columns of *The Times*."

From the *Christian Science Monitor*:

Verify all quotations, especially from the Bible, whenever time will permit.

Use words of one syllable rather than those of many—the latter may serve to show off your learning, but the average reader hasn't a dictionary at his elbow. . . .

Never use expressions that suggest nauseating ideas.

The last sentence contains a thought we could all take to heart.

the contents of the article they surmount." Before you get the wrong idea, it should be pointed out that these canons should not be dismissed as mere platitudes and empty rhetoric. They do represent the first concrete attempt by journalists to strive for professionalism in their field.

When the canons were first released, *Time* magazine held out grandiose hopes for the future of the profession: "The American Society of Newspaper Editors (ASNE) aims to be to journalism what the American Bar Association is to the legal fraternity." *Time* was overly optimistic. The legal fraternity, through its powerful bar associations, has the power to revoke a member's license to practice. Journalists have fiercely resisted any idea that resembles licensing as a restriction on their First Amendment rights. The ASNE has never proposed licensing or certifying journalists for this reason. In fact, the ASNE has never expelled a member in its history, even though it has had ample reason to do so. To illustrate, just one year after the canons were adopted, our old friend Fred Bonfils (see Chapter 4) of the *Denver Post* testified that he had accepted $250,000 to suppress stories about the Teapot Dome oil-lease scandal that was then plaguing the administration of President Warren G. Harding. (Ironically, Harding himself was a former newspaper editor.) Rather than expelling Bonfils, the ASNE decided to stress voluntary compliance with its canons.

Fifty years later, Sigma Delta Chi, the Society of Professional Journalists, adopted a Code of Ethics for those working in the news media. Intended for journalists in all media, the code was modeled after the ASNE canons. The Sigma Delta Chi code has five main sections: responsibility, freedom of the press, ethics, accuracy, and fair play. Some of the guidelines are fairly specific. Under fair play, for example, one notes that "the media should not pander to morbid curiosity about the details of vice and crime." And under ethics is to be found the following guideline: "Gifts, favors, free travel, special treatment or privileges can compromise the integrity of journalists and their employers. Nothing of value can be accepted." In 1975, the Associated Press Managing Editors Association (APME) adopted a code that also discussed responsibility, accuracy, integrity, and conflicts of interest. As with the ASNE's canons, adherence to these codes is voluntary and neither Sigma Delta Chi or APME has developed any procedures to enforce the codes.

Broadcasting and Film

For many years, radio and television broadcasters followed the National Association of Broadcasters (NAB) Code of Good Practice. This code first appeared in 1929 and was revised periodically over the years. It was divided into two parts, one covering advertising and the other general program practices. In 1982, however, a court ruled that the code placed undue limitations on advertising and the NAB suspended the advertising part of its code. The next year, in order to forestall more legal pressure, the NAB officially dissolved the code in its entirety.

Although the code is gone, its impact lingers on. In 1990 the NAB issued voluntary programming principles that addressed four key areas: children's TV, indecency, violence, and drug and substance abuse. The new guidelines were stated in a broad and general way, e.g.: "Glamorization of drug use and substance abuse should be avoided." "Violence . . . should only be portrayed in a responsible manner and should not be used exploitatively." In order to stay out of trouble with the Justice Department, the NAB declared that there would be no interpretation or enforcement of these provisions and that the standards were not designed to inhibit creativity.

In the broadcast journalism area, the Radio and Television News Directors Association has an eleven-part code that covers everything from cameras in the courtroom to invasion of privacy.

Codes of conduct in the motion picture industry emerged during the 1920s. Scandals were racking Hollywood at that time (see Chapter 11), and many states had passed or were considering censorship laws that would control the content of movies. In an attempt to save itself from being tarred and feathered, the industry invited Will Hays, a former postmaster general and elder of the Presbyterian church, to head a new organization that would clean up films. Hays became the president, chairman of the board of directors, and chairman of the executive committee of a new organization, the Motion Picture Producers and Distributors of America (MPPDA). In 1930, the Motion Picture Production Code was adopted by the new group. The code was mainly proscriptive; it described what should be avoided in order for filmmakers to get their movies past existing censorship boards and listed what topics should be handled carefully so as not to rile existing pressure groups. The 1930 code is remarkable for its specificity; it rambles on for nearly twenty printed pages. The following are some excerpts:

> The presentation of scenes, episodes, plots, etc. which are deliberately meant to excite [sex and passion] on the part of the audience is always wrong, is subversive to the interest of society, and is a peril to the human race.

> The more intimate parts of the human body are the male and female organs and the breasts of a woman.

> a. They should never be uncovered.
> b. They should not be covered with transparent or translucent material.
> c. They should not be clearly and unmistakably outlined by garments. . . .

> There must be no display at any time of machine guns, sub-machine guns or other weapons generally classified as illegal weapons. . . .

> Obscene dances are those: which represent sexual actions, whether performed solo or with two or more; which are designed to excite an audience, arouse passion, or to cause physical excitement.

A few years after the Production Code was drafted, a Roman Catholic organization, the Legion of Decency (see box on page 444), pressured the industry to put teeth into its code enforcement. The MPPDA ruled that no company belonging to its organization would distribute or release any film unless it bore the Production Code Administration's seal of approval. In addition, a $25,000 fine could be levied against a firm that violated this rule. Because of the hammerlock that the major studios had over the movie industry at this time, it was virtually impossible for an independent producer to make or exhibit a film without the aid of a member company. As a result, the Production Code turned out to be more restrictive than many of the local censorship laws it was designed to avoid.

The Production Code was a meaningful force in the film industry for about twenty years. During the late 1940s, however, changes that would ultimately alter the basic structure of the motion picture industry also scuttled the code. In 1948, the Paramount case ended producer-distributor control of theaters, thus allowing independent producers to market a film without the Production Code seal. In addition, economic competition from television prompted films to treat more mature subjects. The industry responded during the 1950s by liberalizing the code; however, despite this easing of restrictions, more and more producers began to ignore them. Nonetheless, the code, outdated and unenforceable, persisted into the 1960s. A 1966 revision that tried to keep pace with the changing social attitudes of the 1960s proved to be too little too late. In 1968, the motion picture industry entered into a new phase of self-regulation when the Production Code seal of approval was dropped and a new motion picture rating system was established. Operated under the auspices of the Motion Picture

After World War I, during the roaringest part of the Roaring Twenties, the films that grossed the most money had titles like *Red Hot Romance*, *She Could Not Help It*, *Her Purchase Price*, and *Plaything of Broadway*. One movie ad of the period stated breathlessly: ". . . brilliant men, beautiful jazz babies, champagne baths, midnight revels, petting parties in the purple dawn. . . ." It wasn't long before public opposition to such sensational movies began to form. The appointment of Will Hays, the creation of the Motion Picture Producers and Distributors of America, and the adoption of the Motion Picture Production Code were designed, in part, to forestall this public criticism. Much of the code was suggested by a Roman Catholic layman, Martin Quigley, and a Roman Catholic priest, Father Daniel Lord. Despite the existence of the code, however, sensational films still appeared in significant numbers. This trend was most disturbing to many segments in society, particularly the Catholic church. Keep in mind that at this time the United States was in the midst of a severe economic depression. Many individuals, including prominent Catholics, connected the country's economic poverty with the nation's moral bankruptcy as evidenced by the films of the period. Additionally, an Apostolic Delegate from Rome took the film industry to task in a blistering speech before the Catholic Charities Convention in New York. In April of 1934, a committee composed of American bishops responded to the speech and to the general tenor of the period by announcing the organization of a nationwide Legion of Decency, whose members were to fight for better films. The Legion threatened to boycott those theaters that exhibited objectionable films and sometimes made good on their threats. The Chicago chapter of the Legion enrolled half a million members in a matter of days and was matched by equal enrollment in Brooklyn. Detroit Catholics affixed "We Demand Clean Movies" bumper stickers to their cars. Other religious groups joined the Legion—Jewish clergy in New York, Lutherans in Missouri. Pope Pius XI praised the Legion as an "excellent experiment" and called upon bishops all over the world to imitate it.

There were 20 million Catholics in the United States in 1934, and naturally the film industry took this group seriously. The Production Code Administration was set up with the power to slap a $25,000 fine on films released without the administration's seal of approval. The Legion's boycotts hurt enough at the box office to force many theaters to book only films that the Legion approved. In Albuquerque, New Mexico, seventeen out of twenty-one theaters agreed not to book a film condemned by the Legion. In Albany, New York, Catholics pledged to avoid for six months each theater that had screened the condemned film *Baby Doll*. Producers, frightened by this display of economic power, began meeting with Legion members to make sure there were no lascivious elements in their films.

By the 1960s, however, the Legion was losing most of its clout. The restructuring of the film industry allowed independent producers to market their films without code approval. Many producers did just that and demonstrated that some films could make money even without the Legion and Production Code approval. The increasingly permissive mood of the country encouraged an avalanche of more mature and controversial films. Moreover, the Legion, renamed the National Catholic Office for Motion Pictures, painted itself into a corner when it condemned artistically worthwhile films like Bergman's *The Silence* and Antonioni's *Blow Up* and endorsed films like *Godzilla vs. the Thing* and *Goliath and the Sins of Babylon*. By the 1970s, this group had effectively lost all its power; it was essentially disbanded in 1980. Nonetheless, during its prime, the Legion of Decency was the single most effective private influence on the film industry.

Association of America (successor to the MPPDA), the National Association of Theater Owners, and the Independent Film Importers and Distributors of America, this new system, commonly referred to as the **MPAA system**, places films into one of five categories:

- G: suitable for general audiences
- PG: parental guidance suggested
- PG-13: some content may be objectionable for children under 13 (a new category added in 1984)
- R: restricted to persons over seventeen unless accompanied by parent or adult guardian
- NC-17: no children under 17 admitted. (This category replaced the X rating in 1990. The MPAA made the change in response to several producers who argued that adult-themed, daring, but nonpornographic films should not be lumped into the same category as porno films.)

Unlike the old Production Code, which regulated film content, the new system leaves producers pretty much free to include whatever scenes they like as long as they realize that by so doing, they may restrict the size of their potential audience. One possible repercussion of this system may be the steady decline in the number of G-rated films released each year. Producers evidently feel that movies in this category will be perceived as children's films and will not be attractive to a more mature audience. During the first eleven years of the rating system's existence, the percentage of films in the G category dropped, while the percentage of films in the R category increased. X- or NC-17-rated films have never accounted for more than 10 percent of the total number of films submitted for review (of course, many low-budget, hardcore pornographic films are never submitted for classification). In 1990, about 95

The Motion Picture Association of America's rating is a prominent part of motion picture advertising. (The Photo Works)

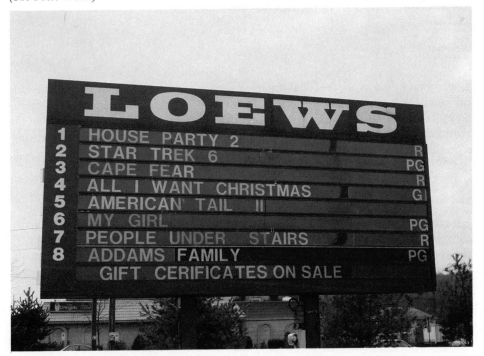

percent of all movies released by the well-known studios and independent producers fell into the PG and R categories; only 1 percent was G rated.

In order for the MPAA rating system to work, producers, distributors, theater owners, and parents must all cooperate. There is no governmental involvement in the classification system; there are no fines involved. Moviemakers are not required to submit a film for rating. People evidently think that the system is a good idea. An industry survey done in 1988 disclosed that 67 percent of the adults surveyed considered the ratings to be "very useful" guides for children's attendance. How often parents actually pay attention to these classifications is still a bit unclear. One survey done in the 1970s found that only 35 percent of a sample of parents could name a movie that their teenage sons and daughters had recently seen and only 17 percent knew the film's rating.

Other Media Codes of Performance and Ethics

There are several other codes of ethics that are involved in regulating the media. The comic book industry, for example, through the Comics Magazine Association, has developed a forty-one-point code. This code, developed in order to forestall governmental regulation of the industry, tries to discourage excessive violence, nudity, and horror in comic book content. Like the codes in the other media, this one is also voluntary. Publishers whose material is approved display the code seal on their comics.

In the advertising industry, several professional organizations have drafted codes of performance. The American Association of Advertising Agencies first adopted its Standards of Practice in 1924. This code, which covers contracts, credit extension, unfair tactics, and the creative side of advertising, contains provisions prohibiting misleading price claims, offensive statements, and the circulation of harmful rumors about a competitor. The Advertising Code of American Business, developed and distributed by the American Advertising Federation and the Association of Better Business Bureaus International, covers much the same ground. Memberships in these organizations and adherence to the codes are voluntary. In public relations, the Public Relations Society of America adopted its first code in 1954 and revised it during the 1970s. As with the other codes enforcement is essentially voluntary, and the society has no control over a practitioner who is not a member.

● ● ● ●

INTERNAL CONTROLS

Codes established by professional organizations and individual ethics are not the only informal controls on media behavior. Most media organizations have other internal controls that frequently come into play. Written statements of policy can be found in most newspapers, television, radio, and motion picture organizations. In advertising, a professional organization for self-regulation has existed since 1971.

Organizational Policy: Television Networks' Standards and Practices

For many years, the major television networks maintained a large department that was usually labeled "Standards and Practices" or something similar. Staff members in these departments would make literally thousands of decisions each season on the acceptability of dialogue, plot lines, costumes, and visual portrayals. The network budget cuts of the late 1980s, however, took their toll on these departments and most were scaled back dramatically. Currently, for most series, the networks will pay close attention to the first few episodes to see if there are any questionable areas. After that, for most series, the networks will rely on the judgment of the series producer as far

"The Material Girl" in the video that MTV wouldn't show. Madonna's "Justify My Love" was considered too racy, even for MTV. (Luc Novovitch/Gamma Liasion)

as standards of acceptability are concerned. Series producers, for their part, have a general notion about how far they can go without arousing network displeasure. Some shows that have a history of dealing with controversial or sensational content get closer scrutiny. *Saturday Night Live* and *LA Law*, for example, are two series that NBC pays close attention to. When controversial comedian Andrew Dice Clay hosted *Saturday Night Live* in 1990, the show, usually done live, was broadcast with a five-second tape delay as insurance against obscene language.

The networks also prescreen commercials and movies for scenes that might be in bad taste. Most recently, ABC edited out scenes from *A Fish Called Wanda* that might have been offensive to those who stuttered. Cable networks, MTV in particular, will also bar content that they feel will offend their audiences. In perhaps the most publicized case, MTV declined to carry Madonna's video "Justify My Love" in 1990 because of its sexual content. Interestingly enough, this decision probably guaranteed that more people would see the video than would have had it been aired normally (see box on page 448).

In addition to these network efforts, most local stations also have what is known as a **policy book**. This book typically spells out philosophy and standards of operation and identifies what practices are encouraged or discouraged. For example, most television and radio stations have a policy against newsroom personnel functioning as commercial spokespersons. Radio stations typically have a policy against airing "homemade" tapes and records. Other stations may have rules against playing songs that are drug oriented or too suggestive. Commercials that make extravagant claims or ads for questionable products and services might also be prohibited under local station policy.

Organizational Policy: Newspapers and Magazines

Newspapers and magazines have policy statements that take two distinct forms. On the one hand, there are **operating policies** that cover the everyday problems and

Justify My Ratings

MTV rejected the Madonna video "Justify My Love" because the video didn't measure up to MTV's standards of acceptability. Of course, it's a major news event in the entertainment world when MTV thinks something is unacceptable, and the resultant commotion got the video and the programs that went ahead and aired it a great deal of publicity. Excerpts from the video were shown on the nationally syndicated *Entertainment Tonight* and boosted that show's rating above its normal figures. *CNN Showbiz Today* showed two minutes of excerpts from it and got its highest rating of the week. The syndicated *The Howard Stern Show* showed the uncut video and got its highest rating ever. *Saturday Night Live* showed 90 seconds of excerpts from the clip and got its highest rating of the season. Madonna even showed up as a guest on *Nightline*, where "Justify My Love" was shown uncut and uncensored. *Nightline*'s rating was the highest it had been all year. Sometimes rejection isn't so bad.

situations that crop up during the normal functioning of the paper. On the other, there are **editorial policies** that the newspaper follows in order to persuade the public on certain issues or to achieve specific goals. Both policies can exert some control over what a particular newspaper or magazine publishes.

Operating policies will vary from paper to paper. In general, however, these policies might cover such matters as accepting "freebies," using deception to gather information, paying newsmakers for a story or exclusive interview (checkbook journalism), junkets, electronic surveillance, use of stolen documents, outside employment of reporters and editors, conflicts of interest, accepting advertising for X-rated films, and deciding whether or not to publish the names of rape victims. Here, for example, are excerpts from the *Rules and Guidelines* used by the *Milwaukee Journal*:

> Free tickets or passes to sports events, movies, theatrical productions, circuses, ice shows, or other entertainment may not be accepted or solicited by staff members.

> A gift that exceeds token value should be returned promptly with an explanation that it is against our policy. If it is impractical to return it, the company will donate it to a charity.

> Participating in politics at any level is not allowed, either for pay or as a volunteer. Public relations and publicity work in fields outside the *Journal* should be avoided.

Some newspapers and magazines are liberal; some are conservative. Some support Democratic candidates; others support Republicans. Some are in favor of nuclear energy; others against. These and other attitudes are generally expressed in the editorial pages of the newspaper. Editorial policy is generally clear at most publications. The *Chicago Tribune* has traditionally expressed a conservative point of view. The *New York Times* has a more liberal policy. The editorial policy of a paper will exert a certain amount of control over the material that is printed on its editorial pages. This, of course, the paper has a perfect right to do. There may be times, however, when the editorial policy of the paper spills over onto its news pages, and this might cause a problem with the paper's reputation for objectivity, responsibility, and integrity.

One problem that crops up periodically is called "boosterism," a procommunity philosophy that sometimes causes not-so-good news to go unreported. In Flint, Michigan, when the local Fisher Body plant closed, TV networks and newspapers across the country announced the bad news that Flint was about to lose 3600 jobs. When it covered the story, the local Flint paper didn't mention the job loss until the eleventh paragraph on an inside page. "Good news," however, got prominent play. A story about new shrubs being planted at the local Buick facility got front-page coverage while a story about the Civil Rights Department charging the Flint Chamber of Commerce with sex discrimination got covered on page fourteen of the paper's third section.

In 1988, a Pasadena, California, paper carried a column that criticized the city's extravagant and expensive preparations for the Tournament of Roses Parade. A few days later, under pressure from civic leaders, the paper's executive editor apologized in print for the remarks. Two days later the column was permanently dropped. Similarly, when one of the networks asked its local Detroit affiliate to transmit a report about "Devil's Night," a pre-Halloween event that encourages vandalism and arson, the station refused, stating that it wasn't going to do a hatchet job on the city.

Owners and publishers can exert editorial control over news policy in several ways. They can hire only those people who agree with their editorial views. (For example, the *New Orleans Times-Picayune* ran an ad in a trade magazine for a business reporter. One of the qualifications was a "probusiness philosophy.") They can also fire those people who produce stories that the owner doesn't like, or they can issue orders to downplay some topics while paying large amounts of attention to others. Walter Annenberg, when he owned the *Philadelphia Inquirer* and the *News*, reportedly became so upset with the management of the Philadelphia 76ers pro basketball team that he limited coverage of them to two paragraphs after a win and one paragraph after a loss.

What is the significance of these examples for the news-consuming public? For one thing, we should point out that the above cases are probably exceptions to the norm rather than the norm itself. Nonetheless, they do illustrate the potential hazards of relying on only one source for news. The intelligent consumer of news and information should rely on several different media to get a more complete picture.

Editorial Policy and What's "Said": Time Magazine and the Presidents

The problem of editorial policy affecting straight news coverage was never a dilemma for *Time* magazine under the direction of Henry Luce. When it was founded in 1923, *Time*'s editors argued that objectivity in presenting the news isn't possible and that *Time* reporters shouldn't hesitate in making a judgment in their articles. More often than not, these judgments were in line with *Time*'s editorial policy. One subtle way of injecting editorial judgment into ostensibly factual news stories is to choose carefully the synonyms used for the word "said" when reporting someone's conversations and speeches. An article by John C. Merrill in a 1965 issue of *Journalism Quarterly* documents that *Time* employed this technique in its reporting about Presidents Truman and Eisenhower.

President Harry S Truman was no favorite of the magazine. When Truman spoke he seldom "said" anything; instead, he "sputtered," "barked," "droned," "preached," or "popped a gasket." When he finally "said" something, he said it "curtly" or "coldly" or said it "flushed with anger" or "grinning slyly." President Dwight D. Eisenhower, however, was liked by the magazine. When he spoke, he "chatted amiably," "pointed out cautiously," "talked with a happy grin," or "spoke warmly." Or, when he preferred not to say anything, he "skillfully refused to commit himself."

Self-Criticism

Some informal control over media content and practices comes from within—but not much. Compared to the amount of investigative reporting and critical analyses that newspapers, magazines, television, and radio conduct about other facets of society, the amount of internal criticism that they do seems insignificant. True, there are some exceptions. Newspapers and magazines employ critics who comment on films and TV programs, but it is debatable if this criticism has any influence. In the news area, there are several journalism reviews that regularly criticize media performance. The *Columbia Journalism Review* is the best known, but its circulation is only 35,000. Television and radio news operations seldom do a serious job of criticizing themselves. Newspapers do a bit more in this area, and the *Wall Street Journal* has occasionally run an in-depth study of the problems facing the newspaper industry. In film, the industry newspaper *Variety* has sometimes published an article critical of the film industry. *Billboard*, the trade publication of the sound recording industry, has run analytical, if not critical, pieces on the recording industry.

Some newspapers have tried to incorporate an idea from Scandinavia into their operations in order to provide some internal criticism. An individual employed by the paper (called an **ombudsperson**) is assigned to handle complaints from readers who feel that they have gotten a raw deal and to criticize in general the performance of the paper's staff. The ombudsperson with the Louisville, Kentucky, newspapers handled between 500 and 1000 complaints during the first three years the paper had this system. The idea, however, has not made a big splash nationwide, and only a few papers maintain such a person. (One of the problems might be the difficult-to-pronounce title, "ombudsperson." The Louisville papers reportedly get letters addressed to the "Omnibus person" or to "Dear Omnipotent.")

Professional Self-Regulation in Advertising

In 1971, the leading advertising professional organizations—the Council of Better Business Bureaus, the American Advertising Federation, the American Association of Advertising Industries, and the Association of National Advertisers—formed the National Advertising Review Council. Its objective is to sustain high standards of truth and accuracy in advertising. The Council itself is composed of two divisions: the National Advertising Division (NAD) and the National Advertising Review Board (NARB). When a complaint about an ad is made by a consumer or competitor, the complaint goes first to the NAD, where it is evaluated. The NAD can dismiss the complaint as unfounded or trivial or it can contact the advertiser for an explanation or further substantiation. If the NAD is satisfied that the ad in question is accurate, it will dismiss the complaint. If the NAD is not satisfied with the explanation, it can ask the advertiser to change the ad or discontinue the message. If the advertiser disagrees, the case goes to the NARB, which functions as a court of appeals. Ultimately, if the case has not reached an acceptable solution, the NARB could call it to the attention of the Federal Trade Commission or other appropriate agencies. Most advertisers, however, are willing to comply with NARB's wishes. Note, however, that the National Advertising Review Council depends totally on moral forces to accomplish its goals. It cannot order an advertiser to stop running an ad, impose a fine, or kick anybody out of the profession.

To give you some idea of the kinds of complaints handled by the NAD, here is a sampling taken from the early 1990s:

Case One: An ad for Bisquick Shake 'n' Pour pancake mixes stated that the product made "50 percent more pancakes than other shake mixes." A competitor challenged the claim and the company responded that it referred only to Aunt Jemima's brand and not to all other mixes. Bisquick agreed to modify the ad.

paragraph on an inside page. "Good news," however, got prominent play. A story about new shrubs being planted at the local Buick facility got front-page coverage while a story about the Civil Rights Department charging the Flint Chamber of Commerce with sex discrimination got covered on page fourteen of the paper's third section.

In 1988, a Pasadena, California, paper carried a column that criticized the city's extravagant and expensive preparations for the Tournament of Roses Parade. A few days later, under pressure from civic leaders, the paper's executive editor apologized in print for the remarks. Two days later the column was permanently dropped. Similarly, when one of the networks asked its local Detroit affiliate to transmit a report about "Devil's Night," a pre-Halloween event that encourages vandalism and arson, the station refused, stating that it wasn't going to do a hatchet job on the city.

Owners and publishers can exert editorial control over news policy in several ways. They can hire only those people who agree with their editorial views. (For example, the *New Orleans Times-Picayune* ran an ad in a trade magazine for a business reporter. One of the qualifications was a "probusiness philosophy.") They can also fire those people who produce stories that the owner doesn't like, or they can issue orders to downplay some topics while paying large amounts of attention to others. Walter Annenberg, when he owned the *Philadelphia Inquirer* and the *News*, reportedly became so upset with the management of the Philadelphia 76ers pro basketball team that he limited coverage of them to two paragraphs after a win and one paragraph after a loss.

What is the significance of these examples for the news-consuming public? For one thing, we should point out that the above cases are probably exceptions to the norm rather than the norm itself. Nonetheless, they do illustrate the potential hazards of relying on only one source for news. The intelligent consumer of news and information should rely on several different media to get a more complete picture.

Editorial Policy and What's "Said": Time Magazine and the Presidents

The problem of editorial policy affecting straight news coverage was never a dilemma for *Time* magazine under the direction of Henry Luce. When it was founded in 1923, *Time*'s editors argued that objectivity in presenting the news isn't possible and that *Time* reporters shouldn't hesitate in making a judgment in their articles. More often than not, these judgments were in line with *Time*'s editorial policy. One subtle way of injecting editorial judgment into ostensibly factual news stories is to choose carefully the synonyms used for the word "said" when reporting someone's conversations and speeches. An article by John C. Merrill in a 1965 issue of *Journalism Quarterly* documents that

Time employed this technique in its reporting about Presidents Truman and Eisenhower.

President Harry S Truman was no favorite of the magazine. When Truman spoke he seldom "said" anything; instead, he "sputtered," "barked," "droned," "preached," or "popped a gasket." When he finally "said" something, he said it "curtly" or "coldly" or said it "flushed with anger" or "grinning slyly." President Dwight D. Eisenhower, however, was liked by the magazine. When he spoke, he "chatted amiably," "pointed out cautiously," "talked with a happy grin," or "spoke warmly." Or, when he preferred not to say anything, he "skillfully refused to commit himself."

Case Two: An ad for Trek bicycles claimed that the bikes were designed and manufactured in the United States. A competitor, Schwinn, complained to the NAD that only twenty-two of twenty-eight Trek models were made in the U.S. Trek replied that the statement referred only to the bikes that were shown in the ad but agreed to modify the ad in the future.

Case Three: The marketers of the reading system "Hooked on Phonics" agreed to modify their ad copy which stated that "any kind of reading problem" would be helped by their program. The NAD noted that "Hooked on Phonics" had presented no evidence that it could help those with reading disabilities.

• • • •

OUTSIDE INFLUENCES

The larger context that surrounds a media organization often contains factors that have an influence on media performance. This section discusses four: economics, pressure groups, press councils, and education.

Economic Pressures

Another factor that has influence over media gatekeepers is a potent one—money. In commercial media, the loss of revenue can be an important consideration in controlling what gets filmed, published, or broadcast. Economic controls come in many shapes and forms. Pressure can be brought to bear by advertisers, by the medium's own business policy, by the general economic structure of the industry, and by consumer groups.

Pressure from Advertisers. Films and sound recording are financed by the purchase of individual tickets, albums, and tapes. They earn virtually no money from advertisers and consequently are immune from their pressure. On the other hand, in the print media, newspapers depend on advertising for about 75 percent of their income, while magazines derive 50 percent of their revenues from ads. Radio and television, of course, depend upon ads for all their income. The actual amount of control that an advertiser has over media content and behavior is difficult to determine. To keep the issue in perspective, it is probably fair to say that most news stories and most television and radio programs are put together without much thought as to what advertisers will say about them.

Occasionally, however, you may find examples of pressure, particularly in recent years when advertising revenue has been hard to come by. A few illustrations:

In 1988, a Wisconsin weekly, under pressure from a large pesticide company that bought a lot of ads in the paper, fired an editor who had written a story about the dangers of pesticide poisoning. The 1991 edition of *Best of Business Quarterly* reprinted a collection of outstanding business articles that had originally appeared elsewhere. In one of the original articles, Xerox was identified as one of about a half-dozen companies that had caused problems in Mexico during their search for cheap labor. When the article was reprinted, the other companies were named but Xerox was omitted. Not coincidentally, Xerox is the corporate sponsor of *Best of Business Quarterly* and ran twenty-two pages of ads in the issue. Finally, a sports writer for a Carbondale, Illinois, paper wrote a column in which he compared the pitching staff of the St. Louis Cardinals to a bunch of used car lemons polished up for sale by slick and shady dealers. The next day the paper carried a fourteen-paragraph apology by the paper's publisher scolding the writer for using an obsolete stereotype, defending the honesty of used car dealers and urging readers to continue to patronize them. Not coincidentally, used car dealers spend a lot of money on newspaper advertising.

A case of advertiser pressure on network TV occurred in late 1991 when NBC learned that several advertisers were considering pulling their ads from an episode of

Public Relations Society of America Code of Professional Standards for the Practice of Public Relations

Declaration of Principles

Members of the Public Relations Society of America base their professional principles on the fundamental value and dignity of the individual, holding that the free exercise of human rights, especially freedom of speech, freedom of assembly, and freedom of the press, is essential to the practice of public relations.

In serving the interests of clients and employers, we dedicate ourselves to the goals of better communication, understanding, and cooperation among the diverse individuals, groups, and institutions of society, and of equal opportunity of employment in the public relations profession.

We pledge:

To conduct ourselves professionally, with truth, accuracy, fairness, and responsibility to the public;

To improve our individual competence and advance the knowledge and proficiency of the profession through continuing research and education;

And to adhere to the articles of the Code of Professional Standards for the Practice of Public Relations as adopted by the governing Assembly of the Society.

Articles of the Code

These articles have been adopted by the Public Relations Society of America to promote and maintain high standards of public service and ethical conduct among its members.

1. A member shall deal fairly with clients or employers, past and present, or potential, with fellow practitioners, and the general public.

2. A member shall conduct his or her professional life in accord with the public interest.

3. A member shall adhere to truth and accuracy and to generally accepted standards of good taste.

4. A member shall not represent conflicting or competing interests without the express consent of those involved, given after a full disclosure of the facts; nor place himself or herself in a position where the member's interest is or may be in conflict with a duty to a client, or others, without a full disclosure of such interests to all involved.

5. A member shall safeguard the confidences of present and former clients, as well as of those persons or entities who have disclosed confidences to a member in the context of communications relating to an anticipated professional relationship with such member, and shall not accept retainers or employment that may involve disclosing, using or offering to use such confidences to the disadvantage or prejudice of such present, former or potential clients or employers.

6. A member shall not engage in any practice which tends to corrupt the integrity of channels of communication or the processes of government.

7. A member shall not intentionally communicate false or misleading information and is obliged to use care to avoid communication of false or misleading information.

8. A member shall be prepared to identify publicly the name of the client or employer on whose behalf any public communication is made.

9. A member shall not make use of any individual or organization purporting to serve or represent an announced cause, or purporting to be independent or unbiased, but actually serving an undisclosed special or private interest of a member, client, or employer.

10. A member shall not intentionally injure the professional reputation or practice of another practitioner. However, if a member has evidence that another member has been guilty of unethical, illegal, or unfair practices, including those in violation of this code, the member shall present the information promptly to the proper authorities of the society for action in accordance with the procedure set forth in Article XII of the bylaws.

11. A member called as a witness in a proceeding for the enforcement of this code shall be bound to appear, unless excused for sufficient reason by the judicial panel.

12. A member, in performing services for a client or employer, shall not accept fees, commissions, or any other valuable consideration from anyone other than the client or employer in connection with those services without the express consent of the client or employer, given after a full disclosure of the facts.

13. A member shall not guarantee the achievement of specified results beyond the member's direct control.

14. A member shall, as soon as possible, sever relations with any organization or individual if such relationship requires conduct contrary to the articles of this code.

Public Relations Society of America. Used by permission.

Quantum Leap that told the story of a gay military cadet who considers suicide after he is persecuted by antigays. Fearful of lost revenue, NBC asked the show's production company to help cover the cost of any lost ad dollars. Eventually, a revised episode of the show was produced.

Business Policies. Economic pressure on media content is sometimes encouraged by the business practices of the media themselves. Some newspapers and broadcasting stations might not report all the details of a news story or might delete certain items in an attempt to give a break to their advertisers. When the Supreme Court of Massachusetts ruled that a creditor could be sued for harassing those who owed money, the Boston newspapers declined to identify the retail store involved in the suit. The store had allegedly made late-night calls to those behind in their payments and threatened them with credit revocation. Why was the name of the store not mentioned? Perhaps because the store in question spent a lot of money on advertising space in the papers. In another example, a TV station taped out the brand names of toys that were being used to demonstrate potentially hazardous playthings. (Toy advertisers spend a lot of money on TV ads.) In San Francisco, two daily papers deleted the names of local companies named in a study of air pollution in the area.

Then there is the problem of what a prominent editor called "revenue-related reading matter." This crops up when a new shopping center or movie theater or department store opens in town and receives heavy news coverage, perhaps more than is justified by the considerations of ordinary journalism, in return for advertising revenue. At WLUP in Chicago, talk-show hosts ad-libbed mentions of items they saw in the *Chicago Tribune* but neglected to tell their listeners that the paper paid for each plug. In St. Paul, Minnesota, during the 1987 Christmas season, a local paper treated its readers to dozens of articles about Santabear, a promotional toy sponsored by the Dayton Hudson Company, a department store chain. The paper even published a sixteen-page educational supplement about the toy. Dayton Hudson was the paper's largest advertiser.

Scott Bakula portrayed a gay military cadet in an episode of Quantum Leap. *The show's content made NBC afraid that some advertisers might cancel their spots in the show. (Photo by, Ron Tom, courtesy NBC, Inc.)*

The early 1990s have witnessed an era when many newspapers and broadcasting stations now treat auto dealers with kid gloves. Newspapers have started including automotive sections whose purpose is not to report objectively on the industry but to provide a better editorial environment for auto advertising. In Birmingham, Alabama, after the local paper published several stories critical of local auto dealers, two dealerships pulled their advertising from the paper, costing it about $500,000 in revenue. Not too much later, the stories stopped and the paper started a "Wheels" section designed to lure back some of the lost dollars. In Minneapolis, Minnesota, a TV reporter broadcast a report on how to save money when buying a new car. In response, many car dealers shifted their ad dollars to a competing station. A reporter at the competing station had put together a story about car thefts from local dealers, but management killed the story, partly because they were afraid of antagonizing local dealers.

Magazines have also become more advertiser friendly. In one well-publicized example, *Family Circle* covered contributing editor Martha Stewart's reconstruction of one of her country houses in a three-part article. Stewart is also a lifestyle and entertainment consultant to K Mart. Interestingly, K Mart helped to finance the reconstruction and also bought $4 million worth of ads in the magazine, many for products used in renovating homes. A survey of magazine editors done by *Folio*, the magazine of magazine management, found that 40 percent of them reported that the advertising department had asked them to do something that seriously compromised the editorial content of the publication.

Lastly, the above illustrations are not meant to criticize or impugn the reputation of any medium or profession. There are probably countless, less publicized examples of situations where newspapers, magazines, television, and radio stations resisted advertising and economic pressure and printed or broadcast what they thought should be publicized. What you should learn from this section is the close relationship that can sometimes exist between advertiser and media and the pressures that can result. Most of the time, this will cause few problems. When professional judgment is compromised by the dollar sign, however, then perhaps the economic pressures are performing a dysfunction for the media.

Pressure Groups

Various segments of the audience can band together and try to exert control over the operation of mass media organizations. These groups sometimes use the threat of economic pressure (boycotts) or sometimes simply rely on the negative effects of bad publicity to achieve their goal. In radio and television, pressure groups (or citizens' groups, as they are often called) can resort to applying legal pressure during the license-renewal process. Because of broadcasting's unique legal position, it has been the focus of a great deal of pressure-group attention. In 1964, for example, a group of black citizens, working with the Office of Communication of the United Church of Christ, formed a pressure group and attempted to deny the license renewal of a TV station in Jackson, Mississippi, because of alleged discrimination on the part of station management. After a long and complicated legal battle, the citizens' group was successful in its efforts. This success probably encouraged the formation of other groups. John Banzhaf III headed an organization called ASH (Action for Smoking and Health), which was instrumental in convincing Congress to ban cigarette advertising from radio and television. A local group in Texarkana, Arkansas, negotiated an agreement with a local television station whereby the station would alter some of its programming and employment practices in return for the group's dropping of its legal action. Several Mexican-American groups were successful in persuading the Frito-Lay Company to remove its cartoon character, the "Frito Bandito," from its ads. At about the same time, perhaps the most influential of all the pressure groups interested in broadcasting was formed: Action for Children's Television (ACT). From a modest start, this group was successful in achieving the following:

1. persuading the networks to appoint a supervisor for children's programming

2. eliminating drug and vitamin ads from kids' shows

3. instituting a ban on the host's selling in children's programs (Captain Kangaroo cannot sell bicycles, e.g.)

4. reducing the amount of advertising during Saturday morning programs

5. helping a bill concerning children's TV pass Congress in 1991.

ACT disbanded in 1992. In its final press release, the organization said its major goal had been achieved with the passage of the 1990 Children's Television Act and that people who want better television for kids now "have Congress on their side."

In the mid-1970s, other special-interest groups whose primary interest was not broadcasting began to get involved with television programming. The American Medical Association stated that televised violence was harmful to a person's mental health and sponsored research to measure the amount of violence in network shows. The national Parent Teachers Association (PTA) also criticized TV violence and working with another citizens' group—the National Citizens Committee for Broadcasting—identified the most violent TV shows and publicized the companies that advertised during those programs. Implicit in the PTA's listings was the threat of a boycott against companies that sponsor violence. In fact, several companies changed their ads when confronted with the PTA's results.

The National Organization for Women (NOW) has also been active in campaigning against discrimination in hiring practices and for a more representative portrayal of women in the mass media. NOW has not limited its attention to the broadcast media. It has also been concerned with the elimination of sexist language in all media, the image of women in advertising, and the lack of significant women's roles in popular films. In 1985, Mothers Against Drunk Driving (MADD) was instrumental in getting the TV networks to modify their policies toward portraying alcohol use in their programs. In 1989, a one-woman letter-writing campaign directed against the Fox network's *Married . . . with Children* prompted some big advertisers, including Procter & Gamble and Coca-Cola, not to run ads in the show. (The campaign had little effect on the program and it went on to become one of Fox's big hits, but this episode illustrates how sensitive advertisers are to viewer complaints.) In 1993, the American Family Association, led by the Reverend Donald Wildmon, attempted to pressure ABC network affiliates to refrain from showing the controversial *NYPD Blue*. About fifty stations refused to air the premiere episode of the series.

Perhaps the most successful of all pressure groups was the National Legion of Decency, discussed earlier in this chapter, which exerted a surprising amount of control over the motion picture industry during the 1930s and 1940s, primarily by using the threat of a boycott. Individual films have upset other groups. *The Godfather* was deemed offensive by some Italian-American groups. The 1988 film *The Last Temptation of Christ* inspired threats of picketing and demonstrations even before it opened. The film eventually took in about $9 million, a little better than it would have done without all the controversy.

Pressure groups organized along political lines have also exerted control over media content and practices. One particularly vicious example occurred in the 1950s during the "Cold War" period when a massive "communist scare" ran throughout the country. A self-appointed group called Aware, Inc., tried to point out what it thought were communist influences in the broadcasting industry. Performers whose background was thought to be even the least bit questionable were "blacklisted" by the organization and were unable to find employment in the industry until they "rehabilitated" themselves by going through a rigid twelve-step process. The blacklist went to the heart of the commercial broadcasting system. Its founders threatened to boycott the products of advertisers who sponsored shows with suspected communists. The investigation techniques of Aware, Inc., were slipshod and deficient. Many innocent persons were put on the blacklist and had their careers permanently damaged. Finally, one performer, John Henry Faulk, sued Aware for libel. After hearing the evidence at the trial, the jury was so aghast at the techniques and tactics used by Aware that they awarded Faulk a record $3.5 million in damages. (Faulk, however, was able to collect only a small part of this sum since the chief defendant died shortly after the trial.)

Disregarding extremist groups like Aware, Inc., we might sum up by saying that there are both positive and negative aspects in the activities of these citizens' groups. On the one hand, they probably have made some media organizations more responsive to community needs and more sensitive to the problems of minorities and other disadvantaged groups. Citizen-group involvement with media organizations has also probably increased the feedback between audience and the media industry. On the other hand, these groups are self-appointed guardians of some special interest. They are not elected by anyone and may not be at all representative of the larger population. In addition, many of these groups have exerted unreasonable power and some, like Aware, may actually abuse their influence and do more harm than good.

Press Councils

The idea of **press councils** was imported from Europe. A press council is an independent agency whose job it is to monitor the performance of the media on a day-to-day basis. The American press councils generally follow the model used in Great Britain, where a council has been operating since 1963. The British council consists of people with media experience and some lay members. It examines complaints from the public about erroneous or deficient press coverage. The council has no enforcement powers; if it finds an example of poor performance, the council issues a report to that effect. Unfavorable publicity is the only sanction the council can bring to bear.

In the United States the National News Council was in existence from 1973 to 1984. In its approximately ten-year existence, the council considered 242 complaints against the news media and found that about half of them were unwarranted. During its tenure, however, the National News Council never won the support of the press. Its proceedings received little publicity and many influential news-gathering organizations refused to cooperate with it. With the National News Council gone, there are only a few local news councils across the country that evaluate press performance.

Education

Education also exerts informal control over the media. Ethics and professionalism are topics that are gaining more and more attention at colleges and universities.

In fact, there has been a recent upsurge in the interest of teaching ethics at many schools of journalism and mass communication. About 40 percent of the schools in the United States offer a special ethics course to their students. More than half of the approximately forty books specifically devoted to mass media ethics have been published since 1980. Numerous workshops and conferences on how to teach ethics were held during the late 1980s and early 1990s. Most of the experts in this area agreed that instead of teaching specific codes of ethics to students, a systematic way of thinking about ethics should be stressed, so that individuals can consider things and arrive at decisions rationally.

Even this book can be thought of as a means of informal control. After reading it, it is hoped, you will bring a more advanced level of critical thinking and a more sensitive and informed outlook to your media profession or to your role as media consumer.

● ● ● ●

SUGGESTIONS FOR FURTHER READING

The books listed below represent a good starting point if you want to find out more about informal controls on the media.

CHRISTIANS, CLIFFORD, KIM ROTZOLL, AND MARK FACKLER, *Media Ethics*, New York: Longman, 1991.

FARBER, STEPHEN, *The Movie Rating Game*, Washington, D.C.: Public Affairs Press, 1972.

FINK, CONRAD, *Media Ethics*, New York: McGraw-Hill, 1988.

GERALD, EDWARD, *The Social Responsibility of the Press*, Minneapolis: University of Minnesota Press, 1963.

HOHENBERG, JOHN, *The News Media: A Journalist Looks at His Profession*, New York: Holt, Rinehart and Winston, 1968.

HULTENG, JOHN, *The Messenger's Motives*, Englewood Cliffs, N.J.: Prentice-Hall, 1985.

LINTON, BRUCE, *Self-Regulation in Broadcasting*, Washington, D.C.: National Association of Broadcasters, 1967.

MEYER, PHILLIP, *Ethical Journalism*, New York: Longman, 1987.

MONTGOMERY, KATHRYN, *Target: Prime Time*, New York: Oxford University Press, 1990.

PATTERSON, PHILLIP, *Media Ethics*, Dubuque, Iowa: William C. Brown, 1991.

RIVERS, WILLIAM, AND WILBUR SCHRAMM, *Responsibility in Mass Communication*, New York: Harper & Row, 1980.

RUBIN, BERNARD, *Questioning Media Ethics*, New York: Praeger, 1978.

MASS MEDIA AUDIENCES

AUDIENCE CHARACTERISTICS AND PATTERNS OF USE

t's 11:30 P.M. on Friday, and outside the movie theater the line for the midnight show is already forming. One glance, however, tells the casual passerby that this is no ordinary movie line. Several people, dressed in hooded black robes, resemble executioners. Others are wearing skullcap wigs; still others are decked out in eyeshadow and motorcycle grease. The most popular costume, however, worn by both males and females, is high heels, black stockings, a short black slip, whiteface, and lipstick.

Once this crowd is inside the movie theater, it is quickly apparent that this is not the typical movie audience. The film seems secondary, and the audience is intent on entertaining itself. As a wedding scene unfolds on screen, showers of rice cascade from the audience. When one of the film's characters proposes a toast, a dozen slices of cold toast come frisbeeing from the audience toward the screen. On screen the cast of the film engages in a dance called "The Time Warp." At least two dozen audience members dance along in the aisles, their movements choreographed to those on screen. At one point, the "hero" of the movie exclaims, "Great Scott!" A half-dozen rolls of toilet tissue streamers (Scott's, one would presume) unravel toward the screen. And so it goes . . . another routine screening of *The Rocky Horror Picture Show*. (In 1990, the *Rocky Horror Picture Show* celebrated its fifteenth anniversary by appearing on videocassette. Its distributing company, CBS/Fox, thought that it would be a hot rental film but that few people would want to own it. Consequently, they priced it at $89.98, way above the normal $20 to $25 range for most sell-through videos. The folks at CBS/Fox underestimated the wonderfully wacky fans of *Rocky Horror*. Despite the steep price tag, all of the 300,000 copies that were made were quickly snapped up— that's another $27 million in revenue for a film that's already made more than $60 million in theatrical release. Some desperate *Rocky Horror* fans were renting the tape from their local video store, reporting it "lost" and paying the $89.98. More than a hundred theaters still have regular midnight showings of the film and there's even a book, *The Rocky Horror Rules of Etiquette*, that instructs new members on how to behave properly during the screening. Great Scott!)

It's 5:30 P.M. on New York City's Long Island Expressway (sometimes called the World's Longest Parking Lot); traffic is at a standstill. One frustrated commuter snaps on the car radio just in time to hear a local radio station's traffic copter report. "Avoid the Long Island Expressway if humanly possible," says the voice on the radio. The commuter, along with about a half-dozen others in the immediate vicinity, opens the car window and shakes his fist at the heavens.

It's midnight in the college dorm. One roommate is on the phone talking to a prospective date. The other roommate is trying to read a Faulkner short story for tomorrow's English Lit class. After ten minutes, the second roommate, having heard enough of the phone conversation, turns on the stereo, plugs in a set of earphones and reads Faulkner while listening to Bruce Springsteen.

Do the Time Warp! Sometimes just being in the audience for The Rocky Horror Picture Show *is more important than watching the film. (Flip Schulke/Black Star)*

The above examples, diverse as they are, all illustrate people in the mass communication audience. To say that the audience is the most important part of the mass communication process is an understatement. Without the audience, there would be no mass communication. In addition, as has been pointed out in Chapter 1, the audience is the ultimate source of mass media revenue. If the audience was not there to purchase movie tickets and recordings, subscribe to newspapers and magazines, and attend to radio and TV programs, no mass medium could stay in business.

The nature and content of the mass medium also determine the precise composition of the audience. As mentioned in Chapter 6, controlled circulation magazines will be read by a highly specific audience segment. Radio formats, as mentioned in Chapter 9, are designed to appeal to tightly defined demographic groups. Finally, as we will see in the next chapter, audience characteristics shape the feedback from receiver to source.

● ● ● ●
STAGES OF AUDIENCE EVOLUTION

As communication media develop and evolve, audiences evolve with them. The notion of media and audience evolution has been suggested by several mass communication scholars. The discussion below incorporates and expands upon ideas put forth by John Merrill and Ralph Lowenstein in their book *Media, Messages and Men* and by Richard Maisel in his article "The Decline of the Mass Media," in a 1973 edition of *Public Opinion Quarterly*.

In general terms, we can identify at least four stages in audience evolution:

1. the elite stage

2. the mass stage

3. the specialized stage

4. the interactive stage

In the **elite audience stage**, the audience for the medium is relatively small and represents the more educated and refined segments of society. In this stage, the audience does not represent the "average man" or "average woman." Media content is geared to elite tastes. In the **mass audience stage**, the potential audience consists of the entire population, with all segments of society likely to be represented. Media content is designed to appeal to what has been called the "least common denominator" in the audience. The **specialized audience stage** is typified by fragmented, special-interest audience groups. Media content is carefully designed to appeal to distinct and particular audience segments. In the **interactive audience stage**, the individual audience member has some selective control over what he or she chooses to see or hear. In effect, the audience member joins in the process as an editor or, in some cases, even as a transmitter of information.

Transitions from one stage to the next are subtle and usually occur over long periods of time. Factors that influence the evolution from stage to stage are social (more education, more leisure time), technological (availability of electricity, printing presses, etc.), and economic (more affluence, presence of commercially based media system). In addition, certain media audiences within a single country may be at different levels of evolution, and audiences within different countries may be at different stages. Lastly, as is the case with most generalizations, these evolutionary stages are better exemplified by some media than others, especially when only a single country (the United States) is examined. Nonetheless, this framework is helpful in analyzing mass media audiences and allows us to gain some indication as to the future trends in audience evolution.

The Print Media Audience

The print media seem to exemplify best the stages in audience evolution. Early books, which were lettered by hand, were usually kept chained to a table in a monastery, and only those privileged people who could read could make use of them. We have already seen how the content of early newspapers and magazines was selected to appeal to elite socioeconomic groups: the policymakers, the educated upper class, and the political leaders who had money to spend and who were interested in business news, sermons, speeches, political events, and book reviews. Newspapers began moving into the mass stage when Benjamin Day realized that technological, economic, and social conditions were right for the penny press in general and his *New York Sun* in particular. Magazines entered the mass stage more gradually. During the late nineteenth century, *McClure's* and *Ladies' Home Journal* took the first steps in this direction, and the success of *Reader's Digest*, *Life*, and *Look* signaled that the mass stage was firmly established by 1930. Of course, not all magazines and newspapers were aimed at a mass audience; some continued to cater to the elite, while others went after more specialized audiences. The point is that we can generally identify consistent patterns in the way audiences change over the years.

Both newspapers and magazines now appear to be in the specialized stage. Magazines in particular illustrate this trend. Almost every occupational and special-interest group has a publication directed at it. In fact, there are only two general-interest magazines left: *TV Guide* and *Reader's Digest*. Although newspapers are not yet as specialized as magazines, the trend toward special supplements, zoned editions, and inserts indicates movement in that direction. Although the print medium has yet to enter the interactive age, some movement in that direction is evident. Many newspapers have "telephone polls" in which readers can call in and leave a comment or a message. Other newspapers are publishing a "faxpaper" to those who request it. Some magazines

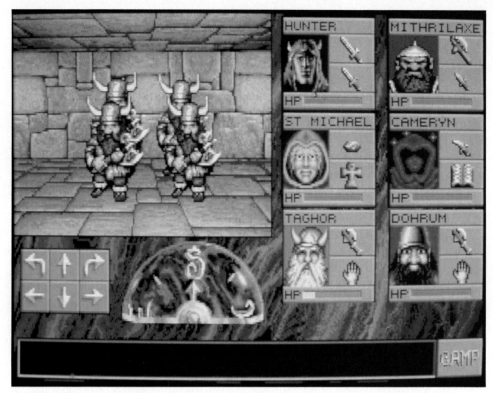

Interactive computer games, such as Eye of the Beholder, *put the audience member in charge of the action. (Strategic Simulations, Inc.)*

and newspapers have set up 900 numbers with special informational messages for consumers with particular interests. In the book publishing industry, many children's and young people's novels are written so that the reader actually selects the various plot options and constructs the story as he or she reads along. In addition, there are a large number of role-playing or interactive fiction computer programs which literally put the reader/player in charge of the story.

The Radio and Sound-Recording Audiences

Because of its early adoption of the commercial system of support, radio passed briefly through the elite stage. During this period, a large proportion of early broadcast music consisted of classical selections, and educational programs were numerous. The birth of the networks in 1927 and the decline in the number of educational stations signaled radio's passage into the mass-appeal stage. By the 1930s, with the tremendous popularity of programs such as *Amos 'n' Andy* and *The Lone Ranger*, radio was truly attracting a mass audience. The coming of television pushed radio rather forcefully into the specialized stage. Radio programming turned to distinctive formats, and its audience fragmented into many smaller groups.

The sound-recording medium's transition from elite to specialized stage is less easy to trace. When the recording industry was in its infancy, record players for home use were fairly expensive, and only the more affluent could afford them. Hence a significant proportion of early recordings featured opera stars or selections of classical music, two content forms that appealed to this elite audience. It is difficult to pinpoint the passage of sound recording into the mass-audience stage; however, the tremendous popularity of jukeboxes and the surge of record sales during the 1930s made this decade the most likely transitional period. Then, with the emergence of a youth culture

Active Viewing Required

One possible way of making the television medium more interactive was recently unveiled at an international TV programmers convention. A German company shot two versions of the same film, each from a different perspective. The idea is to have each version aired simultaneously on two channels with the viewer encouraged to switch back and forth between them.

The film, shot in English, is called *Murderous Decisions*. It tells the story of a TV talk show host, his assistant, and her lover, who come into conflict when the host interviews a killer. Viewers who watch one channel, for example, will see a scene with two characters in the foreground, whose dialogue can be heard, and two characters in the background, whose dialogue is muffled. Viewers who switch to the other channel can find out what the background characters are saying and how it fits into the plot. The two stories parallel each other in this way, with one becoming a traditional thriller while the other is more of a whodunit in the Alfred Hitchcock tradition. In any case, the producers are hedging their bets. Each of the versions can stand alone and be sold separately if the channel-switching idea doesn't catch on.

When radio entered the mass-audience stage during the 1930s and 1940s, young crooner Frank Sinatra developed a national following. (Brown Brothers)

and the birth of rock and roll, the young audience quickly became a distinct consumer segment. More and more records were designed to appeal to this new market. Today, the many variations of rock music currently available on record stands—in addition to the heightened popularity of rap, country, jazz, and folk music—indicate the establishment of various specialized consumer groups. Although the passage of radio and recording into the interactive stage appears to be in the somewhat distant future, the growth of call-in radio programs seems to indicate a step in that direction.

The Film and Television Audiences

It is equally difficult to pinpoint the movement of the motion picture medium from the elite to the mass stage. In the United States, the very roots of the industry were embedded in film's mass-audience appeal. *The Great Train Robbery*, for example, was certainly not designed to be played to an elite crowd. If one were to look overseas, however, one might find evidence of an elite stage in the history of films from other countries. Some scholars have suggested that during the period between 1920 and 1933, German and Russian films went through what might be termed an elite stage. Perhaps the lack of a comparable elite period in American film development is a quirk stemming from the unique economic and social conditions that prevailed during the motion picture industry's development in this country. In any event, by 1920 motion pictures were firmly entrenched in the mass-audience stage. As with radio, it was the arrival of television that brought about change and forced films to specialize.

A glance at the movie section of any big-city newspaper will show that films still try to appeal to a specialized audience. There are films geared to teens (*Bill and Ted's Bogus Journey*), to kids (*Beauty and the Beast*), to blacks (*Boyz 'N' the Hood*), to horror fans (*Friday the 13th*, part whatever), to fans of foreign films (*My Father's Glory*), to action addicts (*Terminator 2*), etc. Most films are still geared to the 18–30 crowd, but recently Hollywood has noted that some films with a more general appeal such as *Home Alone*, *Prince of Tides*, and *Dances with Wolves* also do well at the box office. The interactive stage has started to arrive with home video. Thanks to the VCR, a viewer can fast forward through the slow spots and rewatch the good parts.

Television passed through the elite stage in the 1950s when TV sets were so expensive that only the affluent could afford them. Consequently, prestige drama such

It Can Pay to Watch TV

The Game Channel plans to syndicate an interactive TV game show called *Tele-Quest* in which viewers and on-air contestants can win money.

Viewers over eighteen must pay a one-time $3 fee to The Game Channel. Then, during the live broadcast of the show, registered players can call an 800 number and play as many as four games per show at the cost of $3.50 per game. An MC asks multiple-choice trivia questions with six possible answers and viewers punch in their answers on the phone. A computer tallies up the number of right answers and

the winning viewer gets about 20 percent of the game-entry fees. Thus if 3 percent of an average audience of 50,000 play the game, the winner would pocket $1000. (Of course, if only 1000 watched the program with 3 percent playing the game, the winner would make about $21.) The viewing contestants with the highest scores are invited to come to the show to be an on-air player.

Only three TV stations initially agreed to carry the show, but the Game Channel has high hopes for its future.

as *Studio One* enjoyed popularity during these years. As sets became less expensive and within the reach of everyone, mass appeal programs such as westerns and situation comedies predominated. Television is now moving into the specialized stage. The audience shares of the major networks are declining as viewers tune more to specialized cable channels such as ESPN, MTV, and HBO. New programming services, such as the Automotive Channel and the Cowboy Channel, indicate that this trend is apt to continue.

TV is also moving closer to the interactive stage. Pay-per-view allows viewers to choose their own programming; VCRs let the audience watch programs at more convenient times. Some TV game shows, such as *Wheel of Fortune*, are available in an interactive format.

● ● ● ●
PRECONDITIONS FOR MEDIA EXPOSURE

Not every individual is a member of a media audience. In order for a person to be included, certain economic and personal preconditions must be fulfilled. These preconditions vary from medium to medium.

Time

One major personal precondition is, of course, time. If a person has little free time, it is unlikely that he or she will be a heavy consumer of media offerings. Certain media, however, are less affected by the time precondition than others. To illustrate, an audience member can listen to radio or recordings while doing something else: eating, working, driving, even studying, as noted in one of the opening examples of this chapter. Newspapers, magazines, and books, on the other hand, provide a written record that audience members can put aside or pick up at their convenience. Videocassettes can also be viewed when convenient.

Mobility of a media channel is an important factor in establishing the time precondition. Because radio and, to a lesser extent, record players and tape players are portable, they can accompany an audience member to the beach or to a sporting event. Printed publications are also portable and can be read while traveling on the subway or on a long plane trip. It is difficult to read, however, while performing more demanding activities since reading requires a higher level of concentration. Television is basically stationary. Usually, the audience watches TV in the home, although some viewing is possible while participating in other activities. The medium most affected by the time precondition is that of motion pictures. To see a film, an audience member must leave his or her house, travel to a theater, and have available at least two hours of free time. Films also demand a high level of attention; it is difficult to do anything else (except munch popcorn) while watching a movie.

Economics

Furthermore, in order to become an audience member, an individual must have access to media content. Accessibility may, in turn, have a significant impact on economic preconditions. For instance, if a person is unwilling to make the extra effort needed to travel to a library or to borrow reading material from a friend, then an economic precondition exists. The person must be able to afford the purchase price of a single copy of a newspaper or magazine or the price of a subscription. Publishers are acutely aware of this economic factor and attempt to price their products so that their potential audience is not unduly limited by economic barriers. Note that in the print media, audience members pay only for content; no special receiving equipment must be purchased. Since, apart from adequate hearing ability, the sound-recording audience needs no special skills, the main precondition is also an economic one. Ruling out borrowing, an audience member must be able to afford the cost of reproduction equipment (which can run into a substantial sum for a sophisticated system) in addition to the cost of the content itself (a record or tape). Many people thought that one possible cause of the slump in record sales during the late 1970s was the spiraling prices of records and tapes. Radio may be the medium most accessible to audiences because its preconditions are minimal. No special skills are needed and the cost of the receiving equipment is not great, especially in the case of inexpensive transistor radios. Once the audience member has purchased the receiving set, there is no further direct outlay of money for the programming. From the point of view of the radio audience, sports, music, talk, and news content are all free. (Of course, in radio and television the audience supports the programming indirectly. See Chapters 9 and 13.)

The broadcast television audience finds itself in an analogous situation. Once the initial cost of the TV set has been met (with the advent of inexpensive black-and-white sets, this is not as much of a hurdle as it once was), there is no additional direct charge for TV programs. (This fact has prompted some cynics to state that TV programs are worth exactly what we pay for them.) It should be pointed out that the above statements apply to conventional, over-the-air broadcasting. The audience for cable TV (CATV) is limited because of technological barriers (it's impossible to subscribe to CATV if the cable doesn't pass your house) and economic preconditions (a person must be able to afford the installation fee and a monthly fee). There is also an economic precondition, a monthly or per-program charge, for the pay-TV audience. The audience for videocassettes is limited because of the substantial sum necessary to purchase playback equipment. The drop in price of VCRs and the inexpensive rental fee for cassettes have made this less of a problem.

The motion picture audience must meet the economic precondition of the purchase price of a ticket ($7 in many cities, as of this writing) but does not have to invest in special receiving equipment. Moreover, there are certain informal barriers that will restrict the size of the audience for individual films. An NC-17-rated movie, for example, is restricted to those eighteen years of age or older. Lastly, since the movie audience has to travel to the movie theater, audience members must possess physical mobility.

■ ■ ■ ■
DIMENSIONS OF THE AUDIENCE

This section presents a capsule sketch of the characteristics that describe the audiences for the various media, including a great many facts and figures. Most of these will be expressed in some numerical form. The use of numbers is virtually unavoidable since a great deal of information about media audiences is expressed in quantitative terms (see the next chapter). Additionally, when media professionals talk about the audience,

But Will They Show Jaws?

As this chapter has pointed out, the viewing environment for the motion picture is the most highly structured since viewers must travel to a special place to see a movie. The folks in Wellington, New Zealand, are trying to change all of that with their newest idea—a dive-in. It seems that when attendance at the local munic-ipal swimming pool took a plunge, local officials had a stroke of brilliance: They started showing movies on a portable screen while people were swimming. Their first feature, naturally enough, was *Cocoon*, followed by *Raise the Titanic*. What did people think of the idea? Many liked it but a few thought it was all wet.

they tend to speak in numerical terms, for example, circulation, rating, box-office gross, number of records sold, cost of reaching a thousand people, and so on. Students who plan a career in the media might as well start now to become familiar with this perspective.

Many of the generalizations made in this chapter are expressed in terms of averages or other descriptive statistics. It should be kept in mind that this is simply a convenient way to summarize a large amount of information. Convenience, however, does not come without a price. Discussing the average time a person spends with television or any other medium can camouflage the large degree of variability present in audience behavior. There may be no such creature as the "average TV viewer" or the "average newspaper reader." These summary statistics allow us to make only general statements; they do not tell the whole story.

A final note on tables, charts, and graphs. It is not necessary that a student memorize all the information contained in the tabular material that goes along with this chapter. Tables and graphs are like paragraphs; each contains a main point. It is generally sufficient to come away with the main idea(s) or trend(s) illustrated by the table or chart. Remembering that the total circulation of all daily newspapers in 1970 was 62,108,000 seems less important than knowing that total circulation has leveled off and that circulation per 1000 people has actually declined in recent years.

Newspaper Audiences

As of 1991, approximately 63 million copies of morning and evening papers, either purchased at the newsstand or delivered to the doorstep, found their way into American homes every weekday. Daily newspaper circulation, in absolute terms, has been practically steady since 1970, as a glance at Table 19-1 will show. The population, however, has been increasing. To reflect this fact and to provide additional perspective, columns four and five of Table 19-1 present the ratio of circulation to the total adult population of the United States (expressed in thousands). As can be seen, newspaper circulation is not keeping pace with the overall growth of the population. Weekly papers enjoyed a period of growth from 1960 to 1990.

The percentage of adults reading one or more papers every day has declined from about 80 percent in the early 1960s to about 64 percent in 1990. Although this decline in daily newspaper readership encompasses every age group, the most pronounced decline has occurred in the eighteen-to-twenty-nine and thirty-to-fifty-four age groups. Readership also has dropped in all education categories, but the drop is

YEAR	ALL DAILY PAPERS	ALL WEEKLY PAPERS	DAILY CIRCULATION PER 1000 ADULTS	WEEKLY CIRCULATION PER 1000 ADULTS
1930	39,589,000	—	455	—
1940	41,132,000	—	415	—
1950	53,829,000	—	487	—
1960	58,882,000	21,328,000	475	172
1965	60,358,000	26,088,000	451	195
1970	62,108,000	29,423,000	428	203
1975	60,655,000	35,176,000	380	221
1980	62,201,840	40,970,000	360	245
1984	63,100,000	43,100,000	341	235
1990	62,327,962	56,181,047	329	298
1992	60,083,265	55,445,601	321	295

TABLE 19-1 Daily and Weekly Newspaper Circulation

Source: Reprinted by permission from ANPA, "Facts about Newspapers, 1990."

sharpest among those who have not attended college. The overall drop in daily circulation has been most noticeable in urban areas. As Figure 19-1, shows, newspaper circulation in cities with more than a half-million residents has dropped about 39 percent from 1958 to 1990. Conversely, circulation in medium-sized towns with populations from 100,000 to 500,000 has increased 48 percent. Circulation in smaller communities has also increased, up a third in the same period.

Why the decline? Some have attributed it to the increased mobility of Americans, the increase in single-person households, more expensive subscription and per-copy prices, a general decline in the level of reading ability among young people, and inroads made upon leisure time by television viewing. All these factors probably have had some impact, but as we shall see, magazine readership has not dropped off as sharply as newspaper reading, even though magazines should be affected by the same forces (higher prices, competition from TV, decline in reading skills, etc.). Magazines have avoided a drop in audience levels primarily by specialization. Similarly, weekly newspapers may be attracting readers because of their local appeal. Perhaps part of the readership decline of daily newspapers can be attributed to the absence of specialized information that appeals to distinct audience groups, especially younger readers.

Of those who do read the newspaper, three-quarters have the paper delivered to their homes and, not surprisingly, the home is the place where most newspapers are read. Once the newspaper is in the household, it is read by approximately two people, who spend an average of about twenty-five minutes per day reading the newspaper.

FIGURE 19-1 *Fluctuations in daily newspaper circulation by size of city, 1958–1990.*

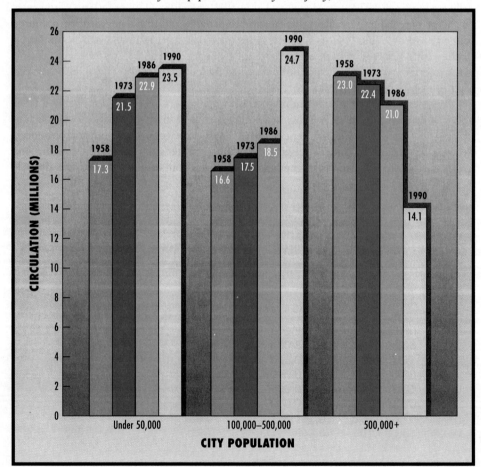

Newspaper vending machines on a Washington, D.C., street corner illustate the variety of choices available, ranging from the special-audience paper, Washington Jewish Week, *through the nationally distributed* Christian Science Monitor *to local and regional papers. (Barbara L. Roche)*

In 1965, the comparable figure was about thirty minutes per day, indicating that not only are fewer people reading the newspaper, but on the average, those who are reading it are spending less time at it. The most popular time of day for newspaper reading is after the evening meal. Those people most likely to read a newspaper are those who are older, more educated, and married.

The Daily Newspaper Nonreader

Not everybody reads the daily newspaper. In general, research has shown that the nonreader tends to be low in education, low in income, and either young (under twenty) or old (over seventy). In addition, nonreaders are more likely to live in rural areas and tend to have infrequent contact with neighbors and friends. Other studies note that the nonreader has little identification with the community, is less likely to own a home, and seldom belongs to local voluntary organizations.

Why don't these people read a daily paper? The main reasons they give are lack of time, preference for another medium for news (usually radio or TV), a general lack of interest in reading a paper, and the fact that newspapers cost too much,

More recent surveys have indicated that the portrait of the nonreader is more complicated than first thought. There appears to be a group of nonreaders that does not fit the typical demographic profile mentioned above. These people tend to be high in income and fall into the twenty-six- to sixty-five-year-old group. These atypical nonreaders are far more likely to report that lack of time and lack of interest in content are the main reasons why they don't read the paper. Editors and publishers are attempting to bring this atypical group back into the fold of newspaper readers by adding news briefs and comprehensive indexes to help overcome the time crunch and by diversifying newspaper content to help build interest.

Although data on the audience for an individual magazine are readily available, information about the total audience for magazines is hard to come by, primarily because of the difficulty in defining what qualifies as a magazine. Nonetheless, some figures are available. In 1990, as reported to the Audit Bureau of Circulations (see next chapter), total magazine circulation exceeded 350 million copies. Of these, about 27 percent were bought at the newsstand while the remaining 73 percent were delivered as part of a subscription. The 1990 figure represented a 32 percent increase over 1979. If we examine circulation figures per 1000 people, as we did with newspapers, we find that magazine circulation has exceeded the growth in the adult population during the 1970s, 1980s, and 1990s.

It was mentioned earlier that the audiences for magazines have become more and more specialized. Approximately 40 percent of all magazines have circulations under 150,000. Only four (*Reader's Digest*, *TV Guide*, *Modern Maturity*, and *National Geographic*) have what might be called mass circulations of more than 10 million copies. In fact, even specialized magazines are becoming specialized. There is now a magazine for *new* lawyers, another for *young* doctors, and one for *Southern* brides. This specialization is further reflected in the growing numbers of magazines that are available to the audience. From 1970 to 1990, as reported by the Audit Bureau of Circulations, the number of general consumer magazines increased 75 percent. (These figures do not include thousands of professional and scholarly publications sponsored by nonprofit organizations.)

Mentioning specific examples of this increasing specialization might be the most effective way of documenting this trend. *Casket and Sunnyside* is a magazine that is widely read among funeral home directors. *Poultry Times* is a big seller among chicken farmers. Other magazines with a tightly focused audience appeal, such as those aimed at hunters, audio buffs, or wrestling fans, have also been successful in attracting an audience.

Specialization is apparent in another area as well. Many magazines have become *regionalized*—that is, they appeal to an audience living in a well-defined geographic area. "City" magazines, such as *Los Angeles*, *Philadelphia*, and *The Washingtonian*, are geared toward specific urban dwellers. *Yankee* directs its appeal to New Englanders, while *Southern Living* is aimed at a regional audience in the South. Even magazines with a national circulation such as *Outdoor Life*, *McCall's*, and *Nation's Business* create special content for several regional editions.

It appears that almost everybody does some type of magazine reading. In an average month, 94 percent of U.S. adults read at least one copy of a magazine. Most read more. One study reported that adults read or look through an average of ten magazines a month. About 28 percent read a magazine on an average day, and the typical adult spends about twenty-five minutes daily reading magazines. About three-quarters of the audience keep magazines on hand for future reference, and about the same proportion reported that they reread something or referred back to an article or ad. As far as demographics are concerned, the typical magazine reader is more educated and usually more affluent than the nonreader. Magazine readers also tend to be joiners. One survey found them far more likely to belong to religious, science, and professional organizations than nonreaders.

Of course, certain magazines seek out a particular demographic group. For example, some magazines have traditionally appealed to either a male or female audience. Automotive, motorcycle, and golf magazines usually have about an 80 percent male readership. At the other end of the scale, *Family Circle*, *Harper's Bazaar*, *Vogue*, and *Glamour* have readerships that are more than 80 percent female. Literary magazines and general-interest publications such as *Reader's Digest* and *TV Guide* have a readership split about evenly between men and women. Within male–female groupings, certain magazines appeal to discrete age groups. Among men, almost half of the readers of motorcycle and automotive magazines are between the ages of eighteen and twenty-four, with a median age of twenty-five. By comparison the median age of men who read business magazines is forty. Among women, approximately half of the readership of *Seventeen* and *Glamour* is under twenty-five.

Book Audiences

Despite competition from television, the book-reading audience has actually increased from 1955 to 1990. In the mid-1950s, about 14 percent of a national sample of adults reported reading a book on the day prior to the survey. Thirty-five years later, the comparable figure was 22 percent. The person most likely to be a book reader was a college-educated female thirty-five to forty-nine years old.

Radio Audiences

There are more radio sets in this country than there are people. In fact, there are about twice as many. As of January 1990, there were more than 535 million radio receivers scattered around the United States, with car radios accounting for about one-third of this number. Virtually every household in the country is equipped with at least one working radio set. On a typical day at least three-fourths of all adults will listen to radio, and the average person will listen, or at least have the radio on, for about three hours. Most people listen to radio in the early morning when they are getting ready for and driving to work and in the late afternoon when they are driving home. These two "day parts," as they are called by those in the industry, consisting roughly from 6 A.M. to 10 A.M. and 4 P.M. to 7 P.M., are called "drive time."

Perhaps the biggest change in the audience for radio over the past fifteen years has been the steady increase in listeners for FM stations. In 1973, only 28 percent of the listening audience was tuned to FM stations. Today the figure is 72 percent, as FM listenership surpassed that of AM. The largest increase in FM audiences has occurred among teenagers. Probably because of the trend toward Top 40, album rock, and progressive rock apparent among FM stations, the percentage of teens who reported listening to FM stations from 1977 to 1984 mentioned above more than tripled, increasing from 24 to 90 percent. As far as demographics are concerned, the average listener, regardless of age, sex, or educational background, listens to radio about three hours a day. Of this group, females and young listeners are slightly more represented.

Perhaps the best way to talk about the radio audience is to examine radio station formats and describe the type of audience each attracts. Contemporary Hit stations draw an audience composed primarily of twelve- to twenty-four-year-olds, with females outnumbering males by about a three-to-two margin. Album and progressive rock attract eighteen- to thirty-four-year-olds, with about equal proportions of men and women represented in their audience. Middle of the road, beautiful music, classical, and all-news formats generally attract an older crowd, with most of their audience coming from the forty-five-and-over age groups. Country music stations seem to have a general across-the-board appeal to those over twenty-five.

As a person gets older, he or she tends to evolve out of the audience for one format and move on to another. For example, as a young person leaves the teenage years, he or she will probably listen less to Contemporary Hit stations and more to stations that play progressive, album rock. As that same person continues to get older, he or she will probably tune more to Adult Contemporary stations or even to progressive country formats. A little later, this person might tune to "good music" or talk stations. (Of course, it is also true that music styles are changing along with the individual. What is considered progressive rock today might fall into the good music category twenty years from now.) Table 19-2 attempts to summarize some areas of peak listener appeal for selected station formats.

Sound-Recording Audiences

Information regarding the audience for sound recording (records, tapes, and CDs) is somewhat difficult to uncover, partially because the recording industry is supported by audience purchases and not by advertising. This means that recording companies concentrate on compiling statistics relating to overall sales figures and that detailed demographic information about the audience is typically not sought after. True, some record companies have sponsored market research to find out more about their audiences, but the results of these studies are usually not made available to the general public. We know that by the early 1990s there were approximately 85 million stereos, with perhaps an equal number of tape playback units and 20 million CD players in use. It has been estimated that more than 90 percent of all the households in the country have some means of playing a record, tape, or CD. In the early 1990s, this audience was buying more than 850 million tapes and discs every year.

In general, those people who have a sound system have paid about $500–$800 for their equipment and have a typical collection of about seventy albums and approximately thirty singles. They listen to discs and tapes about an hour a day.

Record buying is related to age and sex. Older consumers are accounting for more record purchases. In 1990, people over thirty accounted for about 35 percent of the total dollar value spent on prerecorded music, a 5 percent increase from 1988. At the same time, consumer spending by those aged nineteen and under declined from 32 percent to 30 percent. This aging of the audience is partly accounted for by record stores that also rent movies. The video rentals attract an older crowd who frequently buy a CD or tape along with their rental. Males account for about 56 percent of the dollar values of all purchases and this percentage has increased about 7 percent in the last three years. Record sellers explain that this shift is a result of males acquiring CD players at a faster rate than females.

Motion Picture Audiences

Much like the data on the sound-recording audience, information on the motion picture audience is sketchy. Hollywood seems to put little faith in detailed audience study, preferring instead to concentrate on the "bottom line," the amount of money a film brings in. Thus although there is considerable financial information, precise audience data are hard to come by. In general terms, we know that after a slump during the early 1970s, movie attendance picked up. Average weekly attendance has

TABLE 19-2 Appeals of Selected Radio Station Formats			
FORMAT	**AGE**	**SEX**	**REGION**
Adult Contemporary	24–54	Female	All
Album-Oriented Rock	18–24	Male	Urban
Beautiful Music	35+	Both	All
Contemporary Hits	12–34	Both	All
Country	18–49	Both	Rural
Middle of the Road	35+	Both	All
News/Talk	25–54	Both	Urban
Religious	55+	Female	Rural
Urban Contemporary	12–34	Both	Urban

been steady for about the last twenty years (see Figure 19-2). Attendance, however, is nowhere near the levels of the 1930s and 1940s, when film was in its heyday.

The movie audience is a young audience. As Figure 19-3, on page 476, indicates, three out of every four moviegoers are under thirty. Teenagers are a significant part of the movie audience. Although teens make up only 20 percent of the population, they make up nearly 30 percent of the film audience.

The movie audience has changed in recent years. Older fans are now more likely to go out to a theater than they were five years ago. For example, the proportion of forty- to forty-nine-year-olds in the audience has increased 18 percent; fifty- to fifty-nine-year-olds, 26 percent; and those over sixty, 50 percent. Attendance by those under thirty, meanwhile, dropped by about 2 percent. Despite these changes, as Figure 19-3 indicates, nearly seven out of ten moviegoers are still under thirty and teens still account for a significant part of the audience.

Frequent moviegoers (those who see at least one film a month) account for 87 percent of all film admissions. These frequent fans are generally single, within the sixteen-to-twenty age group (going to the movies continues to be a popular dating activity; only 6 percent of the audience goes to a movie alone), more educated, from middle-class families, and from urban areas.

The audience for movies is largest in July and August and smallest in May. The worst two weeks of the year for moviegoing are the first two weeks in December, when attendance drops 30–50 percent.

What films have attracted the largest audiences? Some indirect information is available if we examine what the industry calls "film rental fees." This is the money that the theater pays to the distribution company to show the film. If we assume that films that earn large rental fees are attracting large audiences (a seemingly reasonable assumption), a list of the most popular films can be compiled. Table 11-1, page 272, contains such a list as of 1991. Probably the main reason for the large number of recent releases on such a list is the fact that Hollywood now aims for the "super grosser," the film that will draw huge audiences and earn for the company what the industry calls "megabucks."

FIGURE 19-2 *Average weekly film attendance in the United States. (Motion Picture Association of America. Used by permission.)*

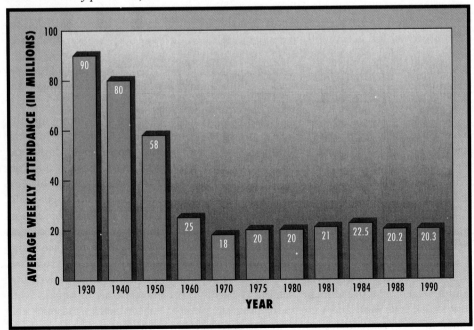

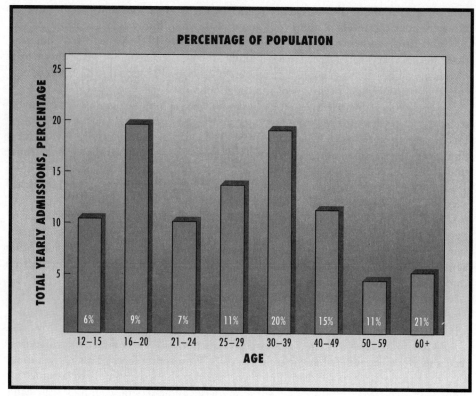

FIGURE 19-3 *Age and movie attendance. (Motion Picture Association of America. Used by permission.)*

Television Audiences

The TV set has become firmly entrenched in the life of Americans. As of 1991, some 99 percent of all homes in the country had at least one working television set. About 65 percent had more than one. Cable television (CATV) had more than 54 million subscribers in 1991, roughly 59 percent of all TV households.

Television rating services report that the set in the average household is on for about seven hours a day, with each individual watching an average of more than three hours daily. The TV audience changes throughout the day, steadily growing from 7 A.M. until it reaches a peak from 8 to 11 P.M., Eastern Standard Time. These hours are typically labeled "prime time." After 11 P.M., the audience drops off dramatically. Figure 19-4 details this pattern of audience viewing.

Not surprisingly, the television audience is largest during the winter months, December through March, and smallest during July and August, when people spend more time outdoors. The composition of the television audience changes during the day. Preschoolers and females tend to predominate during the daytime hours from Monday to Friday. On Saturday mornings, most of the audience is under thirteen. Prime time is dominated by those in the eighteen- to forty-nine-year-old age group.

Not everybody is alike in their TV viewing habits. Various demographic factors such as age, sex, social class, and education affect viewership. For example, teenagers watch the least. People in low-income homes generally watch more television than their middle-income counterparts. People with more education tend to watch less, and women watch more often than men. Cable subscribers are younger, have more children, and are more affluent than the average viewer. They also are dissatisfied with traditional television and want more program variety. Subscribers to the pay-cable

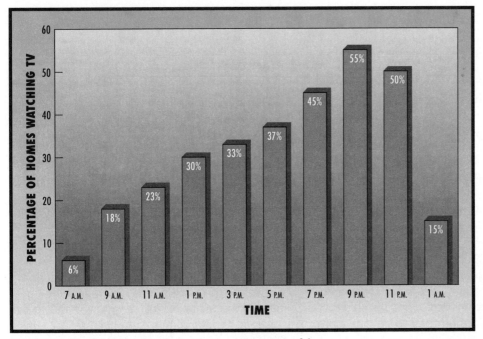

FIGURE 19-4 *Household viewing of television at various times of day.*

channels had younger heads of households, were more affluent, and watched more TV than families in noncable homes.

By the end of 1991, VCRs were in more than 72 percent of all TV households. A higher percentage of cable homes than noncable homes had VCRs. VCRs are used 4.7 hours per week for playing prerecorded tapes and 2.4 hours for recording TV programs. Three-quarters of the playback time is used for rented or purchased tapes, the remainder for playback of home-recorded tapes. Most videotaped playbacks occur during the weekend. Prime-time programs, movies, and soap operas are recorded the

A Glaring Success?

Up in the sky! It's a bird! It's a plane! No! It's Hoodman . . . a new superhero representing the latest technology in giving TV a place in the sun.

Hoodman is actually the creation of three California brothers who realized that TV will never be truly portable until the audience is able to view it outside. The sun's glare, however, is a big problem and can totally obscure the picture. The answer: a sun shade that clips on to any portable TV set, from the two-inch Watchman up to a 21-inch monitor. And what's the best way

to get attention for this product? Hoodman, a superhero from the planet Glare dressed in flowing cape and tights and wearing a huge hood on his head.

So far the sun shades are selling well among industrial customers but are moving slowly among the general public. Hoodman, in contrast, has become somewhat of a local hero at local California college campuses. Getting your picture taken with the hooded hero seems to be the trendy thing to do.

The Television Nonviewers

In the typical household the TV set is on for more than seven hours every day. The average individual watches about three hours a day. TV sets are found in about 99 percent of all households. Given this massive penetration of television into the fabric of the daily lives of Americans, it seems hard to believe that there are people who don't watch it. But there are at least a few who could be called nonviewers. What are these unusual people like?

The best answer to that question is that they are hard to characterize. It is known that nonviewers differ from viewers on specific demographic characteristics. For example, research has shown that nonviewers are more likely to be women, childless, and apparently less religious than viewers. There are no differences between viewers and nonviewers in terms of age and race. Nonviewers also tend to be more educated than viewers. Additional research has discovered that nonviewers are less satisfied with family life, belong to more groups and organizations, and socialize more frequently with friends outside their neighborhoods. All of these facts are difficult to fit together. Nonviewers do not seem to be affected by economic deprivation since they are more likely to be employed and to be more educated than viewers. They do not appear to be socially isolated since they belong to organizations and visit frequently with friends. Perhaps the most intelligent conclusion we can draw is that not watching TV is a complicated behavior (or nonbehavior). People evidently avoid television for a variety of reasons and, as a result, are exceedingly difficult to pigeonhole.

most. Of interest to advertisers is the fact that about one-third of VCR owners delete the commercials while recording off the air and of those that don't delete, about half say they fast forward to skip the commercials during playback.

One striking fact about the television audience is its great size. Ninety-nine million people saw the final episode of *Roots* in 1977, and 125 million saw the farewell episode of *M*A*S*H*. A typical prime-time program might reach as many as 20 million households. What shows are most popular with the audience? Table 19-3 shows the prime-time series that have appeared most often in the top twenty programs of any given year.

RANK	PROGRAM TITLE	YEARS IN TOP 20
TABLE 19-3 Most Popular Prime-Time Series, 1950–1991		
1	I Love Lucy/Lucy/Here's Lucy/The Lucy Show	17
2	Red Skelton	16
	Gunsmoke	16
3	The Ed Sullivan Show	13
4	Bonanza	12
	Disneyland/Wonderful World of Disney	12
5	60 Minutes[a]	11
	Andy Griffith/Mayberry RFD	
6	All in the Family/Archie Bunker's Place	10
7	Beverly Hillbillies	8

[a] Still on the air as of 1992.

TABLE 19-4 Source of Most News (Answers in Percentage)[a]

"I'd like to ask you where you usually get most of your news about what's going on in the world today—from the newspapers or radio or television or magazines or talking to people or where?"

SOURCE OF MOST NEWS	1959	1961	1963	1964	1967	1968	1971	1972	1974	1976	1978	1980	1982	1984	1987	1988	1990
TV	51	52	55	58	64	59	60	64	65	64	67	64	65	64	66	65	69
Newspaper	57	57	53	56	55	49	48	50	47	49	49	44	44	40	36	42	43
Radio	34	34	29	26	28	25	23	21	21	19	20	18	18	14	14	14	15
Magazines	8	9	6	8	7	7	5	6	4	7	5	5	6	4	4	4	3
Other people	4	5	4	5	4	5	4	4	4	5	5	4	4	4	4	4	7

[a] Note: Columns do not add up to 100 because multiple responses were allowed.

Source: The Roper Organization, Inc., *America's Watching*, 1991. Used with permission.

●●●●
INTERMEDIA COMPARISONS

In this section we present responses from people who were asked during the course of several surveys to rate the various mass media on a variety of dimensions. The first of these is a series of polls dealing with news.

Since 1959, the Roper Organization, Inc., has conducted periodic surveys asking people to (1) choose their main source of news and (2) name the one medium that they perceive as most credible as a new source. Tables 19-4 and 19-5 summarize the results of these surveys.

Since 1963, television has been named most often as the source of most news. Its lead over the second-place medium, newspapers, has been growing more or less steadily. The percentage naming radio has declined sharply since 1959, while the percentage naming magazines, never high to begin with, has also slightly decreased. In terms of trends in credibility, TV became the most believable medium in 1961 and now has a two-to-one advantage over the newspaper in that department. Radio and magazines, chosen by a small proportion of the survey, have shown a slight decline.

Before leaving this topic we should point out that some individuals have suggested that the actual wording of the Roper question on the source of most news might give a distorted picture of the results. The phrase "what's going on in the world today" might prompt people to think about international and national events, an area in which

TABLE 19-5 Relative Credibility of Media (Answers in Percentage)

"If you got conflicting or different reports of the same news story from radio, television, the magazines and the newspapers, which of the four versions would you be most inclined to believe—the one on radio or television or magazines or newspapers?"

MOST BELIEVABLE	1959	1961	1963	1964	1967	1968	1971	1972	1974	1976	1978	1980	1982	1984	1987	1988	1990
Television	29	39	36	41	41	44	49	48	51	51	47	51	53	53	55	49	54
Newspapers	32	24	24	23	24	21	20	21	20	22	23	22	22	24	21	26	22
Radio	12	12	12	8	7	8	10	8	8	7	9	8	6	8	6	7	7
Magazines	10	10	10	10	8	11	9	10	8	9	9	9	8	7	7	5	4
Don't know	17	17	18	18	20	16	12	13	13	11	12	10	11	9	11	13	13

Source: The Roper Organization, Inc., *America's Watching*, 1991. Used with permission.

TV network news and CNN seem dominant, and as a result, people tend not to mention the newspaper, whose focus is usually more local.

This fact is apparent in the second survey we will examine. The American Society of Newspaper Editors (ASNE) sponsored a 1985 survey that focused on media credibility. The results indicated that newspapers were considered more reliable than TV, 72 to 66 percent, in the coverage of local news. The ASNE respondents were also asked a question similar to that used in the Roper surveys. If given conflicting reports of events, about half said that they would believe TV and about 25 percent said the newspapers. Another question asked respondents to rank the honesty and ethical standards of people in twelve different occupations. Members of the clergy, doctors, and police were ranked as having the highest standards. TV news anchors and TV reporters ranked fourth and sixth, while newspaper editors and newspaper reporters were seventh and eighth, with advertising executives and used-car salespersons finishing at the bottom. These results prompted newspaper and TV executives to examine new ways to improve their credibility.

● ● ● ●

THE SOCIAL CONTEXT

In Chapter 1, we saw that the mass communication audience was large, heterogeneous, spread out over a wide geographic area, self-defined, and anonymous to one another. During the early part of the twentieth century, these characteristics prompted sociologists and mass communication researchers to regard this audience as a collection of isolated individuals who responded in essentially the same way to a message presented via the media. The viewpoint, called the **hypodermic needle approach**, persisted for many years. It was subsequently discovered that audience members do not exist in a social vacuum. They can be placed in definable social categories based on such common characteristics as age, sex, political affiliation, occupation and education, which will also have an impact on their media behavior. In addition, an audience member's social relationships will have an impact on media use and effect. For example, even though political candidates might spend millions of dollars on commercials, an individual's personal voting choice might be influenced more by the opinions of people in his or her interpersonal communication network—family members, co-workers, boss, or peers.

The relationship of the audience and its social context has great relevance for determining the effects of mass communication, as we shall see in Chapters 21 and 22. In fact, one of the classic theories of the persuasive effects of mass communication, the **multistep flow model** of influence, suggests that mass media alone will be unlikely to change audience opinions on important issues precisely because the media's influence is filtered through a social network of opinion leaders. For our immediate purpose, it is important to note that, in addition to its persuasive aspect, social context also plays a significant role in other areas of media behavior. For example, one study of radio listening among grade-schoolers showed that youngsters with few friends tended to listen more than did their more popular classmates. Other studies suggest that popular teenagers are apt to see more movies than their less popular peers (perhaps because they date more often and attend films as a dating activity). Social characteristics such as occupation and socioeconomic status also affect newspaper and magazine reading. College students frequently develop new musical or film tastes because they are encouraged to sample different offerings by their roommates and friends. Some media activity—attending *The Rocky Horror Picture Show*, for example—has become a social rather than a solitary event. Even such seemingly isolated audience members as those who listen to car radios or recorded music over headphones may have been influenced somewhat by their own social context. ("I have to listen to all-news radio

One of the most important determinants of media usage is a person's age. Exposure to the various mass media changes as each of us gets older. The chart below attempts to profile how our media behavior fluctuates with age. Note that the sound media (radio, records, and tapes) tend to be most used during preteen and teen-age years; movies tend to peak around the early twenties. As time devoted to sound recording, radio, and moviegoing begins to decrease during the thirties, forties, and fifties, newspaper and magazine usage begins to pick up. After the teenage years, TV viewing tends to increase.

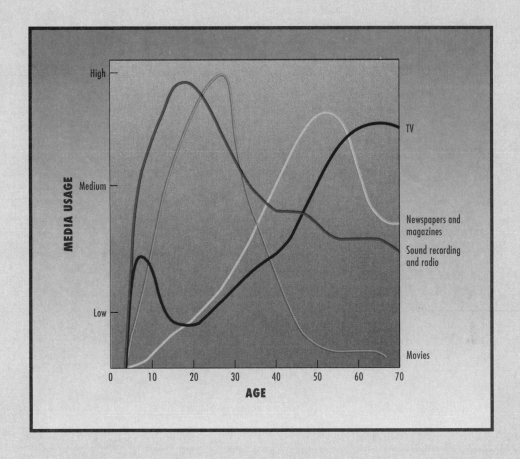

because my boss expects me to know about current events," or "I never liked Bruce Springsteen until my friend explained his music to me.") In any case, even though mass media audiences may be scattered about and isolated from one another, the impact of the individual's social context on his or her media behavior should not be minimized.

• • • •

SUGGESTIONS FOR FURTHER READING

These sources can be consulted for more information on mass communication audiences.

AMERICAN NEWSPAPER PUBLISHERS ASSOCIATION, *Facts about Newspapers*, 1991.

AUSTIN, BRUCE, *Immediate Seating, A Look at Movie Audiences*, Belmont, Calif.: Wadsworth, 1989.

BRYANT, JENNINGS, *Television and the American Family*, Hillsdale, N.J.: Lawrence Erlbaum, 1990.

DEFLEUR, MELVIN, AND SANDRA BALL-ROKEACH, *Theories of Mass Comunication*, 5th ed., New York: Longman, 1989.

JEFFRES, LEO, *Mass Media: Processes and Effects*, Prospect Heights, Ill.: Waveland Press, 1986.

STEINBERG, COBBETT, *TV Facts*, New York: Facts on File, 1985.

——, *Film Facts*, New York: Facts on File, 1980.

STERLING, CHRISTOPHER H., *Electronic Media*, New York: Praeger, 1984.

STONE, GERALD, *Examining Newspapers*, Newbury Park, Calif.: Sage Publications, 1987.

20

MASS MEDIA FEEDBACK SYSTEMS

Many people who follow the fortunes of the television industry are aware of the Nielsens, the ratings that help measure a show's popularity, but very few people are aware of the unique TV ratings called the Van Dorps. It's about time this unsung hero of audience measurement received due recognition. George J. Van Dorp, a water commissioner for the city of Toledo, Ohio, during the early 1950s, happened to develop his own original system for rating TV shows. Van Dorp noticed that during the course of an evening, Toledo's water pressure would suddenly plummet and then, after a few minutes, would zoom upward again. This curious activity baffled Van Dorp until he noticed that the dips in the water pressure were correlated with the commercials and station breaks in evening television programs. Evidently, people were waiting for these opportunities to take care of natural habits that involved the use of Toledo's water supply. When such an opportunity occurred, Toledo's water pressure dropped dramatically. Van Dorp began charting the peaks and valleys in the water pressure and was able to rank in order Toledo's favorite TV shows. After he announced his findings, other major cities also noted this same link between TV shows and water pressure. Unfortunately for Van Dorp, this novel way of obtaining audience feedback was not greeted with enthusiasm by the TV industry, and the Van Dorps never sent the Nielsens down the drain. Nonetheless, this pioneer ratings expert deserves a place in the audience-measurement hall of fame; his feedback technique was certainly among the most inexpensive ever developed.

It's probably obvious by now that this chapter will deal with mass media feedback systems. As noted in Chapter 1, feedback refers to those responses of the receiver that attempt to affect subsequent messages of the source. It was stressed that feedback in the mass communication setting was more limited than in the interpersonal situation and was usually delayed.

As mentioned in Chapter 19, audience characteristics and feedback are closely related. Feedback helps a mass medium know who is in the audience and aids the source in structuring messages designed to interest that audience. Audience characteristics also determine the exact form of the feedback. For example, audiences for mass media are large, too large to be surveyed in their entirety; therefore, some representative samples must be examined. The audience is scattered geographically; therefore, it takes time to gather feedback. The audience is anonymous; therefore, demographic data are collected to give the audience some identity. Let us now take a more detailed look at feedback mechanisms as they relate to mass media.

FORMS OF FEEDBACK

We will begin by distinguishing between two different forms of feedback. The first, **audience-generated feedback**, occurs when one or more audience members attempt to communicate their opinion or point of view to a mass medium. In this form of feedback, the media are receivers of messages initiated by audience members. This type of feedback is set in motion by the receivers of the message; it requires extra effort on the part of the audience to send but little effort on the part of the media to receive. Some typical examples of audience-generated feedback are letters to the editor of a newspaper or magazine (or to the managers of radio and television stations), petitions delivered to media organizations, phone calls to radio talk shows, cancellations of a newspaper or magazine subscription, and reviews of films and TV shows by critics.

The second form, **media-originated feedback**, consists of information about the audience that media industries must go out of their way to gather. The original impetus for this form of feedback comes from the media organization itself. Reactions from the audience are solicited by the media or related organizations acting on their behalf. Examples of media-generated feedback are ratings in television and radio, circulation figures as charted by the Audit Bureau of Circulations, record popularity as compiled by industry publications such as *Billboard* and *Cashbox*, film box-office revenue as reported in *Variety*, surveys done by broadcasting systems, readership surveys sponsored by newspapers, and lists of best-selling books.

Feedback Characteristics

Table 20-1 lists the general characteristics of audience-generated and media-originated feedback. It is important to separate these two forms (1) because their characteristics are different and (2) because usually, but not always, media-originated feedback is more effective in altering subsequent messages.

First, audience-generated feedback is generally not sent by people who are typical of the entire audience. For instance, the person who writes a letter to the editor of a

---

Audience-generated feedback during Elizabethan times. The crowd lets the actors know exactly how the play is doing. (Historical Pictures Service)

TABLE 20-1 Characteristics of Feedback in Mass Communication

AUDIENCE-GENERATED	MEDIA-ORIGINATED
1. Generally not typical of entire audience.	**1.** Tries to examine a representative cross section of audience.
2. Travels directly to a media organization.	**2.** Gathered by a third party.
3. Expressed qualitatively.	**3.** Expressed quantitatively.
4. Audience determines form and channel.	**4.** Media organizations determine form and channel.
5. Delayed.	**5.** Delayed.

newspaper or magazine is usually older (over thirty), likely to be a professional, better educated, and earning more money than those in the general population. Individuals who write letters to radio and television stations also tend to be older, better educated, more interested in public affairs, and more likely to live alone than others in the community. A survey of people who phone radio call-in programs found that the callers were older, less mobile, lived alone more often, and had lower socioeconomic status than the general population. Petitions to broadcasting stations are typically presented by special-interest groups. Published reviews of media content represent the view of only one person (the critic), and in many cases a film or a TV series that receives a bad review will be immensely popular. A media organization that relied only on audience-generated feedback would not get a clear picture of its entire audience.

In contrast, media-originated feedback strives to examine a representative cross section of the audience. Television and radio rating firms sample randomly from across the country or from within a specified market. Readership surveys sponsored by newspapers and magazines also are based on random selection. (A large sample, perhaps around 1000 people, chosen at random will usually mirror the characteristics of the larger community fairly accurately.) Surveys of movie attendance and record popularity attempt to examine markets that are reflective of the entire moviegoing and record-buying public.

Collecting and Expressing Data

Second, audience-generated feedback is collected directly by the media organization. Letters to the editor are read by newspaper or magazine employees, and a few are selected for publication. The rest may or may not be kept on file. Phone calls to a radio or TV station are usually logged, and perhaps a rough record is made of their content (e.g., nine people objected to the program; three praised it). On the other hand, a third party, usually a large organization, gathers and records media-originated

Next Time They'll Try a Phone Call

Here's a prime example of audience-generated feedback. In Michigan, two workers for the local cable TV company were surprised by two cable subscribers carrying a shotgun and a rifle. The couple held the cable workers at gunpoint for about ten minutes while they complained about the cable company's poor service. After the couple left, the workers informed police, who went to the couple's home and questioned them. According to police, the couple admitted threatening the workers but saw nothing wrong with their actions.

feedback. In television and radio, stations and networks do not collect their own ratings data. Instead, they rely on firms such as the A.C. Nielsen Company and Arbitron. Newspaper and magazine circulation figures are compiled by the Audit Bureau of Circulations. Information about movie box-office revenue is collected by the trade paper *Variety*, in association with the Standard Data Corporation; record popularity is tabulated by the trade publication *Billboard;* book sales by *Publishers Weekly.*

Next, audience-generated feedback is usually expressed in qualitative rather than quantitative terms. The TV or film critic reports his or her personal reactions to a movie or TV show. The critic does not take a sample of viewers and report what the majority liked or disliked about what they saw. A letter from a reader or viewer generally reports only the qualitative opinion of one person—the writer. In addition, media organizations generally evaluate audience-generated feedback in qualitative terms. An organized letter-writing campaign that produces a thousand identical letters to a TV network is apt to be less influential than a hundred literate and evidently spontaneous letters. True, there are instances when the quantity of audience responses is noted (as in the case when the number of pro and con calls are tabulated), but the qualitative aspects of the responses will also be considered. To illustrate, the TV series *Designing Women* was saved from cancellation one season because the network received letters from fans of the show. It was not so much the number of letters that impressed CBS executives as the fact that they were from intelligent, well-educated, and apparently affluent viewers. By contrast, in media-originated feedback the emphasis is on quantitative information. Every medium relies upon a numerical form of feedback. Newspapers and magazines rely on circulation data, a compilation of how many people buy a newspaper or magazine at a newsstand or have a regular subscription. Book publishers rely on sales figures. In radio and television, program viewing is expressed as the percentage of people viewing or listening. The film and sound-recording industries rely on box-office figures and sales data as the two main forms of feedback, and both are expressed in numerical terms.

Messages and Channels

Each feedback system offers a different choice between feedback forms and channels to the media audience. In the audience-generated situation, the audience determines what form and channel their message will take. If an audience member is upset about a particular TV program, for example, he or she can choose to (1) write a nasty letter to the station, (2) phone the station, or (3) start a petition among other viewers to present to the station manager.

In media-originated feedback, the precise form that information about the audience takes is determined by media organizations. Newspapers and magazines rely on detailed circulation and readership data. Magazines collect elaborate information that identifies the demographic makeup of their audience and even classifies them by the products that they use. Television and radio usage is expressed in the percentages of total people or total households that are viewing or listening. The audience is further subdivided into various demographic groups whose behavior is of interest to advertisers and other media planners. In sound recording and film, the industries choose to collect sales information rather than actual headcounts of their audience. Thus box-office revenue data are gathered about the motion picture audience, and the industry looks at the bottom-line dollar figures and not at individual behavior. In the eyes of the motion picture media, it matters little if twenty different people paid $6 each to see a film or if ten people paid $6 on two different occasions to see the same film twice— the amount of revenue collected in each situation is the same. Similarly, the recording industry collects sales data on records and tapes and also monitors their play on radio stations as a gauge of popularity. In all cases, the media have adopted the precise form of feedback that is most valuable to them and to their advertisers.

Lastly, audience-generated and media-originated feedback have one characteristic in common: In both systems, feedback is typically delayed. As pointed out in Chapter 1, it takes time for a letter, phone call, petition, or canceled subscription to reach the appropriate office or individual in the media organization. Likewise, media-originated feedback takes time to collect. Circulation figures supplied to the Audit Bureau of Circulations are revised only once or twice a year. Box-office and record-popularity information is generally two weeks old by the time it is published. Ratings information is generally from two weeks to several months old by the time it is disseminated (however, many of the larger markets are measured with computer-assisted devices so that overnight ratings are possible).

In the rest of this chapter, we will examine the most common forms of feedback in each of the various media.

• • • •

FEEDBACK: THE PRINT MEDIA

Letters to the Editor

The most prevalent form of audience-generated feedback in the newspaper and magazine industries is the letter to the editor. This is probably the oldest of all the feedback mechanisms that we shall talk about; letters to newspaper and magazine editors were common during Ben Franklin's time. The *New York Times* started publishing letters in 1851, only a few days after it was founded. Evidently, letters are popular feedback mechanisms with readers since newspapers receive a large number of them. Every year about 8 million people write letters to their local newspapers. Most papers receive at least 100 letters a year; more than half get 500 or more. Many get far more than that. The *Honolulu Star-Bulletin* receives about 3000. The *Seattle Times* about 7000. The *New York Times* gets about 40,000. Papers vary in the amount of letters they can print. Large metro papers will publish less than 10 percent of their letters. The *New York Times*, for example, prints only 5 percent. Smaller papers might use about 70 percent. Written feedback from readers does not provide an accurate picture of the print media's audience, however. We have already noted that the people who write these letters tend to be atypical of general newspaper readers. Nor is it clear whether the letters that finally do get into print are representative of all mail received.

The ABC

The best known media-originated feedback system in newspapers and magazines is that connected with the **Audit Bureau of Circulations (ABC)**. During the early 1900s, with the growth of mass advertising, some newspaper and magazine publishers began inflating the number of readers for their publication in order to attract more revenue from advertisers. In an effort to check this deceptive practice, advertisers and publishers joined together to form the ABC in 1914. The organization's purpose was to establish ground rules for counting circulation, to make sure that the rules were enforced, and to provide verified reports of circulation data. The ABC audits about three-fourths of all print media in the United States and Canada, about 2600 magazine, farm, and business publications and daily and weekly newspapers.

The ABC functions in the following manner. Publishers keep detailed records of circulation data. In the case of a newspaper, these records would include such information as the number of copies delivered by carriers, the number of papers sold over the counter, and the number delivered by mail. Twice a year, publishers file a circulation statement with the ABC, which the ABC in turn disseminates to its clients. Once every year, the ABC audits publications to verify that the figures that have been reported are accurate. An ABC representative visits the publication and is free to

Measuring Ad Readership in the Print Media: The Starch Reports

One of the things that an advertiser needs to know is how many people are exposed to his or her ad in a newspaper or magazine. Since the early 1920s, the Starch organization (formal name: Starch INRA Hooper, Inc.) has been providing this form of feedback to the advertising industry. Every year Starch measures approximately 100,000 ads in more than 100 publications, including consumer magazines; business, trade, and industrial publications; and newspapers. Each Starch readership study is based on interviews done with a representative sample of 100–150 readers of the publication under study. Once it has been determined that a respondent actually has read a publication, a Starch interviewer then goes through a copy of the magazine or newspaper ad by ad and asks whether the person can recall seeing the ad and its various components (headline, illustration, copy, etc.).

After all questions are asked, each respondent is classified into one of four categories:

1. Nonreader: a person who didn't remember having seen the ad.

2. "Noted" reader: a person who remembered having previously seen the ad.

3. "Associated" reader: a person who not only "noted" the ad but also saw or read some part of it that clearly indicated the brand or advertiser.

4. "Read-most" reader: a person who read more than half of the written material in the ad.

A Starch Readership Report includes a copy of the publication in which labels have been attached to all of the ads under study. These labels report the readership score of the entire ad as well as reading scores for each of the ad's component parts. For example, for one particular ad, 19 percent of the sample might be classified as "noted" readers, 16 percent as "associated " readers, and 6 percent as "read-most" readers. In addition, the Starch data would also tell the advertiser that 20 percent saw the illustration that went with the ad, 13 percent read the headline, and 11 percent read some of the ad copy, and so on.

By using the feedback provided by the Starch organization, advertisers can compare one ad campaign against another to see which was more effective, compare the scores of their ads with the scores of competitors' ads, and isolate what layout and copywriting factors are related to high readership.

---

examine records and files that contain data on pressruns, invoices for newsprint, and transcripts of circulation records. In an average year, the ABC's field staff of ninety travels approximately 300,000 miles and spends about 135,000 audit hours in verifying the facts on member publications' circulation. The cost of the ABC's services, about $5 million per year, is financed through member dues and service fees. As far as fees go, an individual newspaper or magazine audited by the ABC pays an hourly rate of about $50 for the amount of time it takes to do the audit. Most audits take fewer than forty working hours to complete, which means the total tab would be less than $2000. Figure 20-1 is a sample newspaper audit.

Business magazines and trade publications are audited by the Business Publication Audit (BPA), which uses methods similar to the ABC.

Total Audience Data

In addition to circulation figures, organizations that provide audience feedback in the magazine industry report total audience figures. The total audience is composed of

PRINTED AND RELEASED
BY ABC NOVEMBER, 1991

Audit Bureau of Circulations

AUDIT REPORT: *Newspaper*

THE STAR (Evening & Sunday)
Peekskill (Westchester County), New York

TOTAL AVERAGE PAID CIRCULATION FOR 52 WEEKS ENDED MARCH 31,1991:

	Evening (Mon. to Sat.)	SUNDAY
1A. TOTAL AVERAGE PAID CIRCULATION (BY INDIVIDUALS AND FOR DESIGNATED RECIPIENTS):	6,316	8,709

1B. TOTAL AVERAGE PAID CIRCULATION (BY INDIVIDUALS AND FOR DESIGNATED RECIPIENTS) IN NEWSPAPER DESIGNATED MARKET:
(See Par. 1E for description of area)

NEWSPAPER DESIGNATED MARKET

	Population	Occupied Households
1980 Census:	41,475	14,030
#12-31-89 Estimate:	44,900	16,200

	Evening (Mon. to Sat.)	SUNDAY
Carrier Delivery office collect system, See Pars. 11(b) & (c)	3,014	3,154
Carriers not filing lists with publisher	1,536	1,749
Single Copy Sales	1,487	3,509
Mail Subscriptions	5	2
School-Single Copy/Subscriptions, See Par. 11(d).	31	
Employee Copies, See Par. 11(e).	50	50
TOTAL NEWSPAPER DESIGNATED MARKET.	6,123	8,464

CIRCULATION OUTSIDE NEWSPAPER DESIGNATED MARKET

	Evening (Mon. to Sat.)	SUNDAY
Carriers		
Single Copy Sales		
Mail Subscriptions	170	227
	23	18
TOTAL CIRCULATION OUTSIDE NEWSPAPER DESIGNATED MARKET	193	245
TOTAL AVERAGE PAID CIRCULATION (BY INDIVIDUALS AND FOR DESIGNATED RECIPIENTS)	6,316	8,709
Days Ommitted from Averages, See Par. 11	48	6
1C. THIRD PARTY (BULK) SALES	None of record	None of record

S&MM Estimate. See Par. 11(a).

FIGURE 20-1 *Sample of an ABC audit report. (Reprinted with permission of the Audit Bureau of Circulations.)*

the **primary audience**, those people who subscribe to the magazine or buy it at the newsstand, and the **pass-along audience**, those people who pick up a copy at the doctor's office, while traveling, at work, and so on. The two major companies that measure magazine readership are the **Simmons Market Research Bureau (SMRB)** and **Mediamark (MRI)**. Because the magazine-reading audience is highly segmented, both companies must select a large random sample of households so that the audience for each magazine will be statistically meaningful. Personal interviews are then conducted with the residents to get an "exposure score" for a large number of magazines. The interviewer shows the respondent a deck of cards bearing the logos of anywhere from 100 to 200 different magazines. The respondent is then asked to sort the cards into three piles according to whether he or she read, may have read, or didn't read the publication. (Since a respondent is sorting a large number of magazines, it's inevitable that some error creeps into the system. Readers frequently forget or confuse the names of magazines they have read. One study of the sorting technique found that a large number of respondents reported reading a publication called *Popular Sports*. Unfortunately, this magazine never existed.)

At this point, the measurement techniques of the two companies diverge. SMRB shows respondents a stripped-down version of the magazine and readership is again verified by asking if the respondent has read or looked through that particular issue. The interviewer also asks about the place where each magazine was read. Additional data are gathered about ownership, purchase, and use of a wide variety of products. MRI measures recent reading by requesting respondents to go through each card in their "read" or "may have read" piles and asking if the respondent has read the magazine within the last week or month, depending on the publication schedule of the magazine. Since they use different techniques, the results of the two companies are frequently at odds; resolving the differences in their estimates for various magazines has become a vexing problem for the industry.

The reports issued by SMRB and MRI are extremely detailed and encompass many volumes. They contain such specific information as what percentage of a particular magazine's readers earn more than $25,000 per year and detailed product use data such as how many readers used an upset-stomach remedy in the last month. A small portion from an MRI report is reproduced in Figure 20-2.

Best-selling book lists are based on several sources of information. The list compiled by *Publishers Weekly* is based on publishers' reports of books shipped and billed to bookstores, libraries, and wholesalers. The *New York Times* best-seller list is compiled from figures taken from a sample of 1600 bookstores, including all the chain outlets.

● ● ● ●

FEEDBACK: RADIO AND SOUND RECORDING

Radio is supported by the sale of advertising time; the sound-recording industry depends upon the sale of tapes and discs for support. Radio stations are licensed by the Federal Communications Commission and as such are subject to a number of rules and regulations. The sound-recording industry is not subject to these restrictions. Because of these differences, the feedback systems that exist in these two media are somewhat dissimilar.

Radio Audience Responses

In the radio industry, there are several sources of audience-generated feedback. First of all, listeners write letters to the station concerning the station's programming practices. Some stations have installed telephone recording devices attached to a special phone number. Listeners are encouraged to dial that number and present their opinions and points of view. These comments may then be spliced together and aired as a public-affairs program. Other stations have call-in shows in which people are asked to present their views on the air (usually with a seven-second tape delay for insurance).

Another form of audience-generated feedback usually comes into play around license-renewal time. The 1934 Communications Act states that an audience member may file a petition to deny the renewal or transfer (sale) of the license of a radio or

BASE: FEMALE HOMEMAKERS	TOTAL U.S. '000	ALL				HEAVY & MEDIUM 3 OR MORE				LIGHT LESS THAN 3			
		A '000	B % DOWN	C % ACROSS	D INDEX	A '000	B % DOWN	C % ACROSS	D INDEX	A '000	B % DOWN	C % ACROSS	D INDEX
ALL FEMALE HOMEMAKERS	85323	6628	100.0	7.8	100	4397	100.0	5.2	100	2231	100.0	2.6	100
MONEY	2719	*310	4.7	11.4	147	*214	4.9	7.9	153	*95	4.3	3.5	134
MOTOR TREND	499	*18	.3	3.6	46	*2	-	.4	8	*16	.7	3.2	123
MUSCLE & FITNESS	1109	*99	1.5	8.9	115	*86	2.0	7.8	150	*13	.6	1.2	45
NATIONAL ENQUIRER	11898	1134	17.1	9.5	123	770	17.5	6.5	126	*364	16.3	3.1	117
NATIONAL GEOGRAPHIC	12588	692	10.4	5.5	71	*416	9.5	3.3	64	*276	12.4	2.2	84
NATIONAL GEOGRAPHIC TRAVELER	889	*19	.3	2.1	28	*7	.2	.8	15	*13	.6	1.5	56
NATIONAL LAMPOON	*313	*21	.3	-	-	*21	.5	-	-	-	-	-	-
NATURAL HISTORY	662	*76	1.1	11.5	148	*6	.1	.9	18	*70	3.1	10.6	404
NEWSWEEK	8286	637	9.6	7.7	99	*447	10.2	5.4	105	*190	8.5	2.3	88
NEW WOMAN	3214	*206	3.1	6.4	83	*129	2.9	4.0	78	*77	3.5	2.4	92
NEW YORK MAGAZINE	728	*117	1.8	16.1	207	*87	2.0	12.0	232	*30	1.3	4.1	158
NEW YORK TIMES (DAILY)	1355	*67	1.0	4.9	64	*31	.7	2.3	44	*36	1.6	2.7	102
NEW YORK TIMES MAGAZINE	2087	*159	2.4	7.6	98	*116	2.6	5.6	108	*43	1.9	2.1	79
THE NEW YORKER	1189	*81	1.2	6.8	88	*51	1.2	4.3	84	*30	1.3	2.5	96
OMNI	975	*102	1.5	10.5	135	*47	1.1	4.8	94	*55	2.5	5.6	216
1,001 HOME IDEAS	3610	*315	4.8	8.7	112	*290	6.6	8.0	156	*25	1.1	.7	26
ORGANIC GARDENING	1904	*35	.5	1.8	24	*28	.6	1.5	29	*6	.3	.3	12
OUTDOOR LIFE	1864	*121	1.8	6.5	84	*107	2.4	5.7	111	*15	.7	.8	31

FIGURE 20-2 *Excerpt from an MRI report. (Copyright © by Mediamark Research Inc.)*

television station. The person or group filing such a petition must cite factual evidence proving that granting the renewal or transfer would not be in the public interest. In recent years, most petitions to deny license renewals have been filed by groups representing women and minorities. These petitions typically allege that the station has not lived up to its obligations under the Equal Opportunity Employment guidelines or that the station has failed to provide programming that adequately serves the minority community. One recent result of contact between petitioners and stations is the negotiated agreement. In this arrangement, the group agrees to drop its petition to deny in return for assurances from the station that the practices that prompted the original petition will be changed. These agreements continue to be an effective (if somewhat drastic) method of settling specific disputes. Much to the relief of broadcasters, a general trend toward deregulation has meant that petitions to deny have lost some of their former power.

Arbitron and the Diary Method

In the radio industry, media-originated feedback is provided by ratings conducted by professional research organizations. The major company that measures the radio audience is **Arbitron,** a subsidiary of Control Data Corporation, manufacturers of computer hardware and software. Arbitron surveys radio listening in approximately 262 markets across the United States and reports its results to broadcasters and advertisers. Large markets (New York, Los Angeles, Boston, Chicago, Detroit, Philadelphia, San Francisco) are measured at least four times a year, while smaller markets may be examined only once in the same period. All markets are measured during April and May.

Within a given market, Arbitron chooses people at random from a listing of all telephone numbers in the market. Individuals who agree to participate in Arbitron's survey are sent a pocket-sized diary. This diary is designed to travel with a person in order to measure both in-home and out-of-home listening. Participants are instructed to fill in the diary on a day-to-day basis, noting the time spent listening to radio and identifying the station. The back of the diary asks respondents to provide basic demographic data. Approximately 3000–4000 of these diaries are mailed in a given market, and Arbitron follows up with several reminder calls to persons in the sample. Nevertheless, only 45–50 percent of the diaries are returned in usable form. Figure

4

THURSDAY

Time			Station			Place			
			Call letters or station name	*Check (✓) one*		*Check (✓) one*			
	Start	Stop	*Don't know? Use program name or dial setting.*	AM	FM	At Home	In a Car	At Work	Other Place
→ Early Morning (from 5 AM)									
→ Midday									
→ Late Afternoon									
→ Night (to 5 AM Friday)									

If you didn't hear a radio today, please check here. ☐

FIGURE 20-3 *Sample of an Arbitron radio diary.* (Arbitron Ratings: Your Radio Ratings Diary. *Copyright © Arbitron Ratings Company. Reprinted by permission.)*

20-3 is an example of an Arbitron radio diary. Once all the diaries have been returned, Arbitron begins an analysis that typically takes three to four weeks. The end product of this process is a ratings book, which is sent to participating stations. A sample page of such a book is reproduced in Figure 20-4, on page 493.

Measurements of radio and television audiences gathered by the diary method are usually expressed in terms of two related concepts: (1) ratings and (2) share of the audience. A **rating** is simply the ratio of listeners to a particular station to all people in the market. To illustrate, suppose that in a market with 100,000 people, 20,000 listen to radio station KYYY from 9:00 A.M. to 9:15 A.M. The rating of KYYY would be 20,000/100,000, or 20 percent. A **share of the audience** is the ratio of listeners to a particular station to the total number of radio listeners in the market. For example, again suppose that 20,000 people are listening to KYYY from 9:00 A.M. to 9:15 A.M. and that in the total market 80,000 people are listening to the radio during the same period. KYYY's share of the audience would be 20,000/80,000, or 25 percent. Shares of the audience divide the listening audience among all stations in the market. When they are summed, shares should total 100 percent. Table 20-2 contains another illustration of the technique of computing shares and ratings. Ratings books are important to stations because they are used to establish what rates stations will charge advertisers. In the smaller markets, where only one survey is done a year, their importance is even greater since the station will be using them to set rates for the next twelve months.

Target Audience
PERSONS 18-34

	MONDAY-FRIDAY 6AM-10AM				MONDAY-FRIDAY 10AM-3PM				MONDAY-FRIDAY 3PM-7PM				MONDAY-FRIDAY 7PM-MID				WEEKEND 10AM-7PM			
	AQH (00)	CUME (00)	AQH RTG	AQH SHR	AQH (00)	CUME (00)	AQH RTG	AQH SHR	AQH (00)	CUME (00)	AQH RTG	AQH SHR	AQH (00)	CUME (00)	AQH RTG	AQH SHR	AQH (00)	CUME (00)	AQH RTG	AQH SHR
WAJI																				
METRO	35	221	3.4	13.8	49	225	4.8	17.4	42	232	4.1	17.9	14	130	1.4	13.2	17	140	1.7	10.2
TSA	55	339			73	352			55	370			18	226			27	264		
WBTU																				
METRO	16	79	1.6	6.3	14	57	1.4	5.0	9	58	.9	3.8	2	29	.2	1.9	8	52	.8	4.8
TSA	97	380			89	295			53	377			16	191			35	295		
WBYR																				
METRO	30	234	2.9	11.9	38	227	3.7	13.5	36	248	3.5	15.4	18	156	1.8	17.0	17	161	1.7	10.2
TSA	92	552			114	642			81	642			31	341			64	540		
WDJB																				
METRO	26	141	2.5	10.3	26	136	2.5	9.2	22	167	2.2	9.4	10	104	1.0	9.4	17	142	1.7	10.2
TSA	26	151			30	166			23	178			12	149			21	185		
WGL																				
METRO	5	22	.5	2.0	13	37	1.3	4.6	4	27	.4	1.7	1	9	.1	.9		9		
TSA	5	22			14	47			4	27			1	9				9		
WQTX																				
METRO						5														
TSA						5														
A/F TOT																				
METRO	5	22	.5	2.0	13	37	1.3	4.6	4	27	.4	1.7	1	9	.1	.9		9		
TSA	5	22			14	47			4	27			1	9				9		
WIFF																				
METRO													*							
TSA																				
WIFF-FM																				
METRO	1	3	.1	.4	1	3	.1	.4	1	3	.1	.4		7						
TSA	1	3			1	3			1	3				7						
A/F TOT																				
METRO	1	3	.1	.4	1	3	.1	.4	1	3	.1	.4		7						
TSA	1	3			1	3			1	3				7						
WJFX																				
METRO	12	63	1.2	4.7	18	59	1.8	6.4	15	63	1.5	6.4	10	45	1.0	9.4	7	53	.7	4.2
TSA	12	63			18	59			15	67			10	45			7	53		
WJLT																				
METRO	4	46	.4	1.6	10	60	1.0	3.5	6	64	.6	2.6	4	29	.4	3.8	5	43	.5	3.0
TSA	5	58			11	94			7	75			4	29			6	54		
WMEE																				
METRO	52	299	5.1	20.6	39	238	3.8	13.8	32	285	3.1	13.7	18	169	1.8	17.0	36	230	3.5	21.6
TSA	96	629			86	486			67	602			34	390			73	534		
WOWO																				
METRO	5	50	.5	2.0	2	43	.2	.7	3	47	.3	1.3	2	38	.2	1.9	3	33	.3	1.8
TSA	17	142			9	93			5	71			5	72			14	78		
WOWO-FM																				
METRO	1	14	.1	.4		14								13			3	25	.3	1.8
TSA	1	14				14							1	25			3	25		
A/F TOT																				
METRO	6	64	.6	2.4	2	57	.2	.7	3	47	.3	1.3	2	46	.2	1.9	6	58	.6	3.6
TSA	18	156			9	107			5	71			6	91			17	102		
WQHK																				
METRO	7	36	.7	2.8	6	32	.6	2.1	9	31	.9	3.8		8			2	26	.2	1.2
TSA	7	36			6	32			9	31				8			2	26		
WXKE																				
METRO	39	230	3.8	15.4	41	204	4.0	14.5	32	238	3.1	13.7	12	136	1.2	11.3	22	141	2.2	13.2
TSA	52	311			66	289			43	311			17	211			27	197		
WJR																				
METRO		4				8			1	9	.1	.4	3	13	.3	2.8	1	17	.1	.6
TSA	1	19				8			3	29			4	22			2	32		
WLW																				
METRO		10								5			2	8	.2	1.9		9		
TSA	9	70			12	47			10	60			9	44			6	52		
WMRI																				
METRO	1	5	.1	.4						5				9			1	10	.1	.6
TSA	2	20			3	35			2	29				9			1	25		
CKLW																				
METRO																				
TSA																				
METRO TOTALS	253	898	24.7		282	806	27.6		234	916	22.9		106	625	10.4		167	814	16.3	

Footnote Symbols: ✱ Audience estimates adjusted for actual broadcast schedule. ✦ Station(s) changed call letters since the prior survey - see Page 5B.

FIGURE 20-4 *Excerpt from an Arbitron radio ratings book.* (Arbitron Ratings—Radio. *Reprinted by permission.*)

TABLE 20-2 Calculating Ratings and Share of Audience

Market size:	500,000 people
Stations:	WALL, WISK, WONT, WENT

Listening at 9 A.M.:

WALL:	15,000
WISK:	20,000
WONT:	50,000
WENT:	30,000
Total listening:	115,000

RATING	SHARE
$\text{WALL} = \dfrac{15,000}{500,000} = 0.03 \text{ or } 3\%$	$\text{WALL} = \dfrac{15,000}{115,000} = 0.13 \text{ or } 13\%$
$\text{WISK} = \dfrac{20,000}{500,000} = 0.04 \text{ or } 4\%$	$\text{WISK} = \dfrac{20,000}{115,000} = 0.17 \text{ or } 17\%$
$\text{WONT} = \dfrac{50,000}{500,000} = 0.10 \text{ or } 10\%$	$\text{WONT} = \dfrac{50,000}{115,000} = 0.44 \text{ or } 44\%$
$\text{WENT} = \dfrac{30,000}{500,000} = 0.06 \text{ or } 6\%$	$\text{WENT} = \dfrac{30,000}{115,000} = 0.26 \text{ or } 26\%$
	$\text{TOTAL} = 1.00 \text{ or } 100\%$

Sound-Recording Audience Responses

Few people write letters to record companies, although some fan mail directed to recording artists provides a rather crude gauge of popularity. Another indirect form of audience-generated feedback is attendance at personal appearances and concerts. In general, feedback is concerned with the bottom line—sales figures.

Media-originated feedback in the sound-recording industry is characterized by stars, triangles, and bullets. These are the common symbols used in *Billboard* magazines's charts of popular records. Stars stand for recordings that are "movers"; they are on their way up in the charts. Bullets go to singles that are one-million sellers; triangles go to two-million sellers. Every week disc jockeys, program directors, and record company executives scan the *Billboard* charts, the most important channel of feedback in the sound-recording industry.

What determines the award of stars, triangles, and bullets? How is the *Billboard* chart put together? In general, the *Billboard* charts are based on two components: (1) exposure and (2) sales. For the Hot 100 Chart, for example, sales information is

Buying a Rating?

The headline pretty well summed it up: "This is a BRIBE." Radio station KELI, AM 1430, in Tulsa, Oklahoma, ran a newspaper ad in which all those with Arbitron diaries were asked to fill out the diary so that all of their listening time was to KELI. In return for this favor, the station would give the diary owner a check for $14.30. KELI was disturbed by the fact that the Tulsa ratings were based on diaries from a sample of only 900 people. KELI's competitors pointed out the ad to Arbitron, and the company, as is its custom, placed advisories in its Tulsa book to warn advertisers of the unusual circumstances surrounding the ratings survey.

gathered in the following manner. *Billboard* selects the top fifty markets in terms of total record sales in the United States (these markets are among the most populous), and within these markets the magazine subjectively chooses the most influential recording outlets. These can be retail record shops, record departments in department stores, and suppliers to jukebox operators. *Billboard* then hands out reporting forms on which sales data for the hottest-selling discs and tapes are recorded. About 185 outlets are surveyed weekly.

In order to measure exposure, *Billboard* surveys the playlist of leading radio stations. The survey includes approximately 240 stations that are weighted by audience reach (i.e., being the number-one record on a 50,000-watt station in New York City is worth more than being number one at a 5000-watt station in a rural area). Note that another mass medium, radio, plays an important part in the feedback mechanism for sound recording. In addition, radio stations with a music format rely on the *Billboard* charts to determine what records they should play. Thus sound recording functions as a feedback mechanism for radio. This reciprocity is another example of a symbiotic relationship between media (see Chapter 1).

When all the sales and exposure data have been collected, *Billboard* combines the two measures and winds up with a final index number for each album or single release. These rankings are then translated into the Hot 100 pop singles chart.

Other charts are prepared in basically the same way, but there are some differences according to format. The pop and country albums charts use electronically-gathered sales data from ninety-nine markets. The Adult Contemporary chart is based on airplay, as is the Album Rock chart.

Figure 20-5, page 496, reproduces one of *Billboard*'s charts. It contains several pieces of information: the record's standing for the current week and thé week before; number of weeks on the chart; title of song and the artist; the producer, writer, and label number (important information for ordering a record); and, if necessary, the distributing label. *Billboard* publishes a chart for almost all formats of popular music. For example, each issue will contain popularity rankings for not only pop singles but also jazz albums, Latin albums, country albums, country singles, classical albums, middle-of-the-road singles, R and B albums and singles, and a chart that lists hit records all over the world. For example, in late 1990, "Tattoo," by Akina Nakamori, topped the charts in Japan while "Yeke Yeke," by Mory Kante, was a big hit in West Germany and Michael Jackson's "Dirty Diana" was number one in the Netherlands.

● ● ● ●
FEEDBACK: TELEVISION AND FILM

Feedback mechanisms in television resemble those used in radio, while feedback systems in the film industry are similar to those used in sound recording.

Television Viewer Responses

In television, audience-generated feedback typically takes the form of telephone calls and letters to the station's management. Since TV stations tend to be more visible and reach a larger audience than most radio stations, they generally attract a larger volume of mail and calls. Television networks also draw a great deal of mail; one estimate places NBC's audience mail at between 50,000 and 75,000 letters yearly. Many of these, however, are generated by letter-writing campaigns organized by special-interest groups. Another significant portion of audience letters to the networks comes from people protesting the cancellation of their favorite show. Cancellations can spark massive volumes of mail, as evidenced by the 150,000 or so angry letters that NBC received when it canceled *The Monkees* in 1968 or the 85,000 letters received by ABC when *The Lawrence Welk Show* was dropped in 1971.

Billboard® HOT 100® SINGLES™

FOR WEEK ENDING SEPT. 25, 1993

COMPILED FROM A NATIONAL SAMPLE OF TOP 40 RADIO AIRPLAY MONITORED BY BROADCAST DATA SYSTEMS, TOP 40 RADIO PLAYLISTS, AND RETAIL AND RACK SINGLES SALES COLLECTED, COMPILED, AND PROVIDED BY SoundScan

THIS WEEK	LAST WEEK	2 WKS AGO	WKS. ON CHART	TITLE PRODUCER (SONGWRITER)	ARTIST LABEL & NUMBER/DISTRIBUTING LABEL
1	1	1	8	★★★ No. 1 ★★★ DREAMLOVER (3 weeks at No. 1) M.CAREY,D.HALL,W.AFANASIEFF (M.CAREY,D.HALL)	◆ MARIAH CAREY (C) (D) (M) (T) (V) (X) COLUMBIA 77080
2	2	3	18	WHOOMP! (THERE IT IS)▲ TAG TEAM (TAG TEAM)	◆ TAG TEAM (C) (M) (T) (X) LIFE 79001/BELLMARK
3	5	6	11	RIGHT HERE (HUMAN NATURE)/DOWNTOWN ● B.A.MORGAN,G.PARKER (B.A.MORGAN,J.BETTIS,S.PORCARO,G.PARKER,K.ORTIZ,G.GOMEZ)	◆ SWV (C) (T) (V) (X) RCA 62614
4	3	2	20	CAN'T HELP FALLING IN LOVE (FROM "SLIVER")▲ UB40 (G.D.WEISS,H.PERETTI,L.CREATORE)	◆ UB40 (C) (V) VIRGIN 12653
5	4	4	10	IF J.JAM,T.LEWIS,J.JACKSON (J.JACKSON,J.HARRIS III,T.LEWIS)	◆ JANET JACKSON (C) (T) (V) (X) VIRGIN 12676
6	6	9	9	THE RIVER OF DREAMS D.KORTCHMAR,J.NICOLO (B.JOEL)	◆ BILLY JOEL (C) (V) (X) COLUMBIA 77086
7	8	7	11	WILL YOU BE THERE (FROM "FREE WILLY") M.JACKSON,B.SWEDIEN (M.JACKSON)	◆ MICHAEL JACKSON (C) (V) MJJ/EPIC SOUNDTRAX 77060/EPIC
8	7	5	16	RUNAWAY TRAIN ● M.BEINHORN (D.PIRNER)	◆ SOUL ASYLUM (C) (X) COLUMBIA 74966
9	9	8	16	LATELY ● D.SWING (S.WONDER)	◆ JODECI (C) (T) (V) UPTOWN 54652/MCA
10	10	12	17	BABY I'M YOURS C.MARTIN (C.MARTIN,M.GAY)	◆ SHAI (C) (M) (T) (V) (X) GASOLINE ALLEY 54574/MCA
11	14	21	13	ANOTHER SAD LOVE SONG L.A.REID,BABYFACE,D.SIMMONS (BABYFACE,D.SIMMONS)	◆ TONI BRAXTON (C) (M) (T) (X) LAFACE 2-4047/ARISTA
12	12	18	13	I GET AROUND D.J.DARYL (T.SHAKUR,D.ANDERSON,R.TROUTMAN,L.TROUTMAN,S.MURDOCK)	◆ 2PAC (C) (M) (T) INTERSCOPE 98372
13	17	22	8	BOOM! SHAKE THE ROOM ● MR.LEE (SMITH,HAGGARD,WILLIAMS,MAYBERRY,WEBSTER,PIERCE,NAPIER,MORRIS)	◆ JAZZY JEFF & FRESH PRINCE (C) (M) (T) (X) JIVE 42108
14	18	19	9	CRYIN' B.FAIRBAIRN (S.TYLER,J.PERRY,T.RHODES)	◆ AEROSMITH (C) (V) GEFFEN 19256
15	13	13	16	ONE LAST CRY B.MCKNIGHT,B.BARNES (B.MCKNIGHT,B.BARNES,M.BARNES)	◆ BRIAN MCKNIGHT (C) MERCURY 862 404
16	16	14	10	RAIN MADONNA,S.PETTIBONE (M.CICCONE,S.PETTIBONE)	◆ MADONNA (C) (D) (M) (T) (V) (X) MAVERICK/SIRE 18505/WARNER BROS.
17	15	11	16	I'M GONNA BE (500 MILES) ● P.WINGFIELD (C.REID,C.REID)	◆ THE PROCLAIMERS (C) (V) CHRYSALIS 24846/ERG
18	11	10	16	IF I HAD NO LOOT ● TONY!TONI!TONE! (R.WIGGINS,J.BAUTISTA,W.HARRIS)	◆ TONY! TONI! TONE! (C) (T) (V) WING 859 056/MERCURY
19	20	20	12	INSANE IN THE BRAIN ● D.J.MUGGS (L.FREESE,S.REYES,L.MUGGERUD)	◆ CYPRESS HILL (C) (M) (T) (X) RUFFHOUSE 77135/COLUMBIA
20	19	15	18	I DON'T WANNA FIGHT (FROM "WHAT'S LOVE GOT TO DO WITH IT") C.LORD-ALGE,R.DAVIES (S.DUBERRY,LULU,B.LAWRIE)	◆ TINA TURNER (C) (V) VIRGIN 12652
21	32	39	7	REASON TO BELIEVE P.LEONARD (T. HARDIN)	◆ ROD STEWART (C) (D) (V) WARNER BROS. 18427
22	30	34	8	SWEAT (A LA LA LA LA LONG) I.LEWIS,T.HARVEY,R.LEWIS (I.LEWIS)	◆ INNER CIRCLE (C) (T) (V) BIG BEAT 98429/ATLANTIC
23	29	32	11	WHEN I FALL IN LOVE (FROM "SLEEPLESS IN SEATTLE") D.FOSTER (E.HEYMAN,V.YOUNG)	◆ C. DION & C. GRIFFIN (C) (V) EPIC SOUNDTRAX 77021/EPIC
24	21	24	9	ALRIGHT ● J.DUPRI (J.DUPRI,W.MARAGH)	◆ KRIS KROSS FEATURING SUPERCAT (C) (M) (T) (V) (X) RUFFHOUSE 77103/COLUMBIA
25	27	31	11	BREAK IT DOWN AGAIN T.PALMER,R.ORZABAL,A.GRIFFITHS (R.ORZABAL,A.GRIFFITHS)	◆ TEARS FOR FEARS (C) (D) (V) MERCURY 862 330
26	37	37	5	SOUL TO SQUEEZE (FROM "CONEHEADS") R.RUBIN (A. KEIDIS,FLEA,J.FRUSCIANTE,C.SMITH)	◆ RED HOT CHILI PEPPERS (C) (D) (V) WARNER BROS. 18401
27	22	17	23	WEAK▲ B.A.MORGAN (B.A.MORGAN)	◆ SWV (C) (T) (V) RCA 62521
28	38	51	5	HEY MR. D.J. 118TH STREET PRODUCTIONS (GIST,BROWN,CRISS,ZHANE,BAHR,WARE,GREY)	◆ ZHANE (C) (T) FLAVOR UNIT 77121/EPIC
29	23	23	22	WHOOT, THERE IT IS▲ THE BASS MECHANICS (J.MCGOWAN,N.ORANGE)	◆ 95 SOUTH (M) (T) (V) WRAP 0150*/ICHIBAN
30	49	52	3	★★★ POWER PICK/SALES ★★★ TWO STEPS BEHIND (FROM "LAST ACTION HERO") WOODROFFE,COLLEN,ELLIOTT,SAVAGE,CAMPBELL (J.ELLIOTT)	◆ DEF LEPPARD (C) COLUMBIA 77116
31	28	27	12	OOH CHILD DINO (S.VINCENT)	◆ DINO (C) (T) EASTWEST 98398
32	24	29	9	CHECK YO SELF ICE CUBE,D.J.POOH (ICE CUBE,E.FLETCHER,M.GLOVER,S.ROBINSON,C.CHASE)	◆ ICE CUBE FEATURING DAS EFX (M) (T) (X) PRIORITY 53830*
33	33	33	10	HEY JEALOUSY J. HAMPTON,GIN BLOSSOMS (D. HOPKINS)	◆ GIN BLOSSOMS (C) A&M 0242
34	31	25	38	DAZZEY DUKS▲ PARAGON PRODUCTIONS (L.A.SNO,CREO-D,BAMBATTA,ROBIE,BAKER,ALLEN,MILLER)	◆ DUICE (C) (T) TMR 3089/BELLMARK
35	26	26	23	WHAT'S UP ● D.TICKLE (L.PERRY)	◆ 4 NON BLONDES (C) INTERSCOPE 98430
36	34	28	26	SHOW ME LOVE ● A.GEORGE,F.MCFARLANE (A.GEORGE,F.MCFARLANE)	◆ ROBIN S. (C) (M) (T) (X) BIG BEAT 10118/ATLANTIC
37	35	38	12	VERY SPECIAL BIG DADDY KANE (W.JEFFERY,L.PETERS)	BIG DADDY KANE FEAT. SPINDERELLA, L. WILLIAMS & K. ANDERSON (C) (D) (T) COLD CHILLIN' 18437/REPRISE
38	36	30	27	I'LL NEVER GET OVER YOU (GETTING OVER ME) ● G.ROCHE (D.WARREN)	◆ EXPOSE (C) (M) (X) ARISTA 1-2518
39	25	16	18	SLAM▲ C.PARKER,JAM MASTERS JAY (SCRUGGS,TAYLOR,PARKER,JONES)	◆ ONYX (C) (M) (T) (X) JMJ/RAL 77053/CHAOS
40	39	41	11	RUFFNECK M.RILEY,A.DAVIDSON,W.SCOTT (MC LYTE,A.DAVIDSON,M.RILEY,W.SCOTT)	◆ MC LYTE (C) (M) (T) FIRST PRIORITY 98401/ATLANTIC
41	50	57	5	WHAT IS LOVE HALLIGAN,TORELLO (D.HALLIGAN,TORELLO)	◆ HADDAWAY (C) (M) (T) (X) ARISTA 1-2575
42	41	35	22	THAT'S THE WAY LOVE GOES▲ J.JAM,T.LEWIS,J.JACKSON (J.JACKSON,J.HARRIS III,T.LEWIS)	◆ JANET JACKSON (C) (T) (V) (X) VIRGIN 12650
43	52	58	4	HOPELESSLY G.STEVENSON,R.ASTLEY (R.ASTLEY,R.FISHER)	◆ RICK ASTLEY (C) RCA 62597
44	40	36	14	CREEP S.SLADE,P.Q.KOLDERIE (RADIOHEAD)	◆ RADIOHEAD (C) (V) CAPITOL 44932
45	43	43	17	FIELDS OF GOLD H.PADGHAM,STING (STING)	◆ STING (C) (X) A&M 0258
46	42	40	25	KNOCKIN' DA BOOTS▲ B.BURRELL (SHAZAM,DINO,GI,STICK,R.TROUTMAN)	◆ H-TOWN (C) (M) (T) LUKE 161
47	44	46	20	DRE DAY ● DR.DRE (DR.DRE,SNOOP,C.WOLFE)	◆ DR. DRE (C) (M) (T) DEATH ROW 53827/INTERSCOPE
48	68	—	2	I'D DO ANYTHING FOR LOVE (BUT I WON'T DO THAT) J.STEINMAN (J.STEINMAN)	◆ MEAT LOAF (C) (V) MCA 54626
49	48	45	24	COME UNDONE DURAN DURAN (DURAN DURAN)	◆ DURAN DURAN (C) (V) (X) CAPITOL 44918
50	53	72	6	SOMETHING IN YOUR EYES L.A.REID,BABYFACE,D.SIMMONS (K.EDMONDS)	◆ BELL BIV DEVOE (C) (V) MCA 54725
51	57	67	6	NO RAIN R.PARASHAR,BLIND MELON (BLIND MELON)	◆ BLIND MELON (V) (X) CAPITOL 15994*
52	46	44	17	SOMETHING'S GOIN' ON J.PENN II (J.POWE,D.PEETE,J.CLAY)	◆ UNV (C) (V) MAVERICK/SIRE 18564/WARNER BROS.
53	60	68	5	SUNDAY MORNING M.WHITE (WHITE,REYNOLDS,WILLIS)	◆ EARTH, WIND & FIRE (C) (D) REPRISE 18461
54	47	48	17	ONE WOMAN V.BENFORD (V.BENFORD,R.SPEARMAN)	◆ JADE (C) (M) (T) GIANT 18606
55	64	74	6	BETTER THAN YOU S.BERNARD (L.KEITH,K.THOMAS)	◆ LISA KEITH (C) PERSPECTIVE 7430/A&M
56	56	53	6	LOVE FOR LOVE A.GEORGE,F.MCFARLANE (A.GEORGE,F.MCFARLANE)	◆ ROBIN S. (C) (M) (T) (V) (X) BIG BEAT 98382/ATLANTIC
57	51	47	14	I'M FREE E.ESTEFAN,JR.,C.OSTWALD,J.CASAS (J.SECADA,M.A.MOREJON)	◆ JON SECADA (C) (D) (V) SBK 50434/ERG
58	58	56	12	CHIEF ROCKA K-DEF (A.WARDRICK,D.KELLY,M.WILLIAMS,K.HANSFORD)	◆ LORDS OF THE UNDERGROUND (C) (M) (T) PENDULUM 64631/ELEKTRA
59	62	69	4	TOO MUCH INFORMATION DURAN DURAN,J.JONES (DURAN DURAN)	◆ DURAN DURAN (C) (V) (X) CAPITOL 44955
60	88	—	2	★★★ POWER PICK/AIRPLAY ★★★ PINK CASHMERE PRINCE (PRINCE)	PRINCE (C) (D) (V) PAISLEY PARK 18371/WARNER BROS.
61	63	77	4	COME INSIDE N.HODGE (K.GREENE,C.WIKE,N.HODGE)	◆ INTRO (C) ATLANTIC 87317
62	73	89	3	EVERYBODY HURTS S.LITT,R.E.M. (BERRY,BUCK,MILLS,STIPE)	◆ R.E.M. (C) (M) (V) (X) WARNER BROS. 40992
63	61	49	14	RUN TO YOU (FROM "THE BODYGUARD") D.FOSTER (A.RICH,J.FRIEDMAN)	◆ WHITNEY HOUSTON (C) (D) (V) ARISTA 1-2570
64	54	54	8	MEGA MEDLEY R.TROUTMAN (R.TROUTMAN,L.TROUTMAN,N.WHITFIELD,B.STRONG)	ZAPP & ROGER (C) (M) (T) (X) REPRISE 18420
65	90	—	2	JUST KICKIN' IT J.DUPRI (J.DUPRI,M.SEALS)	◆ XSCAPE (C) (T) SO SO DEF 77120/COLUMBIA
66	59	55	12	CHATTAHOOCHEE K.STEGALL (A.JACKSON,J.MCBRIDE)	◆ ALAN JACKSON (C) (V) ARISTA 1-2573
67	55	50	13	WHAT'S UP DOC? (CAN WE ROCK) ● K-CUT (R.ROACHFORD,J.JONES,L.MATURINE,K.MCKENZIE,S.O'NEAL)	◆ FU-SCHNICKENS WITH SHAQUILLE O'NEAL (C) (M) (T) (X) JIVE 42164
68	92	—	2	ALL THAT SHE WANTS D.POP,JOKER/BUDDHA (JOKER/BUDDHA)	ACE OF BASE (C) (M) (T) (X) ARISTA 1-2614
69	71	80	4	COME BABY COME J.GARDNER,K7 (K7,J.GARDNER)	◆ K7 (C) (M) (T) (X) TOMMY BOY 7572
70	65	60	13	BELIEVE L.KRAVITZ (L.KRAVITZ,H.HIRSCH)	◆ LENNY KRAVITZ (C) (V) VIRGIN 12662
71	66	59	15	GIRL U FOR ME/LOSE CONTROL K.SWEAT,R.MURRAY (K.SWEAT,R.MURRAY)	◆ SILK (C) KEIA 64643/ELEKTRA
72	69	70	10	HAPPY BAG,SNOWMAN (A. BAGGE,M. BECKMAN)	◆ LEGACY OF SOUND FEATURING MEJA (C) (T) (X) RCA 62538
73	67	64	20	CRY NO MORE R.WHITE,K.JACKSON,D.WILEY (R.WHITE,K.JACKSON,D.WILEY)	◆ II D EXTREME (C) (M) (T) (V) (X) GASOLINE ALLEY 54650/MCA
74	74	75	19	DON'T TAKE AWAY MY HEAVEN S.LINDSEY (D.WARREN)	◆ AARON NEVILLE (C) (V) A&M 0240
75	75	82	5	I'M IN LUV J.DIBBS (J.DIBBS,B.ALLEN,T.DENSLOW)	◆ JOE (C) (T) MERCURY 862 462
76	70	63	13	GET IT UP (FROM "POETIC JUSTICE") D.AUSTIN,TIM & BOB (PRINCE)	◆ TLC (C) (M) (T) LAFACE/EPIC SOUNDTRAX 77059/EPIC
77	77	84	5	DELICATE T.T.D'ARBY (T.T.D'ARBY)	◆ TERENCE TRENT D'ARBY (C) COLUMBIA 77128
78	76	73	7	OH CAROLINA J.R. ALLEN (O.BURRELL,W. RILEY)	◆ SHAGGY (C) (T) (V) VIRGIN 12672
79	84	—	2	BREAKADAWN DE LA SOUL,PRINCE PAUL (K.MERCER,D.JOLICOEUR,V.MASON,P.HOUSTON,WONDER)	◆ DE LA SOUL (M) (T) (X) TOMMY BOY 586*
80	72	62	17	CAN'T GET ENOUGH OF YOUR LOVE R.CLIVILLES,D.COLE (B.WHITE)	◆ TAYLOR DAYNE (C) (M) (T) (V) (X) ARISTA 1-2582
81	81	79	9	LICK U UP B.BURRELL (SHAZAM,DINO,GI,STICK)	◆ H-TOWN (C) (M) (T) LUKE 163
82	85	83	8	WHAT MIGHT HAVE BEEN J.STROUD,C.DINAPOLI,D.GRAU (P.HOWELL,D.O'BRIEN,B.SEALS)	◆ LITTLE TEXAS (C) (V) WARNER BROS. 18516
83	80	66	10	THE WAYS OF THE WIND P.M.DAWN (A.CORDES,J.MITCHELL)	◆ P.M. DAWN (C) (T) (V) (X) GEE STREET/ISLAND 862 475/PLG
84	NEW ▶		1	★★★ HOT SHOT DEBUT ★★★ ANNIVERSARY TONY!TONI!TONE! (R.WIGGINS,C.WHEELER)	◆ TONY! TONI! TONE! (C) (V) WING 859 566/MERCURY
85	79	78	7	STREIHT UP MENACE (FROM "MENACE II SOCIETY") MC EIHT,DJ SLIP (A.TYLER,T.ALLEN)	◆ MC EIHT (C) (M) (T) JIVE 42154
86	78	61	12	STEP IT UP STEREO MC'S (R.BIRCH,N.HALLAM)	◆ STEREO MC'S (C) (T) (X) GEE STREET/ISLAND 862 308/PLG
87	NEW ▶		1	LET ME RIDE DR.DRE (DR.DRE,SNOOP)	◆ DR. DRE (C) DEATH ROW 57128/INTERSCOPE
88	98	—	2	HUMAN WHEELS J.MELLENCAMP,M.BURN,D.LEONARD,M.WANCHIC (J.MELLENCAMP,G.GREEN)	◆ JOHN MELLENCAMP (C) (V) MERCURY 862 704
89	86	88	7	FOR THE COOL IN YOU BABYFACE,L.A.REID,D.SIMMONS (BABYFACE,D.SIMMONS)	◆ BABYFACE (C) (T) (V) EPIC 77109
90	95	85	9	THE BONNIE AND CLYDE THEME POCKETS,Q.D.III,ICE CUBE (YO-YO,ICE CUBE,POCKETS,QUINCY D.III)	◆ YO-YO (C) (M) (T) EASTWEST 98394
91	91	87	9	IN THE HEART OF A WOMAN J.SCAIFE,J.COTTON (K.HINTON,B.CARTWRIGHT)	◆ BILLY RAY CYRUS (C) (V) MERCURY 862 448
92	89	86	19	BY THE TIME THIS NIGHT IS OVER W.AFANASIEFF,D.FOSTER (M.BOLTON,D.WARREN,A.GOLDMARK)	◆ KENNY G WITH PEABO BRYSON (C) (X) ARISTA 1-2565
93	83	76	11	IT'S FOR YOU (FROM "THE METEOR MAN") M.A.SAULSBERRY,E.KIRKLAND (S.WILSON,M.A.SAULSBERRY,E.KIRKLAND)	◆ SHANICE (C) (T) MOTOWN 2207
94	82	71	11	STAY FOREVER S.BARRI,T.PELUSO (J.LAWRENCE,A.L.BACON,A.SHALLIT,N.BACON)	◆ JOEY LAWRENCE (C) (V) IMPACT 54653/MCA
95	97	90	11	EVEN A FOOL CAN SEE D.FOSTER,P.CETERA (P.CETERA,M.GOLDENBERG)	PETER CETERA (C) WARNER BROS. 18561
96	NEW ▶		1	INDO SMOKE (FROM "POETIC JUSTICE") WARREN G. (R.TRAWICK,W.GRIFFIN III)	◆ MISTA GRIMM (C) EPIC SOUNDTRAX 77256/EPIC
97	94	—	2	HEAVEN KNOWS L.VANDROSS,M.MILLER (L.VANDROSS,R.VERTELNEY)	◆ LUTHER VANDROSS (C) (T) (V) LV 74996/EPIC
98	100	92	3	WORLD (THE PRICE OF LOVE) S.HAGUE,NEW ORDER (G.GILBERT,P.HOOK,S.MORRIS,B.SUMNER)	◆ NEW ORDER (C) (M) (T) (X) QWEST 40966/WARNER BROS.
99	96	97	17	ABC-123 G.LEVERT,E.NICHOLAS (G.LEVERT,E.NICHOLAS,T.SCOTT)	◆ LEVERT (C) (D) (V) ATLANTIC 87366
100	93	91	8	THAT'S WHAT LITTLE GIRLS ARE MADE OF C.ELLIOTT (C.ELLIOTT,M.ELLIOTT)	◆ RAVEN-SYMONE (C) (T) MCA 54625

◯ Records with the greatest airplay and sales gains this week. ◆Videoclip availability. ● Recording Industry Assn. Of America (RIAA) certification for sales of 500,000 units. ▲ RIAA certification for sales of 1 million units, with additional million indicated by a numeral following the symbol. Catalog number is for cassette single. *Asterisk indicates catalog number is for cassette maxi-single; regular cassette single unavailable. (C) Cassette single availability. (D) CD single availability. (M) Cassette maxi-single availability. (T) Vinyl maxi-single availability. (V) Vinyl single availability. (X) CD maxi-single availability. © 1993, Billboard/BPI Communications.

FIGURE 20-5 *Excerpt from* Billboard*'s Hot 100 chart. (© 1993 by Billboard Publications Inc. Compiled by Billboard Research Department and reprinted with permission.)*

Because of the delayed nature of feedback in the industry, letters and calls generally have little impact. By the time the viewer protests get to the network, the show has long been canceled and the cast has scattered to other jobs. There are times, however, when audience reaction can influence network behavior. Viewers for Quality Television, a citizens' group that tries to keep worthwhile TV shows on the air, was instrumental in CBS's decision to renew such programs as *Cagney and Lacey* and *Designing Women*.

At the local level, many television stations set aside segments of the newscast for reading viewer letters over the air. Other stations may have a call-in program entitled something like *Let Me Speak to the Manager* in which audience members are encouraged to express their views. Certain cable television systems have set aside one or two channels, called public-access channels, whereby viewers can appear on television, usually either free or at a nominal cost, and state their opinions on a topic of their choice. There are limitations, however, on these forms of audience-generated feedback. Since stations have a limited time set aside for reading viewer letters, only a few can be presented over the air. Not all stations have programs where viewers are encouraged to call. Relatively few cable systems have access channels, and in those systems that do, few people seem to understand their purpose and fewer still watch the channels. Consequently, at the local level, feedback opportunities in television are somewhat limited. Television broadcasters, however, generally pay very close attention to the feedback they do receive and tend to treat it seriously.

Since television stations are licensed by the FCC, they are also subject to audience-filed petitions to deny renewal or transfer of a license. Stations faced with petitions to deny have accumulated substantial expenses in responding to this extreme form of negative feedback; sometimes these expenses total more than $100,000. Similar to the situation in radio, the emphasis on broadcasting deregulation has made it more difficult for groups to effectively pursue petitions to deny.

Measuring TV Viewing

This section will first examine how the ratings for network TV shows are compiled and then examine how ratings are gathered for local stations.

Network Ratings. The A.C. Nielsen Company, the biggest market research company in the world, provides the networks with audience data through its Nielsen Television Index (NTI). To compile these ratings, Nielsen uses a device called a Peoplemeter, introduced in the late 1980s. The Peoplemeter consists of a "people monitor," an apparatus about the size of a clock radio that sits on top of a TV set and a hand-held device that resembles a TV remote control unit. Demographic data are gathered from each household member and then each is assigned a number. While they are watching TV, each family member is supposed to periodically punch in his or her number on the hand-held device to indicate viewing. These data are stored in the monitor until they are downloaded into Nielsen's computers. Peoplemeters can be used to tabulate all viewing: network, syndicated shows, and cable and can even tabulate VCR playbacks. There are 4000 households in the Nielsen Peoplemeter sample and usable data are obtained from more than 90 percent of the meters. The sample is replaced every two years. The Peoplemeter service is not cheap. Networks pay millions of dollars annually for the service.

Reaction to the Peoplemeter has not been all positive. The ratings for network shows took a curious drop in the first quarter of 1990, which cost the networks a significant sum in advertising revenue. Many industry executives blamed the drop on the introduction of the Peoplemeters. In addition, children's viewing levels have plummeted. Most agree that young people are not reliable users of the Peoplemeter.

A happy Nielsen family using the Peoplemeter. (Courtesy Nielsen Media Research)

A-4

Nielsen NATIONAL TV AUDIENCE ESTIMATES

EVE. TUE. NOV. 17, 1992

TIME	7:00	7:15	7:30	7:45	8:00	8:15	8:30	8:45	9:00	9:15	9:30	9:45	10:00	10:15	10:30	10:45
HUT	59.1	60.9	61.6	62.9	64.4	65.7	65.8	66.5	66.9	67.5	66.1	65.4	60.6	59.0	57.5	54.2

ABC TV

Metric	7:00	7:15	7:30	7:45	8:00	8:15	8:30	8:45	9:00	9:15	9:30	9:45	10:00	10:15	10:30	10:45
Program					FULL HOUSE		HANGIN WITH MR. COOPER		ROSEANNE		COACH (PAE)		GOING TO EXTREMES →			
HHLD AUDIENCE% & (000)					16.7	15,550	15.5	14,430	22.4	20,850	19.3	17,970	9.0	8,380		8.3*
T4%. AVG. AUD. 1/2 HR %					19.5		17.8		25.6		21.7		13.7	9.6*		
SHARE AUDIENCE %					26		23		33		29		15	16*		15*
AVG. AUD. BY 1/4 HR %					15.9	17.5	14.9	16.1	21.5	23.2	19.4	19.1	10.4	8.8	8.5	8.1

CBS TV

Metric	7:00	7:15	7:30	7:45	8:00	8:15	8:30	8:45	9:00	9:15	9:30	9:45	10:00	10:15	10:30	10:45
Program					RESCUE: 911 →				CBS TUESDAY MOVIE — OVERKILL →							
HHLD AUDIENCE% & (000)					15.2	14,150	15.9*		15.4	14,340	14.8*		16.5*		16.7*	
T4%. AVG. AUD. 1/2 HR %					20.8				23.4							
SHARE AUDIENCE %					23		24		25		21*		27*		30*	
AVG. AUD. BY 1/4 HR %					14.0	14.9	16.0	15.7	13.9	13.7	15.2	14.5	16.5	16.6	17.1	16.2

NBC TV

Metric	7:00	7:15	7:30	7:45	8:00	8:15	8:30	8:45	9:00	9:15	9:30	9:45	10:00	10:15	10:30	10:45
Program					QUANTUM LEAP-TUE →				REASONABLE DOUBTS →				DATELINE NBC →			
HHLD AUDIENCE% & (000)					8.9	8,290	8.8*		8.1	7,540	7.9*		11.6	10,800	11.7*	
T4%. AVG. AUD. 1/2 HR %					12.9		9.1*		10.5		8.2*		17.6	11.6*		
SHARE AUDIENCE %					14		13*		12		12*		20	19*		21*
AVG. AUD. BY 1/4 HR %					9.0	8.6	9.1	9.0	7.8	7.9	8.1	8.3	11.5	11.9	12.0	11.2

FOX TV

Metric	7:00	7:15	7:30	7:45	8:00	8:15	8:30	8:45	9:00	9:15	9:30	9:45	10:00	10:15	10:30	10:45
HHLD AUDIENCE% & (000)																
T4%. AVG. AUD. 1/2 HR %																
SHARE AUDIENCE %																
AVG. AUD. BY 1/4 HR %																

INDEPENDENTS (INCLUDING SUPERSTATIONS EXCEPT TBS)

Metric	7:15	7:30	8:00	8:15	8:30	9:00	9:15	9:30	9:45	10:00	10:30
AVERAGE AUDIENCE	15.4 (+F)	15.5 (+F)	12.1 (+F)	12.1 (+F)	12.1 (+F)	11.6 (+F)	11.6 (+F)	11.9 (+F)	11.9 (+F)	11.4 (+F)	9.9 (+F)
SHARE AUDIENCE %	26	25	19	19	18	17	17	18	18	19	18

PBS

Metric	7:15	7:30	8:00	8:15	8:30	9:00	9:15	9:30	9:45	10:00	10:15	10:30
AVERAGE AUDIENCE	2.0	2.3	3.4	3.4	3.8	3.2	3.2	3.5	2.6	2.2	2.7	2.3
SHARE AUDIENCE %	3	4	5	5	6	5	5	5	4	4	4	4

CABLE ORIG. (INCLUDING TBS)

Metric	7:15	7:30	8:00	8:30	9:00	9:30	10:00	10:30
AVERAGE AUDIENCE	11.2 (+F)	13.1 (+F)	13.4 (+F)	13.9 (+F)	12.9 (+F)	12.9 (+F)	12.6 (+F)	10.4 (+F)
SHARE AUDIENCE %	19	21	21	21	19	20	21	19

PAY SERVICES

Metric	7:15	7:30	8:00	8:15	8:30	9:30	10:00	10:30
AVERAGE AUDIENCE	1.7	1.7	3.4	3.5	3.6	2.6	2.7	2.9
SHARE AUDIENCE %	3	3	5	5	5	4	4	5

U.S. TV Households: 93,100,000

For explanation of symbols. See page B.

FIGURE 20-6 *Excerpt from Nielsen's NTI report. (The Pocketpiece, Nielsen Television Index, National TV Ratings. Copyright © Nielsen Media Research. Used by permission.)*

Faced with these problems, the networks have asked for a new system that relies both on Peoplemeters and diaries to collect data.

Potential competitors have also noted the dissatisfaction with the current system. Arbitron has announced it will compete with Nielsen, using a new system called ScanAmerica. Under this arrangement, a sample of about 5000 families will be measured using Arbitron's version of the Peoplemeter. Additionally, these families will also use a scanning wand to electronically record the Universal Product Code on their supermarket, drugstore, and department store purchases. Subscribers to Arbitron's service will be given viewing data and product consumption information, a combination that advertisers would find most attractive. Arbitron started a preliminary version of this system in 1992.

Nielsen is also looking at improvements. The most ambitious plan uses a passive meter and remote image recognition. Families agreeing to participate in this arrangement will be photographed and their facial features stored digitally in a black box atop the TV. At prearranged intervals, a tiny camera located in the black box takes a picture of a 120-degree arc in front of the TV and matches the faces of anyone watching the set with the faces stored in its memory. The greatest problem with this system is whether families will permit themselves to be scanned by this device or whether they will look upon it as an invasion of privacy.

Local-Market TV Ratings. Ratings of local-market TV stations still depend on the diary and passive household meter. Nielsen had planned to install Peoplemeters in local markets but dropped the plan in 1990 when local stations balked at paying the price tag for installation.

Nielsen and Arbitron provide local-market viewing reports. Arbitron surveys more than 210 local television markets every year, while Nielsen surveys around 220. Both companies use the diary technique to collect viewing data, and both use essentially the same procedures in selecting sample households. In simplified form, the method used by both companies is this. A computer selects phone numbers at random from a listing of all telephone directories in the area. The households selected into the sample are then contacted by letter and by telephone and are asked to keep a diary record of their television viewing.

Households that agree to participate receive one diary for every working TV set in the household. The diary provides a space for entering the viewing of the head of the household as well as any other family members or visitors who happen to be watching television. Participants are asked to record their viewing every quarter-hour. In addition, the respondents are asked to record the sex and age of all those who are watching. At the back of the diary are questions concerning family size, the city where the household is located, and whether the family subscribes to a cable television system. Diaries are kept for seven days, after which they are returned to the ratings company. Both Arbitron and Nielsen report that they are able to use approximately 50–55 percent of the diaries that they send out.

Once the diaries are received, they are checked for accuracy, and diaries from households with more than one set are edited in order to provide an estimate of unduplicated viewing for a household. The handwritten information in the diaries is then keystroked into a form that can be processed by computers. In a few weeks the data are tabulated, and the ratings books, as they are called, are ready to be mailed to subscribing organizations.

In more than twenty large markets, including New York, Los Angeles, and Chicago, both Nielsen and Arbitron maintain a separate sample of households that are hooked up to passive meters which measure when the set is on and to what channel it is tuned. Viewing information from this sample is compiled overnight and sent to subscribers early the next morning. These local meter data are augmented by information from diaries.

Currently, a weak advertising market has many stations that once subscribed to both Arbitron and Nielsen dropping one firm to save money. Most of the time Arbitron has been the one dropped. As a result, Arbitron is looking for ways to cut costs and has suggested cutting back on the number of reports it issues. On another front, local TV stations are studying replacing the household diary with a personal diary that would be sent to all members of a household. The new diary would provide measurement of out-of-home viewing and furnish more detailed demographic data for advertisers.

Television Ratings

Television viewing data are reported for TV in essentially the same way as they are for radio except that the unit of analysis is now expressed in terms of households (or people) viewing TV rather than listening to radio. To illustrate, the following formula is used to calculate the **rating** for a TV program in a local market:

$$\text{Rating} = \frac{\text{number of households watching a program}}{\text{number of TV HH}},$$

where TV HH equals the number of households in a given market equipped with television.

Similarly, the **share of the audience** is found by using the following formula:

$$\text{Share of Audience} = \frac{\text{number of households watching a program}}{\text{number of HUT}},$$

where HUT equals the number of households using (watching) television at a particular time.

The information reported in the Nielsen and Arbitron ratings books is essentially similar. Figure 20-7, page 502, reproduces a sample page from a local Nielsen ratings book. As can be seen, Nielsen reports shares, ratings, and an estimate of the number of people in the audience in various demographic categories for different areas in the market.

Four times every year (February, May, July, and November), both Arbitron and Nielsen conduct a "sweep" period during which every local television market in the entire country is measured. Local stations rely on these ratings to set their advertising rates. Naturally enough, affiliated stations, anxious for the highest ratings possible, pressure the networks for special programming that will attract large audiences. All three networks generally go along with the affiliates' desires. As a result, blockbuster movies and specials are scheduled in competing time slots, leaving many viewers to wonder why all the good programs on TV always come at once.

Determining the Accuracy of Ratings

Because the numbers in the rating books are the basis for spending vast amounts of money, it is important that they be as accurate and reliable as possible. The organization that is responsible for ratings precision is the Electronic Media Ratings Council (EMRC). During the early 1960s, in the wake of the quiz show and payola scandals, Congress took a close look at the broadcasting industry. In response to one congressional committee's criticism of audience-measurement techniques, advertising and broadcasting leaders founded the EMRC. (It was originally called the Broadcast Ratings Council.) The task of the EMRC is basically threefold. It monitors, audits, and accredits broadcast measurement services. The council monitors performance of ratings companies by making sure that reported results meet the minimum standards of performance set up by the EMRC. Audits are performed on a continuing basis. During an audit, the EMRC checks the sample design, data processing, and computer programs and even double-checks the calculations of some ratings to ensure accuracy.

LOS ANGELES, CA

THURSDAY 6:30PM - 8:30PM

WK1 9/26-10/02 WK2 10/03-10/09 WK3 10/10-10/16 WK4 10/17-10/23

METRO HH RTG (1)	METRO HH SHR (2)	STATION	PROGRAM	DMA HOUSEHOLD RATINGS WEEKS 1 (3)	WEEKS 2 (4)	WEEKS 3 (5)	WEEKS 4 (6)	MULTI-WEEK AVG RTG (7)	MULTI-WEEK AVG SHR (8)	SHARE TREND MAY '91 (11)	SHARE TREND FEB '91 (12)	SHARE TREND OCT '90 (13)
1 LT			R.S.E. THRESHOLDS 25+% (1 S.E.) 4 WK AVG 50+%	2 LT	2 LT	2 LT	2 LT	1 LT				
		6:30PM										
6	11	KABC	ABC-WORLD NWS	8	5	6	5	6	11	13X	13	9
4	7	KCAL	IT'S A LIVING	5	4	3	3	4	7	10	8	8
9	17	KCBS	AVG. ALL WKS	6	4	11	18	10	18	10	10	13
4	8		CBS EVE NWS	6	4			5	10			
15	26		NTL CHAMP GME			11	18	14	25			
1	2	KCET	MACNEIL&LEHRER	1	1	2	2	1	2	2X	3	3
6	11	KCOP	AVG. ALL WKS	7	5	5	5	5	10	11	13	9
7	12		STAR TK-GENRTN	7				7	12			
5	10		NIGHT COURT		5	5	5	5	9			
<<		KDOC	HOGANS HEROES	<<	1	<<	<<	<<		1X	1	
3	5	KMEX	NOTICRO UNIVSN	2	2	2	2	2	4	5X	5	5
6	11	KNBC	NBC NITELY NWS	6	6	6	7	6	11	11X	12	12
6	12	KTLA	HUNTER	8	4	6	6	6	11	13X	15	17
7	13	KTTV	STUDS	5	8	8	7	7	13	8	7	7
1	3	KVEA	NOTC TEL CNN	1	2	1	1	1	2	3X	2	2
<<		KWHY	SPANISH PRGMMN	<<	1	<<	<<	<<		1X	1	3
54			HUT/PUT/TOTALS*	55	48	54	60	54		53	62	54
		7:00PM										
6	10	KABC	INSIDE EDITION	8	5	6	6	6	10	13X	11	11
3	6	KCAL	LOVE CONNECTN	3	3	4	5	4	7	10X	11	10
12	22	KCBS	AVG. ALL WKS	8	9	12	18	12	21	15	16	16
8	15		WHEEL-FORTNE	8	9			9	16			
16	28		NTL CHAMP GME			12	18	15	26			
2	3	KCET	MACNEIL&LEHRER	1	1	2	2	2	3	2X	3	3
5	9	KCOP	AVG. ALL WKS	5	5	5	5	5	8	10	13	11
5	9		COSBY SHOW	5				5	9			
5	9		STAR TK-GENRTN		5	5	5	5	8			
<<		KDOC	7 O'CLOCK MOV	<<	<<	<<	<<	<<				
3	5	KMEX	ALCNZR-ESTRLLA	3	2	3	4	3	5	5	5	5
8	14	KNBC	ENT TONIGHT 30	8	8	7	8	8	14	12X	14	13
4	8	KTLA	NOW IT-BE TOLD	4	4	5	4	4	7	9	10	10
11	20	KTTV	MARRIED-CHLDRN	14	10	10	9	11	19	9	7	5
1	2	KVEA	MANUELA	1	1	1	1	1	2	2	1	2
<<		KWHY	SPANISH PRGMMN	<<	<<	<<	<<	<<		1X	1	2
56			HUT/PUT/TOTALS*	57	51	57	62	57		56	64	57
		7:30PM										

STATION	PROGRAM	PERSONS 2+ (15)	PERSONS 18+ (16)	PERSONS 12-24 (17)	PERSONS 12-34 (18)	PERSONS 18-34 (19)	PERSONS 18-49 (20)	PERSONS 21-49 (21)	PERSONS 25-54 (22)	PERSONS 35+ (23)	PERSONS 35-64 (24)	PERSONS 50+ (25)	WOMEN 18+ (26)	WOMEN 12-24 (27)	WOMEN 18-34 (28)	WOMEN 18-49 (29)	WOMEN 25-49 (31)	WOMEN 25-54 (32)	WOMEN WKG (34)	MEN 18+ (35)	MEN 18-34 (36)	MEN 18-49 (37)	MEN 21-49 (38)	MEN 25-49 (39)	MEN 25-54 (40)	TNS 12-17 (41)	CHILD 2-11 (42)	CHILD 6-11 (43)
	R.S.E. THRESHOLDS 25+% (1 S.E.) 4 WK AVG 50+%	1 LT	1 LT	2 1	1 LT	1 LT	1 LT	1 LT	1 LT	1 LT	1 LT	1 LT	1 LT	4 1	2 1	1 LT	2 LT	1 LT	2 LT	1 LT	3 1	1 LT	2 LT	2 LT	2 LT	5 1	4 1	5 1
6:30PM																												
KABC	ABC-WORLD NWS	3	4	1	2	3	3	3	3	5	4	7	5	1	4	3	4	4	4	3	2	2	2	3	3		1	1
KCAL	IT'S A LIVING	2	2	1	1	1	1	1	1	3	3	4	3	1	1	1	2	2	2	1	1	1	1	1	1	1	2	2
KCBS	AVG. ALL WKS	5	6	3	4	4	4	4	5	8	6	11	5	2	3	3	4	4	4	7	6	6	6	6	6	3	2	3
	CBS EVE NWS	3	3			1	1	1	2	5	3	8	4			2	2	2	4	3	1	1	1	1	2		1	2
	NTL CHAMP GME	8	9	6	8	8	8	8	8	10	9	13	6	4	5	5	5	5	5	12	10	10	11	11	11	6	2	4
KCET	MACNEIL&LEHRER	1	1							1	1	2	1						1	1								
KCOP	AVG. ALL WKS	3	3	3	3	3	3	3	3	3	3	2	3	3	3	3	3	3	2	2	2	3	3	3	3	6	4	4
	STAR TK-GENRTN	3	4	4	5	4	4	4	4	3	3	2	2	2	2	2	2	2	2	5	6	6	7	7	6	6	2	
	NIGHT COURT	3	2	3	3	2	2	3	2	3	2	2	3	3	3	3	4	3	3	2	1	1	2	2	2	5	5	5
KDOC	HOGANS HEROES																											
KMEX	NOTICRO UNIVSN	2	2	2	3	3	2	3	2	2	2	2	2	2	2	2	2	2	2	2	3	3	3	3	2	1	2	1
KNBC	NBC NITELY NWS	3	4	1	1	1	2	2	3	5	4	7	4		1	2	2	3	3	4	2	3	3	3	3	1		
KTLA	HUNTER	3	3	1	2	2	2	3	3	4	3	6	4	1	2	3	3	3	3	3	2	2	2	3	3	2	1	1
KTTV	STUDS	5	4	10	8	7	5	5	4	2	2	1	5	15	8	6	4	4	5	4	6	5	4	4	4	10	3	4
KVEA	NOTC TEL CNN	1	1	2	2	2	1	1	1	1	1		1	2	2	1	1	1	1	1	2	1	1	1	1	1	1	1
KWHY	SPANISH PRGMMN													1													1	1
	HUT/PUT/TOTALS*	36	39	29	31	32	32	33	34	44	38	55	40	32	32	33	33	34	35	38	32	32	33	33	34	31	24	24
7:00PM																												
KABC	INSIDE EDITION	3	4	1	2	2	3	3	3	5	4	7	5	2	3	3	3	4	3	3	1	2	2	2	2	1	2	2
KCAL	LOVE CONNECTN	2	2	1	2	2	2	2	2	2	2	3	3	1	3	2	2	3	3	2	1	1	1	2	2	1	1	1
KCBS	AVG. ALL WKS	7	8	3	4	5	5	6	6	10	8	15	7	2	4	4	5	5	5	9	6	7	7	7	7	3	2	3
	WHEEL-FORTNE	4	6	1	1	2	2	2	3	9	5	14	7	1	3	3	4	4	5	4	1	1	1	2	2	1		
	NTL CHAMP GME	9	11	5	7	8	9	9	9	12	10	15	7	2	6	5	6	6	6	14	10	12	12	13	13	5	4	5
KCET	MACNEIL&LEHRER	1	1						1	1	1	2	1				1	1	1	1								
KCOP	AVG. ALL WKS	3	3	3	4	4	3	4	3	3	3	2	3	3	3	3	4	3	4	3	4	4	4	4	4	4	2	3
	COSBY SHOW	3	3	3	3	2	3	3	3	3	4	2	3	3	3	4	4	4	4	2	2	3	2	3	3	4	4	
	STAR TK-GENRTN	3	3	3	4	4	4	4	4	2	2	2	3	3	4	3	3	3	4	3	5	4	4	4	4	4	2	1
KDOC	7 O'CLOCK MOV																											
KMEX	ALCNZR-ESTRLLA	3	3	5	4	4	3	3	3	1	2	1	3	6	5	4	3	3	2	2	4	3	3	2	2	4	3	2
KNBC	ENT TONIGHT 30	4	5	2	3	4	4	5	5	6	6	7	6	3	5	5	5	6	6	4	3	4	4	4	5	2	1	1
KTLA	NOW IT-BE TOLD	2	3	1	2	2	2	3	3	3	3	3	3	1	2	3	3	3	3	2	2	2	2	2	2	1	1	2
KTTV	MARRIED-CHLDRN	7	6	13	10	8	7	6	6	4	4	3	6	14	9	8	6	6	6	5	8	6	6	6	6	16	9	11
KVEA	MANUELA	1	1	1	1	1	1	1	1	1	1	1	1	1	1	1	1	1	1	1	1	1	1	1	1		1	1
KWHY	SPANISH PRGMMN					1															1		1	1			1	
	HUT/PUT/TOTALS*	39	41	34	37	37	36	37	38	44	40	53	43	37	38	38	38	39	39	40	35	35	36	37	38	36	31	34
7:30PM																												

FIGURE 20-7 *Sample of a Nielsen TV ratings book.* (Nielsen Ratings—Television. *Copyright © Nielsen Ratings Company. Reprinted by permission.)*

If the ratings company passes the audit, it is accredited and is allowed to display the EMRC's seal of approval on its ratings reports.

Despite the EMRC's work, broadcast ratings are still subject to widespread criticism. One common complaint, voiced by many who evidently do not understand the statistical theory that underlies sampling, is directed at Nielsen's national survey. How can a sample of only 4000 homes, these critics ask, accurately reflect the viewing of 90 million television households? In actuality, this sample size will generate tolerably accurate results within a specified margin of error (see boxed material, pages 504–505). Other criticisms, however, deserve closer attention.

First, it is possible that the type of person who agrees to participate may have viewing habits different from those of the viewer who declines to participate. Second, in the case of both Arbitron and Nielsen reports (based on about 55 percent of the diaries sent out), it is possible that "returners" behave differently from "nonreturners." Third, people who know that their viewing is being measured may change· their behavior. A family might watch more news and public-affairs programs than usual in order to appear sophisticated in the eyes of the rating company. Fourth, both ratings companies admit that they have a problem measuring the viewing of certain groups. Minorities, particularly blacks and Hispanics, may be underrepresented in the ratings companies' samples. Lastly, the stations that are being measured can distort the measurement process by engaging in contests and special promotions or by running unusual or sensational programs in an attempt to "hype" the ratings. This activity is frowned on by the ratings companies, which usually append a warning label to their ratings books that identifies any unusual promotional activity during the ratings period. The distinction between hype and legitimate programming, however, is somewhat fuzzy. Clearly, the ratings aren't perfect. Nonetheless, despite all their flaws, they present useful information at an affordable price to advertisers and to the television industry. As long as the United States has a commercial broadcasting system, some form of the ratings will always be around.

Questionnaires, Concept Testing, and Pilot Testing

In addition to ratings, there are still other forms of media-originated feedback in the TV industry. The TV networks gather three special types of feedback from the audience to help them predict what television shows will be popular with viewers. The first kind of research consists of questionnaires that attempt to measure audience tastes, opinions, and beliefs. Perhaps as many as 100,000 people per year are questioned in person or over the phone as the networks try to identify what situations and topics might be acceptable for programs.

A second form is called **concept testing**. In concept testing, a one- or two-paragraph description of an idea for a new series is presented to a sample of viewers. who are asked for their reactions. Here's a hypothetical example.

First Down

Sandi and Marcia are two young women enrolled in law school at Southern Methodist University in Dallas, Texas. During the fall season, they must juggle their studies with their jobs as cheerleaders for the Dallas Cowboys. Sometimes this is tough—such as the time Sandi's law books were accidentally locked up in the football team's locker room and she tried to retrieve them at the same time the team came in from practice. Or the time when Marcia was asked to represent the team's star player in tough contract negotiations with the team's owner.

Would you:

_____ definitely watch this series
_____ don't know if I'd watch or not
_____ definitely not watch this series

Many people find it hard to believe that a sample of approximately 4000 homes can adequately represent the viewing of 90 million households. How can a sample that includes only 0.0044 percent of all homes be accurate? Some people might concede that a sample of 4000 from a city of 50,000 might be adequate but surely not for a population of 90 million. This line of reasoning seems to make intuitive sense, but it's off base.

To illustrate why, we'll have to make a brief excursion into what statisticians call "sampling theory." First, two definitions. A **population** is the whole collection of households or persons or whatever it is we're interested in. Thus for the A. C. Nielsen Company, the 90 million U.S. homes with TV sets constitute the population. A **sample** is a segment of the population that is taken to represent the population. Nielsen's 4000 randomly selected households would constitute a sample. Now for an example. Pretend that we had a big urn (a statistician's favorite piece of furniture) filled with 10,000 Ping-Pong balls (the population). Pretend further that 3000 of the Ping-Pong balls (30 percent) were red and 7000 were white. Now let's select 100 Ping-Pong balls at random from the urn (the sample). Clearly, it would be a rare event if we were to draw 100 red Ping-Pong balls (such an outcome is possible but highly, highly unlikely). Similarly it would be unlikely that all 100 would turn out to be white. Moreover, we would not expect our sample to contain *exactly* the same percentage of red and white Ping-Pong balls as the population, that is, 30 red and 70 white. The odds are that we would get a result fairly close to 30 percent, the actual population figure, but we would probably be off by a little bit. As a matter of fact, if we used statistical formulas of probability we could calculate that the odds would be 20 to 1 that the percentage of red Ping-Pong balls in our sample would be somewhere between 21 and 39 percent, a spread of 18 percentage points.

Now let's take a *really* big urn and fill it with 10 million Ping-Pong balls, 30 percent of which are red and 70 percent of which are white, and

draw another sample of 100. Again, we would not expect to get 100 red or 100 white in our sample. Nor would we expect to get exactly 30 red and 70 white. Using the same statistical formulas of probability that we used in the above sample, we would find that the odds would still be 20 to 1 that we would draw somewhere between 21 and 39 percent red Ping-Pong balls— a spread of 18 percentage points and exactly the same as our previous example. The size of the population has nothing to do with the precision (the spread of percentage points) of our results. Assuming that the red–white split stays the same, it's irrelevant if the urn contains 10,000 or 10 million or 90 million Ping-Pong balls.

What does have an impact on precision? The size of the *sample*. If we took a sample of 400 Ping-Pong balls, the odds would be 20 to 1 that we would get somewhere between 25.5 and 34.5 percent red, a spread of 9 percentage points. If we sampled 1600, the odds would be 20 to 1 that we would get between approximately 27.7 and 32.3 percent red, a spread of only $4\frac{1}{2}$ percentage points. The larger the sample, the smaller the spread (statisticians call this spread **sampling error**). To reiterate, it is the sample size, not the population size, that will determine sampling error. Thus a sample of 4000 randomly chosen from the population of Los Angeles will have the same degree of sampling error as a sample of 4000 drawn randomly from the population of the entire world. (The problem, of course, is that the time, energy, and cost of drawing a random sample would increase as the population increases.)

Now let's replace Ping-Pong balls with households. The red Ping-Pong balls become homes watching a particular show and the white Ping-Pong balls turn into homes that are not viewing. Using Nielsen's sample size of 4000 and assuming that for a single week 30 percent of the homes in the sample are viewing (the red Ping-Pong balls), we find that the odds are 20 to 1 that the true value in the population lies between 28.6 and 31.4 percent, a spread of 2.8 points. (A note of caution here. This example is based on a single week's viewing. In actuality, Nielsen may average viewing reports for more than one week—a procedure that reduces the spread or sampling error.) By sampling more people, it would be possible for Nielsen to report more precise results. But increased sample size means increased costs, which would make the ratings more expensive. Consequently, the ad agencies, networks, and production companies that buy the ratings books have settled for this sample size as one that strikes an acceptable balance between precision and cost.

Finally, if after reading this section you are still not convinced of the validity of sampling theory, then make sure you inform your doctor of this fact the next time you go for a blood test.

Show ideas that do well in concept testing have an increased chance of getting on the air.

The third form is **pilot testing**. (A pilot is the first show of a proposed series.) Pilot testing consists of placing a group of viewers in a special test theater and showing them an entire program. The audience usually sits in chairs equipped with dials or buttons that are used to indicate the degree to which audience members like or dislike what is shown. For example, the audience might be told to press a green button when they see something on screen that they like and a red button when they see something they dislike. Networks sometimes do pilot testing themselves or hire private firms to do it for them.

The networks currently favor testing pilots on cable TV systems since that is the closest thing to real TV viewing. In a cable test, several hundred cable subscribers in a certain community are telephoned and are asked to participate in the test. They watch the show on an unused channel of their cable system and then respond by telephone to a questionnaire that asks them about plot, character, relationship, etc. In addition, a company called Marketing Evaluations conducts surveys of program and performer popularity. Viewers in a national panel are asked if they are familiar with a certain program or performer and if that program or performer is one of their favorites. The "TvQ score" is the percentage of people familiar with a show or star who indicate that the star or program is one of their favorites. TvQ data have been

International Perspective: Looking at Viewers in France

As mentioned in the text, Nielsen and Arbitron are at work on a passive meter that will measure television viewing by using an electronic device to scan the area in front of the set and "recognize" the viewers who are out there. The French are way ahead of their American counterparts. Telemetric, a French equivalent to Nielsen, installed its first passive meter, the Motivac, in 1991. Motivac uses a photo sensor to identify those who are watching TV. The camera changes the image into electrical signals and compares them to data stored in its memory. Motivac is programmed to know when a particular viewer is usually home, where he/she normally sits, and what he/she looks like.

One of the advantages of Motivac is that it allows a second-by-second count of the viewing audience. Using this ability, Motivac has confirmed what many have long suspected—viewers, at least in prime time, leave the room in droves when commercials come on. In one show, viewership dropped from 9 million to 3.5 million during the commercial break available since the 1950s and have been influential in many programming decisions. Shows such as *All in the Family*, *ChiPs*, and *Hill Street Blues* were saved from early cancellation in part because they had high TvQ scores.

Film Industry Audience Responses

Audience-generated feedback in the film industry is virtually nonexistent. Motion picture stars do receive fan mail, but people seldom send letters to a director or to a film studio. Feedback that does occur is primarily aimed at local theater owners, and it is questionable whether this information ever gets back to the producer or distributor. Although it is true that film critics provide some qualitative feedback, their opinions are typically less important than box-office figures. As with the sound-recording industry, the critical form of feedback is economic: the amount of money taken in at the box office.

Compiling Box-Office Receipts

Media-originated feedback in the movie industry revolves around the box-office figures compiled and reported in the trade publication *Variety*. Each week, *Variety* reports the top-grossing films across the United States. An example of this listing is reproduced in Figure 20-8.

To compile these data, *Variety*, in cooperation with Entertainment Data Incorporated, surveys approximately 1600 theaters located in about twenty major urban areas across the country. The theaters in this sample usually account for about one-fourth of the total box-office gross in the United States. Most of the column headings in *Variety*'s chart are self-explanatory. Each film's title is listed, followed by the company that is handling distribution. Box-office gross for the listed week and for the previous week are then reported and given a rank ordering. The next four columns show the number and type of theaters showing the film for the listed week and the average revenue per screen. The weeks-on-chart column is followed by the total earnings of the film to date in *Variety*'s sample cities. In order to estimate the film's total earnings in all markets, *Variety* suggests multiplying this column by three or by four. (It varies, depending on the particular release pattern and the appeal of a film. Some movies will die in small towns and do well in urban areas, while a film like *Smokey and the Bandit* will bomb at New York's Radio City Music Hall and yet wind up as Universal Picture's number-seven all-time moneymaker.) Note that this chart reports only a film's gross earnings; it does not show how much, if any, profit a film has made.

The economic feedback contained in *Variety* is extremely important in the movie industry. One or two blockbuster films can improve the financial position of an entire company. Directors who turn out a moneymaker are usually assured of more films to direct (usually with a larger production budget). In addition, a film successful at the box office is apt to inspire one or more sequels and several imitators.

Market Research

Audience research has become more influential in the movie business because of the tremendous cost of motion pictures. In an effort to cut down on financial disasters, many motion picture studios turned toward market research. At most studios the first step is concept testing to find promising plot lines. The next step is an analysis of the script.

One organization, the Emotional Response Index System Company (ERIS), claims that it can forecast whether a movie will be successful before it is even completed. ERIS analyzes a film's shooting script to see if it contains key appeals that audiences usually look for in movies. Based on a sampling of thousands of people, ERIS has concluded that audiences look primarily for the qualities of money, affection, status,

DOMESTIC BOX OFFICE

TITLE/DISTRIB	Reported B.O. Per: 9/10-9/12 (weekend)	Reported B.O. Per: 9/10-9/16 (full week)	Number Theaters This wk	Number Theaters Last wk	Week's Avg $ Per Theater	$ Pct Change	Cumulative Reported B.O.	No. Weeks Release
The Fugitive (WB)	$8,316,440	$10,931,559	2374	2425	$4,605	—45%	$147,152,018	6
Undercover Blues (MGM)	4,379,488	5,577,324	1596	—	3,495	—	5,577,324	1
True Romance (WB)	4,023,420	5,557,178	1254	—	4,432	—	5,557,178	1
The Man Without a Face (WB)	2,922,725	3,920,569	1290	1065	3,039	—41%	17,184,117	4
Real McCoy (WB)	2,705,425	3,639,965	1670	—	2,180	—	3,639,965	1
Jurassic Park (U)	2,104,400	2,793,685	1295	1420	2,157	—41%	320,033,890	14
Hard Target (U)	1,944,650	2,568,890	1691	1967	1,519	—51%	28,150,440	4
In the Line of Fire (Col)	1,611,515	1,938,341	1127	1274	1,720	—48%	100,340,050	10
Sleepless in Seattle (TriStar)	1,579,824	2,071,081	1219	1278	1,699	—38%	115,428,680	12
Needful Things (Col)	1,466,636	1,801,771	1815	1986	993	—61%	13,573,230	3
The Secret Garden (WB)	1,440,497	1,887,223	1194	1332	1,581	—54%	25,797,603	6
Free Willy (WB)	1,249,818	1,550,239	1351	1551	1,147	—54%	69,041,458	9
Rising Sun (20th)	1,228,706	1,692,636	1025	1289	1,651	—51%	58,898,109	7
Fortress (Miramax)	1,196,579	1,588,702	1193	1204	1,332	—66%	6,316,405	2
The Firm (Par)	1,126,548	1,588,831	861	923	1,845	—45%	151,989,625	11
Manhattan Murder Mystery (TriStar)	864,030	1,156,204	347	337	3,332	—51%	8,643,801	4
Rookie of the Year (20th)	773,231	956,187	888	1223	1,077	—46%	50,820,484	10
Robin Hood: Men in Tights (20th)	498,608	653,298	602	801	1,085	—54%	33,216,472	8
Money For Nothing (BV)	491,206	702,996	449	—	1,566	—	702,996	1
Searching for Bobby Fischer (Par)	418,124	571,784	219	219	2,611	—49%	6,150,507	6
Heart and Souls (U)	403,565	524,470	472	907	1,111	—67%	15,279,630	6
Dennis the Menace (WB)	394,818	465,835	568	651	820	—52%	50,721,533	12
The Wedding Banquet (Goldwyn)	375,068	515,856	63	58	8,188	—33%	2,487,730	6
Calendar Girl (Col)	365,123	426,069	1063	1082	401	—79%	2,436,773	2
Son-in-Law (BV)	362,952	487,072	428	481	1,138	—39%	33,614,365	11
Kalifornia (Gramercy)	352,796	546,006	349	359	1,564	—62%	1,980,457	2
Snow White and the Seven Dwarfs (BV)	325,450	418,347	577	727	725	—52%	39,879,205	11
Like Water for Chocolate (Miramax)	301,343	441,187	136	129	3,244	—19%	17,012,564	30
Jason Goes to Hell —The Final Friday (NL)	281,197	354,680	391	494	907	—47%	14,893,604	6
Boxing Helena (BV)	260,456	377,471	153	161	2,467	—61%	1,335,600	2
What's Love Got to Do With It (BV)	233,662	339,934	288	168	1,180	43%	37,842,369	14
Much Ado About Nothing (Goldwyn)	230,714	322,261	130	170	2,479	—40%	20,821,527	19
Aladdin (BV)	223,278	287,980	374	469	770	—51%	216,584,227	43
Cliffhanger (TriStar)	220,224	316,696	248	297	1,277	—30%	82,880,419	16
So I Married an Axe Murderer (TriStar)	211,702	286,296	302	386	948	—42%	11,155,061	7
Hocus Pocus (BV)	197,984	256,791	271	369	948	—52%	35,126,825	8
Joy Luck Club (BV)	159,009	286,274	3	3	95,425	N/A	366,091	2
Father Hood (BV)	157,661	201,089	231	646	871	—81%	3,047,807	3
Only the Strong (20th)	156,651	205,718	136	653	1,513	—78%	2,910,994	3
The Meteor Man (MGM)	131,374	175,915	143	187	1,230	—39%	7,605,779	6
Orlando (SPC)	127,665	189,052	69	70	2,739	—27%	4,607,232	14
Surf Ninjas (New Line)	122,247	150,972	220	426	686	—64%	4,600,147	4
Another Stakeout (BV)	120,208	166,759	177	176	942	—38%	18,920,095	8
King of the Hill (Gramercy Pictures)	99,324	129,907	13	6	9,977	13%	406,567	4
Made in America (WB)	97,013	135,034	320	355	422	—54%	44,942,695	15
The Ballad of Little Jo (Fine Line)	91,129	123,935	36	3	3,443	389%	212,036	4
Menace II Society (New Line)	68,772	89,677	81	75	1,107	—30%	27,139,926	16
Witchboard 2 (Blue Rider Pictures)	65,365	83,350	32	N/A	2,604	N/A	83,350	2
Weekend at Bernie's II (WB)	64,168	83,096	104	129	799	—30%	12,675,471	10
Un Coeur en Hiver (October Films)	54,402	76,960	23	26	3,346	—42%	1,327,616	15
Son of the Pink Panther (MGM)	47,194	66,530	174	983	382	—91%	2,384,626	3
Dave (WB)	35,546	51,982	125	193	416	—53%	63,270,710	19
Carnosaur (Concorde)	32,555	43,224	17	22	2,542	—34%	939,635	15
The Seventh Coin (Hemdale)	31.023	45,145	30	—	1,505	—	45,145	1
Especially on Sunday (Miramax)	29,253	39,491	14	14	2,821	—29%	322,589	5
El Cid (Miramax)	20,127	25,158	10	11	2,516	—30%	200,675	4
Brother's Keeper (Creative Thinking)	17,415	22,847	9	6	2,538	120%	1,311,347	54
Bad Behaviour (October Films)	17,238	26,046	2	2	13,023	—30%	63,297	2
Road Scholar (Samuel Goldwyn)	N/A	43,781	16	12	2,736	—28%	398,896	9

*Estimated by VARIETY **Week is Sept. 10-16. Compiled by EDI and VARIETY

FIGURE 20-8 *Excerpt from* Variety's *report on the fifty top-grossing films. (Reprinted by permission from* Variety.*)*

Silent Night, Deadly Night

Audience-generated feedback sometimes can be very effective in the motion picture industry as demonstrated by the furor surrounding the 1984 Tri-Star movie *Silent Night, Deadly Night*. This picture was about a maniac who disguised himself as Santa Claus and went about carving up his victims. When TV ads for the movie showing a man in a Santa suit swinging an ax at an unlucky victim started appearing around Christmas time, parents across the na-

tion were aghast. The idea of kindly old St. Nick portrayed as a slasher/stalker was evidently too much for them to handle.

When the film opened in New York, picketers stood outside the theater and sang Christmas carols. Tri-Star quickly realized it had overstepped the bounds of propriety and pulled the picture out of distribution less than a week after it opened.

and security in films. If the script appears strong along these dimensions, ERIS claims that it will have a good chance of success.

Once the studio has a rough cut of the finished film, **focus group** sessions are held. A focus group is a small sample (usually about ten to fifteen people) of the target audience, which is asked detailed questions about what they liked or didn't like. With this information, the studio can add or drop a scene, modify the ending, change the musical score, or make other alterations. (The original ending of *Fatal Attraction* was changed because of audience reaction to the rough cut.) Once these changes are completed the move is released for a sneak preview. Audience members fill out preview cards that summarize their reactions to the film, its characters, and its stars. It is possible for the director to make limited changes in the film in response to this feedback, but it is usually too late to make wholesale changes. Consequently, the preview cards are used mainly for fine tuning. Once the movie opens, the studios hire independent research firms to interview members of the audience as they leave the theater. The results of this survey tell the studios if they have a promising or a disappointing film on their hands and allows them to adjust their advertising and marketing plans.

••••

SUGGESTIONS FOR FURTHER READING

Further information about the concepts in this chapter can be found in the books listed below.

BEVILLE, HUGH, *Audience Ratings: Radio, Television, Cable*, Hillsdale, N.J.: Lawrence Erlbaum, 1988.

FLETCHER, ALAN, AND THOMAS BOWERS, *Fundamentals of Advertising Research*, Belmont, Calif.: Wadsworth, 1991.

MEYER, PHILIP, *The Newspaper Survival Book*, Bloomington: Indiana University Press, 1985.

WEBSTER, JAMES, AND LAWRENCE LICHTY, *Ratings Analysis*, Hillsdale, N.J.: Lawrence Erlbaum, 1991.

WIMMER, ROGER, AND JOSEPH DOMINICK, *Mass Media Research: An Introduction*, Belmont, Calif.: Wadsworth, 1991.

THE SOCIAL IMPACT OF MASS COMMUNICATION

EFFECTS OF MASS COMMUNICATION ON KNOWLEDGE AND ATTITUDES

A nyone who watches even a moderate amount of television would probably agree that the world of TV is a fairly violent place. Whereas in the following chapter we will examine the potential link between the portrayal of media violence and aggressive behavior, in this chapter we will concentrate on the impact of mass communication on people's knowledge, perceptions, and attitudes. In particular, we will focus on the extent to which a regular diet of TV mayhem can affect an individual's tolerance of aggression in real-life situations.

To begin, let us look at the results of three studies conducted by a team of psychologists and reported in the Autumn 1975 issue of the *Journal of Communication*. In the first study, forty-four third- and fourth-graders were taken individually by an experimenter to a "new trailer" parked on the school ground. Each child was told that the trailer was used by a kindergarten teacher and his students from a neighboring school and was then given a tour of the trailer's playroom where toys and games were kept. The experimenter made a point of telling each child that the trailer also contained a TV camera that took pictures of the entire room.

After the tour had ended, half of the children were taken to an adjacent gameroom, where they were shown a violent western film. The rest of the children didn't see any film. Next, the experimenter told the child that he (the experimenter) had a problem: He had promised a friend, a kindergarten teacher who was scheduled to work with young children in the trailer playroom, that he would watch the children for his friend over the TV monitor. The experimenter then clicked on the set in the gameroom and showed the child the scene from the empty playroom next door. However, he explained, he had to go to the principal's office for a while and was afraid that the children might arrive while he was gone. The experimenter then asked the child to watch the TV set and keep track of the kindergarten children if they should arrive while he was away. Each child was instructed to come and get the experimenter if the kindergarten children got into any kind of trouble. As he left the room, the adult told the child to begin viewing the monitor.

What the children actually saw on the monitor was a videotape constructed for this experiment. After two minutes, the tape showed an adult and two young children (a boy and a girl) entering the empty room. These two children played quietly for about a minute with a set of building blocks after the adult had left. Then the boy knocked over the structure the girl had built. This act was followed by yelling, pushing, crying, and shoving. Violence between the two escalated until it appeared that the TV camera in the next room had been destroyed. The researchers, of course, were interested in seeing how long the children observing the fight would let it continue before summoning the experimenter. As it turned out, the children who had viewed the violent film waited longer before seeking help than did the children who had seen no film.

A second and a third study were then conducted along the same lines. In the first instance, one group of children watched an aggressive excerpt from a TV detective program, and another group saw an excerpt from an exciting sports event. The results confirmed the findings of the first study: Children who saw the aggressive program were slower to report the alleged fight than were the children who had not been exposed to media violence. The third study was identical to the second, except that older children (fifth-graders) were tested. Like the children in the first two studies, the fifth-graders who had watched the detective program were slower to seek help once the fight began. Although these studies cannot be called conclusive, they do provide preliminary evidence that short-term exposure to televised violence may affect some children's attitudes by increasing their tolerance of violence.

These three studies represent only a tiny sample of the experiments and surveys performed in an effort to evaluate the impact of the mass media on the way people think about and view the world. Sometimes the dividing line between attitudes and behaviors is fuzzy. In many instances, we can only infer that an attitude or perception exists by observing relevant behavior. Thus many of the research studies cited may involve the measurement of *both* behavior and attitudes. Of course, we cannot hope to cover all research on this topic in a single chapter. Therefore, we will examine six topics that seem to best represent those issues that have generated the most research interest:

1. the role of the media in socialization

2. cultivation analysis

3. the impact of TV advertising on children

4. the diffusion of information

5. agenda setting

6. media exposure and cognitive skills

. . . .

THE MEDIA AND SOCIALIZATION

In Chapter 2, we defined socialization as the ways in which an individual comes to adopt the behavior and values of a group, and we briefly discussed the implications of "media socialization." In Chapter 22, we will consider the socializing impact of the media in connection with the acquisition and performance of certain behaviors, most notably, antisocial and prosocial acts. In this chapter we will concentrate on the role of the media in a more subtle area—the socialization of the individual in regard to certain knowledge, attitudes, and beliefs.

Before we begin, we should point out that television is the medium with the greatest potential for transmitting information and beliefs from one group to another. It is particularly influential in the socialization of children. Television is found in almost every American home; it requires only minimal skills and its visual nature makes it particularly appealing to youngsters. (In fact, some studies have reported a form of TV watching in children who are a year old.) Finally, because television attracts large numbers of children, its audience of young people numbers in the millions. For all these reasons, our primary emphasis will be the socializing impact of television on children (the area that has generated the most research interest).

Socialization is a complex process, extending over a number of years and involving various people and organizations. These people or organizations are called **agents of**

socialization, and they all contribute in some degree to the socialization process. Figure 21-1 represents a simplified diagram of some of the more common agencies.

As the figure demonstrates, parents, siblings, school friends, personal experience, and the media are all potential sources of socialization. From each of these sources, the child receives information and learns attitudes and behaviors through formal instruction (being told what to do), through direct experience, or through the observation of the actions of others. This last form of education, known as **observational learning**, can take place when a child observes either someone in real life or a fictional character portrayed by the media.

In many situations, the media's contribution to socialization will be slight. Other primary agents with greater influence might be parents ("Eat your spinach. It's good for you."), friends ("Don't be a tattletale."), or direct experience ("I'd better not take my sister's things, because the last time I did she hit me in the mouth."). On the other hand, the media may play an important role in socialization when it comes to certain topics. Let us now examine evidence pinpointing some of these areas.

The Media as a Primary Source of Information

Learning is an important part of the socialization process, and children acquire information from various sources. There is increasing evidence that the media serve as important sources of information for a wide range of topics, and one such topic concerns politics and public affairs. To illustrate, a survey of sixth- and seventh-graders found that 80 percent named a mass medium as the source of most information about the president and vice president, 60 percent named a mass medium as the primary source of information about Congress, and half named a mass medium as

FIGURE 21-1 *Agencies of socialization.*

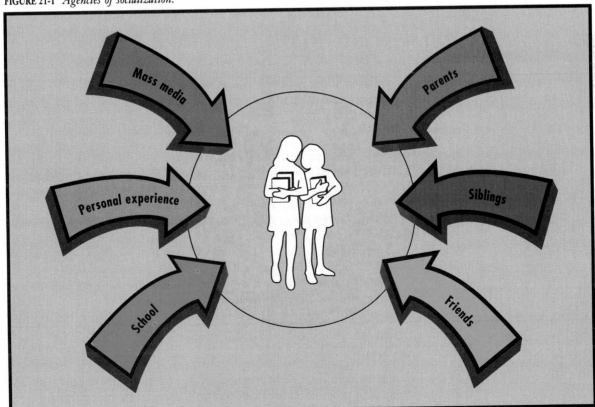

chief information source about the Supreme Court. Similar results were obtained in a study done in the late 1970s concerning junior high school students and their sources of information about political figures and government institutions. About 80 percent named television as their principal source of information about the federal government and the president.

Other research has shown that the media, primarily TV, serve as primary information sources for a wide range of topics. Eight of ten Americans cited television as their primary source of information about the 1991 Persian Gulf War. Television was also named as the source of most information for local and congressional elections. This phenomenon is not limited to political and public affairs information. There is reason to believe that media presentations, including those in entertainment programs, are important sources of information on topics such as occupations, crime, law enforcement, alcohol and drug usage, the environment, and minorities. One recent study of high school students, for example, found that about two in ten students listed rock music as an important source of information about moral values and one out of four specified it as an important source of information about interpersonal relationships.

Shaping Attitudes, Perceptions, and Beliefs

The mass media also play an important role in the transmission of attitudes, perceptions, and beliefs. Several writers have suggested that under certain conditions, the media (especially TV) may become important socialization agencies in determining the attitudes of young people. To be specific, TV will be an influential force when the following factors are operative:

1. The same ideas, people, or behaviors recur consistently from program to program; that is, they are presented in a stereotyped manner.

2. A child is heavily exposed to TV content.

3. A child has limited interaction with parents and other socializing agents and lacks an alternative set of beliefs to serve as a standard against which to assess media portrayals.

All of this means that under certain conditions TV will be an influential force in shaping what children think about certain topics. Complicated though the task is, some researchers have identified some of the conditions, the topics, and the children to which the above theory applies. Moreover, they have specified some of the effects that may result when television does the socializing.

Creating Stereotypes. In studying media socialization, it is helpful to identify consistent themes or stereotypes present in media content. For instance, consider how television programs typically portray law enforcement and crime. Programs about crime and law enforcement are a staple of prime-time television; research has indicated that between 20 and 35 percent of all program time consists of shows dealing with cops and robbers. The popularity of this format means that the large percentage of law enforcement characters portrayed on TV does not accurately reflect the actual percentage employed in this capacity in real life. Similarly, when a suspect is brought to trial in a TV program, that trial is almost always conducted before a jury (as any *LA Law* fan will attest), even though judges decide the majority of cases in real life. Furthermore, on television, at least, crime doesn't pay. One study found that some 90 percent of crimes were solved; real-life law enforcement agencies are not nearly as effective.

Television also overrepresents violent crimes such as murder, rape, and armed robbery. One study found that violent crime accounted for about 60 percent of all TV crimes in one week of programming. To give some perspective to this figure, only 10 percent of crimes are violent in the real world. Lastly, television emphasizes certain

Mass-media portrayals of the Arab world have caused concern among Arab-Americans. They argue that Americans are exposed to stereotyped portrayals, such as the Arab terrorist, that influence our attitudes toward all Arab peoples. (A. Nogues/Sygma)

aspects of the legal system (ask a young fan of any police show to name an arrested suspect's rights), while ignoring others (ask that same young fan what happens at an arraignment or about the functions of a grand jury).

The war in the Persian Gulf also focused attention on the way Arabs had been portrayed in the mass media. Content analyses of TV revealed that Arab men were typically portrayed via three main negative stereotypes: (1) terrorist (although only a minuscule amount of real Arabs fit this category, it is prevalent in the media); (2) oil sheik (not too many fit in here either); and (3) Bedouin desert nomad (only 5 percent of Arabs in real life are Bedouin). Arab women were rarely seen and when they appeared at all were shown usually as belly dancers or members of a harem (harems were never common and none exist today). Arab children were virtually invisible. How many Arab children have you seen on *Sesame Street?* It comes as no surprise then that many of the troops who were stationed in Saudi Arabia were surprised by their contact with Arab culture. Their media exposure did not prepare them for the reality.

It is important to note that although the mass media (particularly television) may influence the shaping of stereotypical images, the media also have the power to change such stereotypes. For example, in one study examining children's perceptions of sex roles, children were shown commercials specially made for "Zing" fruit drink. One set of commercials depicted women in conventional female occupations such as model, file clerk, and telephone operator. A second set of commercials portrayed women in traditional male jobs such as butcher, welder, and druggist. Girls who saw the women in male-dominated jobs were more likely to aspire to these occupations than were girls who saw women in the traditional roles. Some stereotypes, however, were particularly hard to extinguish. In a study done in the late 1980s, children saw a tape portraying the visit of a young child to the office of Dr. Mary and Nurse David. When asked shortly after viewing to describe the tape, a large number of boys reported the tape featured Dr. David and Nurse Mary.

In summary, there appears to be evidence that the TV world often presents images that are at odds with reality. In addition to the field of crime and law enforcement, stereotyping has also characterized sex-role portrayals, and the depiction of occupations, methods of problem solving, portrayals of scientists, and depiction of mental illness.

The Effects of Heavy Viewing. It seems probable that youngsters who are heavy TV viewers should display a pattern of beliefs and perceptions consistent with media portrayals. The earliest research in this area, completed in the 1930s, found that frequent viewing of crime and gangster movies could change attitudes on topics such as capital punishment and prison reform. More recently, other researchers have noted a connection between heavy viewing of violent TV programs and favorable attitudes toward the use of violence in real life. Further, children who were heavy viewers of cops-and-robbers TV programs were more likely to believe that police were more successful in apprehending criminals than were children who were not fans of these shows. This socialization effect is not confined to American children. A study in Great Britain indicated that five- and six-year olds who were heavily exposed to news of the violence in Northern Ireland were more likely to perceive the world as a violent place in which to live than were children who were not so exposed.

In other areas, several studies have linked high levels of television viewing with attitudes favoring traditional sex roles. In other words, children who were heavily exposed to television were more likely to feel, among other things, that men would make better doctors and that women would make better nurses or that raising children was a job for women rather than men.

Socialization by TV can also have positive effects. For example, a television program such as *Sesame Street* can help children develop skills and knowledge that will help them in school. *Sesame Street* is probably the most researched program ever to appear on TV. Findings have indicated that children who watched this program scored higher on tests measuring knowledge of numbers, letters, relationships, and vocabulary—concepts that the series was designed to teach. Similar research indicates that a related program, *The Electric Company*, has also been successful in teaching specific reading skills to youngsters. In addition, there is evidence that *Sesame Street* has also promoted attitudes associated with academic success (such as favorable feelings about school) that were not explicitly mentioned in the show. Finally, *Sesame Street* has been shown to affect general prosocial attitudes that are not directly concerned with school. Children who watched scenes in which white and minority children played together showed more tolerance in their racial attitudes than did children who had not viewed the scenes. Similarly, the TV series *Freestyle, Villa Allegre,* and *Big Blue Marble,* aired on public television, were attempts to create programs that would alter stereotypes about sex roles and ethnic groups. When coupled with in-class discussions, viewing of these series led to a reduction in ethnic stereotyping and a broader acceptance of the different sexes in various occupations. *Square One,* a more recent series from the creators of *Sesame Street,* has been found to help students develop math skills. Another program from the Children's Television Workshop, *The Rotten Truth,* helped promote recycling.

To be fair, we must again stress that this type of research *assumes,* but does not necessarily *prove,* that the mass media play a significant part in creating the attitudes held by these youngsters. Surveys can only highlight associations. It is very possible, for example, that young people who hold traditional sex-role concepts may be more

Big Bird, Telly, and friends learn about similarities and differences. On the air for more than twenty years, Sesame Street *is now educating its second generation of youngsters. (Photo by Richard Termine, Children's Television Workshop)*

inclined to watch television. Although some experimental evidence points to the media as the cause of certain attitudes, we cannot entirely rule out other interpretations. Nevertheless, it is likely that the link between media exposure and certain attitudes demonstrates reciprocal causation. What this means is best shown by an example. Watching violent TV shows might cause a youngster to hold favorable attitudes toward aggression. These favorable attitudes might then prompt him or her to watch more violent TV, which, in turn, might encourage more aggressive attitudes, and so on. At the risk of some redundancy, the two factors might be said to be mutually causing one another.

The Absence of Alternative Information. Although research evidence is less consistent in this area than in others, it appears that, for some young people under some circumstances, television can affect attitudes about matters for which the environment fails to provide first-hand experience or alternative sources of information. To be specific, one survey that examined the potential impact of TV on dating behavior found that teenagers were more likely to turn to TV for guidance when they had limited real-life experience with dating. Another study, conducted in the late 1960s, asked three groups of youngsters—low-income black, low-income white, and middle-income white teenagers—how much they believed that life, as pictured on TV, resembled real life. Low-income black teenagers, the group least likely to have contact with white middle-class society (the world most portrayed on TV), held the greatest degree of belief. Middle-income white teenagers, the group most likely to have direct experience with white middle-class society, showed the most disbelief.

A recent study noted that foreign students who depended most on television for their information about Americans had stereotyped beliefs about Americans. Chinese students who depended primarily on TV for most of their information and who had little interpersonal contact with Americans rated them as more pleasure seeking and

Sesame Street is probably the most successful educational television program ever produced. After its debut in 1969, the show was showered with praise from critics, parents, teachers, and children. Initial research projects indicated that the program was accomplishing its educational goals. However, even something as universally acclaimed as *Sesame Street* did not succeed without generating some criticism.

Seven years after its inception, *Sesame Street* had established itself as an international favorite. The program was viewed regularly in more than forty countries around the world, and Big Bird, Cookie Monster, and Oscar had become household words. Children in Latin America watched *Plaza Sesamo*; in Germany, *Sesamstrasse*; and in Holland, *Sesamstraat*.

With international prominence came international problems. The Spanish-language version, *Plaza Sesamo*, was faced with the difficult task of producing a program that would adequately reflect the diverse subcultures of 22 million Latin American preschoolers. For example, in English there is one form for the second person: *you*. In Spanish, however, there are two choices: the formal *usted* or the more informal *tu*; other South American countries use *vos* and *che*. The rules concerning which form to use differ from region to region. The program ignored the language variations in favor of a standardized approach. Further, although Latin America has many varieties of folk music, the first series of *Plaza Sesamo* contained only one Latin American selection per program; other selections consisted of American rock. Soon critics of the program emerged, charging that *Plaza Sesamo* was submerging local culture and substituting a standardized American-influenced culture in its place.

Another criticism that emerged closer to home complained that *Sesame Street* was teaching too well. One of the program's original goals was to aid the intellectual growth of disadvantaged children, and the show was clearly meeting this goal. However, advantaged children were also watching *Sesame Street* and learning from it, sometimes at a faster pace than their disadvantaged counterparts. As a result, critics noted that *Sesame Street* had done little to narrow the gap between the two groups and, in fact, might even have widened it, thus placing poor children at even more of a competitive disadvantage. Other educators criticized the program's fast-paced format, which contrasted dramatically with the slower-paced classroom environment of local school systems. Such a frenetic format, these educators claimed, might contribute to hyperactivity and other behavioral problems in the classroom.

In recent years *Sesame Street* has tried to address these criticisms. International versions of the show have striven to incorporate greater cultural awareness. In the United States, efforts have been made to narrow the learning gap between advantaged and disadvantaged children, and teachers have been shown how to integrate the program into the classroom to minimize behavior problems.

---

materialistic (two characteristics consistent with TV's portrayal of Americans) than did students who relied more on other sources.

To make these examples more personal, consider your knowledge about prostitutes. In this situation, the media may be a primary source of information. My guess is that the vast majority of people reading this chapter has had little direct experience with prostitutes. Nonetheless, almost everybody has seen news reports about them where they were portrayed negatively, as drug users decked out in heavy makeup and provocative dress, soliciting passersby. We've also seen more gentle portrayals, such as Julia Roberts in *Pretty Woman*, who's just like the girl next door and really has a

Madonna's Message?

Evidence suggests that the media, particularly the electronic media, are potent socialization forces for young people. Socialization is a complicated process, however, and much of its impact depends upon how the audience perceives and interprets the content. This point was well illustrated in a 1990 *Journal of Communication* article summarizing the work of researchers at the University of North Carolina and the University of Denver.

The researchers were interested in examining if there were race and gender differences in audience comprehension of the message in two Madonna music videos: "Papa Don't Preach" and "Open Your Heart." The videos were shown to an audience of college students which included males and females, blacks and whites. The students were asked to give a written explanation as to what the videos were about.

There were dramatic differences in what the viewers saw and there was wide disagreement over fundamental story elements according to race and gender. For example, almost all of the white students thought that "Papa Don't Preach" was about teenage pregnancy. In contrast, most black viewers interpreted the video as being about the relationship between a father and daughter in which the father didn't want his daughter to continue to see her boyfriend.

As for "Open Your Heart," most males thought the video was about a sexual relationship while most females thought it was about a platonic relationship between Madonna and a young boy or between a brother and sister. Another interesting finding from this part of the study was that in their descriptions males were more likely to view Madonna as a sex object. Males often wrote about "Madonna's body" as opposed to "Madonna." No female fans used this construction.

In sum, the socialization messages that a person derives from media content depend on many considerations, a fact that makes determining the socializing impact of the media even more intricate.

---

good heart, or Candice Bergen portraying Washington madam Sidney Biddle Barrows managing her stable of call girls, or Richard Gere as an *American Gigolo*. When it comes time to vote on measures to make the laws regarding prostitution more/less severe, what do we do? What's the reality? How do we find out?

Before closing, we should point out that where media influence is indirect, it is also more difficult to pinpoint. This is particularly true in situations where the media operate simultaneously with other agencies of socialization and where interpersonal channels may outweigh media channels in forming attitudes and opinions. In the area of politics, for instance, the media probably supply youngsters with information and viewpoints that are subsequently commented on by parents and friends. Political beliefs and attitudes evolve out of this double context. In such cases, the socializing impact of parents and other interpersonal sources is more important than that of the media. One study dealing with attitudes toward police found that although children spent a great deal of time watching TV cop shows, friends and family were the important socializing agents. The point is this: The media play a significant role in socialization. Sometimes this role is easy to detect; sometimes it is indirect and harder to see; at still other times, it is apparently slight. Clearly, numerous factors are influential in determining how a child comes to perceive the world. The media (and television, in particular), however, seem to have become important factors in the socialization process.

As the text suggests, the mass media, especially television, play an important role in the socialization of children. But is it possible that television is also changing the experience of childhood itself? Professor Joshua Meyrowitz of the University of New Hampshire, for one, thinks that it is. In fact, he argues in his book *No Sense of Place* that television is subtly putting an end to what we used to call "childhood." Here, in condensed form, is what Professor Meyrowitz suggests.

Back in the nineteenth and early twentieth centuries, children were looked upon as innocent and weak creatures who had to be shielded from the harsher realities of life. Children were dressed differently from adults; they had their own games; there were words and topics that were taboo for children or for adults in conversations around children. The school system consisted of rigid grades that defined what children of certain age should or should not know.

Recently, however, all of that seems to be changing. It is no longer unusual to see kids dressed in designer jeans and three-piece suits and other outfits that mimic adult clothing. At the other end of the spectrum, adults now dress in Superman T-shirts and sneakers and wear Mickey Mouse watches—grownup versions of play clothes. The distinction between children's play and adult play has also been obscured. Adults now zip around on rollerskates and skateboards and attend summer camps. The new "toys" made possible by electronic technology—computer and video games—can be and are being played by both adults and kids. Further, the list of taboo topics unfit for children to know has shrunk and, more importantly, children are learning previously taboo topics at younger and younger ages. Formal programs of sex and drug education, for example, are hampered because young people frequently enter them having considerable experience with the topics and with their opinions already formed. The changing nature of childhood is readily apparent in mass entertainment. The Shirley Temple films of the 1930s have given way to the Macaulay Culkin films of the 1990s.

What has TV had to do with this changing nature of childhood? Professor Meyrowitz contends that TV has changed the pattern and sequence of access to social information. When a society moves from dependence on one medium as a primary information source to another, there are shifts in the ease with which certain information becomes available. For example, in the early part of the century, print was a primary means of communicating social information. Young children had to master complex reading skills before they were able to have access to information in print. Thus young children without the necessary symbolic skills were automatically forbidden access to information contained in books, newspapers, and magazines. Moreover, printed information could be directed at children of different ages simply by varying the complexity of the message.

Television, however, is completely different. It takes little skill to watch television, and the information it provides is available to all who watch it. Thus second-graders, ninth-graders, and adults are all simultaneously exposed to programs about junkies, prostitutes, crooked cops, adulterous parents, and unscrupulous politicians. In fact, with TV, shielding children from such information is extremely difficult. An adult book might be hidden in a drawer or stored on a high shelf, but the TV set is available to everybody. More than half the households in the United States have more than one TV, and many of these sets are located in children's rooms. Even the advisories placed at the beginning of some programs ("This show deals with adult themes and situations. Parental discretion is advised.") can have a boomerang effect by increasing the child's interest in what follows.

Additionally, in a print culture, children were given an "onstage" view of adults. Traditional children's books presented idealized and stereotyped versions of adult behavior. Politicians acted nobly; parents knew what was best; the teacher was always right. In a television culture, children are shown a "backstage" view. Newscasts, situation comedies, and dramatic programs show children crooked politicians, depressed parents, and incompetent teachers long before they get the idealized view. Children also learn that adults play roles. They act one way in front of children and another way when children are not present. This fact also reduces the traditional distance between children and adults.

In short, the information presented on TV immediately thrusts children into the adult world. It is no longer possible to go through the leisurely process of socialization by stages that typified print culture. As Professor Meyrowitz sums up: "In the shared environment of television, children and adults know a great deal about each other's behavior and social knowledge—too much, in fact, for them to play the traditional complementary roles of innocence vs. omnipotence."

CULTIVATION ANALYSIS

Directly related to socialization is an area of research called **cultivation analysis**. Developed by George Gerbner and his colleagues at the University of Pennsylvania, cultivation analysis suggests that heavy TV viewing "cultivates" perceptions of reality consistent with the view of the world presented in television programs. This notion has already been suggested in our discussion of socialization effects. With cultivation analysis, however, Gerbner has expanded his focus to include the possible effects of media content on adults as well as on children. Additionally, cultivation analysis concentrates on the long-term effects of exposure rather than the short-term impact on attitudes and opinions. Gerbner and his associates have been performing cultivation analyses for several years, using large and in some instances national samples of respondents. The results suggest that television may have a subtle effect on the way many of us look at the world.

Methodology

The first stage in cultivation analysis is a careful study of television content in order to identify predominant themes and messages. Since 1967, Gerbner and his colleagues have been meticulously analyzing sample weeks of prime-time and daytime television programming. Not surprisingly, television portrays a rather idiosyncratic world that is unlike reality along many dimensions. To mention a few examples, television's world is usually populated by a preponderance of males. In fact, in an average season, about two-thirds to three-quarters of all leading characters are men. Moreover, in portraying occupations, television overemphasizes the professions and, as previously mentioned, overrepresents the proportion of workers engaged in law enforcement and the detection of crime. Lastly, the TV world is a violent one—around 70 to 80 percent of all programs usually contain at least one instance of violence.

Step two examines what, if anything, viewers absorb from heavy exposure to the world of television. Respondents are presented with questions concerning social reality and are asked to check one of two possible answers. One of these answers (the "TV answer") is more in line with the way things are portrayed on television; the other (the "real-world answer") more closely resembles situations in actual life. An example might help to demonstrate what we are talking about:

What percentage of all males who have jobs work in law enforcement and crime detection?

Is it

_____ 1 percent or _____ 10 percent?

How many lawyers in real life are like Grace Van Owen (Susan Dey) and Tommy Mullaney (John Spencer) of L.A. Law? Cultivation analysis would suggest that for some heavy viewers, TV portrayals of lawyers would influence perceptions of real-life lawyers. (Photo by Alic S. Hall, Courtesy NBC, Inc.)

On television, about 12 percent of all male characters hold such jobs. Thus 10 percent would be the "TV answer." In reality, about 1 percent are employed in law enforcement; thus 1 percent is the "real-world answer." The responses of a large sample of heavy TV viewers are then compared with those of light TV viewers. If heavy viewers show a definite tendency to choose TV answers, we would have evidence that a cultivation effect was occurring.

Research Findings

Is there evidence to suggest such an effect? At the risk of oversimplifying, it appears that most findings suggest that among some people TV is cultivating distorted perceptions of the real world. To illustrate, in one survey done among approximately 450 New Jersey schoolchildren, 73 percent of heavy viewers compared to 62 percent of light viewers gave the TV answer to a question asking them to estimate the number of people involved in violence in a typical week. This same survey discovered that youngsters who were heavy viewers were more fearful about walking alone at night in a city. They overestimated the number of people who commit serious crimes, how often police find it necessary to use force, and how frequently police have to shoot at fleeing suspects. These results are in line with the expected predictions of cultivation analysis.

In addition, results from a national survey of adult viewers indicate that cultivation is not limited to children. In this survey, heavy television viewers evidently felt that TV violence and crime presented an accurate depiction of reality, since they also were more fearful of walking alone at night and were more likely to have bought a dog recently or to have put locks on windows and doors than were light TV viewers. Although the differences in findings between heavy and light viewers were not large in the absolute sense, they were almost certainly not due to chance. Even more intriguing was the finding that heavy TV viewers were more likely to keep a gun in order to protect themselves than were light viewers.

Research has shown that content other than crime and violence might also demonstrate a cultivation effect. One study of college students conducted in 1981 found that heavy soap opera viewers were more likely than light viewers to overestimate the number of real-life married people who had affairs or who had been divorced and the number of women who had abortions (common occurrences in the soap opera world).

Other cultivation research has focused specifically on college students. In one study, students' exposure to pornography was examined to see if stereotyped perceptions were being cultivated. Among males, those who were heavy users of pornography were more apt to report that they had less confidence in females doing certain jobs (e.g., mechanic, mayor). They also tended to agree more with stereotypes of sexuality ("Men have stronger sexual urges than women." "Women say 'no' to sex when they don't really mean it.") than did light users. These relationships stood up even after rigorous statistical controls removed possible influences of other factors. Women showed no such effects from exposure.

Although the results of cultivation-analysis studies are evocative and fascinating, conclusions are clouded by three problems. First, it is difficult to determine cause and effect. Does heavy TV viewing cause people to be fearful of walking alone at night or does being fearful cause them to stay home and watch more TV? Since the problem

The effect of television on young viewers is one of the most thoroughly researched areas in mass communication. (Rick Kopstein/Monkmeyer)

of causation is one that cannot adequately be addressed through the use of only survey data, it is necessary to examine the results of laboratory experiments for added information. In the case of cultivation analysis experiments are difficult to conduct since, by its very nature, cultivation analysis is concerned with long-term effects of exposure to consistent television portrayals.

One experiment that attempted to address the issue of cause and effect manipulated television viewing among college students to create heavy- and light-viewing groups. After six weeks of structured viewing, heavy viewers, who had been exposed to large doses of action-adventure programs, were more fearful and anxious about life in the real world than were light viewers. This result supported the cultivation hypothesis.

Another experiment used specially constructed TV programs to look for a cultivation effect. One group of experimental subjects saw a program in which justice triumphed (the good guy shot the bad guy). A second group saw a version in which injustice won out (the bad guy shot the good guy). In addition, a third group saw a documentary about crime, while a control group watched an episode of *The Love Boat*. It was hypothesized that cultivation of greater anxiety and a perception of increased crime in the world should be greatest among those who saw the version depicting injustice (the bad guy triumphed and was free to strike again). The actual results were not clear-cut. As predicted, subjects who saw the version depicting injustice were more anxious than those in the other conditions. When asked about their perceptions of the frequency of crime, subjects in both the injustice condition and the documentary condition showed a tendency to overestimate its frequency compared to other groups. When the subjects were questioned again three days later, however, the difference had dissipated. Taken together, these two experiments suggest that the cultivation effect is more complicated than previously thought. Both the type of content that is viewed and the time factor apparently influence its potency.

The second problem concerns the fact that heavy and light TV viewers differ in ways other than their TV viewing habits. Consequently, factors other than TV watching might affect the differences in perceptions and attitudes between heavy and light viewers. Analyzing this problem is somewhat difficult. When certain factors that appear relevant to the cause-and-effect relationship (such as age, sex, and education) are statistically controlled, one factor at a time, the association between TV watching and perceptions is evident, but somewhat weakened. When two or more factors are controlled simultaneously (e.g., examining the relationship between TV viewing and anxiety, while simultaneously controlling for effects of both sex and age), some overall relationships disappear. We cannot conclude, however, that a relationship does not exist. In fact, recent research indicates certain subgroups will show a cultivation effect while others won't.

Gerbner and his associates, for example, have detected a phenomenon they have labeled **mainstreaming**, whereby differences apparently due to cultural and social factors tend to diminish among heavy TV viewers. They have also found evidence for what they call **resonance**, a situation in which the respondent's real-life experiences are congruent with those of the television world, thereby leading to a greater cultivation effect.

Third, technical decisions about the way TV viewing and attitudes are measured can have a significant impact on findings. For example, the precise wording of the questions has been shown to be important. In addition, some researchers argue that exposure to a particular kind of program (e.g., violent shows) gives a more accurate picture of cultivation than simply measuring overall TV viewing. Others note that deciding upon the number of hours of viewing that differentiate high and low viewers has a bearing on the magnitude of cultivation.

The recent emphasis in cultivation studies has been on specifying the conditions that are most likely to encourage or hinder cultivation. Although results are not as clear-cut as we might like, cultivation appears to depend on the motivation for viewing.

Individuals who watch TV simply to pass time or because it becomes a habit appear to be more affected than people whose viewing is planned and motivated. Moreover, cultivation appears to be enhanced when the viewer perceives the content of entertainment shows to be realistic. Audience members who look with skepticism on the accuracy of TV shows seem less likely to display the cultivation effect. Finally, some studies have noted cultivation seems to work best when audience members have only indirect or distant contact with the topic. Interestingly enough, this finding seems to run counter to the resonance notion.

To sum up and perhaps oversimplify, it is probably fair to say that although not all mass communication scholars are totally convinced by the reasoning underlying cultivation analysis, a growing body of evidence suggests that the cultivation effect is indeed real for many people. Nonetheless, it's obvious that a lot of research still needs to be done before the cultivation process is completely understood.

●●●●
CHILDREN AND TELEVISION ADVERTISING

If you've ever watched Saturday morning television, you are probably familiar with Tony the Tiger, Captain Crunch, Count Chocula, Ronald McDonald, and Snap, Crackle, and Pop. This is not surprising because by the time you graduated from high school, you had already seen about 350,000 TV commercials. A typical child will see about 20,000 commercials every year, mostly for toys, cereals, candies, and fast-food restaurants. The effects of this massive exposure to TV persuasion became a topic of concern during the 1970s as the citizens' group Action for Children's Television brought this issue to the attention of the Federal Communications Commission (FCC) and the Federal Trade Commission (FTC). By the early part of the 1980s, most people had accepted the notion that children constitute a special audience and deserve special consideration from television advertisers. It has been argued that children constitute a special audience because of the following reasons:

1. Children are a vulnerable audience and should not be exploited by TV advertising.

2. Children, especially younger children, might be deceived by TV techniques that make products appear more desirable than they really are.

3. The long-term effects of exposure of TV ads might have a negative effect on a child's socialization as a future consumer.

Using this threefold division, we will examine some of the many research studies that have investigated the effects of TV advertising on children.

A Vulnerable Audience?

Adults have little problem in distinguishing commercials from regular television programs, and they realize that the purpose of a commercial is to promote some idea, product, or service. But what about children? Can they recognize a commercial and understand its purpose? Research suggests that this ability is related to age. Younger children (five to eight years old) were able to identify commercials, but they had difficulty in separating ads from the rest of the program and had little idea as to the purpose behind them. When asked to differentiate between a TV program and a TV commercial, these youngsters typically responded that commercials were "shorter" or "funnier" than the programs that contained them. These same children did not perceive that commercials were designed to sell things to people. Additionally, it was discovered that ads that used program characters and program hosts to sell the product further confused the distinction between program and ad. They were more persuasive

The typical child sees up to 20,000 commercials in a year, many for popular games and toys. The impact of television advertising and its role in consumer socialization is a popular research topic. (Grover Photography/The Picture Cube)

with youngsters, probably because of the trust and identification children place in these characters.

Older children (nine to twelve years old) were better able to differentiate the ads from the rest of the program and had little trouble in distinguishing between the purpose of an ad and a program. A typical response from a child in this age group was that "programs entertain" and "commercials try to sell things." These older children were also less susceptible to the selling efforts of hosts and program characters in ads.

Partly as a result of these findings, the FCC, in a 1974 inquiry into advertising aimed at children, concluded that some device was needed to clearly separate commercials from programs. Shortly thereafter, broadcasters started using a separation device. This separation device was five to ten seconds long and contained the words "We will return after these messages" and "We now return to (name of program)." Experiments in this area have shown that program separators are ineffective with young children (five and younger). The separators worked better with older children, who were better able to distinguish the difference between programs and commercials if separators were included. Although young children have trouble differentiating an ad from programming even with separators, it is apparent that the broadcasting industry has acknowledged the special nature of the child audience.

Much of our knowledge about the impact of advertising on children comes from surveys or from laboratory experiments. Both sources are helpful but both have shortcomings. The experiment yields information about cause and effect but suffers from artificiality. The survey method is more natural but yields no firm evidence about causation. A technique that helps bridge the gap between them is the field experiment, which gives some information about what causes what and is not as artificial as a lab experiment.

Such an opportunity presented itself in Quebec, Canada. In 1980, a law passed in Quebec eliminated TV commercials directed at children throughout most of the schedule, including Saturday and Sunday mornings and after school. Children in Quebec, however, could still receive all three American networks with their programs that contained commercials. As reported in the November, 1990, *Journal of Marketing Research*, Professor Marvin Goldberg took advantage of this situation and conducted a field experiment. He reasoned that English speaking children would be more exposed to American commercial TV than would French speaking children. Consequently, the impact of commercials aimed at kids might be detectable if these two groups of youngsters were compared.

Professor Goldberg measured two variables designed to gauge ad influence. One was awareness of toys currently on the market and the other assessed how many different brands of cereal were in the children's homes (toys and cereal ads make up a significant portion of commercials during kids' TV). The results showed a definite impact of exposure to commercials. The English speaking children were able to identify fifteen toys currently on the market; the French speaking children could identify about eight. The English speaking children also had significantly more brands of cereal in their home than did their French language counterparts. Income played a role in this relationship but exposure to commercials also had a separate effect.

Professor Goldberg concludes that Quebec's law apparently reduced the French children's exposure to ads for cereals which in turn reduced their cereal consumption. Moreover, reduced exposure to toy commercials left French youngsters unaware of many toys in the market and presumably less inclined to pressure their parents to buy them. It has not been established if a comparable law in the U.S. would have the same effect.

Effects of Special Selling Techniques

When you were much younger, some of you may have had an experience like the following. On Saturday morning, while watching your favorite cartoon show, you may have seen an ad for a toy, perhaps a plastic model truck called "Toughie." In the ad, the truck, with headlights flashing and horn blowing, was shown dumping a load of sand in the middle of a miniature construction site, surrounded by miniature construction workers. The truck was then shown in close-up, practically dwarfing the young child in the background. Excited, you told your parents that "Toughie" was the one thing you wanted most for Christmas. When Christmas arrived and you were lucky enough to find Toughie under the tree, you might have been disillusioned to find that the actual truck was much smaller than it had appeared on TV. The headlights didn't flash and the horn didn't blow because batteries weren't included with the truck. There was no sand, no miniature construction site, and no tiny construction workers. Somehow, it wasn't the same toy that you remembered.

Then again, you might have seen an ad for "Cuddly Carol," a perfectly lovable doll dressed in three or four different outfits, who presided over a miniature tea party furnished with a complete tea set, while an announcer told you that "Cuddly Carol" was the best doll around. If you were fortunate enough to receive "Cuddly Carol," you might have discovered that whenever you tried to stand her up, "Cuddly" had an irritating tendency to fall flat on her face. Further, the several outfits shown on TV were not included, and the miniature tea set was nowhere to be found. Somehow, "Cuddly Carol" looked a lot better on TV.

It's obvious that toys and other products designed for children can be made to look more appealing through the use of special camera angles, lenses, advertising copy, sound effects, animation, and special lighting techniques. The ability of children to distinguish the illusion created by these techniques from the real object has been an area of continuing interest among policymakers and mass communication researchers. Recently, in response to tighter industry guidelines, commercials directed toward children have included disclaimers, messages such as "Some assembly required," or "Batteries not included," or "Accessories sold separately," which are read by an announcer and/or flashed on the screen. Some critics have argued that these disclaimers are not understood by children, and several research studies have examined this area. This section will provide a brief summary of what is known about this issue.

Turning first to the effects of special TV production techniques, we find that there has been relatively little research addressed to this topic. Studies of ads broadcast during children's programs have indicated that animation occurs in about 40 percent of all commercials and in about 80 percent of cereal commercials. Additionally, special visual effects are used to enhance the appearance of the product in about 15–20 percent of children's commercials. Product close-ups occurred in about 40 percent of all ads and were particularly likely to show up in ads for toys. One study indicated that children aged five to eight had trouble interpreting the meaning of a close-up or a zoom that magnified the object. Young children who saw a candy bar in a medium shot followed by a close-up of the candy bar or a zoom into a close-up of the candy bar thought the object itself had gotten larger.

The effects on children of the use of special selling techniques are unclear. One study showed children a particular television commercial that exaggerated the virtues of the product it was promoting, a simple child's game. Young boys who saw only the TV ad were willing to pay a higher price for the game than were boys who saw the actual toy. Interestingly, girls did not show this tendency. In another experiment, a group of children were shown a commercial that purposely exaggerated the appeal of a building-block game. Other children saw a similar commercial that was more modest in its depiction of the toy. Those children who saw the exaggerated version had greater expectations about the game and were evidently disappointed when the real item failed to live up to its promised potential.

Other research has examined the effects of product disclaimers appearing in ads. A disclaimer such as "Batteries not included" was remembered by far more children when it was both mentioned by the announcer and superimposed on the screen than when it was only shown on the screen. Further, the wording of product disclaimers has been shown to be an important factor in their effectiveness. In one experiment, two toy commercials were shown to two groups of six- and eight-year-olds. One used the standard disclaimer, "Some assembly required"; the other contained a simplified disclaimer, "You have to put it together." Results indicated that children who were exposed to the standard "Some assembly required" had no better understanding that the toy must be put together than did children who saw the ad without any disclaimer. In other words, the standard line did nothing to improve comprehension. On the other hand, children who heard the simplified version were far more likely to realize that assembly was necessary. In another study, it was found that a disclaimer stating that a certain cereal was only "part of a balanced breakfast" had little apparent impact on young viewers. Most of the four- to eight-year-olds who saw the commercial didn't know what a "balanced breakfast" was.

In light of the above research, the television and advertising industries have acknowledged the potential of television production techniques to influence children's perceptions of TV commercials. Industry guidelines for toy products now state that audio and video techniques should not misrepresent the appearance and performance of toys and that disclaimers should be used when batteries are needed, when the product must be assembled by the consumer, or when accessory items shown in the ad are not included in the price of the advertised product. The research we've mentioned above also suggests that perhaps these guidelines should be amended to cover the actual language used in the disclaimer.

Children's Ads and Consumer Socialization

Consumer socialization includes all those processes by which children learn behaviors and attitudes relevant to their future behavior as consumers. Like socialization in general, consumer socialization is accomplished by several agents—parents, the school, direct experience, and, more pertinent to our discussion, television advertising. It is obvious to any parent that television commercials teach children the names of certain products, slogans, and jingles and even make celebrities of young performers in commercials (the "cereal that Mikey likes" made Mikey a TV star). In more general terms, the question addressed by many researchers in this area concerns the ultimate contribution that TV advertising makes to consumer socialization. This is not an easy question to answer. Many members of the advertising industry argue that advertising, particularly TV advertising, aids children's general understanding of the American free-enterprise system and helps them learn about products and purchasing skills. On the other hand, critics of advertising for children charge that TV ads help foster materialism in children and promote generally unhealthy social attitudes.

Although relevant research evidence is not clear-cut, primarily because concepts such as consumer skills and materialism are hard to define, certain generalizations can be made. We do know that as a child gets older the influence of parents as a consumer socialization force decreases and the influence of the peer group increases. Mass media influences appear to be small but are constant with age. Unfortunately, there have been no long-term studies demonstrating a link between childhood socialization experiences and subsequent adult consumer behavior. There is evidence, however, that certain effects do occur, at least among five- to twelve-year-olds. One phenomenon that has been observed several times is that as children get older, they begin to distrust commercials and even become cynical about them. In one survey, children of different ages were asked if they believed that commercials always told the truth. About 35 percent of the five- to seven-year-olds said yes, compared with about 15 percent of the eight- to ten-year-olds and only 5 percent of the eleven- to twelve-year-olds. Another study that asked the same question in a slightly different way found that the percentage of youngsters who trusted commercials declined from 65 percent to only 7 percent by the fifth grade. Why do children come to mistrust TV commercials? One reason seems to be that as children get older they find out that products do not live up to the expectations that commercials give. Coupled with this disillusionment is a growing awareness of the actual motives behind commercials. "They're tricky and try to get you to buy things" and "They just want to make money" are some reasons given by youngsters for their mistrust.

Developing Consumer Skills. A second area of research has investigated the contribution of TV ads to the development of children's consumer skills. Consumer skills might consist of abilities such as comparing prices, finding out how well a product will perform, checking several sources of information about a product, and so on. One survey found that although consumer skills increased with age, in most instances exposure to TV commercials seemed to be unrelated to this increase. In those few situations in which viewing of commercials was associated with consumer skills, the association produced negative results. In effect, children who were exposed to many TV ads actually had lower levels of skills than children not so heavily exposed. Other studies have also turned up little evidence of a relationship between viewing ads and consumer skills. In general, then, we might conclude that there is little reason to accept the argument that being an intelligent and skillful consumer is a function of exposure to media advertising. To be fair, however, we should point out that the inability to prove an association might be due to the difficulty in accurately measuring consumer skills. More research in the area is needed before a definitive conclusion can be drawn.

Advertising and Materialism. A third area of socialization and advertising concerns materialism—that is, preoccupation with possessions and wealth. Research has turned up a link between positive attitudes toward commercials and endorsement of materialistic attitudes. For example, adolescents who favorably regarded television ads also thought that money and physical possessions were necessary for happiness. This finding, however, again does not conclusively determine cause and effect. It may be that people who are already materialistic are predisposed to like TV ads.

In one experiment that tried to pin down the direction of causation, young children were divided into two groups. One group watched TV commercials promoting a particular toy; the other group did not. The children were then shown pictures of two boys: one was empty-handed and described as "nice"; the other was holding the toy shown in the commercials and was described as "not nice." The children were then asked which of the boys they would like to play with. In the group that didn't see the commercial 70 percent chose the empty-handed "nice boy," compared with only 35 percent of the group that saw the TV ads. Most of this latter group chose the "not-nice" boy with the toy, thereby suggesting that TV commercials had increased the importance of the material possession. This and similar studies are interesting because they suggest a possible cause–effect relationship between ads and materialism; however, the issue deserves more study before a final verdict can be pronounced.

In summary, we have seen in this brief review that some criticisms voiced by public-interest groups such as Action for Children's Television appear to be supported by research. Some children, especially younger ones, have trouble understanding the basic intent of advertising. As a child matures, repeated exposure to commercials evidently results in disillusionment and cynicism about the merits of advertising. Additionally, family conflicts may result if children respond to the ad with purchase requests directed toward their parents. As is probably obvious by now, this whole topic raises questions of regulation. It is to be hoped that the construction of a public policy dealing with the general issue of advertising for children is a task that organizations such as the Federal Trade Commission and the Federal Communications Commission will accomplish in the near future.

● ● ● ●
THE DIFFUSION OF NEWS AND INFORMATION

One effect of mass media that is so obvious it is almost overlooked is the ability of the media to disseminate information rapidly to a large group of people. Before the emergence of a mass communication system, it took a long time for news and information to reach large numbers of people. As noted in Chapter 2, it took nearly two months for news of the signing of the Treaty of Ghent, which officially ended the War of 1812, to reach America. Ironically, the American victory at the battle of New Orleans occurred two weeks after the treaty had been signed but five weeks before news of the end of the war was received in the United States. Had there been a mass communication system in place in 1815, the course of world history might have been much different.

Contrast that situation with what happened on the night of January 16, 1991, when war broke out in the Middle East. Shortly after the bombs started falling on Baghdad, a CNN crew was on the air reporting live from the scene. Millions of Americans knew about the opening of hostilities only minutes after they happened. Television broadcast live the Scud missile attacks on Saudi Arabia and Israel. Unlike the days when news traveled slowly and went first to a nation's leaders, the rapid diffusion of news now means that political leaders and their constituents get their news at the same time. When he was asked about the early progress of the war, Secretary of Defense Dick Cheney said he was getting most of his information by following CNN.

Mass media researchers have carefully studied how mass communication channels function in the distribution of news and information. This area of study has been labeled **news diffusion** and is defined as the dissemination (spread) of information in a society across time. Three main stages of the diffusion process have been identified. The first stage is called the **newsbreak** and consists of the time it takes for reporters to transmit the essential facts of a story back to a media organization, which, in turn, publishes or broadcasts the news. The second is called the **dissemination stage** and consists of the period during which the news is spreading through the audience and during which the facts are becoming known to the members of some community or society. The last stage, called **saturation**, occurs when most of the population has heard the story and it no longer can be classified as breaking news. For our purposes, we will define saturation as occurring when approximately 90 percent of the population has heard the news.

An example may serve to illustrate these three stages better. When President John Kennedy was assassinated in November of 1963, the event took place at approximately 1:30 P.M. (Eastern Standard Time). The first news bulletins announcing the event were

Antiaircraft fire lights the night sky over Baghdad early in the Gulf War. About two-thirds of the American people learned about the start of the war from television. (Wide World Photos)

broadcast about four to five minutes later. Thus the newsbreak for this story was only four to five minutes long. At this point the dissemination stage began. As would be expected, news of this magnitude spread quickly, with about two-thirds of the audience having heard the facts within half an hour. The saturation stage was reached only one hour after the event.

The Kennedy assassination, however, was not a typical news event. Most news stories do not diffuse as quickly. Studies of more common news events have been fairly consistent in their description of the diffusion process. For these events, the speed of dissemination is a function of the news value of the event. Extremely important events will reach the saturation stage in a matter of a few hours. Important events—those that receive bulletin treatment in radio and television and banner headlines in the newspaper—will typically reach saturation six to twelve hours after the newsbreak. Events of intermediate importance usually require twenty-four to thirty-six hours to reach 90 percent of the population. Less important events may take two or three days to reach saturation, if at all.

If we were to graph the cumulative percentage of people who know about an event and the elapsed time after the event, we would find that diffusion curves for news events of differing importance would have certain similarities. The curves would take roughly an S-shape, indicating a rapid initial spread of information that eventually tapers off with the passing of time. Figure 21-2 illustrates typical diffusion curves for events of three different levels of newsworthiness.

Of course, the particulars of diffusion will vary according to the type of story that is being reported. The dissemination of news for an anticipated event is much faster (and the resulting diffusion curve much steeper) than is the case with an unanticipated story. In some instances, the story might be anticipated and covered live by the media

FIGURE 21-2 *News diffusion curves.*

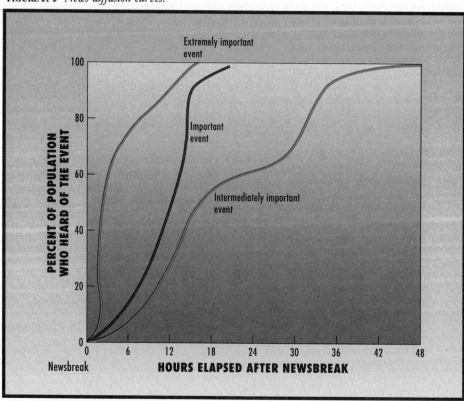

(as is the case with a presidential inauguration or press conference), and the time between the newsbreak and the dissemination stage will be zero.

Moreover, the source of first exposure for a news story will, with some exceptions, be one of the mass media. In most cases, radio or television will serve as the first source of information for approximately 50–70 percent of the population. The remainder will learn about a news story from one of the print media or through interpersonal channels. This same general diffusion pattern occurred in the spread of news about the attempted assassination of Ronald Reagan, the shooting of Pope John Paul II, and the *Challenger* explosion. In the last case, three-fourths of the population was aware of the event only 30 minutes after it happened.

The role of interpersonal channels in supplementing news diffusion has been studied in some detail. Generally speaking, there are apparently two types of events for which interpersonal communication is often the first source of information: (1) those events that are so important that everybody is interested in them; and (2) those events of such minor importance that only a few people are interested in them. (As

International Perspective: Cultivation Analysis

One of the most notable trends in cultivation analysis has been its expansion into other countries and other cultures. Since cultivation was developed with American culture and American media in mind, there are formidable problems in applying it to other countries. In the first place, although extensive data on the content of American TV are available, comparable knowledge about the content of foreign systems does not exist. This is not as much of a problem in countries which depend heavily on U.S. TV for their programming (such as Australia) as it is in countries where U.S. content is rare (such as China). Further, other cultures hold different notions about violence, sex roles, and politics, areas traditionally examined by cultivation analysis. Despite these obstacles, cultivation researchers are active on several continents.

A study done in Australia found that Australian youths who were heavy viewers of American TV action/adventure shows were more likely than light viewers to believe that the world was a violent place and that people ought not be trusted. A study in Israel found that heavy viewers had a more idealized picture of life in the United States. On the other hand, a study in Great Britain found little evidence of a cultivation effect when it came to images of a violent world. This last finding may be due to the fact that there was little violence in British programs and that U.S. shows accounted for only a small portion of British TV.

A more recent study done in the U.S., Argentina, China, and Korea reported the results of similar cultivation analyses examining sex roles. Despite the differences in culture and TV content, the cultivation effect seemed to show through. In the U.S. 27 percent of the high TV viewers agreed with the statement "Women are happiest at home raising children" compared to 17 percent of the light viewers. In Argentina, 66 percent of the heavy viewers and 50 percent of the light viewers agreed. In China, where equality between the sexes is mandated by law, viewers were asked to agree or disagree with the statement "Women should do most household chores." There were so few who agreed with the statement that no differences were found, but high TV viewers were slightly less likely to disagree than were light viewers. In Korea, traditionally a male-dominated society, 53 percent of heavy viewers endorsed the statement "It's better if men work and women stay at home" compared to 46 percent of light viewers, demonstrating a weak cultivation effect. These findings suggest the cultivation effect may be generalizable to other cultures—a finding that demonstrates that, despite all the hardships, international cultivation research holds great promise.

for news events of intermediate importance, interpersonal communication serves as the first source of information for only about 3–5 percent of the population.) Consider what occurred when Kennedy was shot: About one out of every two people (50 percent) who heard the news heard it first from another person, either in person or over the phone. When *Challenger* exploded, about 25 percent heard first from other people. Similarly, events of relatively minor importance—local stories that might be of interest to only a few people—are also more likely to be passed along via interpersonal channels. One survey found that 10–11 percent of the population first heard about such relatively low newsworthy events from other people, about twice the usual percentage.

• • • •

AGENDA SETTING

One influence of mass media that has turned up in many studies of mass communication is called the **agenda-setting effect**. (An agenda is a list of things to be considered or acted upon.) When we say that the media have an impact on agenda setting we mean that they have the ability to choose and emphasize certain topics, thereby causing the public to perceive these issues as important. Or, to paraphrase Bernard Cohen in his book *The Press and Foreign Policy*, the media may not always be successful in telling people what to think, but they are usually successful in telling people what to think about.

Agenda-setting studies typically concern themselves with information media: news magazines, newspapers, television, and radio. Although some studies have examined the role of news magazines, far more attention has been paid to newspapers and television in agenda-setting research. The few studies that have examined radio have found that this medium has little effect on agenda setting. Further, much of the research on agenda setting has been carried out during political campaigns. There are two reasons for this. First, messages generated by political campaigns are usually designed to set agendas (politicians call this tactic emphasizing the issues). Second, political campaigns have a clear-cut beginning and end, thus making the time period for study unambiguous.

To illustrate a typical agenda-setting study, one investigation of the 1968 presidential election asked a sample of voters to rank-order what they believed to be the key issues of the campaign. While this was going on, researchers examined news magazines, newspapers, and television newscasts, and a ranking of campaign issues was prepared according to the time and space the media devoted to each issue. When the media's ranking was compared to the voters' ranking, there was a strikingly high degree of correspondence. In other words, the voters perceived as important those issues that the media judged important, as evidenced by the amount of coverage they received. Similar studies of more recent elections have found similar results. Although such studies strongly suggest a relationship between personal agendas and media agendas, they do not address the question of causation, an issue that we have encountered before. Although it can be assumed that the media's agenda influences the public's agenda, it is also possible that the public's agenda actually influences that of the media.

Additional research upholds the theory that at times the media have formed the public's perceptions. The Clarence Thomas/Anita Hill episode illustrates this pattern of influence. At first, the story received limited coverage, primarily on public radio; then it was featured more prominently in newspapers, magazines, and network television newscasts. However, public concern did not match media coverage until the TV networks began live coverage of congressional hearings. Subsequently, the Thomas/Hill issue began to assume increased importance among the general public.

To complicate matters, additional studies indicate that there are other situations in which the direction of cause and effect is unclear—or will even depend on the

Media coverage of the hostage situation helped keep the topic on the public's agenda for seven years. The freeing of Joseph Ciccipio, Terry Anderson, and Alann Steen marked the formal end of the crisis. (Kessler/ SIPA)

medium under consideration. At least two studies report that newspapers exert a greater agenda-setting effect than does television. In fact, one survey found that during a political campaign television appeared to alter its coverage to conform to voter interest, while newspapers appeared to shape the voters' agendas. Other research studies have attempted to clarify the differences between the influence of newspapers and television on agenda setting. Interestingly enough, newspapers seemed to become more influential as researchers examined more detailed and differentiated levels of an agenda for a particular topic. For example, one team of researchers postulated that there were at least three different levels of agenda setting: Level one consisted of broad issues such as crime; level two consisted of various subissues such as gun control or mandatory jail sentences; level three consisted of specific information about these subissues such as arguments for or against gun control. The findings of the study revealed that newspapers had more influence on agenda setting at all levels than did television, but were especially important at levels two and three. The type of topic being covered will also influence agenda setting. Coverage of a concrete issue (drug abuse, energy) will have a more pronounced effect than coverage of an abstract issue (federal budget deficit, nuclear arms race). Moreover, a person's experience with a certain news topic will also influence the agenda-setting effect. Stories about inflation, a topic that most consumers experience directly, will have little impact on the public's perception of the importance of this issue. On the other hand, coverage of foreign affairs, where most people lack direct experience, has been found to have a considerable agenda-setting effect.

The occurrence of the agenda-setting effect also depends on other factors, namely, a person's interest in the information, age, education, and political involvement, to name a few. In general, however, we can conclude that the mass media, newspapers and magazines in particular, do have an impact on their audience's perception of certain topics and issues. Sometimes, although not always, television will be less influential than newspapers, probably because of the different characteristics of the two media.

TELEVISION AND COGNITIVE SKILLS

Television has been charged with producing a generation of couch potatoes who simply vegetate in front of the tube, showing little sign of intellectual life. What does the research tell us? This section will briefly examine the connections between TV viewing, IQ, and school achievement.

At first glance, the relationship between TV viewing and IQ seems simple enough. Heavy viewers tend to have slightly lower IQs. On closer examination, however, age seems to be a complicating factor. A couple of surveys showed that in children up to the age of ten or eleven, heavy viewing was associated with a higher IQ. Older children showed the opposite pattern. After about age twelve, the familiar negative relationship showed up. (It may be that the general level of TV programming is geared to the level of a bright ten- or eleven-year-old. As these kids get older, they tend to outgrow their attraction to TV.) Note that these data do not establish that TV *causes* a lower IQ. It may be that youngsters with a low IQ are drawn to the undemanding world of TV for entertainment.

The relationship between TV viewing and school achievement became a hot news item in the 1970s, 1980s, and 1990s because of the steep drop of SAT scores. Some critics blamed much of this decline on TV viewing. The research findings in this area suggest that there is a slight negative relationship between school grades and TV viewing. In one study that statistically controlled for IQ, heavy TV viewers tended to

Are You a TV Addict?

There are numerous references to the addictive nature of TV in popular literature: "Turned On, Tuned In, Strung Out" in *High Times*; "Are You a Secret TV Addict?" in *Vogue*; "Turned On but Tuned Out" in *Redbook*; Marie Winn's *The Plug-In Drug*. Is it possible to be addicted to TV the same way some people are addicted to drugs?

A doctoral dissertation by Robin Smith attempted to construct a scale that would measure possible TV addiction. Some of the items follow. (Score yourself 4 if you answer "always"; 3 for "frequently"; 2 for "sometimes"; and 1 for "never.")

1. I feel depressed when I can't watch TV.

2. I lose track of the time while I'm watching TV.

3. I can't walk away from the TV once it is on.

4. When I'm watching TV I feel like I can't stop.

5. I feel nervous when I can't watch TV.

6. I can't think of anything to do on the weekend or the holidays.

7. I'll watch anything that's on TV.

Total your score. If it's above 14, you scored above the average TV watcher.

Professor Smith's research leading to the development of this scale indicated that if there were TV addicts out there, they were hard to find. None of the 491 people surveyed scored high enough to be considered an addict. Smith concluded that the popular conception of TV as a drug was invalid.

score lower on tests of vocabulary and language achievement than did light viewers, but math achievement scores were not linked to amount of TV viewing. Another study noted that the type of TV content was important. Youngsters who watched a lot of news and educational programs did better than kids who watched lots of action-adventure shows.

Studies of the relationship between reading achievement and TV viewing are hard to summarize. Most have found a slight negative relationship between entertainment viewing and reading skills, but this relationship was influenced by such factors as IQ, social class, age, and parental attitudes toward reading. In short, TV is certainly not the biggest culprit behind the slide in SAT scores. Its impact is relatively light. By the same token, the hours that youngsters invest in watching TV don't seem to pay off in better academic skills.

● ● ● ●
SUGGESTIONS FOR FURTHER READING

The books listed below are valuable sources for additional information on the topics discussed in this chapter.

BARCUS, EARL, *Images of Life on Children's Television*, New York: Praeger, 1983.

COMSTOCK, GEORGE, *Television in America*, Beverly Hills, Calif.: Sage, 1980.

COMSTOCK, GEORGE, STEVEN CHAFFEE, NATHAN KATZMAN, MAX MCCOMBS, AND DONALD ROBERTS, *Television and Human Behavior*, New York: Columbia University Press, 1978.

DENTON, ROBERT, AND GARY WOODWARD, *Political Communication in America*, New York: Praeger, 1990.

GRABER, DORIS, *Mass Media and American Politics*, Washington, D.C.: Congressional Quarterly Press, 1989.

GREENBERG, BRADLEY, AND EDWIN PARKER, *The Kennedy Assassination and the American Public*, Stanford, Calif.: Stanford University Press, 1965.

JEFFRES, LEO, *Mass Media Processes and Effects*, Prospect Heights, Ill.: Waveland Press, 1986.

KUBEY, ROBERT, AND MIHALY CSIKSZENTMIHALYI, *Television and the Quality of Life*, Hillsdale, N.J.: Lawrence Erlbaum, 1990.

LIEBERT, ROBERT M., JOHN NEALE, AND EMILY DAVIDSON, *The Early Window: Effects of Television on Children and Youth*, New York: Pergamon Press, 1988.

PALMER, EDWARD, AND AIMEE DORR, *Children and the Faces of Television*, New York: Academic Press, 1980.

SIGNORIELLI, NANCY, AND MICHAEL MORGAN, *Cultivation Analysis*, Newbury Park, Calif.: Sage, 1988.

TAN, ALEXIS, *Mass Communication Theories and Research*, New York: Wiley, 1985.

22

THE EFFECTS OF MASS COMMUNICATION ON BEHAVIOR

manuel Priola was a hard worker. He would spend many long hours at his West Orange, New Jersey, bar, sometimes not closing until well after midnight. But on this particular autumn evening in 1938, he did an extraordinary thing—he closed up early. Hustling the dozen or so customers out the door, Emanuel Priola rushed home to save his wife and children from the Martians who were invading New York. Luckily for Mr. Priola (and, for that matter, the rest of the world), the Martians hadn't landed. He had just been fooled by a CBS radio dramatization of H.G. Wells' *War of the Worlds*.

The Air Lines Pilots Association knew it was a bad idea. Shortly before Christmas in 1966, NBC was planning to broadcast a made-for-TV movie, written by Rod Serling, called *The Doomsday Flight*. In the film, a man hides a bomb that is rigged to an altimeter aboard an airliner. If the plane drops below a certain altitude, the bomb will explode. While the plane is airborne, the man calls the airline and offers to disclose the location of the bomb in exchange for a large sum of money. The Pilots Association was afraid that such a film would prompt some unstable individuals to imitate what they had seen. The pilots were right. Even before the telecast was over, one bomb threat based on the idea in the film was telephoned to an airline. In the days following the broadcast, twelve more similar threats were received. (Ignoring the above, Australian TV broadcast the same film in 1971. The effects were the same. In fact, Qantas Airlines paid out half a million dollars in ransom to a person who called in to report a bomb on one of their planes heading for Hong Kong.)

The manager of the Esplanade Triplex Theater in Oakland, California, was uneasy. Paramount Pictures had chosen February 1979, to release one of its newest pictures, *The Warriors*. The film was about gang warfare in New York City, and the manager had noticed that it had attracted a rather unusual crowd to his California theater. Many in the crowd looked as though they belonged to gangs themselves. The audience was unusually rowdy during the screening of the film, but there were no major incidents and the manager began to breathe a little more easily as the crowd slowly filtered out into the lobby after the film was over. Suddenly, before anybody could tell what was happening, a knife fight, much like the one portrayed in the film, broke out between two rival gangs. Before the manager could stop it, an eighteen-year-old boy was fatally stabbed.

In 1991, history repeated itself—twice. In March, Warner Brothers released *New Jack City*, a violent film about a Harlem drug lord. In New York, two teenagers got into an argument during the movie and went outside to fight. A gunfight broke out; more than 100 shots were fired—some from an automatic weapon—and when it was over, one of the teens was dead. In Chicago, an innocent bystander was shot in the leg when rival gangs exchanged gunshots after seeing the movie. In New Jersey, three police officers and a civilian were hurt when fights broke out during the movie.

Los Angeles police converge on a theater in the Westwood section of L.A. after violence broke out at a showing of New Jack City. *(Wide World Photos)*

Eighteen people were arrested in Las Vegas when a gang brawl erupted during the film.

Five months later, more violence broke out during the premiere of *Boyz 'N' the Hood*. The critically acclaimed film tries to show an alternative to violence as a solution to problems (the film was subtitled "Increase the Peace"). Its opening, however, was marred by brutality. In Chicago, a man was fatally shot after a midnight showing at a local drive-in. Five people were hit by gunfire in Los Angeles. In Minneapolis, the crowd fled when shots were fired inside the theater. As the crowd ran outside, someone in a passing vehicle fired shots at them, wounding six people.

These incidents, drawn from four different decades, highlight the dramatic power that mass media possess—the power to influence a person's behavior. Typically, of course, the media are not this influential. Not everybody who listened to *War of the Worlds* fled for the hills. Not everyone who saw *The Doomsday Flight* phoned in a bomb threat. Probably two million people saw *Boyz 'N' the Hood* during its opening weekend and only a small number were moved to violence. Nonetheless, the mass media have the potential to influence audience behavior, and throughout the years there has been an expression of social concern over the extent of this topic.

As we have seen, some of this concern has been reflected in formal and informal controls over the media. For example, the Supreme Court has recognized that children are a special audience that need protection from exposure to potentially harmful material, such as pornography (see Chapter 17). Additionally, television networks recognize that there may be harmful effects for some people in viewing some program content. Consequently, the networks have standards and guidelines that attempt to minimize any negative impact (see Chapter 18). This chapter will focus on what is known about the media's impact on actual behavior. Our goal is to present a basic overview of the effects of media on how people behave.

• • • •

INVESTIGATING MASS COMMUNICATION EFFECTS

There are many ways to investigate what is or is not an effect of mass communication. Some individuals claim that personal observation is the best way of establishing proof. Others rely on expert opinions and evaluations; still others point to common sense when they wish to support their views. All of these methods have their place, and each can be quite valid. Nonetheless, in an area as complicated as this, many feel that the best sources of information are those derived from scientific study of the media's impact on individuals. Consequently, most of this chapter will consist of a discussion and summary of these studies. You should keep in mind that when it comes to gathering information about media effects, scientists have typically used two main methods:

1. The **survey** is carried out in the real world and usually consists of a large group of individuals who answer questions put to them via a questionnaire. Although the survey is usually not sufficient proof of cause and effect, it does help to establish associations between various factors. A special kind of survey, a **panel study**, allows researchers to be more confident about attributing patterns of cause and effect in survey data. The panel study collects data from the same people at two or more different points in time. As a result, it is possible, for example, using sophisticated techniques that control the effects of other variables, to see if viewing televised violence at an early age is related to aggressive behavior at a later date. Panel studies are expensive and take a long time to complete.

2. The **experiment** is performed in a laboratory and usually consists of the controlled manipulation of a single factor to determine its impact on another factor. A special kind of experiment, a **field experiment**, is conducted in a real-life setting. Field experiments are more realistic than laboratory experiments but they are also harder to control. Experiments are useful because they help establish causality.

• • • •

MEDIA EFFECTS ON BEHAVIOR: A CAPSULE HISTORY

It was early motion pictures that first inspired questions about the impact of the entertainment media on society. After all, children would sit for hours in a darkened theater, away from parental supervision, and watch films produced by the inhabitants of Sin City (more precisely, Hollywood). During the late 1920s and early 1930s, the "gangster" film became quite popular. (Some of these films still show up on late-night TV. Try to watch one if the opportunity arises to see what all the shouting was about.) People were lining up to see movies such as *Me, Gangster* (1928), *Little Caesar* (1930), and *The Public Enemy* (1931). It wasn't long before concerned parents and civic groups began to question the impact of these films on their children.

Consequently, in 1929 the first full-scale investigation into the effects of the entertainment film was begun. The study (actually, there were twelve studies in all) was sponsored by the prestigious Payne Fund. Experiments and surveys were carried out to address such questions as: How do the morés of the movies compare with the morés of America? Do films directly or indirectly alter the conduct of children? Are films related to delinquency and crime? Although these studies did not conclusively prove that movies caused delinquency, their findings brought a tremendous amount of pressure to bear on the government and the industry to take action. As a result, the production code of the Motion Pictures Producers and Distributors of America, a powerful industry group, was strengthened to make sure that films did not portray gangsters in a favorable light.

Growing Public Concern

The potentially harmful effects of gangster and action-adventure radio programs were again the subject of limited research attention during the 1930s. The area that aroused the most research interest, however, was the political impact of the mass media, especially that of radio. Franklin Roosevelt had used radio effectively during his first two terms in office. In Louisiana, Huey Long also used radio addresses to increase his political influence. Many people feared that a skilled political demagogue might use the new radio medium to shape popular opinion to his advantage. As a result, large-scale studies of the voting process were conducted during the 1940 presidential campaign to gauge the extent of media influence. After an interruption caused by World War II, the 1948 election was similarly studied by sociologists and political scientists. Somewhat surprisingly, these researchers found that the media had little direct effect on political decision making. Instead, personal influence was more important, and individuals called "opinion leaders" were thought to be quite important in transmitting political information (recall the discussion of the multistep flow in Chapter 19).

The explosive growth of television in the early 1950s refocused research attention on media impact on young people. Families with children were among the first to acquire TV sets, and children tended to watch a lot of television. Some of the cartoon programs and slapstick comedies that were the staples of early television contained a good deal of violence. Parents were worried that, as had been the case with movies, their children would imitate and adopt some of the violent behaviors they were watching. This concern was translated to the national level when in 1952 Senator Estes Kefauver held hearings into the causes of juvenile delinquency. Part of the hearings examined the effect of violent portrayals on television and in comic books. When this same committee held hearings again during 1954–1955, it concluded that violent programming in large doses could be potentially harmful to children.

Franklin D. Roosevelt effectively used radio as a political communications tool during his "fireside chats" with the nation. The increasing importance of radio as a political tool prompted several large-scale studies during the 1940s. (The Bettmann Archive)

The growing importance of television was also evident in the increased attention given to it by scientists concerned with the effects of mass communication. In the late 1950s and early 1960s three important books discussing the impact of the media, and of TV in particular, were published. Two were somewhat similar in approach. The first of these, *Television and the Child*, appeared in 1958 and discussed the results of interviews with several thousand English youngsters. In this English study, the researchers found that television had an impact on children's values and their perceptions of the world. Three American scientists—Schramm, Lyle, and Parker—reported the results of surveys conducted in ten American cities in their book *Television in the Lives of Our Children* (1961). In many ways their reported findings were similar to those of their British counterparts. The American researchers noted that as children grew older, those with lower IQ scores watched more television than did those with higher IQ scores. They also noted that children who had unsatisfactory social relationships reported heavier viewing. These researchers further reported that although there was no indication that television causes delinquency or violent behavior in most normal children, certain children might be susceptible. In short, Schramm and his colleagues emphasized that the intellectual and emotional characteristics of children were important factors in determining TV's influence.

The third book, *The Effects of Mass Communication* (1960), was written by a sociologist, Joseph Klapper. Its main thesis stressed the social and psychological factors that would "mediate" the direct effects of the mass media. Klapper argued that because of these mediating factors, the media would operate far more frequently to reinforce a person's behaviors, attitudes, and values than they would to change them. Based on his research, Klapper concluded that although the mass media do not necessarily cause viewers to become more apathetic, passive, or aggressive, they might reinforce tendencies already present in the viewers. (Taken together, these three books marked the emergence of the effects of mass communication as an area of scientific research and served to highlight many areas of concern that were to encourage more research. We will have more to say about many of these topics later in this chapter.)

During the 1960s, there was considerable concern over the impact of the mass media, as evidenced by Senate subcommittee hearings on juvenile delinquency conducted in 1961 and again in 1964. The report of this subcommittee warned that violent television content might cause antisocial behavior among young people. The concern was reinforced by the assassinations and civil disorder of the middle sixties, and in 1967 President Lyndon Johnson appointed the National Commission on the Causes and Prevention of Violence. The commission reiterated the need for more significant research in the area and concluded that a "constant diet of violent behavior on television had an adverse effect on human character and attitudes." In addition, the commission studied the role of the news media in creating and aggravating civil disorders by their very presence on the scene.

At about this same time, another national commission was preparing a report on a totally different topic. Because of less stringent laws governing pornographic and obscene materials, "adult-oriented" films, books, and magazines were becoming more prevalent. The National Commission on Obscenity and Pornography was established to examine the potentially negative effects of this material. When it released its report in 1970, it urged, among other things, that all laws prohibiting the distribution of pornographic materials be repealed.

The 1970s: Concern over TV Violence

The big story of 1970, however, concerned the impact of television violence. Through the efforts of Senator John Pastore, the Office of the Surgeon General (the same office that had earlier released a report on the health hazards of smoking) was given a million dollars to sponsor a program of original research to "establish scientifically insofar as possible what harmful effects, if any, television programs have on our children." A scientific advisory committee, composed of distinguished scientists, was to be set up to conduct the research program. Unfortunately, controversy soon developed over the way committee members were selected. (The television networks were allowed to veto potential committee members whom they felt would be "biased" in their outlooks.)

Ultimately, research was completed and the report released in 1972. Consisting of a summary written by the advisory committee and five technical volumes encompassing twenty-three separate research reports and more than forty separate technical papers, the project was the single most concerted research effort directed at determining the effects of violent media content on the audience. More controversy met the release of this report. Several researchers who had contributed technical reports to the series felt that the summary volume, written by the advisory committee (which consisted of two employees in the research departments of NBC and CBS, respectively, and several others who had done consulting work for the networks), did not accurately summarize the results. Not surprisingly, criticism also surrounded the reporting of the research results in the popular press. Newspaper and television reports were based on the summary volume rather than on the technical reports. Critics charged that the summary volume was a "whitewash" that minimized the negative effects of viewing televised violence.

It was unfortunate that so much controversy obscured the findings of this research effort, which was a valuable project, reporting significant results about the effects of televised violence. Using both the survey and the experimental techniques, researchers had concluded that exposure to televised violence could increase the probability of antisocial behavior over both the short and long term. In addition, the researchers announced evidence of a causal link between viewing TV violence and antisocial behavior. This was the first time such a statement had been made by a body of distinguished researchers. Reinforcement for this causal link came a few years later from a study done in England by William Belson. Belson's survey, which examined more than 1500 London youngsters, reported data demonstrating that watching violence on television apparently prompted the commission of serious aggressive acts. In 1982, a follow-up study to the Surgeon General's report confirmed the findings of the original and stated in stronger terms the link between viewing televised violence and antisocial behavior.

In the early 1980s, a considerable amount of attention was given to studying the media's impact on what was called **prosocial behavior** (simply a catchall term that researchers assign to behaviors that are judged to be desirable or worthwhile under the circumstances). The popularity of this topic had declined by the mid-1980s, possibly because of the difficulty in defining precisely what was meant by the concept and the difficulty in finding links between viewing prosocial behavior on TV and real-life prosocial actions.

In the middle 1980s, a great deal of research attention was devoted to investigating the behavioral effects of the new technologies. Several studies examined who first acquired VCRs, teletext, cable, or home computers. Other research analyzed how the new technologies were used by consumers and how much time was spent with each. Still other researchers tried to determine what impact the new media were having on society. In the area of political communication, two topics attracted research attention. The first had to do with the impact of televised debates between presidential and vice-presidential candidates on voting behavior. The second had to do with the effects of exit polling and early projections of winners on the outcomes of elections. (Both of these topics are discussed further below.) In the late 1980s, sparked by the publication of a new federal report on the topic, a considerable amount of attention and controversy were focused on the effects of aggressive and nonaggressive pornography. The results of this research (summarized later in this chapter) were at the center of a scientific and political debate.

In the early 1990s, attention was again focused on media violence because of a combination of events. First, a law sponsored by Senator Paul Simon was passed that enabled the networks and cable companies to cooperate to control the presentation of violent behavior without fear of running afoul of the Justice Department's anticollusion provisions. Simon got interested in the violence issue after he saw what he claims was *The Texas Chainsaw Massacre* on TV in his motel room during his unsuccessful campaign for the Democratic presidential nomination in 1988.

Secondly, an unprecedented surge of violent media content surfaced at about the same time. At the local movie theater were pictures such as *Silence of the Lambs*, about a psychopathic killer, *Die Hard II*, in which 264 people are killed including one unfortunate villain stabbed in the eye with an icicle, and *Terminator 2*, which was bursting with gory special effects. On the bookshelves were books like *American Psycho*, another story about a psychopathic killer, and *Angel of Darkness*, a true-crime novel about a serial killer who murdered 67 people. On TV, there was *Twin Peaks*, a quirky show about the murder of a prom queen, and on CD, there was the Geto Boys' "Mind of a Lunatic," a rap rendition about yet another psychopath, and Guns 'n' Roses' *Appetite for Destruction*, with a cover so offensive that many record stores didn't carry the album.

As a result of this, public concern about media violence was rekindled. One poll showed that two-thirds of Americans thought that media violence was a considerable factor in prompting real-life violence. At the same time, many researchers started to examine seriously the impact of this new round of ultraexplicit violence. When their results become available, perhaps new light will be shed on the repercussions of exposure to media mayhem.

To summarize,

1. As of 1992, the bulk of media research has been concerned with potentially antisocial effects of the mass media on their audiences.

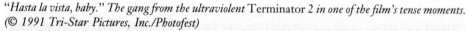

"Hasta la vista, baby." The gang from the ultraviolent Terminator 2 *in one of the film's tense moments.* (© *1991 Tri-Star Pictures, Inc./Photofest*)

2. Research questions deemed important by the federal government have received the major share of research attention (in part because the federal government can make money for research available).

3. Most research into the effects of mass communication on behavior has focused on children and adolescents.

4. Since the 1960s, studies concerning the impact of television have been the most numerous.

We will now examine more closely some of the topics mentioned in this summary. We begin by considering the topic that has generated the most research attention: the effects of TV violence.

• • • •

THE IMPACT OF TELEVISED VIOLENCE

Does television viewing prompt violent or other antisocial behaviors on the part of the viewer? As we have just seen, this question has been debated for the better part of three decades. It is a complicated issue, and the absolute answer has not yet been found. Nonetheless, enough evidence has been gathered so that we can begin to point to some preliminary conclusions. In order to arrive at these conclusions it will be necessary to examine research data from surveys and from experiments.

Survey Results

The following represent abbreviated and modified questionnaire items taken from surveys designed to analyze violent TV viewing and aggressive behavior.

About how often do you watch the following TV programs:

	ALMOST ALWAYS	OFTEN	SOMETIMES	NEVER
Heat of the Night	_____	_____	_____	_____
Cheers	_____	_____	_____	_____
Young Riders	_____	_____	_____	_____
The Cosby Show	_____	_____	_____	_____
Top Cops	_____	_____	_____	_____
Jake and the Fatman	_____	_____	_____	_____

Next, what would you do if these things happened to you?

1. Pretend somebody you know takes something from you and won't give it back. What would you do?

_____ Hit the other person and take my property back

_____ Call the police

_____ Ask the person to return it

_____ Nothing

2. Pretend somebody is telling lies about you. What would you do?

_____ Hit the person and make the person stop

_____ Ask the person to stop telling lies

_____ Nothing

As you can see, with measures like the above (assuming, of course, a questionnaire that was much longer), it would be possible to index a person's viewing of programs that generally contain violence. It would also be possible to measure that same person's tendency to report his or her willingness to use violence in everyday situations. If violent TV viewing does affect behavior, we would expect to find some relationship between reported heavy viewing of violence and an individual's own self-report of aggressive tendencies. If we do not find such a link, we might assume that exposure to media violence has no impact on subsequent aggressive tendencies. If, however we do find a connection, we might conclude that media violence could actually cause aggression. We could not be sure, however, because survey data alone are not sufficient to establish a cause-and-effect relationship. (It might be possible, for example, that aggressive tendencies actually cause people to view violent TV shows, or that some third factor, related to both viewing TV violence and aggression, is the real cause.) We must also keep in mind that there are different ways of measuring exposure to TV violence and aggressive tendencies. In fact, as we shall see, some of the inconsistencies found in survey research might be due to variations in the way that exposure to violence is measured.

Early surveys revealed no significant relationship between general television viewing and aggressive actions. The British surveys reported in *Television and the Child* found no differences in aggressive tendencies among young children who had access to TV sets and those who didn't. Schramm and his co-workers found the same in a survey done among Canadian youths. These researchers also found no differences on scales designed to measure antisocial aggression between young people classified as heavy viewers and others labeled as light viewers. Overall exposure to television, however, is perhaps not the same as overall exposure to *television violence*, a factor that might account for the lack of a relationship.

The Surgeon General's report discusses other surveys that used somewhat different measures of exposure to TV violence. At least two studies in which young people were asked to name their favorite TV programs found a connection between aggression and the number of violent programs named, but at least two other surveys using similar techniques failed to uncover any such association. More recent research suggests why such inconsistencies may have occurred. It appears that classifying individuals on the basis of selecting four or five favorite programs may not be an accurate measure of the total amount of TV violence that they see. Interestingly, most surveys that measure viewing of TV violence by measuring all programs usually watched in a specified time period (the abbreviated form of that particular measurement technique is illustrated in the example preceding this section) have consistently demonstrated a positive relationship between such viewing and measures of aggressiveness. This relationship persists when the effects of other factors (such as sex, school performance, and social class) are statistically controlled.

Viewed as a whole, these studies and other surveys compiled over the years are difficult to sum up. Perhaps the most concise generalization about the results of survey research is one that appears in a recent summary of television research findings. After carefully analyzing all survey results, the authors of this summary state: ". . . we conclude that the evidence to date indicates that there is a significant correlation between the viewing of violent television programs and aggressive behavior in day-to-day life."

Nevertheless, as already mentioned, a relationship is not necessarily evidence of cause and effect. Remember, however, that the special survey technique known as a panel study gives us a little more confidence in making cause-and-effect statements based on survey data. Since panel studies cost a lot and sometimes take years to complete, not many exist. Further, the results from those that are available are not as clear as we might like them to be. One panel study was included in the 1972 Surgeon General's report on television and social behavior. Although its methods might have been stronger, it found evidence that viewing violent TV shows at an early age was a cause of aggression in later life.

Additional survey evidence appeared in 1982 with the publication of *Television and Aggression: A Panel Study*. This book reported the results of a three-year research project sponsored by the NBC television network. Data on aggression, TV viewing, and a large number of sociological variables were collected on six different occasions from children in two Midwestern cities. Eventually, about 1200 boys in grades two through six participated in the main survey. Exposure to TV violence was measured by giving each child a program checklist. Aggression was measured by asking each boy to nominate peers who "hit and punch other people" or "hurt others by pushing or shoving."

Lengthy and detailed analysis of the data suggested that there was no relationship between violent TV viewing and subsequent aggressive behavior. Later, other researchers were given the opportunity to reanalyze the NBC data. One reexamination did find some partial evidence of a causal relationship between TV violence and aggression, but its impact was tiny. In sum, if a causal relationship was present in the NBC data, it was extremely weak and hard to find.

In 1986, an international team of scientists reported the results of panel studies done in five countries: the United States, Finland, Australia, Israel, and Poland. The U.S. study and the Polish study found that early TV viewing was significantly related to later aggression. The Finnish study reached a similar conclusion for boys but found no similar relationship for girls. In Israel, viewing TV violence seemed to be a cause of subsequent aggression among boys and girls who lived in urban areas but not for those who lived in the country. The panel study done in Australia was not able to find a causal relationship. Despite these differences, the five panels were consistent in at least two findings. First, the relationship between the viewing of violence and aggression tended to be somewhat weak. Second, there was a pattern of circularity in causation. Viewing violent TV caused some children to become more aggressive. Being aggressive, in turn, caused some children to watch more violent TV.

What are we to make of all these panel studies? On the whole, they seem to suggest that there is a mutual causal connection between watching TV violence and performing aggressive acts. This connection, however, is small and influenced by individual and cultural factors.

Perhaps at this point we should turn to the results of laboratory studies to aid us further in forming a conclusion about what causes what. In the lab, time order is strictly controlled and possible third factors can be ruled out (because the random assignment of people to experimental conditions would cancel out any extraneous influences). If experimental studies confirm survey results, we could feel more confident about drawing a connection between viewing violence on television and aggressive acts in everyday behavior.

Experimental Results

Imagine the following. It is a cold winter night. As part of the requirements of Psychology 100, a course in which you are enrolled, you are required to serve as a subject in three hours of research. Tonight is your night to fulfill part of your obligation. Thus you find yourself trudging across campus to the Psychology Building. Upon arriving, you join several dozen other students in a large auditorium. Before long an individual enters the room, introduces himself as Professor so-and-so, and tells you that you are about to begin your first experiment of the evening.

Professor so-and-so has a new IQ test that he is trying to develop and needs your cooperation. The test booklet is passed out and you are told to begin. As soon as you start the test, you realize that it is unlike any IQ test you have ever seen before. There are questions about advanced calculus, early Greek architecture, and organic chemistry, which you have no idea how to answer. In a few minutes, Professor so-and-so starts making sarcastic comments: "You'll never finish college if this simple test takes you so long"; "It looks as if this group will certainly flunk out"; "High school students have finished this test by now." Finally, with an air of exasperation, the professor says, "There's no hope for you. Hand in the papers. Since most of you won't be in school after this semester's grades, let me say goodbye to you now." With that, the professor storms out of the room.

A few minutes go by and then another individual enters the room and calls out two lists of names. Each group is assigned to another room down the hall. When you report to your assigned room, you find another professor already there. She tells you that this is the second experiment you will participate in tonight. It is a study to see how much people remember from films. You are going to be shown a brief excerpt from a film, and then you will be asked questions about it. The lights go out, and all of a sudden you are watching an eight-minute fight scene from a Kirk Douglas film called *The Champion*. In the movie, Douglas, playing a boxer, gets the stuffing beaten out of him as he competes for the championship. (Unknown to you, that other group of students is also seeing a film. At the same time you're watching Douglas get battered, they're viewing a totally different scene from *Canal Boats in Venice*.) When the film ends, you are asked several memory questions about its content.

You are then directed to yet another room. Once in this cubicle, you are told that the third and last experiment is to begin. You are seated in front of a rather strange-looking machine with a dial that can be moved from a setting of one to eleven. You also notice a button and a light connected to something behind the machine. The researcher explains that you are to be part of an experiment designed to investigate memory. In another room, but wired up to this same machine, is a student who is learning a word-association test. Every time this other student makes a mistake, you are to punish him by giving him a shock. The dial on your panel determines the intensity of the shock; when you press the button, it will be administered. You can choose any level you like; you can hold the button down as long as you like. The experimenter then gives you a level-two shock to show you what it feels like. You jump and wonder why you didn't take botany instead of psych. Your thoughts are interrupted, however, when the little light on the panel flashes on. The other student has made a mistake. It's your job to administer punishment. Your hand reaches for the dial. . . .

The Catharsis vs. Stimulation Debate

The above is an abstracted, simplified, and condensed version of the prototype experimental design used in several key studies to investigate the impact of media violence. The idea behind this experiment is to test two rival theories about the effects of watching violence. The first theory is thousands of years old; it is called the **catharsis theory** and can be traced back to Aristotle. This theory holds that viewing scenes of aggression can actually purge the viewer's own aggressive feelings. Thus a person who sees a violent television program or movie might end up less likely to commit violence. The other theory, called the **stimulation theory**, argues just the opposite. It suggests that seeing scenes of violence will actually stimulate an individual to behave more violently afterward.

As you may realize, in the above hypothetical experiment everybody was first insulted and presumably angered (this part of the experiment gave you some hostility to be purged); one group saw a violent film while the other saw a nonviolent film. Both groups were then given a turn at the punishment machine. If catharsis is right, then the group that saw *The Champion* should give less intense shocks; if stimulation is correct, then *The Champion* group should give more intense shocks.

The catharsis vs. stimulation debate was one of the earliest to surface in the study of mass media's effects. One early study seemed to point to catharsis, but a series of studies carried out by psychologist Leonard Berkowitz and his colleagues at the University of Wisconsin found strong support for the stimulation hypothesis. Since that time, the bulk of the evidence seems consistent: Watching media violence tends to stimulate aggressive behavior on the part of the viewer. There is little evidence for catharsis.

Bandura's Experiment

The catharsis vs. stimulation question was only one of several topics that sparked early experimental work in the investigation of the effects of the media. Another controversy arose over the possibility that TV and movies were serving as a school for violence. Would children imitate violent behavior they had just observed in films or TV programs in their own real-life play behaviors? A series of experiments conducted by psychologist Albert Bandura and his colleagues during the 1960s indicated that, in fact, films and TV might teach aggressive behaviors.

Preschool children were shown films in which a model reacted violently to a large rubber doll (called a Bobo doll). When children were placed in a play situation similar to the one they had just observed, they mimicked the behaviors they had just seen, performing far more aggressively toward the unfortunate Bobo doll than did children who had not seen the film. It was further determined that children would behave more aggressively if they were rewarded for doing so or if they saw the model in the film

A series of still photographs of the famous study by Bandura, Ross, and Ross (1961). In this experiment children watched adults act aggressively toward a Bobo doll. When allowed to play in the same room, these children imitated the behavior of the adult models. (Courtesty of Albert Bandura)

rewarded. Of course, as you are probably aware, there is a big difference between hitting an inanimate doll and hitting a human being. To account for this, more recent studies have substituted a human being dressed as a clown for the faithful Bobo doll. Although more children were willing to hit the rubber doll, a large number also physically assaulted the human clown. This reaction did not occur among children who had not seen the violent film.

Complicating Factors

Of course, there are many complicating factors that might influence the results of such experiments. To begin with, many of these studies used specially made films and videotapes. In laboratory situations, the experimental "program" may not be able to duplicate the impact of real-life TV or films. In those films and tapes produced especially for laboratory use, the violence is concentrated in a short period; there is usually a clear connection between the violence and its motivations and consequences. Contemporary films or TV shows are not this direct, and violence is usually embedded in a larger story line. Punishment for violence may not occur until the end of the program. Motives may be mixed or unclear.

Further, it is likely that a person's age, sex, social class, and prior level of aggression will influence the ultimate effect of viewing televised violence. Boys, for example, tend to be more affected by TV violence than girls. Children who come from homes where there are no explicit guidelines condemning violence also seem to be more strongly affected. Evidence concerning age and social class is not as clear-cut. It also appears that a similarity between the setting and circumstances surrounding televised violence and the situation in which a person finds himself or herself immediately after viewing is an important factor. The more alike the two settings, the more aggressively the person is likely to behave. (Recall the example of *The Warriors* mentioned in the beginning of this chapter. Also, see box on page 552.)

Finally, the presence or absence of others and their reactions directly influence aggression. If children were watching an aggressive film in the company of an adult who made positive comments about the media violence, they acted more aggressively than children who viewed with a silent adult. Conversely, children who heard the on-screen aggression condemned committed fewer aggressive acts. It has also been shown that children who view violence in pairs act more aggressively than children who are alone.

Field Experiments

Recall that field experiments are experiments that take place in a natural setting. People are studied in their typical environment, where they probably react more naturally than they do in the lab. On the other hand, field experiments are subject to the contaminating influences of outside events.

The results of field experiments are not entirely consistent but they do suggest some preliminary conclusions. At least two field experiments done in the early 1970s revealed no link between TV and aggression. On the other hand, five field experiments have yielded data consonant with the survey and lab data. Their main conclusion is that people who watched a steady diet of violent programs tended to exhibit more antisocial or aggressive behavior.

One of the more elaborate field experiments involved identifying a Canadian town that was surrounded by mountains and unable to receive a TV signal until 1974. Two similar towns were selected for comparison—one could get only Canadian TV while the other could get Canadian and U.S. channels. The research team gathered data from all three towns in 1974 and again two years later. Children in the town that just got U.S. TV showed an increase in their rate of aggressive acts that was more than three times higher than that of children living in the other two towns. Taken as a

Is Nintendo Hazardous to Your Health?

The Japanese computer game giant, Nintendo, has been one of the biggest success stories of the last five years. Its games are in more than 22 million American homes; it sells about 50 million game cartridges a year. Nintendo and its competitors market videogames that are strangely addictive. One teenager played Mario Brothers for two days straight. A woman in Indiana played so much she developed "Nintendonitis," a finger inflammation caused by too much pressing and joysticking.

Nintendo and its counterparts have been criticized for the violent content of their games. In Top Gun, players shoot down planes; in Punch-out, they knock out people in hand-to-hand combat; in countless space games, players zap, disintegrate, or otherwise destroy fleets of spaceships. Some videogames have raised questions of taste. One is based on the Intifada and pits Israelis against Palestinians. Another is based on escaping from Nazi prison camps.

No matter the content, many have been concerned that the games spark aggression in the kids who play them. Research into the effects of videogames has turned up little evidence to show that videogame violence leads to real-life aggression. One study done at Auburn University found that playing the games does get kids excited but not aggressive. Another study suggested that the games were so far removed from reality that their impact was minimal. Some even go so far as to suggest that videogames might be good for you. A recent book, *Mind and Media*, even points out that college students who frequently play videogames show an improvement in intellectual abilities. And you thought you were wasting your time with Mario and Luigi.

Children testing their reflexes with a popular videogame manufactured by a company in Japan. Critics have voiced concern over such toys, suggesting that they might encourage aggressive behavior and promote long hours in front of the TV. (Spencer Grant/Monkmeyer)

After an individual has seen a violent film or TV program, his or her aggressive tendencies might remain in low gear unless something in the postviewing environment sets them off. It is possible, for example, that a person who has witnessed scenes of a brutal fight in a movie might not exhibit any aggression immediately afterwards unless that person encounters something or someone that has some association with the filmed fight.

In a series of intriguing experiments, Dr. Leonard Berkowitz and his associates at the University of Wisconsin studied one circumstance that seems important in triggering violent behavior: the similarity between the victim of the screen violence and the potential target of the viewer's aggression. In one experiment, similar in design to the simplified experiment reported in the text, college students were insulted by a confederate of the experimenter who was posing as another subject. The confederate was introduced to one group of subjects as a "speech major" and yet to another group as a "college boxer." The insulted subjects were then shown either a violent film of a boxing match (the fight sequence from *The Champion* in which star Kirk Douglas gets beaten up) or a nonviolent film. Afterwards, all participants were given a chance to administer electric shocks to the confederate (the one who had earlier insulted them) as part of an alleged learning experiment. What group gave the larger number of shocks? The group that had seen the boxing film and that had been insulted by the "college boxer."

In a follow-up study, Berkowitz linked the film's victim and the potential target by giving them the same name. Again, two films were used—the boxing film starring *Kirk* Douglas and another nonviolent but exciting film of a track race. One group of subjects was insulted by a confederate called "Bob." Another group of subjects was insulted by a confederate named "Kirk," the same name as that of the victim in the movie, a "coincidence" that was pointed out by the experimenter. Each group then saw either a violent or nonviolent film and was given a chance to administer electric shocks to the person who had recently insulted them. What group gave the most shocks? As you might have already surmised, the group that saw the boxing film and that had been insulted by "Kirk."

We can conclude from the above experiments that one important condition for the triggering of violent behavior is the availability of an appropriate target who resembles the victim in the media portrayal of violence.

whole, although the results from the field experiments are not as striking as they might be, they tend to support the notion that violent TV viewing fosters aggressive behavior.

Let us now try to summarize the results of these surveys and experiments. Although no single survey or experiment can provide a conclusive answer about the effects of media violence and although every single study can be criticized for certain shortcomings, there appears to be a thread of consistency running throughout these studies. Surveys and panel studies have indicated that there is a relationship between viewing violent programs and aggressive behavior. Lab and field experiments also have shown that watching violence increases the possibility of behaving aggressively. Taken as a whole, these results encourage a tentative acceptance of the proposition that watching violence on television increases aggressiveness on the part of at least some viewers. This conclusion, however, should be qualified.

Viewing TV violence is only one of many factors that might prompt a person to behave aggressively and, in relative terms, its influence is not particularly strong. But is a weak relationship an inconsequential relationship? Much of the recent debate about TV violence has centered on this question. In statistical terms, researchers gauge the strength of any relationship by the amount of variability in one measure that is accounted for by the other. For example, height and weight are two factors that are related. If I know how tall you are, I can make a better guess about your weight than if I didn't know your height. I may not get your weight exactly right, but at least I'll be closer to the correct figure. Consequently, height "explains" some of the variability associated with weight. If two factors are perfectly related, one explains 100 percent of the variability of the other. If two factors are strongly related, one might account for 60–70 percent of the variability of the other. If two factors are not related, for example, weight and IQ, one would explain 0 percent of the variability of the other. As far as TV violence and aggression are concerned, exposure to TV violence typically explains from about 2–9 percent of the variability of aggression. In other words, about 91–98 percent of the variability in aggression is due to something else. Given these figures, is the impact of TV violence really that important in a practical sense?

The answer to this question is more political and philosophical than scientific, but research does provide some benchmarks for comparison. In psychology, the relationship between undergoing psychotherapy and being "cured" of your mental ailment is only slightly stronger than that between TV violence and aggression. Psychotherapy explains about 10 percent of the variability in cure rates. In relative terms, however, this means that psychotherapy increases the success rate from 34 percent to 66 percent of patients, hardly an outcome to be labeled inconsequential. Moreover, the effect size for TV violence's impact on antisocial behavior is only slightly less than that of the effect size between viewing *Sesame Street* and readiness for school. *Sesame Street*, of course, was regarded as a great success. Furthermore, the Food and Drug Administration has released for general use several drugs whose therapeutic effect was about as great or even less than the size of the effect between TV violence and aggression. Thus, although the size of the effect is not great, it is not too different from effects in other areas that we treat as socially and practically meaningful. Even though the effect might be small, it is not necessarily trivial.

● ● ● ●
ENCOURAGING PROSOCIAL BEHAVIOR

Most of the early research into the effects of mass communication dealt with the negative or antisocial effects of the media. Increasing violence in society and rising crime rates were important social issues that attracted attention. Toward the end of the 1960s, however, sparked perhaps by the success of public television's *Sesame Street*,

therapysomething

ABC's yuppie show *thirtysomething* was a TV show that was sometimes used in psychological therapy. This is not surprising since most of the show dealt with characters discussing their inner conflicts, frustrations, unfulfilled needs, and hidden feelings. Therapists have prescribed viewing the program to get people more in touch with their own emotions. Sometimes, counselors have shown specific scenes that are similar to problems faced by their cli-ents in real life. Especially popular are the episodes dealing with Nancy and Elliot's marital problems and Michael and Hope's adjustments to a new baby. Therapists report that although some people are initially skeptical about TV therapy, the show does provide them with a common ground to allow them to talk about their feelings.

Unfortunately, ABC canceled *thirtysomething* after the 1990–1991 season. It seems that ABC's ratings were also in need of therapy.

researchers realized that many positive behaviors could be promoted by television programs. (These behaviors are generally referred to by the umbrella term of **prosocial behavior** and can include actions such as sharing, cooperating, self-control, and helping.) For the sake of simplicity, we will divide our discussion into three parts; each part will examine one specific area of prosocial behavior that has received research attention.

Therapeutic Effects

If film and television can have adverse effects on some people, it is possible that they might also encourage positive attitudes, such as courage, in children. Early studies demonstrated that these media could help children overcome psychological childhood phobias. For example, many children are afraid of dogs (caninophobia). In an early experiment, some fearful children viewed films of children playing with dogs while other fearful youngsters saw a different film. Subsequent to the film viewing, the youngsters exposed to the film portraying the play of youngsters and dogs were more willing to pet and play with dogs than the other group. There is even evidence that exposure to specially made TV programs can help overcome a very potent fear in young children—fear of going to the dentist (dentophobia). In this particular experiment, a film showed an eight-year-old boy climbing fearlessly into the dentist's chair while a nervous four-year-old looked on. As the film progressed, the younger child became more courageous until, when her turn came, she climbed fearlessly into the chair to be treated. This particular film was then shown to phobic youngsters. After viewing it, these same youngsters were far more likely to visit the dentist than were other fearful children who had not seen the film. Lastly, experiments done in a nursery school indicated that withdrawn children became more outgoing after watching films depicting appropriate nursery-school behavior. This is a rather dramatic finding when we consider that ordinarily such behavior change would have occurred only after rather intensive psychological therapy.

Developing Self-Control

Laboratory experiments have also shown that films and TV programs can affect a young child's self-control. These studies typically use a brief television program to depict a particular aspect of self-control. This program is shown to one group of children, while other groups see a different program or perhaps no program at all. To illustrate, one study was designed to examine children's resistance to temptation. Five-year-olds were brought into a room containing several attractive toys and a dictionary. The boys were told they could not play with the toys but could look at the dictionary (not exactly a five-year-old's idea of fun). These boys were then divided into three groups. One group saw no film; a second group saw a film in which a boy played with these toys and was even joined by his mother (this was called the "model-rewarded" condition). In yet a third condition, youngsters saw a film in which a boy played with the toys but was scolded for doing so when his mother entered the room (this was the "model-punished" condition). Each boy was then left alone in the room, and hidden observers measured how much time each spent playing with the forbidden toys and how long it took to disobey. As you might expect, those boys who saw the model-punished film resisted temptation for a longer period of time and spent less time playing with the toys. (As it turned out, most boys who had seen the model-punished version didn't even attempt to play with the forbidden toys; also, as you might expect, the boys who saw the model-rewarded film played with the toys the longest.)

Cooperation, Sharing, and Helping

Experiments that have investigated sharing behavior usually use the same basic approach as described above in the self-control experiments. In this instance, however,

The long-running Mister Rogers' Neighborhood *is a good example of a show that promoted prosocial values. (Courtesy Mister Rogers' Neighborhood/Family Communications, Inc.)*

children watch a film depicting a model playing a game and receiving a prize for winning (usually money). A film model then donates part of his or her winnings to charity. The child then wins at the same game and is also given the option to donate some money to charity. In general, the many experiments in this area indicate that observing a generous model prompts young people to behave more generously. Other experiments have shown that children are willing to imitate cooperative behavior that they have seen portrayed in a television program. One study showed children a segment of *The Waltons* in which cooperation was depicted. These children were more willing to help one another in a subsequent game-playing situation than were those who did not view that particular episode.

Survey Data

In comparison with the survey research examining antisocial behavior, there is little comparable survey research analyzing prosocial behavior. Apparently, the research effort in this area has just begun. Some data exist, however. Research on the CBS series *Fat Albert and the Cosby Kids* revealed that about 90 percent of approximately 700 children were able to express at least one prosocial theme from episodes of the series. Other research indicated that children who watched *Sesame Street* were able to identify accurately the cooperation messages contained in that program. Thus it appears that the prosocial messages are at least perceived. Do these messages influence the day-to-day behavior as measured in real life? One large-scale survey found little relationship between viewing prosocial programs and performing prosocial acts in school, when all other variables were statistically controlled.

Judging from this study, we can say that it is apparent that the relationship between viewing and prosocial behavior is much weaker than that between viewing and aggressive behavior. Closer examination indicates why this should be the case. Violent behaviors as portrayed on TV and in films are blatant, easy to see, and physical; prosocial behaviors are subtle, sometimes complicated, and largely verbal actions. Because children learn better from simple, direct, and active presentations, aggressive behaviors may be more easily learned from media content. Further, it is possible that

Problems in Prosocial Messages

It looked harmless enough. The TV spot showed a boy and a girl running across a playground to reach a vacant swing. They get there at the same time and tussle a bit as each claims to have gotten there first. Then, one of them suggests that they take turns and the spot ends with the kids playing happily on the swing and with the announcer's voice encouraging cooperation.

This was a spot sponsored by an agency of the United Methodist Church that was designed to use TV to promote prosocial values. Its message certainly looked to be positive and noncontroversial. Interestingly, this innocent looking spot sparked a great deal of controversy. An article in the *New York Times* criticized the ad as an example of mind control via the media. Was it moral to create a TV spot in which the prime purpose was to influence kids' behavior? What values should be taught? Should kids growing up in a ghetto be taught to stand up for their own rights rather than cooperate? Should we instead be teaching kids to be tough, independent, and vigorous? All of these concerns make it difficult for TV to function as a prosocial force.

since most children are taught early in life that they should be friendly, helpful, and cooperative, media content may only reinforce what children already know. On the other hand, aggressive behavior is usually punished at home and at school, and frequent viewing of it on TV might serve to overcome children's inhibitions against performing this discouraged behavior. It appears that much more research evidence is necessary in this area before the total impact of the media on prosocial behavior is known. Unfortunately, at present only a few researchers are studying this topic and results are accumulating slowly.

To summarize:

1. When presented in a controlled environment, film and television can promote the learning of prosocial attitudes and behaviors, particularly among young people.

2. In everyday situations, the impact of prosocial TV programs and films is much harder to detect.

OTHER BEHAVIORAL EFFECTS

Political Behavior

The effect of the mass media on political behavior is a complicated one. It first came into prominence in 1940 when sociologists and political scientists feared that a particularly skilled demagogue might use the media to achieve political power. These early studies found surprisingly little impact due solely to the influence of mass communication; interpersonal sources were found to be more powerful. Interest in the unique effects of the media was rekindled by the 1960 Kennedy–Nixon debates and by the subsequent emergence of a group of political consultants who served as media imagemakers. (You might read Joe McGinniss' book *The Selling of the President 1968* for a vivid account of the activities of these consultants.)

Trying to summarize the many studies that have been conducted about the influences of the media on politics would require far more space than we have available.

Smiles and the Presidency

Can a newscaster's smile influence your vote for president? This was the intriguing question asked by Brian Mullen and his colleagues. Briefly, here's what they did.

Twelve hours of network newscasts were videotaped. Segments in which the anchorperson referred to one of the major 1984 presidential candidates (Reagan or Mondale) were edited to a separate tape. With the audio turned down, subjects were then asked to judge the facial expression of the anchorperson to see if anyone exhibited positive or negative expressions toward the candidates. Tom Brokaw and Dan Rather exhibited no apparent bias toward either candidate, but subjects judged that ABC's Peter Jennings exhibited a strong positive bias toward Reagan, apparently displaying a subtle smile when he referred to him.

Could Jennings' smile have influenced the way people voted? The researchers surveyed about 140 people who were frequent viewers of the networks' newscasts. The proportion of people who watched NBC and CBS who voted for Reagan was compared with the proportion of ABC viewers who voted for him. If the smile was having an impact, more ABC viewers should have voted for Reagan. The results: 75 percent of the ABC viewers voted for Reagan compared with 63 percent of the CBS and NBC viewers, a result that was statistically significant.

You can find the full study reported in *Journal of Personality and Social Psychology* (1986), Vol. 51, pp. 291–295.

Consequently, we will restrict our discussion to the more central findings. Keep in mind that throughout our review our focus will be on the political *behavior* of the individual as it has been affected by the media. Chapter 21 summarized the impact of the media on a person's political knowledge, attitudes, and perceptions. At the core of our current discussion will be an examination of the individual's most important political behavior, the ultimate payoff in any political campaign, namely, voting behavior.

Studies of Voter Turnout. Voter turnout in presidential elections generally increased from 1924 to 1960 (if we discount the war years). From that time, however, the trend has been reversed, and fewer people have voted in presidential elections. Have the media had an impact in this area? The data are not conclusive, and many people have different viewpoints. At least one political scientist has argued that part of the increased voter turnout from 1930 to 1940 was due to the impact of radio. As this new medium reached those who were less educated and less politically involved and beyond the reach of printed media, it apparently stimulated greater interest in politics and increased the tendency to vote. The parallel emergence of TV did not have such an impact, although many argued that the visual dimension of TV would make the political process more vivid and so further increase participation. But turnout has decreased, starting with the 1964 election (interestingly enough, this was the first election in which the first "TV generation" would be eligible to vote). A current explanation for this drop holds that the unique characteristics of TV news are in part responsible. TV news, it is argued, presents the news in such a way that it is hard to avoid messages about the opposition. Seeing an opponent making a good case for his or her position will rarely convert a voter, but it might make that voter less sure of his or her own views and more confused. As a result, these voters might simply tune out and become less interested in politics and voting.

Data from presidential elections from 1960 to 1976 indicate that the frequency of reading a newspaper was strongly related to voter turnout, but radio and television exposure were not. These data suggest that the recent decline in newspaper reading among those of voting age might be part of the cause of the low turnout rather than the alleged confusion that might result from viewing TV news. Obviously, the relationship between media exposure and turnout is complicated, and it is likely that the future will bring more evidence to help us better understand the situation.

One area of voter turnout that has been studied in some depth is the effect of exit polls. An **exit poll** is conducted on election day at a polling place among voters who have just cast their ballots. These polls enable the TV networks to project winners early in the day, before the polls have closed. Although common sense suggests that people won't turn out to vote if they think their vote is meaningless or if their candidate has already been declared a loser, the research suggests the impact of exit polling is much more complicated. First, the closeness of the race is important. If exit polls simply confirm a landslide predicted by preelection surveys, their impact might be different from that of exit polls which confirm a close race or show that preelection surveys were wrong. The most recent evidence suggests that exit polls are most influential when they change perceptions about the closeness of a race. Second, only those potential voters who have yet to vote and who hear an election being called can be affected. People who haven't voted by the time a call is made are usually not very interested in politics and are not likely to be exposed to election calls. Third, in some states the polls may close shortly after a call is made, whereas in other states the polls may be open much longer. Finally, a lot of extraneous factors, such as bad weather, early concession speeches, and close local races will also affect turnout.

Taking all these complications into account, the consensus of research in this area suggests that in an election where exit polls predict a clear winner in a race that had previously been thought close, election calls based on exit polling decrease voter turnout about 1–5 percent if the polls are open more than an hour after the call. In other situations, any effect will be hard to find.

In the 1988 election, the networks agreed to limit their coverage and projections in a state until the polls had closed in that state, limiting some of the impact of early calls. Of course, if Congress passes a uniform poll-closing bill, the whole issue will become academic.

The 1988 presidential campaign was notable in its use of negative political advertising. Although there is no standard definition of this term, most political experts interpret it as a personal attack on the opposing candidate or an attack on what the opposing candidate stands for. There was much speculation that negative advertising would turn off voters, make them distrustful of politics, and make them less inclined to participate in the political process. Both survey and laboratory research suggested that most of these fears were unfounded. When compared with those who did not view negative ads, voters who were exposed to negative ads were just as likely to vote, were just as involved, and showed little difference in the amount of trust they placed in the political system. There was a tendency, however, for negative advertising to be related to more polarized attitudes, but this polarization didn't seem to have much impact on political behavior.

Effects of the Mass Media on Voter Choice. When it comes to choosing a candidate to vote for, the mass media function along with many other factors, both social and psychological, to affect a person's choice. Still, some tentative generalizations can be made. First of all, it would appear that conversion (changing your vote from Republican to Democrat, for example) is unlikely to occur because of media exposure. Conversion seldom occurs because it is difficult for the media to persuade someone whose mind is already made up to change to an opposing view and because it appears that most people (roughly two-thirds) have already made up their minds before the political campaign begins. Far more common are two effects that have a direct bearing on voter choice: **reinforcement** and **crystallization**. Reinforcement means the strengthening or support of existing attitudes and opinions. Crystallization means the sharpening and elaboration of vaguely held attitudes or predispositions. One key factor that would influence whether reinforcement or crystallization occurs is a person's partisan leanings. If a person approaches a campaign undecided or neutral, then crystallization is likely to occur. If the person has already made up his or her mind, then reinforcement will probably take place.

In recent national elections there has been an increase in ticket-splitting (supporting one party's candidate for president and another's for governor, for example). This phenomenon may be due to crystallization, which in turn results from exposure to mass media. The flow of information during the campaign evidently crystallizes a vague voting intention that these individuals may have and, in many instances, these choices do not square with party loyalty. On the other hand, when partisan voters are exposed to the media, reinforcement is likely. A study of the 1948 election found that people who chose their candidate early were more likely to expose themselves to media content that supported their chosen candidate and reinforced their initial view. Further, results from at least six studies of the 1960 debates showed that people who had already made their vote choice declared their candidate to be the winner far more often than the opponent.

These findings do not necessarily mean that the media are not influential. A key factor in winning any election is to keep the party faithful loyal (reinforcement) and to persuade enough of the undecideds to vote for your side (crystallization) in order to win. Thus even though widespread conversion is not usually seen, the media are still influential. Even more important, the media may have significant indirect influence on the electorate. By serving as important sources of political news, by structuring "political reality," and by creating an image of candidates and issues, the media may have a potent effect on a person's attitudes about the political system. Furthermore, our discussion has been mainly concerned with the effects of the media in national elections. Local elections present a somewhat different picture. Most research evidence indicates that the media, especially local newspapers, might be highly influential in affecting voter choice in a city, county, or district election.

The Debates. A basic knowledge of the effects of mass media on politics would not be complete without an examination of the presidential debates of 1960, 1976, 1980, 1984, 1988, and 1992. Thirty-one different studies were done on the Nixon–Kennedy debates to gauge their impact. As mentioned above, reinforcement of voter choice seemed to be the main effect since many had already made up their minds prior to the debate. There was also evidence of crystallization in that independent voters became more favorable to one or the other candidate throughout the course of the debates. Significantly, more independents shifted to Kennedy. All in all, the number of voters actually influenced appeared rather small. The 1960 election, however, was decided by a tenth of a percentage point. Thus even a relatively small effect in terms of numbers might have an enormous social impact. The 1976 Carter–Ford debates showed a more pronounced media effect. Consistent viewers of the debates put more weight on differences over issues in determining their vote. This group was also the group that showed a greater tendency to change their vote choice. Declines in party loyalty and identification made reinforcement a less likely effect and suggested an even more important role for the media.

Because of the last minute scheduling of the 1980 presidential debate between Jimmy Carter and Ronald Reagan, few detailed studies evaluating its impact were conducted. Public opinion polls taken after the election showed that Reagan benefited most, picking up the previously undecided vote by a two-to-one margin. The two debates between Ronald Reagan and Walter Mondale in the 1984 campaign were

Television coverage is an integral part of today's political conventions. In fact, most conventions are planned to take advantage of TV's presence. (A. Tannenbaum/Sygma)

studied more extensively. Surveys showed that Mondale did better in the first debate, with even Reagan supporters conceding that he performed better than their candidate. The polls showed that Reagan scored a narrow victory in the second debate. In any event, the debates had apparently little effect in determining the final outcome. Reagan had a lopsided lead all through the campaign, which was translated into a landslide victory on election day. If anything the 1984 debates again demonstrated the reinforcement effect. After the debates, about 85 percent of the moderate Mondale supporters and 75 percent of the moderate Reagan supporters made their final decision to vote for their candidate. The 1988 debates between George Bush and Michael Dukakis showed the same pattern, as did the 1992 debates.

Television and the Political Behavior of Politicians. On a general level, it is clear that the emergence of television has affected the political behavior of politicians and political campaigns. A comparison of pre-TV practices with those occurring after TV's adoption reveals the following:

1. Nominating conventions are now planned with television in mind. They are designed not so much to select a candidate as to make a favorable impression on public opinion.

2. Television has increased the cost of campaigning.

3. Television has become the medium around which most campaigns are organized.

4. Campaign staffs now typically include one or more television consultants whose job it is to advise the candidate on his or her television image.

Research into the effects of obscene and pornographic material is not as advanced as it is in the other areas we have examined. The most concerted effort in this area was conducted by the Commission on Obscenity and Pornography, which sponsored a three-year study of the impact of such material. The writing of this commission's report was immersed in many political considerations, and the commission was unable to issue a unanimous statement. Nonetheless, the major research findings are of interest. The commission found that the most frequent users of pornography were middle-class and middle-aged males. It found no evidence to indicate that viewing pornography was related to antisocial or deviant behavior and attitudes. Further, the commission even stated that pornographic material served a positive function in some healthy sexual relationships. The majority of this commission went so far as to make the politically unpopular recommendation that all laws prohibiting the sale of this material to adults should be repealed. The Nixon administration repudiated the recommendations of this body in 1970, and since that time this report has been largely ignored.

During the next decade, however, pornography became more abundant and more extreme. In addition, the results of new research cast doubt on the conclusions of the earlier commission. Consequently, a new National Commission on Pornography was appointed in 1984 and released its report in 1986. Surrounded by political considerations, the new commission concluded that pornography, particularly violent pornography, was harmful and that its distribution should be curtailed. More recent studies have found that sexual arousal might be linked to subsequent aggressive behavior if other outlets for release are not available. Other research has indicated that the responses of males and females to this content are becoming more alike.

In addition, several studies done in the mid-1980s found a disturbing link between exposure to pornography and feelings of callousness toward women. In one experiment, college students were divided into three groups. One group saw thirty-six erotic films over a six-week period. A second saw eighteen erotic and eighteen nonerotic films over the same period, while a control group saw thirty-six nonerotic films. After the viewing period was over, all groups were questioned concerning their attitudes toward pornography, rape, and women in general. The group that received the heaviest dose of pornography was less likely to think that pornography was offensive, had less compassion for women as rape victims, and was less supportive of women's rights than were the other groups. In a similar study, males viewed five movies showing both erotic and violent behavior toward females. The subjects were questioned about their perceptions of violence after viewing just one film and again after viewing all five. The results indicated that after seeing all five films the subjects had fewer negative reactions to the films and perceived them as less violent and less degrading to women, suggesting a desensitization effect of this material.

The most recent debate in this area is over the relative effects of violent versus nonviolent pornography. Several studies have noted a link between exposure to films that were both violent and pornographic and feelings of sexual callousness toward women. But is it the violence or the pornography that is the cause? At least one study has found the same result after viewing nonviolent pornography but others have failed to replicate this finding. This topic has assumed added importance after recent research disclosed that sexually related violence might be more accessible than previously thought. A content analysis of R- and X-rated adult videos revealed that, on a percentage basis, R-rated videos contained more episodes of sexual violence against women than did the X-rated videos (R-rated videos also contained more nonsexual violence as well). This suggests that the current concern over violent pornography might be masking what potentially may be more harmful material.

• • • •
TELEVISION AND BEHAVIOR DISORDERS

The role that TV plays in various dysfunctional behaviors has been the research focus of social scientists, psychiatrists, physicians, and health care workers. In recent years, TV has been linked to such behavior disorders as suicides, drug and alcohol use, eating disorders, and sex offenses. Obviously, conducting research on topics such as these is difficult and the findings are not as clear as we might like them to be. Nonetheless, it's an area of some importance and this section will summarize research done on two of the most widely researched subjects: eating disorders and suicides.

The evidence regarding the relationship of TV watching to obesity is clear: The more people watch TV, the more likely they are to be overweight. Studies done with national samples in three different decades have shown that this relationship occurs in adolescents as well as adults and in men as well as women. In one study of 6000 adult males, men who watched three hours or more of TV daily were twice as likely to be obese as men who watched less than an hour. Another study suggested that as much as 25 percent of the recent increase in obesity among adolescents is due to TV viewing.

What accounts for this relationship? Clearly, TV watching is a sedentary activity and viewers burn few calories while they watch. Another probable factor is all the TV ads for food and snacks, many of questionable nutritional value, that encourage viewers to eat while they view. A third consideration is that viewers see a lot of thin characters on TV shows and in ads who eat and never seem to get fat. This might lead to unreal expectations concerning eating habits and weight.

What's unclear in all this research is whether TV viewing causes obesity, or whether obesity simply causes you to watch more TV, or whether maybe some other factor, like not exercising, leads to both. Although all of the answers are not in, the conclusion endorsed by many researchers is that the relationship is mutual. People who are obese may turn to TV for relaxation and this, in turn, causes them to become even more obese.

The relationship between other eating disorders, such as anorexia and bulimia, and TV viewing is hard to find. Despite fears that TV programs that emphasized leanness might be encouraging these disorders, there is no compelling research evidence that links these activities to TV.

Chapter 10 noted the concern over the possible influence of rock music lyrics and suicides. The research summarized in this section is related to the imitation phenomenon investigated by Bandura. The central question is whether media portrayals and news of suicides prompt others to commit suicide. As you might imagine, this topic is exceedingly difficult to study. There are problems with measurement and causation and even in defining what exactly is a suicide. Despite these difficulties, more than twenty studies in the last decade or so have examined this topic.

The typical study usually scans media coverage or medical examiner reports in the period of time following a well-publicized suicide or media program that depicts suicide to see if there are any unusual increases in the suicide rate. The most common finding from this type of research is that suicides do indeed increase after media exposure. For example, in a study reported in the *New England Journal of Medicine*, researchers found that the suicide rate among teenagers increased about 8 percent in the seven days following the televising of a news story about suicide. This relationship persisted even after statistical corrections for season, day of the week, holidays, etc. A second study published in the same journal found a similar effect after the broadcasts of TV movies dealing with suicides.

Another study using similar methods and looking at news coverage of suicides from 1973 to 1984 ascertained that although there was no relationship between news stories about suicide and suicides among adults, such a relationship was found among

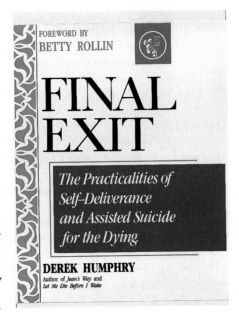

The controversial how-to book about suicide: The book sparked renewed research interest concerning the media's role in suicides. (The Hemlock Society/ Carol Publishing Group)

teenagers for the period 1973–1980. Then, interestingly enough, the trend disappeared. The researchers suggested that increased sensitivity to the problem of suicide might have helped teens become more resistant to the effects of TV.

Other studies done in Europe also show an imitative effect after a TV movie about a suicide. As social learning theory would predict, those most prone to imitate the TV suicide were those whose age and sex were closest to those of the actor on TV who committed suicide.

These findings, however, need to be qualified. They are correlational in nature; there is no definitive evidence that TV viewing caused the suicidal behavior. Indeed, in these studies there is no direct evidence that the victims had even seen the newscasts or the TV programs in question. In fairness, there is some anecdotal evidence from some people who were unsuccessful in their attempts that they had gotten the idea from watching TV, but there is no way to know how generalizable these reports are. Another explanation of these findings argues that medical examiners are influenced by TV portrayals of suicide so that when they come upon an ambiguous case (a death that may have been accidental or may have been a suicide) they tend to declare it a suicide.

It is evident that much more research needs to be done before television's impact on suicides is fully understood. As of now, it is clear that there is enough evidence to cause some concern. Indeed, it is probable that the whole issue of suicide and the media will be examined with more intensity than ever. Two recent stories involving doctors who helped patients commit suicide got wide national coverage, and in late 1991 the book *Final Exit*, described as a how-to book on how to commit suicide, made the *New York Times* best-seller list.

● ● ● ●

SUGGESTIONS FOR FURTHER READING

The books and articles listed below represent good sources of further information.

BAKER, R. K., AND S. J. BALL, eds., *Violence and the Media. A Staff Report to the National Commission on the Causes and Prevention of Violence*, Washington, D.C.: Government Printing Office, 1969.

BRYANT, JENNINGS, AND DOLF ZILLMANN, *Perspectives on Media Effects*, Hillsdale, N.J.: Lawrence Erlbaum, 1986.

COMSTOCK, GEORGE, STEVEN CHAFFEE, NATAN KATZMAN, MAXWELL McCOMBS, AND DONALD ROBERTS, *Television and Human Behavior*, New York: Columbia University Press, 1978.

DE SOLA POOL, ITHIEL, "Why Don't People Vote?" *TV Guide*, October 14, 1976, p. 6.

HARRIS, RICHARD, *A Cognitive Psychology of Mass Communication*, Hillsdale, N.J.: Lawrence Erlbaum, 1989.

HUESMANN, L. ROWELL, AND LEONARD ERON, eds., *Television and the Aggressive Child*, Hillsdale, N.J.: Lawrence Erlbaum, 1986.

JOSLYN, RICHARD, *Mass Media and Elections*, Reading, Mass.: Addison-Wesley, 1984.

KLAPPER, JOSEPH, *The Effects of Mass Communication*, New York: The Free Press, 1960.

LIEBERT, ROBERT M., AND JOYCE SPRAFKIN, *The Early Window: Effects of Television on Children and Youth*, 3rd ed., New York: Pergamon Press, 1988.

LOWERY, SHEARON, AND MELVIN DeFLEUR, *Milestones in Mass Communication Research*, New York: Longman, 1987.

SCHNEIDER, CY, *Children's Television*, Lincolnwood, Ill.: NTC Publishing, 1991.

SPRAFKIN, JOYCE, AND ELI RUBINSTEIN, "Children's Television Viewing Habits and Prosocial Behavior: A Field Correlational Study," *Journal of Broadcasting*, Vol. 23:3 (Summer 1979), pp. 265–276.

U.S. GOVERNMENT, *Report of the National Advisory Commission on Civil Disorders*, New York: Bantam, 1968.

———, *Television and Social Behavior, Reports and Papers* (5 volumes), Washington, D.C.: Department of Health, Education and Welfare, 1972.

WILLIAMS, TANNIS, ed., *The Impact of Television*, New York: Academic Press, 1986.

MASS
COMMUNICATION
AND THE FUTURE

23

MASS MEDIA IN THE FUTURE

This chapter will briefly review the innovations that will greatly influence the media's evolution in the next few years, consider the social impact of these developments, and then scan the horizon for developments in the more distant future. As you read this chapter, keep in mind that making predictions is a risky business. Economic, political, and social forces that are difficult to foresee sometimes have great impact in determining what technology succeeds or fails. Moreover, there are probably some things that will occur that you and I probably can't think of right now. After all, twenty-five years ago, who would have predicted that we would routinely get cash from walls, make telephone calls from airplanes, rent movies from a store on the corner, and watch them while eating popcorn prepared in a device that uses super high frequency energy waves to cook food? Nonetheless, in the near future, here's where I think we're going.

PRINT MEDIA: NEWSPAPERS, MAGAZINES, AND BOOKS

As we mentioned in earlier chapters, the computer has had enormous impact in publishing. Video-display terminals have replaced the traditional typewriter; manuscripts can be electronically edited; and whole pages can be laid out with computer assistance. Electronic pagination is expected to save the industry about $2.5 billion in the next decade. Satellites now transmit whole pages of copy to outlying printing plants where the actual paper is put together.

Currently under development are systems that allow the editor to have complete control of the newspaper content—changing makeup, digital photography (a computer-assisted method of displaying photos on the printed page), which allows electronic cropping of photos, and headline construction. This new system means that the current method of photocomposition, page paste-up, photographing the page, and then making plates can be simplified with all the information going straight to the computer and having the plates made directly from electronically stored information. Ink jet printers, which "paint" each letter with microscopic drops of ink, will allow papers to be printed more quickly, and it is hoped, more cheaply.

New ways of assembling newspapers will make them more similar to magazines and will allow them to become even more specialized. As mentioned in Chapter 6, magazines print demographic editions, which are designed for a particular group of readers. The development of new insertion and assembly equipment will enable papers to insert special sections and supplements into the paper at about the same speed that the paper is printed. To illustrate the reason behind this idea, consider the business section of the typical paper. Surveys indicate that only one-third of the audience reads this section, and as far as the other two-thirds of the audience is concerned, the

Technicians at NBC studios fine-tuning new robotic cameras that the network uses to broadcast its newscasts, including NBC Nightly News with Tom Brokaw. *(David Rentas/New York Post Photo)*

business section could be eliminated from the paper, and it would not be sorely missed. It would seem to make sense, then, from a marketing viewpoint, to supply the business pages only to those who actually want them. Similarly, the sports section might be inserted only in those copies of the paper going to readers who are interested in sports. The use of high-speed assembly equipment lets a newspaper tailor each copy for the individual subscriber. To illustrate, a subscriber would pay a basic fee for the core of the paper but would be required to pay extra for any customized inserts that he or she wished to read. The paper might offer as many as a dozen special inserts including "Food," "Business," "Society," "Sports," and "Entertainment." Each reader's choices would be recorded and stored in a central computer. Specific quantities of each combination would be printed, address labels attached, and the copy delivered to the subscriber's doorstep. This technique would ultimately be more efficient in its use of paper and allow advertisers to buy space in a section that would reach a well-defined reader group. Manufacturers of business products would advertise in the business section and be reasonably certain that their messages would go only to those interested in their products.

Newspapers are also looking ahead to the day when a shortage of paper and paper substitutes makes alternative delivery systems a viable possibility. In addition to the video newspaper editions now available on Prodigy and CompuServe and similar services, some publishers are looking at a system in which the traditional carrier delivers a VCR cassette or computer disc to the doorstep that contains the day's news, personalized for the subscriber. When finished, the cassette or disc is picked up by the carrier and used again, eliminating waste. A more intriguing plan has each household producing its own paper using a miniature ecosystem. Consumers would place used paper, leaves, and grass clippings into a device that would shred, heat, and compress the mixture into paper that would be fed into a laser printer. The printer would be hooked up to a home computer where the consumer could print all or some parts of the day's news.

A screen from CompuServe: Subscribers can search for the stories that they are interested in. CompuServe had about 800,000 subscribers in 1991. (© CompuServe, Inc.)

The future of teletext and videotex (see Chapter 7) is hard to predict. Most media companies have backed away from further developing these services. Many experts think that videotex and teletext will be used to compile large data bases and will ultimately serve a small, specialized audience such as the financial or scientific community. Another scenario suggests that telephone companies will become the leader in this area and use it to store their directories and other specialized data. A 1991 court decision favoring the entry of telcos in this field makes this scenario more likely.

Another printed medium likely to be around quite a while is the magazine. A safe prediction is that many new and special magazines will appear and that some of these will survive and others won't. New businesses, hobbies, and leisure-time activities will produce new magazines. Market research will spur the inception of others as publishers try to reduce some of the risks involved in starting new publications. Since market research aims at attracting a relatively affluent, relatively young, college-educated crowd, many future magazines will reflect the interests of this group, especially topics concerned with lifestyles, self-improvement, and self-fulfillment. There are limits, of course, to the degree of specialization that can be achieved without overspecializing the magazine out of the market. Some critics have suggested, only somewhat jokingly, that in the future we'll have magazines like *Sweatsox and Leash*, a magazine for joggers who own poodles, and *Smashed Scissors*, the magazine for barbers and hairdressers who have also been run over by a bus. Clearly, specialization can be taken too far.

Other technological advances promise to improve the magazine's production process, making color photos easier to reproduce and more colorful to the eye. Editorial copy will be transmitted by satellite, enabling publishers to speed up printing and delivery.

Likewise, we can probably expect more specialization from the book publishing industry. The continuing trend in job specialization will probably prompt growth in the professional and educational areas. In addition, the market for children's and juvenile books appears to be a growth area as many publishers realize that this age group can be wooed away from the TV screen. Further, several children's books are now being marketed in combination with related videocassettes. The cross-media symbiosis that is apparent in other areas will probably become more important in book publishing as well.

In textbook publishing, many companies are now publishing "customized" books. This allows the professor to integrate some of his/her own material with articles and information from other sources to produce a book designed specifically for that course. Such a book can be produced in forty-eight hours thanks to new printing technology.

Finally, many reference books—dictionaries, encyclopedias, almanacs, first aid guides, and the like—have been transferred to compact disc. A video compact disc player displays the information requested.

●●●●
RADIO AND SOUND RECORDING

The most important word for both of these industries is "digital." Digital Audio Broadcasting, once a home is found for it in the spectrum, may erase the AM-FM sound quality disparity. Since there is little interference using digital signals, more radio stations could serve the same area. Local radio stations might also be competing with national services delivered direct to your radio by satellite. New digital receiving sets will make it possible to program your radio to receive only the formats you like. Some have even suggested that the new sampling technology makes it possible to have computer-generated, synthetic DJs equipped with logic circuits to handle announcing chores.

The recent legal agreement on digital audio tape (DAT) makes it possible that the traditional tape cassette might be on its way out. If the DAT players become competitive in price, DAT may become the listening and recording medium of choice in American households. Thanks to big companies like Sony, DAT is already acquiring fans in Japan where sets are on sale.

●●●●
HOME COMPUTERS

As of 1990, computers were in 15 percent of U.S. households, but surveys showed that the number who planned to buy a computer in the near future was dropping. It appears that any drastic reshaping of our lifestyle because of the home computer is still somewhat in the future.

One of the prime uses for tomorrow's home computer will be information retrieval via a technology known as CD-I, Compact Disc-Interactive. CD-I uses the same technology found in audio CDs but in addition to sound, CD-I stores video, text, graphics, and animation. One CD-I five-inch disc can store volumes of written material or up to 7000 still photos or 72 minutes of video or 19 hours of digital sound or any combination of the above. All of this material can be accessed in any order. In addition to the obvious—illustrated dictionaries and encyclopedias—CD-I can also be used for high-powered games, travelogues (imagine a video-audio tour of the Sistine Chapel), training (a step-by-step illustration of how to program your VCR), education (high school students in New York now study poetry on CD-I and can choose several different people to read a poem; the disc even contains a section on the similarities of poetry and rap music), and entertainment (movies and TV shows could be released on CD-I along with expert analysis and commentary about their production methods or themes).

Another thing is certain. Computers will become easier to use. In late 1991, the two computer giants, Apple and IBM, announced plans to team up in the personal computer business. Their first goal: make personal computers more user friendly. Only 25 percent of the U.S. population regularly use computers. The other three quarters find them too difficult to use or too limited in their applications. Computer

The many people who made fevered predictions about the burgeoning communications revolution of the early 1980s and then, much to their dismay, discovered that their predictions didn't actually pan out needn't feel so bad. Many other expert predictions didn't come about either. Consider:

Thomas Edison totally misread the future of the phonograph. He thought it could be used as a sort of telephone answering machine or a device for recording the last words of prominent persons before they died.

A Massachusetts newspaper predicted that the telephone would be primarily used to transmit music and news.

When the telegraph was first perfected, people thought the new device would make the whole world into one neighborhood and become "a sublime force for preserving morality."

A prominent magazine, flushed with the potential of radio, predicted that radio's biggest use would be person-to-person communication. It also predicted several other bizarre uses for radio, including radio-powered roller skates.

(Of course, if a person waits long enough, sometimes even a wayward prediction comes true. A recent invention, cellular radio, uses radio technology to create a system of mobile telephones used in person-to-person communication. So far, however, there's been no word of radio-powered roller skates.)

programmers are trying assiduously to reach those in the audience who haven't a clue when they see the C> prompt on their computer screens. Several schemes are on the drawing board. One includes a computer that "reads" ordinary handwriting. Another uses voice-recognition technology and allows the computer to respond to spoken commands, much like the computers on *Star Trek*. (This same speech-recognition capability will also be built into appliances so that when you get up in the morning you can simply say "Brew" to your coffee maker and it will. Or you can tell your phone to dial the local pizza delivery service. Or your microwave oven to pop some popcorn. This development will give a whole new meaning to "machine-assisted" communication.)

In late 1993, Apple unveiled Newton, its new personal digital assistant, a hand-held device that can do calculations, list phone numbers, display appointments, and send and receive faxes. Newton has no keyboard. Instead, the user simply writes plain English commands (like "Fax to Bob") with a special pen on Newton's screen. The development of personal digital assistants illustrates how computer companies are trying to solve their biggest problem, the same one that was confronted in years past by the radio, film, and sound-recording industries. What is the personal computer good for? Most available programs are for business uses, home education, or games. What is lacking is one compelling application that appeals to everyone. As one analyst stated: "Before the home computer becomes *the* appliance of the . . . 1990s, it has to make living easier, less expensive or allow people to do something they couldn't do before." Of course, someday, someone (maybe you) will solve that problem and revolutionize the industry . . . and become quite rich and famous in the process.

● ● ● ●

THE FUTURE OF MOTION PICTURES

Although the demise of the motion picture industry has been predicted several times, somehow or other it has always managed to survive. Hollywood is likely to stay in

A reporter covers a press conference using a lightweight, lap-top PC. The story can be stored in the computer and then sent via modem over telephone lines back to the newspaper. (Courtesy Compaq Computer Corp.)

business in the near future, but there will be major changes in film production, distribution, and exhibition. In the production sector, as evident in *Terminator 2*, computer-assisted graphics have revolutionized the special-effects area. Further, the distinction between film and television will become blurry as video technology begins to replace more and more material that used to be confined to film. For example, in one new system employing high-definition television, scenes that would ordinarily be shot on film are shot on videotape. The tape can be played back immediately, thus eliminating the time it takes for film processing. A computer-assisted editing system makes the tape as easy to edit as film. Further, a greater variety of special effects are possible with video, and they can be done less expensively. This system will ultimately save the motion picture industry money since there are no costs for film developing and processing. Finally, by using a laser scanner, the finished videotape is transferred to thirty-five- or seventy-millimeter film, and the film is then shipped to theaters where it can be shown over conventional projectors. Eventually, even this last conversion to film may be eliminated, once high-resolution TV systems that project either videotape or live signals received via satellite have been installed in motion picture theaters.

As we saw in Chapter 12, the biggest change prompted by the new technologies in the motion picture industry has been the new distribution channels made possible by videocassettes. Movies on cassette have already become an important source of income for the industry and pay-per-view promises to become an important revenue source. The symbiosis between motion pictures and TV will become even closer in the years to come.

What impact will the coming of videocassettes and pay-per-view have on motion picture exhibitors? If people can see movies less expensively in their homes, will anybody still go to the motion picture theater? The answer is yes, some people will still go the movies. Remember that in Chapter 19 we pointed out that for many people movie-going was more of a social experience than a media experience. Going to the movies will continue to be an important dating activity for teens who seek to avoid the confines and supervision of the house and for other young adults seeking relatively low-cost recreation. It is quite probable that movie theater owners will start to stress the social aspect of moviegoing. Single seats may be replaced by couches; movie theaters may be merged with restaurants, bars, and even nightclubs. Live entertainment might precede the film (sort of a throwback to vaudeville). Since the movie-going audience will continue to be composed primarily of young people, motion picture theaters might become part of an entertainment complex geared to this age group with skating rinks, electronic games, and miniature golf.

Other theater owners may attempt to attract a somewhat older crowd. New ultra-swank theaters with plush seats, improved soundproofing, and concession stands stocked with Perrier, croissants, and frozen yogurt are already springing up in Southern California.

Other changes that will also affect the exhibition segment of the industry will be innovations in the way films are screened. Sound systems will become more sophisticated. Quadraphonic or quintaphonic systems seem well suited for movie sound and will be especially appropriate for soundtracks recorded by means of the digital method. Although the age of experimentation with giant screens and multiple screens may be over, some theaters will probably attempt new projection methods. One possibility that has already been tested involves putting the spectators in steep balconies and projecting a film simultaneously on two screens, one lying on the floor and the other standing vertically. Another arrangement puts the audience on a device resembling a merry-go-round and turns them toward different screens at different times. A third idea is the interactive movie, in which audience members are given a small device on which they vote for a particular plot option and the film proceeds accordingly. (The problem with this technique is that a large amount of film has to be shot to cover all the possible permutations and combinations.) Some of these ideas might catch on, but it is probable that the traditional motion picture screen will persist into the immediate future. On the home video front, some industry experts predict the ultimate decline of the local video rental store as pay-per-view becomes more common on cable systems. They predict viewers will watch the latest hits on pay-per-view and only rent older films or specialty tapes at stores.

Merging Media

One pretty safe bet about media in the future is that they will become harder to tell apart. Motion pictures might be shot in HDTV, reference books will be read on computer screens using compact discs, and newspapers will exist in print and electronic versions. Another example of this convergence is illustrated by a new "TV magazine" that is meant to be recorded on a VCR. A publisher of a singles magazine in Phoenix has started a service called Pageburst Personals. This video magazine consists of 330 pages of pictures and text about eligible singles and is broadcast in only sixty seconds over a local TV station. Viewers must videotape the sixty seconds and then play the tape back frame-by-frame to see the information. How does the "videozine" make any money? Viewers who wish to respond to an ad can call a 900-number at a charge of $1.49 a minute.

● ● ● ●

TELEVISION: ON THE HORIZON

Several new developments will influence the way TV looks and acts in the future: HDTV, DBS, signal compression, and interactive TV.

Already available in Japan, **High-Definition TV (HDTV)** will significantly increase the picture quality of television to a point where it will be comparable to the quality of 35-mm motion picture film. Television picture clarity is a function of the number of scanning lines that make up the TV picture. The United States developed TV back in the 1940s and the highest number of scanning lines that was technically feasible back then was 525. (If you've ever seen TV in Europe, you're probably aware that the pictures on European TV are a little sharper and crisper than what you are used to. This is because European TV developed later than American TV, when electronic technology made it possible to have 625 scanning lines.) HDTV will replace the 525-line standard with 1125 to 1150 lines, depending on the exact system of HDTV that is chosen. HDTV sets also have a different aspect ratio. Current TV screens are three units tall by four units wide; the new HDTV sets are nine units tall by sixteen units wide, more like the current motion picture screen.

The exact time of HDTV's introduction will be affected primarily by economic and administrative factors. On the economic front, conversion to HDTV will be

Engineers are currently working to perfect an HDTV system. The United States was slow to enter the race to develop HDTV and lagged behind Japanese and European companies. Recent breakthroughs in digital transmission, however, have given the U.S. system an edge. (Zenith Electronics Corp.)

expensive as networks, stations, and production companies will have to replace cameras, recorders, transmitters, editing equipment, and studios. NBC estimated that it would cost them about $500 million to convert their New York and Hollywood production units to HDTV. Broadcasters and cablecasters are worried about how they will pay for the conversion. Many are afraid that HDTV programs will not draw big enough audiences and advertising revenue to cover their costs.

The administrative factors include settling on an engineering standard for HDTV. As of 1992, a half-dozen different systems were being considered. Plans call for a system that would be compatible, initially at least, with conventional TV receivers. The FCC scheduled tests throughout 1992 in the hope of choosing a standard by 1993. At the same time, international standards will be under study. As is probably obvious, a company whose standards are adopted worldwide will make a bundle of money. Consequently, intense lobbying for one system or another is currently going on all over the world. After a slow start, the United States is firmly in the race to develop an HDTV standard thanks to recent breakthroughs in digital transmission.

Another consideration has to do with the spectrum space that is needed to transmit HDTV. Although advances in compression are being made every year, the HDTV signal still requires more than the six-megahertz chunk of spectrum space given to TV stations. As one engineer put it, trying to get HDTV into the conventional space is like trying to get twenty-five pounds of something into a five-pound bag. One possible plan involves assigning more space to TV stations somewhere else in the spectrum to accommodate the additional information for HDTV. Unfortunately, where this new space will come from is not exactly clear since the spectrum is already cluttered with other telecommunications services such as mobile telephones, satellites, military communications, etc. Note that cable companies, which do not use the over-the-air spectrum, would have less of a problem sending HDTV. HDTV VCRs don't have the spectrum problem either. Direct broadcast satellites might also be used to transmit the new signals.

From the point of view of the consumer, you would have to purchase a new set to fully appreciate HDTV. Although no sets have been put on the general market as yet, initial prices will probably range from about $2000–$5000. Whether consumers will pay this price is yet to be established.

The ultimate fate of HDTV may be closely entwined with that of **direct broadcasting by satellite (DBS)**. DBS differs from the service that people now pick up through their backyard dishes in that DBS is not meant for retransmission. People with satellite dishes are really intercepting signals meant for some other distribution agency. True DBS is designed to go directly to viewers' homes. From a satellite or two in a stationary orbit 22,300 miles above the equator, a DBS operator could theoretically broadcast multiple programming services to every home in the country that was equipped with the small, inexpensive DBS receiver.

After some false starts in the 1980s, interest in DBS was renewed in the early 1990s. Thanks to advances in technology, the cumbersome backyard or rooftop antennas once needed to receive DBS signals have been replaced by new models barely bigger than a page of notebook paper that perch on a window sill. Unlike the backyard dishes, which sell for about $2500–$4000, these new miniature receivers retail for about $300–$500. In addition, advances in signal compression have made it possible for new satellites to provide 100 or more channels of video and audio.

Despite the tremendous start-up expenses that must be incurred by a DBS operation, companies are still eager to test the market. In June of 1991, Hughes Communication and the United States Satellite Broadcasting Company announced a $100 million deal to start a DBS system in the U.S. by 1994. The proposed system would offer free, subscription, and pay-per-view TV, CD-quality stereo audio, and HDTV. Total cost for the system is estimated at about a billion dollars. In addition to the Hughes plan, companies such as SkyPix, Sky Cable, and K-Prime (backed by Time Warner and

It's not another piece of laundry: A DBS dish coexists with the clothesline outside a Tokyo suburban home. (© Dennis Gray)

G.E.) have systems in the planning stage. (DBS systems are already operating in Great Britain and Japan.) Of course, the recession of the early 1990s may postpone some of these ambitious designs, but many entrepreneurs are convinced that in the future DBS will battle cable for TV viewers.

Signal Compression

In early 1993, TCI, the nation's biggest cable company, announced the development of a new technology, called digital compression, that would enable it to provide 500 different cable channels to subscribers. What sort of programming will fill these new channels? Initial indications suggest that television in the future will more and more resemble the magazine industry. On the drawing boards are plans for such specialized offerings as the golf channel, the auto channel, the love story channel, and the game show channel. In addition, companies such as HBO and Showtime are planning to expand to several channels (maybe as many as ten) and run popular movies at staggered starting times.

Another chunk of channels will be devoted to pay-per-view offerings. Sophisticated interactive technology might allow viewers to access a huge library of current and classic movies that can be seen at any time the viewer wants.

And if 500 channels aren't enough, fiber optic technology will eventually make it possible to deliver literally thousands of TV channels to the home. Stay tuned.

Interactive TV

If you've ever wanted to be a TV director or match wits with the contestants on *Jeopardy*, **interactive TV (ITV)** might be just what you've been waiting for. Two ITV systems, one in Montreal and one in Massachusetts, are currently undergoing tests. Both systems are based on the same principle. Four different cable channels are used and the viewer can instantaneously switch back and forth among them. For example, a viewer can choose the angle from which to view a favorite sporting event. In the U.S. test market, TV watchers could in effect serve as TV director for a football game. By pressing buttons on a hand-held keypad, they could choose a view from a camera in the end zone, one from high in the stands, one that had a close-up of a key player, or one that stayed with the ball. In Montreal, viewers had comparable options with a hockey game. Additionally, subscribers can build their own TV newscast. During a traditional TV news show audience members are given the opportunity to get more information on selected stories by tuning to one of the other available channels. Another feature allows subscribers to play along with *Jeopardy* contestants. After listening to the question (well, actually in *Jeopardy* it's the answer but you get the idea), viewers key in their responses from a multiple choice display on the screen. Their choices are tabulated on the cable company's computer and high scores are eligible for prizes.

This sort of TV has been tried before, most notably with the QUBE system in Columbus, Ohio, and has never caught on. Nonetheless, Videotron, the company behind the Canadian tests, is optimistic about ITV's future. A study by an ad agency predicted that 40 percent of homes in Canada and the U.S. will be equipped for interactive TV by the year 2000. Videotron is also betting that the additional monthly charge for ITV on the subscriber's cable bill, estimated at $24–$40 per month, will not scare off potential customers. The company also notes that for new generations raised on Nintendo and video games, ITV will not be looked at as a novelty but as a logical progression of TV viewing.

● ● ● ●

TELECONFERENCING AND TELECOMMUTING

Teleconferencing substitutes telecommunications for transportation. Larger corporations spend more than $100 million every year on business travel, and the cost of travel is constantly increasing. As a result, many organizations investigated alternatives to travel. One promising substitute was the **teleconference**, a system by which individuals in different cities could interact by means of television. At its most sophisticated level, here's how a teleconference works. Let's assume that individuals in three different cities are involved. Each conference site is equipped with two-way video and audio equipment. Signals are sent by microwave using communications satellites. Thus, the people in location one can make a presentation over TV complete with graphs and visual aids to the people in the other two locations. In turn, the participants in the other cities can ask questions of the people who made the presentation. Personnel in a central control room direct the conference. They decide what scene to show on the TV monitors and what audio signals are to be transmitted.

Teleconferencing was enjoying a boom as the decade began. There were more than 12,000 satellite receiving sites at corporations and other organizations. Big hotel chains like Hilton and Holiday Inn had their own private networks for video meetings. Big companies are optimistic about this technology. In 1985, the Compaq Computer Corporation used a videoconference to introduce two new models to dealers in the United States, Canada, and Europe by means of an elaborate setup using three different communication satellites. About 3000 people saw the finished product—at a cost of more than a quarter of a million dollars, a tidy sum but less than it would have cost to bring all the participants to Compaq's base in Texas. Other companies have embraced the technique. Apple Computer Inc. has five videoconference facilities in the U.S. and one in Paris. The Hewlett-Packard Company has twenty-nine videoconference sites worldwide. You don't have to be part of a big company, however, to use teleconferencing. Sprint has a satellite TV network, called the Meeting Channel, that is open to the general public. Business is good. Sprint reported a 30 percent increase in usage in the first part of 1991. International videoconferencing grew about 50

At work at home. Although tele-commuting won't work for every-body, about 2 million Americans now work at least two days a week at home linked to the office via telephone, fax, and computer. (Sarah Putnam/The Picture Cube)

percent from 1990 to 1991. It appears that the long-term prospects for teleconferencing are excellent.

Telecommuting is another example of substituting communication for travel. The majority of the labor force in the United States has jobs concerned with transmitting or manipulating information. A lot of this work involves computer terminals and word processors. With the proper communication links, a lot of this work could be done at home, saving employees the expense and trouble of commuting to work.

Telecommuting systems have three basic parts: (1) a central computer that distributes the work to be done and receives the finished product; (2) a computer terminal where the person actually performs the work to be done; and (3) a communication link, usually over phone lines, that connects the terminal to the central computer. The most appropriate work for telecommuting involves computer programming, data analysis, and word processing. The most common kind of remote work stations are quite simple: a computer, a printer, and some file cabinets located in a study, bedroom, or kitchen. A more flexible alternative is the portable work station. Thanks to light-weight, lap-sized computers, an employee can move from place to place, hooking up with the central computer only when it's necessary to transmit work or to receive further assignments. The typical telecommuter works about two days at home; full-time telecommuting is not desirable since people tend to lose touch with the organization and feel isolated. In addition, top managers can seldom telecommute nor can employees who require a good deal of supervision.

The Age of Multimedia

The word heard most when experts discuss the future of computers is "multimedia." In its simplest terms, multimedia means the blending together of the computer, TV set, and telephone into one all-purpose, supersophisticated communication device. The limits of multimedia have yet to be established. As one IBM executive put it, "Defining multimedia only limits its scope." Nonetheless, some of the possibilities might include:

- viewing movies and other entertainment programming from interactive compact discs

- telephones that can transmit voice, data, and pictures

- computers that construct custom-made media menus

Let's elaborate a bit on that last possibility. Upon purchasing a multimedia device (a catchy name for this product has yet to surface), you will tell the computer that you like Chuck Norris movies, are a fan of the Chicago Cubs, invest in mutual funds, and are thinking of buying a new car. While you are away from the set, the computer will scan the input of the 150 or so cable channels that come into the device and select those items that you have a personal interest in. When you are ready to view, you call up a menu that tells you that the computer has taped two Chuck Norris movies, a Cubs baseball game, forty-seven new car ads, a program on auto safety, and a dozen news items about the performance of mutual funds. You can then select what items you want to view and watch at your leisure.

Both Apple and IBM are already working on hardware and software for this new multimedia age and both are trying to figure out how it will develop. The president of Apple's U.S. division put it this way: "[Multimedia] is going to generate some new types of business. I wish I knew what they all were."

As it currently stands, about 500 U.S. companies have some type of telecommuting program employing about 2 million telecommuters. Consider some specifics. Blue Cross and Blue Shield of South Carolina has installed personal computers in the homes of its data entry clerks, who earn from four to ten cents per line for their work. The Grumman Corporation has about forty engineers working at a satellite office in Florida. They telecommute to Grumman's New York office because the company couldn't persuade them to relocate there. Boston-based USTeleCenters has 100 employees who telecommute.

The field has grown so fast that there's now a monthly newsletter, *Telecommuting Review*, devoted to it. As the technology improves and more workers and companies discover the benefits, some experts predict that by the year 2000 at least 15 million people will be telecommuters.

It's easy to see the potential of telecommuting and teleconferencing for higher education. For better or worse, much of the instruction that takes place in college uses the lecture method—a technique that has shown little change since medieval times. There is nothing inherently wrong with the lecture method, but there is no compelling reason why lecturer and lecturees have to assemble in the same place to get the thing done. Instead of traipsing across campus in a rainstorm to get to a dreary lecture hall filled with 150 other bodies where you take your seat in front of someone with a chronic sinus problem, it would be far easier for students (and professors) to do the whole thing over interactive TV. At the appointed hour, a student could tumble out of bed, switch on the TV, and there, in living color, would be the professor talking about today's topic. As the session went on, the professor could call up films, tapes,

TV graphics, and other visual devices far superior to chalkboards and overhead projectors. If a student had a question, he or she would merely press a button on the keypad, and the instructor's console would light up, thus alerting him or her that a student had raised a question. The student then would ask the question by switching on a small microphone on top of the TV screen. The professor would hear the question and could then answer it. Would you need to take notes with such a system? You could, but it might make more sense to make a videotape of the whole session for later review. Many feel that the above arrangement would be a big improvement over the present system.

• • • •

VIRTUAL REALITY

The phrase *virtual reality* is an oxymoron, a contradiction of terms. *Virtual* means not in fact; *reality* means in fact. Virtual reality then means not in fact fact. The semantic problems caused by this phrase shrink in the face of some of the social implications of the technology it describes. **Virtual reality (VR)** makes us reconsider what exactly is real.

VR uses computer-generated images to create made-to-order realities (or worlds or environments or spaces) that the user (viewer? inhabitant?) can move through and interact with. To experience VR, a person must wear a helmet-like device that includes a set of miniature goggle-mounted screens which display the images created by a powerful computer. Since each eye sees a slightly different image on the computer screens, the illusion of 3-D is created. Reality (as we know it) is blocked out and a computer-designed world is substituted. If the person turns his/her head to the left, the image shifts just as though he/she were looking at a real scene. Newer VR systems also include a pair of pressure-sensitive gloves that mimic the movement of your own hands as you move them in front of your eyes. The gloves also allow you to manipulate things in VR reality with the sensation of feeling something solid.

The VR system has been in development for about a decade. NASA and the Defense Department used similar systems to train astronauts and pilots. Recently, however, some virtual reality hardware and software have appeared on the marketplace. Using VR equipment, an architect can take a client on a VR tour of a building before it's actually built, allowing for easy correction of mistakes or changes in design. VPL Research, of Silicon Valley, California, has developed RB2 (Reality Built for 2) in which two people can inhabit the same virtual world. VR can be used by the medical profession: Real surgeons can practice on virtual patients. VR would easily solve the dilemma of those students who object to dissecting real frogs in college biology classes. Don a VR helmet and dissect a virtual frog. In that same connection, VR could easily revolutionize education. You could learn how to juggle in a VR world that slows down time until you learn the proper movements. Instead of reading books about dinosaurs, VR could permit students to walk around with dinosaurs or even virtually become a dinosaur, letting them experience what it would be like to be a tyrannosaurus rex battling a stegosaurus.

The possibilities for entertainment would also be mind-boggling. Imagine starring in a virtual movie with Clint Eastwood or Kim Basinger, or dancing with a virtual Michael Jackson, or pitching to a virtual Babe Ruth. One plan under consideration is a series of "experience boutiques" in which visitors would pay a fee to enter precreated worlds with others under the direction of performance artists who would structure the experience. Indeed, although the inventors working to perfect virtual reality don't talk about it much, virtual sex is a possibility.

VR's potential is still off in the future. The early manifestations that exist today are characterized by shockingly high price tags (one super-deluxe VR setup could cost about $225,000). Some early versions of VR systems creating aerial battles are available

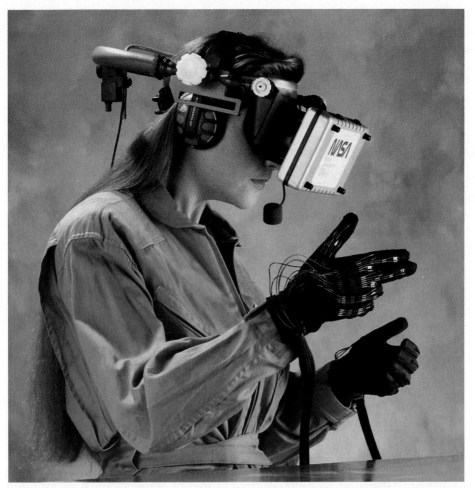

Is it real or is it Memorex? Virtual-reality gear as developed by NASA. Will alternative, computer-generated realities be more attractive than the real thing? (Courtesy NASA—Ames Research Center)

at coin-operated arcades in Great Britain. The cost is about $2 per play. The company that markets the arcade is developing a home system that would eventually retail at less than $50,000. Obviously, VR is a long way from a mass medium.

Nonetheless, philosophers are pondering the questions raised by this new technology. Many people might find VR much more attractive than the basic reality we all know. Will we have to contend with a generation of VR addicts who are always off in some other reality? If we can enter a world where we can do anything or be anything we like, why would we want to bother with plain old reality?

Maybe this is a good place to stop and consider some of the crucial issues that all of this media progress might raise.

● ● ● ●

MASS COMMUNICATION IN THE FUTURE: CRITICAL ISSUES

Examining the breakthroughs in media hardware just over the horizon is exciting and it's always fun to speculate on the neat things that the latest media gadgets can do, but that should not distract us from asking some relevant questions about the impact of all this technological change. Advances in media technology usually have both an up and a down side. The telephone, for example, made communication at a distance much more convenient. It also meant that we could be interrupted, awakened, or bothered at any hour of the day or night. Television brought us immediate access to news and entertainment but also encouraged the growth of couch potatoes. Let's consider some of the possible issues raised by new communications technology.

Privacy

Cellular and cordless phones have greatly expanded the communications potential of the telephone. Instead of being a device tied to the end of a wire, the new phones can go anywhere: to the supermarket, in the car, to a restaurant, wherever. Although we're still not quite to the point of the personal communicators worn by Spock and Kirk, the telephone is moving in that direction. On the down side, keep in mind that cellular and cordless phones are simply miniature radio stations and anybody with the right equipment, such as a scanner, can pick up all your conversations. (In fact, you can pick up cordless phone calls on some rather low-tech electronic hardware. People have reported that neighbors have overheard phone conversations on toy walkie-talkies and baby monitors.)

Computers are now common in the workplace. Word processing programs have improved efficiency and made the typewriter obsolete. Data base programs have made it possible to analyze and manipulate large amounts of data. Computers, however, have opened up other threats to privacy. Some systems allow supervisors to monitor every keystroke of their employees as a way to observe productivity. Electronic mail (E-mail), no matter how personal, can be read by those with access to the system. Consumers who subscribe to computerized data services (such as Prodigy) run the risk of having their personal files examined by unauthorized persons.

In the past, spying on our personal habits was made more difficult simply because the information was scattered about in different places. Now computers store huge amounts of information about us in one centralized place, the computer's memory, that is easily accessed from anywhere over phone lines. We willingly provide a lot of this information when we apply for a credit card, buy a car or a house, take out insurance, file a lawsuit, claim unemployment benefits, etc. What many consumers don't know is that a lot of this information is sold to other organizations for other purposes. This is one of the reasons why many of us are hit with barrages of junk mail from organizations we've never heard of. It's also possible that someone could tap into the system and have access to highly personal information. In one memorable example, a "techie" journalist was able to tap into the credit records of the vice president of the United States.

On the horizon are computer scanning systems for use at the checkout counters of supermarkets, drug, and discount stores that would record your every purchase. Such information would be invaluable to marketers. The makers of Mylanta could offer discounts to people who regularly buy Tums to get them to switch to their product. Bumblebee Tuna could send free samples to Chicken of the Sea buyers. Although this is great for marketing purposes, it is troubling for consumers. If you're like the rest of us, there are some purchases you make that you might like to keep private. Do you want everybody to know what kind of birth control method you use?

In an effort to control the problem, the European Community passed new privacy laws in 1991. Consumers would have to approve each release of private data. The United States was also considering legislation in the area. One proposal would create a federal Data Protection Board that would regulate government and business use of personal information. Whatever happens, it's a pretty safe bet that the new communications media will make privacy even harder to safeguard.

Fragmentation and Isolation

As has been pointed out many times in this book, the mass media are serving more and more the needs of specialized audiences. Magazines, radio stations, and cable TV networks, with their highly targeted niche audiences, are the best examples of this trend but the other media are moving in this direction. The media are increasingly encouraging individuals toward more selective content exposure. If this trend continues, it might result in a generation of consumers fragmented into smaller and smaller interest groups with little in common with the rest of society. If people are over-specialized in their interests, they may run the risk of being ignorant about the rest of the world.

This phenomenon has been labeled the "cocoon effect" by sociologists. From their perspective, it refers to the process, already evident in the 1990s, whereby people surround themselves with only the political and social information that they find comforting, appealing, or acceptable. It's as though people retreat into their informational cocoon to escape some of the uncertainty of modern life and to help reduce the multitude of choices that have to be made in today's society. It seems possible that this cocooning could generalize into cultural and recreational use of knowledge as well.

One of the functions of the media for the individual as discussed in Chapter 2 is conversational currency, giving people some common ground with which to start a conversation. What happens when one person who reads only magazines devoted to wrestling, watches only the wrestling channel on TV, and reads only books written by wrestlers meets another person who reads only magazines about knitting, watches only the knitting channel on cable, and only reads books about knitting? What will they have to talk about? Will fragmented audiences mean the loss of the common values and common knowledge that help hold society together?

Moreover, as telecommuting becomes more popular, more and more people will have little need to leave the house. A home computer, a fax machine, and a TV set can allow a person to shop, bank, work, and be entertained at home. With worries over personal safety mounting daily, will it be more attractive in the future to just stay at home?

Add to these concerns the fact that the new communication media are not free. The typical monthly cable bill in the U.S. can range anywhere from $20 to $80. Pay-per-view events cost $25 to $35 each. DBS will also be expensive. High quality programming might make the switch to pay and cable channels, leaving "free" TV with an inferior product. Computer information services have time charges that can mount up swiftly. Some special interest magazines can cost $4 to $5 per copy. In the long run, we run the risk of creating segments of society that are "communication rich" and those that are "communication poor." Children who grow up in households that can afford computers, educational tapes and videodiscs, cable TV, and pricey magazines and books might have an insurmountable head start in school over those children not so privileged, further increasing the fragmentation of society. Would taxpayers be willing to subsidize "information stamps," much like they do food stamps, to aid the underprivileged?

Overload in the Information Society

As is fairly evident, the United States and a good portion of the rest of the world have entered the information age. News, data, and entertainment have become the most important products of society as we move into the postindustrial age. This transition means that the individual is faced with a literal plethora of choices for knowledge and recreation: thousands of magazines, 150-channel cable TV systems, dozens of radio stations, thousands of books, print and electronic newspapers, movies on videocassette, pay-per-view TV, direct broadcast satellites, computerized information services, etc. The world's knowledge is doubling every eight years. A study done in Japan found that the production of information is growing at a rate that is four times faster than the consumption of information. Some observers have said we are creating an "infoglut." How can an individual manage this flood of information without drowning in it?

It's likely that those who succeed in the future will be the ones who can maximize the efficiency of their information-seeking behavior. Since there is a finite amount of time in a day, it makes sense to examine the media menu available to us and to select only those items that will fulfill our most important needs. It's not too early for you to start this process. Analyze your own patterns of media consumption. How well do they stack up against your own long-term needs and requirements? (Surveys suggest that on a typical day the average college student watches more than three hours of TV while reading textbooks for about half an hour. How do your media habits compare?)

Escape

This issue has been around almost since the time that the mass media were invented. Many parents and educators were worried that young people would much prefer to spend time in the media world instead of the real world. Social critics have painted bleak pictures of mesmerized children attending to various forms of media: radio, movies, TV, and Nintendo. In the future, this concern might have more validity since the media realities that are available are becoming more and more lifelike. Motion pictures are projected on large screens with Dolby surround-sound. Home theaters that duplicate the theater experience with VCRs are already on the market. Big-screen HDTV sets with stereo sound and interactive features will soon be available. Manufacturers of videogames are experimenting with ways to make their displays three-dimensional. And who knows what advances will be made in the virtual-reality area? What happens when it's far more fun to be in some media-generated reality than in real life? In fact, virtual-reality simulations raise the question of what exactly is "real" life anyway. Will large numbers of us abandon socially relevant pursuits for a romp in the media world? (Are you still reading this or have you gone to play Super Nintendo?)

● ● ● ●

THE FAR FUTURE

The laser has already been widely used in medicine, engineering, and data transmission. In the field of mass communication, the area of laser application with the most promise appears to be **holography**. Briefly defined, holography is three-dimensional (3-D) lensless photography done with laser light. In the following section, we will briefly explore the promise and current problems of holography.

Lasers and Coherent Light

The theory of holography was developed during the late 1940s by Dennis Gabor, a Hungarian physicist. Gabor discovered that if interference patterns created by coherent light waves reflecting from an object were captured on a photosensitive material, they could be reconstructed to form a three-dimensional image. Familiar sources of light such as the sun and electric light bulbs emit light irregularly. As a result, the light waves have different frequencies and travel in different directions. Coherent light, on the other hand, is made up of light waves of the same wavelength, emitted in a coordinated way so that they move "in step" much like soldiers in a close-order drill. Gabor tried using a mercury arc lamp, but although the results demonstrated the validity of his theory, they were not impressive.

An actual demonstration of holography had to be postponed until someone created a reliable source of coherent light. By 1962, someone had created such a source—the laser. A laser emits a constant stream of light waves at a uniform frequency. This beam of radiated light is very intense and it is coherent; since it is almost perfectly parallel, it does not spread out or diffuse as it travels. If you pointed a flashlight at the moon, the light waves would eventually reach the moon but would be so scattered that it would be hard to detect their arrival. A pencil-thin beam of laser light, however, would arrive at the moon in essentially the same form as that in which it left the Earth—the beam would be about the same thickness (Fig. 23.1).

With the invention of the laser, physicists could now conclusively demonstrate Gabor's theory of holography. In 1962, two scientists at the University of Michigan, Emmitt Leith and Jaris Upatnieks, put Gabor's theory to the test by using a laser as the light source for creating 3-D images. Their experiments confirmed that Gabor's theory was correct. In 1971, Dennis Gabor received the Nobel Prize in physics for his theory of holography.

Holograms

The three-dimensional image created by holography is called a **hologram**. It is important to recognize that a hologram is not the same kind of three-dimensional image created by viewing two slightly different images through polarized or colored glasses (the method used for 3-D movies and TV commercials). You do not need glasses to see a hologram. The image is truly three-dimensional and can be viewed from different positions and different angles. You can even see around or behind objects. In fact, objects in the foreground of the image will eclipse objects in the background as your position changes. In short, the hologram is an accurate three-dimensional representation of the scene it records.

A hologram generates a three-dimensional image by rebuilding the original light waves that are reflected from an object. The simplest method of creating a hologram involves splitting a laser beam into two parts. One beam, the reference beam, bounces off a mirror directly onto a photographic plate; the other, the object beam, reflects off the object or scene being photographed. The photographic plate is located so that it will be struck where the two beams meet and form an interference pattern composed of light waves from one source mingling with light waves from the other. A similar effect occurs when two stones are dropped into a pool of water and the two concentric rings of ripples converge. This interference pattern, captured in the photographic emulsion, is the hologram.

To view a hologram, a person looks directly at the highly sensitive photographic plate while it is illuminated with laser light (or in some cases, ordinary white light). The photographic film or plate becomes a "window," and the three-dimensional object appears to float in space either behind or in front of the window, depending on the technique used to create the hologram. The three-dimensional illusion occurs because the observer perceives the waves as coming from the actual object rather than from the hologram. Figure 23-1 on this page is a simplified version of how a hologram is created.

There is a certain amount of shock associated with one's initial viewing of a hologram, for the sight of an image popping off the photographic plate toward the viewer is somewhat disconcerting. (The feeling may resemble what moviegoers of the 1880s felt when they first saw moving pictures.) The natural urge is to reach out and touch the object hanging there in space. Naturally, a person's hand passes right through the image since the object isn't really there but exists only in the person's optical system and brain.

During the 1970s, the United States underwent a surge of interest in holography. RCA, General Electric, and IBM, among others, spent large sums on holographic

FIGURE 23-1 *A common arrangement for producing a hologram: The laser beam is split into two parts. One, the reference beam, is reflected from a mirror so as to strike a photographic plate. The other, the object beam, reflects off the object being photographed. The hologram is produced by the interference pattern formed where these two beams meet and are recorded on the photographic emulsion.*

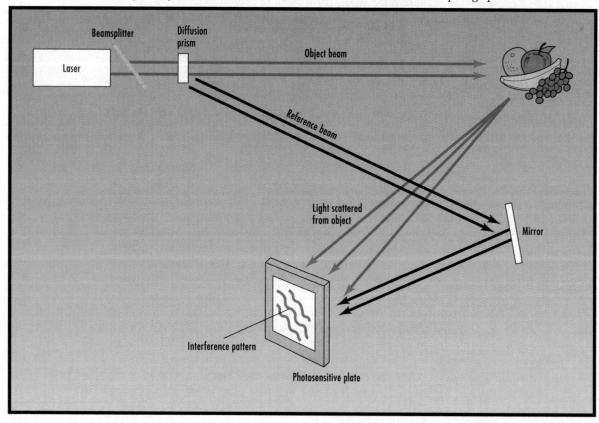

research. The 1970s saw the birth of holographic motion pictures that could be viewed by using ordinary white light. Although these early films were short and crude-looking, they convincingly showed that holographic motion pictures were possible. Advertisers were also interested in holograms, and publishers of medical books began binding holograms of various organs and tissues into their texts.

The increased interest in holography also uncovered some major technical problems that will have to be overcome before holography can become a true mass medium. First, it is difficult to make holographic movies that can be shown to large audiences; "projecting" a hologram poses special problems. Second, no one has yet invented a way to match a soundtrack to holographic film. Third, a hologram that yields true-to-life colors is still awaiting development—most current holograms are tinged with yellow, red, or green. Finally, holograms are still extremely expensive to produce.

Some progress toward solving these problems was being made in the 1980s. A group of Russian scientists was developing a specially constructed, seven-foot-wide holographic screen that could display holographic motion pictures to an audience of about 400 persons. A New York company developed a way to increase the size of the viewing window and magnify the image size so that the viewer would see the 3-D image floating several feet in front of the frame.

Holography has made other advances in the 1980s. It is now routinely used by many industries to test stress loads on such things as airplane and automobile parts.

Holographic technology has now advanced to the point where it is fairly easy to reproduce holograms on paper as evidenced by these pages from National Geographic. *The hard part will be developing holographic movies and TV. (Eric Sander/Gamma Liaison)*

Holograms can now be mass produced, and credit card companies are placing holograms on their plastic cards to guard against counterfeits. There are now holographic greeting cards. Holograms of scenes from *ET* were placed in bags of Reese's Pieces candy as a promotional device. *National Geographic* became the first magazine to put a hologram on its cover. (The magazine sold an additional 400,000 copies of that issue.) More recently, Michael Jordan, *Sports Illustrated*'s Athlete of the Year in 1991, showed up in holographic form on the magazine's cover.

Thanks to the development of a pulse laser, holographic portraits can now be done in a fraction of a second. Astronomer Carl Sagan, Gloria Steinem, Chicago Bears' coach Mike Ditka, and David Byrne (a Talking Head whose portrait was a floating head) are just some of the many celebrities who have posed for the 3-D portrait. (The price is not cheap. One Illinois company charges $950 for a five-by-seven-inch picture.)

The biggest breakthrough in the early 1990s was the creation by scientists at MIT of the synthetic hologram. Instead of making a hologram of a real-life object, such as a flower or chess piece, synthetic holography uses a computer to generate the image and then makes a hologram of it. Thus a person sitting at a computer screen can draw a house and then see it in three dimensions as a hologram. Fittingly enough, one of the first holograms produced by this system depicted the starship *Enterprise*. The biggest problem with this technique is that it uses so much computer space that only supercomputers can handle it. The scientists at MIT say such a system would have uses in architecture, medicine, defense, and engineering, not to mention its entertainment possibilities. As one MIT scientist said, "We're only inventing the future, not predicting it."

Holography When Perfected

Holography in the early 1990s is about at the same point that motion pictures were at in the 1880s or television in the 1930s. Significant problems have to be solved, but there appears to be no essential reason why holograms cannot be made into whatever form we desire. Skeptics might say that holography is an interesting phenomenon that will remain merely a curiosity and that it will never amount to much. (Other skeptics made the same comments about early radio, TV, and movies.) It will take time, but holography appears on its way to becoming an important mass communication medium.

Snap, Crackle, and Holograms

You never know where holograms are apt to turn up next. They're already on magazine covers, credit cards, and costume jewelry. Now a firm called Dimensional Foods Corporation has developed a process that will make it possible to put holograms on some types of food. Usually the printed version of a hologram is re-created by reflecting light off a photographic emulsion or foil. Dimensional Foods has turned these photographic emulsions into molds that create microscopic ridges on food that reproduce holographic images when hit by ordinary light. The company is betting that kids will go crazy for breakfast cereals and candy that have holograms of their favorite heroes on them.

When perfected, the first application of holography will be as a substitute for motion pictures. New theaters will have to be developed since a holographic film will not take place on a flat plane but will occur out toward the audience. The "holofilm" theaters will probably be horseshoe shaped, with a viewing area thrusting out into the spectators' seats. Of course, all the conventional aesthetics of the flat screen will no longer work for 3-D movies, and a new set will have to be worked out for this art form. After holographic motion pictures, the next step will be holographic TV or perhaps laservision (LV?). Home architecture will have to accommodate 3-D viewing, and a whole wall of a room in a house will be converted into a holographic viewing window. Family members will sit along the walls to watch the action, which will appear to occur in the middle of the room. If a person wants to peer around the edge of the scene, he or she will simply get up and walk to the far corner to see what can be seen. For example, suppose you were watching the twenty-first-century version of *The Tonight Show* and wondered what things were kept on the table behind the guest's chair. You could get up, walk to the edge of the screen, and look in back of the chair and see for yourself (provided the optical system was sophisticated enough).

In its early stages, holographic TV will be expensive to produce. This means that it will have to attract large audiences in order to be commercially successful either as an advertiser-supported or pay medium. Consequently, the content of "holovision" will be general in its appeal, and the mass audience, now in a state of fragmentation, may be resurrected by holographic TV.

What lies farther down the road with holography? Now we are dealing with sheer speculation—but sometimes sheer speculation has an interesting tendency to come true. One plan calls for affixing a tiny electrical charge to the surface of the holographic image as it is suspended in space. When a person's hand touches the surface of the hologram, the tiny electrical charges will stimulate the nerve endings of the fingers and the person will be fooled into thinking that he or she is touching something solid. Holography would then be extended into another sense realm, and the distinction between image and reality would be obscured. The perceptual problems this would create would be staggering since it would be difficult to distinguish your real friends from their holograms.

● ● ● ●

THE FARTHER FUTURE

After holograms, what next? Now we are in the realm of science fiction, but it's still worth thinking about. Aldous Huxley, in *Brave New World*, suggested the "feelies," a system in which viewers of a motion picture were hooked up with electrodes and had the appropriate brain center stimulated electrically so that they would "feel" what they were seeing on screen. Science fiction writer Ray Bradbury, in his short story "The Veldt," suggests a system of audience-participation media in which viewers suddenly find themselves transported through the screen and actually become part of the media world, interacting with the media characters. (In Bradbury's story the media world becomes a little too real, and some audience members don't survive their "trip.") In William Gibson's *Neuromancer*, people plug computer chips, called "stims," right into their brains. Stims provide experiences for all the senses, usually preprogrammed, but there is also the possibility of becoming a "rider," shifting yourself into another person's reality and experiencing the world as the other person experiences it. Is this the way we're headed? Alternate realities hard-wired into the cerebral cortex?

In any event, perhaps the best way we might close this chapter is to quote scientist and science fiction writer Arthur C. Clarke. Someone once asked Clarke what kind of communication systems we will likely have in the future. Replied Clarke, "Whatever kinds we can think of."

• • • •
SUGGESTIONS FOR FURTHER READING

The sources listed below contain additional information on the future of mass media.

CLARKE, ARTHUR C., *Voices from the Sky*, New York: Pyramid, 1965.

GIBSON, WILLIAM, *Neuromancer*, New York: Ace, 1984.

GROSS, LYNNE SCHAFER, *The New Television Technologies*, Dubuque, Iowa: William C. Brown, 1986.

KASPER, JOSEPH, *The Hologram Book*, Englewood Cliffs, N.J.: Prentice-Hall, 1985.

"The Media Decade," *Next*, February 1981, pp. 27–63.

RICE, RONALD, *The New Media*, Beverly Hills, Calif.: Sage Publications, 1984.

SINGLETON, LOY, *Telecommunications in the Information Age*, Cambridge, Mass.: Ballinger, 1986.

YOUNGBLOOD, GENE, *Expanded Cinema*, New York: E. P. Dutton, 1970.

GLOSSARY

A.C. Nielsen Company. The world's largest market research firm, best known for network TV ratings.

Acculturation. In a media context, the tendency of reporters or other media professionals to adopt the ideas and attitudes of the groups they cover or with which they have a great deal of contact.

Agenda-Setting Effect. The influence of the mass media created by emphasizing certain topics, thus causing people to perceive these same issues as important.

Agents of Socialization. The various people or organizations that contribute to the socialization of an individual.

AM. Amplitude modulation of radio waves.

Arbitron. The professional research organization that measures radio and TV audiences.

Audience Flow. Scheduling TV programs so that the audience attracted to one show naturally carries over to the following show.

Audience-Generated Feedback. Feedback that occurs when one or more audience members attempt to communicate their opinions or points of view to a mass medium.

Audit Bureau of Circulations (ABC). An organization formed by advertisers and publishers in 1914 to established ground rules for counting circulation data.

Authoritarian Theory. The prevailing belief that a ruling elite should guide the intellectually inferior masses.

Backmasking. Technique used to hide a message in a record or tape so that it can be heard only by playing it backward.

Barter Deal. In TV syndication, the program syndicator keeps most of the available commercial minutes to sell in the syndicated program.

Billboard. The sound-recording industry trade publication that tabulates record popularity.

Block Booking. A policy of major film studios that required theater owners to show several of a studio's low-quality films before they could receive the same studio's top-quality films.

Brownlines. Sample copies of the final edition of a magazine.

Business-to-Business Advertising.   Advertising directed not at the general public but at other businesses.

Campaign.   In advertising, a large number of ads that stress the same theme and appear over a specified length of time.

Carriage Fee.   In cable TV, a fee per subscriber paid by the local cable company to cable programming services.

Cash Plus Barter Deal.   In TV syndication, a station pays cash to a syndication company and gives up some commercial minutes to the company to sell nationally.

Catharsis.   A release of pent-up emotion or energy occurring as a function of viewing certain art forms, such as theater or music.

Catharsis Theory.   A theory that suggests that viewing aggression will purge the viewer's aggressive feelings.

CATV.   Cable television system introduced in the 1950s in order to extend conventional television signals to fringe areas.

Cease-and-Desist Order.   A Federal Trade Commission order notifying an advertiser that a certain practice violates the law. Failure to comply with a cease-and-desist order can result in fines being levied against the advertiser.

Channel.   The pathway by which a message travels from sender to receiver.

Churn.   In cable TV, the tendency of subscribers to cancel shortly after signing up for cable services.

Circulation.   The total number of copies of a publication delivered to newsstands, vending machines, or subscribers.

Clock Hour.   Radio format that specifies every element of the program.

Cold Type.   A process in which the elements of a newspaper page are pasted down and photographed; the finished product is then transferred onto a plate for the printing press.

Commercial Television System.   Local stations whose income is derived from selling time on their facilities to advertisers.

Communications Act of 1934.   Act of Congress creating the Federal Communications Commission.

Compact Disc (CD).   A sound system using laser technology that reproduces audio quality very precisely.

Comprehensive Layout.   The finished model of a print ad.

Concept Testing.   A type of media-originated feedback in which a one- or two-paragraph description for a new series is presented to a sample of viewers for their reactions.

Consent Order. Federal Trade Commission order in which the advertiser agrees to halt a certain advertising practice.

Consumer Advertising. Advertising directed at the general public.

Contagion Effect. In a media context, the theory that reports of violence can instigate new violence.

Controlled Circulation. A type of circulation in which publications are sent free or distributed to a select readership, such as airline passengers or motel guests.

Conversational Currency. Topic material presented by the media that provides a common ground for social conversations.

Copy. Headlines and message in an ad.

Corantos. Sheets of foreign and commercial news that originated in Holland around 1620 and were the forerunners of newspapers.

Corporation for Public Broadcasting (CPB). The network office of the Public Broadcasting Service.

Counter programming. Airing a program designed to appeal to a different segment of the audience than those on competing stations.

Creative Boutique. Advertising organization that specializes in the creative side of advertising.

Credibility. The trust that the audience holds for media that perform surveillance functions.

Crystallization. The sharpening and elaboration of a vaguely held attitude or predisposition.

Cultivation Analysis. An area of research that examines whether television and other media encourage perceptions of reality that are more consistent with media portrayals than with actuality.

Cycle. In all-news radio, the amount of time that elapses before the program order is repeated.

Decoding. The activity in the communication process by which physical messages are translated into a form that has eventual meaning for the receiver.

Demo. A demonstration tape used to sell a musical performer.

Demography. The study of audience characteristics such as age, sex, and socioeconomic status.

Developmental Journalism. Type of journalism practiced by many Third World countries that stresses national goals and economic development.

Digital Audio Tape (DAT). High-quality audiotape that uses digital audio technology to achieve fidelity comparable to that of a compact disc.

Direct Broadcasting by Satellite (DBS). A system in which a home TV set receives a signal directly from an orbiting satellite.

Dissemination Stage. In a news diffusion study, the period of time during which news spreads through a particular society.

Distribution System. The actual cables that deliver the signals to CATV subscribers.

Diurnals. Seventeenth-century daily publication of domestic and local events.

Double Feature. Practice started by theaters in the 1930s of showing two feature films on the same bill.

Dummy. A plan or blueprint for upcoming magazine issues that shows the contents in their proper order.

Dysfunction. Consequences that are undesirable from the point of view of the welfare of society.

Editorial Policies. Guidelines followed by a media organization with regard to certain public issues or political positions.

Electronic News Gathering (ENG). Producing and airing field reports using small, lightweight portable TV equipment.

Elite Audience Stage. A stage of audience evolution in which the audience for the medium is relatively small and represents the more educated and refined segments of society.

Encoding. The activity in the communication process by which thoughts and ideas from the source are translated into a form that may be perceived by the senses.

Equal Opportunities Rule. Part of the Communications Act of 1934. Section 315 allows bona fide candidates for public office to gain access to a broadcast medium during political campaigns.

Exit poll. Survey technique in which voters are asked whom they voted for as soon as they leave the polling booth. Used to make computer projections of election winners.

Experiment. A research technique that stresses controlled conditions and manipulates variables.

Fair Use. Under copyright law, people can use copies of the protected work for legitimate purposes.

Federal Communications Commission. A regulatory agency, composed of five individuals appointed by the president, whose responsibilities include broadcast and wire regulation.

Feedback. The responses of the receiver that shape and alter subsequent messages from the source.

Field Experiment.   An experiment that is conducted in a natural setting as opposed to a laboratory.

First Amendment.   The first amendment of the Bill of Rights, stating that Congress shall make no law . . . abridging the freedom of speech, or of the press.

First Sale Doctrine.   Motion picture companies make a profit on only the first sale of a videocassette. The studios make no additional money from cassette rentals.

Flexographic Printing.   A printing technique that cuts paper waste and makes ink less likely to rub off on a reader's hand.

FM.   Frequency modulation of radio waves.

Focus Group.   A group of ten to fifteen people led by a moderator that discusses predetermined topics.

Format.   Consistent programming designed to appeal to a certain segment of the audience.

Format Wheel.   A pie chart of an hour divided into segments representing different program elements.

Four-Walling.   A practice that allows the distributor to rent a theater at a specified fee for a predetermined length of time and to keep all box-office receipts.

Franchise.   An exclusive right to operate a business in a given territory.

Freedom of Information Act.   Law that states that every federal executive branch agency must publish instructions on what methods a member of the public should follow to get information.

Full-Service Agency.   An ad agency that handles all phases of advertising for its clients.

Functional Approach.   A methodology that holds something is best understood by examining how it is used.

Gag Rules.   Judicial orders that restrict trial participants from giving information to the media or that actually restrain media coverage of events that occur in court.

Galleys.   Sheets of paper used to display typeset copy.

Gatekeeper.   Any person (or group) who controls what media material eventually reaches the public.

Gramophone.   A "talking machine" patented in 1887 by Emile Berliner that utilized a disc instead of a cylinder.

Graphophone.   A recording device similar to the phonograph, but utilizing a wax cylinder rather than tinfoil.

Grazing.   Method of TV watching in which a viewer rapidly scans all the available channels using a remote-control device.

Head End.   The antenna and related equipment of the CATV system that receives and processes distant television signals so that they may be sent to subscribers' homes.

Heavy-Metal Sound.   Counterculture musical trend of the 1960s–1970s, characterized by a vaguely threatening style and heavy utilization of amplification and electronic equipment.

Hertz (Hz).   The basic unit of frequency. Named after German physicist Heinrich Hertz.

Hicklin Rule.   A longstanding obscenity standard based upon whether a book or other item contains isolated passages that might deprave or corrupt the mind of the most susceptible person.

High-Definition Television (HDTV).   High-resolution television system that uses over a thousand scanning lines as compared with traditional 525-line system.

Hologram.   The three-dimensional image created by holography.

Holography.   Three-dimensional lensless photography by means of a laser beam.

House Drop.   The section of the CATV cable that connects the feeder cable to the subscriber's TV set.

Hypodermic Needle Approach.   A sociological view that regarded the mass communication audience as a collection of isolated individuals who responded in essentially the same way to a message presented via the media.

Independents.   Radio or TV stations unaffiliated with any network.

Injunction.   A court order that requires an individual to do something or to stop doing something.

Instrumental Surveillance.   A media function that occurs when the media transmit information that is useful and helpful in everyday life.

Interactive Audience Stage.   A stage of audience evolution in which the individual audience member has some selective control over what he or she chooses to see or hear.

Interactive Television.   An arrangement whereby signals can be sent from the cable company to the home and also from the home to the cable company. Also known as two-way TV.

Interpersonal Communication.   A method of communication in which one person (or group) interacts with another person (or group) without the aid of a mechanical device.

Jazz.   A form of popular music that emerged during the Roaring Twenties era and was noted for its spontaneity and disdain of convention.

Jazz Journalism. Journalism of the Roaring Twenties era that was characterized by a lively style and a richly illustrated tabloid format.

Joint Operating Agreement (JOA). In order to preserve editorial competition, two newspapers merge their business and printing operations but maintain separate newsrooms.

Joint Venture. Method of movie financing where several companies pool resources to finance films.

Kenaf. A shrub whose pulp is being tested as a replacement for paper.

Kinetoscope. The first practical motion picture camera and viewing device, developed by William Dickson in 1889.

Libel. Written defamation that tends to injure a person's reputation or good name or that diminishes the esteem, respect, or goodwill due a person.

Libel per Quod. Written material that becomes libelous under certain circumstances.

Libel per Se. Falsely written accusations (such as labeling a person a "thief" or a "swindler") that automatically constitute libel.

Libertarian Theory. The assumption that all human beings are rational decision makers and that governments exist to serve the individual.

Limited partnership. Method of movie financing in which a number of investors put up a specified amount of money for a film.

Linkage. The ability of the mass media to join different elements of society that are not directly connected by interpersonal channels.

Linotype Machine. A machine for molding lines of type from hot metal.

Low-Power Television (LPTV). A TV station that broadcasts with lower power than the normal broadcast station and that has a coverage area of twelve to fifteen miles in radius.

Machine-Assisted Interpersonal Communication. A method of communication involving one or more persons and a mechanical device (or devices) with one or more receivers. Possibly separated by time and space.

Macroanalysis. A sociological perspective that considers the functions performed by a system (i.e., mass media) for the entire society.

Magazine. In colonial times, literally storehouses of material gathered from books, pamphlets, and newspapers and bound together under one cover.

Mainstreaming. In cultivation analysis, the tendency of differences apparently due to cultural and social factors to disappear among heavy TV viewers.

Management by Objectives (MBO). Management technique that sets observable, measurable goals for an organization to achieve.

Mass Audience Stage.   A stage of audience evolution in which the potential audience consists of the entire population, with all segments of society likely to be represented.

Mass Communication.   The process by which a complex organization, with the aid of one or more machines, produces and transmits public messages that are directed at large, heterogeneous, and scattered audiences.

Mass Media.   The channels of mass communication.

Mechanical.   Completed paste-ups (of magazine pages) ready to be taken to the camera room.

Media Buying Service.   Organization that specializes in buying media time for advertisers.

Media-Originated Feedback.   Feedback consisting of information about the audience that media industries go out of their way to gather.

Media Vehicle.   A single component of a mass medium, i.e., a newspaper or TV network.

Mediamark (MRI).   Company that measures magazine readership.

Message.   The actual physical product in the communication process that the source encodes.

Microanalysis.   A sociological perspective that considers the functions performed by a system (i.e., mass media) for the individual.

Mix-Down.   The process of reducing multiple recording tracks down to a two-track stereo master.

Motion Picture Patents Company (MPPC).   An organization formed by the nine leading film and film equipment manufacturers in 1908 for the purpose of controlling the motion picture industry.

MPAA Rating System.   The G-PG-PG-13-R-NC-17 rating system for movies administered by the Motion Picture Association of America.

Muckrakers.   Term coined by Theodore Roosevelt to describe the reform movement undertaken by leading magazines in the 1890s. Corrupt practices of business and government were exposed to the general public by crusading members of the press.

Multiple System Operator (MSO).   A cable company that owns more than one cable system.

Multistep Flow Model.   A classic theory suggesting that the persuasive effects of mass media alone will be unlikely to change audience opinions on important issues because the media's influence is filtered through a social network of opinion leaders.

National Advertiser.   Advertiser who sells a product all across the country.

Network.   An organization composed of interconnecting broadcasting stations that cuts costs by airing the same programs.

News Diffusion.   The spread of information through a society over time.

Newsbreak Stage.   The time it takes for reporters to transmit the essential facts of a story back to a media organization, which in turn publishes or broadcasts the news.

Newshole.   The amount of space available each day in a newspaper for news.

Nickelodeon.   A popular name for the many penny arcades and amusement centers that emerged around the beginning of the twentieth century and specialized in recordings and film.

90–10 Split.   Common method of dividing motion picture box office revenue. After the exhibitor subtracts operating expenses, the distributor takes 90 percent of what's left and the exhibitor keeps 10 percent.

Noise.   In communication, anything that interferes with the delivery of a message.

Noncommercial Television System.   Those stations whose income is derived from sources other than the sale of advertising time.

Nonduplication Rule.   FCC rule passed in 1965, stating that an AM–FM combination may not duplicate its AM content on its FM channel for more than 50 percent of the time.

O and Os.   VHF broadcasting stations owned and operated by each of the three commercial networks.

Observational Learning.   A form of education in which individuals learn by observing the actions of others.

Offset Plate.   In the newspaper printing process, a plate is made by placing a photographic negative between glass and a sheet of photosensitive metal and exposing the plate to light.

Offset Printing.   A process that transfers an image of a newspaper page captured on a photosensitive plate to a rubberized blanket and then to the surface of paper.

Oligopoly.   An economic situation in which a few mutually interdependent firms dominate the market.

Ombudsperson.   An individual in a media organization assigned to handle complaints from audience members.

One-stops.   Individuals who sell records to retail stores and jukebox operators who are not in a position to buy directly from the record company.

Operating Policies.   Guidelines that cover the everyday problems and situations that crop up during the operation of a media organization.

Option Contract.   An exclusive right to put into effect an agreement for rights or services over a fixed period of time.

Page Proof. A page-size piece of paper with all the elements—type, photos, and illustrations—positioned in their proper places.

Paid Circulation. A type of circulation in which the reader must purchase a magazine through a subscription or at a newsstand.

Panel Study. A research method in which data are collected from the same individuals at different points in time.

Parasocial Relationship. A situation whereby audience members develop a sense of kinship or friendship with media personalities.

Pass-Along Audience. That portion of a magazine's total audience composed of individuals who pick up copies of a magazine while at the doctor's office, at work, traveling, etc.

Pay-per-View (PPV). A system that allows cable TV subscribers to pay a one-time fee to view one specific program or movie.

Payola. Bribes of gifts and money paid to DJs by record companies in order to gain favorable airplay for their releases.

Penny Press. Term that describes the mass-appeal press of the early nineteenth century.

Peoplemeter. A mechanical device used to measure TV viewing that electronically records individual TV watching data.

Percentage Split. Method by which exhibitor and distributor divide the box office receipts of a motion picture.

Persistence of Vision. Quality of the human eye that enables it to retain an image for a split second after the image has actually disappeared.

Phi Phenomenon. Tendency of the human perceptual system to perceive continuous motion between two stationary points of light that blink on and off. Basis for the illusion of motion in motion pictures.

Phonograph. A "talking machine" developed by Thomas Edison in the late 1870s. The hand-cranked device preserved sound on a tinfoil-wrapped cylinder.

Photocomposition Machine. High-speed, computerized device tht translates electronic impulses into images and words.

Pickup. A technique of financing a motion picture.

Pilot. The first episode of a projected television series.

Pilot Testing. A process that involves showing a sample audience an entire episode of a show and recording their reactions.

Policy Book. At radio and TV stations, a book that spells our philosophy and standards of operation and identifies what practices are encouraged or discouraged.

Political Press. A polarization of the press into factions advocating specific political views; reached its extreme around 1800–1820.

Portfolio. A collection of one's personal work.

Positioning. In advertising, stressing the unique selling point of a product or service to differentiate it from the competition.

Press Council. An independent agency whose job it is to monitor the day-to-day performance of the media.

Press-Radio War. A series of confrontations between newspaper publishers and radio station owners caused by economic competition in the 1930s.

Primary Audience. That portion of a magazine's total audience made up of subscribers or those who buy it at the newsstand.

Prime-Time Access Rule. Rule adopted in 1970 intended to expand program diversity by barring network programs from the 7:30-8:00 P.M. (E.S.T.) time slot.

Prior Restraint. An attempt by the government to censor the press by restraining it from publishing or broadcasting material.

Programming. In radio and TV, deciding what programs to produce and where to place them in the schedule.

Property. A creative idea submitted to a film producer.

Prosocial Behavior. A general term used by researchers to describe behaviors that are judged to be desirable or worthwhile under the circumstances.

Public Broadcasting Act of 1967. Congressional act that established the Public Broadcasting Service.

Publicity. Placing stories in the mass media.

Rack Jobbers. Individuals who service record racks located in variety and large department stores by choosing the records to be sold in each location.

Radio Act of 1927. Congressional act establishing the Federal Radio Commission, a regulatory body that would issue broadcasting licenses and organize operating times and frequencies.

Rating. The ratio of listeners to a particular station to all people in the market.

Receiver. The target of the message in the communication process.

Reinforcement. Support of existing attitudes and opinions by certain messages.

Resonance. In cultivation analysis, the situation in which a respondent's life experiences are reinforced by what is seen on TV, thus reinforcing the effect of TV content.

Retail (Local) Advertiser. Business that has customers only in one trading area.

Rough layout. Early version of a print ad.

Satellite News Gathering (SNG). Using specially equipped vans and trucks to transmit live stories from any location via satellite.

Saturation Stage. In news diffusion, the stage at which most of the population has learned of an event and the story is no longer classified as news.

Sedition Act. Act of Congress passed in the late 1790s that made it a crime to write anything "false, scandalous or malicious" about the U.S. government or Congress; it was used to curb press criticism of government policies.

Sell-through Market. In home video, movies on cassettes that are meant to be bought by consumers rather than being rented from a video store.

Share of the Audience. The ratio of listeners to a particular station to the total number of listeners in the market.

Shield Laws. Legislation that defines the rights of a reporter to protect sources.

Signal Compression. Electronic technique using digital signals that makes it possible to squeeze more information through a coaxial cable or optical fiber.

Simmons Market Research Bureau (SMRB). The organization that offers the most comprehensive feedback about magazine readership.

Slander. Spoken defamation. (In many states, if a defamatory statement is broadcast, it is considered to be libel, even though technically the words are not written. Libel is considered more harmful and usually carries more serious penalties.)

Sliding Scale. An arrangement whereby as the box-office revenue for a motion picture increases, so does the amount of money that the exhibitor must pay the distributor.

Social Responsibility Theory. The belief that the press has a responsibility to preserve democracy by properly informing the public and by responding to society's needs.

Social Utility Function. In psychological terms, the social integrative needs that spring from an individual's compulsion to affiliate with family, friends, and others in our society.

Socialization. The ways in which an individual comes to adopt the behavior and values of a group.

Source. The originator of a thought or idea subsequently transmitted to others in the communication process.

Specialized Audience Stage. A stage of audience evolution that is typified by fragmented, special-interest audience groups.

Status Conferral. A process by which media attention bestows a degree of prominence on certain issues or individuals.

Stimulation Theory. A theory that suggests viewing violence will actually stimulate an individual to behave more violently.

Storage Instantaneous Audimeter (SIA). A small device hooked to a television set that allows rapid computer retrieval of viewing information.

Storyboard. A series of drawings depicting the key scenes in an ad.

Straight Cash Deal. In TV syndication, a station pays a fee to a syndicator and retains the right to sell all the commercial spots in the program.

Strategic Planning. Management technique that sets long-range goals.

Surveillance. The news and information function of the mass media.

Survey. A technique of gathering data that typically uses a questionnaire.

Symbiotic Relationships. In mass media, relationships of mutual benefit between industries; for example, television and film, radio and the record industry.

Tabloid. Heavily illustrated publication usually half the size of a normal newspaper page.

Tactical Planning. Management technique that sets short range goals.

Target Audience. In advertising, the segment of the population for whom the product of service has an appeal.

Telecommuting. Using computers, modems, and phone lines to transmit information and data from the home to the office instead of commuting.

Teleconference. System in which individuals in different cities interact via TV.

Teletext. Electronic news delivery system in which the viewer uses a computer to select information from a broad spectrum of electronic pages that can be viewed on a TV screen.

Tie-in. Releasing a message in one medium to coincide with some other media content. For example, books released along with motion pictures, record albums along with TV shows, etc.

Timeshifting. Recording programs off the air and playing them back when more convenient.

UHF. The ultra-high-frequency band of the electromagnetic spectrum. Channels 14–69 on the TV set.

Underground Press. A type of specialized reporting that emerged in the mid- to late 1960s, with emphasis on politically liberal news and opinion and cultural topics such as music, art, and film.

Uses-and-Gratifications Model. A model proposing that audience members have certain needs or drives that are satisfied by using both nonmedia and media sources.

Variety.   The entertainment industry trade publication.

VHF.   The very high frequency band of the electromagnetic spectrum. Channels 2-13 on the TV set.

Video-Display Terminal (VDT).   An electronic display keyboard widely used for the composition and printing of news copy. It is capable of storing typed information that can later be called out on the viewing screen for further design and editing.

Videotex.   Electronic news delivery system in which the viewer interacts with the computer in selecting the exact content choice desired.

Virtual Reality.   System in which a person dons special headgear and gloves and interacts with a computer-generated alternate reality.

Vitascope.   An early motion picture projector developed by Thomas Edison.

Warning (Beware) Surveillance.   A media function that occurs when the media inform the public of short-term, long-term, or chronic threats.

Yellow Journalism.   Period of sensationalized journalism during the 1890s noted for its emphasis on sex, murder, popularized medicine, pseudoscience, self-promotion, and human-interest stories.

Zoned Edition.   Newspaper that has special sections for specific geographic areas.

INDEX